AGING & SOCIETY

AGING & SOCIETY
A Canadian Perspective

Third Edition

MARK NOVAK

San José State University

formerly of the
University of Manitoba

I(T)P® Nelson

an International Thomson Publishing company

Toronto • Albany • Bonn • Boston • Cincinnati • Detroit • London • Madrid • Melbourne • Mexico City
New York • Pacific Grove • Paris • San Francisco • Singapore • Tokyo • Washington

I(T)P® **International Thomson Publishing**
The ITP logo is a trademark under licence

Published in 1997 by

I(T)P® **Nelson**

A division of Thomson Canada Limited
1120 Birchmount Road
Scarborough, Ontario M1K 5G4

Visit our Web site at **http://www.nelson.com/nelson.html**

Canadian Cataloguing in Publication Data
Novak, Mark W.
    Aging and society : a Canadian perspective

3rd ed.
Previous ed. published under title: Aging & society.
Includes bibliographical references and index.
ISBN 0-17-605622-X

1. Aging – Canada. 2. Aged – Canada. 3. Aged – Canada. – Social conditions. 4. Gerontology – Canada. I. Title.
II. Title: Aging & society.

HQ1064.C2N68 1997   305.26'0971   C97-930157-2

Publisher and Team Leader   Michael Young
Executive Editor   Charlotte Forbes
Senior Production Editor   Bob Kohlmeier
Project Editor   Evan Turner
Production Coordinator   Brad Horning
Art Director   Angela Cluer
Designer   Ken Phipps
Interior Designer   Alicja Jamorski
Senior Composition Analyst   Alicja Jamorski
Illustrator   Eric Colquhoun

Printed and bound in Canada
    3 4 (BG) 00 99 98

Contents

Preface

Many changes have taken place in Canadian gerontology since the second edition of this text was published. More researchers have entered the field of aging and have produced many new studies. The government has released many reports that summarize studies of health, disability, and social supports. And new consortia of researchers and research centres have begun studies that will shape social policy into the next century.

As Canada moves into the twenty-first century, the study of aging will increase in importance. Our country's population will have more older people than ever before. These people will make new demands on Canada's health care, retirement income, and housing resources. They will also bring to old age new interests, new skills, and a new perspective on aging. People young and old will need to understand the process of aging.

I set the same goals for the third edition of this book as I did for the first two. To begin with, I wanted a readable book—one that students could read without stumbling over social science jargon and dense academic prose. I have defined most technical terms within the text so that students will not have to flip to a glossary or interrupt their reading by looking at footnotes. I also present examples, charts, or graphs to illustrate difficult points. This edition also includes key terms and study questions that students can use to review and test their knowledge. I hope that these techniques will free students to think about what the text says.

Second, I wanted a text that presented aging in the context of Canada's history and social life. In the past I have used U.S. texts in my aging courses, and each year I have had to delete large sections of the text from the assigned readings. Canadian students don't need to know how many older people live in Arizona, the workings of the U.S. Social Security system, or the differences between aging black, white, and Hispanic Americans. These are interesting topics, but Canada has its own geographic regions, social policies, and mix of culture and ethnic groups. Canadian students should first learn about aging in their own country.

Third, I wanted a text that described Canada's social institutions—its health care, income, and housing systems, as well as its family and community life. Canadian students should know, for example, that their health care system provides free health care benefits to all older people and that the retirement income system provides a basic income to older Canadians. These systems create a social safety net for older people and provide the basis for a decent old age today.

Canadian students should also know that their society has problems. Many Canadians hold negative stereotypes about older people (my own children put me down by telling me I am getting old); the fast pace of modern society often pushes older people to the sidelines (imagine trying to cross a six-lane street if you have arthritis in your legs); and some groups of older people (many of them very old women) still live in poverty. Canadian society needs improvement. Students need to know what parts of the social system work for older people and what parts work against them. *Aging and Society: A Canadian Perspective* gives students the facts about aging and helps them sort through and understand the issues surrounding aging today.

This new edition has a fourth goal: to improve on the second edition. Many instructors and students across the country have used the second edition. They have commented on what they liked and did not like about the text. I have used their comments in revising the text.

As in earlier editions, this one contains the most up-to-date information available on aging in Canada. For example, I have added many new exhibits that present case studies of older people today or discuss current issues in the field. This edition also has some new sections that reflect new research in the field of aging. Chapter 1 contains new information on crime and older people. Chapter 2 includes new material on applied research, dialectical theory, and qualitative methods. Chapter 5 has more information on technological aids than was present in the second edition; Chapter 6 discusses recent psychological research on wisdom and new studies of competency and intervention in cases of cognitive impairment. Chapter 7 provides a new section on the self and on spirituality in later life. Chapter 8 discusses health care reform. This includes a discussion of community-based models of long-term care. Chapter 9 describes the proposed new "Seniors Benefit" that may replace the current Old Age Security and Guaranteed Income Supplement. Chapter 12 contains an expanded section on education in later life. Chapter 13 has expanded sections on caregiver burden. Chapter 15 contains a discussion of generational equity issues in Canada and Chapter 16 includes new material on careers in gerontology. In addition, each chapter has more discussion of theories as they apply to specific topics.

ORGANIZATION

This book begins by describing large-scale (macroscopic) changes in society. It then shows how these changes affect people and social institutions. It concludes by showing how individuals respond to these changes and how individuals' actions give new direction to society. The structure of the book reflects a dialectical model of social change.

Part 1, Gerontology Today (Chapters 1 and 2), introduces students to the field of aging. It shatters many of the myths people have about aging and shows the range of topics gerontologists study. It also describes the theories and methods gerontologists use when they study aging.

Part 2, Historical Change (Chapters 3 and 4), looks at the changes in Canada's history and demographic structure that led to population aging (the increased proportion of older people in the population). It also places aging in Canada in a world context.

Part 3, Maturational Change (Chapters 5, 6, and 7), looks at individual aging—the physiological, psychological, and developmental changes that come with age.

Part 4, Institutional Change (Chapters 8 through 14), examines Canada's institutions—the health care, social security, and housing systems as well as the family, the community, and the institutions responsible for death and dying.

Part 5, Societal Change (Chapters 15 and 16), looks at Canada's political structure, political action, and the effects of aging on Canadian society in the future.

Together these chapters give students a broad understanding of how aging affects the individual and society.

SPECIAL FEATURES

A number of features will make this both a useful and easy-to-use book. First, the chapters are organized into topics that most instructors cover in their courses. Each chapter represents a unit of study and presents the facts and issues related to one topic (e.g., housing, health care, etc.). This will allow instructors to use this text in either a one- or a two-term course. Instructors of a two-term course will be able to use the entire book, while those teaching one-term courses can assign specific chapters and know that a topic will be covered in depth. A one-term course, for example, might include those chapters that deal specifically with population aging and Canada's social institutions (i.e., Chapters 1, 3, 4, 8, 9, 10, and 11).

Second, each chapter starts with an outline of the chapter's contents and an introduction to its main themes.

Third, in each chapter the text is supplemented by exhibits, including graphs, charts, and excerpts from other publications. Some of the exhibits present controversies in the literature; others contain case studies that show the human side of aging. Most graphs and charts have accompanying explanations that describe them and show their relation to the text.

Fourth, each chapter concludes with a series of main points that summarize the text, a list of study questions, and an annotated list of important sources students can consult for further reading.

Fifth, the book concludes with a reference list of all the sources referred to in the text, in alphabetical order by author surname. Each listing has beside it a number (or series of numbers) that corresponds to the chapter(s) in which the reference appears. A student will find this list helpful when doing a research paper. All the references in Chapter 11 (Housing and Transportation), for example, have an "11" beside them. A student who decides to do a research paper on housing can quickly pick out all the references for housing and transportation.

Acknowledgments

Charlotte Forbes, Executive Editor in the Market and Product Development Department at ITP Nelson, guided me through this project. She contacted instructors throughout the country for comments on the second edition and worked diligently to get the book out on time. Like all good editors, Charlotte cleared away editorial problems so that I could focus on the research and writing. I thank her for her support. I also thank Evan Turner, Project Editor at ITP Nelson, for her careful work and creative suggestions.

Jerry Holcombe helped me gather permissions for this edition and Erlinda Yanez helped with the preparation and printing of the final draft of the manuscript. Maureen Forrest and Sharon Cancilla coordinated secretarial assistance on my behalf. I thank all of them for their hard work and attention to detail.

My wife, Mona, helped me by reading the chapters and preparing the summary points, key terms, and study questions at the end of each chapter. She has made the book more useful to students. My son Jonathan helped with the preparation of the bibliography. I thank both of them for their help.

Many Canadian colleagues in the field of gerontology sent me their papers and research reports. I cannot thank them all here, but I want to acknowledge that they helped make this a better text. A few people deserve special mention. Neena Chappell, my friend and colleague, discussed many of the ideas in the text with me. Nora Schwarz of Concordia University and Herbert C. Northcott of the University of Alberta reviewed and commented on the book, and I have tried to honour their efforts by incorporating their suggestions in the text whenever I could. Victor Ujimoto, C.G. Gifford, and Wayne McVey also commented on specific chapters in the first edition. Professor McVey also kindly supplied me with charts and data on demographic change. These people all took time from their busy schedules to help me with this text, and I thank them for their efforts. I alone take responsibility for the text's shortcomings.

I owe special thanks to Leroy Stone, a good friend and tireless worker, who taught me the importance and the limits of demographic research. Two close friends, John Hofley and Hans Mohr, inspire all of my work. I can never repay them, only thank them, for their support and friendship.

I dedicate this book to my family—my wife, Mona, and my sons, Christopher, Jonathan, Sean, and Daniel. All of them deserve credit for lightening my spirits with their good humour and love.

Gerontology Today

What Is Gerontology?

INTRODUCTION

Everyone needs to know about aging. First, all of us are getting older. While some of us are over 65 already, most adults not yet 65 will become part of the older population between now and the year 2030.[1] We will want to make old age as good a time of life as it can be. Second, when those of you who are younger students reach middle age, your parents, aunts, uncles, neighbours, and older friends will have grown old. You will want to know about aging so that you can help them live the best old age possible.

Third, more people work with the elderly than ever before, and more will find themselves working with the elderly in the future. Canada now has about 3.2 million people aged 65 and over. Older Canadians make up more than one-tenth of the population today (11.6 percent in 1991), and experts predict that this proportion will grow to 22 percent by the year 2031 (Norland 1994). Nurses, social workers, teachers, family counsellors, and even travel agents will have more and more older people as clients.

An older population will also put new demands on Canada's **social structures.** Sociologists define a social structure as a relatively stable pattern of social interactions (Abercrombie, Hill, and Turner 1984, 198–99). The family, the education system, and the health care system all fit this definition, and they will change in the following ways as Canadian society ages:

- More Canadians will live in three- and four-generation families. And many people will become grandparents while they are still active in their careers.

- Schools and universities will attract more older students than ever before. These students will want flexible schedules. They will also need different kinds of teaching methods and different grading schemes than younger students.
- The health care system will also change. The current system favours treatment of acute (short-term) illness, but older people tend to have chronic ailments like arthritis, hearing problems, and diabetes. An aging society needs to prevent illness before it occurs.

Gerontology is the discipline that studies aging systematically. It looks at the subject from two points of view: how aging affects the individual and how an aging population will change society. This chapter describes (1) attitudes toward aging today and myths about aging, (2) the history and structure of the field, and (3) approaches to the study of aging in Canada.

ATTITUDES TOWARD OLD AGE

People hold many **stereotypes** about old age. Sociologists define a stereotype as "a one-sided, exaggerated and normally prejudicial view of a group, tribe or class of people" (Abercrombie, Hill, and Turner 1984, 209). People who hold a stereotype do not check it to see if it is true. If they meet someone who does not fit the stereotype, they think he or she is an exception. Stereotypes often have some basis in truth, but they exaggerate and distort the truth. Often they lead to discrimination.

When it comes to old age, we hold both positive and negative stereotypes: the wise old farmer and the kindly grandmother; the dirty old man and the sex-starved spinster. Hendrick et al. (1988) asked female undergraduates to estimate how well an "average" younger and an "average" older woman would do on a group of psychological tests. The students gave the older woman a lower score than the younger woman on measures of psychomotor speed and memory. At the same time, the students were "unrealistically generous in their perceptions of cognitive abilities, particularly in the case of older women" (Hendrick et al. 1988, 197). Ryan and Heaven (1988) studied the attitudes of 120 adults toward older people in 40 situations. The people in this study assigned older people less often to situations that required competence and more often to those that called for benevolence. These adults thought of older people as kinder but less able than younger people.

Many of our stereotypes consist of negative views of older people and old age. Knox and Gekoski (1989) asked undergraduate students in an experimental study to compare young, middle-aged, and older people. The study found that students gave older people lower ratings than those who were middle-aged on such qualities as autonomy, effectiveness, and personal acceptability.

Even older people sometimes hold negative views about old age (Harris 1975). Studies of identity show that some people try to distance themselves from aging. They call people their own age old and refer to themselves as middle-aged (Bultena and Powers 1978; Matthews 1979).

Gerontologists call prejudice against older people **ageism.** Butler (1969) says ageism comes about because the young and the middle-aged feel distaste for aging. They see old age as a time of weakness, sickness, and dying. Ageism also comes about because people know little about old age, and because what they know is based on myth and fear.

In Canadian society today, people learn to be prejudiced against the old. These negative views come from many sources. Berman and Sobkowska-Ashcroft (1986, 1987) reviewed the treatment of older people in great books from the Bible to those of the twentieth century. They found that comedies almost always make fun of older people. Overall, in philosophy, literature, and the theatre, they found that "negative traits outnumber positive traits by about two to one" (Berman and Sobkowska-Ashcroft 1986, 141). Towler (1983) analyzed five hundred of the most popular current books for children (kindergarten to grade 6 students) and fifty of the most popular TV shows. He found fewer older people in them than expected and only a shallow development of their characters. He concluded that the media gave children a biased and misleading view of old age. Meadows and Fillmer (1987) conducted a study of basal readers from the 1960s and 1980s. They found that the readers gave a generally positive view of older people, but the readers underrepresented them. Also, when older people did appear, they played only minor roles in the stories.

Exhibit 1.1

What Is It Like to Be Old?

No one can know the answer to this question until they reach old age themselves. But Professor Paul Baker of the University of Victoria set out, at age 33, to learn about aging first-hand. In the story that follows he describes his experiment with old age.

"You're too young to be a gerontologist. How can somebody who's only 33 know what it's like to be 83?" This reaction from one of the few older students in my course on the sociology of aging bothered me. My first instinct was to haul out my academic/scientific defences and claim that you don't have to be an X to study X's (be they old, female, black or handicapped).

But I was left with the uncomfortable feeling that maybe she was right, maybe I was missing some of the more subjective and emotional aspects of aging by working only with "hard," "objective" data. Then I ran across John Griffin's classic book, *Black Like Me*, written in 1961. Griffin dyed his skin black and passed as a black man in the southern United States for a month. His book showed how different the world was for a black man, and made a lot of white people realize what racism meant at the human level.

So, how could I become old? The answer was obvious: the same kind of makeup that turned Dustin Hoffman old in *Little Big Man* might work for me, and with the help of a makeup artist in Vancouver, plus some old clothes, a cane, and a grey wig, I made the transformation. The makeup took several hours to apply, and hurt like hell going on and coming off, but it worked.

My main interest was in experiencing society's reactions to an old man. I walked around in Victoria and Vancouver about a dozen times, in different places, at night and during the day. And what I found was pretty much what I expected; a few people go out of their way to help the old, a few turn their backs, and most people simply ignore them.

One "young" woman (my own age) waited patiently for me as I struggled up the stairs at the Victoria Institute of Gerontology, held the door open, and said "have a nice day." I felt very uncomfortable:

I was really a young, healthy male but was masquerading as a decrepit old man; I actually felt like I was a "burden" and almost told her I could open doors for myself, even if I was old.

On the other hand, I was shoved off the sidewalk in front of the Empress Hotel by a large, noisy bunch of tourists. It may have been accidental, but I felt angry and frustrated. On crowded streets I could no longer stride along and know that other people would move aside. I had to be on the defensive, anticipating others' moves. Crossing busy streets became a totally different experience. I hung back so that the crowds could bolt across as soon as the light changed, and then I shuffled along, keeping my eye on the cars, which seemed like racehorses just itching for the gates to open. The lights always started flashing "DON'T WALK" before I was across. What was I supposed to do, the bunny hop?

I experimented with getting in and out of cars and using buses. The basic lesson I learned was that the world gets bigger and faster for an old man, and I became acutely aware of this dramatic change because I was really young, and hadn't gradually accepted the inevitable changes of aging.

I discovered a sense of comradeship of the old, who had the time to sit and talk. I also found a subtle difference between old Victoria and big Vancouver: it seemed easier to be old here, partly because of the size and pace, but maybe also because in Victoria we have so many old people. I think we have learned to be a little more patient.

Would I do it again? Probably not ... pretending to be old hurt my back, my legs, my feet. It was hard to explain to friends and neighbours what I was doing. I think I'll wait for old age to creep up on me slowly, and in the meantime, I think I have gained a better understanding for my old friends.

Source: Paul M. Baker, "Old Before My Time," videotape distributed by the Centre on Aging, University of Victoria, Victoria, B.C. V8W 2Y2, 1983b. Reproduced with permission of the author.

Other mass media also foster prejudice against older people. Newspaper stories, for example, sometimes point to older people as the cause of rising health care costs in Canada. Harding and Neysmith (1984) say that this practice overlooks the deeper reasons for rising health care costs and creates a negative image of older people. Ageism even influences retail sales staff. One woman, in a National Advisory Council on Aging study of attitudes toward older people, said that "salespersons can be impatient if you are choosing something and are not swift enough." Another woman said that "salespeople will talk to me rather than to my mother who is 85" (NACA 1993, p. 20).

Jokes give a negative view of old age and older people as well (Davies 1977). Demos and Jache (1981) studied humour in birthday cards. They found that cards often focused on physical or mental decline connected with aging. The cards also focused on age concealment, and most took a negative view of aging. Palmore (1971) studied attitudes to older people in humour. He looked at 264 jokes taken from ten popular joke books. He found that one-quarter of the jokes took a positive view of aging and about one-fifth took a neutral view, but more than half of them showed a negative attitude to aging or the aged. He also found a double standard in jokes about age: jokes about women, more often than those about men, portrayed older people negatively.

These jokes project our own fears about aging onto older people. But do these fears have a basis

---

Exhibit 1.2

Profile: Rose Ouellet

Journalist Mary Nemeth (1994, 26) says that "old stereotypes [of aging] are under assault." Advertisers, for example, have begun to present a more positive image of older people. And when they do they often turn to actress and comedian Rose Ouellet.

She is liable to show up just about anywhere. In a TV commercial she sits vampishly on the hood of a pick-up truck ... Another time, another channel and there she is, persuasively pushing beer. Or on a billboard high above a Montreal street, her image hustles cars. "I always wanted to do something outside the theatre and now I've done it. ... Now, I have done everything."

She probably has, for at age 90, La Poune—an affectionate but untranslatable nickname picked by her agent decades ago—has been entertaining audiences longer than any other stage personality in French Canada. She entered professional vaudeville in 1917 when she was only 14 because she had become bored with amateur productions.

Ouellet lives by herself at Maison des Artistes, a retirement home for theatre people on Montreal's downtown St. Denis Street. She gets up anywhere from 7 a.m. to early afternoon and, when she's not working, sometimes visits old folks' homes. "Everyone laughs because they're all younger than me," she says. Her only visible concession to vanity is her hair; when it began to go grey while she was fairly young, she had it dyed red—and has kept it that way.

She walks a lot and smokes whenever she feels like it. "I listen to my body," she says. "If I eat something and it doesn't agree with me, I notice. If it happens a second time, I won't eat that food again. I think people can control their health. Mine is good. I don't even know what a headache feels like."

At the same time, says La Poune, "I never think about death. Why worry about it? I know someone who lives in my building and it's just terrible how she worries about death. I keep telling her, 'What's the point? You got yourself all worked up about it yesterday and you're still here! Are you going to worry all of today, as well?'" When her time comes, adds Ouellet, "it will be an interesting voyage to a place I've never visited before."

Source: Mary Nemeth, "Amazing Greys," *Maclean's*, January 10, 1994, pp. 32–33. Reprinted with permission.

in fact? Studies of older Canadians show that they do not. A study by Health and Welfare Canada (1988a), for example, found that only 30 percent of people aged 65 and over said that life was very or fairly stressful, compared with 52 percent of people aged 55 or younger. Also, 92 percent of people aged 65 and over said they were either pretty happy or very happy, which is about the same proportion as for the 55–64-year-olds (93 percent) (see also Thompson 1989). Between 90 and 95 percent of seniors in another study said they felt satisfied with their families, marital status, friends, and housing (Gauthier 1991). A study by the Commonwealth Fund (1993) looked at aging in five developed nations (Canada, the United States, the United Kingdom, western Germany, and Japan). The study found that 58 percent of older Canadians said they felt "generally very content." This surpassed the other countries in the study (except the United States with 61 percent). Northcott (1982) studied 440 Edmontonians and found that older people reported higher life satisfaction than those who were younger. Also, more often than younger people, they said they felt no pressures. Northcott concluded that "old age looks far more attractive than stereotypes suggest."

MYTHS AND REALITIES OF AGING

Gerontology has two goals. First, scholars and researchers work to produce accurate knowledge about aging. Second, professionals who work with older people apply this knowledge to create a better life for their clients. Academic gerontologists try to decrease prejudice and stereotyping in society by writing about the facts of aging today. Consider the following myths and the facts that gerontologists have found to replace them.

Myth: People feel lonely and lost in retirement. They often get sick and die shortly after they retire.

Reality: Few people face sickness or loneliness due to retirement (McDonald and Wanner 1990). Given the chance to retire with a decent income, most people do so as soon as they can. McDonald and Wanner (1990) report that retirement has little, if any, effect on health, social activity, and life satisfaction or happiness. Streib and Schneider (1971) found that the health of some workers

improves when they retire. Many start new careers, take up volunteer work, or go back to school.

Myth: People in older age groups face a higher risk of criminal victimization than people in younger age groups.

Reality: Older people report more fear of crime than younger people. Podnieks and her colleagues (1989, 12) report that nearly 20 percent of a random sample of older Canadians said they felt "somewhat fearful of being out alone in their neighbourhood." Brillon (1986), in a Montreal study of 210 people aged 60 and over, found that 53 percent of men and women said they felt afraid of burglary; 53 percent of the men and 69 percent of the women in this study reported a fear of being attacked at home; and 47 percent of men and 69 percent of women said they feared an attack away from home.

The General Social Survey (Statistics Canada 1993, cited in Trainor, Normand, and Verdon 1995) studied people's feelings of safety. The study found that older people showed the greatest fear of walking in their neighbourhood. For example, 57 percent of women aged 65 and over compared with 41 percent of women aged 45–64 felt totally unsafe walking in their neighbourhood after dark.

Men aged 65 and over, compared with younger men, showed a greater fear of walking in their neighbourhood. Nineteen percent of older men, compared with 11 percent of men aged 45–64, felt totally unsafe walking alone in their neighbourhood after dark. Some studies report that older women with low incomes and fair-to-poor health, and who live alone, reported the most fear (Kennedy and Silverman 1984–85; Podnieks et al. 1989). Loss of social networks due to retirement, widowhood, and staying home may lead to increased fear of crime. But this fear of crime does not fit the facts about crime against the elderly.

Podnieks and her colleagues (1989), for instance, found that only 6 percent of their sample had property or money stolen from them by a stranger since turning age 65. Studies in Britain, the United States, and Canada show that older people run less risk of victimization than any other age group. A 1993 Canadian survey found that older people made up only 3 percent of victims of violent crimes (Statistics Canada 1994b). Older people had only one-sixth the rate of assault of

Exhibit 1.3

A New Myth about Aging

A student passed the following story along to me. She said she heard it from someone who heard it from a Nova Scotia fisherman. Maybe it will become a part of our Canadian mythology about aging.

The ferry between Cape Breton and St. John's was having a rough passage. The seas were so rough that the captain decided that it was too dangerous to take the boat right to the dock. Instead, he anchored in the harbour. He maneuvered the boat so that passengers could get off, but he kept the boat far enough from the quay walls to keep the boat safe. The crew set up a makeshift gangway made of wood planks and a rope handrail on either side. The heaving of the boat and the springiness of the planks made the passengers reluctant to cross to the shore.

The crew and shore personnel persuaded and encouraged the passengers to get them to cross. At last, a small, frail-looking old lady came from below. She hesitated to cross the gangway, but finally she worked up her courage and inched across. Many people watched her make her way and the people on shore almost carried her the last few feet. People began to cheer as she set herself on the shore. Then she turned to face the boat, she cupped her hands and called, "It's all right, Mother. You can come down now."

Exhibit 1.4

Facts on Aging Quiz

Try the following quiz to see how much you know about aging in Canada. The quiz is based on Palmore's "Facts on Aging: A Short Quiz" (1977), but it incorporates suggestions made by Canadian researchers who have revised Palmore's work (Matthews, Tindale, and Norris 1985). The answers are at the bottom of page 15. You will find the facts to support these answers throughout this book.

True or False?

1. A least 15 percent of the aged in Canada are living in long-stay institutions (i.e., nursing homes, mental hospitals, homes for the aged).
2. British Columbia has a higher proportion of older people in its population than any other province.
3. Older people today have less contact with their families than older people in the past.
4. Older people stand a higher risk of criminal victimization than people in other age groups.
5. Memory declines with age.
6. A decline in sexual vigour in older men is usually due to hormone deficiencies.
7. Retirees more often feel depressed, bored, and ill than those who keep working.
8. Most older people in rural areas depend on public transportation.
9. The body's systems go into a steady decline from age 40 on.
10. The majority of older people have incomes below the poverty level (as defined by the federal government).

people aged 25–34 and about one-third the rate of personal robbery of people aged 25–34 (Statistics Canada 1994b). Brillon (1987, 10) says that "elderly people are largely under-victimized, proportionately, for all types of crime." The Canadian Urban Victimization Survey (Solicitor General of Canada 1983, 3) sums up these findings, stating that "contrary to popular belief ...

elderly people are relatively unlikely to be victimized by crime ... In fact, the actual sample counts of sexual assault and robbery incidents for those over 60 were so low that estimated numbers and rates are unreliable."

Older people do face relatively high rates of certain kinds of crimes. For example, compared with younger people, they run a higher risk of being victims of fraud. The National Advisory Council on Aging (Plouffe 1991) consulted 125 older people on consumer fraud. About a fifth of these people claimed that a salesperson or company had tried to cheat them. Fourteen percent said that advertising had misled them. Ten percent said they knew a senior who had lost money through fraud. NACA reported a number of conditions that create a higher risk of fraud among older people. These included: lack of information, social isolation, and lack of wariness in business relations.

Myth: Most old people live in institutions.

Reality: Only a small percentage of older people live in **special-care homes** for the aged—nursing homes, hospitals, or asylums—at any given time. Norland (1994) reports that in 1991 4.2 percent of older men and 8 percent of older women lived in special-care homes. The likelihood of institutionalization increases with age. Only 1.4 percent of men and 1.7 percent of women aged 65–74 years lived in special-care homes. But this figure jumps to one-quarter of men and more than one-third (36.3 percent) of women aged 85 and over (Norland 1994).

Institutionalization rates have slowed for men aged 85 and over and have decreased for both sexes aged 80–84 (Stone and Frenken 1988). Most institutions house the very old, sick, and frail elderly—people with few social supports, who cannot live on their own. Current moves in Canada toward increased community care may lead to less institutionalization in the future.

"One antidote to ageism," Butler (1993, 77) says, "is knowledge, the primary intervention." Research shows that stereotypes about old age decrease with increased education. Palmore (1977) devised a "Facts on Aging Quiz (FAQ)." (See Exhibit 1.4.) Researchers and educators have used this quiz with people from a variety of backgrounds. Studies report that scores improve with education. People with a high-school education or

less, for example, average 57 percent correct. Undergraduates do somewhat better, averaging 64 percent. Gerontology students and faculty on average score 83 percent (Palmore 1988). A study in Canada by Greenslade (1986, cited in Palmore 1988) found that nurses with no gerontology training scored 61 percent correct, but a group with training in geriatrics scored 83 percent.

Matthews, Tindale, and Norris (1985) gave a modified version of Palmore's quiz to public health nurses and also to students and faculty at Guelph University (see Exhibit 1.5). (They found that the people with the most knowledge about aging scored best on the quiz. Undergraduate students just completing a gerontology course scored highest. Introductory students in a human development course scored lowest. Their results suggest that when people learn about aging, their concept of old age improves.

Knox, Gekoski, and Johnson (1984) and Gfellner (1982) studied undergraduate students. These studies found that positive contact with older people in general leads to better attitudes. So does voluntary, frequent contact between a younger person and an older person he or she knows well. Stereotyping decreases when older and younger people see each other as individuals with good and bad traits (Hooyman and Kiyak 1993).

Dooley and Frankel (1990) studied a friendly visiting program where adolescents visited a specific senior each week. They found that adolescents who had a positive perception of the person they visited made a favourable attitude change toward seniors in general. This evidence supports the idea that knowledge about aging and satisfying contact with older people can relieve fears and replace negative stereotypes with a more positive view of old age (Butler 1989). Kenyon (1992, 4) says that "all people in an aging society need to be sensitive to their own assumptions ... of aging."

The study of aging shows that old age has its compensations. Older people in Canada have guaranteed incomes, subsidized housing, and free medical care. They also get reduced rates on buses, hotels, and car rentals. Other bonuses include tax breaks, free tuition at many universities, and financial support for recreation programs.

Marshall and McPherson (1993) say that Canadian society has an ambivalent view of aging. Ageism exists alongside care and concern for older people. They say that Canada has "been called an ageist society, yet no societies in world history have provided a larger proportion of societal wealth to provide income security, health care, and shelter for the aged" (7). Atchley (1985, 6) declares that in North America today the positive results of aging "outnumber the negative by at least two to one."

The study of aging shows that the attitudes of others cause many of the worst problems older people face. Canada's National Advisory Council on Aging studied how older people feel about society's view of aging (NACA 1993). One person told the NACA that "some people confound aging with illness." Another said: "People confuse the 90% of older people who are able with the 10% that are not." Finally, "I get tired of the 'good for you' attitude, as if it were surprising that someone 65+ can be involved in a number of physical, intellectual and volunteer pursuits" (NACA 1993, 10–11).

Slaughter-Defoe, Kuehne, and Straker (1992) found that children from varied backgrounds (Canadian and U.S.) held ageist views of older people. But some evidence suggests that educators and writers have begun to present a more balanced view of older people to children. Janelli (1993), for example, studied 37 children's books published between 1985 and 1990. She compared this sample with children's books published between 1966 and 1984. She found that authors still stereotyped grandparents. But grandmothers wore more modern hair styles and clothes. They also engaged in more physical activity and drove cars. Grandfathers were often involved in teaching activities.

Research shows that people aged 50–70 have good incomes, little or no mortgage, and no children. These people have money to spend and active lifestyles. The National Advisory Council on Aging (1990, 2) says that older consumers want to buy "experiences rather than objects." Recreation programs, education, and travel services appeal to this group (Fletcher 1990). Some companies now market services to the needs of these busy seniors.

Luttropp (1995) reports that Oil of Olay skin lotion has a new ad campaign that presents healthy, happy women in their 40s. One woman says she is "looking forward to being the best-looking grandmother on the block" (Luttropp 1995, 5). Other cosmetics companies like Clinique have removed ageist language from their ads. Nemeth (1994, 27)

says that "advertisers now poke fun at the aged only at their peril." For example, a Doritos tortilla chip TV ad showed a steamroller squashing a confused older woman into wet cement. The company faced public outrage after it aired the commercial. "The contrite manufacturer," Nemeth says, "delivered cases of free chips to a food bank" to soothe public anger.

Today, compared with the past, the mass media present an image of healthier, more active older people (Dail 1988). Television shows like *The Golden Girls*, *Murder She Wrote*, and *Who's the Boss* feature single, independent, older women. Bell (1992) reviewed the opening sequences of five TV shows that star older people (*Murder She Wrote*, *The Golden Girls*, *Matlock*, *Jake and the Fatman*, and *In the Heat of the Night*). He found that these sequences portrayed the older stars as powerful, affluent, and quick-witted. Movies like *Cocoon*, *The Karate Kid*, and *Driving Miss Daisy* present positive images of older people, as do the afternoon soaps. The Rolling Stones, now in their 50s, tour and produce albums. Jane Fonda and Cher promote fitness through aerobic exercise videos.

The mass media have begun to present more varied images of older people. And David Poltrack, an executive vice president at CBS, says that when the baby boom generation reaches its 50s it "will demand television that serves their needs and is directed at them" (S.C. Taylor 1995). But the media may create a new stereotype: the sophisticated, successful, beautiful senior. Bell (1992) found that the TV shows he reviewed ignored issues of sexuality, family relations, and social problems that older people face. New images of aging may lead to new forms of ageism that will marginalize the very old and older people with disabilities. The media can change public attitudes toward aging and older people, but it must pay attention to the content of its programs. A number of sources (NACA 1993; Nuessel 1982) propose that the media set up guidelines on ageist language and the portrayal of older people.

Gerontologists study various topics, such as retirement, housing, and the media. They gather facts about aging today and attempt to replace prejudice with knowledge. Gerontology can help overcome ageism by presenting a more balanced view of aging and older people.

THE HISTORY OF GERONTOLOGY

Gerontology comes from the Greek words "geron" (old man) and "logos" (reason or discourse). Writings about aging can be found in the scriptures of the Far East, biblical sources, works by the Greek philosophers, and medical writings of the Middle Ages (Cole and Winkler 1994). One list of works on aging written before the nineteenth century totalled 1800 titles (Freeman 1979, 81). Freeman describes the earliest of these works (from the first written records to those of the seventeenth century) as the products of perceptive individuals. These writings reflect their authors' biases and fears as well as the attitudes of their time. Not until the seventeenth century, with the rise of the scientific method, did researchers look at the facts about aging. These researchers' backgrounds were usually the natural sciences and medicine.

Francis Bacon, credited as the founder of the scientific method, wrote one of the best-known early books on aging, *Historia Vitae e Mortis* (*The History of Life and Death*, 1623). Bacon wanted to use systematic observation to learn the causes of aging, but his own work echoed the biases of the past. The following passage, for example, could have come straight from Aristotle 2000 years earlier: "Men of age," Bacon says, "object too much, consult too long, adventure too little, repent too soon, and seldom drive business home to the full period, but content themselves with a mediocrity of success" (cited in Freeman 1979, 38).

By the eighteenth century the scientific method began to change the way researchers studied aging. Mathematicians and scientists began to use the mathematical techniques of natural science to study aging. Astronomer Sir Edmund Halley constructed the first table of life expectancy.

In the nineteenth century, Quetelet, a Belgian astronomer-mathematician, conducted studies of birth rates, death rates, and other statistics that looked at how crime and suicide varied with age. In *On the Nature of Man and the Development of His Faculties* (1835), Quetelet described how human traits like strength and weight varied with age (Birren and Clayton 1975, 18).

In the early twentieth century scientific interest in old age grew more intense. In 1903 Elie

---

Exhibit 1.5

Controversy: Do We Live in an Ageist Society?

David Schonfield says that introductory gerontology texts often give "the impression that a negative attitude toward elderly people is rampant in the United States and presumably, also, in other western countries" (1982, 267). He goes on to say that these texts exaggerate the amount of prejudice against older people in North America. Review articles and studies by well-known gerontologists find little evidence for this supposed prejudice. Studies show that older people maintain good relations with their families, receive many services from the government, and get preferred treatment from restaurants, banks, and airlines.

Schonfield's own research shows that people have both positive and negative attitudes toward old age and aging. He found that between 20 and 77 percent of his sample agreed with stereotypes about older people, but many of these same people said that the statement applied to only a portion of the older population. He says that "at most one in five participants could be convicted [of stereotyping]" (269). Schonfield concludes that "some acts portray ageist attitudes, but these are insufficient to justify the generalization that ours is an ageist society. On the other hand, there seems to be ample evidence to contradict the generalization" (270).

Schonfield's research shows the danger of generalizing about attitudes toward older people. Still, his research shows that some proportion of people (as many as one in five) do stereotype older people. More education and information about aging might improve attitudes toward older people.

Can you find examples of ageist attitudes or behaviours in your environment? Can you find examples of positive attitudes or behaviours toward older people? Do you agree with Schonfield's conclusion that gerontologists sometimes exaggerate the extent of ageism in Canadian society?

Metchnikoff at the Pasteur Institute in Paris first used the term "gerontology" (Freeman 1979, 16). He wrote one of the first modern books on aging, entitled *The Problem of Age, Growth and Death* (1908). In 1912 the Society of Geriatry was formed in New York—one of the first groups in North America to study aging.

Research and writing on aging grew quickly after 1950. A study of the literature published between 1950 and 1960, for example, found as many publications in those ten years as there had been altogether in the previous 115 years (Birren and Clayton 1975). A bibliography of sources on aging for the years 1954–1974 listed 50 000 entries (Woodruff 1975). Research in gerontology now goes on in many disciplines, including biology, psychology, and sociology. Researchers now have access to the latest gerontology research through the use of CD-ROM bibliographies and on-line databases.

CANADIAN DEVELOPMENTS IN GERONTOLOGY

Historical Overview

Gerontology in Canada grew slowly from 1950 to 1980. In 1950 the government set up the first of a series of committees to study aging. This committee—the Joint Committee on Old Age Security of the Senate and House of Commons—studied the effects of aging on Canadian society and on individuals. It focused on income security, but also collected information on housing, health, and welfare services (Health and Welfare Canada 1982b, vii).

In 1963 the Senate appointed a special committee to study the services, facilities, and preventive programs available to older people. At that time Canada had no national body devoted to research on aging, so the committee had to gather its own facts. It used Dominion Bureau of Statistics (now Statistics Canada) census data, research reports published by the Department of National Health and Welfare, and submissions by scholars, researchers, and agencies across the country. The committee collected the most up-to-date information on aging, and its report gives a good overview of aging in Canada at that time.

In this report the committee refers again and again to the lack of social scientific research on aging. Gaps were found in many fields (like the study of retirement in Canada), and the quality of the research in others was judged to be poor. Response to a questionnaire sent by the committee to government departments, universities, and voluntary organizations across the country indicated a lack of coordinated gerontological study. Only 78 out of 118 organizations answered the questionnaire, and less than one-third (24) reported any research on aging from 1950 to 1963. The committee learned of only 129 research projects started in Canada from 1950 to 1963—71 by universities, 38 by voluntary organizations, and 20 by provincial and federal governments—an average of only ten research projects per year throughout the country (Senate of Canada 1966).

The committee traced the slow rate of growth in Canadian research to a lack of research funds. Federal health grants to support aging research averaged less than $75 000 per year for the ten-year period from 1955 to 1965. Only four provinces (Quebec, Ontario, Saskatchewan, and British Columbia) received these funds, and three institutions in Quebec received more than 77 percent of the total (Senate of Canada 1966).

Other groups—the federal departments of Labour and Veterans Affairs, and a number of volunteer agencies—supported research in the 1950s and 1960s. The Ontario Department of Public Welfare, for example, started the "Longitudinal Study of Male Workers, Ontario, 1959–78." This study focused on social, economic, and health changes in male workers and offered a rare look at changes in workers over time. It also looked at the adjustments men made to aging and the kinds of services they used as they aged (Senate of Canada 1966). A number of researchers have continued to use this data set into the present (Hirdes and Brown 1994; Hirdes and Forbes 1993). A recent analysis of this data set (Forbes, McPherson, and Shadbolt-Forbes 1989, 65) found that it contained reliable data and that it "represents an exceptionally good longitudinal study." These researchers said that the data can be used to study how health behaviours at the start of the study affected respondents' health at the end.

Canadian research activity increased during the 1960s and 1970s. In 1971 Manitoba began a province-wide survey of the needs of the elderly. Researchers set out to measure both the needs of older people and how well present resources met these needs. They questioned 3558 people who lived in the community and 1247 older people who lived in long-term care facilities—a total of 4805 people over the age of 65 (Government of Manitoba 1973). The province repeated this survey in 1976 and in 1983. The results of the three surveys (along with three follow-up surveys of survivors) make this the largest, most complete longitudinal study of aging in Canada. An annotated bibliography of results from this study lists over 100 publications written between 1971 and 1983 (Rempel 1987). A number of other Canadian longitudinal studies began in the 1970s and early 1980s (Havens 1995c).

In 1973 the Canadian Council on Social Development (CCSD) sponsored a nation-wide study of elderly persons' housing. The council's report, *Beyond Shelter* (Canadian Council on Social Development 1973), shaped housing policy in Canada for at least the next decade. The government also formed the Special Senate Commission on Retirement Age Policies. The commission's report, *Retirement without Tears* (Senate of Canada 1979), described the major issues facing retired Canadians and suggested social reforms.

In 1971 Canadian researchers and scholars formed the Canadian Association on Gerontology (CAG). The CAG presents position papers to the government on issues related to aging, keeps track of research activities across the country, and sponsors an annual Scientific and Educational Meeting. The CAG publishes proceedings from these meetings and also publishes the *Canadian Journal on Aging*. (In the late 1970s the journal's title was *Essence: Issues in Death, Dying and the Process of Aging*.) The CAG has a computerized database of over 2000 resource people in Canada.

In 1980, recognizing the need for more stable support for gerontology research, the Social Sciences and Humanities Research Council of Canada (SSHRC) for the first time awarded over $1 million to researchers through its Strategic Grants Division program on Population Aging. The council also set aside funds to sponsor five new gerontology centres in Canada. These centres, at St. Thomas University (New Brunswick), the University of Guelph, the University of Toronto, the University of Manitoba, and Simon Fraser University, conduct and encourage research, keep local researchers informed about national and provincial research activities, and sponsor forums and seminars on aging.

By 1980 Canadian gerontology had begun to come of age. In that year Victor Marshall (1980a) published the first collection of gerontology writings by Canadian scholars, *Aging in Canada*. This collection includes papers on various topics, from demography to health care to housing, as well as articles that take a sociohistorical view of aging and others that look at intergenerational conflict. These articles show Canadian gerontology's links to European and British traditions of critical social science. Other articles show Canadian gerontology's links to U.S. research. Marshall (1980a) noted in his introduction that in 1980 Canada still lacked basic research on aging—research on family life, biological research, and studies of mental functioning in later life. He spoke of the small number of Canadian researchers as pioneers, many of whom "have worked, of necessity, virtually alone, without the benefit of colleagues who share their research interest in gerontology" (Marshall 1980a, 6).

Developments in Francophone Gerontology

During the late 1970s and 1980s research activity in gerontology also increased steadily among francophone social scientists. In 1976 the Quebec Department of Health set up one of the first Canadian gerontology centres (the Laboratoires de gérontologie sociale) at the Université Laval. Two years later a group of Quebec gerontologists formed L'Association québécoise de gérontologie (Béland 1988), and in 1980 they set up a research committee. The association has held symposiums on professional issues each year since 1979 and since 1980 has held an annual scientific meeting. Proceedings of these meetings keep members of the association up to date on francophone research.

The Association québécoise de gérontologie research committee compiled a list of gerontologists who worked in the field from 1977 to 1982. The list included 635 people. Of these, 122 had permanent positions that allowed them to do full- or part-time research (Zay et al. 1984, cited in

Béland 1988). These researchers had conducted 128 projects, about one-third of which dealt with topics in administration, psychology, sociology, or political science. Béland (1988) reports 800 articles published from 1975 to August 1986 by franco-phone authors. These appeared in peer-reviewed journals, symposium proceedings, policy reports, and elsewhere.

Béland (1988) surveyed the content of this research and found that it focused on three topics: psychosocial topics, demography, and program evaluation. He also found that francophone researchers prefer to use qualitative research meth-ods. Bernardin-Haldemann (1988) traces these themes and the use of qualitative methods to the social and political context of Quebec in the 1970s. At that time, the government of Quebec defined the growth of the older population as a social prob-lem. This led gerontologists to study demography, older people's psychosocial conditions, and their service needs.

In the 1970s the rise of Quebec nationalism led to an interest in Québécois identity, and geron-tologists took up this theme in their studies. Researchers focused on the everyday lives of older people, their world views, and the issues of *"inter-generational relationships* and *socio-cultural continuity"* (Bernardin-Haldemann 1988, 329, italics in the original).

Béland (1988) posed the question of franco-phone gerontology's significance in the subtitle of a literature review: "An Obscure Originality or a Deserved Obscurity?" Anglophone Canadians have often overlooked francophone research, as have other North American scholars. Béland (1988) points out that francophone researchers often publish their work in French and tend to publish in research reports rather than in refereed journals. For these reasons, their work has not reached the wider North American academic community. But, as Béland's review shows, fran-cophone researchers have conducted community studies that could interest a wider audience. They have also conducted social-psychological studies that speak to important issues like the loneliness and isolation of the elderly. Anglophone gerontol-ogists could benefit from wider exposure to this research.

The Current State of Canadian Gerontology

In 1982 the CAG published the first issue of the *Canadian Journal on Aging (CJA)*. The *CJA* since then has gained international recognition. Higgs (1994) reports that the *CJA* ranks ninth in the world (out of 389 journals) in the rate at which researchers cite the journal. Higgs (1994, 8) says that this points to the journal's quality, "consider-ing that it emphasizes Canadian research, and therefore presumably has a smaller readership than most American journals."

In the year that the *CJA* first appeared, 1982, the program of the association's 11th Annual Scientific and Educational Meeting contained 129 abstracts (these included media presentations, symposium, and discussion groups, as well as papers). By 1995 over seven hundred researchers and practitioners presented papers at the annual meeting. They presented their findings in over one hundred sessions (including symposiums and discussion groups). The meeting also included a series of pre-conference workshops and dozens of technical, educational, and media exhibits.

Still, more research on aging needs to be done. A review of the CAG annual meetings in 1995 shows that researchers presented more papers on health-related issues than on any other subject. We still know too little about healthy older people, even though most older people live healthy, active lives. We also need to know more about the social conditions that lead to good aging. What do people of different ethnic backgrounds need as they age? Do the needs of people in rural areas differ from those of people in cities? Do older people have unique educational needs? How do they learn best? And what do they want to know? Researchers have begun to turn to these and other questions about aging.

SUMMARY

1. The growth of the older population in Canada has made aging a major social issue—one that will affect all of us.
2. Gerontology has two goals: first, to increase our knowledge about old age and, second, to improve the quality of life in old age. In Canada today these goals take the form of scholarly

research and the practical application of research findings.

3. Canadians have both positive and negative images of aging and older people. Many of these stereotypes have little basis in fact. Gerontology tries to replace stereotypes with facts, information, and a clearer understanding of aging.
4. Canadian research has grown rapidly in all parts of Canada since the early 1970s. This growth has led to more scholarly publications, new research programs, and more projects to improve the lives of older people.

STUDY QUESTIONS

1. Why should students know about aging? How will an aging population affect social structures like education, health care, and the family?
2. What is ageism? Where do negative attitudes toward aging come from? How can people develop a more positive attitude toward aging?
3. Define the term "gerontology." What are the two main goals of this discipline?
4. State three common myths about aging. Explain why these myths are false.
5. Explain why older consumers have become a major force in the marketplace. What types of products do older consumers prefer? How has the image of the older consumer changed in the past few years?
6. What issue occupies the most attention of researchers in Canada today? What other topics concerning aging in society need more study? How can these studies help society in the future?

KEY TERMS

ageism   prejudice against older people.

social structures   a relatively stable pattern of social interactions.

special-care homes   nursing homes, hospitals, or asylums.

stereotypes   "a one-sided, exaggerated and normally prejudicial view of a group, tribe or class of people" (Abercrombie, Hill, and Turner 1984, 209).

SELECTED READINGS

Binstock, R.H., and L.K. George, eds. *Handbook of Aging and the Social Sciences*. 4th ed. San Diego: Academic Press, 1996.

This handbook contains state-of-the-art reviews of the literature in the field. It includes articles on changes in the field, migration patterns of the elderly, family life, and social supports. A basic resource for social gerontologists.

Laforest, Jacques. *Introduction à la gérontologie. Croissance et déclin*. Montréal: Hurtubise HMH, 1989.

This introductory text, from a francophone scholar, takes an interdisciplinary approach to gerontology. It views aging as a process of decline and growth. The author sees old age as a time of existential crisis in which identity, autonomy, and belonging all come into question.

Marshall, V.W., and B.D. McPherson, eds. *Aging: Canadian Perspectives*. Toronto: Broadview Press/Journal of Canadian Studies, 1994.

Many of these articles appeared in a special issue of the *Journal of Canadian Studies* devoted to aging. The book includes articles from francophone as well as anglophone writers. Topics include: aging and the environment, technology, retirement and work, and social policy. The collection gives a sampling of work by some of the best-known scholars in Canadian gerontology.

Novak, M.W., ed. *Aging and Society: A Canadian Reader*. Toronto: Nelson Canada, 1995.

A collection of topical articles by Canadian gerontologists. This collection brings together articles published in professional journals, government reports, and chapters from books. Topics include: myths and realities of aging, cultural diversity, health care, housing, income, and retirement. The readings reflect Canadian concerns about aging like living in winter cities and Aboriginal health care.

NOTE

1. The terms "old," "elderly," "aged," and "senior" in this text refer to people aged 65 and over unless another age is given.

Answers to Exhibit 1.4:
All ten statements are false.

Theories and Methods

INTRODUCTION

In 1980 the Gerontological Society of America (GSA) and the Association for Gerontology in Higher Education (AGHE) set out to define the discipline of gerontology (Foundations Project 1980). They asked 111 scholars, researchers, and professionals in the field to describe a basic education program in gerontology. These experts came from such different disciplines as biomedicine and economics, and their descriptions of the exact content and boundaries of gerontology varied. But they did agree on their most significant conclusion, that three broad areas of study should make up the core of a gerontology curriculum: biomedicine, psychosocial studies, and socioeconomic-environmental studies.

The first area, biomedicine, looks at the changes in physiology and health that come with age. This area includes studies of the biochemical causes of aging, studies of reaction time and stress, and studies of dementia. Experts disagreed least about the curriculum content for this area; this may be due to the long tradition of biomedical research on aging.

The second area, psychosocial studies, examines the changes that take place within individuals and between individuals and groups. This includes psychological studies of memory, learning, and personality, as well as studies of friendship and recreation.

The third area, socioeconomic-environmental studies, concentrates on the effects of aging on social structures like health care and education. It also looks at the effects of social structures on the aging individual, and includes the study of income policies, health care systems, and formal social supports.

Exhibit 2.1

Time-Lines

These time-lines show three dimensions of aging. Line A refers to the biomedical changes that take place with age. Biomedical aging takes place at different rates for each person, and at different rates for each system of the body. Still, we can describe the aging process in terms of some general trends that take place in the physiology over time.

Line A

Line B

1 — 18; peak of sexual vigour

2 — 30; onward; decline of 1 percent per year on average

3 — 40; physical decline shows up as greying hair, wrinkled skin, balding, loss of stamina

4 — 47; menopause

5 — 70; high risk of heart disease and stroke

6 — 73.9; (1990) life expectancy at birth for males

7 — 80.5; (1990) life expectancy at birth for females

8 — 120; (estimated) life span

1 — 16; legal driving age

2 — 18; legal voting age

3 — 18; fluid intelligence high (e.g., ability to visualize objects in space)

4 — 25; first marriage

5 — 50; last child leaves home

6 — 65; crystallized intelligence high (e.g., ability to define words)

7 — 65; pensionable age (under rules of most pension plans)

8 — 65; person may begin a second career

Line B refers to psychosocial and socioeconomic-environmental changes that take place with age. Most psychologists and social psychologists agree that human beings develop through a series of stages (though different psychologists list different stages and different patterns of aging). Sociologists say that culture (societal values, norms, and expectations) all play a role in shaping the individual's development. This time-line lists some of the basic events in the life course in Canada today.

Only time-line A shows aging as a constant decline with age. Line B shows aging as a complex series of changes—some abilities like fluid intelligence decrease, while others like crystallized intelligence may increase. Also, a person may experience declines on one dimension (e.g., physical stamina), but increases on another (e.g., more involvement in recreation in retirement). Some changes that come with age, like a second career, can only develop in later life.

Line B also reflects the social structures of society. These structures can change, and they are changing today. The Canadian government, for example, has begun to allow a choice of retirement ages for people who get benefits from the Canada Pension Plan; this will allow people to retire before or after age 65 if they choose.

The Canadian Association on Gerontology today has six sections: general, biology, health sciences, psychology, social sciences, and social policy and practice. The way this association has organized itself reflects the increase in research activity and the greater specialization of research in biology and health sciences. It also reflects gerontologists' desire to apply their knowledge. The social policy and practice section, in particular, focuses on programs and practices that can improve the lives of older people.

Social gerontology includes psychosocial, socioeconomic-environmental, and practice-related research. It looks at aging from the points of view of both the individual and the social system. Social gerontologists often take an interest in physical and health care changes that come with age. But the focus of the social gerontologist differs from that of the physiologist or biochemist. When social gerontologists look at biological or physical change in old age they ask how these changes affect the individual's social life or society as a whole.

Social gerontologists, for example, will want to know how diseases in old age affect hospital costs or how changes in lung capacity affect a person's ability to work. They will also want to know how a social norm like retirement affects an older person's health, how changes in family life in Canada affect the psychological well-being of the elderly, or what counselling methods work best with new retirees. Social gerontology has grown in importance from the 1950s to the 1990s in Canada.

This chapter will look at: (1) the theories that gerontologists use to guide their research and to interpret their findings, (2) the methods researchers use to gather data, and (3) current developments in Canadian research on aging.

THEORIES OF AGING

Social gerontologists use theory to guide research and to interpret the results of their studies. A good theory helps a researcher choose research methods, questions, and samples. Cockerham (1991) says that "theories specify relationships between concepts and provide a framework for explaining why certain things happen the way they do." For instance, research shows that women get more of their retirement income from public pension sources than men. Why does this difference exist? And is this an important finding or a trivial fact? Theory offers an explanation and an understanding of research findings. Feminist theory, for example, would trace this difference to gender inequalities in the workplace. Women have less opportunity to pay into private pension plans during their middle years. This forces them to draw on public pension sources in old age.

Theory gives an interpretation to the facts. But no one theory in gerontology can explain all the facts about aging (Moody 1988b). And sometimes a researcher will use several theories to explain the results of a study. Authors often select theories to fit their sense of how the world works. If you know the assumptions that underlie a theory, you know the costs and benefits of using that theory. And you know the biases that each theory brings to the facts. More than one theory can often explain a set of research findings. The theory used depends on how the researcher makes sense of the data.

Social gerontologists have generally used sociological or social-psychological theories in their

work. Sometimes they have adapted these theories to fit the study of aging.

Two Levels of Theory

Theories describe all sorts of human activity and relationships, from individual attitudes to societal structures. The following discussion categorizes theories by placing them into a framework and it also gives examples of how gerontologists apply these theories in their work.

Gerontologists often classify theories into two categories: (1) micro-level and (2) macro-level.

Micro-level theories focus on individuals and their interactions and are used to explain phenomena like the relationship between adult children and their parents, changes in memory with age, and the effect of negative attitudes on older people. **Macro-level theories** focus on "social structure, social processes and problems, and their interrelationships" (McDaniel 1989, 51). Such theories explain phenomena like the effect of industrialization on older people's status, the history and impact of public pensions, and how gender and income affect older people's well-being. Critics of micro-level theories say they focus too much on people's actions. They ignore or take little account of economic conditions and social policies (Estes 1979). Critics of macro-level theories say that this approach tends to minimize people's ability to act and overcome the limits of social structures.

Three Theoretical Perspectives

Both micro- and macro-level theories can take one of three perspectives: (1) the interpretive perspective, (2) the functionalist perspective, or (3) the conflict perspective.

The Interpretive Perspective

The **interpretive perspective** focuses almost exclusively on the micro-level of social life. It looks at how people define situations, how they create social order, and how they relate to one another in daily life. Social gerontologists have made the least use of this perspective, though it can provide insights into everyday interactions. The exchange, symbolic-interactionist, and social phenomenological theories that grew out of the work of Homans (1961), George Herbert Mead (1934), and Max Weber (1978), respectively, exemplify the interpretive perspective. Mead (1934), for example, said that objects and events have no meaning in themselves. People give them meaning through everyday interaction. Grey hair, for example, can be a sign of wisdom in one society but a sign of decline in another. People give meanings to objects and then base their actions on these meanings. Some people will refuse to wear a hearing aid because to them it symbolizes decrepitude and weakness. Weber (1978) said that to understand a social phenomenon the researcher needs to understand the meaning that people in the situation attach to events and actions.

The interpretive perspective views the individual as a creator of social order and organization. This perspective asks the question, "How does a recognizable, predictable social order come about?" (Berger and Luckman 1967; Garfinkel 1967; Schutz 1967). The interpretive perspective can give a good understanding of how people interpret their social world, how they interact with one another, and why they do what they do. Gerontologists have used this approach in studies of the self in later life (Chappell and Ohrbach 1986), death and dying (Marshall 1986), and successful aging (Novak 1983).

Gubrium (1986) used the interpretive perspective to study Alzheimer's disease, and his findings show some of the strengths of this approach. Writers have called Alzheimer's disease "the disease of the century," and television shows have depicted the struggle spouses and children face when they have to care for a confused parent. Studies describe the signs and symptoms of the illness, but Gubrium takes all of this information and these facts as social constructions. He focuses on the way that members of the Alzheimer's community—physicians, family members, social service workers—create this disease through their discussions, writings, and interactions (Novak 1988).

Gubrium attended scientific conferences on Alzheimer's disease, meetings of the Alzheimer's Disease and Related Disorders Association (ADRDA), and caregiver support group meetings. He studied scholarly reports, monographs, the popular literature on the disease, and media reports. He studied the Alzheimer's community as an anthropologist might study a strange culture.

He treated its members' speech and artifacts as the products of a unique subculture.

Gubrium shows that the members of the Alzheimer's community work together to make sense out of the disease's many contradictions. A caregiver, for example, "tries to make sense of what it is she deals with from day to day, in order to organize what, to her, seem to be reasonable courses of action in response" (Gubrium 1986, 69). Other members—neurologists, nurses, support group leaders—have their own reasons for making sense of the disease. And each one of these actors uses different methods and bits of information to create a sensible account of the illness. Biologists see the disease as a puzzle. They use bits of tissue and slides of brain cells to make sense of it. The ADRDA sees it as an enemy and uses terms like fight, war, mission, and conquest to define members' activities and goals.

Gubrium's study shows the way that interested people create an entity, called Alzheimer's disease, that they can understand and talk about. He also shows how they form a linguistic community and a culture around the disease they have created. His study questions the meaning of common-sense concepts like aging, disease, and treatment and asks gerontologists to pay attention to the social construction of reality that they often take for granted. Phenomenological studies like this one can sensitize all of us to the many meanings that aging can have. They also show that people play a vital role in creating the social world they live in.

The interpretive perspective has weaknesses as well as strengths. Like all perspectives it gives only one point of view on social life. Cockerham (1991) says that this perspective makes too little of the connections that exist among interactions, interpretations, and macro-level social phenomena like the economics of the health care system. This means that it cannot answer many of the questions gerontologists ask. The interpretive perspective, for example, cannot tell us how health care policies will have to change to serve an aging society. It also says little about power and conflict between social groups. For example, it cannot explain income inequality between men and women in old age or the effects of ethnicity on social status in later life. Fortunately, the functionalist and conflict perspectives do look at these questions.

The Functionalist Perspective

The **functionalist perspective** holds that "social order is based on cooperation, interdependence, and shared values, adjustment by the individual to society, and societal equilibrium" (McDaniel 1989, 52). Wilson (1970) contrasts this functionalist perspective with that of the interpretive. While the interpretive perspective asks "How do people create their social world through interaction with one another?" the functionalist asks "What is the structure of the society that people live in and how do the parts of this structure function?"

The structural-functionalist theories (Parsons 1937, 1951) that grew out of Émile Durkheim's work in nineteenth-century France best express the functionalist perspective. Durkheim's studies, *The Division of Labor* and *Suicide*, serve as models for this approach. Structural-functionalist theories treat society as a system that consists of social institutions like the family, the military, and educational institutions. These systems keep society in a dynamic equilibrium. They adjust to one another as the system responds to internal and external pressures. For example, the increased number of women in the labour force has led to a decrease in the number of full-time family caregivers for frail older people. This, in turn, has led to more community care programs sponsored by government health services. The health care system has changed to meet new family demands, and this change serves the useful function of restoring society's balance.

Structural functionalism sometimes draws the analogy between society and a living organism. Just as our bodies, for example, will adjust to an increase in our blood sugar, so will society adjust to changes in its internal condition. An increase in the number of older people, for example, may lead society to increase funding to health promotion programs. Structural functionalism predicts that society will attempt to create an orderly transition to a new, stable state.

Structural functionalism also assumes that shared norms and values shape individual behaviour. People conform to these norms through social pressure, but also through belief in society's underlying value system. The values expressed in the commandment "Honour thy father and mother" show up in everyday behaviour and in social policies. Failure to honour a parent may lead to informal sanctions, like criticism from a sister or brother. Extreme neglect may lead to the charge of elder abuse and legal sanctions. Functionalism draws connections between large-scale (macro) social structures and individual action.

Finally, structural functionalism assumes that society changes or evolves in a positive direction. It explains social problems as dysfunctions, and it proposes to correct these dysfunctions through the use of experts in planning and the helping professions (McDaniel and Agger 1982)

Gerontologists have used the functionalist perspective more than any other perspective in their study of aging. Gerontology's most influential theories, disengagement theory (Cumming and Henry 1961), activity theory (Neugarten, Havighurst, and Tobin 1968) (both discussed in Chapter 6), and modernization theory (a theory that describes the transition from traditional to modern society, discussed in Chapter 3) (Cowgill and Holmes 1972) all rely on structural-functionalist assumptions. Riley (1971, 1987; Riley, Johnson, and Foner 1972; Riley, Foner, and Waring 1988) also produced a dominant theory based on structural-functionalist principles: age stratification theory.

Age stratification theory focuses on the flow of age cohorts through the life cycle. Gerontologists define an age cohort as a group of people born in the same period of time. All of the people born between 1945 and 1954, for example, form an age cohort. According to age stratification theory, people in each cohort move or flow through society's predetermined age grades as they age. (An age grade is a period of life defined by society. Childhood, adolescence, and young adulthood, for example, are all age grades in Canada.)

People born in the same period experience the transitions from one stage to another at roughly the same time. They also experience the same historical events at the same time in their life cycle. People who are in their 40s today, for example, experienced the cultural changes of the 1960s in their teens and early 20s. These people still have an interest in the music of that period, and easy-listening or soft-rock radio programs cater to this large group. People in their 30s today lived through the 1960s as children. They may recall the events of that decade, but the cultural, social, and political turmoil of those years had less effect on them.

Riley (1987) says that society also changes as people age. So, the norms and roles learned by each new cohort change as society changes. The norms of adult behaviour that people learn in their childhood, for example, may no longer fit when these same people reach adulthood. Many older people today, for example, learned in their childhood that sex outside of marriage was immoral. Now, due to widowhood or the influence of the changed values of their children and grandchildren, many older people have had to rethink this point of view. Younger people will similarly have to make changes in their own values as they age and as society changes.

Age cohorts constantly move along as if on an escalator. As one group leaves an age grade, a new group takes their place. Each age grade (youth, young adulthood, and so on) places expectations on its members and offers people new roles. Also, each cohort brings new norms and values to its age grade.

This leads to a dialectic between individuals and societal structures. Changes in norms and values lead to changes in social organizations. These changes, in turn, shape the process of aging. For example, new cohorts of older people, with interests in travel and education, will bring changes to the traditional programs offered in senior centres. Some senior centres may close because they cannot meet the demands of these new seniors. Others may remain open by adapting their programs to serve newer cohorts of older people. These changes in programs will also change the way younger and middle-aged people think about later life.

Age stratification theory relies on many of the assumptions of the structural-functionalist approach to aging (Estes, Wallace, and Binney 1989). First, it assumes that norms and values influence individual aging. Second, it describes the relationship between the individual and society as a feedback loop. Change begins with the individual cohort or with large-scale historical or social change. These changes then lead to change in other parts of the social system. Third, it tends to see society as a homogeneous set of structures and functions that all people experience in the same way.

This perspective has its limits. For example, people of the same age do not all experience the world in the same way. The age stratification theory overlooks each person's interpretation of the world (Passuth and Bengtson 1988). The theory also makes little reference to the tensions and conflicts between social groups in society. It says little, for example, about the differences between growing old as a poor woman compared with growing old as an upper-middle-class man. Streib and Bourg (1984) have criticized this theory for the latter reason. They say it overlooks inequality within age cohorts (e.g., social class differences between people aged 30–39 years old) and that such variations within cohorts may have a greater influence on people's lives than the norms and values related to their age grade. A person's race or gender will lead to different behaviours and to different responses to sociohistorical events even for people in the same age cohort. A policy change, like a decrease in government pension payments, will have different effects on poor and wealthy seniors.

Cockerham (1991, 60) sums up this critique when he says that "a weakness of age stratification theory is that differences within, not just between, age cohorts are not given sufficient consideration. Besides socioeconomic factors, gender, race, and ethnicity may also shape the aging experience within cohorts, and age stratification theory does not account for such differences." Still, age stratification theory has made a major contribution to our understanding of aging. It orders many complex phenomena and accounts for the relationship between the individual and society.

The Conflict Perspective

Few gerontologists have used the conflict perspective in their work. But a new interest has developed in social conflict and aging. Researchers have begun to study the causes of poverty in later life, women and gender discrimination, the ideology of aging as a social problem, and pensions and policies (McDaniel 1989). The conflict perspective holds that society consists of conflicts between dominant and subordinate social groups (McDaniel and Agger 1982).

The **political economy theory** that grew out of the work of Karl Marx exemplifies the conflict perspective. This theory focuses on conflict and change in social life. It traces this conflict to the struggle between social classes and to the resulting dominance of some groups and the subordination of others in society.

Marxist theory, for example, predicts that because older workers work more slowly and have less stamina, they will become less useful to industry as they get older. Companies will tend to fire or retire older workers and hire younger, faster workers at lower wages.

Work on the political economy of aging looks at aging in the modern state. Gerontologists have looked at the influence of global economics on the treatment of older people in developing nations (Hendricks 1982), the impact of retirement and pensions on aging (Myles 1984), and social policy in an aging society (Estes 1979; Guillemard 1983).

The political economy approach traces the origins of older people's problems to the political and economic structure of capitalist society. It also looks at how social programs and policies for older people serve the interests of middle-aged, middle-class professionals.

Myles (1984) used the political economy approach to study pensions in Canada and other liberal democracies. He traces the development of modern, state-run pension plans to the struggle between labour and the owners of the means of production. Workers today expect pensions to form part of their wage package, but employers resist paying this money. For this reason employers support government pension programs. This allows them to pay less into workers' pension programs.

Myles (citing Murphy 1982) says that for this reason Canada's Old Age Security Act of 1951 gained the support of industrialists. More recently, labour unions have played an important role in deciding pension entitlements. Myles (1984) reports that increased labour union organization leads to better public pensions, as do increased political power of working class parties, and the right to strike. He also found that the electoral process itself leads to better pensions. Political

parties pay attention to have-not voters when an active electoral process exists.

Myles's (1984) work shows the strengths of the political economy approach to aging. First, it places the study of aging in the context of large political, historical, economic, and social forces. Second, it views public pensions as the outcome of a struggle between competing groups. Third, it predicts that economic and political forces will shape future changes in public pensions. Myles says that

> both the right to retire and the rights of the retired are the outcome of a political process. Thus, politics, not demography, determines the size of the elderly population. The social, legal, and political constituency we now call the elderly was created and given form by social, political, and economic forces; it can be destroyed or transformed by these same forces. (1984, 120)

The political economy approach looks beyond the individual to understand the forces that shape individual aging today. It broadens gerontologists' understanding of aging and offers another way to interpret the origins and effects of social policies. Estes (1979), for example, shows how welfare programs lead to more middle-class jobs for service workers, but often fail to help older people.

The political economy approach emphasizes the impact of history and economics on individuals, but it sometimes overemphasizes the poverty and problems older people face. It also tends to view the individual as the product of political and economic forces and pays little attention to individuals' interpretations of social life. It says little about the ways in which individuals shape their world through their interactions with others. Still, the political economy perspective presents a valuable way to understand the impact of society on the individual.

The Future of Gerontological Theory

Baum and Baum (1980) have summed up the characteristics of gerontological theories. First, they say that in most cases gerontologists have adapted their theories from other social sciences. Social scientists, for example, have used modernization theory for many years to describe the transition from a rural, traditional society to an urban, modern society in developing nations. They have also used interactionist theory and the political economy approach to study relationships and institutions in modern society.

Second, Baum and Baum (1980) say that most gerontological theories describe relationships between age groups. **Disengagement theory,** for example, views retirement as a way to create a smooth transition from one generation to the next. Political economy theory studies the conflict between age groups over the use of economic resources.

Third, all of these theories try to make sense of the complex, multidimensional fact of aging. They show that no single explanation of aging can account for everything we know.

What theoretical ideas will emerge in social gerontology in the years ahead? Moody (1988b), Kenyon (1988), and others support the wider use of interpretive theories in gerontology. **Dialectical theory** (one type of interpretive theory), for example, says that aging has many dimensions (physical, psychological, social, and historical). Dialectical theory focuses on the asynchronies that exist between these dimensions. For example, a sudden illness (a physical change) or the death of a spouse (a social loss) can lead to a psychological crisis. Dialectical gerontology highlights the crises and tensions in individual and social life. It argues that these moments of crisis force a person to reflect critically on his or her own life and on the social environment. This reflection on life crises and our responses to them lead to growth and development. Dialectical theory and other interpretive theories (hermeneutic and critical theories) work to foster self-understanding and personal development.

Future theorists may look to the natural sciences for new theoretical insights. Some theorists, for example, have already used the general systems, catastrophe, and nonequilibrium systems theories, which are based on biological, mathematical, and thermodynamical research, respectively (Schroots 1988). Gerontological theories offer many explanations of aging. Their variety reflects the many dimensions of gerontological research. Each of these perspectives gives us a different insight into what it means to age.

RESEARCH ISSUES AND METHODS

Research Issues

Gerontologists use a variety of theories to direct their research and explain their findings. They also use a number of methods that help them to study the process of aging. The proper use of these methods ensures that researchers come up with reliable and valid findings. Improper use can lead to biased and confusing results. The following discussion will give a glimpse of the methodological issues that gerontologists face.

Hendricks and Hendricks (1981) say that studies done on aging in the 1960s, for example, supported many of the negative stereotypes of aging. These studies often focused on sick and institutionalized older people. They used nonrandom samples of people to draw conclusions about all older people.

Also, many studies done in psychology until the 1960s used a **cross-sectional research design.** This type of method studies people from many age groups at one point in time. These studies found that older age groups, compared with younger age groups, scored lower on intelligence tests. This research supported the view that people get "simple-minded" as they get older. But these studies tended to confuse differences *between age groups* (differences due to when a person was born) with *changes due to aging.* Baltes and Schaie (1982), for example, found that younger people had more education than older people. This, they say, may account for a large part of the differences in younger and older people's test scores.

Much of the early research on aging used the cross-sectional method. This method allowed researchers to gather data in a short time at a low cost. This allows policy-makers to assess and meet the needs of different age groups fairly quickly. Most researchers still use this method. Researchers in a single study can ask a broad range of questions. This gives a detailed snapshot of a group of people at one point in time (Charness 1995).

Still, this method causes problems. As the early intelligence studies show, cross-sectional studies confound environmental effects (such as lower education levels in older cohorts) with age changes (e.g., changes in intelligence due to increasing age). The findings from cross-sectional studies cannot tell us whether aging (maturation) leads to changes in intelligence, health, or any other variable that changes over time.

Longitudinal research designs attempt to overcome this problem. A longitudinal study looks at a single group of people at two or more points in time. For example, a longitudinal study of how aging affects intelligence might test the same group of people at ten-year intervals. These results give a truer picture of the effects of age on intelligence, because this kind of study avoids the problem of trying to compare different cohorts (e.g., people with different educational backgrounds due to the historical conditions in their childhood) (Hirdes and Brown 1994). Gerontologists use longitudinal studies when they want to learn about age changes, but this method also creates problems. Environmental changes—historical events, changes in the economy, or changes in political values—can confound changes due to aging. Havens (1995a) says that longitudinal studies of older people face special problems. These include: loss of people in the study due to death, illness, and moving; inability to respond due to chronic illness or cognitive decline; and a shift in the sex ratio due to the deaths of more men than women in later life (see also Hirdes and Brown 1994).

These examples show the kinds of problems gerontologists face when they search for the causes of change in later life. Gerontologists generally place changes in old age into one of three categories:

1. **Age effects** due to physical decline. These changes appear with the passage of time. They include an increase in the body's fat-to-muscle ratio, less lung elasticity, and decreases in bone density. They also include environmentally caused changes like wrinkled skin and cataracts caused by the sun.

2. **Cohort effects** related to the time of a person's birth. A cohort refers to a group of people born around the same time (usually within a five-year period). People born in a certain cohort often share a common background and view of the world. People born just after World War II, for example, were the first cohorts exposed to large doses of television. This shaped their entertainment habits and lifestyles.

3. **Period effects** due to the time of measurement. This includes historical effects on measurement, like an ongoing war, or changes in health habits, like increased exercise. These effects have different influences on different age cohorts.

Gerontologists try to disentangle these effects to understand the causes of aging. Maddox and Campbell (1985, 20) call this the "age/period/cohort (APC) problem." Gerontologists use a number of research designs to look at these three effects and understand change in later life.

A third method, **time-lag comparison,** tries to overcome the problems raised by simple cross-sectional and simple longitudinal designs. Time-lag studies look at different groups of people of the same age at different points in time (e.g., 70-year-olds in 1960, 1970, and 1980). This type of study tries to measure differences between cohorts. Like cross-sectional and longitudinal methods, the time-lag method also presents problems. It confounds cohort effects with environmental ones. If a research study finds that 70-year-olds in 1980 visited doctors less often than 70-year-olds did in 1960, this may be due to the better health of 70-year-olds in 1980 (a cohort effect) or it may be due to some change in the health care system like higher costs to users (an environmental effect).

Each type of study creates problems when it comes to interpreting results. In addition, longitudinal and time-lag studies pose practical problems. First, they often take many years to complete—years during which researchers must wait before they can show results to granting agencies or to the public. Second, they are expensive to maintain. This can force the researcher to apply for new grants for each wave of the research. The researcher must compete with all other applicants, but cannot tailor sample size or limit the research to fit new funding conditions (Havens 1995a). Third, subjects in longitudinal studies drop out (or die), biasing results in later rounds of the study (Birren 1968, 549). Fourth, longitudinal studies require institutional support. The time needed to complete a longitudinal study means that researchers may die or move before the study ends. A research centre or university can see the study through and provide a home for the data (Havens 1995a).

Exhibit 2.2

Longitudinal vs. Cross-Sectional Designs

The chart below shows the difference between cross-sectional and longitudinal designs. The cross-sectional study took place in 1930. It studied three age groups (10-, 20-, and 30-year-olds) in that year. The longitudinal study also began in 1930. But it measured the 1930 birth cohort three more times (in 1940, 1950, and 1960) at three different ages (10, 20, and 30 years old). The time-lag study measured 30-year-olds at four different times (1930, 1940, 1950, and 1960).

Cohort Time Measurement

Source: Adapted from "Life Span Developmental Psychology: Introduction to Research Methods" by P.B. Baltes, H.W. Reese, and J.R. Nesselroade. Copyright © 1977 Brooks/Cole Publishing Company, Pacific Grove, CA 93950, a division of Thomson Publishing Inc. By permission of the publisher.

Gerontologists have solved some of these problems by turning simple cross-sectional and simple longitudinal designs into sequential designs. Birren (1968) describes a sequential design as a series of cross-sectional studies during a longer longitudinal study. The cross-sectional studies allow for quick data collection. The longitudinal study provides a check on cross-sectional findings. These two methods together also provide time-lag data on the sampled members of same-aged groups at different times.

The Aging in Manitoba study (Government of Manitoba 1973) offers this kind of option to researchers by providing comparable data on health and health care needs for a random sample of older people in the province at different points in time. This type of study allows researchers to compare the needs of different age groups in a given year (e.g., 66–75-year-olds and 76–85-year-olds in 1971) (Havens 1980). It also allows researchers to study the changes in these groups' needs over time (whether the needs of the sample of 75–84-year-olds have changed in the ten years from 1971 to 1981). It also allows researchers to see whether social changes have affected all age groups (e.g., whether all groups of older people used hospitals more in 1971 than in 1981). Researchers can then separate period effects—effects due to social conditions at the times of measurement (e.g., new medical care policies)—from effects due to aging (such as the need for more medical care as a person ages).

Botwinick (1984) shows that these complex designs still do not unconfound time of measurement, age, and cohort effects, though they do give researchers more information about the group under study. He concludes that unconfounding variables takes a great deal of time and effort. Without the effort, the researchers could make a fundamental error in understanding, but even with it, the researcher still has to explain, for example, what specific historical events led to changes in health care use or how these events translated themselves into different behaviours. "Separating the confounds," he says, "is not the end of the line, it is but the beginning" (1984, 400). Whatever method the researcher chooses, Botwinick's final comment on methods still holds: "Common sense and logic," he says, "must accompany the analysis separating the confounded variables" (1984, 403).

Types of Research Methods

Gerontologists use psychological tests and surveys to study aging, but they also use other research methods. Researchers in each dimension of aging (biomedical, psychosocial, socioeconomic-environmental) have their preferred methods.

Pharmacologists, chemists, and neurophysiologists, for example, use laboratory techniques and controlled experiments to study aging; historians use libraries, archives, diaries, and even paintings (Fischer 1978; Aries 1962); literary scholars use plays, novels, and poetry (Berman and Sobkowska-Ashcroft 1985, 1986, 1987; de Beauvoir 1978; Manning 1989). Some studies require more than one method—a questionnaire survey of a large population, for example, may include a psychological test, and an anthropological field study may include the study of a society's literature and history as well as a measurement of the people's physical condition.

Researchers have recently expanded their interest in certain research issues. Statistics Canada publications for general use, for example, now routinely include separate information on age groups over age 65 (e.g., groups aged 65–74, and 75+) (Statistics Canada 1990e). This presentation of data recognizes that age cohorts among the 65+ group often differ from one another. It also recognizes that we need more information about the growing population of very old people. Researchers also focus more now on the differences between men and women as they age. Studies of retirement, widowhood, and social life, among other topics, all show the importance of gender differences in later life (Streib and Binstock 1990). Sociohistorical methods and critical analyses of data have developed with the growth of a political economy approach to aging. Studies of retirement policies (Myles 1984; McDonald and

Wanner 1990), for example, have used this approach. Gerontologists' interests continue to grow and expand. As this happens, researchers will develop and use the methods that best answer their questions.

GERONTOLOGY TODAY

Research on aging in Canada has increased in the last ten to fifteen years, and it will continue to increase as the population ages. One series of monographs presents a detailed review of research in Canada on selected topics. The monographs include studies of demographic change (McDaniel 1986), ethnicity (Driedger and Chappell 1987), retirement (McDonald and Wanner 1990), and family ties (Connidis 1989a). The federal government has conducted a series of General Social Surveys that focus on topics like health and social supports. Reports from this research (Statistics Canada 1987b; Stone 1988) give a detailed look at family and social supports throughout Canada.

Chappell (1995) says that research has recently begun to play an important role in policy and program development. Applied research has gained new status. In December 1987, for example, experts from various disciplines conducted the first national study of Alzheimer's disease and other dementias. Health and Welfare Canada funded a Collaborative Study Centre to conduct the study. The centre linked the University of Ottawa's Department of Epidemiology with the federal Laboratory Centre for Disease Control and with researchers at universities across the country.

The study took place in five parts of the country: British Columbia, the Prairie region, Ontario, Quebec, and the Atlantic region. Each region contains a consortium of researchers who work through a total of eighteen study centres. Each study centre conducted the core study, but most also focused on a single topic of interest to researchers in that region. This study produced the first national picture of the incidence and impact of dementia in Canada. It also produced some of the first nation-wide data of this kind in the world (Eastwood et al. 1992).

In May 1988, the Canadian Strategy for Science and Technology (Innov-Action) spent $240 million to establish Networks of Centres of Excellence (NCE) across Canada. The program set up fifteen national networks with a total of over 500 scientists to "promote fundamental and long term applied research and to provide an opportunity for the nation's best researchers to work together in support of Canada's long term industrial competitiveness" (Inter-Council 1988, 1).

The NCE sponsored the Canadian Aging Research Network (CARNET), which began in 1990. CARNET has four research programs based at the universities of Toronto, Guelph, and Manitoba. Research in this program includes studies of formal supports, new products to enhance independent living, work and eldercare, and cognitive function. CARNET has also developed relationships with corporate partners to develop useful products and technology.

Three national longitudinal studies began in the early 1990s: the Canadian Study of Health and Aging, 1991; the Survey of Labour and Income Dynamics, 1993; and the National Population Health Survey, 1994 (Havens 1995a). The Canadian government also conducts a General Social Survey of social well-being each year and other surveys related to issues like health care, activity, and fitness (Black 1995). These studies and the others noted above show a trend toward large-scale, interdisciplinary research. They also show that Canada's pool of gerontologists has grown in size and in expertise. Collaborative studies save money by pooling researchers' skills and resources. They also create interdisciplinary teams that can carry out sophisticated analyses of large data sets.

This research and the many other studies conducted by researchers throughout Canada expand our understanding of aging. They also help governments, social service agencies, and professionals to plan better programs for older people.

Chappell (1982b; 1995) suggests a number of strategies for improving communication between researchers and practitioners:

1. Each partner (researcher and practitioner) should recognize and respect the other's contribution to the research project.

2. Partners in research must have an ongoing dialogue. Researchers must meet with nonresearch partners at the start of a project and when it comes time to analyze the data. This takes time, but makes both parties feel that they own the findings.

3. Researchers need to write simply. One researcher I know had a sign above his desk that read, "Eschew obfuscation." This humorous saying reminded him to avoid jargon in his writing.

4. Service delivery organizations that fund research can set up meetings between researchers and service delivery staff. Staff members can then use the latest research results to benefit their clients.

5. Researchers should circulate drafts of research reports widely. Get input from interested non-researchers. This often leads to better analysis of findings and gives the research a better chance of having practical value.

6. Researchers should present their findings at public forums to shape policy for the elderly. They should get to know and have frequent contact with policy-makers and practitioners.

This collaboration between researchers and practitioners also opens researchers to new research questions. Practitioners can tell researchers about their concerns and the concerns of their organizations. Researchers can help practitioners shape their concerns into a research question. Older people themselves can play an active role in the research process. They can serve on advisory boards to research centres, they can share views on the meaning of research findings, they can attend research forums, and they can encourage governments to sponsor more research to meet their needs.

Chappell (1995) says that the 1990s have brought a new recognition of applied research. In the past, some social scientists thought of applied research as tainted and biased. But Canadian researchers have shown that they can do rigorous research on issues of practical concern. Studies of social networks (Strain and Payne 1992), housing (Joseph and Martin-Matthews 1993), and recreation (Cousins 1995a) have all shown the value of applied research.

Today, government funding agencies encourage researchers with applied research interests. Health Canada's Seniors Independence Research Program (SIRP), for example, funds studies that can help older people stay independent. SIRP supports multidisciplinary, collaborative research on diseases and disabilities like Alzheimer's disease and osteoporosis. These diseases affect the independence of older people. SIRP funded a national study of Alzheimer's disease. It also encourages the use of varied research methods (SIRP 1991). For example, SIRP funded an academic conference on research methods and applied research (Matthews 1995).

Universities, colleges, and technical schools have begun to add gerontology courses to their programs. Many universities also sponsor certificate programs in gerontology. These programs allow professionals who work with the elderly—nurses, social workers, dentists, policy planners—to learn more about the latest research on aging. Nearly all provinces also have a social services division that directs programs for the elderly and a provincial gerontologist or a gerontology consultant who helps create new programs based on the latest research (Health and Welfare Canada 1982b). All of this activity makes gerontology one of the fastest-growing and most exciting fields today.

THE FUTURE OF GERONTOLOGICAL THEORY AND METHODS

What theories and methods will gerontologists use in the future? First, gerontologists will create new and more sophisticated **quantitative methods.** These include structural equation models, longitudinal factor analysis, and multivariate effects models. These will emerge as computer power increases and as gerontologists apply methods used in other social sciences. These methods will allow gerontologists to test new and more complex theories.

Second, gerontologists would like to link the micro- and macro- levels of theory. The age stratification theory comes closest to doing this now, though it has its limits. Like other theories that try to explain a great deal, it remains abstract. Passuth and Bengtson (1988) support the further development of political economy and phenomenological theories. These theories, they say, allow gerontologists to stand back and analyze social processes. Both approaches reveal hidden sides of aging. Both approaches challenge the myths of aging. And both approaches explore ways to create a good old age.

Third, **qualitative methods** will continue to play a role in gerontological research. Qualitative methods can explore the experience of aging at a

time when more and more people will want to know about that experience. Qualitative methods can also reveal the diversity of later life. Still, only a small number of researchers will use these methods. Achenbaum (1993) found no reference to qualitative research in the *Encyclopedia of Aging* (Maddox 1987), the *Handbook of the Biology of Aging* (Schneider and Rowe 1990), or in the *Handbook of Aging and the Social Sciences* (Binstock and George 1990). The positivist paradigm that dominates gerontology gives less value to qualitative study. This makes it riskier for researchers to build a career on this kind of work.

Fourth, studies in the humanities will add new methods to gerontological research. This will include linguistic analysis, the study of paintings and photos, and autobiographical analysis. New topics of interest in the future will lead to new approaches to the study of aging.

Researchers will develop new methods as they work to answer new questions about aging. Chappell (1995, 26) says that "the research question ... should drive our methodological approach and not vice versa." Researchers should choose the method that best suits their needs. A bias for or against one research method or another only stifles the search for knowledge. A more open approach to varied methods will lead to a better understanding of aging in the future.

SUMMARY

1. Three broad areas make up the field of gerontology: biomedicine, psychosocial studies, and socioeconomic-environmental studies. Social gerontology includes psychosocial and socioeconomic-environmental studies. It also includes practice-related research.

2. Gerontologists use theory to guide their research and to interpret their results. Micro- and macro-level theories exist. These include interpretive, functionalist, and conflict theories. Each theory gives a different and valuable insight into aging.

3. New theoretical approaches draw on current thinking in the natural sciences (general systems theory and catastrophe theory) and the social sciences (dialectical theory).

4. Gerontologists have developed methods to disentangle age effects (changes due to age)

from changes in groups due to differences in cohorts, historical events, and the effects of repeated testing.

5. Gerontologists also borrow methods from traditional disciplines like biology, chemistry, history, philosophy, and anthropology. Researchers have begun to shift their interests as their knowledge grows. New statistical reports now present separate statistics for the oldest age groups. New critical methods of analysis have also emerged as gerontology has grown.

6. Today gerontologists often apply the methods of natural science to the study of aging. Researchers refer to this type of science as positivism. Positivism assumes a nonreflective object of study. Critical gerontologists use other methods to study aging. They use in-depth interviews, observation, and policy analysis. These methods expose some of the forces that shape older people's lives.

7. New research thrusts in Canada will provide national data on Alzheimer's disease, caregiver burden, and the application of research to creating products for older people.

8. Gerontology today is one of the fastest-growing fields of study. It can make old age a better time of life by increasing knowledge about aging and by modifying or creating social structures that meet the needs of older people.

STUDY QUESTIONS

1. List and describe the three main areas that make up the field of gerontology. What areas does social gerontology include? Compare the major focus of the social gerontologist with the focus of the medical gerontologist.

2. Explain the function of a sociological theory. Gerontologists classify theories into two categories. Define these two types of theories and the three perspectives that these theories can take. Critique each of these perspectives.

3. State the major characteristics of gerontological theories. What theoretical ideas may emerge in social gerontolgy in the future? Where will future theorists look for new theoretical insights?

4. What is the most significant problem with using a cross-sectional method to gather gerontological data? How can researchers overcome this problem?

5. What method do gerontologists use to overcome the age-period-cohort (APC) problem?

6. List at least six methods that gerontologists use to study aging.

7. How does gerontological research benefit society? Suggest a number of strategies for improving communication between researchers and practitioners. How can this improve the benefits that society gets from the study of aging?

8. Define the new field of critical gerontology. How does critical gerontology differ from traditional gerontology? What methods do critical gerontologists use to obtain data?

KEY TERMS

age effects   an effect on a person's life due to physical decline. These changes appear with the passage of time.

cohort effects   an effect on a person's life related to the time of a person's birth.

cross-sectional research design   a design that studies people from many age groups at one point in time.

dialectical theory   a type of interpretive theory. It says that aging has many dimensions (physical, psychological, social, and historical). Dialectical theory focuses on the asynchronies that exist between these dimensions.

disengagement theory   views disengagement from activity (e.g., retirement) as a way to create a smooth transition from one generation to the next.

functionalist perspective   this perspective holds that "social order is based on cooperation, interdependence, and shared values, adjustment by the individual to society, and societal equilibrium" (McDaniel 1989, 52).

interpretive perspective   focuses almost exclusively on the micro-level of social life. It looks at how people define situations, how they create social order, and how they relate to one another in daily life.

longitudinal research design a design that looks at a single group of people at two or more points in time.

macro-level theories these theories focus on "social structure, social processes and problems, and their interrelationships" (McDaniel 1989, 51).

micro-level theories these theories focus on individuals and their interactions and are used to explain phenomena like the relationship between adult children and their parents, changes in memory with age, and the effect of negative attitudes on older people.

period effects an effect on a person's life due to the time of measurement. This would include historical effects on measurement, like an ongoing war, or changes in health habits, like increased exercise. These effects have different influences on different age cohorts.

political economy theory a theory that grew out of the work of Karl Marx. It focuses on conflict and change in social life. It traces this conflict to the struggle between social classes and to the resulting dominance of some groups and the subordination of others in society.

qualitative methods these methods include in-depth interviews, analysis of the content of documents or artifacts, and observation (Reinharz and Rowles, 1988).

quantitative methods these methods include census data, national social surveys, and epidemiological studies. Quantitative research uses statistical methods and mathematical models to analyze data.

time-lag comparison time-lag studies look at different groups of people of the same age at different points in time (e.g., 70-year-olds in 1960, 1970, and 1980).

SELECTED READINGS

Birren, James E., and Vern L. Bengtson, eds., *Emergent Theories in Aging*. New York: Springer, 1988.

Reviews of social scientific theories as they apply to gerontology, traditional gerontological theories, and new theoretical perspectives. This book shows the growing richness of theoretical work on aging today.

Cole, T.R., D.D. Van Tassel, and R. Kastenbaum, eds., *Handbook of the Humanities and Aging*. New York: Springer, 1992.

Articles discuss aging in ancient Greece and Rome, the meaning of aging in the major religions, and creativity in later life. The editors include discussions of aging in literature, history, and philosophy. This handbook shows how the scope of gerontological research and scholarship has broadened in the past few years.

Matthews, Anne M., ed., (1995). "Methodological Diversity." *Canadian Journal on Aging*, 14(1) (1995). Special issue.

This issue contains articles by English- and French-Canadian gerontologists. The articles discuss both quantitative and qualitative research issues. These include an analysis of feminist methodologies, longitudinal research, and action research. A good look at the diversity of methods used by Canadian gerontologists.

P A R T   2

Historical Change

C H A P T E R 3

Aging Then and Now

INTRODUCTION

In Laurel Creek, West Virginia, old men retire to the porch. They watch the traffic go by, they talk to friends and neighbours, and they arrange for part-time work. Life on the porch in the early years of retirement allows a man to keep in contact with the community. When a man gets older and his health fails, life on the porch allows him to draw on his social credit. People stop to check on him, and they make trips to the store to get his groceries. If bad health keeps him indoors, his absence from the porch alerts people that he may need extra help. When a man nears death he may come out to the porch to receive last visits from friends and neighbours. Life on the porch keeps a man part of the community until he dies (adapted from *Human Behavior Magazine* 1977).

Life on the porch matches an ideal we have of late old age. It reminds us of another time—a time when people grew up and died in the same town, when neighbours knew one another well, and when the young respected the old. Today many people feel that old age has become devalued. We push old people aside in retirement, advertisers tell everyone to "think young," and even birthday cards make fun of aging. One card reads, "Roses are red, violets are blue, thank goodness I'm not older than you." It seems that in the past people enjoyed old age, but that in modern society this is less so because older people get little respect or attention.

Has old age become worse over time? Did simpler societies offer a golden age to the old? Or do we just like to believe things were better in the past?

Social gerontologists try to answer these questions. They take two approaches: some gerontologists study past societies to see how such societies viewed and treated older people; others study modern societies to see how different social structures lead to different experiences of old age. This chapter will examine both points of view. It will look at: (1) how aging differs in different types of societies, (2) how social structures affect aging, and (3) how aging today differs from aging in the past.

FOUR TYPES OF SOCIETIES

Sociologists Gerhard and Jean Lenski (1974) describe four stages of sociocultural evolution. These stages correspond to four types of societies: hunting and gathering, horticultural, agricultural (agrarian), and industrial. They also list specialized types of societies including herding and fishing societies. Recently, sociologists have described a new sociocultural stage: **post-industrial society.** This chapter will look at four major societal types: (1) hunting and gathering, (2) agricultural, (3) industrial, and (4) post-industrial societies. Each type of society has a unique social organization. And each type exists today. But they also represent a historical evolution from the simplest to the most complex forms of social life. A look at these societies will show the impact of social organization on the status and treatment of older people. This review will also give a picture of how aging has changed over time.

Hunting and Gathering Societies

Humans lived in hunting and gathering bands for a million years or more and only settled into agriculture between ten thousand and twenty thousand years ago. People in hunting and gathering societies survive by gathering wild plants and by stalking or trapping wild game. These groups (sometimes as few as twenty people) move constantly from place to place in search of food. They resemble an extended family. Their technology is simple, consisting mainly of bows, spears, and fire, and they have no permanent settlement.

Most simpler societies have undergone rapid change in the past few years. Industry has destroyed many of their habitats. And some groups find themselves confined to reservations. Other groups have adapted to new technologies and new opportunities. They now work for the large companies and government projects that use their land. These contacts have led to changes in traditional nomadic life. The discussion below refers to traditional hunting and gathering life as it existed in the past and where it exists in the present. Where possible, the discussion below compares traditional life with life for these people today.

Archaeologists estimate that people in hunting and gathering societies had a normal life expectancy of about eighteen years (Lerner 1970; Cutler and Harootyan 1975; Howells 1960). Cowgill and Holmes (1972) report that these societies defined a person as old by age 45 or 50; and Simmons (1970; 1960), in a study of seventy-one contemporary simple societies, says that people in these societies were considered old at 50 or 60 years of age. He estimates, on the basis of scarce data, that these societies rarely had more than 3 percent of their people over age 65. Therefore, when the terms "old" and "elderly" are used here in connection with simple societies, they refer to people 50 to 60 years old.

Cowgill (1972), and Press and McKool (1972) present four conditions that lead to support for an older person in simple societies. First, the person needs an important role to play in social life; second, the older person must live near and fit into his or her extended family; third, he or she must control some important material or informational resource; and fourth, the group must value collective rather than individual development (Sokolovsky 1990). Few simple societies fulfil all of these conditions. So, treatment of older people varies among them.

Amoss and Harrell (1981) say that one condition more than the others leads to a good old age in primitive societies. They say the old have high status when their contribution to subsistence outweighs their cost to the group. Older people do well when they still have a valued role to play in the culture. Their ability to give to the group depends on two things: first, the culture must offer alternative roles for older people to play as they lose their strength, and, second, the older person must have good health.

The Inuit (Eskimo) of Canada serve as a good example of a present-day hunting and gathering society. They live in a climate that demands physical strength to survive, but they love and respect their elders and allow their older members to take part in social life as long as they can (Holmes and Holmes 1995). Men, for example, "retire" slowly from work. As a man loses his strength, younger male members of the community or household do more of the winter hunting. The older man may then take shorter hunting trips or teach the young how to hunt. Older Inuit women have an easier time moving into old age than do men (this is true of women in most nomadic societies). They pass the heavy work on to younger women and spend more time taking care of the children. "Because women's work is less demanding … the decreasing physical capability of a woman does not appear so obviously or so dramatically" (Guemple 1974, 205, cited in Holmes and Holmes 1995).

Older men and women find their own ways to adapt to decreases in their strength. Older men will start to hunt early in the spring in order to stockpile food for the winter. They may also strike a bargain with a young hunter—the older man may fix the gear while the younger man hunts. Older women sometimes adopt children. The Inuit allow their elders to play new roles in society as their health and strength decline. For example, the Inuit value their old as much for their knowledge and wisdom as for their work. A person still gives something to the group when he or she recalls and passes on the knowledge of Inuit lore. This social role makes the old person useful to the group and improves his or her status and treatment in the community (Holmes and Holmes 1995).

Not all groups make these arrangements for older members. The Chipewyan, for instance, who live in Canada's northern prairies, have no roles for older men to play. The Chipewyan do not place a high value on knowledge of tribal lore or craftwork. A man has status when he succeeds at hunting, but when he stops hunting he loses respect and power in the group—people label him "elderly." Men will do anything to avoid this label. Some continue to hunt even when their health fails. Sharp (1981) reports the case of a man who had

Exhibit 3.1

Do Nomadic People Abandon Their Elders?

In any nomadic society, if people live too long and become decrepit or demented, the group may abandon or kill them.

Jacob Bronowski (1976) shows this in his film series and book *The Ascent of Man*. In Iran, he follows a nomadic group called the Bakhtiari on their yearly journey to their summer pastures. The tribe climbs over six mountain ranges, through high passes and snow, until it reaches the Bazuft River.

Bronowski says the test for the group comes at the river. The Bazuft, a trickle in summer, swells each year with melting snow and spring rain. The group—men, women, and animals—must swim across. For the young, crossing the Bazuft stands as a test of adulthood. For them, life begins, but for the old, Bronowski says, life ends. The camera records in detail the struggle to cross the river. The current batters horses, donkeys, sheep, goats, and people. The young men swim for their lives and help the animals get across. But then the camera pulls back to focus on two figures among the rocks—a dog and an old man. The dog races back and forth looking from the man to the group below. The man sits silently with his back against the rocks watching the tribe cross the river. No emotion shows on his face. He no longer has the strength to cross the river, and the tribe will go on without him. "Only the dog is puzzled to see a man abandoned," Bronowski says. "The man accepts the nomad custom; he has come to the end of his journey" (1976, 64).

Life in many nomadic cultures demands this kind of choice. The tribe must move on to survive, and the old, who cannot keep up, get left behind. This man accepts his fate. He may have left his own parents to die in the same way. This dramatic case shows the dark side of life in primitive society. "In a vigorous community," Turnbull (1961, 35–36) says, "where mobility is essential, cripples and infirm people can be a handicap and may even endanger the safety of the group."

A study by Maxwell and Silverman (1977, 37) found that 80 percent of the societies that did not value the elderly lived as nomads for at least part of the year. The harsher the environment, the greater the chance a group will kill or abandon its aged. Killing the aged shows up most often in societies that have irregular food supplies, move often, and live in severe climates (Simmons 1970, 240).

just recovered from a heart attack and had emphysema, but still went into the bush alone. His wife worried that he would kill himself through over-exertion, but he would rather have risked his life than be called old. The Chipewyan offer fewer options to older men than do the Inuit.

Most of these simpler societies have changed in the recent past due to contacts with the modern world. Elders on Holman Island in Canada "now watch color televisions in the comfort of heated homes equipped with running water and electricity" (Condon 1987, 5, cited in Holmes and Holmes 1995). They no longer rely on their contribution to group survival. They now get government pensions. Graburn (1969, cited in Holmes and Holmes 1995) found that pensions freed elders from economic dependence on their families. This gave elders new status as well as a source of income for their children. But, at the same time, the cash economy led to less respect for older people. Modernization has decreased the role of elders as educators and caregivers to their grandchildren. In some cases grandchildren (who learn English in school) cannot understand their grandparents' language.

Researchers report that hunting and gathering societies distinguish between two different stages of old age. In the first, a person retires from the heavy work of middle age, but he or she still has good health. In the second stage, the older person gets sick or becomes demented or frail. Simmons (1960) calls people in this second group the "overaged."

In Inuit society, for example, older people keep their status as long as they do some useful work for the group. Their status drops if illness makes them dependent. People make fun of the frail elderly, say nasty things to them, or ignore them. The "over-aged" get the worst cuts of meat, have little money, and have to do without trade goods. A stranger may take in an Inuit who outlives his or her spouse, children, and close relatives, but this person will get little respect and will have to do the worst work (Guemple 1977).

The Inuit also abandon their aged when they become liabilities to the group. They do this as a last resort, and they encourage the older person to make the decision (Guemple 1980). But sometimes the group will withdraw its support rapidly, thus hastening death (Glascock and Feinman 1981; Holmes and Holmes 1995).

Glascock and Feinman found this same ambivalence to old age in fifty-seven simple societies they studied. They found that in 35 percent of the societies younger people treated older members well, and in 80 percent young people showed respect for the aged. Many of these same societies abandoned and killed their elderly (Koty 1933; Maxwell and Silverman 1977). Glascock and Feinman (1981) found nonsupportive treatment (abandoning and killing the aged) in some form in 84 percent of the simple societies they studied. This, they say, contradicts the idea that all simpler societies support the aged. Research shows that simpler societies vary in how they treat the aged and that treatment of the aged often depends on how much an older person contributes to or takes from the group.

Agricultural Societies

People in agricultural societies live on food produced from farming the land. These societies have more complex technologies than hunting and gathering societies. They also have more complex social structures, including social classes and bureaucracies.

Humans settled into villages and cities for the first time in the Middle East, China, and India about ten thousand years ago at the end of the last Ice Age. For the first time in human history, societies gathered a surplus of food. In these societies older people often owned property, and they used property rights to get support from the young. "Property rights," Simmons (1970, 36) says, "have been life-savers for the aged ... The person who controlled property was able to get more out of life and to get it much longer. Indeed, the importance of property for old age security can hardly be overrated."

As a general rule, in agricultural societies, those with land command the most respect, those without land the least. All over the world, property rights create a legal dependence of the young on the old (Amoss and Harrell 1981). Old people among the Gwembe Tonga of Zambia today, for example, get power by owning livestock and land (Colson and Scudder 1981). Older people among the Etal Islanders of Micronesia gain respect when they own property. The Etal look down on old people who hold on to all their land, but they think of a person as foolish if he or she gives it all away. The land serves as an inheritance bribe (Nason 1981).

Americans in the past also used property to hold power in old age. Fischer (1978) studied aging in the United States from 1607 to the present. He found that young men had to wait to inherit their fathers' land before they could start families. In the 17th and 18th centuries that meant a son might reach age 40 before he owned the farm. Fischer (1978, 52) calls the land "an instrument for generational politics"; parents used it to ensure good treatment in their old age.

Fischer (1978) also found that this kind of coercion bred hostility. The diaries of Colonel Landon Carter, for example, report signs of growing anger between the younger and older generations. One night in 1776, Colonel Carter reports, his son, Robert Wormeley Carter, invited friends over for gambling with cards. When the enraged Colonel ordered the game to stop, his son exploded and called his father a tyrant. The two men almost came to blows. After that the Colonel carried a pistol with him in the house. He wrote in his diary, "Surely it is happy our laws prevent parricide ... Good God! That such a monster is descended from my loins!" (Greene 1965, 250, 310, 315, 713, 763, 1004, 1102, cited in Fischer 1978, 75).

Other agricultural societies in the past also expressed their dislike for the aged, some more openly than Americans. The Greek playwright Aristophanes mocked the old in his plays; Aristotle derided the way most people grew old (though he thought a philosopher could live a good life even in old age); and in the Renaissance Machiavelli portrayed the old man as a lecherous fool in his play *La Clizia*. Tension between the generations sometimes surfaced in song. An Austrian folksong (Berkner 1972, cited in Fischer 1978, 69) says:

> Papa, when will you give me the farm?
> Papa, when will you give me the house?
> When will you finally move to your little
>   room
> And tend your potato patch?

Studies of English Canadians in the late 19th century show the same tensions between the young and the old. Historical accounts indicate that parents gave a great deal of thought to how they would pass their land down to their children (Gagan 1983b; Mays 1983), and the children, who worked to improve the family farm, sometimes into their thirties, expected to get it as a reward for their work. In 1853 Susannah Moodie wrote that "death is looked upon by many Canadians more as a matter of ... a change of property into other hands, than as a real domestic calamity" (Moodie 1853, cited in Gagan 1983b, 185).

Ontario farmers kept intergenerational tension low by passing the land down before they died. Synge (1980) says that the older people stayed on the land with the inheriting child and his family. The young or the old couple built a new house nearby. "They [the parents-in-law]," one woman says, "stayed on in the house till they built a place out back for them" (Synge 1980, 138). Getting the land early in life must have reduced some tensions between the generations, but it created others. Selling the land to the young, for example, risked the older generation's old-age security. Parents, when they did sell the land to their children, often kept a few acres for themselves to maintain their independence in old age (Mays 1983).

The content of farmers' wills also suggests some worry about future security. Wills stated exactly what the inheriting son was to do for his parents. One will describes in detail the kind of food ("flour, pork and butter and milk, potatoes and other vegetables"), the kind of firewood ("plenty of good wood ready for use"), the transportation ("a horse and buggy"), and the cash ("$100 a year") that a son had to give his mother for the rest of her life (Gagan 1983b, 186).

Inequality in Old Age in Agricultural Societies

Treatment of the aged in agricultural societies differed by social class. The elderly who owned land in these societies had power until they died. For this reason, older people who owned land commanded the greatest respect in societies from Canada to traditional China (Ikels 1981). The poor and landless lived less well and got little respect.

"To be old and poor and outcast in early America," Fischer (1978, 60) says, "was certainly not to be venerated but rather to be despised ... Old age seems actually to have intensified the contempt visited upon a poor man. A rich old man was the more highly respected because he was old, but the aged poor were often scorned." A New Jersey law in 1720 ordered police to search ships for old people and to send them away. In one case the crew of a ship placed a poor, sick old man on a barren island and left him there to die (Fischer 1978).

Fischer also describes drunk, crippled old men who hid in cellars and roamed the wharves at night looking for food. Poor old widows had low status too, but their womanhood made old age and poverty worse (as it did in most countries). Without money a woman was degraded and left to depend on others for support. Neighbours sometimes forced old widows to move away to keep poor rates down. Even their own children sometimes turned them away. "If the aged poor were only a small minority [in early America]," Fischer (1978, 61) says, "their misery was great."

Laslett (1976) reports that in Elizabethan England the Poor Law of 1601 made children responsible for their aged parents—but only their parents. This excluded other relatives from aid by law. The existence of a law that spells out the relations between the generations suggests that custom bound children to their parents less than we may have thought. Laslett says that in some cases a parent who lived with his or her children got listed in official records as a "lodger, receiving parish relief" (1976, 95). In other cases the children moved into the family cottage and left their widowed mothers and sisters in poorhouses.

Stearns, in a study of customs in France, says that "older women were treated horribly in the popular culture of traditional society" (1977, 119). Villages expected widows over age 45 to stay single, and literature made fun of older women. Even the grandmother role got little prestige. Other historians have also documented the suffering of the aged poor in the past and in less industrialized societies (Hufton 1975). The large numbers of poor people and their misery argue against the idea of a golden age in pre-industrial society.

Agricultural society, in its treatment of older people, looks like a mirror image of primitive society. In the simplest societies the old had no wealth, but they received respect as long as they gave to the group. The !Kung San, for example, roam the Kalahari desert throughout their lives and have little property. The young revere their elders as storytellers, spiritual leaders, and healers (Biesele and Howell 1981). In agricultural societies the elderly get the most respect if they own property and keep it from their children until late in life or until they die. In agricultural society "a firm hold on the strings of a fat purse," Simmons (1970, 46) says, "was one effective compensation for declining physical powers" (see also Cowgill 1986, 108). The old may be respected in this kind of society, but they are not often loved by the young (Fischer 1978).

Modern Industrial Society

The agricultural revolution created a new form of society. Agriculture produced a surplus of food and gave rise to the first cities. It created social classes and based status on ownership of property. This kind of society dominated until the middle of the eighteenth century, when three interrelated changes began to reshape social life: (1) industrialization, (2) urbanization, and (3) the demographic transition.

These changes took place over two hundred years, and they still affect society today. They began at various times in different places, and sometimes one type of change—economic change, demographic change, a change in values—had more influence on a society than another. Scholars still argue over which change came first in which society, but taken together these three changes revolutionized social life and led to a new age of older people.

Industrialization

By the 19th century most of Europe had begun to industrialize. Industry began to use steam and water power to increase productivity; the factory system gathered workers and raw materials in cities; and transportation systems spread the production of factories to all classes and countries. Some countries industrialized before others, and some more quickly, but by 1850 industrialization had changed the shape of European society (Stearns 1967).

Industrialization both caused and resulted from the breakup of rural life. Cottage industry, in which small groups of workers in villages produce mostly for local needs, failed as the factories produced more and cheaper goods. At the same time, parents could no longer keep their sons on the farm with the promise of future inheritance. As death rates declined, families had too many sons who wanted the land. The younger sons had to move to the city to find work, and the city welcomed them as a cheap source of labour. The new pace of work and life in the city freed young people from traditional ties and beliefs (Stearns 1967) and led to a decrease in the status of older people.

Industrialization decreased the status of older people in another way: companies looked for ways to get the older, supposedly less effective, older worker out of the workplace. In the United States in the 1920s, for example, some companies used physical exams to screen out older workers (Holmes and Holmes 1995). Also, retirement rules, supported by both labour and management, forced older workers out of work. Management liked retirement because it allowed them to release workers who were costly because they had seniority. Unions supported retirement because in return they won seniority rights (first hired, last fired rules) from management (Haber 1978). In short, unions traded older workers' right to work for younger workers' job security. Retirement expressed in a formal rule the decline of the older person's status in industrial society.

Urbanization

Canadian society changed from a rural to an urban one between 1851 and 1950 (Biggs and Bollman 1991). During the 19th century both men and women migrated to the cities. Cross (1983) found that Montreal attracted large numbers of young women from the crowded countryside. Bradbury (1983) describes Montreal in 1871 as a city in transition from pre-industrial to industrial life. Accounts of this time say little about the elderly.

Katz (1975) gives one of the few reports on what life was like for older people in a Canadian town. He studied Hamilton, Ontario, between 1851 and 1861. In a report on 597 land-owning men in 1851, he counted only 26 men aged 60 or over out of 597, or about 4 percent of the population. (Men among the poorer classes died younger and probably made up a smaller portion of the population than the landowners.) Men who owned land had the most security in old age, and men aged 60 and over were the largest group of landowners. However, after age 60, Katz shows, a man's power began to decrease, and men over 60 had a greater chance of having less land from one year to the next than any other group. Men 60 and over were also the least likely to have a servant (a sign of wealth). After age 60, Katz (1975, 163) says,

men often "decline[d] into difficult circumstances."

Synge (1980) says that in small businesses and on farms older people could adjust their work to suit their health and strength, but in industrial cities older people had to meet the demands of the workplace or quit. No public pensions existed in the 19th century, and many older people in the cities had no private savings. In addition, they often had to take the lowest forms of work, move into public homes for the aged, or live in poverty, especially if they were without children (Haber 1983; 1993).

In North America, urban life undermined traditional society in another way. The cities supported a market system in which individuals could accumulate wealth outside the family structure. Inequality in society began to grow as some individuals gathered wealth for themselves through trade. Those who were successful turned from public affairs to private concerns. This focus on the self broke the individual's communal bonds, including those that linked the older to the younger generation (Fischer 1978).

Synge (1980), who studied working-class families in Ontario in the early 20th century, found that city life made old age an uncertain time. Young people earned their own wages and gave money to their parents while they lived at home. But when these children grew up and moved out, parents lost this income. Few social services existed for older people, and an unmarried daughter often looked after her parents as they aged. Families sometimes passed the job of care from one child to the next. Synge reports the case of one old woman who lived for periods of time with each of her children for her last twenty-five years.

Katz (1975) found that few older people in Hamilton lived with their married children, and the poorest households were least likely to house an older relative. Only 8 percent of households in 1851 and 10 percent in 1861 had adults of two or more generations. "Only when old age and loneliness were combined," Katz (1975, 254) says, "would a parent move in with her children."

Katz (1975) also found that 58.8 percent of women aged 60–69 were widowed, almost double the rate of men. Women of the poorest social class (Irish Catholic women) faced an eight-times greater chance of widowhood than women of the highest class (Canadian-born Protestant women).

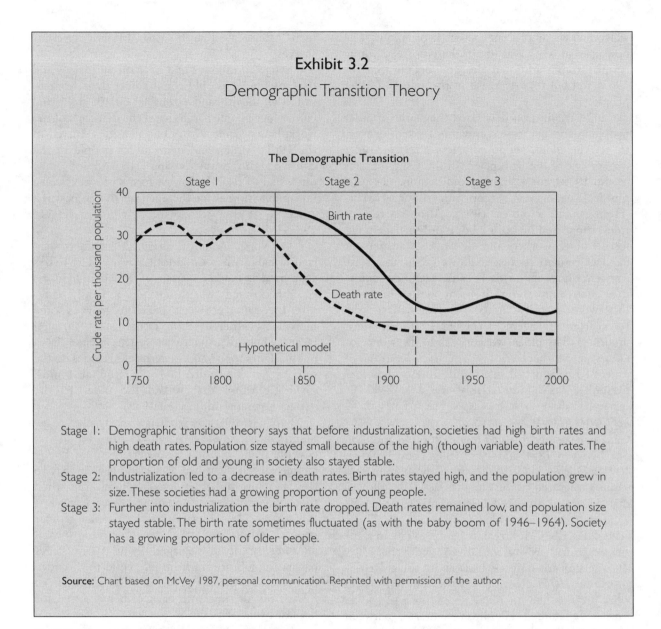

Exhibit 3.2

Demographic Transition Theory

The Demographic Transition

Stage 1:   Demographic transition theory says that before industrialization, societies had high birth rates and high death rates. Population size stayed small because of the high (though variable) death rates. The proportion of old and young in society also stayed stable.
Stage 2:   Industrialization led to a decrease in death rates. Birth rates stayed high, and the population grew in size. These societies had a growing proportion of young people.
Stage 3:   Further into industrialization the birth rate dropped. Death rates remained low, and population size stayed stable. The birth rate sometimes fluctuated (as with the baby boom of 1946–1964). Society has a growing proportion of older people.

Source: Chart based on McVey 1987, personal communication. Reprinted with permission of the author.

Poor widows had little or no savings and no pensions from their husbands. The poorest women, especially those without children, would finally be recipients of charity (a special charity, the Ladies' Benevolent Society, grew up to help them) or live in a "house of refuge and industry" (Katz 1975; Synge 1980).

On the surface the new freedom and equality in urban industrial Canada made all people more alike, but for the old they meant a decrease in status. "A really democratic ethic," Cowgill (1986, 51) says, "is incompatible with any system of stratification based on ascribed statuses ... You cannot

have gerontocracy [rule of the eldest] and democracy at the same time."

The Demographic Transition

The demographic transition refers to the changes in population that led to a high proportion of older people among the developed nations (of Europe and North America). This transition, which took place in North America at the end of the 19th century along with industrialization and urbanization, was a three-stage process. The stages outline how European and North American societies shifted from a youthful to an older population structure.

Stage 1: 1300–1750. Before the 18th century, population had been relatively stable. High birth rates were balanced by high death rates. French studies of the 17th century estimate that there were about eight children to a normal marriage and that about 70 percent of the households had children. Children made up 45 percent of the French population at that time (compared with half that rate in industrial societies today) (Laslett 1965).

Only a small number of people lived to old age in pre-industrial society. Figures exist only for scattered populations before 1800, but they give some idea of the proportions of people 65 and over. A national census in Iceland in 1703, for example, reported 4.6 percent of the population was 65 or over; Belgrade in 1733 reported 2.1 percent; and Nishinomiya, Japan, in 1713 reported 6.6 percent. A listing of counties in England from 1599 to 1796 showed people aged 65 or over made up between 1.4 percent and 6.4 percent of the population. Charbonneau (1970, cited in Lavoie 1992) estimates that in Tourouvre-au-Perche in France, people born between 1720 and 1770 had a life expectancy of only thirty-three years. Those born between 1670 and 1719 had a life expectancy of only twenty-five years. Rarely in any of these places did the 65-or-over population top 10 percent, and Laslett (1976) cautions that past the age of 60 people tended to exaggerate their age.

Stage 2: 1750–1850. Three phenomena caused rapid population growth in Europe from 1750 on, and also changed the proportion of young and old people in society. First, the death rate decreased, because war fatalities decreased; the cycle of epidemics ended; improved hygiene in cities led to better health; border controls stopped the spread of disease; and food supplies increased due to better climate and more open land (Braudel 1981; Stearns 1967).

Second, the birth rate stayed high and in some cases increased. New lands opened and allowed earlier marriage in the countryside. Young people in the cities, who did not have to wait for their parents' land, married young. Better nutrition and more opportunity led people to have more children.

Third, more people lived to old age, and the proportion of older people in the population began to grow. In France, the first society in Europe to have an aged population, the proportion of the elderly rose from 7.3 percent of the population in 1776 to 10.1 percent in 1851 (Laslett 1976).

Stage 3: 1850–Present. The birth rate and death rate in Western Europe had both declined by 1900. This completed the transition to an aging population. The biggest change in death rates came from improvements in the general standard of living. Diet and hygiene in the cities improved. Clean underwear, soap, coal for heat, and glass in the windows all helped people stay healthier. Improved housing and more efficient treatment of water and sewage decreased disease. As the standard of living rose, the virulence of disease—and so the death rate—declined.

These changes led all social classes to decrease the number of children per family (Stearns 1967). Middle-class families led the way. They had smaller families to ensure that their children would have the money needed to enter the middle class themselves. Rural families followed later in order to ensure that each of their children would get a good portion of land. Children had a different meaning in agricultural and industrial societies. In an agricultural society children are an economic asset: they help produce food, care for the farm, and increase a family's wealth. In an urban society children are an economic liability. They cost the individual family money to raise, and the family gets little economic benefit from them. These facts led to a decreased birth rate.

From 1850 onward the proportion of older people in the developed nations grew. Longer life expectancy meant that more people lived into old age. But more than anything else, it was the decrease in the birth rate after industrialization that led to a higher proportion of older people in society.

The three trends mentioned previously—industrialization, urbanization, and the demographic transition—put an end to almost all of the following conditions, each of which had supported the high status of older people:

1. ownership and control of property

2. a monopoly on special knowledge

3. ancestor worship and a high value placed on tradition (where the old provide a link to the gods)

4. society organized around kinship and extended family

5. small, stable communities

6. high mutual dependence of group members

7. small numbers of older people

8. special roles for the aged (Rosow 1965; Eisdorfer 1981)

In the past two centuries the economy, the structure of family life, and the relations of the old to the young changed. Old age became more common, but it also lost its privileged status (Fischer 1978).

Modernization Theory

Some researchers believe that a sharp break took place as societies moved from an agricultural to an industrial way of life. This break, where it occurred, affected all social institutions and social relations.

Cowgill and Holmes (1972) refer to the shift from agricultural to urban society as a process of modernization. Modernization, according to Cowgill (1974, 127), is "the transformation of a total society from a relatively rural way of life based on animate power, limited technology, relatively undifferentiated institutions, parochial and traditional outlook and values, toward a predominantly urban way of life based on inanimate sources of power, highly developed scientific technology, highly differentiated institutions matched by segmented individual roles, and a cosmopolitan outlook which emphasized efficiency and progress."

Cowgill and Holmes (1972) theorized that the status of older people decreases with increases in modernization. They reviewed studies of fourteen contemporary societies from around the world. These ranged from a study of the Sidamo of southwestern ethiopia to two studies of Israeli society (one of a kibbutz) to a study of the aged in the U.S.S.R. They found that small numbers of older people, ancestor worship, low social change, extended families, a value system that emphasized the importance of the group, stable residence, and low literacy (where the group values the old for their knowledge) all lead to high status in old age. In modern societies, where such conditions are reversed, older people have low status (Cowgill and

Holmes 1972). The authors concluded that these trends support **modernization theory.**

Other research supports this theory. Palmore and Whittington (1971) studied the change in status of the elderly in the United States between 1940 and 1969. They used a "similarity index" to compare the status of the aged (65 and over) and the non-aged (14–64 years old) and found a decrease for the aged in the weeks and hours worked as well as a decrease in income and education level compared with younger people. They found improvements only in the health status of the elderly. They conclude that even with improvements in health and health care, the elderly lost status relative to the young over the thirty years they studied.

A later study by Palmore and Manton (1974) also supports the idea that status drops in old age in modern society. The authors compared people 65 and over with people 25–64 in thirty-one countries. They used an "equality index" (EI) to compare these groups. This index measured employment status (employed or not employed), occupation for those employed, and years of education completed for each group. The researchers then computed the similarity of the young and the old in each country. EI scores ranged from the 90s for underdeveloped countries like Iran to the 50s for developed nations like the United States or Canada. (A score of one hundred means perfect equality.) "This indicates," the researchers write, "that the socioeconomic status of the aged is almost equal that of younger adults in some underdeveloped countries, but has apparently declined to about one-half of equality in some of the modernized countries" (Palmore and Manton 1974, 207). Bengtson and his colleagues (1975) studied more than 5000 men in six developing countries and found that negative views of aging increased with increased modernization.

Other writers, many of them historians, have criticized modernization theory. Laslett (1976) says that the theory compares the present, with its problems, with an idealized past. He shows, to the contrary, that the treatment and status of the aged varied from time to time and from place to place before modernization (as it varies today among simpler societies). O'Rand (1990) says that modernization theory cannot account for the complexities of social change. It misses the differences within the older population based on age cohort differences, socioeconomic differences, and historical conditions. Within a single society, researchers often find ambivalent feelings toward the aged (Vatuk 1982; Trexler 1982).

Most people think of Japan, for example, as a country that reveres its aged. Traditional tenets urge respect and honour for the elderly, and the Japanese try to follow this rule (Plath 1972). But Plath found a second view of aging in Japanese culture—*obasute* or "discarding granny." This theme of abandoning the old, he says, runs through Japanese literature from the 6th to the 20th century. Even within industrial societies the treatment and status of the aged has differed from class to class and between women and men (Achenbaum and Stearns 1978; Quadagno 1980).

A study by Cherry and Magnuson-Martinson (1981) also questions the simple application of modernization theory to all developing nations. They propose that researchers look at the country's political economy to understand the status of the aged. These writers studied the status of older people in modern China. They learned that China had a tradition of great respect for the elderly based on authority, power, and prestige, but that this system of age stratification had declined in recent years. They did not find, however, that industrialization, urbanization, education, demographic change accounted for the decreased status of the old. Instead, their research showed that the decline in older peoples' status came about as a result of government social and economic policies.

Communist laws, for example, ended arranged marriages, which was one way in which the old had maintained power over the young, and gave married couples more autonomy. Land reform also led to less control of property by the old and less leverage for fathers over sons. The Chinese government emphasized equality between the generations. Older people would now get recognition for helping their families with child care, housework, or industrial work.

Cherry and Magnuson-Martinson (1981) suggest some modifications to modernization theory be made based on their work. First, the theory needs to take into account social policies that affect age-group relationships. Second, a society can alter the status of the aged directly (through political action) rather than through processes of modernization. Third, some groups in a society will experience a greater change in status than others (e.g., men compared with women).

Some research describes a middle ground between the pro- and anti-modernization camps. Cohn (1982) found that the status of the old does drop at the start of modernization. Changes in education, leading to more professional and technical jobs, cause this drop. But, as modernization increases, the educational and occupational gap between the old and the young decreases. The modern welfare state, Maddox (1988, 3) says, has "tended to treat older adults rather generously." Improved retirement benefits, more adult education, and job retraining will raise the status of the aged in the future.

Post-Industrial Society

Today some people in the developed nations still live badly in old age—they have poor housing, poor nutrition, bad health, and little money. Studies also show that some people still hold negative attitudes toward the aged. Baker (1983a) studied Canadian university students' attitudes toward various ages. He found that the youngest and oldest ages received the lowest ratings. Middle-aged people received the highest ratings. He found the same pattern in attitudes regardless of the social class, gender, or age of the people making the judgment. He describes the findings as an inverted U with status low early in life, rising to mid-life, and falling in old age.

Graham and Baker (1989) replicated this study with a sample of older people (mean age 67). Their results showed that the older people gave less negative ratings to all age groups, and they rated the young and old less negatively compared with the middle-aged. Still, the researchers discovered the same inverted U-curve in the older sample's ratings as was found in the earlier university student sample. The researchers say that these similar findings from two diverse samples support the idea that Canadians see old age as a time of low status.

Knox and Gekoski (1989) studied 1400 undergraduates' judgments and attitudes toward age. They studied two different approaches to making judgments. The researchers found that regardless of their rating method students gave older people

Exhibit 3.3

The Dega and the Nacirema: Then and Now

About 30 years ago, an anthropologist named Horace Miner described some of the peculiar body rituals among a tribe called the Nacirema. Most of his writing concerned the repressive sexual attitudes and primitive medical practices of that culture. Very little was said about the position of older people among the Nacirema. However, an unpublished manuscript was recently discovered which describes the relationship between the Nacirema and another tribe called the Dega. This manuscript was written in 1958 by Dr. L.N. Rekab of Adanac University, and portions of it are presented below.

I believe this material is vitally important because it gives us an eyewitness account of the abuses inflicted upon the Dega by the Nacirema culture, and because it offers a historical baseline by which we can judge the progress which has been made since that time.

For some time now, members of the Dega tribe have been migrating into the village occupied by the Nacirema. Relations between the two cultures are far from cordial. Perhaps the best way to describe the situation is that the Nacirema treat the Dega like visiting relatives who have overstayed their welcome. The Nacirema prohibit the Dega from taking any active part in the economy, except for some childcare work, or tending the sick and the lame among their own group. This work is called *gnireet-nulov* and is never rewarded with pay or goods. The Nacirema explain that the Dega refuse to accept compensation because that would take away the honor of *gnireet-nulov* and turn it into mere labour. The Dega told me they had never been offered any pay.

The Dega appear to be slaves to the Nacirema, although neither group seems aware of the relationship. The Dega are not subjected to long days of hard labour, but are kept in a state of enforced idleness. They are given a meagre allowance for food and clothing, called a *noisnep*, which gives them a standard of living not much better than the poorest Nacirema. Some of them are permitted to live in their own individual huts, but many of the Dega are forced to live in group quarters called *gnisrun* homes. They are confined to small rooms, usually shared with another Dega, all their personal possessions are taken away from them, and they are tended by apprentices of the village witch doctor.

The daily life of the Dega is occupied mainly by sedentary activities. The Nacirema encourage them to play children's games and to do some weaving, but the articles they produce are given away, not sold in the market. A favorite pastime of the Dega is a sport called *flog*. Small white rocks are hit with a stick, over a large area of long grass, sand pits, and ponds. The aim of the game is to find the rock after you hit it. Each player has to buy a dozen special rocks from the Nacirema who makes them, who is called the *orp*. The player who returns at the end of the day with the most rocks is given free drinks by the other players. Sometimes the wealthy Nacirema also play *flog*, but never on the same day as the Dega. The Nacirema complain that the Dega take too long to finish the game. One of the Dega told me that the reason they played so slowly was that they had nothing else to do anyway, so enjoyed the company and the fresh air ...

The temple is the major gathering place for the Dega. They attend the religious ceremonies regularly, but conversations with the priest and the Dega revealed a curious discrepancy. While the priest was sure that they believed fervently in the religious teaching, most of the Dega said that they did not really believe, but like to see their friends and listen to the music.

The temple is also used for activities which are a major source of excitement for the Dega. The most popular activity is a game of chance called *ognib* which consists of chanting by the priest and the creation of magic geometric shapes by the Dega. At the end of each chant, one of the players shouts the name of the game and jumps up and down with great excitement. The priest inspects the magic shape to see if it has been done correctly, and if it was, presents a clay pot to the winner ...

The sexual practices of the Dega are either nonexistent, or are very well-hidden. No births have ever been observed among the Dega, so it may be inferred that they are beyond their reproductive years. However, there seems to be no sexual activity at all. I asked one Nacirema warrior if he had ever heard of such activity among the Dega, but he just laughed loudly, saying that would be like two rocks

(continued)

Exhibit 3.3

The Dega and the Nacirema: Then and Now (cont.)

trying to lay an egg!' When I asked if any Nacirema had sexual relations with the Dega, he turned pale, spat on the ground, and told me he would rather sleep with a wild pig. Even though some of the Dega are very good-looking, the Nacirema consider them all as sterile, sexless individuals.

What will become of the Dega? Their future looks bleak, but I observed that new members arrive almost daily from the forest outside the village. Because of this immigration, there seems to be an increase in their numbers each month. When food was scarce, there was some talk among the young Nacirema warriors of attacking the Dega, but this was discouraged by the older warriors, who seemed more sympathetic to them.

The total population in the village seems to be kept in check by the disappearance of the Nacirema warriors after the ceremony of the gold sundial. This ceremony occurs only among the oldest of the

Nacirema, who are given a small sundial and sent off into the forest to rest before they battle with the great spirits. Only one warrior ever returned while I was in the village, and he had gone crazy. He came back and began embracing the Dega, crying out 'Brother! Sister!' ... He was put out of his deluded misery by a young warrior.

What has happened in the quarter century since Dr. Rekab wrote this account? Well, the Dega have not died out. In fact, their numbers have increased dramatically since then, and most of the abuses put upon them by the Nacirema have disappeared. The *gnisrun* homes have been improved, the *noisnep* plans are providing a better standard of living for the Dega, and the Dega themselves are taking on a more active role in Nacirema society. To be sure, there are still some problems that need solving. However, it is a sure bet that the Dega will never again be second-class citizens.

Source: Reprinted by permission of Transaction Publishers. "The Dega and the Nacirema," by P. M. Baker, in B. Hess and E. Markson, eds., *Growing Old in America*, 3d ed. (New Brunswick, NJ: 1987).

the lowest rating on two of three scales—effectiveness and personal acceptability.

A study of selected Canadian literature for children (de Vries 1987) found some loving portrayals of older people. "Older characters always have their annoying side," de Vries (1987, 43) says, "but attempts are made to appreciate their point of view." A study of novels over four decades found both positive and negative views of old age. Matthews and Thompson (1985) studied forty novels—half of them winners of the Governor General's Award for Fiction. They found that most older characters had high self-esteem and high life-satisfaction, but they also concluded that more recent novels treated the aged as comic figures and saw this as a possible sign of growing negative attitudes to the old.

These studies show that in Western society people feel ambivalent toward old age. Kastenbaum and Ross (1975) call this an "approach–avoidance dilemma." They say that

limited resources and the physical decline that comes with old age make it unattractive in all societies. On the other hand, most people know and like older individuals, and at all times in history younger people have cared for and loved their aged relatives and friends.

In spite of some negative attitudes toward old age, older people as a group in North America live materially better lives than older people at any time in history. Schulz (1980) reports "major breakthroughs" in private and public programs that deal with economic problems in old age.

He cites as proof the increase of private pensions, property tax relief, and a rise of almost 100 percent in U.S. Social Security benefits from 1970 to 1980 (Schulz 1980). He could also have included in his list improvements in Canadian Old Age Security benefits, the Canada Pension Plan, and Canada's free nation-wide health care coverage for the elderly. All these programs increase older people's independence and freedom.

Some writers predict an age-irrelevant society in the future (Fischer 1978; Neugarten 1980). This kind of society will treat individuals on the basis of what they can do, rather than on the basis of sex, race, or age. This fits with the trend in North America today to eliminate racism and sexism. Fischer (1978) points to the end of mandatory retirement as a sign of this trend, and Atchley (1980) cites better treatment of old age on television as a sign of improved attitudes toward and treatment of the elderly in industrial nations.

AGING IN THE WORLD TODAY

In the year 2000 about 18 percent of the population of the developed nations (like the United States and Canada) will be over age 60 (Salas 1982). Cockerham (1991, 35) says that "Australia and the world's entire northern tier of countries, including Canada and the United States, all of Western Europe (less Turkey), Eastern Europe and the Soviet Union, and Japan, will have at least 13 percent of their populations age 65 or older." Europe will have a greater proportion of older people than any other continent. One projection estimates that Great Britain, for example, will have 36.4 percent of its population aged 60 or over in the year 2020 (Eurolink Age Bulletin 1992, cited in Schmidt 1993). This increase in the older population will be caused mostly by a decrease in birth rates and, to a lesser extent, by increased longevity. These countries will see increases in health care and pension costs. They will try to find ways to reduce costs and yet provide services to their aging populations (Henripin 1994; Secretariat 1992).

The developing nations (such as the Latin American, African, and Middle Eastern countries) make up three-quarters of the world's population, and they too will see changes in their population structures. These countries have relatively young populations, with large numbers of children and proportionately few older people—some with as few as 2 percent of the population aged 65 and over (e.g., Ivory Coast and Afghanistan) (Araba 1988). But the death rates in these countries have begun to fall and many more people now live into old age.

The low proportion of people aged 65 and over in the developing nations, compared with that in the developed nations, tells only part of the story of aging in these countries. First, the United

Nations (UN) projects that between the years 2000 and 2025 the world population of older people will nearly double to 828 million people. And most of these people will live in the developing nations (86 percent of the older people in the developing world will live in Asia). Second, the less-developed nations will show the greatest percentage increase of older people (United Nations 1992). These nations will also see increases in their oldest old populations. Third, the developing nations have few public services to meet the needs of their aging populations.

Many developing countries will face a crisis due to these future large numbers (Cockerham 1991). Africa, for example, will see a large increase in its population aged 60 and over between 1980 and 2025. The UN projects an increase in this age group by a factor of 4.4—from 22.9 million in 1980 to 101.9 million in 2025 (Araba 1988). The UN projects an even greater rate of increase in older people in Latin America, with an increase in people aged 70 and over from 9.4 million in 1980 to 80 million in 2025 (DeLehr 1988).

In South Asia the older population will grow 174 percent from the year 1980 to 2000. In Japan it is expected to grow from 15 million people in 1980 to 33 million by 2025—from 12.7 percent to over 25 percent of the total population in forty-five years (Salas 1982). Also, the less-developed nations make up nearly 75 percent of the world's population (Population Reference Bureau 1980). The greater number of people surviving to old age in developing nations, added to the already large number of older people in the developed nations, will swell the world's aged population.

In 1950 about 200 million people in the world were aged 60 or over. By 1975 that population had grown to 350 million, and projections estimate that there will be one billion people aged 60 and over by 2025. This population will have grown by 224 percent in about fifty years, while the total world population will have grown by only about 102 percent. By 2025 the world population of the elderly (60+) will be about 14 percent of the total world population (Salas 1982).

Sixty percent of the world's elderly (60+) will live in the developing nations by the year 2000, and by 2025 that figure will climb to almost 75 percent. China alone in the year 2025 will have as many people aged 60 or over as the entire population of the United States (Sokolovsky 1990, citing

Nusberg 1982). For poorer nations, with few of the resources and with little of the social machinery needed to meet older people's needs, these changes will create problems never seen before (Salas 1982).

When nations develop, the young often move to the cities (Holmes and Holmes 1995). This leaves the aged in rural villages with little family or social support. These villages lack communications, transportation, supplies, and services that the elderly need. Older workers sometimes return to their home countries after years of working in another country. They have no work, no skills, and no pensions, and will grow old in poverty (DeLehr 1988). In rural settings, DeLehr (1988, 7) reports, old people must work as long as they have the strength. In larger centres a growing number of older people survive by "scratching out a living from rubbish dumps or peddling goods on the streets." She predicts things will get worse unless

these countries develop basic services to help older people.

Sennott-Miller (1994) says that developing nations need more information about their older populations. And they need to plan for an aging society. Countries with social programs and pension plans in place will need to adapt these programs to serve more older people (Sheppard and Streib, 1985). Gerontologists need new theories of aging to explain the changes taking place in these countries (see Exhibit 3.4) and new plans for social change that fit the needs of an aging world.

Solutions that fit Western industrialized countries do not necessarily fit the developing nations (Gillin 1986). These countries have neither the social services nor the economic resources to help the elderly poor. Nor can these countries afford the housing, health, or welfare services for the old that Western nations have set up. China, for example, had 65.2 million seniors in 1988—more than

Exhibit 3.4

Controversy: Modernization vs. Dependency Theory

Modernization theory views developed industrial societies as the model for less-developed nations and proposes that less-developed nations set up policies for older people like those used in developed countries (Neysmith and Edwardh 1983). But developed nations' solutions often do not fit the needs of developing societies. Some theorists propose an alternative theory of aging—dependency theory.

Dependency theory uses a critical Marxist approach to the study of aging. It says that the social and economic structures in a society create the status of the old and that to understand the developing world gerontologists have to understand aging in terms of the economic relations between nations. Dependency theory looks at the societal and worldwide forces that decide the fate of older people (Hendricks 1982).

Dependency theory begins with the fact that structured inequality exists between developed and less-developed societies. Less-developed or peripheral nations now depend on the developed or core nations for their economic well-being. The peripheral nations of Latin America, Africa, and Asia produce

raw materials, crops, and manufactured goods for the core nations. The core nations decide what a peripheral country should grow or make for its markets. This keeps the peripheral country dependent and poor, and disrupts the country's economic, familial, and political life.

Younger people in developing countries move off the land to work in the cities. Also, the gap between rich and poor people in these nations grows. Families, for example, grow less food for their own use. They begin to grow cash crops for export. This makes it harder for them to support large families that include older members (Gillin 1986). Older people also lose status in these societies because their knowledge does not serve the core nation's needs (Hendricks 1982). "Old people do not simply become out of date," Hendricks (1982, 343) says, "they are made obsolete. If one goal of gerontology is to upgrade the quality of life for older people in any given society, then it must first understand the structural imperatives that have shaped their control over potential resources." Dependency theory adds this understanding to the study of aging and society.

double the population of Canada. India had 32.7 million seniors (4 percent of its population). Krishnan (1990) says that even a basic pension of 100 Indian rupees would cost $3 billion Canadian and the Indian States cannot afford to provide even this small pension.

Sokolovsky (1990) reports that some of the world's poorest countries have public pension systems, but only one-third of the working population can get benefits. Often these benefits come to only small amounts, and few rural people can expect much from public pensions. One case that shows the kinds of problems people face in these countries was described in *The Globe and Mail* (1983, B8): "After 35 years as a farm labourer, Feliciano Rodriguez has retired. The Peruvian Social Security system is giving him a pension equivalent to 10 cents (U.S.) a month. All is not lost, however ... He gets an extra 2 cents a month because he is married."

CONCLUSION

Did older people live better lives in the past than they do today? Can we learn something about aging from past societies? Will aging in the future differ from aging today?

Older people's status in the past differed from time to time, from place to place, and from class to class. Some societies treated their aged badly, some treated them well, but all of these societies had fewer older people than societies today. We cannot look to the past for ways to create a good old age today. The large number of older people in the world today is a new phenomenon. And Laslett (1976, 96) says, "it calls for invention rather than imitation."

In the future, as in the past, aging will differ from society to society. The wealthier nations will have the best chance of creating a materially satisfying old age for their people. The poorer societies will struggle under the burden of more people—old and young. One thing, however, seems certain: aging populations will challenge all countries in the world. The economy, the political system, the culture, the level of development, and the age structure of a society will all affect how a society responds to this challenge.

Canada, like other countries, cannot copy past societies in its treatment of older people, but it can learn something from the past and from simpler societies. The !Kung San elders heal the sick through dance and music. In traditional Chinese culture the older woman works as a matchmaker. Among the Coast Salish tribe of British Columbia the old serve as ritual leaders. Wherever older people have had valued roles to play in their societies they have lived respected and purposeful lives. Canada can make this a goal of its policies for older people.

SUMMARY

1. Culture, custom, and the economic life of the group all influence how a society treats its older members. A study of three types of societies—hunting and gathering, agricultural, and industrial—shows that treatment of the aged differed in the past from time to time and from place to place. None of these societies created a golden age for older people.

2. Like most societies, past and present, modern Western societies show an ambivalence toward the aged. Negative stereotypes exist, and some discrimination against the aged takes place. Modern societies also offer older people independence, a high standard of living, and many opportunities for life satisfaction.

3. The developed nations have a high percentage of older people. They will have to shift resources to serve the changing needs of their populations. Post-industrial societies show an ambivalence toward older people. They provide pensions and services, but they also show prejudice toward older people. Some writers predict that this prejudice will end and that post-industrial societies will be "age-irrelevant" societies in the future.

4. Modernization theory predicts a decline in the status and treatment of the aged in modern society compared with societies in the past. Some studies that compare developed and developing nations today support modernization theory, but critics of the theory argue that it oversimplifies life in the past, ignores differences in treatment of the elderly within a society, and undervalues the opportunities for a good old age today.

5. The developing nations have large numbers of older people, even though older people make up a small percentage of their populations. This increase in the numbers of older people poses service delivery, economic, and health care support problems for developing nations.

6. Population aging has become a worldwide challenge. The response a nation makes to the challenge of aging will depend on its traditions, culture, level of development, and economic strength.

STUDY QUESTIONS

1. Identify and describe the four major types of societies. How were older people treated in each of these societies?

2. What are the four conditions that lead to support for an older person in simpler societies? How do these conditions determine the way these societies treat older people? How has modernization affected the status of elders?

3. How did older people command status and respect in agricultural societies? What kind of tension did this create?

4. Define the process of modernization. What three changes created the modern industrial society? How did these three things influence the status and treatment of older people? Why do some researchers criticize modernization theory?

5. Explain why older people in the developed nations live better materially now than at any time in the past.

6. How will an increase in the older population of the developing nations pose a problem for them?

KEY TERMS

post-industrial society societies like Canada that have gone through the industrial revolution and have become service-based, complex societies.

modernization theory this theory holds that a shift to urban life, with high technology and complex institutions, leads to a decrease in the status of older people.

SELECTED READINGS

Albert, S.M., and M.G. Cattell. *Old Age in Global Perspective: Cross-Cultural and Cross-National Views*. New York: G.K. Hall, 1994.

The authors use field research and national surveys to describe aging around the world. The book discusses older peoples' living arrangements, social relationships, and the life course. The book also looks at the effects of modernization on old age.

Cole, Thomas R. *The Journey of Life*. New York: Cambridge University Press, 1992.

The author, a historian, traces the meaning of aging from the Middle Ages to the present. He focuses his more recent analyses on the United States. Cole shows different views of aging—as a personal problem, as something to manage and control, and as something to deny. He suggests that today we need a full picture of life that includes aging and death. He suggests that our view of aging today needs to include notions of spiritual growth, a legacy, and wisdom. Cole shows how one society—the United States—has grappled with the meaning of aging over time.

Sokolovsky, J., ed. *The Cultural Context of Aging: Worldwide Perspectives*. Westport, CT: Greenwood, 1990.

This book focuses on aging in a variety of cultures. Articles include research on supports for older members of the Kung San of Botswana, grandparenting among Native Americans, and the elderly in modern Japan. A picture of the diversity of aging worldwide.

Synge, Jane. "Work and Family Support Patterns of the Aged in the Early Twentieth Century." In Victor W. Marshall, ed., *Aging in Canada: Social Perspectives*. Toronto: Fitzhenry and Whiteside, 1980.

A close look at intergenerational relations in Ontario in the early 1900s. One of the few studies of aging in Canada in the past.

Aging in Canada

INTRODUCTION

When people think about aging, they think of wrinkled skin, grey hair, and false teeth. But societies age too. From 1901 to 1991 Canada's population grew five times in size (Norland 1994). During this same period the older population grew by almost twelve times—more than twice the rate of the general population. The proportion of people aged 65 and over rose from 5 percent of the total population in 1901 to 11.6 percent of Canada's population in 1991. This makes Canada's population one of the oldest in the world, and demographers expect Canadian society to age even more in the next fifty years (Norland 1994; Statistics Canada 1989a; Stone and Frenken 1988).

This chapter will look at: (1) why Canadian society has aged, (2) the population structure of Canada today, and (3) the impact of population aging on health care and pension programs.

AGING AROUND THE WORLD

The United Nations groups the ages of societies by the proportion of their populations aged 60 years and over. It defines a country as "young" if less than 4 percent of its population is aged 60 and over; "youthful" if between 4 and 6 percent of its population is in this age group; "mature" if 7 to 9 percent of the population is in this age group; and "aged" if 10 percent or more of the population is aged 60 and over. Exhibit 4.1 presents proportions of older people for a sample of countries.

Most studies, including some United Nations reports, use the population aged 65 and over to measure population aging. We will use this figure most of the time in this text. This allows for a comparison of different societies, past and present.

European countries that went through demographic transitions first have the largest proportions of older people. Almost a century ago more than 7 percent of the populations of France and Sweden were aged 65 or over (France had 8.2 percent in 1900; Sweden had 8.4 percent in 1900). England and Wales, along with Germany, became mature societies around 1930; both had 7.4 percent of their population aged 65 or over in 1930 (Laslett 1976). The high **death rates** for young men and the low **birth rates** during World War II speeded up societal aging in these countries. By 1985 12.4 percent of France's population was over age 65; that of England and Wales was 15.1 percent; and Sweden had a 16.9 percent rate—the highest percentage in the world (U.S. Census Bureau 1987).

Canada is a relatively young nation compared with these European countries. Until 1900 less than 5 percent of its population was aged 65 and over. The country aged gradually through the first part of this century. Canada had 7.8 percent of its population over age 65 in 1951 (Statistics Canada 1984b). By 1991 Canada had 3 170 000 people, or

Exhibit 4.1

Percentages of Population Aged 60 Years and Over, Selected Regions and Nations, 1990, 2010, and 2030

Regions	1990	2010	2030
World	9.2	10.7	15.7
Africa	5.0	5.2	7.1
Latin America/Caribbean	7.2	9.6	15.9
North America	16.6	18.4	25.4
Asia	7.6	9.7	16.0
Europe	18.1	21.3	28.1
Oceania	12.9	14.8	20.3
Canada	**15.5**	**19.0**	**26.7**
China	8.6	11.7	21.1
Egypt	6.3	7.6	13.2
France	19.1	22.4	28.9
Israel	12.4	13.7	19.1
Jamaica	6.8	6.7	12.4
Japan	17.4	28.3	32.9
Kenya	4.5	3.7	5.7
Mexico	5.8	8.4	15.6
Russian Federation	16.0	18.5	25.1
Sweden	22.8	24.6	28.1

Sources: *World Population Prospects: The 1994 Revision* (United Nations publication, Sales No. E.95.XIII.16). Reprinted with permission.

11.6 percent, of its population aged 65 and over. By the year 2031 the portion of Canada's population aged 65 and over could be almost one-quarter (22.7 percent) of the total population—almost five times the proportion of older people in 1900 (Desjardins 1993). (See Exhibit 4.2.)

What caused Canada to age in the 20th century? What will keep it aging in the years ahead? And what effect will population aging have on Canadian society? A look at Canada's population—past and present—will answer these questions.

CANADA COMES OF AGE

Demographers study three conditions that affect a population's size and structure: immigration, death rates, and birth rates. Each of these demographic forces caused the Canadian population to age from the mid-1800s to the present (Beaujot and McQuillan 1982).

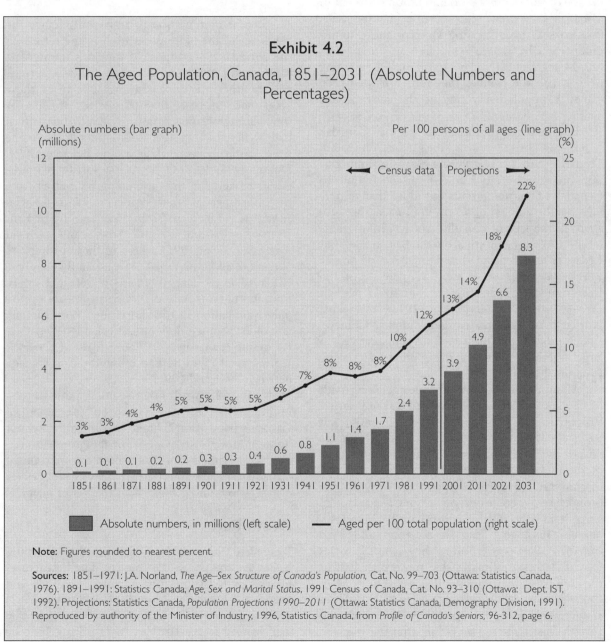

Exhibit 4.2

The Aged Population, Canada, 1851–2031 (Absolute Numbers and Percentages)

Absolute numbers (bar graph) (millions)

Per 100 persons of all ages (line graph) (%)

Census data | Projections

Absolute numbers, in millions (left scale)
Aged per 100 total population (right scale)

Note: Figures rounded to nearest percent.

Sources: 1851–1971: J.A. Norland, *The Age–Sex Structure of Canada's Population*, Cat. No. 99–703 (Ottawa: Statistics Canada, 1976). 1891–1991: Statistics Canada, *Age, Sex and Marital Status*, 1991 Census of Canada, Cat. No. 93–310 (Ottawa: Dept. IST, 1992). Projections: Statistics Canada, *Population Projections 1990–2011* (Ottawa: Statistics Canada, Demography Division, 1991). Reproduced by authority of the Minister of Industry, 1996, Statistics Canada, from *Profile of Canada's Seniors*, 96-312, page 6.

Immigration

Of the three demographic forces—immigration, birth rates, and death rates—immigration played the smallest part in the aging of Canada's population. It also affected different parts of Canada in different ways. Waves of immigration in the early 20th century brought new groups of young adults to Canada. Between 1901 and 1911 1.5 million people arrived in Canada—as many as in the previous forty years combined. Immigration in the first decade of this century accounted for 44 percent of Canada's total population increase in those years (Statistics Canada 1981a). Most of these immigrants came to Canada as children or young adults (20–34 years old) (Northcott 1988). These young people (and the families they raised) helped keep Canada's population young at the start of this century (see Exhibit 4.2).

Immigration continued to add to Canada's population until the start of the Great Depression. From 1901 to 1931 successive waves of immigration brought from 3.5 to 4.5 million people to Canada. These immigrants did more than simply increase the number of people in Canada; they also changed the face of Canadian society. Immigrants before 1900 came mostly from the British Isles, but Leacy (1983) reports that Canadians of "other European" origin rose from 37 percent of the European-born population in 1881 to 43 percent of the same population in 1911. Germans, Norwegians, Mennonites, Doukhobors, Chinese, and Southern and Eastern Europeans arrived in large numbers. Most of these immigrants were young males.

Many of the Eastern Europeans, along with Icelanders and Mennonites, settled on the Prairies. Provinces like Manitoba in the 1880s and Saskatchewan around 1911 had high birth rates due to the large number of young immigrants in their populations (Henripin 1972). This large wave of immigration partly explains the drop in the proportion of people over age 65 in Canada from 5 percent in 1901 to 4.7 percent in 1911 and 4.8 percent in 1921. This same group added to Canada's older population as they aged. Statistics Canada (1981a) estimates that more than half of the country's older immigrant population came to Canada before 1929 (see also Norland 1994). More and more older immigrants came to Canada during World War II and the first years after the war.

Foreign-born older people made up 26.7 percent of Canada's older population in 1991. This proportion dropped steadily due to decreased immigration from a high of 38.8 percent in 1961 (Norland 1994). The proportion of foreign-born people in the older population may increase somewhat in the next few years. A major wave of immigration in the early 1950s accounts for about 6 percent of Canada's growth from 1946 to 1978. These immigrants have begun to increase the size of the foreign-born older population (McDaniel 1986).

Recent immigration patterns will change the character of the older population in the future. In the period 1956–60 most of Canada's immigrants came from the United Kingdom, Central Europe, and Southern Europe. Immigrants from these areas made up more than 60 percent of Canada's total immigrant population. By 1989 this pattern had changed. Very few immigrants today come from Eastern Europe (Dumas and Bélanger 1994; Dumas 1994). In 1989 the largest portion of immigrants came from the developing nations of Asia, the Caribbean, South America, and Central America—46 percent from Asia and 15 percent from the Caribbean, and South and Central America (Logan 1991). Many of these people (44 percent of all immigrants) came as family members of Canadian residents (Dumas and Bélanger 1994). Still, immigrants have only a small impact on the older population in the short run. For example, few older people immigrate. Norland (1994) says, for example, that in 1991 "only 2.0% of Canada's seniors aged 75 to 84 had immigrated to Canada between 1981 and 1991."

Compared with other demographic forces, immigration has little effect on the aging of Canada's population (Dumas 1990). Fertility, not immigration, causes population aging or rejuvenation. But immigration does alter the makeup of Canadian society, and it creates new challenges for organizations and groups that serve older people.

Death Rates

By the late 19th and early 20th centuries, death rates began to drop across the country. The best figures for this period come from Quebec. Henripin and Peron (1972, cited in Beaujot and McQuillan 1982) say that the crude death rate in Quebec dropped by half from 24 per 1000 in 1871–75 to 12.9 by

1921–25. These figures probably overestimate the drop in death rates for Canada as a whole. Historians say that Canada's large cities still suffered from high death rates (Gagan 1983a; Cross 1983; Torrance 1981; Artibise 1977), but a steady, if not dramatic, decline did take place. Life expectancy at birth rose from 41.9 years for men and 44.2 years for women born in 1851 to 60.0 years for men and 62.1 years for women in 1931. Life expectancy at age 65 had increased to 78 years for men and 78.7 years for women in the same eighty years. This meant that more people lived longer and that more lived into late old age (Lavoie and Oderkirk 1993; Legare and Desjardins 1976, cited in Beaujot and McQuillan 1982; Nagnur 1986).

Life expectancy increased steadily for men and women at all ages between 1941 and 1981, but infants gained the most years (see Exhibit 4.3). **Infant mortality rates** (the death rates of children less than a year old) decreased by about 78 percent for both males and females from 1953 to 1986 (Statistics Canada 1990e). By 1986 less than 1 percent of children died before their first birthday (compared with about 10 percent in 1921) (Parliament 1987; Dumas and Bélanger, 1994).

Control of childhood disease, better prenatal care, and improved nutrition account for most of this change. Between 1931 and 1981 the death rate for children under 5 decreased by 90 percent (Parliament 1987). Lavoie and Oderkirk (1993; see also Lavoie 1992) say that in the mid-19th century epidemics of cholera (in 1832), typhus (in 1846–49), and smallpox (in 1885–86) led to high infant and child mortality. Nagnur and Nagrodski

Exhibit 4.3
Evolution of Life Expectancy by Age and Sex, Canada, 1921–1990

Year	At Birth Males	Females	At Age 65 Males	Females	At Age 85 Males	Females
1921*	58.8	60.6	13.0	13.6	4.1	4.3
1931	60.0	62.1	13.0	13.7	4.1	4.4
1941	63.0	66.3	12.8	14.1	4.1	4.4
1951	66.4	70.9	13.3	15.0	4.3	4.7
1961	68.4	74.3	13.6	16.1	4.6	5.0
1971	69.4	76.5	13.8	17.6	5.0	5.9
1981	71.9	79.1	14.6	18.9	5.2	6.6
1990	73.9	80.5	15.4	19.6	5.2	6.7

*The 1921 life table excludes Quebec.

This table shows a steady increase in life expectancy at birth, at age 65, and at age 85 from 1941 to 1990 for both sexes, with one exception: life expectancy at age 85 for men seems to have levelled off for 1990. Note that until 1990, women gained more in life expectancy than men at birth and at age 65 in each time period. This may be due to differences in lifestyles, habits, or environmental conditions (e.g., working conditions). The most recent figures show a change in this trend. Men at birth and at age 65 gained more years in life expectancy than women between 1981 and 1990. Changes in work patterns and lifestyles for men and women may account for this reversal.

Source: Dhruva Nagnur, *Longevity and Historical Life Tables 1921–1981 (Abridged) Canada and the Provinces*, Statistics Canada, Cat. No. 89-506 (Ottawa: Minister of Supply and Services Canada, 1986); Statistics Canada, *Canada Year Book 1990*, Cat. No. 11-402E/1990 (Ottawa: Minister of Supply and Services Canada, 1989); Statistics Canada, *Health Reports, Supplement No. 13*, Vol. 2, No. 4, "Life Tables, Canada and Provinces 1985–1987," Cat. No. 82-0038 (Ottawa: Minister of Supply and Services Canada, 1991). Adapted with the permission of the Minister of Industry, 1996, Statistics Canada.

(1988, 26) report that "infectious and parasitic diseases, including tuberculosis, accounted for almost 15% of deaths in 1921; in 1986, however, only about half of one percent of all deaths were the result of these diseases." Life expectancy at birth increased from 1931 to 1990 by 13.9 years (from 60.0 to 73.9) for men and by more than 18 years (from 62.1 to 80.5) for women (Perrault 1990; Dumas 1990).

Canada since 1951 has also seen a drop in the most common causes of death in adulthood—cardiovascular disease (including ischemic heart disease, strokes, arterial disease, hypertension, and rheumatic heart disease) (Parliament 1989). Due to these changes, men aged 65–69 showed a 19 percent decrease in mortality rate between 1951 and 1986. Women in this age group showed a 43 percent decrease during this same period.

People in the oldest cohorts show some of the greatest improvements in life expectancy. Dumas (1990, 64), for example, says that "the most spectacular progress [in the extension of life expectancy has been] realized at very advanced ages: the probability of living 10 years beyond one's 80th birthday rose from 28% in 1966 to 41% in 1986, or nearly 50 per cent in 15 years." As a result of this trend, between 1981 and 1991 the proportion of Canadians aged 75 and over increased by 22 percent and the proportion aged 85 and over increased by 31 percent (Government of Canada 1993).

Better medical care, a safer environment, and a higher standard of living mean that 98 percent of all children born in Canada today can expect to live through infancy; 90 percent can expect to live to age 50; 66 percent to age 70; and 40 percent to age 80 (Statistics Canada 1981a). This gives Canada—along with Sweden, Denmark, Norway, and the United States—one of the highest life expectancies in the world (73.1 years for males at birth and 79.7 years at birth for women). And this means that more people than ever will enter old age in this country (Government of Canada 1993).

Birth Rates

A population ages when its proportion of younger people declines. Quebec in the 1700s, for example, had a young population and one of the highest birth rates ever recorded. From 1700–30 women averaged births of one child every two years until they reached age 30. Women who reached the age of 50 averaged eight or nine children. In the middle of the 18th century the average was thirteen children apiece (Henripin 1972). During this time the birth rate ran two to six times higher than the death rate. Quebec's population grew twenty times from 1608 to 1765, and by one and a half times again by 1851 (Kalbach and McVey 1979). Death rates in Quebec began to decline after 1780, but despite this the province's birth rate was still high and the population stayed young (Kalbach and McVey 1979; Henripin 1972).

Frontier regions in Ontario also had high birth rates. McInnis (1977) and Henripin (1972) report rates similar to Quebec's in rural Ontario in the mid-19th century. A writer of the time reported that children "in Canada [are a man's] greatest blessing, and happy is that man who has a quiver full of them" (Philpot 1871, cited in Gagan 1983b). McInnis says that Upper Canada at the time "had one of the highest birth rates in the world" (1977, 202). Gagan (1983b) estimates that settled Ontario families in Peel County had eight to nine children. New immigrants to Canada before 1830 often had more.

Around 1850 Canada began its demographic transition when the birth rate decreased. Henripin (1972) shows that the birth rate in Canada as a whole dropped by about 30 percent from 1851 to 1951 (with a sharp drop during the 1930s). Though the provinces all showed the same declining trend, individual rates varied: the Quebec birth rate dropped least, by about 20 percent from 1851 to 1921; Ontario showed a sharp drop of about 50 percent during this same time; Manitoba between 1881 and 1921 showed a drop of more than 60 percent; and Saskatchewan showed a similar drop between 1901 and 1921 (Henripin 1972). This drop in the birth rate, more than any other demographic change, led to the aging of Canadian society.

Baby Boom and Baby Bust

Two phenomena affecting the birth rate—the **baby boom** and the **baby bust**—account for the greatest changes in Canadian population from 1951 to the present.

From 1946 until about the early 1960s Canada went through a baby boom. Between 1941 and 1961 the total **fertility rate**, defined by Beaujot and McQuillan (1982, 220–21) as "the average

Exhibit 4.4

Median Age* of the Population, Canada, 1881–1991 (Excluding Newfoundland)

Year	Median Age	Year	Median Age
1881	20.1	1961	26.5
1891	21.4	1966	25.6
1901	22.7	1971	26.4
1911	23.8	1976	27.8
1921	23.9	1981	29.6
1931	24.7	1986	31.6
1941	27.0	1991	33.5
1951	27.8		

* Half the population is older and half is younger than the median age.

Canada's median age, according to the table, rose 13.7 years from 1881 to 1992. The table shows a jump in the median age of 3.7 years between 1931 and 1941. This reflects the sharp drop in the birth rate during the Depression years. The table also shows a steady rise in the median age throughout this century until 1951, followed by a drop from 1952 to 1966. During these years the rise in the birth rate (the baby room) led to a decrease in the median age by 2.2 years to 25.6 years. In 1976 the median age rose again to its 1951 high of 27.8. By 1981 more than half the population was over the age of 30. The aging of the baby boom cohorts will increase the median age in the years ahead. Statistics Canada projects a continued increase in the median age into the middle of the next century.

Sources: Dominion Bureau of Statistics, *Census of Canada (1961 Census)*, Bulletin 7:1–4 (Ottawa: Queen's Printer, 1964); Statistics Canada, *1966 Census of Canada*, Vol. I (1–11) (Ottawa: Queen's Printer, 1968); Statistics Canada, *Census of Canada (1971 Census)*, Bulletin 1:2–3 (Ottawa: Information Canada, 1973); Statistics Canada 1978b, cited in Warren E. Kalbach and Wayne W. McVey, *The Demographic Bases of Canadian Society*, 2d ed. (Toronto: McGraw-Hill Ryerson, 1979), 161, Table 6:3; Mary Sue Devereaux, "Aging of the Canadian Population," *Canadian Social Trends*, Winter, 1987, 37–38; Craig McKie, "Population Aging: Baby Boomers into the 21st Century," *Canadian Social Trends*, Summer, 1993, 2–6; M.V. George, M.J. Norris, F. Nault, S. Loh, and S.Y. Dai, *Population Projections for Canada, Provinces and Territories 1993–2016* (Ottawa: Minister of Industry, Science and Technology, 1994); Statistics Canada, *Annual Demographic Statistics* (Ottawa: Minister of Industry, Science and Technology, 1994). Adapted with the permission of the Minister of Industry, 1996, Statistics Canada.

number of children that would be born alive to a woman during her lifetime if she were to pass through all her childbearing years conforming to the age-specific fertility rates of a given year," rose from 2.83 to 3.84. The **age-specific birth rate** (the number of births in a given age group per one thousand women in that age group) nearly doubled for 15- to 19-year-olds, going from 30.7 to 58.2 (Statistics Canada 1978c, cited in Beaujot and McQuillan 1982). Total births soared from 264 000 in 1941 to almost 476 000 in 1961 (Statistics Canada 1978c, cited in Beaujot and McQuillan 1982). The baby boom reversed a general trend of decreased fertility rates that had begun in the 19th century (Henripin 1972). It also reversed a century-long trend in population aging (excluding the years 1911 to 1931) that began in the late 19th century.

After 1961, Canada went into a baby bust cycle. The total fertility rate dropped from 3.84 (children per woman) in 1961 to 2.81 in 1966—a rate below that of 1941. It dropped further to 1.71 in 1992 (the rate averaged 1.7 from 1970 to 1992) (Beaujot and McQuillan 1982; Dumas and Bélanger, 1994; Lachepelle 1988; McKie 1993; McVey 1987; Statistics Canada 1989a; Perreault

1990). Lavoie and Oderkirk (1993) say that Canada's low fertility rate today falls below the level (2.1) needed to replace the population.

Low fertility led to a sharp drop in the number of young people in Canada. Between 1976 and 1991, for example, the population of young people 0–14 years old decreased from 5.9 million to 5.7 million, which was a 5 percent decrease, from 26 percent to 21 percent of the population (McKie 1993; Statistics Canada 1989a). Statistics Canada projects a continuing decline in the proportion of the population made up of younger people as we move into the next century. A medium growth projection by Statistics Canada estimates that the younger population (under age 18) will fall to 19 percent of the population in 2041, while the older population will grow to 23 percent of the popula-

tion (from 11.6 percent in 1991) (George et al. 1994; McKie 1993; Romaniuc 1984; Statistics Canada 1990e).

This decrease in the birth rate, especially the sharp drop since the 1960s, speeded up the rate of population aging in Canada. Between 1961 and 1991 the population aged 65 and over rose by four percentage points, moving from 7.6 to 11.6 percent of Canada's population (Norland 1994). The older population will increase sharply again in the first decade of the 21st century when the baby boom generation moves into old age. Demographers project an increase in the older population of 168 percent from 1992 to 2036. They project that the group aged 90 and over will multiply five times during this same time (McKie 1993; Romaniuc 1984; Statistics Canada 1990e).

Exhibit 4.5

Canada's Oldest Seniors

Canada has more very old people (aged 80 and over) in its population than ever before. And demographers predict a growing number of very old people in the future. Few studies have looked at this age group. The National Advisory Council on Aging (NACA) talked with Canada's oldest seniors to learn something about their lives and how they see the world. The excerpts below show the varied perspectives very old people have on aging and on living in late old age.

"It is very peculiar being over 100 … and fun. I'm a rare breed, a museum piece. They bring people in to look at me. I would say that I have had a very good life. There have been bad times but I am happy now, although my health is slowly deteriorating. Last night, I went to hear my grand-daughter and her husband in a Gilbert and Sullivan musical. I was an actress and singer when I was young. They must get it from me." (101-year-old widow living in a long-term care facility)

"You shouldn't be congratulated for living too long. It's a question of endurance. … Nothing works properly in my body, from teeth to toes. … Old age is a form of punishment. The more you go on, the more you endure. I hate every minute of it." (87-year-old single woman living in a long-term care facility)

"I really mourn the loss of my friends. I miss most of all having someone to share news or encounters, reports of the day when I return from shopping or an outing. I sometimes find myself saying 'I must tell Mary about that,' and then I remember that she is no longer around. We used to be a close group of six and now I am the only one left." (87-year-old widow living in a seniors' housing complex).

"I was born blind and have been living here for 40 years. Last year, I married a fellow resident who has cerebral palsy. I am happier than I have ever been in my life because I am so much in love. Life is good to me now." (80-year-old woman living in a long-term facility)

Source: The National Advisory Council on Aging, *The NACA Position on Canada's Oldest Seniors: Maintaining the Quality of Their Lives* (Ottawa: NACA, 1992). Reproduced with the consent of the National Advisory Council on Aging (NACA) and with the permission of the Minister of Public Works and Government Services Canada, 1997.

Exhibit 4.6

How to Read a Population Pyramid

Population pyramids graphically portray a society's population structure at a certain point in time and allow researchers to compare societies at a glance. Most pyramids have the same design:

The title: The title contains the name of the country and the year this "snapshot" was taken. The title answers the questions: What? Where? When?

The centre line: The centre line divides the pyramid by sex—males on the left, females on the right.

The base: The horizontal axis can represent absolute numbers or percentages. The pyramids for Canada, 1986–2036 (see Exhibit 4.7), use absolute numbers. The centre line marks 0, and each point on the baseline marks 200 000 people (males to the left of the centre, females to the right).

The tiers: Each tier or level of the pyramid stands for an age cohort (conventionally a five-year group).

The lowest tier stands for the youngest age cohort (0–4 years old), and as one moves up the pyramid the cohorts get older. The top cohort (90+ in the Canadian pyramids) contains everyone over a certain age. (Note that this large top tier takes in a larger age span than the other tiers. It includes people from age 90 to over 100.)

Pyramids allow a viewer to compare age cohorts within a country (e.g., the size of young cohorts can be compared with the size of older cohorts), to compare sex differences within cohorts (by comparing the size of a tier to the right and left of the centre line), and to see unusually large or small cohorts at a glance. Gerontologists also use population pyramids to study population change over time and to compare one country with another.

Summary of Population Aging in Canada

Canada's demographic transition took place from before 1850 to the present in three stages. In the first stage, before 1850, Canada had both high death and high birth rates, and, in Ontario and the Maritimes, a high rate of immigration. These forces kept the average age of Canadians low. Gagan (1983a) says that in Ontario in the mid-19th century half the population over the age of 15 was made up of men under the age of 30. Statistics Canada data put the median age of Canadians in the mid-19th century at around 20 (compared with a **median age** of almost 34 in 1992 (McKie 1993).

The second stage of the transition began after 1850 as major declines in birth and death rates took place (Kalbach and McVey 1979). This stage differed from the second stage in Europe's demographic transition, where death rates declined and birth rates stayed high for some time before they dropped to complete the transition. In Canada both birth and death rates dropped (with some important fluctuations in birth rates) until the present. These changes transformed Canada from a young nation (under 4 percent aged 65+) in the late 1800s to a mature nation (with about 7 percent of the population aged 65+) by 1950.

Today, in the third stage of the transition, Canada has low death rates, low birth rates, and an aging population. Into the next century Canada's population pyramid will change from that of a wide-based, triangular shape to a more rectangular one (see Exhibit 4.7).

AGING IN CANADA TODAY

Older people differ by age, sex, marital status, and health. They come from different ethnic backgrounds, have lived through varying historical events, and live in diverse parts of the country. These differences make older people one of the most heterogeneous age groups in the country.

The Aging of the Older Population

The older population itself has aged in the past eighty years. In 1901 people aged 85 and over made up 5.1 percent of the older population; by 1991 they made up almost 9.0 percent of the older population (Norland 1994; George et al. 1994). Desjardins (1993) projects that the 85-and-over

Exhibit 4.7

Population Pyramids by Age Group and Sex, Canada, 1993, 2016, and 2041

a estimate based on 1991 census

b low = population = growth projection based on 1991 census data

These pyramids show at least three important trends: the dramatic growth in size of the older age cohorts (aged 40+); a continued higher proportion of women compared with men in the oldest cohorts; and the movement of the baby boom cohorts into old age. The 2041 pyramid is top-heavy, with small younger age groups below a large older population.

Source: M.V. George, M.J. Norris, F. Nault, S. Loh, and S.Y. Dai, *Population Projections for Canada, Provinces and Territories 1993–2016* (Ottawa: Minister of Industry, Science and Technology, 1994). Reproduced by authority of the Minister of Industry, 1996, Statistics Canada.

population will equal 14.7 percent of the older population in 2036. In the 1980s Canada's oldest age groups grew at a faster rate than did corresponding age groups in the other developed nations. The number of males aged 90 and over, for example, doubled in size from 1966 to 1986, and the number of females aged 90 and over tripled in size (Statistics Canada 1990e). George et al. (1994) say that the 85-and-over group will double in size between 1993 and 2016 and will grow fivefold by 2041. Longer life expectancy and larger numbers of people entering this group account for this growth. Stone and Frenken (1988) say that this trend will lead to "a veritable population explosion among seniors of advanced age" (Stone and Frenken 1988, 35).

An Ontario White Paper says that "the increase in the number of elderly citizens, and particularly the older elderly, is creating a new generation of issues" (cited in Stone and Frenken, 35). These issues will influence social policy and the use of resources in the future. For example, the group aged 75 and over, compared with people aged 65–74, shows higher rates for institutionalization, disability, and poor health. They also show a greater need for daily support (Norland 1994; Statistics Canada 1987b). This group will, therefore, need more institutional supports, medical care, household maintenance, and community health care supports in the future.

At the same time that the oldest cohorts grow in size, the younger cohorts 65 and over will also get larger. Projections show more than a doubling in the population aged 65–74 from 1991 to 2041 (George et al. 1994). This large number of older Canadians will make new demands on society. The younger elderly will change retirement patterns by retiring early or by staying at work past age 65. This group will want more recreational and educational opportunities. Services like job bureaus, schools, and counselling programs will also be needed to serve these people.

Programs for all types of older people will cost taxpayers more money. In 1986–87, for example, Canada spent $54 billion on its social security system (compared with $42.9 billion in 1982–83). More of this money went to older people than to any other age group. The single largest amount of this money went to the **Old Age Security** program (including the **Guaranteed Income Supplement** and the **Spouse's Allowance**). These

programs cost about one-quarter of the total spent on social security programs (Statistics Canada 1989a). During this same time (1986–87), the retirement payments for the Canada/Quebec Pension Plans increased 97 percent (Statistics Canada 1989a). If the proportion of older people more than doubles in the next fifty years as expected, will the public be willing to pay out even more of the country's income for older people? Or will the costs lead to resentment and a crisis in Canadian society? We will discuss these issues in more detail later in this chapter under the topic of dependency ratios.

Ethnicity

In 1986 people of British background made up almost half (45.9 percent) of Canada's older population, people of French background made up a quarter (22.5 percent), and the rest came from a wide variety of backgrounds including non-French and non-British European, African, and Chinese cultures (Statistics Canada 1986a). Older people made up almost 18 percent of the foreign-born Canadian population in 1991 (compared with 9.6 percent of the native-born group) (Norland 1994).

These figures reflect the high immigration rates of the early 1900s and the recent immigration of older family members who join their families in Canada. In the mid-1980s, more than half of immigrants aged 65 and over come from non-British and non-French backgrounds (Statistics Canada 1986a). In the past these non-charter-group immigrants came mostly from Eastern Europe. But newer immigrants tend to come from Asia, South America, and the Caribbean (Dumas 1990).

In 1987, for example, slightly more than 20 percent of all immigrant seniors came from India (10.5 percent) and the Philippines (10 percent) (Government of Canada 1989). As these people age, they will create a new mix of ethnicities among the older population. Many of these people, who learned a language other than English in their native countries, continue to use this language at home. Having now reached old age, they make the older population today a more ethnically diverse group.

Some ethnic groups have a higher proportion of older people than others. Exhibit 4.8 shows the proportion of people aged 65 or over within each ethnic group. Note that 23 percent of people who

Exhibit 4.8

Population 65 Years and Over as a Percentage of the Total Population for Selected Ethnic Groups, 1981

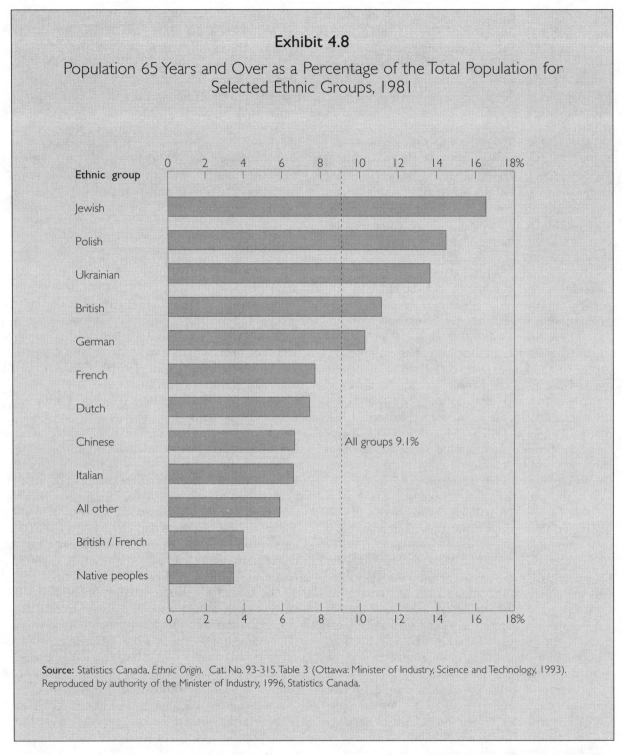

Source: Statistics Canada, *Ethnic Origin.* Cat. No. 93-315. Table 3 (Ottawa: Minister of Industry, Science and Technology, 1993). Reproduced by authority of the Minister of Industry, 1996, Statistics Canada.

claim Ukrainian ethnicity, 20 percent of people who claim Jewish ethnicity, and 19 percent of people who claim Polish ethnicity are aged 65 or older. These are three of the "oldest" ethnic groups in the country. At the other extreme, a relatively small percentage of people who claim Chinese, East Indian, or Portuguese ethnicity are aged 65 or over. North American Native peoples have a very "young" population with about 4 percent of their population aged 65 and over. The high proportion of Ukrainian, Jewish, and Polish older people shows the effect of low fertility rates on the aging of these populations. The small proportion of older North American Indians shows the effect of high fertility rates on their population (Statistics Canada 1993).

Gerber (1983) reports that both the size of an ethnic group and the proportion of older people in the group determine the institutional supports that older people can expect from their group. A large group with a moderate proportion of its population aged 65 and over can provide a more complete community life for its elderly. A small group with a high proportion of older people may be able to offer little support. Also, the concentration of the group (how close to one another members live), their location (urban or rural), the proportion of old-old to young-old, family size, and cultural values all affect the number of supports older people can draw on.

People of Finnish background, for example, tend to live in rural areas and have small families. This can lead to hardship in late old age if a person needs health care services or informal (family) supports. As these people age, spouses and friends die, and their social networks get smaller. This can lead to a lack of care and support in late old age. People of Italian background, on the other hand, have large families, tend to live in cities, and tend to live with their children. Older Italians have more access than members of smaller groups to community resources and family support in old age.

This brief look at ethnicity and aging shows that ethnic groups vary in their size, their location, their proportion of older people, and their institutional completeness, a term that refers to the amount of community support they offer their older members. For this reason Driedger and Chappell (1987, 75) say that "ethnicity can have significant implications for care and supportiveness in old age," and so policies for older people from different types of groups (large, small; rural, urban) will have to vary. Driedger and Chappell (1987) advise planners and policy-makers to take ethnicity into account, along with socioeconomic status and physical mobility, when designing programs for older people. (See Chapter 7 for a more detailed discussion of ethnicity and aging).

Geographic Mobility

Older people follow internal migration patterns similar to those of younger people, but they are less mobile than the non-aged (Norland 1994; Northcott 1988; Statistics Canada 1990e). Statistics Canada (cited in Norland 1994) reports that between 1986 and 1991 people aged 25–29 had a mobility rate of 76 percent (this means that more than three-quarters of people in this age group moved in those years). This rate declined to 35 percent for people aged 45–49 and 24 percent for people aged 65–69. The oldest group (age 85 and over) had a mobility rate of 21 percent. The majority of older movers (52 percent) moved within the same census subdivision. Only a small percentage (7 percent) of older people moved between provinces. Interprovincial moves by older people have only a small impact on provincial populations. B.C., for example, received 35 percent of all interprovincial older movers, but older in-migrants represented only 3.8 percent of older people in the province (Norland 1994).

Litwak and Longino (1987) describe three stages of later life when people may choose to move. The first is the retirement stage, when freedom from the need to live near work allows people to move to a more pleasant climate and to have a more relaxed lifestyle. Some of these people move out of the country to the U.S. sunbelt (see Exhibit 4.9). Others move to Canadian retirement sites like Niagara-on-the-Lake and Victoria (see Exhibit 4.10). In the second, or disability stage, physical limitation may lead the older person to move closer to children or others who can give them help. The likelihood of this type of move increases with age (Moore and Rosenberg 1994). The severe disability stage is the third phase, and it requires the older person to move to a nursing home or other institution.

Northcott (1988) reports a peak in migration among older age groups around retirement age (60–69 years). This corresponds to Litwak and Longino's retirement stage. Many of these people moved out of their locality, and they most often relocated to improve their quality of life (Northcott 1988). British Columbia showed the greatest rates of gain in older migrants, according to the 1991 census. The Northwest Territories and the Yukon, Quebec, Manitoba, and Saskatchewan showed the greatest rates of loss (Northcott 1988).

Exhibit 4.9

Canadian Snowbirds: Are They a Grey Peril?

Some older Canadians stay in place, others move within Canada. But, some choose a third option. They migrate south for the winter. These "snowbirds" settle in Florida, Arizona, Texas, and other southern states. Most of them stay in the United States for less than six months of the year because the Canadian health system requires at least six months' residence in Canada. These seniors move to their winter homes when the snow falls and return to Canada again in the spring.

Longino (1988b) found that Florida attracts more older Canadians (60+) than any other nonborder state. He also reports that many Floridians along with other Sunbelt natives have a "gray peril mentality" (Longino 1988a). They fear that older seasonal migrants will place a burden on local social and health care services.

To test this idea, Longino and a group of Canadian and U.S. researchers conducted a survey of Canadian seasonal migrants in Florida. They asked about Canadians' background, health, social life, and migration patterns. This survey included the responses of 2731 (mostly English-speaking) Canadians who lived in Florida in 1986 (Tucker and Marshall 1988; Tucker et al. 1988). The people who answered the survey had a median age of 69.2 years, more than half (57 percent) were between 65 and 74 years old, and about a fifth (21 percent) were aged 75 or older. Nearly all of them (89.6 percent) were married. More than half had graduated from high school, and most reported former middle- to upper-middle-class occupations (Tucker and Marshall 1988). Most of them had children, siblings, or friends who lived in Florida (Longino et al. 1991). And most of them (80 percent) still owned homes in Canada (Tucker et al. 1992).

Marshall and Longino (1988) reviewed the health status of these people. More than 80 percent of them reported excellent or good health (see also Martin et al. 1992). Only about 10 percent of any age and gender group reported any sick days. Less than 10 percent of the sample had recently consulted a family doctor or other health professional. And few of these people used any health or social services in Florida.

Most of the snowbirds in this study reported good physical and psychological health, good social supports, and high life satisfaction (Mullins et al. 1989). A third of them said that they had better health when they visited Florida. One respondent said, "My wife finds that her bronchitis is ... considerably better in Florida, as a result of the sun and warmth" (Tucker et al. 1988, 227).

This study shows that Canadian seasonal migrants make few demands on Florida's health care or social service system. The large majority of these people live healthy, active lives. Marshall and Tucker (1990) report that Canadian snowbirds spend about $1200 per month during their typical five-month stay. They also create demands for housing, goods, and services. Most of them (89 percent) moved to Florida for the climate or for the lifestyle (67 percent). A later study of French-Canadian snowbirds in Florida suggests that they too use few local health care services. French Canadians tended to be younger as a group and to have a larger family network to rely on (Tucker et al. 1992). Longino (1988a, 451) says that "the search for [an] ... impact on specialized services for the aging by seasonal migrants has turned up disappointingly little evidence for the gray peril."

A larger than average group of older people in the Atlantic provinces have moved there from another province (Health and Welfare Canada 1983; Northcott 1988; Statistics Canada 1984b). These people may have migrated because they sought a certain lifestyle in the Atlantic provinces. Overall mobility trends in Canada show a higher concentration of older people in certain places (e.g., older people tend to move westward and tend to concentrate in Ontario and British Columbia) (Northcott 1985).

Migration patterns also show a multidirectional flow. But some trends do appear. Litwak and Longino's (1987) second and third stages of migra-

Exhibit 4.10

Enjoying the Good Life

Older Canadians who move after retirement often choose to live on the West Coast. The warm weather and the large number of older people with similar interests make this a good retirement spot. The cases described below fit the type of migration that Litwak and Longino (1987) call "amenity migration." This often begins with a couple vacationing in a spot for a number of years. The couple then decides to settle there after retirement. Reporter James Deacon describes the amenities and social life that attracted the Perrigos and their neighbours to Qualicum Beach, British Columbia.

A brilliantly sunny morning in late July greeted Ladies' Day at the Qualicum Beach Memorial Golf Club. As the first groups finished their rounds, they gathered in the clubhouse to add up their scores. Nearly all of the women were in their 60s, and most had moved to the Vancouver Island community from somewhere else in Canada. One of the golfers, Beth Perrigo, 64, said that she first visited Qualicum Beach 13 years ago, while vacationing from Ottawa with her husband Howard and their two children. Perrigo said that she was strongly attracted by the town which overlooks the Strait of Georgia 40 km north of Nanaimo. "We bought a lot and just sat on it," she says. In 1989, Howard Perrigo retired from his job with the federal government. The couple had already decided that they did not want to stay in Ottawa ("My husband got tired of shovelling snow."). The Perrigos considered wintering in Florida, but in the end chose Qualicum Beach, attracted by the mild climate and relaxed lifestyle that has made the province the most popular retirement region in the country.

According to federal census figures, during the 12-month period to June, 1991, almost 4,600 new arrivals from elsewhere in Canada were over 65. The temperate West Coast climate has traditionally attracted older Canadians to such cities as Vancouver and Victoria. Now, provincial officials say that migrating senior citizens have made smaller communities on the east coast of Vancouver Island, including Nanaimo, Qualicum Beach, Parksville and Comox, into some of the province's most popular retirement areas. Other pensioners, including many Albertans, favor communities in the mainland's south-central Okanagan Valley. ...

As in many retirement communities, Qualicum Beach's municipally owned golf course is a busy social centre. Sitting with Perrigo at a table overlooking the golf course and the strait beyond, Wilma Bleakley, 66, and Gladys Morton, 70, discussed the area's mild climate as being one of the main attractions for senior citizens. "There may be two weeks when we can't play golf," said Morton, who moved to Qualicum Beach from the central B.C. mining town of Hendrix Lake. "But that's about it."

Patricia and Conrad Nadeau lived in an ocean-view home in Lions Bay, 30 minutes northwest of Vancouver, but were lured to the Island by its weather and the abundance of recreational opportunities. Conrad Nadeau, a semi-retired insurance executive, and Patricia, a keen gardener, bought a two-bedroom condominium alongside Morningstar Golf Course, six km east of Qualicum Beach, and moved in eight months ago. Surveying her flourishing garden, which backs onto the golf course, Patricia Nadeau said, "Don't think we could do any better than this." Clearly, that judgment is shared by the thousands of retirement-aged Canadians who have responded to the attractions of British Columbia.

Source: James Deacon, "Enjoying the Good Life," *Maclean's*, August 24, 1992, p. 50. Reprinted with permission.

tion help explain these trends. Older people, for example, tend to move from farms to towns or cities, and most older movers (60 percent) relocate within their local area. People probably move in order to live closer to their children or to the services that towns and cities offer. Provinces and towns with increased numbers of older people will face new challenges in the future.

Increased Numbers and Proportions of Older Women

The death rates for older women have decreased faster than they have for older men through most of this century. Between 1921 and 1976 the death rate of Canadian women aged 70–74 decreased by 50 percent, while men in this age group showed only a 10 percent decrease (Statistics Canada 1979a). In 1931 the life expectancy for a 65-year-old woman was 13.7 years; in 1961 it was 16.1 years; and in 1990 it was 19.6 years (for a 65-year-old man it was only 13.0 years in 1931, 13.6 years in 1961, and 15.4 years in 1990) (Statistics Canada 1987c; Health and Welfare Canada 1983).

As a result of these changes, the proportion of older women in the population has grown. At the turn of the century there were 105 men for every 100 women aged 65 and over, and in the mid-1950s older men still outnumbered older women, but by the 1960s the pattern reversed itself. By 1991 there were 72 men for every 100 women aged 65 and over (Norland 1994). Projections show that the ratio of men to women aged 65 and over will decrease until 2011 and then level off at 72 men per 100 women in 2031. But for the age group 85 and over, the ratio of men to women will decrease until 2011 (from 44 in 1991 to 39 in 2011). It will then rise to only 42 in 2031 (Norland 1994).

This means that policies and programs for older people will have a greater impact on women than on men. Women will live longer and so be affected by programs for older people for more years. This is especially true of health care, housing, and income support programs. We will study these programs in detail in the chapters ahead. For now, we will look at the overall impact of population aging on Canada's economy.

THE IMPACT OF POPULATION AGING

The Dependency Ratio and the Cost of an Aging Population

Concern about the increasing numbers of older people typically pits the old against the young. The Science Council of Canada (Auerbach and Gerber 1976, 3) called an older population of between 13 percent and 15 percent "a significant social burden." And some writers say that an older population could lead to intergenerational conflict (Tindale and Marshall 1980). An editorial in *The Globe and Mail* (1993) calls the baby boom generation "a massive unfunded liability." "It's probable," the editorial goes on to say, "that those in the baby boom's wake will rebel at paying ... to subsidize the retirement of a generation that may well be better off than they are." These sources assume a high dependence of older people on the young, and they suggest that the young will rebel or resent the burden of a large older population.

Gerontologists use a figure called the **overall dependency ratio** to gauge the burden that the old and the young place on people in middle age. Experts arrive at this ratio by adding the number of people under age 18 to the number of people aged 65 and over. They then compare this figure to the population aged 18–64:

$$\frac{(\text{Population aged } 0–19) + (\text{Population aged } 65+)}{\text{Population aged } 20–64}$$

(Some writers use ages 0–14 or 0–17 as the age span for the younger group.)

Denton and Spencer (1980) used the dependency ratio to look at dependency in Canada. They found that while the ratio of people aged 65 and over to those aged 20–64 will nearly double from 1976 to 2031, the proportion of young people will decline. When they combined these projected changes in the young and old populations, they found that this led to "a somewhat lower overall dependency ratio for the remainder of this century and throughout the first decade of the next, as compared with 1976, and then a pronounced increase in the following two decades or so" (Denton and Spencer 1980, 24–25; see also Perrault 1990). In spite of this increase, in 2031 (when the baby boom will have created large increases in the over-65 population) the overall dependency ratio may not be much higher than in 1976 (Chawla 1991).

Exhibit 4.11 shows Statistics Canada dependency projections based on moderate demographic change. This box introduces the concept of the elderly and youth dependency ratios. The **elderly dependency ratio** refers to the number of people aged 65 and over divided by the population aged

Exhibit 4.11

Dependency Rates for Canada, Selected Years 1901 to 1986, with Two Projections for Selected Years 1991 to 2031

Year	Elderly Dependency (65+/20–64)	Youth Dependency (0–19/20–64)	Overall Dependency
1901	.10	.89	1.17
1921	.09	.84	.94
1941	.12	.67	.79
1961	.15	.83	.98
1981	.17	.55	.72
1991	.19	.46	.65
2011	.24	.39	.63
2031	.41	.40	.81
2036	.42	.40	.82

These figures show a fairly steady increase in the elderly dependency ratio over the years shown here. The figures also show a fairly steady decrease in the youth dependency ratio (except for the sudden jump during the baby boom years around 1961).

The overall dependency decreases until early in the next century. It then increases only to the 1941 level in the years after 2030. These figures suggest that an older population will not create an undue burden on Canadian society.

Note: Projections assume modest increases in life expectancy of .8 years per five-year period, a total fertility rate of 1.8, and immigration of 250 000 gradually decreasing to 200 000 by the year 2011.

Source: B. Desjardins, *Population Ageing and the Elderly.* Cat. No. 91-533E (Ottawa: Minister of Industry, Science and Technology, 1993). Reproduced by authority of the Minister of Industry, 1996, Statistics Canada.

20–64. The **youth dependency ratio** refers to the number of people aged 0–19 divided by the population aged 20–64. These ratios show how these two subgroups contribute to the total dependency ratio.

Denton, Feaver, and Spencer (1986, 86) say that figures like these should reassure "those who are concerned about the possible inability of the economy to support its dependent population— young and old—in the decades ahead." But the Ontario Ministry of Treasury and Economics says that the **crude dependency rates** presented tell only part of the story. These rates tell us little about the economic burden of an older population (Stone and Fletcher 1980). Chawla (1991), for example, projects roughly the same dependency

ratio in 2030 as in 1965. But in 1965 people aged 65 and over made up only 19 percent of the dependent population. Chawla (1991) projects that in 2030 people aged 65 and over will make up 55 percent of the dependent population. This will give Canada a dependency ratio with one of the largest proportions of older people of any country in the world (Chawla 1991).

A study by Canada's Treasury Board Secretariat (1977) estimated that in 1976 government expenditures for people aged 65 and over came to two and a half times the amount for people aged 0–17. Burke (1991; see also O'Higgins 1988, cited in Easterlin 1996) reports roughly the same figure for 1980. And Denton and Spencer (1995), in a recent study, project large increases in government expenditures as society ages. They report, for example, that by the year 2011 social security costs (for the old) will surpass education costs (for the young) as a percent of the gross domestic product. Social security costs will triple between 1986 and 2041, while education costs will increase by about 10 percent. Likewise health care costs will more than double between 1986 and 2041. Denton and Spencer project a steady increase in the total cost of health care, education, and social security between 1986 and 2041. Population aging accounts for most of this increase.

The Ontario Ministry of Treasury and Economics (1979) calculated **effective dependency rates** based on these differences in the costs for older and younger age groups. It concludes that with a crude total dependency ratio in 2031 that is about the same as the crude rate in 1976, but with more older people and fewer younger people in the population, the effective total dependency rate in 2031 exceeds the 1976 rate by 43 percent (Ontario Ministry of Treasury and Economics 1979).

A study by Denton, Feaver, and Spencer (1986) also concludes that service costs may rise as the population ages. They projected dependency ratios from 1980 to 2030, and then estimated the changes in government program and service costs in the future. They report two trends. First, they predict a shrinking labour force in the years ahead. This could lead to a decline in the gross national product (GNP) from 2010 to 2030 and an increase in service costs above growth in the GNP for these two decades.

Second, they predict a shift in government service costs. They also project a decrease in education expenses of about 15 percent between 1980 and 2030, but forecast a tripling in social security payments and almost a doubling of health expenditures for this period. They also note that, given present arrangements, the federal government will bear most of the cost of social security and health care increases. This will lead to tensions between the provincial and federal governments and to a shifting of responsibilities for health care services to the provinces. Some recent changes in funding arrangements suggest that this has already begun (Canadian Council on Social Development 1990).

Burke (1991) says that in the years between 1980 and 2040 pension costs will rise more than any other expense and projects a 204 percent increase over this time. If this comes to pass, pensions will "account for 38% of social spending, up from just 24% in 1980" (Burke 1991, 7). At the same time, health care costs will increase by 118 percent and account for 33 percent of social spending (compared with 29 percent in 1980). These trends would lead to an increase in social spending of 87 percent in Canada, which is quite high compared with predictions of 65 percent for the United States and 40 percent for Japan.

Researchers may disagree about the specific impact of an aging population on health and income resources. But nearly all of them agree that more health care and income resources will go to serve older people and that this will cost more money. This shift in resources to the older population will force Canadians to make some hard choices. Burke (1991, 8), for example, says that "Canadians will most likely have to choose between increasing tax rates and social security contributions or lower levels of social benefits." The next fifty years will see increased debate over the allocation of health and income resources.

Reports on the future look gloomy, but dependency ratios tell only part of the story. Myles and Boyd (1982, 259) say that "alarmist exercises in futurology ... have produced more oversight than insight" when it comes to the issue of dependency in the future. Even small changes in Canada's economy and social norms, for example, could lead to large decreases in the effective dependency rate (Chen 1987). Denton, Feaver, and Spencer (1986, 90) say that "non-demographic forces [e.g., changes in the demand for services, increases in per capita worker output, or changes in the federal government's commitment to fund programs] could easily be more important quantitatively than demographic ones in their effects on government expenditures."

Most projections, for example, assume a traditional retirement age of 65 (when people become entitled to Old Age Security payments). But government policy could change and this age could be raised. Northcott (1992, 15) says that society could deal with "the social 'problem' of population aging" by defining it away. A change in the retirement age could also affect the age when a person would get free health care.

Also, because more middle-aged workers today have private pension plans and savings, they may rely less on government pension supplements when they reach old age than pensioners do today. More flexible retirement plans will allow some people to work full- or part-time after age 65. The Canada Pension Plan has changed its rules to make both early and late retirement more attractive. All of these trends will change current dependency patterns and alter future projections (Chen 1987).

A stronger economy would also ease the dependency burden. Even a small improvement in the income of middle-aged people, compared with costs for services to the old, would significantly decrease the effective dependency rate. The Ontario Ministry of Treasury and Economics (1979) found that if income for working people increased even 1 percent faster than dependency costs, the effective dependency rates would be less than in 1976. In a strong economy, higher costs for services to the elderly may not create a burden for the middle-aged.

Weller and Bouvier (1981) point to one of the greatest weaknesses of using dependency rates to project into the future. They say that dependency rates focus too narrowly on the costs of having more older people in society. They remind us that an older population will also bring benefits, such as a lower crime rate, a lower auto accident rate, and increased concern for fitness, diet, and disease prevention. Higher numbers of older people may also improve the economy: they will likely spend their savings to consume the services of travel agencies, restaurants, and professionals (McDaniel 1986). These trends may reduce some waste of social resources and create a higher quality of life for people of all ages.

McDaniel (1986) says that dependency ratios lead to demographic determinism. Demographic determinism assumes that population dynamics determine the future of social relations and social institutions. But, McDaniel says, social policies have the greatest effect on the dependence of older people. Retirement policies today, for example, encourage retirement at age 65. Ironically, countries with the highest elderly dependency ratios encourage older people to leave the work force early. They appear to encourage and may even

demand economic dependency by the older population.

Demographers need to study the connections between demographic facts, political realities, and social change. How much choice do countries have in how they will respond to demographic change? What determines the choices a country makes? Are there models of preferred adaptation to an aging population? Countries like Sweden and Norway could serve as models for Canadian policy. Already, more than 14 percent of the populations of these countries are over age 65, and they have not faced crises as a result. Progressive programs have been put in place to serve older people, and citizens pay more in taxes to support them. These countries show that the transition to an older society can come about without social conflict and distress (Myles 1982).

Canadian society has its own history, its own mix of ethnicity, age/sex ratios, economic institutions, and values. Canada also faces its own demographic issues. The baby boom generation, for example, has gotten used to society's meeting its needs (for housing, child care, etc.). Will this generation demand an unreasonable level of social support as it ages? Or will the baby boomers develop a broader view of their relationship to society and moderate their expectations?

Canada will face unknown political, economic, and social challenges in the years ahead. So, Canada will have to discover its own responses to population aging. The Science Council of Canada says that the adjustments necessary to an older society "can be done"—and done without social upheaval (Auerbach and Gerber 1976, 3). These changes will take planning, thought, and creative social action, and all of us will play a part in this societal transformation.

SUMMARY

1. Canada has a younger population than most of the other developed nations. It had about 11 percent of the population aged 65 and over in 1986. Demographers project that this population will more than double by 2031 and will equal almost 24 percent of the total population.
2. Canada went through a demographic transition between 1850 and 1950. During this time

immigration increased, the death rate decreased, and, most important, the birth rate decreased. Between 1850 and 1950 the older population grew from about 4 percent of the population to over 7 percent.

3. Canada today has a diverse older population. Older people differ by ethnicity, sex, income, education, and marital status. They also differ by age. Longer life expectancy in old age has given rise to a wide range of age groups within the older population. Large increases in the very old population will place new demands on health care and social service resources.

4. Ethnic groups vary in their size, location, proportion of older people, and the amount of community support they offer older people. Researchers and policy-makers will have to take ethnicity, socioeconomic status, and physical mobility into account when designing programs for older people.

5. The growth of the older population (and the decrease in the younger population) has led some people to predict an economic crisis due to the large numbers of dependent older people. Gerontologists measure the dependence of young and old people on middle-aged people and call this measure the overall dependency ratio (or rate).

6. Experts look at dependency rates to project the future costs of an aging society. Future dependency rates will depend on a number of social conditions. A weak economy, low birth rates, low immigration rates, and a rise in costs of services for the old (compared with per capita income for the middle-aged) will increase the burden on middle-aged people. A strong economy, higher birth rates, more immigration, and a rise in per capita income for middle-aged people (compared with costs in services for the old) will mean less burden on middle-aged workers. Changes in social values and retirement ages as well as better preparation for old age by middle-aged people today could also decrease effective dependency rates.

7. Dependency rates focus on the costs of an aging society. But an aging society may have a lower crime rate, a lower accident rate, and more concern for lifelong health and fitness. These changes would decrease the waste of social and economic resources and improve the quality of life in Canada.

8. Canada can grow old without upheaval and conflict; most of the developed nations have done so. But the transition to an aging society will take planning, thought, and creative social action.

STUDY QUESTIONS

1. List the three demographic forces that caused Canada's population to age from the 1850s to the present. How did each force affect societal aging?

2. What developments helped increase the life expectancy of men and women in Canada during the past century?

3. What two factors account for the greatest changes in Canadian population from 1951 to the present? How did these factors affect Canada's population?

4. State three ways in which an increase in the number of older people affect public policy.

5. How does ethnicity affect the care and support of older people?

6. Where in Canada do older people tend to live? Why? What types of environments do they prefer?

7. Describe the changes that brought about the growth of the large older female population today. What implications does this increase have for older women?

8. What do gerontologists mean by the "overall dependency ratio?" How do gerontologists calculate this ratio? How might a higher percentage of older people affect the economy in the future?

9. What steps can we take to help reduce the potential economic cost of an older population in the future?

KEY TERMS

age-specific birth rate the number of births in a given age group per 1000 women in that age group.

baby boom the sharp rise in the fertility rate in Canada from about 1946 to the early 1960s.

baby bust the sharp drop in the fertility rate from the mid-1960s on.

birth rates the number of births in a population per 1000 women in the population.

crude dependency rates rates based solely on the numbers of people in each age group.

death rates the number of deaths in a population per 1000 people.

effective dependency rates rates based on differences in the costs for older and younger age groups.

elderly dependency ratio the number of people aged 65 and over divided by the population aged 20–64.

fertility rate "the average number of children that would be born alive to a woman during her lifetime if she were to pass through all her childbearing years conforming to the age-specific fertility rates of a given year" (Beaujot and McQuillan 1982, 220–21).

Guaranteed Income Supplement an income security program for the poorest older people.

infant mortality rate the death rate of children less than a year old.

median age half the population is older and half younger than the median age.

Old Age Security Canada's basic retirement income program. Nearly all older people in the country get the OAS.

overall dependency ratio experts arrive at this ratio by adding the number of people under age 18 to the number of people aged 65 and over. They then compare this figure with the population aged 18–64.

Spouse's Allowance an income security program for spouses of pensioners who receive only OAS income.

youth dependency ratio the number of people aged 0–19 divided by the population aged 20–64.

SELECTED READINGS

McDaniel, Susan A. *Canada's Aging Population.* Toronto: Butterworths, 1986.

A good overview of aging and demography in Canada. This book covers basic demographic concepts like dependency ratios, population pyramids, and population age/sex structure. It also examines current issues in population aging, including aging in a world context, policy implications of population aging, and the future of aging in Canada. Well written, with up-to-date sources throughout the text.

Northcott, Herbert C. *Changing Residence: The Geographic Mobility of Elderly Canadians.* Toronto: Butterworths, 1988.

A detailed analysis of older people's geographic mobility. The book presents concepts related to mobility, facts about moving within Canada, and a discussion of mobility patterns across the life cycle. It also compares Canadian mobility with mobility in other developed countries.

Statistics Canada. *Canadian Social Trends.* Cat. No. 11-008E. Ottawa: Minister of Supply and Services, Annual.

Statistics Canada publishes this journal four times a year. Articles report on data from recent government studies in a readable magazine format and are accompanied by charts and graphs that help to interpret the statistics. Each issue contains useful and up-to-date information on topics like demography, living arrangements, and aging in Canada. A good resource for professionals and students of aging.

Maturational Change

CHAPTER 5

Personal Health and Illness

INTRODUCTION

Jean Calment of Provence, France, turned 121 years old on February 21, 1996. This made her the oldest person in the world and one of the longest-lived people ever. To celebrate her birthday Ms. Calment released a four-song CD album. The songs mix rap and techno music with stories from her life (for example, she met Vincent Van Gogh in her childhood). Money she earns from the CD will go to pay for a minibus for her nursing home (Mitchell 1996).

How did she live so long? For one thing, Ms. Calment has stayed active throughout her life. She lived on her own in a second-floor apartment until age 110 and she rode a bicycle until age 100 (Glass 1995). Other centenarians also attribute their long life to an active lifestyle. Some add that they like regular sex, never worry, or drink a shot of whisky before bed. One 100-year-old man claimed that eating a pound of peanuts a day led to his long life.

Scientific research supports some of these methods for longer life: moderate drinkers live longer than teetotallers (though no one knows why) (Woodruff 1982); a simple diet low in fat, salt, and sugar can decrease disease; and exercise leads to good health and possibly a longer life (Aussman and Russell 1990). But even with good habits, a good diet, and a good environment, physiological aging takes place. Older people on the covers of

Exhibit 5.1

Controversy: The Long-Lived People of Abkhazia

"Work hard and never worry," say the Hunza people of Pakistan. The Hunza claim to produce some of the longest-living people in the world. They say they live such long lives because they have good water and a good climate, and they stay happy. The Vilcabambans of Ecuador also claim long lives (Mazess and Forman 1979). About 1 percent of them claim to live past the age of 100 (compared with about 1 in 10 000 in North America). The Abkhazians, one of the best-known and most-studied of the long-lived peoples, live in the Caucasus mountains of the former Soviet Union. The Soviet census in the early 70s reports that 70 percent of Soviet citizens 110 years old or over live in this region (Benet 1976, 7).

Some Abkhazians (like the Hunzas and Vilcabambans) claim to be 120, 130, and even 160 years old. Pitskhelauri reports that the oldest man in one district of Abkhazia is 139 years old. This man, he says, works as a farmer and has "150 children, grandchildren, great-grandchildren, great-great-grand-children" (1982, 53).

Stories like this have led journalists, television crews, and researchers from all over the world to study and visit the Abkhazians, but few Western scientists believe their claims. Hayflick (1974, 43) says that researchers have "reported these claims without sufficiently emphasizing the meager evidence for the allegations. … Claims of superlongevity should be taken with as much skepticism as any claim unsupported by proof."

Careful studies of the Abkhazians' ages reveal that "only 38 percent of the 115 [people] thought to be over 90 were actually verified as being over 90 … Furthermore, none of those reevaluated were found to be actually over age 110" (Palmore 1984, 95; see also Medvedev 1974). A study of census data by Bennett and Garson (1986) found that only a small fraction of the number of Abkhazians who claim to be over 100 years old have actually reached that age. These studies have put an end to the myth that a long-lived people exists, but the latest research leaves open two important biological questions. First, why do so few humans in any society live past 100 years of age, if humans have a potential life span of 110 to 120 years? Second, what are the causes of biological aging?

health and nutrition magazines beam good health—but they still have white hair, brown spots on their skin, and wrinkles, like older people all over the world.

Gerontologists distinguish between the **maximum life span** (the maximum number of years a member of a species can live) and **life expectancy** (the number of years at birth an average member of a society can expect to live). Scientists think that the maximum human life span of somewhere between 110 and 120 years has stayed the same for the past 100 000 years. Kraus (1987), for example, reports 114 years as the oldest authenticated age ever recorded in Canada. Human life expectancy at birth, on the other hand, has increased in the past 2000 years from an average of 22 years in ancient Rome to around 70 years today. Technology and biomedical science continue to extend life expectancy (Stone and Fletcher 1986; Parliament 1987), and if this trend continues, more and more people will live close to the maximum human life span (Botwinick 1984). This means that more people will live to old age and more will live longer in old age than ever before.

The study of personal health and illness has two goals: to understand changes in the body that come with age and to apply this knowledge to extend and improve human life. This chapter will look at (1) what effects aging has on health, behaviour, and everyday life; (2) how older people cope with physical change; and (3) future changes in health and illness.

Researchers have asked two questions about the effects of physiological aging on the older person's well-being. First, do health problems increase with age? Second, does physiological aging limit the older person's activities?

CHANGES IN HEALTH STATUS

The 1991 General Social Survey asked a sample of 11 611 community-dwelling Canadians aged 15 and over about their health (Statistics Canada 1994a). The study asked about limits to activity, psychological well-being, health service use, and **chronic health problems.**

Older people in this study reported more chronic illness than the younger population. They reported high rates of arthritis, rheumatism, hypertension, diabetes, and heart disease (Statistics Canada 1994a). (See Exhibit 5.2.)

Statistics Canada (Statistics Canada 1994; 1995a) reports that specific groups among the older population report high rates of chronic conditions. Women, for example, reported higher rates of hypertension, arthritis, and rheumatism

than did men. Also, Chappell, Strain, and Blandford (1986, 44a) report that women "have more days per year of restricted activity, more days of bed disability, more doctor's visits, higher expenditures for health care and higher rates of institutionalization than men" (see also Statistics Canada 1994a). These figures may reflect the continuation of a pattern of health care use by women during their middle years. The figures may also reflect a denial of health problems by men, or they may reflect the fact that a greater proportion of men are married and have someone to care for them outside of an institutional setting.

Researchers report that low income leads to poor health in later life (Wolfson et al. 1993). People with lower incomes show poorer health by ages 45 to 64. Health differences between people with low and high incomes shows up at all ages in

Exhibit 5.2

Percentages of Population in Each Age Group, by Sex, Self-Reporting Selected Health Problems, Canada, 1991

Health Problem	Both Sexes	15+ Males	Females	65 + Males	75 + Females
Arthritis/ Rheumatism	21	46	59	49	65
Hypertension	16	31	41	27	42
Heart Trouble	7	25	24	30	30
Emphysema	8	19	18	19	21
Diabetes	4	11	9	13	9

The proportion of men and women who report health problems increases with age. Males aged 65 and over, compared with all adults, reported more than twice the rate of arthritis/rheumatism, emphysema, and diabetes. They reported more than three times the rate of heart trouble. Women aged 65 and over showed a similar pattern. But, compared with older men, they reported higher rates of arthritis/rheumatism and hypertension. The oldest age groups show the same pattern of illness.

Source: Statistics Canada, *General Social Survey Analysis Series.* Cat. No. 11-612 E, No. 8, Table 2-1 (Ottawa: Minister of Industry, Science and Technology, 1994). Reproduced by authority of the Minister of Industry, 1996, Statistics Canada.

later life. Poor nutrition, poor-quality housing, and lack of information all lead to poor health among low-income people.

Lifestyles as well as poverty lead to poorer health. Lower-income older people also report more trouble getting to sleep (Tait 1992). This may explain their greater use of sleeping pills. Also, older people who live in households with low income show a greater likelihood of smoking and tranquillizer use. Low-income smokers reported

the least intent to quit. This places their health at risk as they age. Also, people with poor education, the unemployed, and unskilled workers report poor health (Roberge, Berthelot, and Wolfson 1995; Schoenborn 1993).

Studies show that the oldest age groups among people aged 65 and over have more health problems than the younger groups. Some researchers (Chappell and Havens 1980) divide the older population according to differences in their health

Exhibit 5.3

HIV/AIDS in an Aging Society

Few people think of the elderly when they hear the word AIDS. The media have linked AIDS (Acquired Immune Deficiency Syndrome) to gay men, intravenous drug users, and sexually active young people. And the data support this view. People aged 30–44 had a higher number of deaths from AIDS (723 deaths) than any other age group in 1992. The group aged 60 and over had only 42 deaths from AIDS in Canada in that year (Dumas and Bélanger 1994). Still, older people can and do get AIDS. And the numbers of older people with AIDS has begun to climb.

Celia Gibbs, a researcher at the Lakehead University Northern Education Centre for Aging, reports that one in ten Canadians with AIDS (926 people) is over age 50. Heterosexuals make up only a small percentage of older people (aged 50 and over) with AIDS. But this number may increase as AIDS spreads among younger heterosexuals. Older people can get AIDS the same way younger people do: through sexual relations, intravenous drug use, and blood transfusions. Gibbs says that "many older people do not know they have the disease, they do not expect to get it, but unknown to them, they are spreading it" (cited in Paul 1994).

What explains this projected increase in AIDS among older people?

First, a person can have HIV (Human Immunodeficiency Virus, the cause of AIDS) ten years or more before the body's immune system breaks down and AIDS appears (Riley, 1989). Intravenous drug users, for example, may get infected with HIV in

their younger years, but may not show signs of the disease until old age. More people in the future will come into old age with the AIDS virus.

Second, some people have gotten AIDS from contaminated blood.

Third, any sexually active adult can get HIV. HIV spreads when bodily fluids like semen or blood pass from one person (who has the disease) to someone else. Because older women have thinner uterine linings than younger women, they are more susceptible to HIV if they have sexual contact with an HIV carrier. About one older person in ten with AIDS got the disease through heterosexual activity. The person with AIDS will spread the disease to other partners. Older people may stand a greater chance of getting HIV through sexual contact because they have weaker immune systems. AIDS also progresses faster in an older person for this reason.

Fourth, older people tend to know less about safer sex practices or to think about using a condom to prevent AIDS.

Fifth, medical professionals may misdiagnose AIDS because older people have a low risk of getting AIDS.

Gibbs (cited in Paul 1994) says that as many as 4000 older people have HIV, but have not yet gotten AIDS. These people may need long-term health care in the future. A larger older population will include more older people with AIDS. The spread of AIDS among older people could lead to heavy use of health services.

status. For women they describe three groups: young-old (aged less than 75), middle-old (aged 75–84), and old-old (aged 85 and over); for men they describe two groups: the young-old (aged less than 80) and the old-old (aged 80 and over). Studies report that chronic conditions increase with age.

Slightly more than 20 percent of the group aged 65–69 reported no chronic conditions, but this dropped to only 16.5 percent for the group aged 70 and over. Almost 35 percent of the 70 and over group reported three or more chronic conditions compared with only 29 percent of the group aged 65–69 (Health and Welfare Canada and Statistics Canada 1981). Chronic illness may lead to functional decline, decreasing an older person's quality of life. Strain (1993) found, for example, that nearly half of older people (43 percent) define good health as the ability to do their daily activities.

LIMITS ON ACTIVITY DUE TO PHYSICAL DECLINE

Chappell, Strain, and Blandford (1986, 36) define functional disability as a "functional limitation on the performance of normal daily role activities as a result of illness or injury." This measure looks at the effects of illness on a person's everyday life.

Statistics Canada (Dunn 1990) asked about the activity limitations faced by a sample of Canadians chosen from the 1986 census. All of the people in the sample said that they had a disability. The sample included only people who had problems managing their daily living activities due to their disability and people who had had a disability for at least six months.

The study found that people aged 65 and over made up about 40 percent of the disabled population aged 15 and over. Also the disability rate increased with age (Statistics Canada 1990b). The group aged 0–14 years had a 5.2 percent disability rate; people aged 35–64 had a 15.7 percent rate; the group aged 65–74 had a 37 percent rate; and people aged 85 and over had a rate of 82 percent (Nessner 1990). The study found that 45.5 percent of people aged 65 and over had a disability. Women made up more than half (60 percent) of this group (Statistics Canada 1990b). Women tend to have activity limitations earlier in life and live for more years with these limitations. Also, poor older

people have the highest rates of disability regardless of gender (National Advisory Council on Aging 1996b). Older disabled people tended to have more than one disability and they usually had a severe disability (Nessner 1990).

Disabilities impaired some functions more than others. Disabled seniors most often said they had trouble with mobility (e.g., walking from room to room or standing for a long time). They also had trouble with agility (e.g., bending, dressing, or grasping things) and hearing (Statistics Canada 1988; Norland 1994). Fifty-nine percent of them needed help with heavy chores; 55 percent needed it for housework; and 49 percent needed help with meal preparation. Community services sometimes helped them, but these disabled seniors reported that they could have used more help (Dunn 1990).

The need for help also increases with age. Older people at all ages reported the need for help with heavy housework. But the proportion who need help increased from 63 percent for people aged 65–74 to 86 percent for people aged 85 and over. Likewise, the proportion of people who need help with shopping increased from 29 percent for people aged 65–74 to 71 percent for people aged 85 and over (HALS Report 1990, cited in Chappell 1993a).

Chappell, Strain, and Blandford (1986, 37) compared the rate of chronic illness with the influence of illness on daily activity. They found that both the number of chronic conditions and the extent of functional disability tend to increase with age. However, chronic conditions do not necessarily translate into functional disability. That is, while over three-quarters of elderly persons have at least one chronic condition, only about half experience some functional disability. Even fewer, about one-fifth, require assistance with basic activities.

Gerontologists study the effects of functional disability on **activities of daily living (ADLs)** and **instrumental activities of daily living (IADLs)**. ADLs include bathing, moving from a bed or chair, dressing, getting to and using the toilet, eating, and walking (Leon and Lair, 1990). IADLs refer to home management activities like using the phone, shopping, and doing light housework. Limitations may range from a mild problem like trouble dialing the phone to more serious problems like the inability to eat or use the toilet (Leon and Lair, 1990). A drop in the ability to care for oneself signals a drop in quality of life and in the number

Exhibit 5.4

Testing the Limits of Ability in Later Life

Jean Cleator, age 67 in 1994, quit running at age 55 and turned instead to downhill ski racing. Cleator shows that older people can cope with disability and even excel in physical activity as they age.

In 1981, at age 55, Jean Cleator set a world record for 55-to-60-year-olds in the 5,000 m, but she quit running the following year because it was wrecking her knees. Now 67 and a widow, she restricts herself to competitive alpine skiing, camping, hiking and backpacking in summer, swimming in the Pacific Ocean and working an eight-hour day at the Vancouver ski service centre she owns with her son Barry. "It's a little harder to stay motivated when you get older," she says. "You have to force yourself a little bit more."

This winter, Cleator—a skier for more than 40 years—competes in the 60-to-70 age category for downhill racers, mostly at B.C.'s Whistler Mountain and in the Rockies. She talks animatedly about life on the slopes, lacing her conversation with skiing terms—Nordic, bindings, alpine, slalom, ski faces, gates, moguls, snow conditions. When the snow disappears from the low ground later this year, Cleator will head for the wilderness regions of the province's Tweedsmuir park, pitch a tent and set up her propane stove. Then, she will spend a month as a parks department guide, noting where visitors come from, how long they plan to stay and what they want to see. "If anybody wants to know what it's like up ahead, I tell them," she says.

For Jean Cleator, life at home is no less active. Example: "Yesterday, I slept in and woke up at 7. Normally, I'm up at 6:30. I'm not a great early riser." Or: "I would love to have done it, but I have not taken up scuba diving or board-sailing. It came along a little bit late for me and besides, I'm a bit of a coward." In addition to swimming, she has also water skied but admits that "it took me a long time to get up on one ski."

Along with the lifestyle is a philosophy. "If you feel like doing it and you can do it, you do it. What's age got to do with it?"

Source: R. Corelli, "Over What Hill?" *Maclean's,* January 10, 1994, 30–33. Reprinted with permission.

of active years a person will live (Prohaska et al. 1993).

Penning and Strain (1994) studied 1406 people between the ages of 65 and 104. They found that 55 percent of these people reported problems with at least one ADL or IADL. And women reported more disability than men. But they also reported getting more help from other people (National Health and Welfare 1993). Most older people cope with declines in their health. They accept the health changes that come with age, adjust their expectations about their activities, and gradually make changes in their lives to cope with physical decline (Chappell, Strain, and Blandford 1986). The Canadian National Survey of Ageing and Independence (NSAI) asked older people with disabilities about their ability to cope. Eighty-five percent said that they cope "very well" or "fairly well" (National Health and Welfare 1993). Even among the most disabled seniors, those in institutions, 21 percent report that they go shopping, and 18 percent manage their own finances (Statistics Canada 1993, cited in Norland 1994).

COPING WITH PHYSICAL CHANGE

The research on physical functioning, reaction time, and health makes old age seem like a time of loss and suffering. But older people vary on these measures. Studies show that 80 percent of old people live without functional handicaps on certain activities (like toileting and bathing) (Branch and Jette 1981). And in one Canadian survey of older people in the community 72 percent said that compared with other people their age they had good to excellent health (Statistics Canada 1991, cited in Norland 1994; see also Keith and Landry 1992; National Health and Welfare 1993). Even among people aged 75 and over, 68 percent said they had good to excellent health. The survey also found that 85 percent of people aged 65–74 years old and 83 percent of people aged 75 and over said they felt satisfied to some degree with their health. Nearly all of the older people in the survey (95 percent) reported some degree of life satisfaction. And Hirdes and Forbes (1993) report that high life satisfaction predicts future good health.

These studies suggest that older people adapt to changing physical problems, in part, by adapting their expectations and activities. Cape and Henschke (1980, 299) report that "only beyond the age of 80 does this picture begin to change significantly."

Studies of reaction time, for example, show that groups of older people make more varied responses than groups of younger people (Botwinick and Thompson 1968), and some older subjects do just as well as younger subjects on these tests. A study by Surwillo (1963) found that age accounted for only about 4 percent of the variance in reaction time. In studies of real-life performance based on many years of practice (like typing), older people did as well or almost as well as younger people (Bosman 1993; Dixon, Kurzman, and Friesen 1993; Salthouse 1984, cited in Spirduso and MacRae 1990).

Studies show that exercise (Botwinick and Thompson 1968), practice (Murrell 1970), and motivation (Botwinick, Brinley, and Robbin 1958; 1959) all decrease the differences in reaction time between young and old people (though they do not entirely eliminate age group differences) (Spirduso and MacRae 1990). Welford suggests that exercise, for example, may increase cardiovascular fitness, which leads to better blood flow to the brain and to better mental functioning (Welford 1984). And Spirduso (1980; 1982) suggests that muscle activity in exercise may directly improve the structures of the central nervous system.

Older people can also make up for declines in the senses, muscles, and organs as they age. More than one-third of seniors with a hearing disability, for example, use a hearing aid. Eighty-two percent of seniors with a seeing disability wear glasses. And 31 percent of seniors with a mobility disability use a mobility aid (most often a cane, wheelchair, or walker) (Statistics Canada 1990b). The more mobility problems a person has, the more likely that he or she will use a mobility aid (Zimmer and Chappell 1994). Older people can hire homemakers to help with heavy housework, and they can change their diet to make up for slow digestion and poor food absorption. Three responses to aging can decrease the effects of physiological decline: changes in environment, improvements in technology, changes in lifestyle.

Changes in the Environment

Sense thresholds, the points at which a person can begin to perceive a stimulus, begin to increase as early as age 30, and by age 60 most people notice changes in their senses. Hearing aids and glasses can help correct some of these problems, but hearing aids amplify all sounds, even background noises. In one case an elderly man with a hearing aid in a university class showed up to take the course a second time. Surprised, the professor asked him why. The man said that students talking behind him, a bus depot across the street, and a noisy heating system all made his hearing aid useless. Some days he left it at home or shut it off and tried to read the professor's lips. "I only got half of what you said last time," he told the professor. "So I've come back to get the rest." This man needed a quieter classroom setting.

Fozard (1990, 165) says that "the elderly appear to benefit as much as or more than younger adults from good context." Older people need to make educated guesses at the meaning of sensory inputs due to a decline in the senses. A beneficial environment can help the older person live a fuller life.

Charness and Bosman (1990, 446) say that the motto for good design should be "know the user." Designers, architects, and planners need to use knowledge about older people when they design environments for them. A number of manuals exist to guide planners and designers today. These guides give advice based on research and experience with older people.

Charness and Bosman (1990) say that researchers need to conduct more research on the anthropometry (the measurement of the shape, size, and movement capability) of older adults. They also suggest that designers use low-technology solutions, where they can. This includes easy-to-use door handles, cabinets, and clothing (Haber 1988, cited in Chappell 1993a; also Fernie 1994). These often cost less than high-technology solutions, and older people have less trouble adapting to them. Zimmer and Chappell (1994), for example, found that older people tend to use simple assistive devices (like canes and handrails) only when they have no other option. And they sometimes solve problems by changing their environment. Older people who cannot walk stairs may choose to live in a one-floor home. Changes in the environment—including changes in the way other people speak to or treat an older person—can help that person cope with physical decline.

Mann (1994) reports that many older people say they need an assistive device. But many people do not have the devices they say they need. The National Advisory Council on Aging (NACA) (1995c) says that older people need more information about existing technologies. More knowledge might lead to more use of technologies that would enhance older people's lives. For example, older people need to know how to use technological aids. Also, professionals need to select devices that suit the individual's ability and self-image. Mann (1994) found that some people do not use devices because they call attention to the user or make a task harder to do.

NACA reports that the cost of technological aids keeps some older people from using them. Provincial health programs do not cover all technologies. For example, some programs do not

---

Exhibit 5.5

Good Settings to Live In

The Manitoba Health Services Commission published the *Planning Guide for Personal Care Homes in Manitoba* in 1980. The guide suggests environmental changes that help older people cope with sensory loss. The commission based the guide on years of informal research in more than one hundred rural and urban personal care homes in the province. It gives examples of the kinds of things that designers need to keep in mind when they design environments for older people.

Lighting

The commission recognized that older people on average see less well than younger people and in the guide warns against pockets of light that create an uneven effect on walls and floors of hallways. This can lead a person to misjudge the floor's height or the distance to a wall. It can also increase a person's fear of falling and thereby decrease the older person's movement in the home. The guide also suggests soft indirect lighting at entrances, since direct lighting can create too great a contrast between the outside and the entry of the home.

Sound

Sounds from TVs, radios, and intercoms can blend into an audio mush that can distract and tire residents. In the guide, the commission warns against "a constant source of meaningless sound in social areas." Designers can use fabric textures, pile carpets, and soft drapes to dampen background noise, making it easier for people to hear one another. Also, small lounges or quiet areas allow people to communicate.

Decoration

Designers should avoid rough surfaces on walls, as they can cause skin abrasions. Patterned carpets or vinyl blocks can lead to optical illusions. Zigzags or stripes, for example, give the illusion of movement, and sharp contrasts in colours suggest a change in depth. People may try to step up or down and lose their balance. This can lead to frustration and cause people to avoid public space and withdraw to their rooms.

Personal care homes house only a small percentage of older people, but acknowledging these principles of design can improve the quality of their lives.

cover batteries for wheelchairs and lifting devices. But even low-cost items often go unused. Charness and Bosman (1994) call for more research on the technology needs of disabled, minority, and poor older people.

Improvements in Technology

Benjamin Franklin invented bifocals in the 18th century. He cut his glasses in half when he found he needed to watch the speakers' expressions at the French court. Today technology helps older people cope with aging in dozens of ways. Some people wear electronic pacemakers to regulate their hearts; people with severe arthritis can have joint replacement surgery; and in some cases a person can have a childhood problem corrected in old age.

One woman lived her first sixty years with her hip bones outside their sockets. Her muscles and ligaments allowed her to walk, but she limped and tired quickly. Her muscles weakened as she aged, and her doctor said she would have to spend the rest of her life in a wheelchair. She searched for and found a doctor who agreed to operate on both of her hips. He told her it would endanger her life, but she decided to try the operation. She now has both hips in place in their sockets and she stands two inches taller than in her youth.

Technological aids to older people range from the simple (e.g., a thick piece of rubber tubing that fits over a wooden spoon handle to help a person with arthritis or a weak grip) to the complex (e.g., a Century tub with a cranelike lift and a swinglike seat that lifts an immobilized or frail older person into a stainless steel tub. Water and pre-measured amounts of soap come out of jets at the sides of the tub. The person sits up to his chest in the water, while it swirls him clean). Technological aids range from the common (e.g., rubber strips for the bottom of the bathtub to prevent slipping) to the unusual (e.g., a chair with a seat that lifts a person to a standing position when she press a button). In the future, computers may also allow housebound older people to order groceries, get their mail, or play Scrabble with a grandchild across the country.

Haber (1986) says that in the future robots may help older people with their daily chores. They might also be used to help bathe and feed people in nursing homes. Voice-activated robots will pick things up or move them around (Korba et al. 1992). Robots may also help patients do passive exercises, help them walk, or bring them something they need. Haber argues that robots could free nursing home staff from unpleasant work and allow them more enjoyable time with patients. He says that voice-activated robots would give aware, but immobilized, older people a feeling of control over their environment, thereby increasing their life satisfaction. Research will have to be done to see whether robots further dehumanize institutional settings; whether older people (or institutions) can afford complex machines; and whether people will use high-tech equipment if they have the chance.

A group in the United States has designed a "smart house." This house will have a cable system to handle power, audio, video, and data. The smart house can turn lights on and off when you enter or leave a room. It can signal the coffee maker to go on when you get out of bed in the morning. It can turn on the TV to your favourite news channel. It can learn how warm you like your house and turn up the heat just before you get home. You can call the smart house any time and through the phone tell your applicances what to do (Davis 1991). A smart house will make life easier for people with or without disabilities. It will "make a home a safer, more comfortable, and more secure environment for an elderly person" (Davis 1991, 84).

LaBuda (1990) cautions that designers will have to make complicated technology easy to use. Computer manufacturers may need to adjust their products to serve an older market. Charness and Bosman (1989) found, for example, that middle-aged and older adults showed the best performance on computers with black-on-white screens. They also found that older people could learn a software package as well as younger adults, but that older people took longer to complete the test on their knowledge and needed more help from the experimenter. The older people also learned well in pairs (Zandri and Charness 1989).

Lowe (1990) reports that only 6 percent of people aged 65 and over could use a computer, compared with 82 percent of 15–19-year-olds. And only 3 percent of seniors had computers at home, compared with 35 percent of 15–19-year-olds. When compared with nonowners in their age group, computer owners aged 65 and over tended to have higher incomes and higher levels of education. These figures suggest that future generations of older people may feel comfortable with computerized solutions to everyday needs. But many people in the current generation of older people need aids that use simpler technologies.

Present transportation technology helps solve many disabled seniors' problems. But sometimes the technology does not meet seniors' needs. The Health and Activity Limitation Survey (HALS) (Dunn 1990), for example, found that 92 percent of disabled seniors engage in leisure activities outside their homes. But these seniors report problems with boarding and leaving planes, long-distance buses, and trains. They also have problems with local transportation, finding it difficult to get to and wait at bus stops. Kline (1994) reports that older drivers often have trouble seeing signs in time to react to them. He proposes larger, better lit signs in higher-contrast colours.

The HALS also found that 8 percent of people who need mobility aids do not have them; 31 percent who need a hearing aid do not have one; and 10 percent of people who need a visual aid do not have one. Seniors often report that they cannot afford the aids they need. Government programs cover only some aids and government support differs from province to province. For example, Chappell (1993a) says, government programs often provide medical equipment, but they do not always provide devices that help a person stay active and live safely.

The National Advisory Council on Aging (NACA) (1988) says that for technological aids to be useful, (1) people have to know about them, (2) people have to understand their usefulness, and (3) products have to be affordable and physically accessible. NACA also says that manufacturers should set up norms and standards of safety and suitability for new products.

Chappell (1993a) places the use of technological aids in a social context. She says that we know little about what type of older people use technological aids and about when they choose or reject these aids. We also know little about the effects of aids on a person's social life. A simple self-administered blood sugar test, for example, can cut down on the cost of a nurse's visit. But this may remove an important social contact for the older person. And the older person may prefer to see a nurse. We know little about whether technology can have side effects like social isolation. Technology can also create

dependence. Does an electric wheelchair help a woman who has trouble using a walker or does it put an end to her ability to walk (Strain, Chappell, and Penning 1993)? Researchers have begun to address these and other questions as they look at the impact of technology on older people's lives.

Changes in Lifestyle

People can also change their habits to cope with biological aging. Heavy smoking and drinking put wear and tear on the body; overeating can increase a person's risk of heart disease and diabetes; and long exposure to the sun increases the risk of skin cancer. People can cut back on such activities and habits that speed the process of aging.

Some recent figures show that people have already begun to change their habits. McKie (1987) compared the findings on cigarette smoking from the 1978–79 Canada Health Survey and the 1985 General Social Survey. The data show that in 1985, compared with 1978–79, every age group of men and women (except women aged 65+) showed a decline in the proportion of people who reported regular cigarette smoking. Men aged 65 and over showed the greatest proportion of any age or gender group (49 percent) who had given up smoking, while less than 20 percent of older women reported having given up smoking. People can also begin activities that improve their physical condition.

O'Brien and Vertinsky (1991) say that much of what people accept as aging falls into the category of **hypokinesia,** or disuse. This causes decline in muscle and bone mass, and a loss of function.

Studies show that exercise can slow the aging process, improve health, and improve physical function. Goldberg and Hagberg (1990) list dozens of benefits from exercise in later life. They include reduced body fat, greater muscle mass, greater strength, improved cardiac output, improved endocrine-metabolic function, lower blood pressure, decreased hypertension, decreased heart disease, and decreased osteoporosis.

These studies point the way to a new view of aging. Science cannot stop or reverse the process of aging, but individuals can improve their environment and can delay chronic problems through lifestyle changes and exercise. O'Brien and Vertinsky (1991) say that physically active women, for example, have a physical condition ten to twenty years younger than women who do not exercise. Older athletes, who take part in special national and international competitions into their 70s, can match the ability of sedentary people in their 20s. Even sedentary people can gain benefits from exercise. Studies report that three months of training can bring a sedentary person's condition up to that of active people (National Advisory Council on Aging 1994c). Leo and Blonarz (1981) report on one medical expert who says that "the body is now felt to rust out rather than wear out." Over time organs lose their reserve capacity, the amount of work they can do under conditions of great demand. But "if loss of reserve function represents aging in some sense, then exercising an organ presents a strategy for modifying the aging process" (Leo and Blonarz 1981).

THE COMPRESSION OF MORBIDITY HYPOTHESIS

Statistics Canada (cited in Norland 1994) developed the concept of **health expectancy** to describe disability and independence in later life. Health expectancy refers to the number of years a person can expect to live with some type of disability. A man at age 65 in 1986, for example, could expect to live 14.9 more years, a woman, 19.1 years. They can expect to live about half of those years (54 percent for a man and 49 percent for a woman) disability free. A man can expect to live 3.4 of his years with some, moderate, or heavy dependence, a woman about 5.8 years with dependence. A man can expect to live about 1 year in an institution, and a woman can expect to live 2.3 years in an institution. In other words, both men and women can expect to spend about a quarter of their later years in a state of moderate to heavy dependence due to disability.*

What will a longer life for Canadians mean? Will it mean more years of health and activity with a short period of illness at the end? Or will it mean a slow decline in health with more years of disability? Will we wear out quickly like Oliver Wendell

---

* Statistics Canada defines "some dependence" as help with heavy housework or groceries; "moderate dependence" as help with going out, light housework, or making meals; and "heavy dependence" with personal care and mobility at home (Norland 1994).

Holmes's "one hoss shay" that fell apart all at once? Or will we rust out over many years like an old Chevrolet? How many people will want to live 120 years, if they know that they will spend their last 30 in a nursing home with dementia or paralysis due to a stroke?

Fries (1980) gave an optimistic answer to the question of what a longer life would mean. He predicted three things: first, that more people would live a life that approached the hypothetically fixed life span of 110–120 years; second, that longer life would come about primarily through the reduction of chronic illnesses like heart disease, cancer, and stroke; and third (Fries and Crapo 1981), that severe chronic illness would occur for a short time near the end of life (the **compression of morbidity hypothesis**). Researchers have challenged all three of these predictions. A closer look at Canadian figures will show the reasons for researchers' doubts.

Challenge 1: Canadians' life expectancy has increased over the past half-century. This trend gives the impression of rectangularization of the survival curve. Exhibit 5.6 illustrates this trend, using the example of Canadian women at three time periods.

Note that according to Exhibit 5.6 cohorts born more recently die off at a slower rate than those born earlier. Also, note the drop off in numbers at later ages for the most recent cohorts. This begins to make almost a right angle on the chart and gives the name **rectangularization or squaring to the survival curve.** Fries and Crapo (1981) conclude from these curves that a finite life span exists and that modern populations have begun to approach this limit.

Note something else in Exhibit 5.6. The tail of the most recent cohort does not come as close to the zero point as the tail for earlier cohorts. This means that the oldest older women show a decreasing mortality rate. This suggests that the life span may have a flexible rather than a finite limit. It also creates a "derectangularizing" of the curve as the tail moves further to the right (Myers and Manton 1984). Simmons-Tropea and Osborn (1987, 410) conclude from this type of evidence that "although natural limits to the life span may exist, these limits are as yet unknown."

Researchers report similar findings in the United States (Schneider and Brody 1983) and in

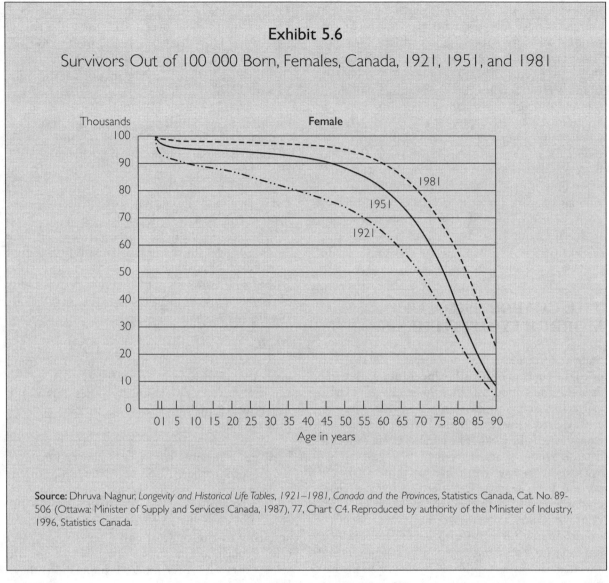

Exhibit 5.6

Survivors Out of 100 000 Born, Females, Canada, 1921, 1951, and 1981

Thousands   Female

Source: Dhruva Nagnur, *Longevity and Historical Life Tables, 1921–1981, Canada and the Provinces*, Statistics Canada, Cat. No. 89-506 (Ottawa: Minister of Supply and Services Canada, 1987), 77, Chart C4. Reproduced by authority of the Minister of Industry, 1996, Statistics Canada.

England and Wales (Grundy 1984). A model developed by Manton (1982) in the United States shows that a lower rate of chronic illness leads to lower mortality, but also to longer life expectancy. This finding goes against Fries's notion of a fixed life span. Canadian research by Kraus (1987, 59) reports a two-year increase in the "usual life span" ("the age to which only 1 percent of a birth cohort lives")—more than 100 times Fries's prediction. "Age-sex specific mortality rates in Canada in the 65–69, 70–74 ... 85+ age groups," he says, "declined from 11 percent to 18 percent in males and from 11 percent to 21 percent in females between 1974 to 1984" (Kraus 1988, 62). This trend runs counter to the rectangularization prediction.

Challenge 2: Fries (1990) says that longer life expectancy has come about through the decrease in chronic illnesses like smallpox, whooping cough, and diphtheria. In the future, he says, decreased rates of chronic illness in old age—lung cancer, stroke, and heart disease—will lead to longer life. Fries (1986) says that this indicates the possibility of a postponement of illness until late old age ("the compression of morbidity") and implies a longer and healthier life.

But some writers challenge this optimistic view of the future. Simmons-Tropea and Osborn

(1987, 411) say that "the major causes of morbidity are not necessarily related to the major causes of mortality." Manton (1986) found that in the United States chronic conditions that cause death (like heart disease) produce only small amounts of disability. Manton (1986) goes on to say that chronic degenerative (but not necessarily fatal) conditions cause the most disability. These conditions include the most common illnesses reported by older people—diabetes, respiratory problems, and arthritis/rheumatism. People live with these last few diseases for many years (Statistics Canada 1987b). Manton (1986, 680) concludes that "the numbers of disabled elderly adults can be expected to increase as the number of survivors to later ages increases due to mortality reduction."

Colvez and Blanchet (1981) report on U.S. statistics from 1966 to 1974 that show increases in the proportion of people 45 years and older who report "main activity [occupational activity, housework, etc.] impossible." As these people enter old age they will add to the proportion of older people with disabilities. Canadian data show a similar trend. In Canada from 1951 to 1978 life expectancy increased 4.5 years for men and 7.5 years for women. For this same time period, disabled years increased by 3.2 years for men and 6.1 years for women. This means that as life expectancy increased, so did the years of disability. Canadians made only small gains in disability-free years (Simmons-Tropea and Osborn 1987; see also Roberge, Berthelot, and Wolfson 1995).

Shapiro (1991) reports on a longitudinal study of Manitobans between 1971 and 1983. She concludes that "while the 1983 cohort was living to be older, their physical and mental functioning status was poorer, they had more health problems and a higher rate of hospitalization" (Shapiro 1991, 54). Using this same data Roos, Havens, and Black (1993) found that the number of older people in Manitoba increased by 29 percent between 1971 and 1983. But the number of older people in poor health increased by 73 percent. They found the greatest increase in poor health among the oldest people (aged 85 and over) (Black et al. 1995). These facts run contrary to Fries's predictions. Barer, Evans, and Hertzman (1995) reviewed a number of studies in the United States and Canada. They conclude that "the *proportion* of life spent in a state of disability is increasing" (Barer, Evans, and Hertzman 1995, 219).

Challenge 3: Trends show an increase in survivorship after the onset of chronic disease. New treatments for chronic illness explain part of this increase. Kraus reports knowing of no case in which survivorship has decreased for chronic disease where treatment has taken place. Kraus (1988) studied a representative sample of 500 death certificates of people aged 65 and over in Ontario from 1975 to 1985. He looked at causes of death and the date of death to test Fries's compression of morbidity hypothesis. Not only did he find no statistically significant findings to support compression of morbidity, he also found some findings that were inconsistent with the hypothesis.

Simmons-Tropea and Osborn (1987) sum up recent findings on the compression of morbidity hypothesis. The data, they say, "strongly suggest that the years gained in life expectancy will be largely spent suffering long-term activity limitation. Less than 30 percent of the increased years of life expectancy from 1951 to 1978 can be expected to be free from limitations" (Simmons-Tropea and Osborn 1987, 419). This leads to a pessimistic conclusion. If current trends continue, Canada will have larger numbers of older people with disabilities than ever before. These people will place more demands on health and social services.

Has this debate settled the issue of morbidity compression? Fries (1990) says that healthier habits, training, and health policies can compress morbidity. He also says that the variation in ability among seniors shows room for further compression of morbidity. In other words, if some people live morbidity-free lives into late old age, other people can follow this pattern. The potential for further improvement in well-being among older people has led some authors to study the phenomenon of **successful aging.**

SUCCESSFUL AGING

Biologists' focus on intrinsic processes has led to a more precise description of normal aging. But this research does not explain (nor does it try to explain) the differences in function among older people. It does not deal with the influence of the environment, lifestyles, and habits on physical functioning.

Rowe and Kahn (1991, 21) say that current research has produced a "gerontology of the usual." In addition to the biological focus on normal aging, they recommend the study of successful aging. This approach would look at "people who demonstrate little or no loss in a constellation of physio-logic functions ... [these people] would be regarded as more broadly successful in physiologic terms" (Rowe and Kahn 1991, 22). This research would work to understand the reasons for these people's success.

Thompson and Forbes (1990) see a contradiction in the concept of successful aging. If a person can avoid decline through lifestyle or environmental change, this decline must not be intrinsic or true aging. For this reason, the concept of successful aging may have little use to the biologist. But, for the physiologist, the clinician, and others who work at improving life in old age, the focus on successful aging has some value.

Rowe and Kahn (1991) show that in a variety of studies, including research on metabolism, osteoporosis, cognitive functioning, mortality, and well-being, extrinsic influences like diet, exercise, and social relations can inhibit and sometimes reverse functional decline (see also Molloy et al. 1988; Vandervoort et al. 1986).

Roos and Havens (1991) used the concept of successful aging in a longitudinal study of elderly Manitobans. Their definition of successful aging included the following criteria: the person had survived from 1971 to 1983; the person lived in the community in 1983; and the person received fewer than fifty-nine days of home care services in 1983. The definition also included signs of well-being in measures of health, mobility, and mental ability. They found that 20 percent of the sample aged 65 to 84 fit the criteria for successful aging in 1983. They also found that people with the following characteristics tended to age successfully: spouse maintained his or her well-being; good self-reported health in 1971; did not retire due to poor health; no cancer or diabetes; and good mental status. Successful agers also reported more life satisfaction. These findings show that successful aging depends on good self-reported health and the absence of disease. But it also depends on psychosocial influences like a spouse's well-being and good mental status.

These findings suggest that researchers should use an interdisciplinary approach to the study of aging. Studies should include psychosocial as well as physiological measures of functioning and researchers should look for links between the psychosocial and the physiological findings. Also, attention needs to be paid to the people who function best in each age group, because these people may hold the key to a longer life and a better age for everyone in the future.

CONCLUSION: SCIENTIFIC PROSPECTS FOR LONGER LIFE

People have tried to reverse or stop the process of aging at least since Ponce de Leon set out to find the fountain of youth. Drug companies have looked into the effects of animal glands, sex hormones, and chemical therapy on aging. One company that sells skin cream includes in its formula "proteins from the placentas of black sheep (because they are so resistant to disease)" (Toufexis 1986, 51). These methods can make the skin softer or add water below the skin to temporarily smooth out wrinkles, but they do nothing to increase life expectancy or reverse aging.

Still, the search goes on. Scientists have explored many methods for increasing life span and extending youth. They have found that certain drugs, calorie-restricted diets, and lowered body temperatures (during hibernation) extend the lives of some animals in the laboratory (Schneider and Reed 1985; Aussman and Russell 1990).

Will any of these methods lead to a longer, healthier life for humans in the near future? Neugarten and Havighurst (1979) asked leading biological researchers whether their work would lead to an extension in human life span in the near future. All but two of the researchers they spoke with predicted only small changes in life expectancy. Most predicted a slow increase in life expectancy in the next few years due to better health care, healthier lifestyles, and new medical technology. An end to cardiovascular disease and cancer in Canada, for instance, would add a total of 16.6 years to the life expectancy of women born in 1981 (Nagnur and Nagrodski 1988, 27). The estimated gain in male life expectancy would be 11.9 years. The elimination of the most common causes of death would raise life expectancy at birth in 1981 to about 90 years for men and about 101 years for women (Statistics Canada 1989). These figures still do not approach the currently estimated human life span of 110 to 120 years.

Some scientists propose a more optimistic scenario. Crews (1993, 288), for example, says that "the possibility of human life span extension is real and interventions that postpone human aging are a likely prospect."

Rose (1993, 72) says:

Given enough time and resource, there is no reason to doubt that eventually we will be able to postpone human aging, at least to some extent ... [T]here is the further possibility that increases in the human "health span" could likewise be open-ended ... [E]volutionarily postponed aging involves an enhancement in performance at later ages, not an extended period of debility. The long-term prospect, then, is more of an extension of youth than an increase in longevity, though the latter does occur.

Any of the following changes could increase the length of life and well-being in old age: the discovery and use of gene therapy, the use of human growth hormones, or genetic postponement of aging through natural selection. *These changes would both extend the human life span and increase the number of healthy years people live.* This prospect challenges the morbidity compression hypothesis and the findings of its critics.

But the technical ability to extend life may arrive before we have worked out the social effects of this change. For example, how would personal and social life differ if people on average lived for 120 years? How would this change our ideas about youth, middle age, and old age? Would retirement at age 65 make any sense? Would people and society adjust their life cycles and careers to meet this new schedule?

Studies of people aged 100 years or more throughout the world give some clue about what a long-lived society will look like. These studies report that long-lived people have: good genes, a purpose in life, physical activity, independence, close family ties, friends, good hygiene, a simple balanced diet, low stress, good self-esteem, and a belief in God (Palmore, 1987). In other words, centenarians live balanced lives in supportive social settings.

These findings suggest that we expand the quest for a long life beyond the realm of science and science fiction. We should place the search for a full life where it belongs: within the power of each of us and the society we live in. We can and will extend life through scientific research. But life extension will only put off the deeper question: Can we give meaning and purpose to those added years?

SUMMARY

1. Chronic health problems increase with age. People with a low income have more health problems than those with a higher income.
2. Changes in health in turn lead to changes in activity and in people's ability to function on their own. Declines in ability can lead to the need for help with activities of daily living.
3. Social and health care supports as well as a more supportive environment can all help older people maintain their independence.
4. Technology can help people cope with declines in health. Simple objects like spoons can be adapted for people with arthritis, computers can increase a person's contact with others, and in the future robots may help people bathe, exercise, and do daily tasks. Eyeglasses, hearing aids, and a supportive environment can make up for losses in the senses.
5. Research shows that changes in diet and exercise can slow the aging process. People can even improve their lung capacity and bone density through exercise. This can lead to a longer and healthier life.
6. The compression of morbidity hypothesis says that people will live longer and have more disability-free years in the future. But recent research questions this view, suggesting instead that a longer life may lead to more years of disability.
7. Many older people stay healthy and active as they age. They live without physical handicap and without special help. Studies of successful aging show that people can extend the number years they live in good health. In the future, science may find a way for people to live past the current limits of the human life span.

STUDY QUESTIONS

1. Describe the changes in health that often occur in later life. How does income affect health in old age?
2. What effects does physical decline have on activity in later life? What do older people need in order to maintain their independence? How can older people cope with physical change?
3. Describe three broad responses to physical aging that can improve or maintain physical well-being in later life. Discuss some of the problems that can limit useful responses to physical change. How could these problems be overcome?
4. State the compression of morbidity hypothesis. Briefly present three challenges to this hypothesis.
5. What do biologists mean by successful aging? How can this concept expand our thinking about physical potential in later life?
6. What scientific developments might extend the human life span in the future? What developments might expand the span of good health?

KEY TERMS

activities of daily living (ADLs)   bathing, moving from a bed or chair, dressing, getting to and using the toilet, eating, and walking.

chronic health problems   long-term illnesses like arthritis, rheumatism, hypertension, diabetes, and heart disease.

compression of morbidity hypothesis   the idea that severe chronic illness would occur for a short time near the end of life.

health expectancy   the number of years a person can expect to live with some type of disability.

hypokinesia   physical problems due to lack of movement.

instrumental activities of daily living (IADLs) home management activities like using the phone, shopping, and doing light housework.

life expectancy   the number of years at birth an average member of a society can expect to live.

maximum life span   the maximum number of years a member of a species can live.

reaction time   refers to how fast a person responds to a demand from the environment.

rectangularization or squaring to the survival curve   more recent survival curves make almost a right angle and take on a square shape.

successful aging   the study of "people who demonstrate little or no loss in a constellation of physio-logic functions … [these people] would be regarded as more broadly successful in physiologic terms" (Rowe and Kahn 1991, 22).

SELECTED READINGS

Government of Canada. *Ageing and Independence: Overview of a National Survey.* Cat. No. H88-3/13-1993E. Ottawa: Minister of Supply and Services Canada, 1993.

   A summary of the Statistics Canada national survey on health and the social life of older people. This book presents findings on health status, activity limitation, and stress.

Schneider, Edward L., and John W. Rowe, eds. *Handbook of the Biology of Aging.* 4th ed. San Diego: Academic Press, 1996.

   A review of the latest findings in the field of biology and aging. Topics range from studies of cells to studies of physiological change in later life. Readers with little scientific background may find the chapters difficult to understand, but this is an excellent resource for the latest findings in the biology of aging.

The Psychology of Aging

INTRODUCTION

A few years ago, one of Canada's leading geriatric specialists gave a talk on memory to a group of seniors. He told the group that, in the absence of disease, memory stays about the same in old age as in youth. Young people and old people both forget things, he said, but older people notice it more, because they expect memory loss to come with age. A man stood up at the end of the talk and said, "I respect your views, Doctor. But I know my memory has gotten worse with age. What I want to know is what I can do about it." This response fits with two things research has found out about older people and memory: first, older people believe their memories are getting worse (Dobbs and Rule 1987; Hultsch, Hertzog, and Dixon 1987; Ryan and See 1993), and, second, memory failure upsets them, even if they forget something unimportant (Cavanaugh, Grady, and Perlmutter 1983).

Many people, older people included, accept the stereotype that cognitive decline is a normal part of aging. But recent research on memory, intelligence, and creativity questions this belief (Perlmutter 1988). Studies show that people can learn and grow intellectually in old age as well as in youth. On some measures mental ability may even improve with age. Dramatic declines in mental functioning are due to physiological disorders or distress, not to normal aging.

This chapter will look at: (1) memory and intelligence in later life, (2) creativity, and (3) the psychological problems some older people face.

PSYCHOLOGICAL STUDIES OF AGING

Birren and Schroots (1996; see also Schroots 1995) describe three approaches psychologists take to the study of aging: the psychology of the aged; the psychology of age; and the psychology of aging. The **psychology of the aged,** they say, describes life in old age. It emphasizes the biomedical view of aging as decline or disease. It supports ageism and the view of older people as a social problem. The **psychology of age** focuses on differences between age groups. It uses cross-sectional methods to study differences between age groups. For example, researchers compare the mental abilities of young and old people on measures of memory or intelligence. The **psychology of aging** studies changes in individuals over time. It uses longitudinal methods to study both gains and losses through the life cycle. The sections that follow discuss the psychology of age and the psychology of aging approaches to the study of memory and intelligence.

NORMAL CHANGES IN PSYCHOLOGICAL FUNCTIONING

The brain changes with age. These changes vary from person to person, but, in general, the brain shrinks in size, loses weight, and loses neurons. The brain also develops more abnormalities like **neurofibrillary tangles,** neuronal fibres wrapped around one another. These show up in healthy older brains and in greater numbers in cases of Alzheimer's disease. Still, Scheibel (1996) says, research on the older brain also shows that (1) changes in the brain take place gradually throughout life; (2) people lose more neurons in childhood than in healthy adulthood; (3) the nervous system has a remarkable ability to adapt to change; and (4) most neurons live through the entire life of the person. This allows for continuity and growth throughout life. Recent studies of learning, memory, and intelligence support these conclusions. These studies show that individuals differ in their mental abilities over time. And some mental abilities improve with age.

LEARNING AND MEMORY

Memory is the recall of information after learning has taken place. Most measurement of memory takes place in psychology laboratories. Psychologists in the field of aging have spent more time on the study of memory than on any other topic. Smith (1996, 236) reports that studies of memory and aging made up "34% of all the published papers in the two journals, *Psychology and Aging* and *Journal of Gerontology: Psychological Sciences*." Psychologists show a strong interest in memory and aging for a number of reasons. First, popular stereotypes about aging and early psychological research on memory predict a decline in memory with age. If this is true, studies of memory can trace the causes of this decline. Second, psychologists can study memory in the laboratory under controlled conditions. This makes research on memory relatively easy to do. Third, studies of memory have produced testable models of how the mind works. These models attempt to explain complex processes like learning, forgetting, and the storage and retrieval of information. For all of these reasons the study of memory has dominated the study of psychological aging.

Researchers break the process of remembering into a series of steps. Most researchers today use an information-processing model to guide their work (France 1990). This model includes the following steps: (1) a person perceives information, which psychologists call **sensory memory;** (2) the person acts on this information, transforms it in some way, while the information sits in **short-term memory;** and (3) the person stores the information in **long-term memory,** the storehouse of knowledge that also includes the rules for applying knowledge.

Take the example of looking up and remembering a phone number. You open the phone book and see the number (sensory memory). You repeat it to yourself a few times as your eye moves from the phone book to the dial (short-term memory). You make a rhyme of the number so you can remember it later (long-term memory). The greatest mental work goes on when a person stores information in long-term memory.

Much of the research on memory and aging points to some decline in memory with age (Waugh and Barr 1982; Arenberg 1977). Welford (1958), for example, referred to the decline in learning ability in old age (the decline in retention of information) as an established fact.

Many studies show that older people take longer to learn new information, longer to search for it in memory, and longer to use it when they need it. Cerella (1990) says that latency (the length of time a person takes to process information or make a response to a question) increases with age. Hultsch and his colleagues (1992) studied two groups of older people (one aged 65 on average, the other aged 75 on average). They found that over three years decrements in processing time occurred. They also found that the older group showed more decrement than the younger group.

Foisy (1995) reviewed twenty-two studies of word memory. He found that older people showed the greatest decline in memory on free-recall tests when they had the fewest cues from the environ-

ment. Older people showed the least decline in memory on recognition tests. Foisy says that free-recall probably demands more processing resources. A decline in these resources with age would account for these findings. Cerella (1990) agrees. He says that processing time increases regardless of the content of the task. He calls this process "generalized slowing" and considers this a classical and well-accepted finding in the field of cognitive psychology (see also Craik 1994). Birren and Schroots (1996) say that this finding shows the link between decreased brain integrity and mental ability.

Research shows that some types of memory decline more than others. **Explicit memory,** in which the person intends to remember, decreases more with age than **implicit memory,** in which memory occurs without intention (Hultsch and Dixon 1990). Also, external conditions influence an older person's actual ability to remember. Studies show, for example, that the design of memory tests, their content, and the use of cross-sectional designs (which compare older and younger people at one point in time) may all lead to exaggerated estimates of memory decline in older people. Hundreds of studies have tried to sort out the effects of age on memory.

In particular, the research has focused on differences in learning (acquisition) between younger and older subjects. Psychologists believe that retrieval and acquisition are closely related. How someone retrieves information (how they search for and find information in memory) depends on how they acquired it (the methods they used to organize and store the information).

Laboratory Studies

Some studies have found deficits in memory in older people due to the way they learn and store information (Annon and Lee, 1994). Ska and Nespoulous (1988), for example, studied **encoding** (the process whereby a person takes new bits of information and puts them together with already stored information) and retrieval in a sample of 150 people aged 20 to 84. They found that "elderly subjects reproduced less during the encoding phase and retrieved fewer elements during the recall phase" (1988, 408). Speeded trials appear to increase the learning deficit. More than the young, older subjects miss verbal and pictorial items presented at a rapid rate. They miss late items in a list more than earlier ones, and they encode some items at the expense of others. Waugh and Barr (1982, 190) say that "the older the subject, the less efficiently and the more selectively he encodes—perhaps because ... he simply lacks the time to encode efficiently and comprehensively."

Other studies (Kausler 1982) report that older people do not automatically use **mediators,** the process of picturing a word or finding a rhyme for a word, to help with remembering (Kausler 1982). Sanders et al. (1980) found that older learners take an inactive and nonstrategic approach to memorizing their lists, while younger ones actively organized and categorized their lists as they memorized them (Sanders et al. 1980; see also Howard, McAndrews, and Lasagna 1981).

This research suggests that memory decline in older adults may be due in part to the use of inefficient processing techniques. More recent research on memory in old age questions these conclusions. Light (1990) reviewed the literature on the effects of encoding on older people's memories. She weighed the evidence on inefficient mental processing as the reason for memory decline and reported that, in total, "the literature offers no support for the claim that deficits in semantic processing underlie memory problems in old age." She goes on to say that "the organization of knowledge is quite stable across the adult years" (Light 1990, 281).

Light (1990) traces memory differences between older and younger people to deficits in older people's **working memory.** Working memory stores recent information and also attends to, selects, and manipulates this information. In addition, it processes new information, while temporarily storing other information (Hultsch and Dixon 1990).

A number of studies point to a decrease in working memory as a source of memory deficits in older people. First, older adults remember less well when irrelevant information comes between two things to be remembered. Light and Capps (1986) found that older adults did less well when they added irrelevant sentences between two things to be remembered. Second, older adults have more difficulty remembering when the material they have to remember comes in a scrambled order (Light et al. 1982). If sentences are presented in a scrambled order, the older person will have more trouble holding all the information in working memory and making sense of the information. Third, topic changes place a greater load on working memory and lead to poorer memory in older people. When a topic changes, older people appear to forget relevant information. Salthouse and Babcock (1991, cited in Smith 1996) say that decreased processing ability leads to poorer working memory in older people.

Other factors, besides age, may account for the differences in memory between older and younger people found in laboratory studies. Differences in educational background and verbal ability, for example, may influence results in memory studies. Cavanaugh (1983) studied the recall of TV show content and found that when subjects had low verbal ability older people recalled less than younger people. But when younger subjects and older subjects both had high verbal ability, the study showed no difference between the two age groups' scores. Taub (1979) found that the better a person's vocabulary, the greater their ability to retain pieces of prose in memory. Bowles and Poon (1982) found significant age differences in memory between young and old samples with a low vocabulary, but no age differences in high-vocabulary samples.

Test conditions can also influence older subjects' performance on memory tests. Ross (1968), for example, found that a supportive context improved older subjects' ability to learn paired words. A challenging setting, where the instructor said that she would test the students' intelligence, led to the least efficient learning. Poon (1985) found that when older people could control the pace of their learning they showed less decrement in memory.

Finally, most studies show that older people learn familiar and relevant material better than new and irrelevant material. Barrett and Wright (1981), for example, found that older people did less well than younger people on a list of words unfamiliar to them, but they showed a better rate of recall than younger people on a list of familiar words. These studies show that laboratory tests and experiments put the older learner at a disadvantage.

Laboratory studies raise an important question: how well do the results of memory research predict an older person's ability to remember details in everyday life? The answer: not very well.

Memory studies done under laboratory conditions have poor ecological validity (the transferability of knowledge from lab to life). Older people rarely learn or recall well under pressure, and research shows that they remember best when they learn information relevant and useful to them.

The Contextual Approach

The **contextual view** begins with the insight that many conditions influence memory, including "the physical, psychological, and social context in which the event was experienced, the knowledge, abilities, and characteristics the individual brings to the context, [and] the situation in which we ask for evidence of remembering" (Hultsch and Deutsch 1981, 153).

Charness (1981, 1985), for example, reports on a study of younger and older chess players' problem-solving abilities. He found that older players had more difficulty than younger players at the

---

Exhibit 6.1

Teaching Methods for Use with Senior Students

Hultsch and Deutsch (1981) suggest the following methods to help older people learn better in the classroom. Some of these methods should be used no matter what the student's age (taking breaks, giving immediate feedback on tests), while others apply more to seniors than to other age groups (giving visual and aural cues to help memory, speaking slowly and distinctly).

	Technique	Description of the Technique		Technique	Description of the Technique
1.	Pacing	Remove time pressures. Let people set their own pace.	6.	Feedback	Let people know how they did as soon as possible so they can fix mistakes.
2.	Anxiety Arousal	Decrease anxiety. Decrease competition and testing. Let people get used to new ideas or techniques.	7.	Cues	Give older people visual and aural cues to help them with their work. Use clear diagrams, speak clearly, and repeat questions from the class so that everyone follows the discussion.
3.	Fatigue	Give older students rest breaks or cut down the length of time for each lesson.			
4.	Difficulty	Build people up by starting with simple and moving on to more complex work. Break the work into segments.	8.	Organization	Group information for students. Use memory aids like pictures, mental images, or verbal cues.
5.	Practice	Give people a chance to use what they know in different ways.	9.	Relevance/ Experience	Find out what the older student wants to know. Build on students' past experiences. Show them how to apply what they learn.

Source: Adapted from David F. Hultsch and Francine Deutsch, *Adult Development and Aging: A Life-Span Perspective* (New York: McGraw-Hill), 152. Copyright 1981, reproduced by permission of The McGraw-Hill Companies.

same skill level in recalling positions accurately (see also McIntyre and Craik 1987). He attributes this difficulty to older players' poorer retrieval ability. But when Charness (1981) evaluated game-playing performance, he found that skill level, not age, determined a player's ability. Older players did as well as younger players of the same skill level. "Given the retrieval deficits associated with aging," Charness asks, "why is there no deficit in molar [overall] problem-solving performance?" (1981, 34–35). Charness tentatively concludes that the components of chess playing may vary among people in different age groups. Also, older players may use a more efficient search for alternative solutions.

In a study of the effects of age and skill on bridge players, Charness (1985, 1987) also found that skill compensated for decreases in information processing speed. He found that older subjects reacted more slowly than younger subjects on a novel task (unrelated to bridge). But accuracy in bidding depended only on skill level (not age). Charness (1987, 241) concluded that older players may use "preassembled (and highly efficient) programs to maintain effective performance." Dixon and Backman (1993) propose that older people who maintain their cognitive abilities may compensate for losses. They may put more effort into a task, they may call on a past skill, or they may develop a new skill. Dixon and Backman say that people who have a high level of skill at a task show the greatest likelihood of using these methods.

This study and the previous review of the literature supports the idea that factors other than biological decline can influence mental performance in older people. Research shows that different types of older people (with more or less education or skill) (Bosman 1993), under a variety of conditions (supportive or nonsupportive), and exposed to varying types of materials to learn (relevant or irrelevant) differ in their ability to perform mental tasks or to remember specific information.

Only a few studies have looked directly at what older people remember about the world around them. These studies have found little of the memory deficit reported in laboratory studies. A study of memory of recent public events, for example, found no difference between younger and older subjects (between ages 20 and 80) (Poon et al. 1979). When the researchers asked about

events that occurred from the 1920s to the 1970s, they found that older subjects scored better than younger subjects.

McIntyre and Craik (1987) tested older and younger subjects about their knowledge of Canadian facts. They found that older people had less ability than younger people to recall the source of their facts. But the two groups had about the same ability to recall facts after a week, and the older group had a greater knowledge of facts about Canada at the start of the experiment. The researchers note that this study of knowledge about the world, compared with typical laboratory studies, led to smaller differences in recall between older and younger subjects.

Hultsch and Dixon (1990) reviewed the literature on memory for meaningful events and materials. They found that in some studies younger adults outperformed older people. But in others older adults performed as well as younger people. One study (Hultsch and Dixon 1983), for example, looked at the ability of older and younger people to remember biographical sketches. The study found that younger adults remembered better when the sketch referred to a person known best to the younger adults. The researchers found equivalent recall rates for entertainment figures known to both the younger and older adults. Another study (Backman 1985) found that older people remember as well as younger people when they perform an activity related to the item they have to remember. Poon (1985, 435) concludes a review of the research on memory by saying that "in general, evidence to date shows minimal differences in memory for familiar discourse materials that may be found in the everyday environment."

The research reported to date should end the stereotyping of older people as forgetful. Cerella and his colleagues (Cerella et al. 1993) reviewed the literature and found studies of improvements in cognitive ability with age. These studies report compensation for decline, positive effects of physical exercise on memory, and benefits from training (see Baltes and Baltes 1990). These researchers suggest that gerontologists take a more balanced view of memory loss in later life.

The current literature shows that memory depends on the external environment and the material to be remembered as well as on intrinsic changes in the brain due to aging. Older people may have different learning styles and a different attitude toward laboratory tests than younger people, as well as different abilities on different memory tasks. On some types of tasks they remember less well than younger adults. But, on many everyday tasks and meaningful information, older people remember as well as younger people.

INTELLIGENCE

The research on intelligence in old age parallels the research on memory: early studies assumed that intelligence also decreases in old age as the body declines. More recent research questions this simple connection between senescence and intelligence.

Psychologists use at least two definitions of **intelligence.** First, taking a global view, they refer to it as the "ability to negotiate environmental demands successfully" (Labouvie-Vief 1985, 506). Second, they take a pragmatic view, referring to it as "that which intelligence tests measure" (Labouvie-Vief 1985, 506) or "what the testtaker can do now" (Botwinick 1984, 250). Psychologists most often use this second (more limited) definition when they conduct research on intelligence and aging.

Early research done in the 1930s reported a decline in intellectual ability after age 20 (Miles and Miles 1932; Jones and Conrad 1933; Wechsler 1939). These findings supported the idea that mental ability declines along with the body, and all IQ tests build this expectation of decline into their design. They assume that older people will score less well than younger people, and they correct for supposed age declines in their formulas for calculating IQ. The Wechsler Adult Intelligence Scale (WAIS–R) manual uses this approach. It puts the peak of intelligence at between 20 and 34 years (Wechsler 1981) and assumes that each later age group will show a decline in scores.

The actual scores on WAIS–R scales support this assumption of decline with age, but they also show that decline does not take place uniformly. Scores on the WAIS–R Verbal Scale, for example, decrease steadily from a mean score of 61.42 at ages 25–34 to a mean of 51.50 at ages 70–74 (84 percent of the younger group's score). Scores on the performance scale drop earlier and more sharply from 51.14 at ages 20–24 to a mean score of 30.62 at ages 70–74 (60 percent of the younger group's score) (Wechsler 1981, 26).

Other cross-sectional studies of intelligence show a similar pattern of decline in some abilities and less decline in others (Schaie and Labouvie-

---

Exhibit 6.2

Controversy: Physical Change as the Source of Mental Decline

Cerella (1990, 201) proposes that deficits in cognitive functioning (like memory) "could be interpreted as being distributed throughout the information-processing system rather than being localized in particular stages." He proposes that breakdowns in the neural network of the older person or slower transit time lead to slower processing of information. Each breakdown requires the input to travel a greater distance. The older the person, the greater the neural decay and the slower the processing time. This not only explains the general slowing phenomenon, but also indicates why older people do less well on tests that emphasize speed, or why they may do as well as younger people on skilled tasks that have well-established neural networks.

This model, Cerella (1990) says, offers a simple explanation that replaces the many explanations related to specific tasks (like storage and retrieval). Cerella (1990, 217) also says that through this new theoretical development, "cognitive aging reemerges as a subfield of neurophysiology rather than cognitive psychology." This work challenges current models of cognitive psychology. It needs further development, but, in the meantime, it will stimulate further refinement of our thinking about cognitive ability in later life.

Vief 1974). Researchers generally agree that a significant decline in intelligence scores takes place past age 60 (Schaie 1990a). But researchers argue over the meaning of these findings, disagreeing on at least three issues: (1) the concept of intelligence as a single structure; (2) the methods used to produce these findings; and (3) the potential of cognitive functioning in later life.

Intelligence as Multidimensional

Current research on intelligence supports a multidimensional view of intelligence. The WAIS–R scales themselves point to this multidimensionality. They show what Botwinick (1984) calls the "classic aging pattern." The Performance Scale scores show a much greater decrease with age than the Verbal Scale scores (40 percent vs. 16 percent). "This classic aging pattern, relative maintenance of function in verbal skills as compared to performance skills, has been seen many times with a variety of different populations" (Botwinick 1984, 254). These findings give support to the idea that "both decrement and stability—or even growth—over the adult period [are] the rule" (Labouvie-Vief 1985, 502; see also Schaie 1996).

Horn and Cattell have developed a model of intelligence that explains these results. They describe two types of intelligence—fluid and crystallized intelligence (Horn and Cattell 1966; 1967; Cattell 1963). **Fluid intelligence** refers to reasoning, abstracting, concept formation, and problem solving. It makes little use of knowledge gained through reading, schooling, or work. According to Horn and Cattell, fluid intelligence relies on how well the physical and nervous systems function. Performance tests that demand the use of fluid intelligence ask subjects to manipulate unfamiliar material in new ways mentally, and they sometimes require skill at manipulating objects physically. Verbal tests that demand the use of **crystallized intelligence** depend more on stored information, acculturation, and learning (Horn 1978).

This two-part model helps explain the empirical results on intelligence. Numerical and verbal skill problems measure crystallized intelligence; spatial and reasoning questions measure fluid intelligence. Fluid intelligence may follow the decline of the biological system from the teen years on, while studies of crystallized intelligence show stable intelligence scores and even increases in scores with age.

Schwartzman et al. (1987) conducted a longitudinal study of Canadian World War II male army veterans. The study found declines in spatial problem-solving, or fluid intelligence. But the study found that scores on crystallized intelligence, measured by vocabulary and mechanical knowledge, increased over time. Overall the study found that on both spatial problems and vocabulary problems individual scores changed only slightly (a 16.1 percent loss in spatial problem solving and a 10.5 percent gain in vocabulary) over forty years.

Charness (1982) also found multidirectional changes in older people's mental ability as measured by problem-solving tasks. He reviewed the literature on mental ability and found that older people do less well than younger people on novel problem-solving tasks, but perform about as well as younger subjects on familiar tasks that older subjects know well, like chess or bridge. Botwinick (1984) reports that chronological age accounts for only about one-quarter of the variance in IQ scores. This means that age alone is not a very sound predictor of a person's intelligence score (Schaie 1959). Baltes and Willis sum up the current research: "The striking feature of descriptive aging research, is one of much variability, both between persons and within persons for distinct abilities" (1982, 355).

Longitudinal vs. Cross-Sectional Methods

Like studies of memory, most studies of intelligence use a cross-sectional method to draw conclusions about age changes. These studies ignore the fact that older and younger cohorts differ on more variables than just age. Few studies of intelligence have looked at the variability among individuals (differences like educational level, social class, personal experience) in their samples. Age cohorts differ in education, test-taking ability, and vocabulary. These characteristics depend on when people were born and what they have done in their lifetimes (Schaie 1990a; Schaie 1996). When intelligence tests are used to compare age groups at one point in time, they confound cohort differences with age changes.

Longitudinal and sequential studies of intelligence try to overcome this problem by measuring the same groups of people at more than one point in time. Most longitudinal studies find less decline in intelligence with age than do cross-sectional studies. Schaie (1990b, 114), for example, studied one group over time and found that "virtually none of the individuals … showed universal decline on all abilities monitored, even by the eighties." By age 60, he reports, three-quarters of the people in the study maintained their ability over a seven-year period on four of five measures. Even at age 81 more than half the sample maintained its ability over a seven-year period (Schaie 1990b). These findings support the idea that each person shows unique changes in mental ability with age (Birren and Schroots 1996).

Schaie and Labouvie-Vief (1974) gave intelligence tests in 1970 to 301 people who had been tested in 1956 and 1963. They added new people to their study to make up for those who had dropped out since the first sample. They found that younger people scored better than older people. But they also found that older people got roughly the same scores as they had seven years before. The researchers concluded that cohort differences accounted for most of the variations in test scores between younger and older subjects.

Botwinick (1984) takes a less optimistic view of intellectual functioning in old age. He reviewed the Schaie and Labouvie-Vief (1974) longitudinal study and found that decline set in at about age 53. Earlier cross-sectional research by Schaie (1959) showed declines around age 55. "Thus, the longitudinal sequences and the cross-sectional data are not very different" (Botwinick 1984, 262). Declines in intelligence occur regardless of the method used.

Botwinick (1984, 262) also says that longitudinal studies play down the effects of age on intelligence because people with low intelligence scores drop out of the studies. This leaves more intelligent people at older ages. The longer the study and the greater the number of tests on the subjects who remain, the more the dropout factor affects the results.

A study by Botwinick and Siegler (1980) controlled for dropouts and found that both longitudinal and cross-sectional analyses showed declines in intelligence with age. Labouvie-Vief (1985) responded to Botwinick and Siegler (1980) by noting that they studied people aged 60 and over. She says that cohort differences showed up in Schaie and Labouvie-Vief (1974) mostly for groups aged 60 and under. For subjects past age 70, Schaie and Labouvie-Vief (1974) also found steady declines in intelligence with age. Labouvie-Vief (1985, 505) concludes that decline in intelligence does occur late in life, but that current research at least calls "attention to the fact that significant decrements are considerably delayed into the far end of the 60- to 70-year-old spectrum."

The debate over the effects of age on intelligence continues in the literature. Future research will focus on the causes of differences in intelligence within different age groups and between different cohorts.

Improvements in Cognitive Functioning in Later Life

Some of the latest research on intelligence explores ways to improve older people's intellectual functioning. Charness and Campbell (1988) tested young, middle-aged, and older people's mental calculation skills. They found that older adults gained skill in calculation in the same way that younger adults did. The older group showed "marked improvement" in their ability with practice (Charness and Campbell 1988, 127). And they equalled the starting level of the youngest group before the end of the study. The researchers conclude that the older group's improvement "is testimony to the malleability of the human information processing system, even in old age (128)."

This research shows that older people can improve their performance on intelligence tests. Instruction in test-taking methods and in problem-solving strategies can improve the cognitive performance of older subjects (Labouvie-Vief 1977; Baltes and Willis 1981; Denney and Palmer 1981; Schaie 1990a).

Some of these studies show long-term effects. After one year, Sanders and Sanders (1978) found that trained subjects performed better than untrained subjects or subjects who simply practised similar problems. Schaie (1996) reports that trained subjects compared with control subjects over seven years showed less decline in intelligence. Refresher courses can maintain the benefits of training as people age. These studies show that "the old, like the young, have more potential than is typically measured by the tests" (Botwinick 1984, 271).

Jackson et al. (1990) sum up the research on intellectual ability in later life. "As has been suggested by an impressive body of empirical work," they say, "some abilities decline, some remain the same, and some improve with chronological age" (Jackson et al. 1990, 115). The change that takes place depends on the ability studied and on background factors like education and health (Baltes 1987).

Studies show that people who have good health and who live in a challenging environment score better on intelligence tests than those who do not (Gold et al. 1995; Schaie 1975; Schooler 1990). People who read books and newspapers and who travel and talk with friends keep their minds fresh. Researchers now think of the individual as modifiable. Baltes and Willis (1982, 120–21) conclude that "people can learn to make better use of their minds at any age. The logical approach [to observed decrements in mental functioning in later life] might be the development of compensatory education programs at about the time of retirement." The section in Chapter 12 on education discusses some of these programs in detail.

New Models of Mental Ability in Later Life

Schroots (1995) says that the psychology of aging describes typical changes in psychological function over time. It focuses on the mature organism. This model of aging tends to view life as a hill. Ability increases, plateaus, then declines. But, Schroots says, this view has begun to change. The study of wisdom offers a different view of psychological change in later life.

Paul B. Baltes, director of Berlin's Max Planck Institute for Human Development and Education, has conducted some of the most respected research on intelligence. He says that two concepts have led to recent changes in his thinking about mental ability in later life (Baltes and Baltes, 1990). First, research shows variability between individuals. In general, younger people outperform older people on intelligence tests. But, on a given measure, some older people perform better than younger people. Morse (1993), for example, found the greatest variability among older people on fluid intelligence tasks. Second, research shows **plastic-**

ity for each individual. Each person has a reserve mental capacity. Willis (1990), for example, found this potential up to late old age.

Baltes (1992; 1993) concludes that past research has taken too narrow a view of mental ability in later life. He says that certain types of cognitive processes, what he calls **cognitive mechanics** (similar to fluid intelligence), decline with age. Other types of cognitive processes, what he calls **cognitive pragmatics** (similar to crystallized intelligence), improve with age. Baltes says that knowledge and culture can enrich cognitive pragmatics throughout life.

Baltes set out to explore the "new domain" of cognitive pragmatics in old age. To do this he set up the "Berlin wisdom project." This project defines **wisdom** as "expert knowledge about the important and fundamental matters of life, their interpretation and management" (Featherman, Smith and Peterson, 1990; see also Baltes et al. 1990). The project studies wisdom by asking older people to solve real-life problems. One problem, for example, asked people to respond to a suicidal call from a friend. Another one asked people to give advice to a 15-year-old girl who wants to get married (White 1993).

A person who displays wisdom has insight into life's conditions and shows good judgment. This person gives good advice. Rybash, Hoyer, and Roodin (1986) say that younger people may do better than older people in problem solving in a lab or classroom. They can answer clearly structured problems faster than older people. But older people may do better at "problem finding." Older people have a greater ability to shape and solve a problem in a less defined situation. Baltes (1992) reports that older people get higher scores than younger people on problems related to real-life dilemmas. More than half of the top responses, he says, come from people over age 60.

Wisdom makes older people more skilled at working in everyday life. This could allow older people to play a unique role in modern society. Baltes and his colleagues suggest that a society with more older people will have a greater storehouse of wisdom. Society could use that wisdom to redefine problems that escape rational and technical solution (Featherman, Smith, and Peterson, 1990). More older people thinking and advising about

---

Exhibit 6.3

Five Criteria of Wisdom

Psychologist Paul Baltes compiled a list of five criteria for wisdom based on cognitive psychology and life-span theory. A person who had this knowledge would have "exceptional insight into life matters and good judgment and advice about difficult life problems."

1. Rich factual knowledge about life matters.
2. Rich procedural knowledge about life problems.
3. Life-span contextualism: Knowledge about the contexts of life and their temporal (developmental) relationships.

4. Relativism: Knowledge about differences in values and priorities.
5. Uncertainty: Knowledge about the relative indeterminacy and unpredictability of life and ways to manage.

Source: P.B. Baltes, J. Smith, U.M. Staudinger, and D. Sowarka, "Wisdom: One Facet of Successful Aging?" In M. Perlmutter, ed., *Late Life Potential*, 63–81 (Washington, DC: The Gerontological Society of America, 1990). Reprinted with permission.

---

practical problems could enhance the quality of life for everyone. But, for this to occur, society first has to recognize wisdom in its older people (Baltes 1993). Then it has to have the good sense to make use of it. Baltes's work takes the first step by expanding our view of mental potential in later life.

CREATIVITY

The bulk of research on psychology and aging has focused on changes in memory and intelligence with age. Comparatively few studies have looked at creativity in later life. At least three different measures of creativity exist in the literature (Botwinick 1984). First, some studies measure creative achievement by evaluating the greatness of a work or by counting the number of creative works by an individual. Second, some studies use psychological tests to measure creativity. These tests take place in the laboratory and allow for comparisons of old and young people in a number of dimensions. Third, some studies use a more global definition of creativity. They define creative activity as activity that brings fulfillment to the individual and possibly even to others (though it might not reach worldwide or historical importance). Studies done from each point of view have looked at whether creativity declines with age.

Creativity as Measured by Great Works

Lehman (1953) studied the ages at which scientists, philosophers, mathematicians, painters, inventors, and other creative people produced their greatest works. He selected for his sample people who had already died (because someone still alive could still produce a great work). Lehman found that past and present scientists produced their greatest creative work between the ages of 30 and 40. Most great writers produced their foremost work before the age of 45, and most poets produced theirs in their late 20s and early 30s. Painters peaked between ages 30 and 45. In most fields Lehman found that achievement steadily decreased after age 45.

Lehman (1968) went on to study athletes, chess champions, orators, politicians, businessmen, and atomic scientists. He found that still-living atomic scientists, for example, showed a peak in achievement between ages 25 to 29 and a sharp drop in achievement from age 35 on. He also found that older atomic scientists (aged 60 to 64) made only one-tenth the number of contributions as the younger (25- to 29-year-old) scientists. Lehman found the same pattern for still-living astronomers, mathematicians, and botanists.

Exhibit 6.4

Wisdom in Later Life

Plato, in The Republic, says that he likes to talk to older people. They have gone along a path that all of us will one day follow. So, they have a unique perspective on life and aging. Some might call it wisdom. Consider the following thoughts on aging by some thoughtful older people.

Art Blake, a retired judge from Jamaica, says that last year he attended the funeral of a friend. He flew back to Jamaica and went directly to the church from the airport. His plane had arrived early, so he reached the church before anyone else. "I watched as the people arrived," he says. "Many of them I knew from my childhood, we went to school and grew up together. These are all old people, I thought. Then I thought, I too must look like this. But I couldn't see it in myself. I shave everyday and I don't see my age. But, I could see it in them. ... The mind plays tricks on you."

Art serves as the legal adviser to an education program for older people, and sits on the advisory board of a university certification program. "We want to be young," Art says. "We use creams to smooth out the wrinkles. But this is the most natural process. We cannot help but get old."

Bertrand Russell developed new interests as he aged. He began his career as a mathematician, moved on to philosophy, then in late old age he turned to political and social issues. At age 80, he said,

> The best way to overcome it [old age]—so at least it seems to me—is to make your interests gradually wider and more impersonal, until bit by bit the walls of the ego recede, and your life becomes increasingly merged in the universal life. An individual human existence should be like a river—small at first, narrowly contained within its banks, and rushing passionately past boulders and over waterfalls. Gradually the river grows wider, the banks recede, the waters flow more quietly, and in the end, without any visible break, they become merged in the sea and painlessly lose their individual being. (cited in Puner 1979, 270)

John Holt, an educator who wrote about children and their untapped potential, turned to reflect on education for adults later in his career. Holt took up the cello in late middle age. He wrote about his experience learning the instrument and about his own potential as a person.

> If I could learn to play the cello well, as I thought I could," he wrote in his book *Never Too Late*, "I could show by my own example that we all have greater powers than we think; that whatever we want to learn or learn to do, we probably can learn; that our lives and our possibilities are not determined and fixed by what happened to us when we were little, or by what experts say we can or cannot do. (Holt 1978, 185)

Lehman's research set off a wave of controversy. Dennis (1968), for example, challenged Lehman's conclusions about the decline in creativity with age. First, he said, Lehman's research combined people with different lengths of life. Fewer people live to old age, so there will be fewer people to create great works in later life. Lehman's findings, therefore, might reflect a demographic fact rather than a decline in creativity. Second, Dennis questioned Lehman's approach to the study of creativity. Lehman used the works of critics, historians, and experts to decide on the quality of his subjects' work. Dennis argued that experts may favour the early, groundbreaking work of great people and could find it harder to judge more recent work by a great master.

Dennis (1968) conducted his own research on creativity. He used a measure different from Lehman's to compensate for these errors. First, while Lehman studied the age when creators produced their greatest work, Dennis studied the creative output (the number of works produced) of

---

Exhibit 6.5

Can Older People Be Creative?

Henry Wadsworth Longfellow's poem "Morituri Salutamus" is a salute to creative older people and shows that people can create into late old age.

> Cato learned Greek at eighty; Sophocles
> Wrote his grand *Oedipus*, and Simonides
> Bore off the prize of verse from his compeers,
> When each had numbered more than fourscore years.
> And Theophrastus, at fourscore and ten,
> Had just begun his *Characters of Men*.
> Chaucer, at Woodstock with the nightingales,
> At sixty wrote the *Canterbury Tales*;
> Goethe at Weimar, toiling to the last,
> Completed *Faust* when eighty years were past.

Source: Henry Wadsworth Longfellow, *The Poetical Works of Longfellow* (London: Oxford University Press, 1928).

---

738 people. Second, he selected long-lived subjects, all of whom had lived past age 78, to control for the effects of mixed longevities.

Dennis measured the output of a variety of creative people: artists, scientists, scholars, and dancers. He found that each group produced the least amount of work in their 20s. In almost all fields, creativity (measured by output) peaked between ages 40 and 49, about ten years later than Lehman's finding. Dennis, like Lehman, found that people in different fields peaked at different ages. Artists (dramatists, librettists, architects) peaked earliest and showed the sharpest decline in their 70s. Dennis found that scientists also experienced declines in middle age, but they showed a sharp decline only after age 60. Scholars showed little decline with age. They produced as much in their 70s as in their 40s, and they added to their former number of books by 25 percent between ages 70 and 79.

Dennis's work expands on Lehman's, rather than contradicting it. Dennis shows that differences in the peak age of creativity may depend as much on the social structure of a discipline as it does on a creative person's age. Scholars, for example, reach a peak later than artists and stay productive longer. Dennis explains that the arts,

such as painting or composing, depend more on individual creativity. An artist's output declines if he or she loses strength or becomes ill. Scholars and scientists can get younger colleagues (like graduate students) to help them with their work. They can stay productive even if their strength declines (Dennis 1968).

Later studies by Simonton (1977) on great composers partly supported the idea that creativity declines with age. Simonton found that total productivity peaked between ages 45 and 49 and then declined. Total themes (musical ideas) in composers' works also decreased after ages 30 to 34, though they did not decrease to a point below the totals of the composer's younger years. Studies of Nobel Prize winners (Zuckerman 1977) and high-level chess players (Elo 1965) also report peaks in creativity for people in their mid-30s.

Simonton (1990, 1988a) more recently reviewed the research on creativity and aging. He concluded that in the last decade of a creative person's career, his or her productivity equals about half his or her peak output (given a normal life span). In general, Simonton (1990) says, "if one plots creative output as a function of age, productivity tends to rise fairly rapidly to a definite peak and thereafter tends to decline gradually" (322).

Exhibit 6.6

Portraits of Three Creative Older Canadians

Barker Fairley

Barker Fairley began teaching German at the University of Toronto in 1915. He wrote a book of poems and five books on Goethe during his academic career. When he retired, he turned to painting for creative fulfillment. Six years before his death in 1986 at the age of 99, Fairley was profiled by Hubert de Santana in Today *Magazine:*

He remembers vividly the day he took up painting. "I was in my 45th year and had never made a drawing in my life. My friend, the painter and poet Robert Finch, said that I ought to paint and arranged for us to go on a field trip the following day. I was reluctant and said to my wife, 'I hope it rains tomorrow.' It didn't rain, and we went out and painted, and I did a little watercolor which has the characteristics of my later work. It was all there immediately.

For lack of encouragement Fairley stopped painting for 10 years. He began again in his 60s and has painted ever since. His shows now sell out and the cost of his paintings rose from a few hundred to a few thousand dollars in the three years since he turned 90 (he was 93 in 1980). How does he sum up his long and extraordinary life? ... "Like Goethe, I never toed the line professionally or in any way. I followed my nose, I remained a lover, a Liebhaber, in that sense an amateur. I just did what I chose and liked from first to last."

Hubert Evans

Edith Iglauer, Hubert Evans's friend and neighbour, wrote a short biographical sketch about him in 1980. He was 88 at the time. Hubert Evans wrote more than 200 published short stories, 60 serials, 12 radio plays for the CBC, and seven books of fiction from the 1920s to 1954. When his wife died he stopped writing from 1960 to 1976. Then, says Iglauer,

he broke the long silence ... to produce two new volumes of poetry—*Whittlings* and *Endings*. The poems were so well received—Margaret

Laurence, the writer, called them "sheer wisdom in a lunatic age"—that Evans, regaining confidence, completed a novel that had been simmering on what he refers to as "the back burner" for almost 50 years. *O Time in Your Flight*, published [in 1979], was acclaimed across the country ...

"People are going back to what they can read and enjoy," [he says], "but I am writing to please myself and nobody else. I love my subject, and I like writing. I've got this thing about writers being creative people, that creativity came in a package the night I was conceived. Maybe it was something my mother had for supper. If writers don't write, they'll be like the adipose fin on the salmon. At one time it was quite a big thing, but the salmon didn't use it, and now it's no bloody good to him."

Elisabeth Hopkins

Elisabeth Hopkins held her first painting exhibition at the age of 80. Ann Rhodes described Ms. Hopkins's career and life in a feature for Chatelaine:

Today her paintings sell for up to $1,150. She still lives alone, as she always has. She [was] 89 in April [1983] ... Painting had been a purely private pleasure until, in her mid-70s, she suggested to a Galiano [B.C.] gift-shop owner that her greeting cards might sell for a nickel a piece. For a full-size painting her price was $5, the sum paid for one that came to the attention of the Bau-Xi Gallery in Vancouver, which has shown her work ever since. ...

"Sometimes" [she says], "I've no idea what I'm going to do. The animals and the flowers just appear. I think you might say it is a joy to me." There's joy too in the letters and visits from admirers of her work ...

Pinned up in Elisabeth Hopkins's home is a cartoon clipped from *The New Yorker*. It shows two older women, one clearly weighed down by her years, the other sprightly. The line reads: "Well, I tried old age, but it wasn't my cup of tea."

Sources: Edith Iglauer, "The Unsinkable Hubert Evans," *Today Magazine*, December 20, 1980; Hubert de Santana, "Portrait of the Artist as an Old Man," *Today Magazine*, November 29, 1980; Ann Rhodes, "Five Women Who Defy the Stereotypes of Aging," *Chatelaine*, February 1983. By permission of the authors.

Does the quality of the work also decline with age? In other words, do the creative works of a person's later career decline in quality? Simonton (1990) says that creative people can produce great works at every age. But across an entire career he proposes a **constant-probability-of-success model** (Simonton 1990, 323). This model states that within a career, the larger the number of creative works a person produces in a given time period, the more great works they produce during this period (Simonton 1988b).

Why does creativity decline with age? A decline in health, a decrease in energy, changes in a profession, and different goals and motivations later in life all explain the decline in creative output (Simonton 1988b). But even with this general decline, creativity can continue into late old age. Sophocles, Michelangelo, Goethe, Picasso, Winston Churchill, Grandma Moses, and Georgia O'Keeffe, for example, all remained creative past the age of 80. Lehman reported many cases of creativity in old age. He found that 20 percent of atomic physicists made contributions to their field after age 65 (1968, 100).

Lehman might have argued that most of these people had created their greatest works at younger ages. Still, they continued to contribute to society and culture as they aged. And some types of creativity, like comprehensive historical studies, may be possible only in old age. It may take a historian a lifetime to amass the knowledge and gain the perspective needed to make a great contribution.

Creativity as Measured by Psychological Tests

Lehman (1953; 1968), Dennis (1968), and Pressey and Pressey (1967) studied unique groups of people—people famous enough to have their work noted in history. But what about "average" people—those who carry out most of the work in society? Does creativity change with age? Creativity studies of the general population often rely on psychological tests. Like memory and intelligence studies, most creativity studies show a decline in test scores with age with a peak around age 30 (McCrae, Arenberg, and Costa 1987; Simonton 1990). None of these studies show an increase in creativity in later life (Cornelius and Caspi 1987).

A study by Jacquish and Ripple (1981) found a complex pattern of change in creativity with age. They studied 218 men and women 18–84 years old. They found that the oldest group (61–84) had lower fluency and flexibility scores, but scored as well as the youngest group (18–25) on originality. The middle group (40–60) scored best on all measures. This study suggests that some measures of creativity may decline more than others with age.

A study by Crosson and Robertson-Tchabo (1983) suggests that a person's background and experience may also influence creativity in later life. This study compared two groups of women. One group included 271 women artists and writers aged 23–87. A second group included 76 women aged 26–74 who had not had careers in the creative arts. The study found that the noncreative career subjects over 60 scored significantly lower than the noncreative career people under age 50. But the study found no significant correlation between age and creativity in the creative group. Crosson and Robertson-Tchabo suggest that continued creative work may help a person stay creative longer.

Studies that use creativity tests suffer from a number of problems. First, they often use cross-sectional designs that confound cohort differences with age changes (Collins and Tellier 1994). These studies may measure differences in educational background and test-taking ability as much as creativity. Second, the measures used in these studies have low validity, which means that results on these tests may bear little relation to real-life creativity (Simonton 1990). Creativity can take forms other than great works and scores on tests.

Creativity as Personal Expression

Creativity can refer to a great achievement, a test score, or a form of personal expression. This last perspective treats creativity as a source of individual satisfaction regardless of how other people judge the works produced.

Kenneth Koch, a professional poet and teacher, reported on the value of creative expression for personal well-being. Koch agreed to teach poetry writing to twenty-five people in a nursing home in New York City. He said that on the first day the people looked "old, sick, tired, uncomfortable. Some seemed to be asleep or almost so"

(1982, 210). Other people in the class gazed around the room or showed signs of pain. Koch began with a collaborative poem. In this case he asked each person for a line about their childhood. Some people refused to contribute, but most did, and Koch put their lines together in a poem.

He reported that the group members became "excited at the unaccustomed pleasure of hearing what they said read aloud, and excited at hearing it admired by me and by other students" (1982, 211). Koch (1977) eventually collected these poems in a book titled, *I Never Told Anybody*. These poems represent the first formal creative works produced by these people. But it only hints at the joy writing poetry brought to their lives. Koch's (1977) report shows that older people often lack an opportunity to express themselves creatively.

Crosson and Robertson-Tchabo (1983) say that if older people had more opportunity to express their creativity they would show more creative behaviour. Butler (1974) says that today older people have to become autodidacts—self-teachers. These kinds of people take charge of their own learning, they transform their world in response to their own concerns, and, in the process, create something new. This view of creativity makes later life a time of potential discovery and self-renewal rather than a time of decline.

PSYCHOLOGICAL DISORDERS: ABNORMAL AGING

Studies of memory, intelligence, and creativity describe the normal changes that come with aging, but some people show abnormal changes as they age. They may suffer from psychological problems such as paranoia, anxiety neuroses, and schizophrenia. Experts call these functional disorders because they interfere with how a person functions. These problems have no clear organic cause, and some older people have suffered with them throughout their lives. Other people suffer from organic disorders, diseases of the brain such as Alzheimer's disease, Parkinson's disease, or stroke. All of these illnesses arise from a deterioration of the brain.

Organic Brain Disorders

Organic brain syndrome, senile dementia, or dementia are general terms used to describe a variety of organic brain disorders. Organic disorders lead to confusion, forgetfulness, and sometimes antisocial behaviour. Some individuals with these disorders wander, strike out, or resist help from their caregivers. Dementia cases create stress for both professional care providers and family caregivers.

Hendricks and Hendricks (1986, 238) report that 4 to 6 percent of those aged 65–84 suffer from organic brain disorder, but that 20 percent of people aged 85 and over suffer from these illnesses. Canadian researchers say that dementia will show up in greater numbers as more people live into late old age. "Those managing to stay on till well beyond 85 will form a group with very much higher than average risk of severe dementia (i.e., a prevalence rate in the neighborhood of 25 percent)" (Stone 1986, 31). A study by Robertson, Rockwood, and Stolee (1982) in Saskatchewan supports this estimate. They found moderate to severe dementia in 2.4 percent of people aged 65 to 69, but 29.9 percent dementia in the 85-and-over group. The Canadian Study of Health and Aging in 1990–92 found a dementia prevalence of 28.5 percent among people aged 85 and over (Ebly et al. 1994). Carswell-Opzoomer and her colleagues (1993) studied the prevalence of dementia in nursing homes in the Ottawa-Carleton region. They found that 52 percent of residents (women averaged age 84 and men 78) suffered from dementia. Nursing homes and hospitals in the future will have to care for more and more demented patients.

Canada began its first nation-wide study of dementia in 1990, the largest study of its kind. The study included over 10 000 older people in five Canadian regions and included institutionalized seniors as well as people who live in the community. The study had four objectives: (1) to report on the prevalence of dementias among older Canadians; (2) to assess the risk of someone's getting Alzheimer-type dementia; (3) to describe patterns of care for dementia patients and to measure caregiver burden; and (4) to create a uniform database (Gauthier, McDowell, and Hill 1990). The study also included a number of add-on projects that focused on topics like the genetic origins of Alzheimer's disease.

This study has provided the best estimate yet of the prevalence of Alzheimer's disease. For example, the researchers found that 253 000 people or 8 percent of people aged 65 in Canada in 1991 had some form of dementia. Cases of Alzheimer's disease make up about two-thirds of all dementia cases. The prevalence of Alzheimer's disease increases with age. About half of older people with dementia live in the community. The research projects a threefold increase in the number of dementia cases between 1991 and 2031 (National Advisory Council 1996a).

None of the research so far has produced a method to treat Alzheimer's disease. Physicians cannot even make a certain diagnosis of the disease's presence; they can only rule out other causes of confusion and personality decline like brain tumours, blood pressure problems, or hyperthyroidism. Dozens of other illnesses must be ruled out before an illness can be diagnosed as Alzheimer's (Hermann 1991). Caution prevents doctors from doing so because a patient might have a treatable illness or a problem like overmedication or infection. The inability to diagnose Alzheimer's quickly leaves families in limbo and forces patients to go through dozens of tests.

Organic disorders pose problems for the affected individuals and their families. Family caregivers often feel despair because their care receiver does not recognize them anymore. This can add to their burden. A better understanding of memory loss might help these caregivers cope with their care receivers' illnesses.

People with Alzheimer's disease pose practical problems for their families. Patients sometimes suffer from depression, or may sleep all day and wander all night. Sometimes they leave home and lose their way. This creates stress for caregivers. The Alzheimer Society of Canada plans to create a national "Alzheimer Wandering Registry" to support family caregivers. This registry will contain information that police can use to find and identify missing Alzheimer's patients. Health Canada and the RCMP provided funding for this project. The Ministry of the Solicitor General has funded the creation of a police handbook to advise police on how to deal with Alzheimer's patients (*Seniors Today* 1995).

Sainsbury and Coristine (1986, 99) studied patients with cognitive impairment. They found that patients often could not recognize a relative's picture, but these same patients could choose the relative's picture from a set of four pictures. The researchers said that even though a person loses "recognition memory," "affective memory" remains intact. This finding suggests that cognitively impaired patients may have good feelings toward their relatives, even if they do not seem to recognize them. The researchers added that "the subject may be aware that he knows the visitor but not recall the relationship. Awareness of this fact in conjunction with the knowledge that severely impaired people can yet possess strong affective associations can be of considerable comfort to concerned relatives" (Sainsbury and Coristine 1986, 103). Harrison (1993, 436) says that caregivers can focus "on those positive interests, characteristics and abilities which remain and may be strengthened through thoughtful and personalized interventions."

Kraus and McGeer (1983) studied the care system for people with dysfunctional brain syndrome in Kingston, Ontario. They found that people who suffered from this condition needed more appropriate housing, more complete assessment, and more services to support families. MacFadgen (1987), in a study of Toronto and Peel Region dementia patients, found that families felt they needed more respite beds, more home support, special assessment and treatment services, adult day care, and special units for long-term care in their area. Families identified the need for more respite/relief resources as their most pressing need. Kraus (1984) said that some families felt committed to keeping their care receiver at home. But when a care receiver's behaviour became too difficult to handle, even the best family supports and community care could not relieve caregiver burden. Then families felt they had to institutionalize their relative (Cohen et al. 1993).

MacFadgen (1987) also found that cognitively impaired patients posed problems for health-care workers, social service workers, and public housing managers. Sixty-two percent of the institutional sample in this study needed heavy nursing care. Forty-four percent of clients in the community showed disturbing or disruptive behaviour. Dawson and Reid (1987) found that cognitive deficits led to wandering behaviour in institutional patients. Professional caregivers often feel burdened by the demands of these patients. A study by Novak, Chappell, and Miles-Tapping (1990) found that nursing assistants who were distressed by patient behaviour felt most burdened. Service workers will care for more and more clients with these illnesses in the coming years and will need to understand the basis of the illness and how to treat these clients.

Exhibit 6.7

The Stages of Decline Due to Alzheimer's Disease

Health and Welfare Canada (1984a) described the three stages that an Alzheimer's patient goes through. Some people may go through these stages in a few months; others may take years. The changes that come with Alzheimer's disease begin slowly. Often family members recognize the first signs only when they look back over a year or two of caregiving.

Stage I: A person first shows changes in memory. They forget their keys or their wallet. They may also forget recent events or forget that they did a job around a house. This gets worse in time. The person forgets more often, takes longer to do simple jobs, or begins to recheck work already done.

One woman recalls that her husband, an engineering professor, would spend three or four hours writing a fifty-minute lecture that used to take him an hour to write. Another woman recalls that she first became worried when her husband, a physician, lost his way home from work one night. He planned to stop at a patient's house for a short house call around 5:00 p.m. The patient lived only a few blocks away from their house, so his wife expected him home around six. She began to worry at eight o'clock when she still hadn't heard from him. An hour later he came in exhausted. He had spent the last three hours driving around their neighbourhood looking for their house.

Stage II: The second stage of the disease includes more memory decline, loss of speaking ability, and an end to normal daily activity. The ill person may wander at night, lose control of his or her bowel and bladder, and threaten others. One woman left a knife in her garden after she used it to weed the flower bed. Her husband picked it up and stalked through the bushes into a neighbour's yard, saying to the neighbour, "I'm going to kill you." The neighbour ran inside and called the police. When the sick man's wife came outside to finish weeding, she found the police wrestling her husband into a squad car.

In another case a man walked into a new car dealer and signed a contract for a $20 000 car. His wife found out only after the salesman called her to check on the financing. The owner of the dealership agreed to void the contract, but only after she pleaded and explained about her husband's illness.

This stage of the disease can put stress on the family. Caregivers—most often spouses or children of the ill person—can feel tense, trapped, and exhausted. Members have to take on new roles: wives become chauffeurs or nurses; children become parents or police; and husbands become homemakers (Novak and Guest 1985). Mace and Rabins (1981, 63) report one case of a burdened husband who had to bathe his wife. "She screams for help the whole time I am bathing her. She'll open the windows and yell, 'Help, I'm being robbed.'" One man confessed to Mace and Rabins (1981, 179), "There was a time when I considered getting a gun, killing my wife, and then killing myself."

Stage III: The person in the last stage of Alzheimer's disease needs institutionalization and often twenty-four-hour nursing care. The person can no longer speak or communicate. He or she may wander or move constantly unless restrained. Seizures may occur. Death occurs between two and nineteen years after the disease starts (Health and Welfare Canada 1984a). Death often comes from an illness like pneumonia or heart disease, but death certificates rarely mention Alzheimer's disease as a cause of death. This makes it impossible to know the exact number of deaths caused by Alzheimer's.

Not all Alzheimer's patients show all the above-mentioned symptoms. Some show other symptoms of confusion like depression and crying. But these stages give a general picture of the disease. They also give only a faint idea of the stress that Alzheimer's disease puts on the primary caregiver.

Functional Disorders

Functional disorders disrupt normal life. They include emotional upset, depression, and anxiety. Hendricks and Hendricks (1986) say that 25 to 60 percent of older people in and out of institutions in the United States report mental distress and that 10 to 15 percent have emotional problems that need mental health attention.

The Canada Health Survey (Health and Welfare Canada and Statistics Canada 1981) asked a sample of more than 23 000 people from all over Canada to report their health problems. The study found that, compared with the population aged 15 to 64, people 65 and over had more than two and a half times the rate of self-reported mental disorder (12.3 percent of 65 and over compared with 4.5 percent of people from 15 to 64), and that older women reported mental disorders at almost twice the rate of older men (15.4 percent of women 65 and over compared with 8.5 percent of men). Statistics Canada (1990e) reports that the hospitalization rate for functional psychoses (schizophrenia, paranoid states, and other nonorganic psychoses) increased between 1971 and 1985/86, going up by 47.4 percent for those from 65 to 74 years old and 184.9 percent for people aged 75 and over.

The 1991 General Social Survey (Statistics Canada 1994a) studied affect (emotional well-being) throughout life. The study found that the proportion of people with high positive affect decreases from 20 percent for people aged 45–64 to 17 percent for people aged 65–74, to 11 percent for people aged 75 and over. The Canada Health Survey found that the proportion of an age group reporting frequent symptoms of anxiety and depression goes up slightly throughout adulthood. More than 4 percent of males aged 65 and over and nearly 8 percent of females aged 65 and over (7.7 percent) report frequent symptoms of anxiety and depression. This comes to slightly more than the proportion of males and females aged 45 to 64 who report these problems (3.8 percent for males and 6.9 percent for females). But more than 9 percent of the older group did not respond to this question, two to three times higher a proportion of "unknowns" than the 45 to 64 age group. Health and Welfare Canada and Statistics Canada (1981) estimate that these unknowns would probably add to the proportion of older people feeling distress. Including the unknowns, the distressed group would represent 14 to 17 percent of people 65 and over.

Cappliez (1988) reviewed the literature on depression and found that between 0.8 and 8 percent of people aged 65 and over meet the Diagnostic and Statistical Manual of Mental Disorders (third edition) (American Psychiatric Association 1980) criteria for major depression. Other studies use criteria based on the Depression Scale of the Center for Epidemiological Studies. These studies report a depression rate of 9 to 18 percent in the older population. One well-known study on depression (Gurland et al. 1983) reported rates of depression among older people of 12.4 percent for London, England, and 13 percent for New York. The higher rates include moderate as well as severely depressed cases (see also Gurland and Toner 1983; Murrell, Himmelfarb, and Wright 1983; Cohen 1990).

Cohen (1990) notes that controversy over prevalence rates exists for most mental disorders in later life. He reports that depression can appear as vague physical decline or complaints about more than one physical symptom. These cases would increase the estimated proportion of depressed older people. Studies that include people who have dysphoria, a depression having symptoms of pessimism and dissatisfaction with life, as well as people with clinical depression report rates of 20 to 25 percent.

Cappliez (1988) says that the proportion of older people with depression differs little from the proportion of people with depression in the adult population. In general, studies have found that the risk of depression decreases in later life (Chappell and Barnes 1982). People aged 65 and over have a lower risk than 17-year-olds of first experiencing depression. And those under 10 and over 60 have the least chance of suffering from depression (Gurland 1976). Cappliez cautions that only a few studies have looked at people aged 75 and over as a separate group. This group may face more risk than people aged 65 to 74. Also, current studies compare different cohorts of people. Older people today may reflect less on their feelings than younger people; they may think of their depression as a part of a physical illness; or death and institutionalization may take severely depressed people out of the general population. These conditions may explain the low rates of depression among older people.

People with resources such as social skills, problem-solving ability, and emotional support from family and friends will have less tendency toward depression. A person who appraises a situation as nonthreatening or who copes actively to improve situations will show less depression (Cappliez 1988). This perspective shows that social as well as psychological conditions influence depression. Phifer and Murell (1986), for example, conclude that physical health and social support affect depression.

The "unhappy" Canadian, the Canada Health Survey reports, is likely to be old, female, widowed, low-income, in poor health, and without much education (Health and Welfare Canada and Statistics Canada 1981). The inability to get out and the loss of social supports can also lead to unhappiness or depression. This puts the mental health of many infirm older Canadians at risk.

Social support buffers the effect of poor health and protects a person from feeling depressed. We will look in more detail at the influence of social conditions on psychological well-being in Chapter 7.

Treatment and Intervention

Butler (1975) says that mental health experts often ignore the needs of older people. Most psychiatrists, he says, like to treat young, well-educated, successful people (see also Zivian et al. 1992). A study by Gibson (1970) found that many psychiatrists believe that older people will not improve as a result of therapy. Eaton, Stones, and Rockwood (1986) found that physicians often failed to detect cognitive impairment in older patients. They suggest that doctors receive more training in "geriatric assessment, treatment, and management" during medical school and as part of their continuing medical education (Eaton, Stones, and Rockwood 1986).

A whole range of treatments can help older people cope with psychological problems. Smyer, Zarit, and Qualls (1990) say that the individual's characteristics (including age), the diagnosis criteria used, the older person's adaptation patterns, and the intervention setting (community or institution) all influence the choice of treatment. Chemical therapies exist to treat some reversible organic brain syndromes. Physicians can treat alcoholics in the early stages of Wernicke-Korsakoffs dementia (a neurological disease) with large doses of thiamine. Many more therapies exist for older people with functional problems—problems related to a person's personality or social life. Drug therapy can help older people cope with functional problems like depression; behaviour therapy can help with insomnia; and psychotherapy can help the person who has a personality disorder. Life

review (Butler and Lewis 1982) can help with adaptation to loss, and milieu therapy can help a person to change his or her environment.

Some clinicians suggest the use of pets to help relieve loneliness. Goldmeier (1986) found that older people who had pets reported less loneliness, and that older people who lived with other people, even without pets, showed the least loneliness. Goldmeier says that pets cannot fully substitute for human companionship, but pets can create nonthreatening relationships for people who might otherwise reject therapy or other human contact.

New programs for older people with psychological disorders (LeBlanc 1985) will offer older people more options for treatment in the future. Some of these alternatives will need to take forms—such as day centres or hospital adult day-care programs—that older people already feel comfortable using.

A Canadian government report (Mental Health Division 1988) recognizes the unmet needs of older people for psychiatric help. The report describes a comprehensive response to older people with psychiatric problems. It focuses on four approaches that would improve psychiatric care for older people: assessment, management and treatment, coordination of services, and the use of volunteers. This approach fits with the current thinking about health care service in general for an aging population. Chapter 8 will discuss in more detail this general shift toward a comprehensive health care model.

The Loss of Competency

Psychological intervention can sometimes mean protection of the older person from harm. It can also mean making decisions for people who can no longer decide for themselves. A person with a cognitive impairment, for example, may lose the ability to understand his or her situation and make decisions. But when should another person step in to make decisions for someone else? Checkland and Silberfeld (1993) say that this should occur only after a careful assessment of a person's **competency.**

Saint-Arnaud (1993, 35) defines competency as the ability to "understand information relevant to the decision to be taken, weigh the pros and cons in terms of his/her goals and values" and to be "capable of communicating decisions" (see also Silberfeld 1994). Competency differs from **legal capacity,** "the exercise of rights by all citizens" (Saint-Arnaud 1993). Legal incapacity refers to the loss of civil rights when a person comes into protective care. In this case someone else (a lawyer, family member, or the public trustee) has the legal right to make decisions for the older person. This guardian attempts to follow, to the extent that she knows them, the wishes of the person in her care.

A person's competency gets formally decided through an assessment by a professional (a physician, psychiatrist, or other recognized expert). An assessment attempts to answer the question of "whether or not you can make decisions and whether your legal rights should be removed" (Silberfeld cited in Morantz 1990). An assessment should ensure the same assessment standards for everyone and the absence of an assessor's bias. Also, assessment should take place more than once to assess a person's present and future ability to make decisions (Silberfeld 1992). An assessment of incompetence removes a person's ability to make choices on his own behalf. Writers on this topic urge caution in making this judgment.

Checkland and Silberfeld (1993) say that, even after an assessment of incompetence, others should intervene as little as possible. For example, they say that a person may have lost the ability to handle her finances. But she may still have the ability to live in her own home. A person can have decision-specific capacities. The researchers propose that someone else may make decisions for this person on financial issues, but the person should keep the right to make the decision on where to live. The authors say that competency should rest both on mental ability and on what a person can do. For example, a person may thrive in her own home, but not have the verbal skill to say how she does it. Silberfeld (1994) says that a competency assessment should find this person competent. Also, any view of a person's decision-making ability should take into account her past decisions, her values, and her track record or "characteristic way of making decisions" (Double 1992, cited in Checkland and Silberfeld 1993).

The issue of competency can often come up in cases of older people at risk. An older person may feel able to live on his own. The person's daughter may feel this puts her mother at risk. Older people who want to live on their own may minimize risk and hope all goes well. But "caregivers, who fear the worst, can magnify the risk" (National Advisory Council 1993, 3).

The National Advisory Council on Aging (1993a, 2) presents the following case:

> Mrs. X is an 86-year-old widow who has lived alone with the help of home support services for the past ten years. She is an insulin dependent diabetic with a sweet tooth. During the past two years, she has become increasingly short of memory and confused. She often forgets to eat or eats junk food. Efforts to have her live with her only son and daughter-in-law several miles away have failed. The home care case manager is becoming uncomfortable because, even with the maximum level of home care available, Mrs. X is considered to be at risk. Following a fall, where she fractured her wrist, she was hospitalized. The son, in consultation with home care, decided to institutionalize his mother. Mrs. X is clearly unhappy in the nursing home, objecting to all aspects of her care and continually asking when she can go home.

Has the son acted in his mother's best interests or in his own? Family members may consult the family doctor for a competency assessment in order to carry out their own wishes. This assessment may go along with a desire to assume **legal guardianship** for the older person. But guardianship (where the court appoints someone to make decisions on the older person's behalf) also creates a risk. "Starting from assuredly good intentions [to keep the older person from harm], risk becomes part of an unconscious rhetoric for controlling elderly people" (Silberfeld 1992, 134).

Naglie and his colleagues (1995) point to the importance of careful competency assessment in an aging society. The label of incompetence removes a person's free choice, and experts should apply it with caution. Borovy (1982, cited in National Advisory Council 1993b, 4) says that "when we are talking about the precious freedom to be left alone, then we should insist that it cannot be lost unless there are the most exacting criteria and the most scrupulous procedures."

CONCLUSION

Psychological well-being means more than coping with problems, stress, and loss. It means growth, learning, and a sense of purpose. The research on the psychology of aging shows that older people in good health stay alert, intelligent, and able to learn. They face stresses unique to later life, but they can get through these crises, often with the help of others. Sometimes the biggest block to older people's well-being comes from the prejudices and stereotypes other people have about old age. The research on the psychology of aging has begun to remove the basis for these stereotypes. Studies have begun to explore and describe human potential in later life. More research and knowledge about old age and new cohorts of older people will teach us more about mental potential in old age.

SUMMARY

1. Psychological studies of aging take three forms: the psychology of the aged, the psychology of age, and the psychology of aging. The psychology of aging studies change in individuals over time. This provides a look at the effects of aging on psychological abilities.

2. Early research supported the myth that intellectual ability declines with age, but recent studies show more complex findings, for example, younger people do perform better than older people on some memory and intelligence tests, but the pace of testing, the types of questions asked, and the way older people learn can all decrease their performance.

3. In general, laboratory studies show that memory declines with age, though different types of memory show different amounts of decline. Recent research suggests that a decrease in working memory accounts for poorer memory in older people. Education and background differences between older and younger people may account for differences in performance in memory studies.

4. Test conditions may decrease older people's ability to remember in laboratory studies. Studies of memory in real (not laboratory) contexts show that older people can compensate for memory declines. Studies also show that when compared, younger and older people's recall of historical and social events showed little or no deficit for older people.

5. Early studies used cross-sectional methods to study the effects of aging on intelligence. The results confused cohort differences with age changes. Longitudinal methods show declines in fluid intelligence (problem-solving skills). But they show little change and possibly some increase in crystallized intelligence (skills based on acquired knowledge). Research also shows that older people can improve their scores on intelligence tests through training. Willis (1990) studied intelligence scores in individuals over time. She found that some people showed stable fluid intelligence scores, and others showed decline. Training increased both types of individuals' abilities.

6. New models of intelligence have begun to look at human potential in later life. Researchers have begun to study wisdom—the older people's expert knowledge about life and their good judgment.

7. Studies of both the quality and quantity of creative production show a decline in creativity with age. Comparisons of older and younger people on psychological tests also find greater creativity among younger subjects. Both of these approaches to the study of creativity emphasize the products of creative work. Reports of subjective creative development show that people can create and learn to do so at any age. Education, opportunity, and an interest in a subject can all lead to creativity in later life.

8. The number of cases of organic brain disorders like Alzheimer's disease will increase as more people live to late old age. These disorders place a heavy burden on families, and the people with these diseases often need professional health care at the end of their lives.

9. Functional mental disorders (e.g., anxiety and depression) show up less often in old age than people commonly believe. Older people with these problems can benefit from drug therapies, psychotherapy, or milieu therapy.

10. Older people can lose competence to manage their lives due to organic or functional problems. Researchers, ethicists, and physicians work to clarify the concept of competency. They want to find a definition and assessment

of competency that serves older person's needs and limits restrictions on their rights.

11. The research on the psychology of aging presents a balanced view of aging. Some mental faculties may decline, but others remain stable as long as a person is in good health. More research and knowledge about the process of aging will teach us more about mental potential in later life.

STUDY QUESTIONS

1. State the three psychological approaches to the study of aging. Discuss the benefits and limitations of each approach.
2. What approaches have psychologists taken to the study of memory in later life? State two findings that show up in most laboratory studies. How do laboratory and contextual studies of memory differ in what they conclude about memory in later life?
3. What do psychologists mean when they speak of intelligence as multidimensional? Describe the differences between fluid and crystallized intelligence.
4. Discuss the costs and benefits of longitudinal and cross-sectional studies of memory.
5. What do some of the newest theories about intelligence in later life believe about intelligence and aging?
6. State three ways in which psychologists measure creativity in later life. What do each of these measures find?
7. What do psychologists mean by organic disorders? Give some examples. What do they mean by functional disorders? Give some examples.
8. What responses do psychologists propose for organic disorders? For functional disorders?
9. What issues does the loss of competence raise for the older person? For the person's physician? For the family? Discuss the tension that exists between older people's potential need for protection and their right to make decisions for themselves.

KEY TERMS

cognitive mechanics type of cognitive process that is similar to fluid intelligence.

cognitive pragmatics type of cognitive process that is similar to crystallized intelligence.

competency the ability to understand information that applies to a decision, the ability to think about the pros and cons of the decision, and the ability to communicate a decision.

constant-probability-of-success model this model states that within a career, the larger the number of creative works a person produces in a given time period, the more great works they produce during this period (Simonton 1988b).

contextual view of memory the idea that many conditions influence memory, including "the physical, psychological, and social context in which the event was experienced, the knowledge, abilities, and characteristics the individual brings to the context, [and] the situation in which we ask for evidence of remembering" (Hultsch and Deutsch 1981, 153).

crystallized intelligence depends on stored information, acculturation, and learning.

encoding the process whereby a person takes new bits of information and puts them together with already stored information.

explicit memory case in which the person intends to remember something and does.

fluid intelligence refers to reasoning, abstracting, concept formation, and problem solving. It makes little use of knowledge gained through reading, schooling, or work.

implicit memory case in which memory occurs without intention.

intelligence the "ability to negotiate environmental demands successfully" (Labouvie-Vief 1985, 506); "that which intelligence tests measure" (Labouvie-Vief 1985, 506); or "what the testtaker can do now" (Botwinick 1984, 250).

legal capacity the right of all citizens to take part in the legal process and to have civil rights.

legal guardianship process in which the court appoints someone to make decisions on the older person's behalf.

long-term memory the storehouse of knowledge that also includes the rules for applying knowledge.

mediators picturing a word or finding a rhyme for a word, to help with remembering (Kausler 1982).

memory the recall of information after learning has taken place.

neurofibrillary tangles a sign of Alzheimer's disease in which neuronal fibres wrap around one another and fail to function properly.

plasticity the idea that people vary greatly from one another in intelligence as they age. Also, each person has an untapped reserve of mental potential.

psychology of age a perspective in the psychological study of aging that focuses on differences between age groups. It uses cross-sectional methods to study differences between age groups.

psychology of the aged a perspective in the psychological study of aging that emphasizes the biomedical view of aging as decline or disease. It supports ageism and the view of older people as a social problem.

psychology of aging a perspective in the psychological study of aging that looks at changes in individuals over time. It uses longitudinal methods to study both gains and losses through the life cycle.

sensory memory process in which a person perceives information.

short-term memory process in which a person transforms sensory information in some way.

wisdom "expert knowledge about the important and fundamental matters of life, their interpretation and management" (Featherman, Smith, and Peterson 1990; see also Baltes et al. 1990).

working memory stores recent information and also attends to, selects, and manipulates this information. In addition, it processes new information while temporarily storing other information.

SELECTED READINGS

Jarvik, Lissy F. "Aging of the Brain: How Can We Prevent It?" *The Gerontologist* 28 (1988): 739–46.

A readable article that summarizes research on changes in intellectual function as people age. The author links the research on intellectual change with studies of Alzheimer's disease and normal aging.

Kozma, A., M.J. Stones, and J.K. McNeil. *Psychological Well-Being in Later Life*. Toronto: Butterworths, 1991.

These authors review the research on happiness in later life. They also apply the results of their review to policy issues and to future research directions. The authors review the concept of psychological well-being, measures of well-being, and predictors of well-being. The authors also create a testable theory of psychological well-being. The book will appeal to advanced students in gerontology and psychology.

Smith, Anderson. "Memory." In James E. Birren and K. Warner Schaie, eds. *Handbook of the Psychology of Aging*. 4th ed. San Diego: Academic Press, 1996.

A good, up-to-date review of the literature. Covers the major theories that attempt to account for age differences in memory. Contains references to basic topics in the field like working memory, memory for different types of information (spatial location, nonverbal material), and issues of validity of laboratory testing.

The Social Psychology of Aging

INTRODUCTION

What is a good old age? This question has guided research in the social psychology of aging for more than fifty years. Researchers have found that many patterns of good aging exist. What follows are three cases that show the variety of forms a good old age can take.

Joe Willis, 70, worked as an engineer for an oil company until he retired in 1975. Now he spends January and February playing golf in Florida and spends the summer at his cottage in the Muskokas. His company calls him back two or three times a year as a consultant; he serves on the board of directors of a seniors' centre; and he volunteers as a nursing home visitor. "I visit the old folks once a week," he says. "At Christmas I take them to a show or out shopping." Joe does not see himself as old. He works less now and has more leisure time, but he feels the same as before he retired. He stays active and involved, and has found new ways to give meaning to his life.

Birdie Caldwell's husband died fifteen years ago. She moved out of their house and into a two-bedroom apartment a year after his death. She also went back to work as a secretary—work she had not done since her teens. Now, at age 65, she still lives on her own. She has two daughters who live less than an hour away by car. She visits them a few times a month and sometimes stays for the weekend. She travels, belongs to a bridge group, and enjoys her freedom.

Rose Reitman, 73, also lives by herself in her own apartment. Her husband died three years ago. She has a bad case of arthritis in her legs, which keeps her indoors most of the year. On warm days she walks a few blocks to the local shopping centre. Most of the time she watches TV, knits, or talks to friends on the phone. Rose feels content in her old age. She sometimes talks to ten or fifteen friends and relatives in a week. Nieces and nephews call her from all over the country on her birthday or on holidays. Her daughter lives two and a half hours away by car, and her son lives across the country. She has six grandchildren; their pictures cover her walls and table tops.

Three different portraits of old age: Birdie stays active; Rose lives a quiet life without social demands; Joe has found new roles to replace ones that he had lost. Each of these people show a

different response to the challenges of aging, but they all report high life satisfaction. These cases show only a few of the patterns of successful aging today.

This chapter will look at: (1) theories of human development in later life; (2) the social structural conditions (like membership in an ethnic community) that influence the experience of aging; and (3) some social-psychological problems that older people face in society today.

WHAT IS A GOOD OLD AGE?

Three social-psychological theories of aging—**disengagement theory**, **activity theory**, and **continuity theory**—each claim to describe the ideal way to grow old. Researchers have debated the merits of these theories since the 1960s, and references to them show up in the literature even today.

Disengagement Theory

Rosow (1976, 458) defines a *social role* as a "pattern of activity intrinsic" to a social position. Cumming and Henry (1961) describe old age as a time of disengagement—a time to withdraw from social roles and to decrease activity. They base their theory on a study of 279 people aged 50 to 70 in Kansas City. The study focused on people in good health and with enough money to live comfortably. They found that in this sample social roles and emotional ties decreased with age.

Cumming and Henry (1961) describe disengagement as inevitable, universal, and satisfying to both the person and society. Disengagement, they say, serves an important psychological function: it allows older people to reduce their activity naturally as their strength declines. Disengagement also serves a useful social function: it allows older people to leave social roles before the final disengagement—death. This creates a smooth transfer of power and responsibility from one generation to the next.

Critics attacked disengagement theory on three fronts almost as soon as it appeared. First, disengagement theory supports the stereotype of old age as a time of weakness and decline. Second, the theory assumes that the old perform less well than the young and, therefore, supports the existence of mandatory retirement based on age, rather than on a person's ability to do the job. Third, the theory assumes that all older people respond to the world in the same way—that they all disengage from social roles. More recent research shows that many older people, especially those who have good health and a good income, stay active in later life (Markides and Mindel 1987).

Activity Theory

Neugarten, Havighurst, and Tobin (1968) put forward a second major theory of aging: activity theory. This theory is just the reverse of disengagement theory. It holds that, as people lose social roles in old age, they stay happiest when they replace these roles with new ones. This theory, moreover, blames society for the process of disengagement. Modern society, it says, pushes older people out of social roles. This theory fits the North American view that happiness comes from work and activity.

Neugarten, Havighurst, and Tobin (1968) found three types of active people who reported high life satisfaction. One group started new activities to fill in for lost social roles. The researchers called them "re-organizers." Another group held on to their mid-life roles and stayed active. The researchers said these people were "holding-on." A third group stayed active but narrowed the range of their activities, and this group the researchers called "focused." Most recent studies also find that high activity correlates with high life satisfaction.

Continuity Theory

A third theory of aging says that people feel most satisfied if they continue the roles and activities of their middle years (Atchley 1982). This theory says that old age is a continuation of a person's past (rather than a break with it or a change in direction from it) and that people will choose the lifestyle in old age that is most like the pattern of life they lived in middle age. Mildly active people in their younger years will prefer a mild level of activity in later life and will feel satisfied with this lifestyle. But active people will want to keep up their activity—though activity might take new forms in old age.

Research supports each of these theories. Some studies have found that older people tend to be more passive, more introverted, and less committed to achievement in old age (Riley and Foner 1968; Neugarten 1969). Neugarten,

---

Exhibit 7.1

Men, Women, and Life Satisfaction

Many studies have found differences in life satisfaction and personality when they compared men and women (Lowenthal 1975; Lowenthal, Thurner, and Chiriboga 1975). Connidis (1983b) asked a sample of four hundred older Canadians how they felt about aging. She found that most people had a positive view of later life, though they had a realistic view of the problems that come with aging. She also found that men and women differed in how much they liked, disliked, and worried about old age. For example, 71 percent of men, compared with 56 percent of women, reported no worries about growing older. When the older people in Connidis's sample did complain about old age, men complained more often about physical restrictions while women complained more often about poor health.

Men and women also liked different things about aging. Men more often mentioned good health and freedom from work as things they liked about old age. Women more often mentioned contentment and freedom from family responsibility. These findings probably reflect the different social roles played by this generation of older men and women in their early and middle years. Most of these women had worked at home raising families, while the men had worked in the labour force. In later life they each feel a different kind of freedom—women feel the freedom from child rearing, and men feel the freedom from work. These kinds of responses may change in the future as women today spend time on careers as well as child rearing.

Havighurst, and Tobin (1968, 175) found support for both activity and disengagement theories. They found that many disengaged people report high life satisfaction and have integrated personalities. These people want to live a "rocking-chair" style of aging, and they leave their social roles by choice, living contented lives with few social contacts. Other people, who also report high life satisfaction, either stay active in their middle-life roles or replace these with new roles in old age.

Research by MacLean (1982) supports both activity and continuity theories. He found that men who could continue their activities and interests into later life showed the highest life satisfaction. These findings support the idea that people enjoy old age if they continue the activities and relationships they enjoyed in the past.

These three theories tell part of the truth about life satisfaction in later life, but all of them give too simple a picture of old age. People can disengage from some roles and still have high life satisfaction (Maddox 1970; Palmore 1970; Atchley 1971a); life satisfaction depends on what kind of activity declines. Lemon, Bengtson, and Peterson (1972) found that while a decline in group activities did not lead to lower life satisfaction, a decline in social activity with friends did. Kozma and Stones (1978, 248) conclude that activity or disengagement alone do not lead to happiness, but that "people appear to be happy if most of their experiences are pleasant and their perceived needs are met."

PERSONALITY DEVELOPMENT

Stage Theories

Some psychologists who study the individual in society focus on personality development. A number of researchers describe this development as a series of stages. Erik Erikson (1963), for instance, has created one of the best-known stage models of the life cycle. McCrae and Costa (1990, 11–12) call it "the single most important theory of adult personality development." His model describes eight stages of ego development. At each stage, he says, the person faces a crisis with two possible outcomes. If a person gets through the crisis successfully, growth occurs. As a result, the person reaches a new stage of development. If not, the person experiences some psychopathology that inhibits further development.

Exhibit 7.2

Erikson's Stages of Ego Development

Childhood Stages

Stage 1	Basic Trust vs. Mistrust
Stage 2	Autonomy vs. Shame, Doubt
Stage 3	Initiative vs. Guilt
Stage 4	Industry vs. Inferiority

Adolescence

Stage 5	Identity vs. Role Confusion

Adulthood

Stage 6	Intimacy vs. Isolation
Stage 7	Generativity vs. Stagnation
Stage 8	Ego Integrity vs. Despair

Source: Adapted from *Childhood and Society*, by Erik H. Erikson. Copyright 1950, ©1963 by W.W. Norton & Company, Inc., renewed © 1978, 1991 by Erik A. Erikson. Reprinted by permission of W.W. Norton & Company, Inc.

Erikson (1959) describes five stages that occur during childhood and youth, and three that occur in adulthood (see Exhibit 7.2). The adult stages correspond roughly to early, middle, and late adulthood. Each stage offers the person a specific challenge. The sixth stage, "**intimacy** vs. isolation," requires a specific task: "to lose and find oneself in another" (Erikson 1959, Appendix). Love is the virtue of this stage: the young adult will marry or make some other permanent or semi-permanent bond with another person. The crisis of this stage focuses on the experience of "intimacy." If the person fails to achieve intimacy, he or she will face "isolation."

The task of the middle adult years, Erikson says, is "to make be, to take care of" (1959, Appendix). Here the person's concern turns to what he calls "**generativity**" versus its opposite, "stagnation." This includes the generation of products and ideas as well as having children (Erikson 1976, 7). This stage has its unique virtue: care for oneself, but also care for others and for the world as a whole. In mid-life the person becomes concerned with the "maintenance of the world" and with passing the culture on to the coming generations (Erikson 1976, 15, 27).

The task of late adulthood, Erikson says, is "to be, through having been, to face not being" (1959, Appendix). Wisdom is the virtue of this last stage; it comes when the person achieves "**integrity**" and overcomes the threat of "despair and disgust" (1959, 98). Like other psychoanalytic thinkers (Bühler 1951; Jung 1976), Erikson describes old age as a time of inwardness, a time when a person reflects on the past and brings closure to life. At this point, he says, a person with a healthy personality accepts his life as the product of his own actions within a particular culture. This last stage sums up the seven earlier stages, and when a person achieves integrity, Erikson says, it brings a wholeness to life. A person who displays integrity inspires the young to trust in the culture and to follow its prescriptions for action (Erikson 1982, 63; Erikson 1963, 269).

A number of studies support Erikson's model of adult stages. They find the same order of stages he describes, and they find that the stages follow one another as he predicts (Constantinople 1969; Boyd and Koskela 1970; Ciaccio 1971).

Some writers have expanded on Erikson's outline of middle and later life. Erikson began as a child psychologist, and his life-cycle model reflects his interest in children. In his classic paper "Growth and Crises of the Healthy Personality" (1950), for example, he spends forty-five pages on the first twenty years of life and devotes only five pages to the next fifty to sixty years. Peck ([1955] 1968) modified Erikson's model five years later, adding more stages to it.

Erikson's last stage, Peck said, "seems to be intended to represent in a global, nonspecific way all the psychological crises and crisis-solutions of the last forty or fifty years of life" ([1955] 1968, 88). Peck divided this last stage of life into two periods—middle and old age. He found seven crises a person had to overcome within these periods. At each stage the person gives up the narrow commitments—to the body, to people, to concepts, and finally to the self—that dominated earlier stages of life. Peck's work shows that middle and later life are complex and active periods of development.

Erikson, Peck, and others (Levinson 1978; Gould 1978) propose that a stage model of development best describes middle and later life. Each writer proposes an ideal pattern of aging and development, implying, therefore, that those who follow it live a successful old age, while those who deviate from it face problems and frustrations as they age.

A number of studies question whether a set of universal stages exists. Surveys of large numbers of people, for example, have not found the stages these models predict. Lacy and Hendricks (1980), for example, looked for attitude changes predicted by Gould's work. They used data from a survey of over 9000 people, but could not find attitude shifts to support Gould's stages.

Costa and McCrae (1989), for example, report that a few personality traits change over time. But between ages 20 and 30 most people settle into a personality that they will keep for most of their life. They propose that personality stays stable throughout adulthood.

Braun and Sweet (1983–84) reviewed data from four large surveys to see if passages from one stage of life to another existed. They compared personality differences within and between age groups. While they did find personality differences between age groups, they also found that in studies done at different times and in different countries (the United States and Canada) the characteristics of each age-stage differed. In addition, they found that after a passage around age 19, little developmental change took place in people's attitudes as they aged. These findings, therefore, don't support the stage model of adult development.

Other studies have found only partial support for a stage model of development. McAdams, de St. Aubin, and Logan (1993) developed a measure of generativity. They used this measure in a cross-sectional study to assess generativity in young, middle-aged, and older people. They found that generativity did increase between the younger and mid-life groups. But they found no decline in generativity in the older group, as they expected.

Butler (1975; see also Novak 1985–86) has criticized the stage model of development for another reason. He challenges the idea that a person in old age can only accept who they are and what they have been. "People are locked in by such a theory," he says. They may look healthy from Erikson's point of view, but they suffer because they are trapped by their work, marriage, or lifestyle. "Excessive or exaggerated identity," according to Butler, "seems clearly to be an obstacle to continued growth and development through life and to appreciation of the future … Human beings need the freedom to live with change, to invent and reinvent themselves a number of times throughout their lives" (Butler 1975, 400–401). Blau (1973, 185) warns that adults can "become too well adjusted to society's expectation and insufficiently attuned to their own nature and needs" in old age.

Stage models create a caricature of current conditions. Today people divorce, remarry, have children, start businesses, leave careers, return to careers, and return to school at all ages in adulthood. Studies find many stages in the life cycle and different stages and patterns for men and women. These findings reflect the diversity of the life course in a time of social change.

SELF-DEVELOPMENT IN LATER LIFE

Current criticisms of stage models call for a more flexible model of the **self** in later life. Erikson's last stage of integrity vs. despair and doubt points in this direction. He says that a person in later life can give meaning to past events and experiences. This leads to integrity, a sense of wholeness and well-being. Some social psychologists put this dynamic model of the self at the centre of their studies (Ruth and Coleman 1996).

Breytspraak (1995, 93) defines the self as "the ability to be aware of one's own boundaries and individuality and to reflect upon these." Ritzer (1992, 202) says the self has "the ability to take oneself as an object." It can act as both subject and object.

Breytspraak (1995) says that two motives shape behaviour as people age. First, people try to view themselves positively and to present a good image of themselves to others. Second, people try to maintain their sense of self in the face of a changing social environment. This makes the self a dynamic process more than a state of being. The self constantly shapes interaction and interprets events to achieve these two goals.

Aging poses a number of challenges to the self. These challenges come from at least three sources: social attitudes toward older people, physical decline, and the loss of social roles. Ageism, for example, poses a challenge to everyone in later life. The self's sensitivity to others' perceptions can make ageism a painful experience. It can lower a person's self-esteem. In our society a person must work to combat ageism. A strong social support network will make this easier. For example, friends and family can give a person feelings of worth and importance that combat negative stereotypes.

Physical decline also challenges a person's sense of self. A person who gets her self-esteem from playing sports may feel let down as her ability decreases with age. Our culture links driving with maturity, adulthood, freedom, and self-efficacy. A person who can no longer drive a car may feel a blow to her self-esteem. Even people with Alzheimer's disease, a radical loss of the self, resist giving up driving a car. Sports programs for older people like the Seniors Olympics, or the Seniors Golf Tour help people maintain their self-esteem in the face of physical decline. So do programs that refresh older peoples' driving skills.

Finally, role loss can rob a person of self-worth. Social roles give a person status, purpose, and a sense of achievement. Loss of roles threaten a person's well-being. Retirement, widowhood, and the empty nest all challenge people's sense of self as they age. Most people cope with these role losses and find new sources of esteem. A widow may find self-worth in volunteer work by counselling other widows. A retired machinist may find self-esteem in a second career as a handyman. Sometimes these new roles lead to a more satisfying sense of self. The challenge of role loss demands that the older person search for new meaning in later life.

McAdams (1990, cited in Ruth and Coleman 1996) says that near the end of life the self may live in the present. The person may shift from a rational view of life as a coherent story to a transcendent view. Ruth and Coleman (1996, 317) review studies that describe a "spiritual Me." A person at this point may begin an inward journey. Tornstam (1994, 207–11, cited in Ruth and Coleman 1996) refers to this as "gero-transcendence." The self begins to expand its boundaries and reflect on the meaning of human life.

SPIRITUALITY: THE SEARCH FOR MEANING IN LATER LIFE

Do people become more religious with age? Studies differ in their answers to this question. Studies find that poor health and the lack of transportation lead to declines in formal religious activity. But studies also find that religious attitudes stay stable throughout old age. One study reported that, given the chance to change their commitments, most older people would spend the same time they do now on religious activity. And more than a third of the people in this study said they would spend more time on religion (DeGenova 1992, cited in McFadden 1996).

The search for a good old age can take many forms, including religious faith. Canadian life in the past often centred on the church or synagogue. Religion gave people a common set of values, a community of like-minded people, and a meaning to life. Many older people today still have a strong religious faith (McFadden 1996). Lapierre, Bouffard, and Bastin (1993) studied the goals and aspirations of varied age groups. They found that older people, compared with younger people, more often referred to a good death as one of their important goals.

Older Canadians, compared with other age groups, report the highest rate of attendance at religious services. Forty-two percent of older Canadians say they attend services at least once a week (Baril and Mori 1991). A greater proportion of older women, compared with older men, report activity in their church community. Blazer and Palmore (1976, cited in National Advisory Council 1992b) say that people aged 75 and older show some of the strongest religious belief.

This may, in part, reflect their upbringing at a time when religion played a bigger part in people's lives. It may also reflect the role that religious faith can play as health, income, and social supports decline in late old age. Koenig, George, and Siegler (1988, cited in National Advisory Council 1992b) report that older people use religious belief as a way to cope with stressful events. Coping included prayer, faith in God, and support from clergy and the church community. Religious belief can help a person find meaning in the face of despair.

The diversity of Canadian life, with its many ethnic and cultural groups, leads to many different religious and spiritual perspectives. Most Canadians claim Christianity as their religious belief. Forty-five percent of adult Canadians claim Roman Catholicism as their form of Christianity and 30 percent claim Protestantism (Baril and Mori 1991). Other faiths include Judaism, other Christian faiths, Islam, Buddhism, Hinduism, Sikhism, Confucianism, and Taoism.

Some people express their spirituality outside traditional religious channels. They may feel a oneness with nature or a commitment to the betterment of all life. Religious leaders and caregivers can help older people live their faith. Professionals must understand and respect the religious traditions of the people they serve. Professionals can help a religious community provide support to older members, and they can help older members take part in their religious communities. This can take the form of outreach religious services or car pools to places of worship.

Psychologists like Erik Erikson and Viktor Frankl (1990) teach that later life provides a unique time for spiritual growth. Erikson sees this as a time to discover integrity or wholeness in life. Frankl (1990, 7–10) says that older people can bring in the "the harvest of their lives." Spiritual practices, whether formal religious services or quiet reflection on the past, can bring fullness to later life. McFadden (1996) says that researchers need to learn more about the many expressions of religion and spirituality in later life.

LIFE-SPAN DEVELOPMENTAL PERSPECTIVE

One of the newer perspectives in the social psychology of aging—the **life-span developmental perspective**—sees the individual as continually changing from birth to death (Baltes and Goulet 1970). Unlike stage models, it does not describe an end point or goal of development (like integrity or ego transcendence). Instead, the life-span developmental model treats crisis and change as a constant part of life. "At the very moment when completion seems to be achieved," Riegel (1976, 697) says, "new questions and doubts arise in the individual and in society."

The life-span developmental model sees development as a **dialectical process** in which the individual changes in response to societal demands and society changes in response to individual action and adaptation (Riegel 1975). Life-span developmental theorists find many patterns and stages of aging. They say that people's personalities differ, as do their coping styles and the resources they use in coping with the world. People live in different social classes and come from different cohorts. All of this creates varied patterns of aging. The life-span developmental model also turns the researchers' attention to the social context to explain the differences in the time of onset, direction, and duration of developmental stages (Novak 1985–86).

PERSONALITY AND SOCIAL CONTEXT

Life-span development researchers study three types of environmental effects: (1) **non-normative events** (unexpected events such as illnesses, layoffs, and accidents); (2) **normative, history-graded events** (historical events that shape a person's life, such as the Great Depression of the 1930s or World War II); and (3) **normative, age-graded events** (socially sanctioned events that occur most often at a certain age like marriage or retirement) (Riegel 1975; Baltes, Cornelius, and Nesselroade 1979).

Non-Normative Events

Sociologists define norms as "shared rules or guidelines" that prescribe right behaviour under certain conditions (Robertson 1981, 60). Every society has age norms that prescribe how a person of a certain age should act. University students, for example, can hitchhike across the country with backpacks each summer, travel to Europe with Eurail passes, and sleep in railway stations or open fields. People accept this behaviour from the young, and they even expect students to take time off to travel. Social gerontologists call this a normative life event.

People can also go through non-normative events, including accidents, sudden changes in health, or divorce. Social psychologists call these events non-normative because society does not prescribe that everyone go through these events and because people cannot plan for them.

Non-normative life events or life crises—such as the death of a close friend, widowhood, or illness—can lead to shock and fear. Novak (1985) studied the response to life events in a sample of twenty-five healthy, middle-class, community-dwelling older people in Winnipeg. These people all scored high on a standard test of self-actualization (a measure of personality development). Most of them had gone through at least one major non-normative life event—early retirement, loss of a spouse, or an illness.

Sometimes these events came about because a person felt an inner urge to change (one subject retired early so that he could devote himself to writing and to reading philosophy). Sometimes change came from outside: widowhood or illness forced people to rethink their mid-life roles. Many of these subjects found the process of change painful and frightening.

Novak (1985) reports that these non-normative events had a common pattern. First, a person faced a problem or moment of crisis—a "challenge." These challenges included widowhood, early retirement, and illness. Second, they "accepted" the challenge and interpreted it as a demand for some response. Third, they responded to or "affirmed" their lives in spite of the challenge. This allowed them to enter a new phase of life beyond the roles and responsibilities of middle age.

These people were studied after they had passed through this life event. Did they succeed in affirming their lives because of their self-actualizing, integrated personalities, or did the life events they faced lead these people to a new integrated stage of adulthood? Studies of coping styles suggest that people bring their coping methods with them into later life (Lawton and Nahemow 1973; Lieberman 1975).

History-Graded Events

Non-normative events describe sudden changes in a person's personal life, but history-graded events change the lives of many age cohorts. The term *cohort*, as stated earlier, describes a group of people born at the same point or within the same period (usually five or ten years) of time (Schaie 1968, 559; Marshall 1983, 52).

Older people who were between the ages of 75 and 85 in 1985, for example, were born between 1900 and 1910. These people share the experiences of two world wars and the Great Depression. If you talk to one of them about their past, you will almost always hear stories about the Depression and the world wars. These historic events left their mark on this cohort, shaping their family lives, their work lives, and their values (Hagestad 1990).

Tindale (1980) studied a group of poor old men in a large Canadian city. Most of them lived through the Depression as teenagers, rode the rails as hobos, and picked tobacco or fruit for twenty-five cents an hour. They have little education and few family ties.

Their lives today show the effects of their past. "They were poor before the depression," Tindale says, "poorer still during it, and only a little less poor after it" (1980, 91). These men now live alone on government pensions. They eat and sleep in the downtown missions and Salvation Army shelters. They never had much, and they do not expect much now.

The cohort born between 1945 and 1955 (30- to 40-year-olds in 1985) expect different things from life and from society, based on their experiences. These people belong to one of the largest cohorts in Canadian history. Canada built elementary schools for these people when they were children in the 1950s and 1960s, universities for them in the 1960s and 1970s, and housing for them in the 1980s. They have lived through a relatively peaceful, affluent time in Canada's history, and they expect more from society than do older age groups.

As cohorts age (and members die), cohorts replace one another in society's age structure. Riley, Johnson, and Foner (1972) call this *cohort flow*. As cohorts flow through the age structure they change the size of particular age groups (e.g., the size of the group 20–30 years old will differ in 1940 and 1970). New cohorts also bring new experiences with them as they age. Older people today, for example, have less education than younger cohorts. The 1981 Canada Census reports that almost 60 percent of the cohort born between 1897 and 1906 had less than a Grade 9 education (Statistics Canada 1984b). Younger Canadians have more schooling: in 1981 80 percent of the population under 65 had more than Grade 9, and almost 40 percent had between nine and thirteen years of school (Statistics Canada 1984b). Younger, more educated groups will probably demand more educational opportunities when they reach old age.

Riley, Johnson, and Foner's (1972) model of aging omits a few important concepts about aging and age grading. Historical events, for example, also get filtered through the age stratification system, the system of age grades a society uses (e.g., child, adolescent, young adult). The 1900–1910 cohort went through the Great Depression of the 1930s in young adulthood, and the Depression affected their decision to marry as it did the early years of their careers. The Depression also affected the cohort born between 1920 and 1930, but it had a different effect on these people. They lived through the Depression as children. Some of them may not remember the Depression at all; others may simply have accepted the hard times as "the way things are."

Gerontologists use the term *generation* to describe people who share an awareness of their common historical or cultural experiences, but who may come from different cohorts. The baby boom cohorts born between 1945 and the early 1960s form a generation; they have all lived under the threat of nuclear war, and they have lived in a relatively affluent time in Canadian history.

Braun and Sweet (1983–84) found that a "generational event" theory of personality better explained the differences between age groups than did a theory of life stages. **Generational event theory** says that attitudes form for a generation in their teens. People who grow up at the same time in the same society share the same attitudes. These attitudes stay fairly stable throughout life because of what Neugarten (1964, 198) calls the "institutionalization of personality." People respond in the same ways to life's demands; others expect the same responses of them; and people choose their friends and contacts to support a stable sense of self.

These studies all show the effect of social and historical events on individual personality. Like non-normative events, history-graded events happen without warning, and sometimes the changes they bring about do not show up until years later. Society also shapes personality growth more directly through normative age grading.

Normative Age-Graded Events

Anthropologists report that all societies move people through a series of age grades (Linton 1936). Age grades define certain rights and responsibilities for their members. They give order to the life course and help people judge their own development (Cain 1964).

Males of the Nandi tribe in Kenya, for example, belong to one of seven age groups—two for boys, one for warriors, and four for elders. These groups give males their status and allow them to play certain roles at given times in their lives. Likewise, pre-industrial societies recognized three stages of life—infancy-childhood, mature adulthood, and old age.

Industrialized society today includes the stages of infancy, childhood, adolescence, young adulthood, middle age, and old age. Some writers have now added a new stage, the young-old, after middle age and before late old age. This last stage makes sense in a society where people can expect to live in good health for ten or fifteen years after age 65.

Neugarten, Moore, and Lowe (1968) say that people internalize the age-grade system and know the proper time for a life event to occur. A Canadian middle-class girl who falls in love today at the age of 14 will feel it is too early to marry. A woman graduate student in her early 20s may also feel it is too early to settle down. A single career woman of 40 who wants to get married may feel it is too late.

Someone for whom major life events come early or late—a teenaged mother or a newlywed octogenarian—may feel out of sync with the age-status system. Gerontologists call this **age-status asynchronization**.

Neugarten and Moore (1968) say that a person can be on time in certain ways and late or early in others. They can feel on time when they choose to marry, but late in advancing in their profession. Research shows that occupation, ethnic background, and social class affect the timing of life events.

The lower a woman's social class, for example, the earlier she tends to go through life events like marriage or having her first child (Neugarten and Moore 1968). Neugarten and Moore found that female professionals had their first child an average of six years later than unskilled working-class women. The researchers also report that women go through different life events than men. They found, for instance, that women enter a new phase of life in their late 40s. The last child leaves home, menopause occurs, and many women enter the labour market. This produces "an increasingly accentuated transition period in the lives of women, one that men do not face" (1968, 13).

Neugarten and Moore (1968) conclude that the social groups we belong to regulate our life cycle. Groups expect certain behaviours from their members, and members rely on these expectations to guide their actions. Members also observe the transition times of others and get a sense for when changes should occur (Hagestad 1990). Hagestad (1990) reviewed the literature on the life course, and found that researchers have recently increased their interest in life events, life transitions, and life trajectories.

This new interest may reflect recent changes in the timing and sequencing of life events. For example, many women today delay having their first child until after age 30. More women than ever before enter the workforce and stay at work after they have children. Also, many women find themselves back in school in their 40s and 50s in order to prepare for new careers. The National Advisory Council on Aging (1993c) says that women show more diverse patterns of development than ever before. Changing social values, new career options, more education, and the need for two earners in a family account for this change. This has led to a more flexible life course.

The life-span developmental model accepts the idea that maturation and psychological change affect human development, but it says that a more complete picture of human development requires knowledge of a person's life events and social context. It shows that society and history play important parts in shaping individual development.

ETHNICITY AND SOCIAL SUPPORTS

A person's cultural background, language, and country of origin also affect how he or she will adjust to aging. Immigrants to Canada, especially people who come to Canada in later life, face unique challenges as they age.

Sociologists define an ethnic group as a group of people who see themselves as being alike because of their common ancestry and who are seen as being alike by others (Hughes and Hughes 1952, cited in Driedger and Chappell 1987). Culture and ethnicity form a backdrop for psychological development in old age. Ethnic culture gives meaning to life events and can buffer life crises. The size and age composition of an ethnic community also determine the number of social supports a person has available in old age.

Gerontologists in Canada have done relatively little research on ethnicity, aging, and social supports (Wong and Reker 1985; Ujimoto 1983; Driedger and Chappell 1987), but studies done so far show that older people from different ethnic groups (including those from British and French backgrounds) experience old age differently. Even within one group differences exist. Matsuoka (1993) says that group members can differ by social class, geography, religion, and political beliefs. Some group members have lived in Canada for many years, others have just arrived. Matsuoka says that most surveys miss this diversity. She proposes qualitative as well as quantitative studies in order to describe the texture of ethnic elders' lives.

Most of the Canadian research so far has explored three theories that attempt to explain the ethnic elders' experiences: **levelling theory, buffer theory,** and **multiple jeopardy theory.**

Levelling Theory

According to levelling theory, age levels ethnic differences. A decline in health or loss of a spouse will lead all older people (regardless of their ethnicity) to depend more on their families and on social services for help. These changes outweigh cultural differences in family structure or differences in cultural values of parent-child relations.

Rosenthal (1983) found support for the levelling theory of aging and ethnicity. She studied Anglo- and non-Anglo-Canadian older people in Ontario (Anglo-Canadians here are people who report British background). Modernization theory predicts that Anglo-Canadian families will show weaker family ties compared with non-Anglo-Canadians and that non-Anglos will show more traditional family structures and more support for older people. Rosenthal (1983, 1986a) did not find support for this theory. Instead, she found that older Anglo-Canadians and non-Anglo-Canadians in her study reported similar family structures, similar views of family life, and similar family relations. She did find that slightly more non-Anglo-Canadians lived with their middle-aged children, but this difference disappeared in older age groups. Rosenthal (1983, 14) says "there is a strong suggestion that age levels these differences [between groups]."

Buffer Theory

Buffer theory says that ethnic identity buffers people from role loss as they age (Holzberg 1981). A number of studies have found support for the buffer theory of aging and ethnicity. Strain and Chappell (1984; see also Chappell and Strain 1984) compared the social supports of older Aboriginal people with those of non-Aboriginal people in Winnipeg. They found that Aboriginal people had larger numbers of friends and relatives than non-Aboriginal people. Aboriginal people also reported having two and a half times as many relatives outside their household and six times as many friends as did non-Aboriginal people. (Strain and Chappell [1984] say that Aboriginal people may have a broader definition of friends than non-Aboriginal people.) Aboriginal people also have more weekly contact with their friends and relatives than do non-Aboriginal people.

A third of the Aboriginal people studied, but only 6.4 percent of those who were non-Aboriginal, lived with their grandchildren. Strain and Chappell trace this difference to Aboriginal culture. For example, "one native person explained that it was the duty of her grandparents to raise her. She lived with them and was taught the native way of life, thereby freeing her own parents for other responsibilities" (1984, 12).

Gold (1980) supports this finding. She describes the start of a small senior recreation program that was meant to serve a dozen or so Aboriginal seniors. But the planners found that they also had to include the rest of the senior's family. "The culture demanded that the young serve the old," she says, but it also required that the old look after the very young. "So the food was prepared and served to the old, while the old tended youngsters" (Gold 1980, 3). This program for twelve Aboriginal elders became a program for fifty to one hundred people of all ages. These elders had a role to play in their culture, even if they had low status in white society.

Vanderburgh (1988) reports that in Ontario the Ojibwe Cultural Foundation (OCF) began an elders' program to revive the Aboriginal elders' role as mentors. This program arranges for elders

Exhibit 7.3

The Challenge of Aging among Aboriginal Peoples

Buffer theory says that a culture can buffer the effects of physical decline and loss that come with age. Aboriginal culture, under the best conditions, buffers elders from some of the effects of aging. But Aboriginal culture cannot always buffer people from the lifelong inequalities and conditions that lead to problems in old age.

Margaret Labillois (1994), elder and former Micmac chief, describes the decline in status of older Aboriginal people in her own lifetime. "When I was growing up," she says, "elders were always respected for their knowledge and their experience. They were our teachers, our books, our education, our baby-sitters, our story tellers, and our special helpers—in short, a way of life. ... Today elders are no longer elders, but just old people" (Labillois 1994, 15; see also d'Anglure 1994). She goes on to say that many Aboriginal older people today live in poverty. They have few housing options on reserves, and older people who live off the reserve may live in poor-quality housing. A report by the Ontario Advisory Council on Senior Citizens (1993) says that not one of Ontario's 128 First Nations have a full hospital. These communities have few nursing homes and few counsellors to help people cope with diseases like diabetes.

Modernization accounts for part of this decline in status of Aboriginal older people. Young people get formal education and the mass media provide infor-mation that makes older peoples' knowledge seem obsolete. But ageism and racism throughout life also account for the decline in Aboriginal elders' well-being. Chipperfield and Havens (1992), for example, studied Aboriginal elders' own sense of respect at two points. They found that in both the mid-1970s and mid-1980s Aboriginal elders gave themselves the lowest rating of respect of any ethnic group in Manitoba.

Social scientist James Frideres (1994) says that Aboriginal older people suffer from more health problems than non-Aboriginals. They also have twice the average length of time with a disability in life, compared with non-Aboriginals. Frideres traces ill health in Aboriginals in old age to poor nutrition, poor living conditions, and poverty throughout life (see also Armstrong-Esther 1994). He adds that racism and exclusion kept Aboriginal people outside mainstream society.

Professional care providers may assume that Aboriginal older people get the support they need from their families. But Armstrong-Esther (1994) questions the Aboriginal family's ability to care for older family members today. For example, do older Aboriginal people choose family support? Or do they turn to the family as their only option because formal supports do not exist? And how well can Aboriginal families meet the needs of their older members?

Older Aboriginal people, Frideres (1994, 30) says, "have experienced a double alienation, as they have remained outside the mainstream Canadian institutional structure as well as outside the changing Native community." A recent revival of interest in Aboriginal culture and tradition has restored some older people to the status of elder. But Mussell (1994) reports that most older Aboriginal people do not fill leadership roles or feel that they can help with community issues (see also Tasse 1993). He calls for the development of older Aboriginal people as a resource for their communities. They represent "a wonderful resource that has hardly begun to be explored" (Mussell 1994, 58).

to teach language skills, crafts, and healing methods to the young. This and other programs encourage elders to speak with authority at public gatherings about their experience. This mandate to speak with authority and play a guiding role in community life, rather than chronological age, is what defines elderhood. An Aboriginal person who achieves this status has a buffer against the stress of aging.

Holzberg (1982) also found support for the buffer theory. She started an ethnic history program for Eastern European Jews at the Baycrest Centre in Toronto. These older people believed that they had to preserve their memories of the past for their children and grandchildren and so they decided to write and publish a book of their memoirs. This gave them a purpose in life and increased their self-worth. Holzberg (1982, 253) says that "it was the value of ethnic history to the group rather than the value of life history to the individual as a reaffirmation of self that was the rallying point of collective effort." Working for a higher cultural purpose can buffer people from the threat of meaninglessness that sometimes comes with old age and death.

Multiple Jeopardy Theory

Multiple jeopardy theory says that aging makes life worse for members of an ethnic group. Minority members have low status to begin with, and they often have low incomes too (Markides and Mindel 1987). Aging may add to their troubles (Havens and Chappell 1983).

Wong and Reker (1985) found support for the multiple jeopardy theory. They compared a sample of forty Chinese Canadians and forty Anglo-Canadians in Ontario. The average age of the members of both groups was 68. Wong and Reker asked each group about the kinds of problems they faced and the methods they used to cope with these problems. They found that both groups had about the same number of problems, but the Chinese Canadians viewed their problems as being more serious than those of the Anglo-Canadians. The Chinese Canadians also felt that they coped less well than the Anglo-Canadians, and they had lower well-being scores. Wong and Reker say that these findings support the multiple jeopardy theory (see also Lam 1994). They say that stress due to living

in a foreign culture and minority status add to the problems of physical aging.

Moore (1995) compared Aboriginal and non-Aboriginal older people. She found that Aboriginal men tended to have higher unemployment rates and lower incomes than non-Aboriginal men. Aboriginal men and women, compared with non-Aboriginals, had about one and a half times the low-income rate. Low income leads to poor health and poor housing. These figures show that older Aboriginal people face multiple jeopardy. Older people in visible minorities (non-Caucasian, non-White, non-Aboriginal) show similar characteristics and also face double jeopardy (Chard 1995).

Havens and Chappell (1983) also found support for the theory. They studied the cumulative effects of being old, female, and a member of a minority group. They found that on a standard psychological measure of mental function "old-elderly women of Polish, Russian, and Ukrainian descent are significantly more disadvantaged ... than any of the other groups" (1983, 129). Havens and Chappell found less support for multiple jeopardy when they asked this group whether they felt personally disadvantaged. It seems that older ethnic people do not feel (or do not report feeling) worse off than nonethnic elders.

Statistics Canada also reports multiple jeopardy for ethnic elders. Statistics Canada (1984a), in measuring economic well-being, found that older immigrants have a greater chance than nonimmigrants of living in low-income families (see also Penning 1983). Specifically, the study found that 10 percent of nonimmigrants aged 65 and over lived in low-income families, compared with 11 percent of immigrants who had come to Canada before 1961, 14 percent of immigrants who arrived between 1961 and 1970, and 22.5 percent of the most recent immigrants. This study also found that immigrants get more of their income from the Old Age Security and the Canada Pension Plan than do nonimmigrants (Statistics Canada 1984a). Older members of Asian, African, and Latin American ethnic groups show some of the lowest economic well-being on measures of labour force activity, retirement income, and investment income (Wanner and McDonald 1986). These studies show that being old and an immigrant, especially a recent immigrant from a Third World nation, increases the chance that a person will have a low income. Bagley (1993) also found that recent older Chinese immigrants reported more depression and anxiety than established older Chinese residents of Canada.

Limitations of Ethnicity and Aging Theories

Each of these theories gives some clues about how ethnicity affects social and psychological well-being as a person ages. But each theory has its

---

Exhibit 7.4

Overcoming Barriers: Telling It Like It Is

Elvira Herrera, of the Centre for Spanish Speaking People in Toronto, composed the letter below. Five seniors in the Centre's English as a Second Language program contributed to the letter. This letter shows the tensions that can exist in families that sponsor the immigration of older members in Canada. In particular the letter points to the language barrier that keeps older immigrants from living a normal life. The letter ends on a note of hope for a better life in their new country.

My dear family:

How happy I felt coming to Canada to live with you! I thought all my dreams would come true: Enjoying the company of my children, watching my grandchildren grow up, learning English, having a job, making new friends ... Look at me now ...

　　Oh! if you knew how many times I have tried to write this letter, my dear son, my dear daughter, my beloved grandchildren. But I preferred to hide my feelings in order not to make you suffer, too. Did you ever think of the consequences when you sponsored me to come to this country? Then I could have thought twice before deciding to make this enormous change in my life. Now it's too late. I don't have my house, my friends, my independence, I don't have money I can spend freely, and I think I'm also losing my family!

　　Please do not think I don't value your efforts. I know you have to work hard and don't have much time for housekeeping or taking care of your children. But I did not know you wanted such help from me. It's my pleasure to babysit my grandchildren from time to time, but I didn't think this would be a daily obligation. When I told you that I wanted to learn English so I could go out by myself and feel more secure, your answer was, "Mama, you are very old, you cannot learn English. Beside that, I need you here." For years, I didn't venture to ask again. I thought the least I could do was help you, since I was

already a burden on the family. But, to tell you the truth, I cannot stand it any more! I couldn't even go to church on Sundays, if your husband was tired or not in a mood to drive me there, because you were afraid that I could get lost if I went by bus.

　　You came to this country very young. You have already adapted to the culture and customs here. For me, as a senior, the process is very difficult. I cannot even communicate with my grandchildren because they haven't learned to respect the old ones. When I ask the eldest to go with me to a store, he refuses, because he doesn't want anyone to know that we speak Spanish. He's ashamed to go out with his grandma. I feel so lonely and frustrated ... When I lived in my homeland I used to go everywhere, saying hello to everybody, solving problems, helping people, receiving friends in my home. Now, when your friends come over, I prefer to go to the basement and cry silently in my room, because your friends aren't mine and I do not feel welcome to join you. You don't seem to care about talking in English, although you know I don't understand. And I don't have the confidence to invite over some people I have met at church. This is not my house. I just have a dark little room in the basement...

　　However, things are going to change now. A friend opened my eyes. She asked me, "Why don't you go to school? Why don't you have coffee with us when we invite you? Why do you seem so sad?"

Exhibit 7.4 (cont.)

Overcoming Barriers: Telling It Like It Is

I know you were very surprised when I told you about my registration in a seniors' English class. I know you were mad at me because I wouldn't have lunch ready for the family, or be home to babysit your daughter until you returned from work. But dear one, I need to have a life, too. I can help you. As your mother, I am willing to do that. But, you know I need my own activities and friends, too. I know now that I'm capable of learning English, although you laugh at me and try to convince me not to go back to classes because I'm "wasting my time." Now I ride the bus, I have joined a seniors' club and I don't need anyone to take me to church. Certainly I am old, but I have rediscovered the valuable person inside me. I hope you'll understand.

I want to lead my own life, a life worth living, as long as I am alive. Let me live.

Your loving mother.

Source: "Growing Older, Growing Bolder," *The Moment 21* (1994): 11.

limits. Levelling theory, for example, may hold true only for people in late old age. At that point almost everyone turns to government-run services like home care or institutions for help. Buffer theory describes aging in a culture that holds the old in high esteem, but an ethnic group with a different belief system, or a group with few members in Canada, may find that ethnicity does not buffer the effects of aging.

Hall (1993), for example, studied sixteen elderly Vietnamese immigrants in Lethbridge, Alberta. These people (most of them women who lived with their children) reported dissatisfaction with their living arrangements. They also said they felt isolated and rarely met with other relatives. Sixty-nine percent of these people reported dissatisfaction with their relationships at home. Hall found that for many of these people life in Canada meant boredom, a lack of social contacts, and clashes with children and grandchildren.

The case of Aboriginal people in Canada also calls into question buffer theory. Compared with non-Aboriginal people, they have a lower life expectancy, less formal education, lower income, and are more likely to live in poor-quality housing (Bienvenue and Havens 1986; Senior Citizens' Provincial Council 1988; Statistics Canada 1984b). Blandford and Chappell (1990) found that older Aboriginal people reported lower life satisfaction and more loneliness than non-Aboriginal people. Further research revealed that poor health and lack of help accounted for Aboriginal peoples' lower life satisfaction and loneliness. This example again shows that membership in an ethnic group may not buffer aging even when a group values its elders. Social-psychological well-being in later life also depends on objective conditions like health and social supports.

Research on multiple jeopardy theory shows that ethnic elders rate less well on objective measures than nonethnic older people. But Gibson (1988) argues that the theory oversimplifies the effects of ethnicity on aging. It ignores the personal meaning of aging, the social context, and the availability of personal supports. It also fails to explain some of the findings from health research, such as the possibility that ethnic differences in mortality lessen in late old age. Worst of all, the multiple jeopardy theory compares ethnic group members with those in the majority group and focuses on the negative effects of ethnic membership. Gibson (1988) points out that ethnicity alone does not predict a decrease in well-being in old age.

What can we conclude about the effects of ethnicity on aging from these conflicting theories and research reports? What seems certain is that the effects of ethnicity on aging depend on many things other than membership in an ethnic group. The age distribution of the ethnic group's population (the ratio of younger to older people in the group); the geographic closeness of the group (how easily members can pool their resources); the degree of assimilation of the group into Canadian society (how well members can use available resources); and the time of immigration (recent immigrants have less access to public pension funds) all influence the experience of aging for ethnic elders. These conditions differ for each ethnic group, so that "ethnicity" or membership in an ethnic group can mean many things.

Rosenthal (1986b) points out that many studies of ethnicity fail to take into account the differences between ethnic groups. Eastern and Southern European ethnic groups can differ as much from one another as they do from the British ethnic group. This also applies to immigrants from Asian countries like China, Japan, or Vietnam. These people come from different societies, have different cultural traditions, and different religious beliefs. Also, some older immigrants have lived in Canada for many years. Others arrived only a few years ago. Studies of ethnicity need to specify the social and economic conditions of the groups under study.

The next section discusses a model for understanding the social causes of individual problems in later life. It also describes some of the ways in which social breakdown can be avoided or reversed in the case of immigrant seniors.

SOCIAL BREAKDOWN

Kuypers and Bengtson (1973) say that older people often suffer from psychological breakdown due to inadequacies in the social environment. They call

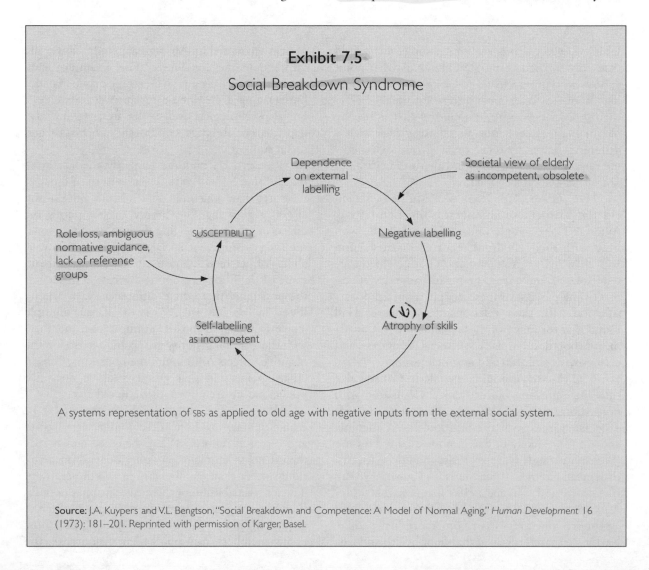

Exhibit 7.5
Social Breakdown Syndrome

A systems representation of SBS as applied to old age with negative inputs from the external social system.

Source: J.A. Kuypers and V.L. Bengtson, "Social Breakdown and Competence: A Model of Normal Aging," *Human Development* 16 (1973): 181–201. Reprinted with permission of Karger, Basel.

this a **social breakdown syndrome,** and they describe it as having the following seven steps (see also Exhibit 7.5):

1. Role loss, lack of norms to guide behaviour, and the loss of friends and relatives as reference groups (i.e., groups that support one's values and behaviour) all make a person susceptible to breakdown.

2. The person begins to depend on external labels for a sense of self. In Canada these labels sometimes have negative connotations (e.g., widow and retiree).

3. Society may view the older person as incompetent. Middle-aged children may begin to take responsibility away from an aging parent. Institutions often leave nothing for older residents to do for themselves.

4. The older person may assume a dependent role in response to this treatment.

5. The older person develops skills that fit the dependent role. People learn to live down to the expectations others have of them.

6. The person loses previous skills. People in nursing homes may lose the ability to make

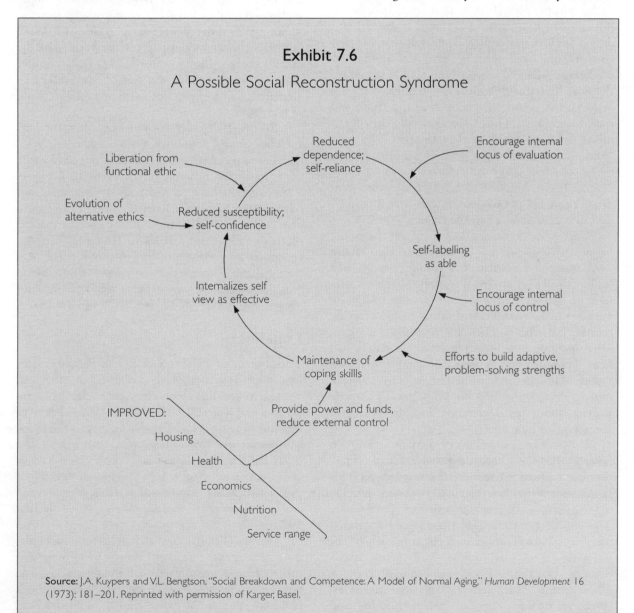

Exhibit 7.6

A Possible Social Reconstruction Syndrome

Source: J.A. Kuypers and V.L. Bengtson, "Social Breakdown and Competence: A Model of Normal Aging," *Human Development* 16 (1973): 181–201. Reprinted with permission of Karger, Basel.

their bed or chop vegetables because they never get the chance.

7. People label themselves as sick and inadequate. This fits the social definition of older people as incompetent and creates a further turn in the cycle of breakdown. It also makes the older person more susceptible to negative labelling.

The case of Carl Teicherow will show how this syndrome can lead to breakdown. Teicherow, 71, worked for Canada Manpower until 1979. He took early retirement at age 63. He says he retired because in the mid-1970s his department began to hire college graduates to fill new jobs. Carl had only a high-school diploma and felt that his new co-workers looked down on him. As his older co-workers retired and more young people joined his division, he felt increasingly isolated. He began to feel that the young workers got all the credit and the promotions. "Those young people they hired didn't know as much as they thought," he says. "Sure they had university degrees, but they had no common sense. They didn't know anything about people. I said, 'the hell with it, if the government doesn't care about this department, why should I?' So I quit as soon as I had the chance."

Carl still feels bitter about work and the young people who joined his department. He doesn't work now, or do much of anything else. He had leadership skills during his working years: his wife says he got elected president of any group he joined. But he quit most of those groups after he retired. Now he watches TV or reads, but these activities give him little pleasure. He had a bad bout of depression a year ago and threatened suicide. His doctor gave him some pills and told him to find something to keep busy. His wife worries about his depression, but she does not know how to help him.

Kuypers and Bengtson (1973) suggest a way to reverse the social breakdown syndrome. They propose a **social reconstruction syndrome.** This syndrome reorganizes the social system to provide older people with new ways to feel worthwhile. This approach includes: (1) a new value system that bases social worth on a person's basic humanity, not on what he or she produces; (2) greater self-reliance; (3) a strong internal sense of control; (4) learning new problem-solving strategies; (5) better-quality services such as housing and

transportation, and better income; (6) maintaining coping skills; and (7) a reduced susceptibility to external judgments. An improvement in any of these areas would increase the older person's quality of life.

THE SOCIAL ROOTS OF PROBLEMS IN OLD AGE

Studies of how history and culture influence aging show that successful aging as well as maladjustment and psychopathology can have social roots. Some maladjustment in later life comes about because society gives older people fewer guides to define correct behaviour than it gives the young. In the case of seniors who have just arrived from another country, for example, the norms and values of Canadian culture may not fit their understanding of old age.

Rosow (1976) says that older people in modern societies occupy a tenuous status—a status or position in the social structure that does not have a role associated with it. A retiree, for example, occupies a status—that of a retired person—but does not have a role to play in society, since retirees are expected not to work, and nothing else is expected of them. The loss of roles in later life, through retirement, children growing up, or arrival in a new culture, excludes older people from taking part in society. It also signals a problem older people have today: finding meaning in later life.

Loneliness

The absence of social roles for older people creates new social-psychological problems in old age. Some studies link loneliness to social isolation (Wood and Guest 1978). Wood (1978) describes loneliness as the loss of social identity—the identity people get from interaction with others and from holding social positions. Loneliness comes about when a person feels a "relational deficit" or gap between the number of relationships desired and the number they have (Weiss 1973; Sermat 1978).

Delisle (1988) found that most older people, though they may live alone, do not feel lonely. But others face a greater risk of loneliness. Delisle concludes that single older people, those without children, people in poor health or bedridden, people with poor education, introverts, neurotics, timid people, or those with low self-esteem face the greatest risk of feeling lonely. Wood (1978) found greater loneliness among older women than older men, among unmarried than married older people, and among older people with no university education. Krause (1993) studied older adults with little education and low income. He found that they often live in run-down neighbourhoods, distrust others, and tend toward social isolation. Other studies have found that older people feel they can do little about their loneliness (Lopata 1969; Abrahams 1972; Gordon 1976).

Perlman, Gerson, and Spinner (1978) suggest two ways to combat loneliness. First, older people should maintain their social contacts with friends and neighbours. Second, since social resources can help older people make these contacts, better transportation, well-designed housing, and more recreational facilities give older people more choice and a stronger sense of control over their lives. Most studies agree that a good old age means more than just the adaptation of older people to what, in some cases, is an inhospitable environment. Older people also need a more supportive social setting to grow old in.

Suicide

The suicide rate in Canada for all age groups (measured in suicides per 100 000 people) increased from the 1960s through the early 1980s. The rate during the 1980s (14.6 per 100 000 in 1986) was about double the rate during the years from 1921 to 1961 (around 7.5 per 100 000). The 1980s rate was the highest ever recorded in Canada (almost one and a half times the rate of the previous high in the 1930s). Rates levelled off in the late 1980s and declined to 13.0 in 1992 (Benetau 1988; Task Force 1994). A greater proportion of men than women commit suicide. Men had a rate of 20.9 per 100 000 in 1992, women had a rate of only 5.5 per 100 000. Men made up the large majority of suicide victims in 1992 (Task Force 1994).

But what do current findings tell us about older people and suicide? Men aged 50–54 had a rate of 26.2 per 100 000 in 1992, while men aged 55–59 had a rate 28.9 per 100 000. The age group 70–74 had the lowest rate of all men aged 15 and over. But the suicide rate for very old men shows a different pattern. The second-oldest group of men

(aged 80–84) had the highest suicide rates in Canada (29.6 per 100 000) in 1992 (Task Force 1994).

Women's rates are much lower than men's at all ages. Women aged 50–54 had the highest rate for women in 1992 (10.0 per 100 000), while those aged 55–59 had a rate of only 5.8 per 100 000. Women aged 85 and over had a rate of 6.2 per 100 000 in 1992—about a quarter of the men's rate in this age group (Task Force 1994).

Why do people commit suicide in old age? Durkheim (1951) proposed that a lack of social integration led to high rates of suicide in modern society. Normlessness or anomie, a lack of connection between the person and society, puts a person at risk. Current research on suicide in later life supports this view. Older people often lose the contacts and links that prevent suicide. Holmes and Rahe (1967), for example, rank "death of a spouse" as the most negative life event. Retirement, the deaths of friends, and a move to a nursing home also weaken the older person's social network (Osgood, Brant, and Lipman 1991). As this network shrinks, the person may lose a sense of purpose and meaning. This increases the risk of suicide.

Reker, Peacock, and Wong (1987) found that older people, compared with middle-aged people, reported stronger feelings of lack of purpose and meaning in life. The researchers say that loss of social roles and social relations may lead people to feel suicidal. A report by Health and Welfare Canada (1977c) supports this view. The report says that loneliness and isolation, widowhood or divorce, retirement, and serious illness all increase the risk of suicide (see also Trovato 1988; Lapierre et al. 1992). Health Canada (1994) reports older people who commit suicide often feel depressed.

Lenaars and Lester (1992) call for some response to the high rate of suicide among older people (especially older men) in Canada. Studies Richarson, Lowenstein, and Weissberg 1989, cited in Health Canada 1994, 22) report that "in the month before committing suicide, three-quarters of elderly suicides visited their physicians, and during the week before, one-third visited their physicians." More awareness by physicians of the signs and symptoms of suicide might prevent some deaths. Also, older people should have better access to psychiatric services, should they need them. The media should make people more aware of the signs of potential suicide in older people. Prevention should also include broader changes in society—such as those that would help older people stay involved in social life.

CONCLUSION

Older Canadians face a number of threats to their social-psychological well-being. But, in general, they report high life satisfaction. They know about the problems of old age, such as widowhood, illness, and physical decline, but they also see many good things about old age. Connidis (1983b) found that older people enjoyed their personal freedom and the chance to do the things they want to do. These advantages, she found, outweigh the problems that come with age. Northcott (1982) found similar results in a study of 440 people in Edmonton. "The elderly," he says, "are more likely than the nonelderly to report no area of life as a major source of pressure and the older the respondent the less pressure reported from all areas of life except health. As pressure falls, satisfaction tends to rise ... In short, the picture one gets of old age is that it is a period of relatively low pressure and relatively high satisfaction, though not without its problems." Each stage of life has its good and bad points, but "old age," Northcott (1982, 77) concludes, "looks far more attractive than stereotypes suggest."

SUMMARY

1. Social psychologists describe at least three models of good aging: disengagement, activity, and continuity. Research shows that each of these patterns can lead to high life satisfaction.
2. Men and women adapt to aging differently, but most older Canadians of both sexes report high life satisfaction. They report that they feel less pressure and enjoy more personal freedom in old age than they did in their middle years.
3. Theories of personality development state that people go through a series of predictable stages as they age. Erikson described eight stages: five for youth and three for middle and old age. Other theorists have found more stages, showing that people go through many

changes in adulthood. Some studies question the universality of these stages.
4. The life-span developmental perspective sees crisis and change as an essential part of life from birth to death. This view states that as people age, they make choices in response to social demands. This perspective allows for many patterns of aging.
5. Self development takes place throughout life. At least two motives shape development: the desire to present a good image of oneself and the desire to maintain a sense of self in the face of change. People face a number of challenges to the self in later life including ageism, physical decline, and role loss.
6. Spiritual development can also take place in later life. Many older people today come into old age with strong religious beliefs. The diversity of Canadian society ensures a diversity of beliefs among older Canadians. Some people express their spirituality outside traditional religious faiths.
7. Life events shape human development. These include non-normative events, normative, history-graded events, and normative, age-graded events. Studies of history-graded and age-graded events show the effects of social structures on personal development.
8. An ethnic group's culture and structure both shape the experience of aging. The group's values, beliefs, and degree of assimilation in part determine how young people treat older members. The group's structure, size, geographic closeness, and age structure also determine the treatment of older members.
9. The life-course perspective provides a more complete view of minority aging. It looks at the effects of social institutions, life events, and social resources on ethnic group members as they age. It looks for continuities and discontinuities in the ethnic older person's life.
10. Kuypers and Bengtson (1973) say that if society views older people negatively, older people can lose confidence in themselves. This can ultimately lead to dependence and psychological distress. They call this process a social breakdown syndrome and conclude that society should judge people by more than their productivity. A change in society's value system, they say, can reverse this syndrome, as can adequate social supports.

11. Members of different ethnic groups will need different forms of social support. Proper support can reverse or avoid social breakdown and lead to a high quality of life. Policy makers need to keep ethnic differences in mind when they plan programs for older people.

12. The way society treats older people can lead to personal problems like loneliness, suicide, and the breakdown of competence. Social psychologists trace these problems to the lack of social supports for older people today.

STUDY QUESTIONS

1. Name and briefly state three of the major social-psychological theories of aging.
2. Name and briefly describe the last three stages of adult development in Erikson's theory of the life cycle. State some of the criticisms of stage models of adult development.
3. What are three challenges that face the self in later life? How can individuals cope with these challenges?
4. What role does religion play in many older people's lives? How and why might religiosity in later life change in the future?
5. Name and describe three types of environmental effects that influence people throughout life.
6. What three theories attempt to explain ethnic elders' experiences? Explain these theories in detail. What does the life-course perspective add to our understanding of ethnicity and aging?
7. Briefly describe the social breakdown and reconstruction syndromes. What role does society play in each of these processes? Why can a person's ethnicity put them at risk of social breakdown?
8. Discuss the sources of loneliness in later life and state at least two ways to combat it.
9. How do suicide rates for older men and women compare with rates for younger people? What might account for the differences in rates between older and younger people?

KEY TERMS

activity theory   this theory holds that people need to stay active to live a satisfying old age. They will need to replace old activities with new ones as they age.

age-status asynchronization   a person can feel on time with respect to certain life events in their life and late or early in others. This can lead to discomfort.

buffer theory   this theory holds that membership in an ethnic group buffers the effects of aging.

continuity theory   this theory holds that people age best when they continue to do the things they have always done.

dialectical process   the individual changes in response to societal demands and society changes in response to individual action and adaptation (Riegel 1975).

disengagement theory   this theory holds that people naturally disengage from activity as they age.

generational event theory   this theory holds that attitudes form for a generation in their teens. People who grow up at the same time in the same society share the same attitudes. These attitudes stay fairly stable throughout life.

generativity   the task of the middle years according to Erikson.

integrity   the task of old age according to Erikson.

intimacy the task of youth according to Erikson.

levelling theory   this theory holds that aging levels differences between people in different ethnic groups.

life-span developmental perspective   sees the individual as continually changing from birth to death (Baltes and Goulet 1970). It treats crisis and change as a constant part of life.

multiple jeopardy theory   this theory holds that membership in an ethnic group increases a person's troubles in later life.

non-normative events   unexpected events such as illnesses, layoffs, and accidents.

normative, age-graded events   socially sanctioned events that occur most often at a certain age like marriage or retirement.

normative, history-graded events   historical events that shape a person's life, such as the Great Depression of the 1930s or World War II.

self Breytspraak (1995, 93) defines the self as "the ability to be aware of one's own boundaries and individuality and to reflect upon these." Ritzer (1992, 202) says the self has "the ability to take oneself as an object."

social breakdown syndrome the idea that people often suffer from psychological breakdown due to inadequacies in the social environment.

social reconstruction syndrome the idea that recreation of a supportive social environment can restore psychological well-being.

SELECTED READINGS

National Advisory Council on Aging. *Mental Health and Aging*. Ottawa: Minister of Supply and Services Canada, 1991.

> A collection of articles that discuss psychological issues in their social context. The authors discuss topics like depression, loneliness, grief, anxiety, and suicide. Readable articles that summarize the literature and focus more on issues than on the presentation of new data.

National Advisory Council on Aging. *Aboriginal Seniors' Issues*. Ottawa: Minister of Supply and Services Canada, 1994.

> A collection of articles that range from a demographic study of Aboriginal people to a personal account of aging by a Micmac elder and former chief. The papers present some of the problems, like poor health care services, that Aboriginal elders face. But some of the papers discuss the important roles that elders played in the past and in some cases still play in their communities. Well-written articles that give many insights into aging among Aboriginal people.

Nichols, Barbara, and Peter Leonard, eds. *Gender, Aging and the State*. Toronto: Black Rose Books, 1995.

> A look at how gender, class, and ethnicity shape the experience of older people. The book makes a strong case for the impact of economic resources on freedom and choice in later life. The contributors often let older people tell their own stories in order to support this view.

Institutional Change

C H A P T E R 8

Health Care

INTRODUCTION

Mrs. Granovetter, 72, lives by herself in a three-room apartment. Until six years ago, she worked as a supervisor in a nursing home, but poor health forced her to quit. She says she has an aortic aneurysm that "looks like a bicycle tire with a bubble in it." She also has arthritis, and her joints get so stiff during the night that, she says, it sometimes takes her until noon to get out of bed. Still, she manages to live on her own. Her daughter, who lives on the other side of town, calls her every day, she talks to or visits with her next-door neighbour daily, and she can still drive. A few times a week she drives to a nearby shopping centre to sit and watch the people go by. She knows just where to park and how far she has to walk to the nearest bench. Last year her children took her on a trip to England. She says they didn't get to walk through the castles, but they toured around in the car and she saw the countryside. With help from family and friends, Mrs. Granovetter stays active and enjoys life.

Like Mrs. Granovetter, a majority of older women suffer from arthritis and almost a quarter of them have heart trouble. But, like her, most of them cope well with some help, and they say they have good health (Statistics Canada 1987). Even among people aged 75 and over, 40 percent who live outside institutions report good health (Roberge, Berthelot, and Wolfson 1995). A Canadian policy statement (Epp 1986, 3) defines health as "a resource which gives people the ability to manage and even to change their surroundings." By this definition, over 90 percent of people aged 65 and over have enough good health that they can live on their own in the community.

Health care refers to the support needed for people to maintain optimum health. The health care needs of Canada's older population range from health promotion and maintenance to long-term chronic care for people with terminal illnesses.

This chapter looks at: (1) the structure and function of the health care system today; (2) how the present system fits the needs of older people; and (3) how the system is changing to meet the needs of an aging society.

THREE MODELS OF HEALTH CARE

Social scientists use models to simplify and describe complex social systems. A model does not perfectly represent the system, but it describes the system's basic structures, functions, and values. Three models of health care have shaped the development of the health care system in Canada: the **medical model,** the **social model,** and the **health promotion model.**

The Medical Model

The medical model focuses on the treatment of diseases and injuries. Treatment most often takes place in the physician's office, in a hospital, or in other health care institutions. The medical model favours surgery, drug therapy, and rehabilitation through physical therapies. Within this model, according to Chappell and her colleagues, "medical care and treatment are defined primarily as technical problems, and the goals of medicine are viewed in terms of technical criteria, such as validity, diagnosis, precision of disease-related treatment, symptom relief and termination of disease process" (Chappell, Strain, and Blandford 1986, 101). Physicians control both the organization of health care and the work of other health care professionals (Torrance 1987). They learn this approach to medicine in medical school and often get little training in other forms of health care such as counselling or long-term community care.

The Social Model

The social model sees medical care as only one part of a complete health care system. This model sees personal and family counselling, home care, and adult day-care programs as part of the health care system. This model of health care tries to keep older people in their own homes. Care within the social model often takes place in the community—in a person's home, at a drop-in centre, or in a counsellor's office. The doctor, in this model, works as part of a health care team that includes nurses, physiotherapists, counsellors, social workers, and other professionals. The social model has grown in importance as more older people need continuing care or long-term care.

Long-term care (LTC) serves people with functional disabilities and few informal supports (Shapiro 1994; 1995). Béland and Shapiro (1994, 245) define long-term care as "all the social and medical services dedicated to the aged who have functional limitations." LTC combines formal services in the home or an institution with family care. It attempts to make up for functional problems and give people as much autonomy as possible. LTC often takes place in the community as an attempt to keep people out of institutions. Home care, for example, offers a range of services that allow people to stay in their homes. Services include meals-on-wheels, homemaker visits, volunteer visits, and physiotherapy (Federal/Provincial 1992).

Béland and Shapiro (1994) reviewed provincial reports on long-term care. They found a number of proposals common to nearly all provinces: (1) decentralized decision-making; (2) a coordinated, single-entry system; (3) a shift from institutional to community services; (4) integration of health and social services; and (5) a continuum of care that includes institutional and community care. Health and Welfare Canada (Federal/Provincial 1992) projects a shift from the medical to the social model of care in the future.

The Health Promotion Model

The health promotion model focuses on prevention and **self-care**. It aims to prevent disease through lifestyle change, increased knowledge about healthy behaviour, and environmental improvement. The Canadian health care system has only begun to use this model. Programs that promote fitness and those that warn about the dangers of smoking or excessive drinking follow this model. This model also includes actions that most people do not associate directly with health care, such as workplace safety regulations, seatbelt legislation, and pollution control for factories.

Each of these models plays a part in the Canadian health care system today. The social model has gained acceptance as a possible alternative to institutionalization. The health promotion model may save the health care system money in the long run by keeping people healthier longer. Recent decreases in heart disease, for example, may have come about through health promotion programs that encourage low-fat diets and discourage smok-

ing. Still, the medical model dominates the system today. Canadians spend more money (much of it through taxes and health insurance programs) on physicians and hospital care than on any other kind of health care (Shapiro and Roos 1986).

THE COST OF CARE TODAY

In 1957 the Canadian government put in place a hospital insurance system that covered the entire population (Chappell 1988). In 1968 the government insured physician services, and by 1972 all provinces belonged to a national medical insurance program. The provincial and federal governments shared the costs for this system of health care. The federal government matched provincial contributions to the program dollar for dollar. The Canada Health Act of 1984 described the principles of the Canadian health care system (Canada Health Act 1984). The system had the following characteristics: universal coverage; access to services; portability (people could get the benefits in their new location when they moved); comprehensive services that include out-patient and hospital care; and administration of the system by a nonprofit public agency (Chappell 1988). According to Russell King, minister of health and community services in New Brunswick, the health care system based on these principles "has become inseparable from our identity as Canadians."

But the national health care system has its limits. For example, though most provinces provide some long-term care insurance, the current system does not fully insure long-term care (Kane 1993). Users often have to pay for programs like adult day care or homemaker services. Also, the system emphasizes medical and institutional care, the two most expensive types of services (Schwenger and Gross 1980). In 1992 Canada had over 1200 hospitals with about 177 000 beds. About 10 percent of these hospitals provided long-term care (Health Canada 1994; Policy, Planning and Information 1993). Canada had about 6000 other health care facilities (including nursing homes). Canada had more than 53 000 physicians in 1992 (up from 31 000 in 1970). This came to about 2 physicians for each 1000 Canadians (National Advisory Council 1994b).

In 1991 Canadians spent $67 billion or 9.9 percent of its gross domestic product (GDP) on

Exhibit 8.1

The Medical Model and the Social Model in Long-Term Care

Medical Model	Social Model
patient	resident, consumer
acute patients	chronic client
physicians and hospitals	community settings and home
patient fits organization	organization fits client, organization will change to fit client if necessary
rigid system boundaries	open system boundaries
high priority to short-term need	high priority to long-term needs
serves long-term care if excess capacity	serves long-term care first
diagnosis, treatment, cure model	assessment of functional capacity, service needs identified, services delivered
organizationally inflexible	organizationally flexible and creative
institutional care	community-based and home care
institutions exclude people in the community	programs include community and may include institution
institution-centred	person-centred
makes little use of informal network	includes informal support
medical/physical assessment	multidimensional assessment (physical, psychological, social needs)
meeting patients' medical needs	helping clients to meet their own needs
patient accepts professional treatment	client plays role developing treatment plan
professional has most power in relationship	client and professional share power
hierarchical organization	flat organization, team approach
expensive resources	lower-cost resources
major share of health care budget	small share of health care budget

These two approaches see and treat the older person differently. Each has a role to play in the Canadian

Source: Adapted from B. Havens, "Long-Term Care Diversity within the Care Continuum," *Canadian Journal on Aging,* 14(2)(1995): 245–62. Printed with permission.

health care (Health Canada 1994). This came to about $2500 per person. Almost three-quarters of health care expenses came from public sources (the federal and provincial governments) (Health Canada 1993). Hospital and other institution costs came to $22.8 billion in 1993, up from $12 billion in 1980 and $6.6 billion in 1975

(Federal/Provincial/Territorial Working Group 1990; Policy, Planning and Information 1993). In 1986–87 Canada spent about $8.4 million per day or $3.08 billion per year on residential care for the elderly (Strike 1989). Both private and public spending on health care increase each year. They rose by about 6 percent in 1990–91 (Policy,

Exhibit 8.2

Selected Nations Ranked by Percentage of Population Aged 65 and Older, Compared with Percentage of Gross Domestic Product (GDP) Spent on Health Care, 1990

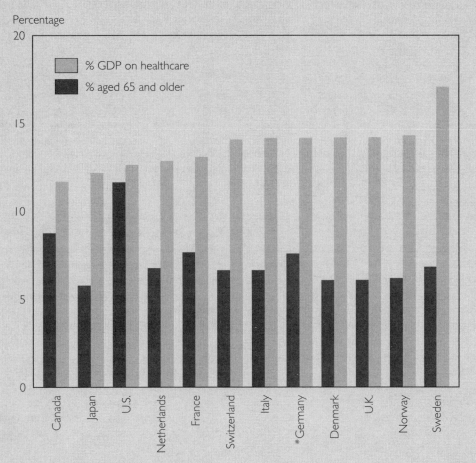

* Both percentages for the Federal Republic of Germany, 1988.

Note that Canada has the youngest population among the developed nations presented here. But it spends a larger proportion of its GDP on health care than any of these nations, except the United States. Also note that the proportion of GDP spent on health care bears no direct relationship to the proportion of older people in a country. Binstock (1993) concludes that the proportion of older people in a country does not explain high health care costs. Instead, public policies that encourage or discourage health care use affect how much money gets spent on health care. So does the increased use of high-tech medical care treatment.

Source: R.H. Binstock, "Healthcare Costs around the World: Is Aging a Fiscal 'Black Hole'?" *Generations* (Winter 1993): 38. Reprinted with permission from *Generation*, 833 Market St., Suite 511, San Francisco, CA 94103. Copyright 1993, American Society on Aging.

Exhibit 8.3

Funding Canada's Health Care System: Danger Ahead

The provincial and federal governments pay most of Canada's medical care bills ($39 billion of the $54 billion dollar total in 1988–89). About $8 billion of the payments come in the form of federal cash outlays to the provinces and territories. The federal funds help poorer provinces to offer a full range of health care programs. These funds also give the federal government some say over provincial health care policies. For example, the threat of removal of federal funds keeps provinces from allowing extra billing by doctors and hospital user fees.

Before 1977 the federal government shared the cost of health care and education on a 50/50 basis with the provinces. In 1977 the federal government began a program of Established Programs Financing (EPF). This program gave "block funding" to the provinces based on a province's population and the gross national product (GNP). Block funding has two parts: one part the federal government pays in cash, the other part the provinces raise through taxes (Canadian Council on Social Development 1990). This program gave the provinces more freedom to use federal funds on community care programs. This program also made the provinces pay for more health care costs.

In 1986 the government reduced the rate of its share of block funds. It agreed to set the rate of increase in block funding at 2 percent below the GNP (instead of equal to the growth in the GNP). In its 1990 budget the federal government announced a freeze in the growth of EPF entitlements until 1992–93. In 1991 it extended this freeze to the end of the 1994–95 fiscal year.

Critics of this policy say that this change in funding will damage the Canadian medical care system. The National Council of Welfare (1991), for example, estimates that by 1994–95 federal EPF support per capita will have dropped below the support level of 1977–78. "In effect," the council says, "a five-year freeze on EPF entitlements would wipe out all the increases in funding made by successive federal governments since 1977" (National Council of Welfare 1991, 15). The new cuts in EPF entitlements will lead to decreasing federal payments for health care. Federal Bill C-69 will end transfer payments to the provinces over time and provinces will need to raise these funds from taxes (Chappell 1993b).

This will have a political as well as an economic effect on the health care system in Canada. Ottawa will have no financial leverage to use in shaping a national health care system. And this could compromise every principle of Canadian medicare: universality, accessibility, comprehensiveness, portability, and public administration. For example, poorer provinces with less money to spend on health care might have to cut back on medical services (an end to comprehensiveness). Some provinces may choose not to recognize the health care plans of other provinces (an end to portability). A two-tiered system may develop where wealthier people will pay for extra services, but poorer people will have to use a reduced basic system (an end to universality).

Planning and Information 1993; Health Canada 1994).

These facts show both the strengths and weaknesses of the health care system today. Canadian medical and hospital insurance matched the most complete coverage in the world, with almost 100 percent of Canadians covered (Statistics Canada 1990a). Older people, for example, receive free hospital and surgical care as well as free access to a range of programs that include chiropractic and optometric services (Health and Welfare Canada 1982b). But Canada also spent more on health care than other countries with comparable systems except the United States (Health Canada 1993; OECD 1993).

The cost of Canada's medical care system grows each year. Denton and Spencer (1995) project that health care expenses will more than double between 1986 and 2041. More older people in the population in part explains these higher costs. Barer and Evans (1989) report that expenditures for special care homes (including nursing homes) rose by nearly 20 percent per year between 1971 and 1982. Hospital expenditures rose by nearly 12 percent per year for that same period (Chappell 1988). Auer (1987) reports that hospital costs accounted for 40 percent of the rise in health care costs between 1961 and 1980. Other sources show that older people as a group use hospitals more often than younger people and that they use them for longer periods (Denton and Spencer 1995; Health and Welfare Canada 1983). Some people fear that an aging population will cause a breakdown in the health care system.

A closer look at the health care system shows that older people account for only a small part of past increases in health care costs (Barer, Evans, and Hertzman 1995; Black et al. 1995). Auer (1987), for instance, says that population change accounts for only about 10 percent of the increases in costs from 1961 to 1980. The Organization for Economic Cooperation and Development (OECD 1988) studied the cost of health care due to population aging. The OECD estimated that between 1960 and 1988 population aging accounted for only about 22 percent of health care cost increases. The study concluded that inflation, growth of the economy, and the organization of health care services accounts for most of the increased costs.

Canada's commitment to the medical model of care explains a large part of the increase in costs. For example, Anderson and his colleagues (1993) report a 317 percent increase in Pharmacare expenditures in British Columbia between 1982 and 1987. They traced one-quarter of the increased costs to increased drug use by older people. Drug costs, more doctors, rising costs for complex treatments, unionization of hospital workers, and more tests to diagnose disease have led to increases in the cost of health care (Binstock 1993; Auer 1987; Feeny 1994; Evans 1984). Barer and his colleagues (1995) say that more older people or more very old people account for little of this increased cost. "Rather," they say, "at each age, more and more is being done for and to each elderly person" (Barer, Evans, and Hertzman 1995, 196).

Some critics of the system today question whether older people need more done to them, or whether they need done to them what currently gets done. Critics question whether the medical model fits the needs of an aging society (Chappell 1988). And they argue that for the same cost Canadians could buy care that more closely fits their needs (Evans 1984). "As a society," Chappell,

Strain, and Blandford (1986, 112) say, "we have not yet dealt with the issue—especially during old age— 'When is health care servicing inappropriate or too much?'"

THE HEALTH CARE SYSTEM AND OLDER PEOPLE'S HEALTH CARE NEEDS

By any standards older people have more health problems than younger people and use more health care services. Statistics Canada (1994c) reports that people aged 65 and over, compared with younger people, see specialists and general practitioners more often. They also have more hospital separations* than younger people and they spend more days in the hospital during each stay. Hospital use increases with age from middle age on. Women aged 75 and over, for example, have a separation rate more than three times the rate of women aged 45–64. They spent 28.7 days in the hospital on average during each stay, compared with 10.7 days for the 45–64-year-old group. Men aged 75 and over had a rate almost four times the rate of people aged 45–64. They spent 20.9 days in the hospital on average during each visit, compared with 10.1 days on average for each stay for the 45–64-year-old group (Statistics Canada 1995).

Statistics Canada (Randhawa and Riley 1995) reports that the hospitalization rate for seniors increased from 1982–83 to 1992–93. People aged 75 and over showed the greatest increases. Statistics Canada (Maclean and Oderkirk 1991) also reports that older people have higher surgery rates than younger people. Between 1975 and 1987 the surgery rate for older people increased at more than triple the rate for people under age 65. Barer, Evans, and Hertzman (1995) report that surgical rates increased for older people by 45.6 percent between 1971 and 1985/86. Older surgery patients also stay in the hospital more than ten days longer on average than younger surgery patients (Maclean and Oderkirk 1991).

* "Hospital separations refer to the discharge or death of an inpatient. They include individual cases separated, not persons separated, that is, an individual may be counted on more than one occasion" (Statistics Canada 1995, 47).

Manitoba Health (1992) reports that the older population in the province (age 65 and over) increased 31 percent between 1971 and 1983. But the number of visits to doctors for this age group increased 79 percent in this time. And referral visits increased 272 percent. Barer and his colleagues (1986) studied the reasons older people use more health care services today than in the past. They wanted to find out whether this increase in costs reflects changes in the diseases older people have today, or whether it reflects the way the system cares for older patients. If the costs reflect older people's increased need for treatment, population aging could lead to a sharp increase in health care costs. But if changes reflect the way the system operates, new approaches to treatment could contain costs. Barer and his colleagues found that little data existed to test the first possibility (that older people have different diseases or more diseases today than in the past); they do suggest that the way the system responds to older people's needs leads them to make heavier use of the medical care system today than in the past.

Black and her colleagues (1995) analyzed Manitoba data to see why older people use more health care now than in the past. They studied consultation visits to specialists. They found that a decrease in the health of older people accounted for only a tiny increase in consultation visits (one-tenth of one percent). Instead, they traced increases in consultations to doctors' increased tendency to make referrals (Black et al. 1995). This, they say, accounts for at least half of added visits to specialists by older people. They go on to say that people in good health account for at least one-third of this increase in visits to specialists. In other words, physicians' tendency to refer older patients to specialists accounts for most of the increase in service use. This has led researchers to link physicians' choice of treatment to health service use.

These findings show that doctors, not patients, have the biggest say in how much and what kind of medical care a person uses. For example, surgical treatment rates vary by province, by county, and even by physician. For one surgical procedure (transurethral prostactectomy), for example, Saskatchewan had a rate ten times that of Prince Edward Island (Statistics Canada 1980c, 1981c). A study in Ontario (Stockwell and Vayda 1979, cited in Roos, Shapiro, and Roos 1984) found that

surgery rates varied widely even within one county. Battista, Spasoff, and Spitzer (1989) say that a physician's practice setting (i.e., whether a physician practises alone or in a group), the availability of new technologies (like CAT scanners), and societal trends (like health promotion) also influence a physician's choice of treatments (see also Shapiro 1991). These findings suggest that how doctors diagnose disease and the type of treatment they choose, if any, play a major part in determining use patterns by older patients.

Chappell, Strain, and Blandford (1986, 100) report that physicians "control approximately 80 percent of health care costs." Only a quarter of this percentage goes directly to physicians, the rest goes to hospital use (half of all health care costs), drugs, tests, and other medical expenses. Doctors control these expenses through the decisions they make about treatment and through their reliance on high technology in hospital settings. Data from Ontario estimate that each doctor costs the system $500 000 a year. Half of this goes to pay for the doctors' services and half goes to other expenses like drugs, lab tests, and hospital admissions (National Advisory Council 1994b). Fewer doctors might lead to lower health care costs. To this end, some provinces have cut medical school admissions by 10 percent. Some provinces limit the number of doctors who can practise and others have capped doctors' billings to the provincial system.

Second, Shapiro and Roos (1986, 165) say that hospital-based care uses "about 60 percent of all health care dollars," but they determined that individual need cannot explain older people's pattern of hospital use. Looking at physicians' "hospitalization style," Shapiro and Roos (1986) found that patients of hospital-prone doctors spent, on average, twice as much time in the hospital as patients of non–hospital-prone doctors. These doctors also accounted for 73 percent of high users who had repeated hospital stays.

Third, the federal government began to insure hospital care in 1957, ten years before it insured the cost of visits to doctors' offices. This encouraged doctors to admit patients to hospitals for treatment, since doing so saved patients money. Gross and Schwenger (1981, 129) blame the high cost of the health care system on "a heavy reliance on institutional care." They compared health care costs in Ontario with those in the United States and found that, when it came to institutional care,

Ontario spent $323 more per year per person aged 65 and over on institutional care. "This amounts to a difference of 31 per cent, some of which can be attributed to inflation and variation in currency. However, the primary reason for Ontario's higher per capita institutional costs is that the province has more of its elderly in institutions" (Gross and Schwenger 1981, 129). Recent reports support this view. A number of studies in Ontario report that 10 percent of acute-care patients and 25 percent of chronic-care patients should not be in institutions (Chappell 1993a). Chappell (1993b) says that Canada has an inpatient-day ratio 25 percent higher than that in the United States. Lower the rate of institutionalization and the costs of health care will come down.

INSTITUTIONAL CARE

Six thousand health care institutions, aside from hospitals, exist in Canada. Most of these institutions house older people. Some of them house only older people. On any given day, 7.5 percent of older people live in these institutions. The proportion of older people under age 85 in institutions dropped between 1981 and 1986 (National Advisory n.d.). In 1986, 17.2 percent of women and 11.8 percent of men aged 80 to 84 lived in institutions. These rates jump to 40.5 percent for women and 28.4 percent for men aged 85 and over (Stone and Frenken 1988). These rates show an increase over 1981 (National Advisory n.d.). Women made up 70 percent of the residents in these institutions (Strike 1989).

Rates vary from province to province. In Alberta in 1986, for example, 50.5 percent of people aged 85 and over lived in institutions. Manitoba, Ontario, and Quebec report that around 40 percent of people aged 85 and over live in institutions, close to the national average of 41.4 percent. These are some of the highest rates in the world (Stone and Frenken 1988).

Most of these people live in nursing homes. These homes go by a variety of names: special care facilities, homes for special care, and personal care homes. The term nursing home, as it is used here, refers to any institution that offers medical care for chronically ill older people but that is not a hospital.

Each province has its own system for classifying patients. The government allocates funds to institutions based on the level of care needed by each patient. Charles and Schalm (1992a; 1992b), for example, describe the development of a new seven-level system in Alberta. Most provinces define four levels of nursing home care. In Manitoba, for example, people in levels 3 and 4 need 3.5 hours of nursing care per day and need help with two to four or more basic activities of daily living such as bathing, dressing, and eating; people in level 2 need 2 to 3.5 hours of nursing care per day and need moderate care and help with at least one basic activity of daily living; people in level 1 need 0.5 to 2 hours of nursing care per day and need personal help only to wash or attend activities (Forbes, Jackson, and Kraus 1987; Shapiro and Tate 1988b).

Shapiro and Tate (1985) report that in a longitudinal study of more than 3000 older Manitobans, 11.7 percent entered a long-term care setting between 1971 and the end of 1977. They also found that people over age 85 had almost a seven times greater chance of using a long-term care bed than people between 65 and 74 (see also Shapiro and Roos 1987; Shapiro and Webster 1984). About one-third of people age 85 and over lived in a nursing home setting in 1986 (National Advisory Council 1993e). Shapiro, Tate, and Roos (1987) say that age, mental impairment, and lack of support play a major role in the decision to enter an institution. Glazebrook and her colleagues (1994) found that poor self-care and incontinence increased the risk of institutionalization. Multiple disabilities also lead to institutionalization (Young, Forbes, and Hirdes 1994).

A more detailed analysis of institution admission calculated the odds of entering an institution given certain conditions in a person's life. Shapiro and Tate (1988b, 238) found that people with the following characteristics—age 85 or over, living without a spouse, "recent hospital admission, living in retirement housing, having one or more [problems with activities of daily living] ... and having a mental impairment"—had more than a three-in-five chance of entering an institution within two and a half years.

Montgomery, Kirshen, and Roos (1988) say that the chance of residence in a nursing home increases dramatically over the four years before a person's death. These studies suggest that as the population ages, the numbers and percentages of older people who spend some time in an institution will increase.

Such increases would be unfortunate: institutionalization can lead to decreased well-being and even death for older residents. Gutman and her colleagues in British Columbia (1986) found a high percentage of deaths among patients within the first six months of admission to a personal care home. They concluded that admission to a long-term care institution in itself causes severe stress to older people (Gutman et al. 1986; Gutman and Herbert 1976; Wershow 1976). Shapiro and Tate (1988a) also found high mortality rates right after admission to a nursing home. They suggest that clinical instability or relocation may account for this high rate (see also Shapiro and Webster 1984). Also, the sickest older people enter institutions. This, in part, accounts for the high death rate for new patients. Still, Chappell and Penning (1979) found that, after matching for levels of health, people in institutionalized settings showed lower well-being than those in the community.

Most people, including government leaders, doctors, nursing home staff, and older people themselves, agree that we should keep older people out of institutions when we can. Still, institutions play a useful role in the continuum of health care services. For example, long-term care institutions reduce the use of hospitalization for residents (Shapiro, Tate, and Roos 1987; Montgomery, Kirshen, and Roos 1988). This can reduce the cost to the health care system, if hospitals close some of their beds. Shapiro and Webster (1984) also report that 15 to 20 percent of people admitted at the two highest levels of care in Manitoba showed improved health even after six years.

Sometimes a person needs to live in a nursing home. Canada's long winters, the great distances between older people and hospitals, the need for constant care, few informal supports, and poverty sometimes make institutional life the only way for people to get the care they need (Forbes, Jackson, and Kraus 1987).

Nursing homes can do some things to decrease the adverse effects of institutionalization (Harbison and Melanson 1987). Brillon (1992), for example, notes that some provinces have no special laws to protect the rights of older people in nursing homes. And some institutions have no clear policies that protect residents' rights. Poirier (1992) proposes three types of rights that institutions should protect: the right to take care of one's own things, the right to respect for one's rights, and the

right to manage one's own life. This last right poses some of the greatest problems. An institution has to serve the collective good as well as ensure the right to manage one's own life. For example, the institution may infringe on the right to privacy as staff enter and leave patients' rooms or provide personal care.

Still, MacLean and Bonar (1983) say, institutions can and should make life in the institution as much like life outside as possible. They call this the **normalization principle.**

First, people should feel the normal rhythm of the day, week, and year. They should get dressed each day, have a weekly routine, and celebrate holidays, birthdays, and anniversaries. Institutions should also include programs that keep residents active. Activity can increase the quality and length of patients' lives (Stones, Dornan, and Kozma 1989).

Second, people should get a normal amount of respect. Sometimes staff forget that patients have a right to decide things for themselves. Buzzell (1981) reports that in one home the staff decided that Edna, a 74-year-old patient, should begin walking again after a hip fracture. Buzzell calls the attempt a "nightmare." First, the staff took her wheelchair away so she would have no choice but to walk. Then, when she tried to walk, the nurses on staff called her "lazy" and threatened her if she moved too slowly. Edna suffered dizzy spells, but an aide tried to force her to walk "non-stop to the end of the corridor, sixty feet." "Edna pleaded for rest," Buzzell (1981) says. But the aide refused to let her rest in her wheelchair and threatened to take her off the active treatment program.

MacLean and Bonar (1983) say that staff should treat the older patient as an adult. They should avoid baby talk, talking down to the person, or making decisions without consulting the patient. Penning and Chappell (1982) found that older residents who felt they had freedom and the ability to make choices showed improved mental health. People who felt most self-motivated showed high levels of psychological adjustment when the institution offered freedom of choice (O'Connor and Vallerand 1994).

Third, people should lead as normal a social life as possible. This should include sexual contact and sexual intimacy if a person has a willing partner. Institutions often allow married couples to live together. Gladstone (1992) reports that when both

Exhibit 8.4

How to Make Visits Count

A person with an older relative or friend in an institution may come to dread visiting day. If the relative has a cognitive impairment or few verbal skills, a well-meaning visitor can find the visit unpleasant and disturbing. Below, Pat Gibbs, consultant to the Ministry of Health in British Columbia, gives some helpful advice on how to make the most of a visit.

Q: My husband is glad to see me when I visit him at the Extended Care Unit, where he has lived for the past two years since I could no longer look after him at home. But he doesn't talk or respond much, and I run out of things to say. Sometimes it's hard to come up with ideas to pass the time during our visits.

A: You have raised a concern that many other caregivers share. Perhaps some of these suggestions might help.

- Bring in photograph albums from home—many pleasant hours can be spent in reminiscing using old photographs.
- Bring in a small tape deck and cassette tapes of music that the two of you enjoyed, and spend a visit listening to music together.
- Include other residents, room-mates, or visitors in social interaction during the visit. For example, if you turn on the T.V. so that your husband can watch a game, invite someone else to join in. This may facilitate your husband's forming relationships with others in the Extended Care Unit.
- Simple grooming activities are relaxing, do not require conversation, provide the soothing contact of touch, and maybe things that the staff have limited time to do for your husband, such as a manicure, or even a massage!
- Try reading out loud—clips of interest from the newspaper, or letters from relatives. Some letters can be read more than once—it doesn't have to be a new one each time.
- Capitalize on all the amenities and resources that the facility has to offer. If possible, change the location of your visits from time to time. Take your husband in his wheelchair down to the chapel, the library corner, the lounge for tea, out to the courtyard for fresh air.
- Incorporate special events going on at the residence into your visiting time with your spouse, such as a family barbecue, or happy hour.
- If appropriate, bring in a pet from home.

Can you think of any other ways to make visiting someone in a nursing home or hospital more rewarding?

Source: P. Gibbs, "How to Make Visits Count," *BC Caregiver News,* 1(5)(1996): 4. Reprinted with permission of Caregivers Association of BC, #170–216 Hastings Avenue, Penticton, BC V2A 2V6.

members of a married couple live in an institution the couple will likely live in the same room. This can improve a person's quality of life. An 87-year-old man says that when his wife had a stroke she spent a year in a hospital. "I lived alone and was terribly depressed," he says. "When we both got accepted here [in a nursing home] I was really glad to be with her again. At least I'm not lonely for her anymore" (National Advisory Council 1993e, 24).

People should also have access to their money, and they should have their own pictures, small pieces of furniture, or pets to make the institution more like their home. MacLennan (1983) says that the institution should also expect patients to socialize and to do as much for themselves as they can. Rattenbury and Stones (1989) found, for example, that reminiscence and current-topic discussion groups increased residents' psychological well-being. Forbes, Jackson, and Kraus (1987, 92) say that older people in institutions "have the right to make decisions about issues which affect them, and to maintain contact with their past life."

Exhibit 8.5

Controversy: The Use of Restraints in Nursing Homes

Many institutions use restraints to cope with residents' behavioural problems (Eaton, Stones, and Rockwood 1986). Restraints include bed rails, belts, geriatric chairs, jackets, and medications. A nursing practice conference in 1980 compared Canadian and British use of restraints. In one Canadian study of 136 patients aged 70 and over, almost 85 percent of patients had a restraint. A similar study of 172 patients in England found that only about 20 percent of patients had restraints (cited in Health Care 1980). The conference members concluded that Canada uses restraints more often than necessary.

Roberge and Beausejour (1988) studied the use of restraints in a sample of thirty-five Quebec nursing homes and chronic-care settings. They found that both types of institutions used restraints on 47 percent of all residents. Institutions that used restraints used bed rails 56 percent of the time; belts and geriatric chairs 16 percent of the time; and jackets 8 percent of the time. Physicians had prescribed some of these restraints (63 percent for the nursing homes and 46 percent for chronic care institutions). In some cases (18 percent) the institutions had policies that required restraints.

But many health professionals disagree with the use of restraints. Mitchell-Pedersen and her colleagues (1985) removed 97 percent of the physical restraints in a hospital setting in one year. They found no significant increase in accidents; they also found that staff attitudes toward their work improved. "Staff became highly creative in looking after patients without the use of restraints and a feeling of pride developed as they were able to provide care that honoured the autonomy of their patients" (Mitchell-Pedersen et al. 1985, cited in Forbes, Jackson, and Kraus 1987, 73).

The use of restraints raises ethical issues. Many institutions say that patients need restraints for their own safety. But patients pay the price for this supposed safety. Forbes, Jackson, and Kraus (1987, 72), for instance, say that physical and chemical restraints disturb older patients and rob them of their comfort and autonomy. Healey (cited in Health Care 1980, 22) asks, "Do we ... have a right to act against their will because we think it's in their best interests? Could it be we are more often than not selfishly protecting our own interests?" The National Advisory Council on Aging (1993e) says that institutions must get informed consent before they restrain a mentally competent resident. A person who refuses restraints would then sign a waiver that absolves the institution of liability.

Roberge and Beausejour (1988) say that institutions should use noncoercive methods to care for patients. They suggest that methods like occupational therapy, music therapy, and more family contacts would help staff reduce behaviour problems. Some institutions use electronic methods to keep track of patients. These include electric locks, tags on patients' clothing that alert staff, and pressure-sensitive strips on chairs that sound an alarm if a person begins to wander (Watzke and Wister 1993). Technologies like these can allow people freedom to move and still provide the safety they need.

The National Advisory Council on Aging (1993e) supports the older person's right to choose or refuse treatment. NACA supports this right even if a choice increases a person's risk of illness or accident. "An ethical course," NACA (1993e, 7) says, "is to restrict individual freedom only if necessary and only as much as necessary."

Sinclair (1984) says that a normalized environment should also include a weekly staff meeting. Meetings allow staff members to talk about problem patients and help them to rechannel frustration into methods for helping patients function better. Devine (1980) found that normalizing encourages nursing staff "to become leaders and teachers of the residents" instead of just caretakers.

She found that staff stopped stereotyping older people as senile and useless because it worked against the goals of the program.

Nursing homes and other institutions will never take the place of a person's own home or apartment. But the changes suggested here can make a nursing home more comfortable for older people who have to live there.

THE NEED FOR CHANGE

Canada's commitment to the medical model accounts for much of the increase in health care costs today (see Exhibit 8.6). Health and Welfare Canada (1984b, cited in Auer 1987) reports that from 1960 to 1982 hospitals and homes for special care accounted for 55 percent of the increase in health care costs; physicians and dentists accounted for 20 percent of increases in health care costs; 11 percent of the increase went to pay for drugs and appliances; and 14 percent went to all other costs.

Some signs suggest that change in the system has begun. Statistics Canada (1993) reports that between 1980 and 1989 acute-care hospital beds decreased from 5.4 to 5.0 per 1000 population. Also, in-patient admissions dropped during this time while out-patient visits increased. Continued reliance on doctors, hospitals, drugs, and expensive treatments will drive up the costs of medical care in the future. Shapiro (1992), for example, says that nursing homes rely too heavily on the medical model. They hire costly registered nurses to give care when most patients need help with activities of daily living (like bathing). "Except for residents who require specialized resources," she says, "even the heaviest care residents are in this category because their heavy dependency on others is primarily for ADL [activities of daily living] help or for supervision due to their cognitive impairment" (Shapiro 1992, 208). Reliance on the medical model also sometimes leads to inappropriate care for the older patients in the community. Chappell (1993, 495), for example, reports that between 25 and 60 percent of doctors' services to older people "are not necessary and do not increase the quality of life."

LONG-TERM CARE: NEW APPROACHES TO COMMUNITY CARE

The current system, Chappell, Strain, and Blandford (1986, 108) say, focuses on "institutional care rather than community care, on acute care rather than chronic care and on medical care rather than health care broadly defined." An aging population, Myles and Boyd (1982, 274–75) say, "requires a qualitative as well as a quantitative change in the health care system. An aging population requires a fundamental restructuring of health care and a redefinition of what constitutes health care." Most provinces have begun this process by shifting health care away from institutions. This has meant an overall decrease in hospital beds, a shift from short-stay to long-stay beds, and hospital and nursing home bed closures in some provinces (Tholl 1994). It has also meant fewer doctors in some provinces and more review of doctors' practices (King 1994). Finally, it has meant the growth of community care services.

The Canada Health Act of 1984, the basis of Canada's health care system, insures hospital and physician care. This system serves acute and chronically ill older people. It protects them from financial ruin in case of a long-term illness. Older people who need other types of long-term care including homemaker help, meals-on-wheels, or transportation must often turn to the social welfare system for help. These programs and services fall on the border between health care and social service (Chappell 1993c; 1994a). The availability of these services varies by province and region. Some communities have a wide range of services, others have few. Havens (1995c, 84) says that "community based long term care is both less universal and less uniform across the country than any other form of health care."

Long-term care programs within the medical model of care get the most funding. Deber and Williams (1995) say, for example, that in 1989–90 Ontario spent almost 80 percent of its $2 billion long-term care budget on institutional care. Shapiro (1994) says that community care gets only 2 to 4 percent of health care funding. And Porter (1991, cited in Chappell 1993a) estimates that only 1.2 percent of Health and Welfare Canada's program budget will go to health services and health promotion. Almost 84 percent will go to pay for health insurance claims (by doctors and hospitals). But the provinces have begun to look more closely at community long-term care. This kind of care looks like a way to cut health care costs and provide appropriate services to older people.

Manitoba Health (1992), for example, reports that it has increased its Support Services to Seniors program from $56 000 in 1985 to $1.45 million in 1991. This program offers support to frail and at-risk older people. The program aims to keep people in their own homes through volunteer services that provide home maintenance, group

Exhibit 8.6

Myths and Realities: Older People and the Use of Health Care Services

Different groups of older people use differing amounts of health care services. Studies that report aggregate data, such as those that use per-1000-population or average-length-of-hospital-stay bases, miss these differences within the older population. "The aggregate statistics," Roos and Shapiro (1981, 656) say, "may reinforce the negative attitudes of health professionals and planners toward the elderly and add fuel to growing feelings that a so-called 'crisis' is looming as the population ages." Roos and Shapiro (1981) and a number of other researchers (Mossey et al. 1981) have used data from the Manitoba Longitudinal Study on Aging (MLSA) to shatter the myth that an older population will inevitably lead to a crisis in health care.

First, the MLSA provides detailed information about individual use of the health care system. The study shows that older people do not form a single group. Some seniors use the system more than others. Residents in senior citizen housing (self-contained apartments built by the government, religious groups, or service clubs for seniors), for example, saw the doctor more often and used more hospital days than people in other kinds of housing. Most older people use a small amount of formal health care service or none at all, and these differences in use patterns stay stable from year to year (Mossey et al. 1981, 557).

Second, the study found that less than one-quarter of Manitoba's older population stays in a hospital in any given year (Roos and Shapiro 1981), and only 5 percent of the older population uses almost three-fifths (59 percent) of the hospital days used by older people in the year (Roos and Shapiro 1981). A small group—2 percent—of older people admitted to hospitals used 20 percent of hospital days in a five-year period. A study in British Columbia found that 2 percent of hospital patients in 1985–86 accounted for 48.5 percent of all patient days (Barer, Evans, and Hertzman 1995). This study found that long-stay older patients took up almost half the hospital beds in B.C. in the mid-1980s. The authors say that "a large proportion of the hospital system had been transformed into 'God's Waiting Room'— and the waiting times were quite long" (Barer, Evans

and Hertzman 1995).

Further work in Manitoba showed that 5 percent of older people who died between 1971 and 1981 used 20 percent of all the hospital days used by older people (Shapiro 1983). Also, only 4 percent of people 85 and over accounted for 32 percent of acute hospital days used by people in this age group, and 9 percent of the 85-and-over group accounted for 57 percent of the acute and chronic hospital days used by people in this age group (Roos and Shapiro 1981).

The study found, too, that the average length of hospital stays for all older people rose between 1972 and 1976. It rose by 15 percent for people 75 years old and over. A closer analysis showed that there were large differences within the older population. The length of stay for seniors who stayed in hospital fewer than 90 days dropped by one day over these years. At the same time, the 75-and-over group who stayed for more than 90 days increased their stays from 117 to 218 days over the same 1972–76 period (Roos, Shapiro, and Roos 1984).

Third, Roos, Shapiro, and Roos (1984) found that older people as a group do not make large numbers of visits to doctors (see also Segall 1987) and do not use large numbers of hospital days. The older population makes only 1.7 more visits to doctors per year than the group aged 15 to 44 and only 0.9 more visits than the group aged 45 to 64. About 20 percent of all age groups, including older people, do not visit a doctor at all in a year (Roos and Shapiro 1981).

The same researchers also found that the very old (aged 85+) use more home care, nursing homes, and hospitals than younger groups, but make the same number of visits to doctors' offices as people aged 65 to 69. They also found that older people get referred to medical consultants at a lower rate than the rest of the population (Roos, Shapiro, and Roos 1984).

These studies show that most older people do not need or use excessive amounts of institutional or medical care. The health care they do need can often be delivered in the community.

Exhibit 8.7

Components of the Continuing Care System

The Federal/Provincial/Territorial Subcommittee on Continuing Care (1992, 25) proposed a list of "major categories of services and settings" that make up the long-term care system. The list below presents programs most often used by older people. It gives a flavour of the mix of services, some medical and some social. This mix can cause confusion for people who need long-term care. Many providers offer these services (government, not-for-profit, for profit); provincial health insurance pays for some services, and other services charge a user fee. Case managers can help make sense of this system and get people the services they need.

1. Meals-on-Wheels

Meals-on-wheels delivers hot, nutritious meals to a person's home. Volunteers deliver the meals. These programs supplement diet to maintain health.

2. Adult Day Care

Adult day care provides personal help, health care services, and recreation in a group setting. People attend for half or full days.

3. Homemaker Services

Nonprofessionals help with personal care or housekeeping. May include help with bathing, cleaning, and cooking.

4. Home Nursing Care

A nurse visits someone's home to provide care. This may cover day and evening care seven days a week. This service usually requires a doctor's referral.

5. Community Physiotherapy and Occupational Therapy

Direct treatment and advice on prevention. These professionals may arrange for equipment to help a person cope with disability at home. They also teach family members how to help clients.

6. Assessment and Treatment Centres and Day Hospitals

Short-term service that diagnoses and treats health problems. This service usually takes place in acute-care hospital. It can include physical and psychiatric assessment.

7. Nursing Home Care

Institutions have a role to play in the long-term care system. Older people, health care professionals, and policy-makers see institutions as a last resort.

8. Chronic Hospital Care

Special care for people with a chronic illness and functional limits. These people do not need all of the services of an acute-care hospital.

9. Other Services

These include programs that provide people with assistive devices, nutrition counselling, and social workers' services.

Source: Adapted from *Future Directions in Continuing Care*, Health Canada, 1992. Reproduced with permission of the Minister of Public Works and Government Services Canada, 1996.

meals, and yard work. The government also increased support for home health care from $25 million in 1985 to $68 million in 1993. The government has shifted funds to community care in order to save money. Manitoba Health reports, for example, that a stay in a teaching hospital cost $775 per person per day in 1992. In this same year home care came to $16.75 per person per day. And the Support Services to Seniors program cost only 51 cents per person per day. These figures show the high cost of inappropriate institutional care. A single day of hospital care saved can provide several weeks of home care.

Other provinces have also taken steps to decrease the use of institutional care. King (1994) reports that New Brunswick, for example, has allotted $6.6 million to expand its single-point-of-entry community care program. This program will serve older people throughout the province. A single-point-of-entry system means that a person can get access to all community social and health care services from one contact point in the system.

Quebec has set up a community health network. This network has 161 **Centres locaux de services communautaires (CLSCs).** CLSCs combine the work of professionals and volunteers to deliver home care services (Nahmiash and Lesemann 1993). The system tries to direct health needs away from hospitals and toward community care. A report on long-term care in Quebec says that the CLSCs need more community resources to help keep people out of hospitals (Garant 1994). Quebec, for example, spends less than half of what Ontario spends on health care ($34 per person compared with $67 per person). CLSC home care costs about $150 per day less than the $490 required per day for hospital care.

Quebec has also regionalized the hospital sector. This decentralizes authority. "The basic purposes of regionalization are to minimize the duplication of services and facilities, to increase access to services, to permit the establishment of efficient referral channels and mechanisms, and to allow communities to become more involved in decision making over their priorities and program development" (Manga n.d., 197). Manitoba has done roughly the same thing.

The use of regional health boards or councils has spread to other provinces as well (National Advisory Council 1995a). Regional boards manage and finance institutional and community health care services. They control costs in a time when the federal government has cut funds to the provinces. This makes regional boards responsible for tough decisions about where to cut services (Deber, Mhatre, and Baker 1994). Critics of these boards fear that administrators and health care professionals will have most of the power on these boards. Also, community control may lead to unequal access to services and varied standards of service. Still, regional boards have knowledge of local needs and can work for the best interests of the community. Health care experts disagree about the value of these boards.

Many provinces intend to shift health services from institutions to community care. But in many cases the development of community care lags behind hospital bed closings. Chappell (1993, cited in National Advisory Council 1995a, 14) warns that "if medical care is cut back without an expansion of community care, seniors are left not with a new health care system, simply a less adequate one." A lack of community supports puts more pressure on community services. And in some cases community care simply means more stress for an elderly spouse or an overworked child caregiver. Some critics of health care reform say that it covers up the government's plan to have family members take on more health care work. Neysmith (1993, 162) says that underfunding community care "tip[s] the dependency scale" toward family and kin. This puts more burden on women as caregivers and leaves poor older people without health care resources.

NACA says that too little community care leads to poor care for patients after they leave the hospital. The Seniors Advisory Council for Alberta (cited in National Advisory Council 1995a) reports that, in at least one city, hospitals discharged older people without setting up community care plans. Older people in rural settings sometimes found themselves without ongoing care. The hospital had made no arrangements with home care agencies or local hospitals to follow up discharged patients.

Typical Community Care Programs

The social model of health care looks for ways to keep people out of institutions. A health care system based on the social model of care would "have at its core a broad definition of health and would make adequate provision for noninstitutionally based chronic care" (Chappell, Strain, and Blandford 1986). Community care programs include hospitals, nursing homes, doctors' services, and community-based services such as geriatric day hospitals, adult day care, and home care.

The programs discussed below, beginning with **geriatric day hospitals,** form a **continuum of care**—from more institutional contact to little or no institutional contact. They show how the Canadian health care system has applied some of the principles of the social model of health care to meet older people's needs.

Three points are worth keeping in mind as you read about these programs. First, some of the evaluations of programs presented here have been done by the same people who run the programs, and this could bias their reports. Second, few evaluations use control groups to see what would have happened to a similar group if they had not used this kind of program. A program that claims to save money by keeping people out of institutions should also show that a similar group of people to those in the program had to enter an institution. If the report cannot show this, then the program may have cost more money than if nothing were done. Finally, evaluation studies often report short-term changes. This makes it hard to judge the long-term effects of a program.

Even with these shortcomings, however, evaluations and reports often provide the only available information about new programs, and give some idea of what these programs do and how well they work.

Geriatric Day Hospitals

Geriatric day hospitals offer a full range of hospital services to people who live in the community. A day hospital will assess an older person's needs and plan a rehabilitation and care program. Services include physical checkups, drug monitoring, dental clinics, diagnosis, treatment, and rehabilitation. Day hospitals can also keep an eye on older patients at risk in the community and ease older acute-care patients back into the community when they leave the hospital (Agbayewa 1990).

Eagle et al. (1987) say that day hospitals can improve patients' physical and emotional well-being. But these programs will add to the cost of the health care system. To contain costs day hospitals should not offer care to a patient for more than two days per week, or for more than six to eight weeks. The day hospital should operate at full capacity to make best use of the facility. And the day hospital must take in patients who would otherwise enter an institution. Eagle et al. (1987) say that at present the health care system should treat geriatric day hospitals as pilot projects that need to prove their benefits and effectiveness.

Adult Day Care

Adult day-care programs "provide noninstitutional support for those unable to remain in the commu-

nity without it" (Chappell, Strain, and Blandford 1986, 121). These programs include hot meals, recreation programs, and a chance for the older person to socialize. The programs also give family caregivers time off to rest, shop, and maintain their own social life. Adult day care offers fewer medical services and more social and recreational services than day hospitals. Some provinces require that people pay for day-care services themselves, while other provinces include the service as part of the provincial health program.

As yet, research has not been able to show a conclusive reduction in the use of other services due to adult day care (or day hospital care) alone (Chappell and Blandford 1987a). Chappell and Blandford (1987a), for example, report on a controlled study of adult day care that included day-care users and nonusers. They found no significant difference between these groups in the use of physician services or hospital use.

Studies do report an increase in participants' well-being (Chappell 1983b; Flathman and Larsen 1976). A study of the first day-care centre for handicapped older people in Victoria, British Columbia, showed that most clients improved their social skills and their self-esteem, and some improved their physical skills. Families reported better family relationships and better health for the client's spouse (Jackson 1983).

Home Care

In 1977 the Canadian federal government started the Extended Health Care Services program to support provincial home care programs. Home care programs differ from province to province, but all of the provinces and territories in Canada have some public home care and nursing services. Some provinces have extensive home care programs that include meals-on-wheels, home repair services, laundry and cleaning help, emergency alert services, friendly visitors, nutrition counselling, and transportation. Private for-profit and nonprofit home care agencies also exist. They most often provide "homemaking, in-home attendance, home health care, nursing and palliative care" (Nahmiash and Reis 1992).

Home care is one of the most important parts of a comprehensive health care system. A report by the National Advisory Council on Aging (1986c) defines community support or home care services as "a co-ordinated and integrated range of services

Exhibit 8.8

Victoria's Quick Response Team:
A Bridge between the Medical and Social Models

Many older people enter acute-care hospitals through the emergency department (Manitoba Health Services Commission 1985). And most older people use emergency care appropriately (Parboosingh and Larsen 1987). A fall, a broken bone, or a stroke, for example, can lead to an emergency admission. After the emergency passes (the medical team sets the bone or the first phase of the stroke passes), the acute-care hospital can do little for the older patient (Eakin 1987). Still, the patient may not be able to return home. Some patients live alone and lose the ability to care for themselves after a stay in the hospital. Some may need more help than a family member can give. Others give up their apartment and sell their furniture because they assume they will never go home again. These people must wait in the hospital for a nursing home bed (Aronson, Marshall, and Sulman 1987), and their health may get worse while they wait.

A report of the Manitoba Health Services Commission (1985) said that acute-care hospitals ought to pay more attention to discharge planning and involvement of home care professionals (see also Fisher and Zorzitto 1983). This might avoid unnecessary admissions. The Capital Regional District (Victoria) in British Columbia has instituted a special program to decrease the number of acute admissions of older people from emergency departments. The Capital Regional District calls this program the Quick Response Team (QRT).

The QRT arranges for community supports at the right time to help the older person return home. A QRT liaison nurse assesses the emergency room patient at a physician's request. Criteria for admission include: acute medical condition, but hospitalization not required; patient aged 60 years old or over; home support possible; and patient nursing needs not over three hours per day.

When a patient meets the QRT criteria, the QRT liaison nurse sets the team in motion. The QRT social worker and home care nurse call the patient's family doctor, arrange live-in homemaker services, transportation, and home nursing as needed. The social worker and nurse assess the patient's home support network and arrange follow-up support like meals-on-wheels where needed. The QRT turns the case over to the regular long-term care program after a maximum of five days.

Mrs. Olive Ross, 86, is one of the QRT's success stories. Mrs. Ross broke her leg and arm in a fall. The QRT moved in a 24-hour homemaker for a month, arranged daily physio- and occupational therapy. Services were cut back as she improved. Mrs. Ross says, "I don't know what I would have done if I had to stay in hospital ... When I broke my hip a while back, I was in hospital for three weeks and ended up losing 15 pounds" (Paterson 1989).

Mrs. Marion Candy, 89, also benefited from the QRT's services. She blacked out and fell in her apartment. Eventually she came around, dragged herself to the door, and screamed for help. She had cut her scalp and needed seven stitches. She got stitched up at a hospital and returned home the same day, but kept losing her balance. "I lurched a lot and grabbed on to anything I could to keep my balance," she said. Her family doctor called the QRT, and the team arranged for an array of services and supports including a homemaker, meals-on-wheels, a walker, a bath seat, and a handrail near the toilet. These supports have allowed Mrs. Candy to stay in the community (Kelk 1989).

The QRT offers the first service of this kind in North America. Eight months after the project began, only eight of the QRT patients had entered a hospital (three of them for palliative care). A report on the QRT says that "this clearly indicates the QRT is a genuine alternative to hospital admission, and is not simply delaying the inevitable" (Quick Response Team n.d., 6).

designed to help people live as independently as possible in the community." A federal government report (Federal/Provincial/Territorial Working Group 1990) describes three goals of home care:

(1) substitution for more costly care in institutions; (2) maintaining a person at home at a lower cost to the system; and (3) prevention of functional breakdown that could lead to institutionalization.

A move to increase home care will require a change in the priorities of the health care system. At present home care accounts for only about 2 percent of the total spent on health care (Federal/Provincial 1990). Ontario, for example, set out "A New Agenda" for health and social services (Van Horne 1986). This plan includes more emphasis on preventive assessments, expanded community programs, and more coordination of services. Still, a government study of home care reports that "home care remains a minor component of the health budget" (Federal/Provincial 1990).

Community care may offer a cost-effective alternative to institutionalization for many older people. This will make community care an important part of the health care system in the future.

HEALTH PROMOTION

So far, this chapter has focused on illness rather than health, but there is no other way to talk about the health care system. We call it a health care system, but it is actually a sickness treatment system. It serves people who are already sick, and it focuses on curing disease. This approach has its limits. Hospitals, doctors, nursing homes, or home care do not prevent disease, but only treat illness after it occurs.

The health promotion model puts health in a social context. The World Health Organization (WHO) (1984, 101) defines health promotion as "the process of enabling people to increase control over, and to improve their own health ... [it is] a mediating strategy between people and their environments, synthesizing personal choice and social responsibility in health to create a healthier future."

Canada's interest in health promotion predates this WHO definition by a decade. In 1974, Marc Lalonde, then the federal minister of health, discussed this and other approaches to Canada's health care system in a report called *A New Perspective on the Health of Canadians* (Lalonde 1974). There he proposed the concept of the **health field.** The health field includes the usual health services, but within it the health care system is one way—not the only way, or even the best way—to improve health. In addition to traditional medical services, the health field also includes improvements in human biology (through basic research), improvements in lifestyle, and improvements in the environment as ways to better health.

An international conference on health promotion that took place in Canada produced *The Ottawa Charter on Health Promotion* in 1986. The charter focuses on the conditions that give rise to health. These include "peace, shelter, education, food, income, a stable eco-system, sustainable resources, social justice and equity" (Hamilton and Bhatti 1996, 2). The *Charter* also proposes actions that (1) build healthy public policy; (2) create supportive environments; (3) strengthen community action; (4) develop personal skills; and (5) reorient health services. Hamilton and Bhatti say that this model challenges researchers and policy planners to link change in underlying social conditions to health. Research, for example, has linked low income and low education to poor health. Likewise, studies of the environment have linked pollution to poor health. These studies support the idea that health promotion must deal with the environment, society, and personal habits.

This model makes sense in Canada today. Studies show that "the majority of the aged remain functionally well until an advanced age" (Health and Welfare Canada 1982b, 43; Statistics Canada 1990e). A study of community-dwelling older people in Ontario, for example, found that only 6 percent of the 65-year-olds in the sample and 35 percent of the 85-year-olds lacked competence in five activities of daily living (Cape and Henschke 1980). Studies of seniors in both Calgary (Research and Planning Unit 1983) and Saskatchewan (Senior Citizens' Provincial Council 1983) found that 60 percent of seniors reported good or excellent health.

A study of rural older people in Alberta found that about three-quarters of the people studied reported few or no health problems and high life satisfaction. This included older as well as younger seniors, men and women, farm and town-dwelling older people, and people who lived alone or with others. The researchers said that older people present "a picture of health not illness" (Thurston et al. 1982, 16).

Health promotion programs in general work to keep older people well. Some of these programs even take place in hospitals. Sulman and Wilkinson (1989) report on a hospital-based geriatric activity group. The staff started the group to help patients who were waiting for placement. The staff had found that the longer these patients stayed in the hospital, the worse they functioned. The program set out to decrease this decline. It involved forty-five minutes of activities at each session, including seated exercises, movies, social interaction, and gardening.

The program highlights the value of health promotion activities in an acute-care hospital setting. "Such programming," Sulman and Wilkinson (1989, 46) say, "also contains the possibility of moving these patients to lighter levels of care, and, in some cases, might prevent the need for placement altogether."

In 1981 Health and Welfare Canada set up a Health Promotion Directorate to "inform and motivate people to adopt and maintain healthy lifestyles" (Hansen and Ledoux 1985). The directorate runs public education and advertising campaigns, publishes health information, and funds health promotion projects (Hansen and Ledoux 1985). Programs supported by the directorate include an Alzheimer's Family Resource Centre, an education program for seniors called "Fully Alive," antismoking campaigns, and a program to help poorer older people stay healthy.

The Future of Health Promotion

Canada now recognizes the health promotion model as a model for the development of future health policy. Jake Epp (1986), as Canada's Minister of Health and Welfare, produced a report titled *Achieving Health for All: A Framework for Health Promotion*. This report defines health as a "basic and dynamic force in our daily lives, influenced by our circumstances, our beliefs, our culture and our social, economic, and physical environments" (Epp 1986, 3). The report provides a framework for health policy in Canada and includes a description of the challenges to health in Canada, health promotion mechanisms, and implementation strategies to achieve health for all (see Exhibit 8.9).

Older people can benefit from improvements in all parts of this framework. For example, some older people already engage in self-care (Segall 1987). Some also eat breakfast regularly and engage in regular exercise (Penning and Chappell 1993; Schoenborn 1993). But a greater proportion of older people (aged 50 and over), compared with younger people, report that they never exercise. And older people (aged 60 and over) more often than younger people said they had no plans to improve their health (Penning and Chappell 1993).

Improvements in self-care through the proper use of medication, a good diet, and exercise can improve older people's quality of life. A more educated older population may also have a better understanding of how to prevent illness (Segall 1987). Likewise, mutual aid programs give people social and emotional support (Fedorak and Griffin 1986). Finally, a healthy environment will include community health services, transportation, and home care.

But will the government support changes in social structures, policies, and allocation of funds? Epp's (1986) report makes no promises. But it does recognize the need for the government to support health promotion. It also gives a good reason for this support. "We believe," the report says, "that the health promotion approach has the potential over the long term to slow the growth in health care costs" (1986, 13). Research at present cannot easily show the direct link between most health promotion programs and decreased health care costs. Strain (1991), for example, found that older people with strong beliefs in health maintenance used more health care services. They may not use a large amount of service, but they use a variety of services.

Glor (1991) reports two problems that health promotion programs face. First, no agreement on quantitative measures of health exists. Second, few programs produce a measurable effect on health where scientists have tried to measure it. Some writers even question the value of helping people to live longer. Evans (1984) says that these programs may lead to higher costs because they keep more people alive long enough to get chronic illnesses in later life.

Gaudette and Roberts (1988) report that, as the rates of cardiovascular disease have fallen, more people have lived into old age. This has led to a rise in the proportion of people who get cancer and die from it. This trend will lead to increased costs for cancer treatment in Canada (due to new treatments and drugs) and a heavier caseload for cancer care units.

Still, disease prevention and health promotion have caught on in Canada among seniors. More than any other age group, people over age 55 say

Exhibit 8.9

Achieving Health for All: A Framework for Health Promotion

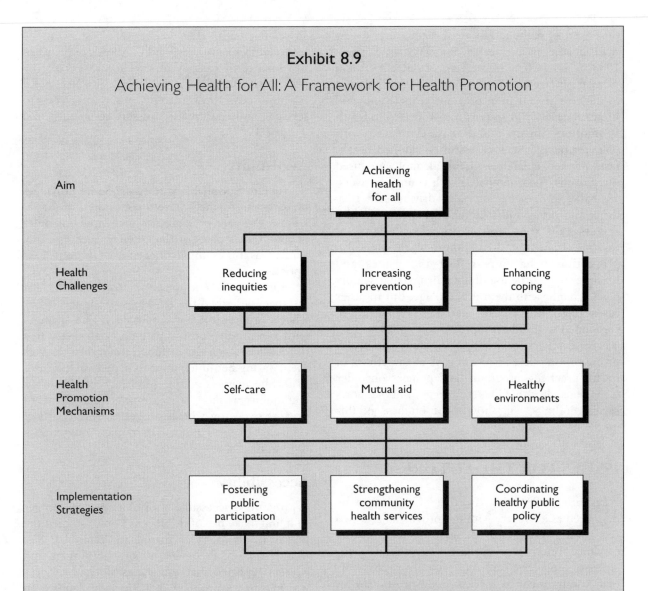

Aim		Achieving health for all	
Health Challenges	Reducing inequities	Increasing prevention	Enhancing coping
Health Promotion Mechanisms	Self-care	Mutual aid	Healthy environments
Implementation Strategies	Fostering public participation	Strengthening community health services	Coordinating healthy public policy

Epp's (1986) health promotion framework calls for improvements in (1) individual behaviour, (2) social structures, and (3) public policy. A useful framework must include all three types of improvement. Changes in individual behaviour, for example, may not be able to overcome health conditions due to income inequities (like poor diet due to poverty). Hirdes et al. (1986) found that a loss in income led to a perceived decrease in self-reported health. The researchers also found that decreased income may lead to decreased purchase of services, poorer nutrition, and poorer living conditions. Epp (1986, 12) says that "we cannot invite people to assume responsibility for their health and then turn around and fault them for illnesses and disabilities which are the outcome of wider social and economic circumstances."

Source: From *Achieving Health for All: A Framework for Health Promotion*, Health Canada, 1986, p. 8. Reproduced with permission of the Minister of Public Works and Government Services Canada, 1996.

they exercise daily, and more of them exercise now than in the past (Health and Welfare Canada 1988b). Also, 30 to 40 percent of older men and women reported eating less fats and less fried food in the past year than in previous years (Stone and Fletcher 1986). A report on Canada's Health Promotion Survey found that, compared with younger people, seniors less often skipped breakfast, smoked cigarettes, drank alcohol, and used illicit drugs. Also, compared with younger drivers, a smaller proportion of older drivers said they drink and drive, and a larger proportion of older drivers said they used seatbelts (Health and Welfare Canada 1988a). Some of these health promotion behaviours reflect the values and lifestyles (e.g., little use of illicit drugs) that seniors have brought with them into old age. But in other cases (e.g., the use of seatbelts) seniors have responded well to health promotion policies.

Researchers will continue to study the health promotion model. They will look at the effects of health practices, programs, and policies on older Canadians' health. This research, if it supports recent findings, will show the usefulness of this model in an aging society.

ISSUES FOR THE FUTURE

Neysmith (1993, 148) says that "Canada can be described as a country with ten provincial and two territorial systems of long-term care." The provinces often agree on the same values and principles of long-term care. But each province has its own commitment to services, its own policies on access to care, and its own funding arrangements for long-term care.

This means that the principle of universality that underlies acute health care does not apply as well to long-term care (Havens 1995a; 1995c). First, clients often must pay for long-term care. Government health benefits may not cover day hospital, respite, or homemaker costs. This may leave the poorest older people without help. Second, Deber and Williams (1995) say that as many as 2000 small agencies deliver services in Toronto. This makes it hard for people to find the help they need. Third, many people fall through the cracks. They may not know about services or may not have access to a service (for example, a religious-based service may serve only people who

share that faith). The health care system of the future will need to respond to these problems in the long-term care system. Three areas of the present system will have to be revised to meet older people's needs: the availability of services, access to services, and coordination of services (Sturdy and Tindale 1985).

Availability

A program is available if it exists. Some provinces or parts of provinces have a continuum of care—from home care to acute hospital care—for older people. Other parts of the country, such as many rural areas, for example, offer only a few home care options.

One rural community care worker, for instance, described the workings of the meals-on-wheels program in her community. She arranges with a local restaurant to pick up a half-dozen to a dozen meals each day at lunch time, then delivers them during her lunch hour to people on her caseload. She marvels at the good luck of city-based community workers, who can refer their clients to existing meals-on-wheels programs. Rural parts of Canada will need more community programs in the future.

Accessibility

A program is accessible if an older person can get to it and make use of it. Havens (1980) studied the unmet needs of older people in Manitoba. She found that in each age cohort both men and women reported that the accessibility of services was more of a problem than their availability. In other words, even where a range of well-designed services existed, older people still found it hard to make use of them. The older the person, the more problems they had with access. Better access requires better transportation and more home-based care for very old seniors.

People with special needs may also have trouble using services. McDonald, Badry, and Mueller (1988) studied the resource use of developmentally handicapped people aged 40 to 65 in Calgary. These people show signs of aging at younger ages than the rest of the population. The researchers found that men who function well physically but have low cognitive ability were most likely to use day-care services. As a group, developmentally handicapped people tended not to use other services available to seniors. The researchers say that "the gerontological social service delivery system has not been prepared to accept these clients" (McDonald, Badry, and Mueller 1988, 145). These people have many of the same needs as seniors, but less access to the system. The researchers say that the rehabilitation and social service delivery systems need to create greater access for developmentally handicapped people.

The National Advisory Council on Aging (1989c) says that new immigrants and seniors from many ethnic groups may need special help to get services. Special dietary requirements, cultural differences, and food preferences can limit ethnic group members' use of community services. Culturally sensitive professionals can help overcome some of these barriers. Wister (1992) reports that people who know about home supports tend to use them. Better information for non-Anglo seniors would provide them more access to services.

Coordination

The health care system needs better coordination and integration (Health and Welfare Canada 1982b; National Advisory Council 1990c; Ontario Public Health Association, 1983). This need will increase with the growth of community care, because community programs decentralize care. They bring together nurses, social workers, and therapists, who often work for different agencies and whose views on how to care for a client will vary.

Sturdy and Tindale (1985) interviewed thirty health care providers in Ontario and found that only 30 percent of them felt that the system of services for older people was well coordinated. Providers saw two problems with the system: first, they said that professionals in different fields try to defend their territories, and, second, that programs in government ministries overlapped. The government lacked policies to decide who should take responsibility for a certain problem. As a result, services often "appear fragmented and the elderly person and his or her family do not know who to go to for what … The elderly person in need of service can fall through the cracks in the system or become frustrated and give up the search" (Sturdy and Tindale 1985, 14).

The National Advisory Council on Aging (NACA) says that a **single-entry model** best coor-

dinates services for older people. It improves "flexibility, continuity and quality of care for clients" (National Advisory Council 1995, 13). It also controls costs. A single-entry model gives personalized help to each client. Staff from a single agency assess clients' needs, coordinate service delivery, and monitor clients' progress. A staff member may arrange for meal delivery, a visiting nurse, and homemaker help in one case. In another case the staff member may arrange for respite care and day hospital use. Many provinces, including Manitoba, Alberta, and New Brunswick, already use this approach. The National Advisory Council on Aging supports further development of single-entry systems throughout the country.

Coordination avoids overlapping between services, and integration unites health and social services into one system. The principle of universality in the *Canada Health Act* ensures that everyone has access to the same services. A more coordinated system will also save time and may save money. But the NACA says that "health reform means more than controlling costs to achieve an affordable health care system. It means providing appropriate and effective care that is responsive to the changing needs of Canadians" (National Advisory Council 1995a, 20). NACA puts response to older peoples' needs at the core of a reformed health care system.

CONCLUSION

Canadians value their health care system. A study by Blendon (1989, cited in Chappell 1993b) found that 56 percent of Canadians think their health care system works pretty well. Only 27 percent of the British felt this way about their system and only 10 percent of Americans. The majority of British and Americans studied say they want a basic change in their health care system. Only 42 percent of Canadians felt this. Most Canadians say that, if they had a choice, they would choose their own system above those of other countries.

Any changes to the health care system will take place in the context of government cutbacks. Some existing programs will get cut. Manitoba's Pharmacare program, for example, now bases rebates on income rather than age. Older people in higher-income families will get fewer benefits from this program. But older people in low-income families with serious illness will get full prescription

Exhibit 8.10

Controversy: User Fees for Health Care

Concern about the rising cost of health care has led some writers to call for new ways to finance health care. Some of these writers suggest that fees for service would improve the health care system (Béland [1995] reports on some of these sources). Some studies suggest that user fees would decrease patients' use of health care services (Manning et al. 1987, cited in Blomqvist 1994). A number of health care researchers disagree.

Evans, Barer, and Stoddart (1995) say that user fees will shift the source of funding health care from taxes to individuals. A shift to user fees benefits people in good health and with high incomes. They will pay less in taxes for the health care system and will only pay for care they use. Evans, Barer, and Stoddart (1995, 362) put this simply: "The wealthy and the healthy gain, the poor and sick lose."

Evans, Barer, and Stoddart (1995, 370) go on to say that Canada's health care costs have not gone out of control. Health care costs have gone up more gradually since the start of Canada's national health care system. Public funding in Canada and in other countries has led to more cost control. Studies of other countries show that user fees create higher costs through higher prices and more service providers. Effective control of costs comes about through limits on the number of hospital beds or the number of physicians. Also, a government-sponsored national system saves administration costs that drive up the cost of health care.

Some supporters of user fees say that fees will create more health care options. Fees would allow people to buy more services if they chose. People may want this as an option to a waiting list for public services. Also, some supporters of fees say they will encourage new services to develop that might improve the public system some day (National Advisory Council 1995b).

But critics of user fees say that such fees will create a second health care system. People who used and paid for services themselves might withdraw support for the public system. People who paid a fee would have a high standard of care. Poor people who could not afford to pay a fee would have to make do with underfunded services. User fees challenge the principle of universality in the *Canada Health Act*. This principle states that everyone should have access to the same package of health care services. But people with more money would clearly gain by being able to afford user fees.

Finally, supporters of user fees say they will discourage overuse or abuse of the system. They will make people think twice before they use a health care service. Studies show that user fees do discourage use. But most people do not know in advance that they do not need a service (Béland 1995). So people get poorer treatment for illnesses they do have, and the quality of health care falls. Also, Evans, Barer, and Stoddart (1995) say that individual decisions account for only about 10 percent of health costs. Hospital stays and visits to specialists account for 90 percent of costs. And doctors, not individuals, decide on these treatments. User fees will have little effect on the total health care budget.

Reduced health care budgets will lead to further cuts in health care services. This will lead to calls for new ways to fund health care. Options will include income tests for services (only the poorest people will get certain services), decreases in the availability of services, and user fees. People need to know the effects of these policies before they can make intelligent choices. Future changes to improve the health care system should focus on appropriateness of treatment (community care to help people stay out of institutions), good management of resources, and accountability to the community. "Health care reforms and cost control are legitimate needs," Béland (1995, 410) says. "But neither should jeopardize acccess to medical care, which is an accomplishment of Medicare."

drug coverage (Krueger 1996). This shift to a need-based system could save the government $20 million a year. Other countries, like Sweden, the United Kingdom, and the Netherlands, have also shifted to need-based programs in order to target programs and save money (Chappell 1993b).

Denton and Spencer (1995) studied the potential for a crisis in health care costs in the future.

They found that government health care costs as a percentage of gross domestic product (GDP) will increase between 1991 and 2041 by about 3 percent. But, Denton, Li, and Spencer (1987) say that projections, based on demographic data, only guess at the future costs of health care. New health care techniques, technological innovation, more efficient use of institutions, and new uses of health care workers (like nurse practitioners) will all influence future costs. And these "factors may be just as important or more important than population change" (Denton, Li, and Spencer 1987, 564; see also Denton and Spencer 1995).

Still, increases in health care costs seem likely in the future. Will this cause a crisis in health care? Denton, Li, and Spencer (1987) say no. They say that costs will grow slowly over time and that Canadian society can plan for this change. They also say that increases in health costs will, at worst, equal the proportion of gross national product (GNP) that West Germany paid for health care in the 1970s, and will come to only a little more than Sweden and the United States paid in that decade (Maxwell 1981; Denton and Spencer 1983). Changes in the system, such as an emphasis on community care and prevention, could help control costs.

The changes taking place today suggest that the health care system will look different in the future. Closer studies of older people's health care needs will allow the system to fine-tune its programs and treatments (Barer, Evans, and Hertzman 1995). The critique of the medical model and growing interest in social models of health care will lead to more community-based services. Also, as the population ages, more people will show an interest in disease prevention and health promotion. More comprehensive models of health care, like the social and health promotion models, will lead to better health care for older people as well as better health at all ages.

SUMMARY

1. Health care needs for the elderly range from maintenance programs for the well elderly to long-term institutional care for those who have severe health problems.
2. Three models of health care exist in Canada today: the medical model, the social model, and the health promotion model. The medical model that dominates the health care system today is concerned with the treatment of illness.
3. The Canadian health care system consists of five basic principles: universal coverage, access to services, portability, comprehensive services, and administration by a nonprofit public agency. The provincial and federal governments share the cost of this system.
4. Canada has one of the most comprehensive health care systems in the world, but it spends proportionately more of its gross national product on health care than do some countries with more comprehensive systems.
5. Research shows that the commitment to the medical model may account for higher than necessary health care costs. Complex medical procedures, increased salaries for medical personnel, and high institutional costs all lead to increasing health care costs.
6. Canada has one of the highest rates of institutionalization in the world. Institutions serve the needs of many older people, and programs exist that can improve the quality of life of institutionalized patients. But sometimes people enter institutions because they cannot get the support they need to stay in the community.
7. The social model of health care supports a continuum of services from institutional care to home care. It calls for health care programs that help older people stay in their own homes. These programs include geriatric day hospitals, adult day-care programs, and home care.
8. Home care programs tailor services to fit the needs of the older person. They provide families with help to relieve caregiver burden. These programs may or may not save money, but they do achieve one goal: they allow people to stay in their homes as long as they can.
9. The health promotion model of health care supports healthy lifestyles and a better environment. It takes a broad view of health care that recognizes a need for changes in the workplace and improvements in socio-economic status.
10. The government will have to deal with three service issues in order to meet the needs of an aging population: availability of services, access to services, and coordination of services.

11. Medical costs will probably rise in the future, but economists say that an increase in the number of older people will not cause a crisis in health care costs. The system will need better use of resources to limit the cost of care.

STUDY QUESTIONS

1. List and describe the three major approaches to health care that exist in Canada today.
2. Explain why the cost of health care in Canada grows each year. How might the government control costs?
3. Discuss three ways in which doctors directly help keep the cost of health care high. How can doctors take steps to lower these costs?
4. Describe the normalization principle. How can institutions use this principle to provide higher-quality care for patients?
5. How can the government restructure the current system to provide better service to an aging society?
6. Describe at least two alternative health care programs that exist today.
7. Explain two of the major approaches to health promotion and give an example of each.
8. Discuss three types of improvements in health care that would improve service to older people.

KEY TERMS

Centres locaux de services communautaires (CLSCs)   centres that combine the work of professionals and volunteers to deliver home care services. This method tries to direct health needs away from hospitals and toward community care.

continuum of care   the current array of services that range from institutional care to little or no institutional contact.

geriatric day hospital   a hospital program that offers a full range of hospital services to people who live in the community. A day hospital will assess an older person's needs and set up a health care plan.

health field   includes the usual health services, but within the health field the health care system is one way—not the only way, or even the best way—

to improve health. In addition to traditional medical services, the health field also includes improvements in human biology (through basic research), improvements in lifestyle, and improvements in the environment as ways to better health.

health promotion model   focuses on prevention and self-care. It aims to prevent disease through lifestyle change, increased knowledge about healthy behaviour, and environmental improvement.

long-term care   Béland and Shapiro (1994, 245) define long-term care (LTC) as "all the social and medical services dedicated to the aged who have functional limitations." LTC combines formal services in the home or an institution with family care.

medical model   focuses on the treatment of diseases and injuries. Treatment most often takes place in the physician's office, in a hospital, or in other health care institutions. The medical model favours surgery, drug therapy, and rehabilitation through physical therapies.

normalization principle   the idea that institutions can and should make life in the institution as much like life outside as possible.

single-entry model   staff from a single agency assess clients' needs, coordinate service delivery, and monitor clients' progress.

social model   sees medical care as only one part of a complete health care system. This model sees personal and family counselling, home care, and adult day-care programs as part of the health care system. This model of health care tries to keep older people in their own homes.

SELECTED READINGS

Béland, François, and Shapiro, Evelyn. (1995). "Policy Issues in Care for the Elderly in Canada." A special issue of the *Canadian Journal on Aging* (Summer 1995).

This volume contains writings on current issues in Canadian health care. Articles range from a discussion of population aging and its impact on health care costs to the role of long-term care in the continuum of care. The collection attempts to answer many questions about the future of the health care system by looking in detail at the use of the system today.

Nahmiash, Daphne, and Frédéric Lesemann. *Home Care ... A Love Affair*. North York, ON: Captus Press, 1993.

A story of the clients and professionals who work within the community health care system in Montreal. At times the book has the feel of a diary. The authors describe death, loss, and illness in old age. They also show how relationships flourish, commitments between people get made, and feelings get shared in the midst of the formal health care system. The authors celebrate a dedicated group of workers and their clients who struggle to humanize health care delivery.

CHAPTER 9

Finances and Economics

INTRODUCTION

Jack Bruckner, aged 65, took early retirement two years ago. He gets a pension from his job and an Old Age Security cheque each month. His wife Betty, 59, never worked outside the home, so she gets no pension.

They live in a small government-subsidized apartment. Last spring Jack and Betty decided to travel east. Jack knew their old car would never make the trip, so he went to the bank for a car loan. "I never thought they'd give me a loan," he says. "I went in thinking they'd just laugh at the idea. But the bank manager looked at my pension income and approved the loan. I can't believe it—I never thought, with the little we make, that we'd be able to buy a new car."

Like many older people, Jack and Betty do not have much, but they feel satisfied with what they have. Both of them lived through the Depression and through lean times when they first got married. They worry less about money now than in the past, and, Jack says, when Betty gets her pension from the federal government in a few years, their financial worries will be over.

Canada's pension system can take most of the credit for the Bruckners' financial well-being. The income of older people adjusted for inflation increased faster than that of younger people (25–64) from the early 1970s to the present. From 1971 to 1986 the income of unattached women aged 65 and over increased by 61 percent and went up by 36 percent for men in this age group. The real average income for women in the 25–64 group grew by only 28 percent and for men by only 13 percent. Family incomes of married older people rose by 35 percent compared with a 27 percent increase for the 25–64 group (Lindsay and Donald 1988). Much of this growth took place during the late 1970s and early 1980s (Statistics Canada 1990c).

The oldest older people gained the most. Families headed by men aged 75 and over had increases in income of 47 percent between 1971 and 1986 (33 percent for families headed by men between 65 and 74). Unattached men aged 75 or over gained 46 percent, while the gain for women of the same age group was 70 percent (single men and women from 65 to 74 had increases of 32 and 58 percent, respectively). The oldest older people still have incomes below that of 65-to-74-year-olds, but the gap is closing. Men 75 and over who headed families had incomes that were 79 percent of the those of 65-to-74-year-olds. Unattached men who were 75 and over had incomes of 87 percent of the incomes 65-to-74-year-olds received. And unattached women who were 75 and over had incomes 90 percent of those who were 65 to 74 (Lindsay and Donald 1988).

Cheal (1983; 1985a; 1985b) looked at intergenerational family transfers—the amount of money that passes from one generation of family members to another—to assess older people's financial well-being. He (Cheal 1985a) found that older people gave (in net value) more than they got and that there was a larger difference between what they gave and what they got than for any other age group. He concludes that older people have more money to spend than earlier studies suggested.

A number of studies and reports like these show that, as a group, older people have better incomes than many people imagine. Compared with other age groups, they show the least **depth of poverty**—the distance between their income and the poverty line (National Council of Welfare 1996b). Older people below the poverty line, on average, have incomes that come to about 85 percent of the poverty line.

Still, the retirement income system has its flaws, some of them serious. While income has risen in the past few years for older people in general, certain groups still have incomes below the poverty line in old age. Older people from lower-income backgrounds, people who cannot speak English or French, people without much education, and people who live in small towns tend to have lower-than-average incomes. Very old people, women, and unattached individuals (a term used by Statistics Canada to describe a "person living alone or in a household where he/she is not related to other household members") often live below the poverty line (Health and Welfare Canada 1988b, 3; National Council of Welfare 1996b). Older women, compared with older men, also show a greater depth of poverty and a smaller proportion of people living well above the poverty line (National Council of Welfare 1996b).

More than a third of the unattached population of older people in 1994 lived in poverty (most of them women). In 1994 about one-quarter (25.2 percent) of elderly unattached men and more than two-fifths (44.1 percent) of elderly unattached

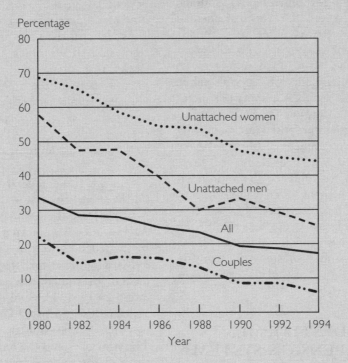

Exhibit 9.1

Poverty Rate, People 65 and Older, 1994

This graph shows the steady downward trend in the poverty rate for all older people. The couples group aged 65 and older saw the most dramatic decline in poverty. Unattached men, compared with unattached women, showed a more dramatic decrease in poverty over these years. Improved public pensions account for most of the decrease in poverty among older people. Still, a high proportion of unattached older women live in poverty. And this rate increases with age.

Source: Adapted from *Poverty Profile 1994*, National.Council of Welfare, 1996, Cat. No. H67-1/4-1994E, Table 4. Adapted with the permission of the National Council of Welfare.

women lived on low incomes. Poor unattached older men had incomes about half those of all unattached older men. Poor unattached older women had incomes 69 percent of those of all unattached older women (Statistics Canada 1995b). Government programs provide about 90 percent of the incomes of poor older people today (Statistics Canada 1995b).

Even reports of average family incomes show lower incomes for older people. Statistics Canada (1990c) reports that in 1989 the average income of families headed by seniors came to 73 percent of the income of families with heads under age 65.

Unattached people aged 65 and over in 1993 had an average income only 71 percent that of unattached people under age 65. For someone who earned an average wage before retirement, the Old Age Security (OAS) will make up about 14 percent of their pre-retirement income. The Canada Pension Plan (CPP) will make up another 25 percent. Therefore, the average wage earner will have to find other means to make up lost income in retirement. People who earn above the average wage will need to make up even more income in order to maintain their standard of living, and those on fixed pensions (i.e., not indexed to the cost of living) get poorer every year because of inflation. Most people, except the very rich and the very poor, will feel a drop in their standard of living when they retire.

Many individuals and groups, including the federal and provincial governments, the National Council of Women, and the Royal Canadian Legion, have suggested changes to Canada's pension system. Their concerns led to the **great pension debate** in the 1980s and more recently to a debate over the **universality** of Canada's public pension system (Myles 1988). A number of sources have proposed income testing for OAS benefits. And a recent government proposed income testing by the year 2001 (Government of Canada 1996a; Myles and Street 1995). The results of these debates have begun to influence the retirement incomes of older Canadians. They will also influence the pensions of future retirees.

This chapter looks at (1) the structure of the Canadian pension system and how it works; (2) the flaws in the system and suggestions for pension reform; and (3) the future of Canada's retirement income system.

HISTORICAL DEVELOPMENTS IN CANADA'S PENSION SYSTEM

Bryden (1974, 19) says that until the 1920s Canadian pension policy reflected the "market ethos." This ethos said that individuals should take responsibility for themselves in old age and that those who need help should get it from their families (Bryden 1974, 20). Bryden reports that city life and industrialization in Canada made this ethos hard to practise. The *Labour Gazette*, for example, stated in 1924 that "high rents, [and] overcrowding in houses, make it difficult for the poor to provide for their aged parents. It has been the experience of social agencies that many of the old men and women in their districts are suffering from the lack of the necessities of life" (*Labour Gazette* 1924, 665, cited in Bryden 1974, 42).

The federal government decided to act to relieve the poverty among older people. A Commons committee issued a report in 1925 that called for a $20 pension to people aged 70 or older who passed a residence requirement and a means test (a test of financial need). The committee proposed that the federal government and the

provinces should each pay half the cost of pension benefits. The plan did not require pensioners to pay anything into the program. The committee saw the program as a supplement to income more than as a pension. The Old Age Pension Act became law in 1927, and all the provinces and the Northwest Territories agreed to the plan by 1936. This plan, for the first time, defined pensions as a right due to all older Canadians. Snell (1993) shows that men, compared with women, had greater access to these pensions. A woman with a younger, employed husband could have her claim rejected. The state expected her husband to support her. Snell traces this type of discrimination to the state's assumption about male dominance in families.

In 1951 the federal government passed the Old Age Security Act and the Old Age Assistance Act to replace the Old Age Pension Act. The Old Age Security Act set up a pension plan run solely by the federal government. The new plan paid up to $40 a month at age 70 without a means test. The federal government increased this pension to $55 a month in 1961. The Old Age Assistance Act set up a means-tested pension for people between 65 and 69 years old who could demonstrate financial need. The provinces and the federal government shared the cost for this program. The plan required no contributions and paid the same pension to all poorer pensioners, including homemakers.

These early programs supplemented the incomes of older people (they offered basic income security). The federal government kept payments low, so people would have an incentive to provide for their own old age (National Health and Welfare 1973, cited in Chappell 1987). In the 1960s the federal government broadened the pension system by setting up the Guaranteed Income Supplement program to supplement Old Age Security. This program was designed to help the poorest older people. In 1966 the federal government and the government of Quebec started the Canada and Quebec Pension Plans. All wage earners in Canada pay a part of their incomes into these plans.

By the 1970s Canada had two types of programs in place: **income security programs** (the Old Age Security and the Guaranteed Income Supplement) and **income maintenance programs** (the Canada and Quebec Pension Plans). These programs form the basis of the Canadian pension system today. The National Council of Welfare (1984a) calls these the anti-poverty and the income-replacement goals of the system, respectively. The federal government designed the first type of program to help people meet their basic needs in retirement and the second type to help people maintain their pre-retirement income and lifestyle.

By the early 1980s federal government transfers (the Old Age Security and the Guaranteed Income Supplement and other transfers paid for from tax revenues) and the Canada Pension Plan accounted for 29 percent of older Canadians' retirement incomes. By 1993 this figure had increased to 36 percent of their incomes. Occupational pensions (those from former employers) made up 20 percent of older people's total income in 1993 (up from 15 percent in 1983), and assets (investments and savings) made up more than 27 percent of retirees' income in 1993 (down from 42 percent in 1983) (Statistics Canada 1996). Federal government transfers and the CPP have made up increasing proportions of seniors' income over the years.

Myles reports that federal government transfers also make up increasingly larger portions of individuals' incomes as they age. "As each year passes," he writes, "the number of wage earners declines, savings are spent and inflation erodes the real value of both savings and private pensions" (1984, 22). This means that older people are more dependent on public policy and programs for their well-being than ever before. And this makes the study of pensions vital to an understanding of old age today.

THE CANADIAN RETIREMENT INCOME SYSTEM TODAY

Canada's complex system of pension plans and programs, along with earnings from work, should create a decent old age for all Canadians, but it does not. Some older people still suffer a sharp loss in income and a shocking change in lifestyle when they retire. Almost every tier and subsection of the Canadian pension system needs improvement. The following discussion will look at the structure and the limits of the Canadian pension system today.

Tier One: Government Transfers

Canada has a three-tiered pension system shaped like a pyramid (see Exhibit 9.2). Government pensions (the first two tiers) make up over one-third of the income of senior families and over one-half the income of unattached older people (National Advisory Council 1993f). The Old Age Security (OAS), the Guaranteed Income Supplement (GIS), the Spouse's Allowance (SPA), and the Widowed Spouse's Allowance (WSPA)—called federal government transfer programs—make up the first tier. Nearly all Canadians aged 65 or over, rich or poor, get the same OAS pension. The GIS goes to people with no income other than the OAS. The SPA goes to spouses between ages 60 and 64 who are married to a GIS pensioner and to widows or widowers of former GIS pensioners. People do not directly contribute to these pension funds; the federal government pays them out of tax revenue. The federal government spent almost $20 billion on them in 1994 (up from $11 billion in 1984). Benefits went to a total of 3.2 million people in 1993 (Statistics Canada 1996). These programs protect older people's incomes—especially those of the very poor—from falling below a specified level. Among seniors, more than one-third of their income on average came from federal government transfers (Lindsay and Donald 1988).

Not surprisingly, poorer people depend on transfers most. Older women, the poorest group of older people, for instance, received 23 percent of their income from transfer payments in 1993. Older men received only 15 percent of their income from these sources (Statistics Canada 1996). Men, compared with women, receive almost four times the proportion of their income from employment earnings and almost twice the proportion of income from private pensions (Lindsay and Donald 1988).

The OAS in the second quarter of 1996 came to $395.55 a month per person (or $4746 per year). It went to 3.6 million people, nearly every Canadian aged 65 and over. The federal government taxes the OAS as income, so pensioners with enough income to pay taxes will pay some or all of their OAS back to the government. The poorest older people, who pay no tax, keep all their OAS benefits.

The federal government indexes OAS payments to the consumer price index or cost of

Exhibit 9.2

Canada's Three-Tiered Pension System

Private Income/
Investments/
Savings

Public Pension Plans
CPP/QPP

Government Transfers
OAS/GIS/SA

Exhibit 9.3

Source of Retirement Income for Tax Filers in Canada, 1993

	Men	Women
Private Pensions	25	14
OAS/GIS	15	23
C/QPP	18	16
Employment	10	4
Investments	24	31
Other	8	12

Source: Statistics Canada, *Canada's Retirement Income Programs: A Statistical Overview*, Cat. No. 74-507-XPB, Tables 1-5 and 1-6. Reproduced by authority of the Minister of Industry, 1996, Statistics Canada.

living, and adjusts the rate four times a year. But in 1983 and 1984 the government capped rises in OAS payments to 6 percent and 5 percent, respectively. This policy had no effect because inflation began to fall before 1983. Full **indexation** began again in 1985. The high cost of the OAS program (about $12.5 billion in 1990) makes it an obvious target for federal government cutbacks (National Advisory Council on Aging 1991). The federal government planned to de-index OAS payments in 1985, but it backed down after seniors and business groups across the country protested.

The GIS goes to the poorest seniors. In 1996 1.4 million people got the GIS (Government of Canada 1996b). GIS benefits in 1996 went to single older people who received less than $11 304 that year from sources other than the OAS. It went to couples in 1991 with a combined (non-OAS) income of $13 187 or less (Government of Canada 1996; National Advisory Council on Aging 1991). The federal government does not tax the GIS, and it indexes GIS payments to the consumer price index, so that they go up quarterly as the cost of living rises. A person (or a couple) gets either full or partial GIS payments based on a yearly income test. In the second quarter of 1996, a single person could receive a GIS of $470.07 per month, while a married couple could get a maximum of $776.25 per month for the two of them (Government of Canada 1996). Widowers or widows could get a maximum of about $9000 per year. Single pensioners, more often than married pensioners, have low enough incomes to need the GIS. Women, many of them widows, make up over 79 percent of all single people who get the GIS (National Council of Welfare 1989b).

The federal government added the SPA program to tier one of the system in 1975. The SPA goes to a low-income pensioner's spouse who is aged 60 to 64 years old. It pays an amount equal to the OAS and the maximum GIS at the married rate. This couple gets the same transfer payments as a poor couple with both spouses aged 65 and over. If the GIS pensioner dies, the spouse continues to get payments. When the survivor reaches age 65, the federal government stops SPA payments and the person then gets an OAS/GIS pension. The vast majority of SPA payments go to women (National Council of Welfare 1989b). Without GIS and SPA benefits, almost half (47 percent) of all older Canadians would live below the poverty line. Eleven percent of all people who receive the GIS are so poor that they get the full amount. About 100 000 older Canadians receive the SPA. This program costs about $400 million a year (Government of Canada 1996b).

Nova Scotia, Ontario, Manitoba, Saskatchewan, Alberta, British Columbia, Yukon, and the Northwest Territories also have provincial or territorial supplement plans to help the poorest seniors. About 10 percent of all seniors receive provincial or territorial supplements. These benefits total about $285 million per year. Most provinces and territories do not index payments to the cost of living, but they do increase the amounts from time to time (National Advisory Council on Aging 1991; National Council of Welfare 1996a).

All provinces reduce taxes for older property owners or give rent rebates to seniors. Newfoundland seniors, for example, get an exemption from local school taxes (either the poll tax or property tax). Manitoba seniors who own homes (and poorer Manitobans aged 55 to 64) get a school tax rebate of up to $175 per household (National Council of Welfare 1989b). These programs play an important part in keeping very old people and even people with occupational pensions at a decent income level.

The National Council of Welfare (1995; 1996a) reviewed the federal government transfer system and concluded that the system keeps many older people out of poverty. Still, the council says, "it is clear that the government programs that make up the first level of Canada's retirement income system are not generous enough to keep all pensioners out of poverty" (National Council of Welfare 1996a, 16). For example, in 1989 the maximum OAS/GIS pension fell $1867 short of the low-income cut-off for a couple living in a large city.* For unattached older people in a large city the gap came to $3393 (National Council of Welfare 1990b). In 1994, 17.2 percent of older people lived below the (1986 base) low income cut-offs (National Council of Welfare 1996b).

---

* Statistics Canada creates low-income cut-offs to classify people into "low income" and "other" groups. Statistics Canada first estimates the average proportion of income that a person or family spends on food, clothing, and shelter. A person or family who spends at least 20

Exhibit 9.4

The Canada Pension System

Pension	Maximum Benefits per Month
Old Age Security	$395.55 (single April 1996)

Requirements and Program Details: 65 years or over; residence requirement; Canadian citizen or legal resident; noncontributory; indexed quarterly.

Guaranteed Income Supplement	$470.07 (single, April 1996)
	$776.25 (couple, April 1996)

Requirements and Program Details: low or no income besides OAS; noncontributory; indexed quarterly.

Spouse's Allowance	$701.73 (April 1996)

Requirements and Program Details: equal to the sum of OAS and maximum GIS at married rate; spouse married to OAS pensioner who gets GIS; spouse between 60 and 64; must satisfy other OAS requirements; noncontributory; indexed quarterly.

Widowed Spouse's Allowance	$774.71 (April 1996)

Requirements and Program Details: paid to any low-income widow or widower (60–64 years old); noncontributory; indexed quarterly.

Canada Pension Plan Retirement Pension	$727.08 (monthly, 1996)

Requirements and Program Details: 5.6% of income paid into plan; half by worker; half by employer (minus a basic exemption (1996—$3500). Up to Year's Maximum Pensionable Earnings (YMPE) 1996—$35 400; indexed yearly. Maximum payment into plan (employer and employee) in 1996—$1786.40.

Canada Pension Plan Survivor Benefits	$436.25 (CPP 1996, spouse 65 and over)
	$399.70 (CPP 1996, spouse 55–64)

Canada Pension Plan Death Benefit	$3540 (CPP, lump sum, 1996)

Program Details: paid to estate of deceased contributor.

Canada Pension Plan Disability Benefit	$870.92 (maximum 1996)

Program Details: paid to contributors with severe and prolonged disability.

Canada Pension Plan Children and Orphan Benefits	$164.17 (CPP 1996)

Program Details: paid to each orphan of contributor.

Source: Adapted from Health and Welfare Canada, *Canada Pension Plan, Family Allowance, Old Age Security, Statement on Current Benefits, 1992.* Current figures: Human Resources Development Canada, *Income Security Programs, April 1996* (Government of Canada, 1996). Reproduced with permission of the Minister of Supply and Services, 1991.

Some policies weaken the universality of the OAS pension. In 1977 the federal government introduced new residence requirements for government pensions. Until 1977, an older person who lived in Canada at least ten years qualified for an old age pension. After 1977, a person earned one-fortieth of his or her pension for each year in Canada after age 18. Anyone with less than ten years in Canada got no benefits. Many immigrants to Canada will now get less than a full OAS when they turn 65. This policy will erode the universality of the old age pension system (National Council of Welfare 1990b).

A new policy has further weakened the OAS's universality. The federal budget speech of April 1989 introduced a **clawback** of OAS benefits from wealthier seniors. This means that seniors who have a net income of over $53 215 per year (in 1993) must pay back 15 cents on every dollar of OAS benefits for every dollar of income they receive that is over this amount (Maser 1995). The government phased in this clawback over three years from 1989 to 1991. In 1989 this meant that a senior with an income of over $76 332 would lose all of his or her OAS pension (National Council of Welfare 1990b). The federal government projected that this would affect only about 4 percent of seniors in 1989 (National Council of Welfare 1989a). Unless the government raises the threshold of $50 000 to keep up with inflation, more and more people (whose retirement incomes will rise with inflation) will face a loss of their OAS payments. Myles and Street (1995, 346) conclude that the "OAS will gradually lose its status as the first tier of the retirement pension system and, along with GIS, become part of the social assistance program for low income seniors."

percent more of their pre-tax income than the average on these items falls into the low-income group. In 1992, for example, a low-income person or family spent 54.7 percent or more of their income on food, clothing, and shelter. A single person, in a city of 500 000 people or more, fell into the low-income group if they earned less than $15 479 in 1994. A couple in a city who earned less than $20 981 fell into the low-income group. Statistics Canada does not refer to these as poverty lines. But some groups like the National Council of Welfare think of them this way (Ghalam 1995; National Council of Welfare 1996b).

Tier Two: The Canada Pension Plan and the Quebec Pension Plan

The Canada Pension Plan (CPP) and the Quebec Pension Plan (QPP) form the pension system's second, smaller tier. Almost 13 million workers (virtually 90 percent of the labour force between ages 18 and 70), their employers, and self-employed people paid about $12 billion into the plans in 1993 (Statistics Canada 1996). The CPP/QPP paid a maximum benefit in 1996 of $727.08 per month (or $8725 per year) and paid out over $12 billion in 1996 to more than three million beneficiaries (Government of Canada 1996b).

It is worth mentioning that the CPP allows a province to opt out of the plan. Quebec chose to do so and set up its own plan. The QPP differs from the CPP in a few details, but in most ways it mirrors it. This text will use the term CPP to refer to both plans.

The CPP does two things: first, it ensures that workers will have some pension beyond the OAS/GIS/SPA when they retire, and, second, it saves the federal government money in GIS and SPA payments in the future. The CPP combines two types of pension plans: a **savings plan** and a **transfer plan.** It works like a savings plan because each worker pays a percentage of his or her salary into it each month. In 1996, for instance, the law required workers to pay 2.8 percent of their wages into the plan (up to a maximum of $446.50 per year for 1996). Their employers paid a matching amount. Self-employed people paid 5.6 percent of their incomes into the plan. Because more people in the future will be eligible for CPP/QPP pensions, the CPP plans gradually to increase the contribution for all workers from 5.6 percent (the total that the employee and employer paid in 1996) to 8.9 percent in 2010 and to 11.68 percent in 2050 (Government of Canada 1996b; National Council of Welfare 1990b). The payments are credited to individual workers and, when they retire, their pension will depend on how much they paid into the plan.

The CPP also works like a transfer plan because the money paid in today does not go into a private account for each person. It goes to pay the pensions of retired plan members today. Pension experts call this a pay-as-you-go plan. Today's workers will get their CPP pensions from workers' contributions in the future. This type of plan does not require that a person spend many years saving for a pension. But it does require that each generation pay for the pensions of the past generation.

The CPP does some things well. First, it protects people from inflation. Personal savings, for example, can decrease in value over time, but the CPP promises that a person will get a pension in the future geared to the cost of living at that time. Second, the CPP covers almost all workers, so most workers will enter retirement with some CPP benefits. Third, the plan is **portable,** which means it moves with workers when they change jobs. In a fluid job market, where people change jobs often, this can mean the difference between having a pension or not.

Fourth, the plan locks in both workers' and employers' contributions from the start. This is called **vesting.** Workers get credit for their total payments (their own and their employer's contributions) even if they move from one employer to another.

Fifth, the CPP promises to pay workers up to 25 percent of their pre-retirement pensionable earnings (to a maximum of 25 percent of the year's average industrial wage) for life.

Sixth, the plan applies the same rules to men and women. Women pay in at the same rates as men, and the plan entitles them to the same benefits. Some occupational plans base benefits on different mortality tables for men and women, so women in some plans get smaller payments because on average they live longer than men.

Seventh, all CPP members get survivor and disability benefits, a vital point because in Canada women often outlive their husbands and many women have no pensions of their own.

Eighth, the CPP calculates a person's pension by adjusting pensionable earnings from past years to bring them up to current wage levels. This adjusts for the fact that inflation makes earlier wage levels a poor basis for calculating a pension today and makes the CPP better than occupational plans that use lifetime earnings to calculate pension payments (National Council of Welfare 1989b).

Ninth, the CPP allows contributors to choose early or late retirement. A contributor can receive benefits as early as age 60 or as late as age 70. The CPP decreases or increases by 6 percent per year for each year a person begins receiving benefits before or after his or her 65th birthday. A person who retires at age 60 would receive 70 percent of his or her normal CPP pension. The retiree will get this lower rate even after the age of 65 (National Council of Welfare 1989b). A person who retires at age 70 will get a 30 percent larger pension than he or she would have gotten at age 65.

Tenth, and not least, the federal government indexes the CPP to the cost of living. It goes up as the cost of living increases, so people do not fall behind each year as they do with a fixed-income pension.

The CPP now pays benefits to more older people than ever before. In 1967, it paid benefits to less than one-half of one percent of older people, but in June 1989 the CPP went to nearly three-quarters of all people 65 and over (National Council of Welfare 1989b). The number of people who get CPP pensions, the size of their pensions, and the total paid out in CPP pensions will all increase in the years ahead.

Still, the CPP has its limits. For instance, it does not help people maintain their pre-retirement income—the second goal of the Canadian pension system. For many older people today—those who retired before 1966 or those who never worked for a wage—the CPP/QPP offers no help at all, and some people who get the CPP find that it does not pay enough.

In 1995, for example, the OAS and CPP paid a maximum of $14 543 to a single person. But the poverty line for a single person in a city of 500 000 or more people came to $16 808. This means that the combined OAS and CPP for a single person in a large city left him or her over $2200 below the poverty line.

These low CPP payments do not replace much of the average person's income. Also, the plan pays low survivor benefits (National Council of Welfare 1990b), and the poorest older people, who get the GIS, lose $1 of their benefits for each $2 they receive from the CPP. As a result of these low rates, most people face a drop in living standards when they retire. People need private pensions or savings to maintain their pre-retirement lifestyles.

The CPP may also face future problems. Today Canada has five workers to pay the pension of each CPP retiree. By the year 2030 this will drop to three workers. This will mean higher contribution rates to the CPP in the future. The government plans to raise CPP contribution rates gradually into the next century. But by the year 2030 workers will need to pay 14.2 percent of their contributory earnings (two and one-half times the current rate of 5.6 percent). A government report asks "whether it is either reasonable or fair to expect younger generations to pay such high contribution rates" (Government of Canada 1996a, 2).

But unless the government raises rates the CPP could face problems. Higher-than-expected payouts of disability pensions, for example, already threaten the CPP two-year reserve fund. At present rates, payouts would use up this fund by the year 2015. The increase in the older population accounts for about a third of the higher projected increase in future payments needed to cover CPP costs in the future. About 45 percent of the increase in future payments comes from higher payouts for disability and enriched benefits. The government plans a review of the CPP in 1996. This could lead to proposed changes in the plan. Some people propose raising the retirement age or limiting cost-of-living increases (Freeman 1994).

Tier Three: Private Pensions, Savings, and Work

Private income makes up the third tier of the Canadian pension system. The OAS/GIS and CPP make up about 40 percent of an average wage earner's pre-retirement income (National Advisory Council on Aging 1991). For some people it makes up even less of their pre-retirement income. In 1995, for example, OAS/GIS and CPP benefits for an unattached person came to $1160 below the poverty line for a single person who lived in a city of half a million or more people. Couples did a little better, but still fell almost $400 below the poverty line (National Council of Welfare 1996a). This means that all workers need private pensions and savings to make up the difference between federal government pensions and pre-retirement income.

How many workers can count on occupational pension plans to help them in retirement? Statistics Canada (1996) reports that about 5.2 million Canadians belonged to an occupational pension plan in 1993. And 1.4 million tax filers aged 65 and over received over $14 billion in pension income. Nearly all (85 percent) public-sector workers (such as government workers,

teachers, nurses) belonged to a plan, but only about a third of private-sector workers belonged (Statistics Canada 1996). Occupational pension benefits in 1993 made up 25 percent of the income of males aged 65 and over, but only 14 percent of the income of females aged 65 and over (Statistics Canada 1996).

Most older people rely on savings to make up for lost pre-retirement income. Investment income makes up about 24 percent of the income of males aged 65 and over and about 31 percent of that of females aged 65 and over. These sources ranked as the second major source of income for males and the major source of income for females (Statistics Canada 1996).

The federal government has encouraged more savings through **registered retirement savings plans (RRSPs)**. As of 1991, self-employed individuals, or employees with no private pension plan, could save 18 percent of their earned income up to a maximum of $11 500 a year without paying income tax on this money. Individuals who belong to a private pension plan can contribute to an RRSP up to this maximum after adjusting for their contribution to their private pension plan.

The federal government increased the maximum contribution to an RRSP to $13 500 for 1996 (Statistics Canada 1996). RRSP members pay tax on the money only when they withdraw it in retirement. This defers taxes to a time when the person has a lower income—and so a lower tax rate. The number of RRSPs grew from 206 000 in 1969 (2.3 percent of tax filers) to 5.1 million in 1993 (26 percent of tax filers) (Statistics Canada 1990d; 1996). In 1993 contributors saved a total of over $19 billion in RRSPs, an increase from $6.2 billion in 1983 (Frenken 1995; Statistics Canada 1996). Proposed higher limits for RRSP contributions could make them even more attractive to middle- and upper-income earners in the future.

Other income in retirement includes earnings, rent subsidies, and tax exemptions. In 1987 earnings accounted for 23.8 percent of family income to households with a male head aged 65 and over, and 44 percent of income for households with a female head aged 65 and over (Statistics Canada 1990e). The federal government allows special tax credits for older people. These include a tax credit begun in 1988 of $550 per year indexed to inflation and a pension income tax credit to a maximum of $170 per year (National Council of Welfare

1989b). Also, corporations offer subsidies for goods and services, like reduced theatre ticket prices or reduced air fares for older people. Stone and MacLean (1979) say that these indirect subsidies could add at least 30 percent to older people's average total income, and this does not count other benefits such as subsidized health care costs and home care services.

How does the private pension system help most people cope with retirement? Not very well on three counts. First, coverage is low: only 42 percent of female paid workers and 47 percent of male paid workers in 1993 had private pension plans (Statistics Canada 1996). This rate of coverage increased for females by 6 percent from 1983 to 1993, but decreased for males by over 5 percent over this same period (Statistics Canada 1996). Women made up 43 percent of pension plan members in 1993, up from 33 percent in 1983. These figures include workers in the public sector (government and Crown corporation workers) and workers in the private sector (workers for private corporations). But the rate of plan membership for men and women differs in each sector. Women made up more than half (53 percent) of public pension plan members in 1993. But men outnumber women in private-sector occupational plans by nearly 2 to 1 (Statistics Canada 1996). Only 31 percent of private-sector workers in Canada in 1993 had occupational pensions (Statistics Canada 1996). People who work part-time, seasonal workers, and those who work for small businesses and at low-paying jobs often have no occupational pensions.

Also, only one worker in ten with earnings either at or below the average industrial wage (AIW) has an occupational pension plan. This means that the poorest people have the least chance to get a private pension. In 1993 only 3 percent of people with incomes under $10 000 per year belonged to an occupational plan that they paid into. Fifty-three percent of people with incomes over $50 000 paid into occupational plans in that year. "It seems unlikely," the National Council of Welfare (1996a, 37) says, "that occupational pension plans will ever be an important source of retirement income to people in low-wage jobs. Coverage by contributory pension plans increases sharply as incomes rise."

Second, in 1986 only 34 percent of all occupational plan members, most of whom worked in the public sector, had some automatic inflation protection. About 67 percent of public-sector workers had some inflation protection, but only 7 percent of private-sector members had inflation protection (National Council of Welfare 1990b; 1996a). In an inflationary economy people on a fixed pension—even a good one—become poorer as they age. At 4 percent inflation, a pension will lose 30 percent of its value over ten years; at 8 percent a $900 pension will be worth only $566 five years after a person retires—more than a one-third drop in their pension's value (Royal Commission on the Status of Pensions in Ontario 1980, cited in National Council of Welfare 1984a).

Statistics Canada reports that in 1993 the average annual income from occupational plans came to $9424 for men and only $4156 for women. In sum, the National Council of Welfare says, "occupational pension plans play a limited role in providing retirement income for Canadians" (National Council of Welfare 1996a, 40; Statistics Canada 1996).

Third, only a small percentage of people who belong to occupational pension plans ever collect a full pension (Senate of Canada 1979). Two things account for this. First, few plans in the past have had early vesting (vesting, as mentioned, is people's right to their own pension contributions and their employer's contributions if they change jobs). Early vesting locks both the employer's and the employee's payments in the plan soon after employment begins. Second, most plans lack portability (portability, as previously mentioned, is the feature of plans that allows workers to transfer their pension money to another plan with a new employer). When workers leave a company today, most of them get either a deferred pension (if their money is vested and locked in) or they get their own (but not their employer's) pension contributions back—sometimes with no interest. The employer's share stays in the fund when workers get their pension contributions back, so each time a person changes jobs he or she loses half of his or her fund and has to start again. This means that even if the whole labour force belongs to occupational pension plans, as long as workers change jobs often (as they do today) only workers with fully vested contributions will ever collect a full pension.

The government started the RRSP program to help people cope with gaps in the private pension system. RRSPs encourage private savings for retirement. RRSP contributors grew from 2.4 million in 1983 to 5.1 million in 1993. Twenty-six percent of all tax filers contributed to an RRSP in 1993 (Statistics Canada 1996).

Anyone can start an RRSP and gain benefits from this program. But, in practice, the program helps people in higher income brackets the most. First, the higher a person's income, the more likelihood that they will pay into an RRSP (Frenken 1995; Maser 1995). Second, people with higher incomes can pay in the most (for a self-employed individual, 18 percent of his or her income to a maximum of $13 500 in 1993). People with high incomes tend to make their maximum contributions. Poorer people simply do not have this much money to put aside. Third, people in higher tax brackets get more money back through the tax deductions received through this program. The higher their tax bracket, the more they get back. For instance, a tax filer in the highest tax bracket got a tax saving of $473 for an RRSP deduction of $1000. But a filer in the lowest bracket got a tax saving of only $269 for the same $1000 deduction. The richer person's higher tax rate leads to more savings.

So, in total, people with more money do better than poorer people under the current system. For example, people with an income of $60 000 or more got an average tax break due to RRSP deductions of $2695. Tax filers who earned under $60 000 got an average tax break due to RRSP deductions of only $806 (National Council of Welfare 1994). Exhibit 9.5 shows the proportion of people from selected income levels who paid into RRSPs and the average amount they contributed.

INEQUALITY IN LATER LIFE

Older people as a group have more income security today than ever before. For example, relatively few older people have incomes in the lowest income group (less than $5000 per year). But most older people live on modest incomes. In 1991, for example, nearly 60 percent of older people had incomes below $15 000 per year. Only 35 percent of people age 25 to 64 had incomes this low (Norland 1994). Income disparity also exists within the older age group.

Myles (1981a) uses a political economy perspective to look at the structural reasons for inequality in old age. For example, he shows that education and former occupational status largely determine income in later life. A person with a high level of education and a high status occupation stands the best chance of a high income in retirement. These people also stand the best chance of maintaining their status after retirement. Norland (1994) shows that, as a group, older people have less education and engage in less work activity than younger people. This largely accounts for their lower incomes in later life. Older people who have access to work, investments, and occupational pensions will have higher incomes. These benefits go to people with higher levels of education and higher job status.

Also, some groups face more financial problems than others in old age. Wanner and McDonald (1986) report that membership in a non-European ethnic group leads to lower income in retirement. Asian, African, or Latin American ethnic group members tend to retire later and have less chance of getting OAS, GIS, or CPP benefits. They also have less chance of getting an occupational pension. This leads to lower income for these older men. Wanner and McDonald (1986), using the political economy perspective, trace these trends to public pension policies and their impact on immigrants. Recent immigrants, for example, receive only partial public pensions.

A small percentage of older people have savings and investments and live on comfortable incomes, but people who live near or below the poverty line in Canada before they retire will stay there in old age. Women, for example, face low incomes in later life and they show higher rates of poverty than men. This reflects differences in men's and women's work careers, salaries, and pension options.

Women and Pensions

The National Council of Welfare (1984b, 24) says that "one conclusion stands out from all the facts and figures [about aging and poverty]: Poverty in old age is largely a women's problem, and is becoming more so every year." In 1987, for example, women aged 65–69 earned only about half the income of men in that age group (Norland 1994; see also Ghalam 1995). The poverty rate of elderly

Exhibit 9.5

RRSP Contributors, by Income Level, 1986

Income Level Contribution	Percentage of Tax Filers	Average
Under $15 000	5	$ 1204
$15 000–$29 999	28	1987
$30 000–$44 999	45	2460

This table shows a clear pattern. The higher the income bracket, the greater the proportion of people who paid into an RRSP. Also, the higher the income bracket, the larger the amounts of money that people in that income bracket paid into a plan. The average contribution for people who earned $50 000 and over was almost five times the amount on average contributed by people who earned less than $10 000 a year. Increases in contribution limits will increase the use of RRSPs by wealthier Canadians and will increase the gap between the contributions of the rich and the poor. The poorest Canadians cannot afford to save in an RRSP.

Source: *A Pension Primer*, National Council of Welfare, 1996, Table 10, p. 43. Reproduced with the permission of the National Council of Welfare.

women was 22 percent, double the poverty rate of elderly men. In that same year, unattached women aged 65 and over (who lived alone or with nonrelatives) made up 6 percent of all women, but 18 percent of poor women. The poverty rate for unattached women aged 65 and over was 56 percent in 1993, seven times the rate of elderly women who live in families (Ghalam 1995). Almost four times as many unattached older women lived in poverty as unattached older men (Statistics Canada 1995b).

The low income rate has declined for all older women from the 1980s to the present. Still, "after a lifetime spent taking care of their spouses and children," the National Council of Welfare (1979, 48) says, many "women who had no opportunity to become financially self-sufficient are now abandoned by the generation that benefited most from their work."

Why do women have such low incomes in old age? First, traditional expectations about women and work lead women to have different work patterns than men. Women often leave a first job to raise children; due to family responsibilities they spend three times longer than men between jobs; and they tend to work at each job for a shorter time than men (Connelly and MacDonald 1990; National Council of Welfare 1984a). Women have increased their presence in the workforce. In 1994 they made up 45 percent of all paid workers (up from 37 percent in 1976) (Almey 1995b). But when women work outside the home, they often take part-time, low-paying jobs. Many working women say they cannot find full-time work. Also, the traditional expectation that women will place family before career leads to part-time work and keeps women from getting high salaries and from storing up pension credits (Almey 1995b).

Second, the structure of occupational and public pensions discriminates against women— sometimes in hidden ways. Women often work for smaller, nonunionized companies with no occupational pension plans, and they also tend to work part-time. For example, 73 percent of women under age 65 worked during 1987 at some time, but 64 percent of them had part-time jobs. Women in part-time jobs often get lower hourly pay than women who work full-time, and they get no fringe benefits. These women often fail to qualify for pension coverage (Government of Canada 1982b; National Council of Welfare 1990a).

Third, women in general are paid less than men and hold lower-status jobs (Connelly and MacDonald 1990; Lavoie and Oderkirk 1993). "In 1988, women made up 44 percent of the total Canadian labour force. That same year, they received 35 percent of all incomes, while men received 65 percent" (National Council of Welfare 1990a). Statistics Canada (1995b) reports that younger, never-married, well-educated women earn about the same incomes as similar men. But Armstrong and Armstrong (1981) report that women more often than men work in low-wage jobs that are defined as unskilled and offer little chance for advancement. In 1994, 70 percent of women worked in "female" occupations: women make up the largest percentage of babysitters, typists, and variety store sales clerks. In 1994 women made up 80 percent of clerks, 56 percent of service workers, and 46 percent of salespersons (Almey 1995b; Best 1995). Poorer women, more often than all women, tended to work in these types of jobs. Women who worked in service jobs, for example, had an average income of only $15 126 per year for full-time year-round work in 1988. They had the second-lowest-paid jobs in Canada. Only female farm workers did worse (National Council of Welfare 1990a).

Women who work in service jobs often work part-time and many of the firms they work for have no pension plans. Only 42 percent of women in paid labour in 1993 belonged to an occupational pension plan (compared with 47 percent of men), and most of these women work for government or for Crown corporations (Ghalam 1995; Statistics Canada 1996). In private industry only 34 percent of women belonged to a pension plan (Statistics Canada 1996).

Even within relatively low-paying fields women find themselves in the poorest-paying jobs. For instance, women tend to work as salaried clerks. Men tend to sell expensive products like cars or appliances. These jobs often pay a commission in addition to a base salary. Women work in service jobs like waitress, hairdresser, or child-care worker. Men tend to work at services like police officer, security guard, or soldier. Armstrong and Armstrong (1984) found that even when women work at the same job as men they may get lower pay. A report on women and poverty (National Council of Welfare 1990a) says that in 1987 women received 31 percent of the average benefits received by men from occupational pension plans.

Low pay means that these women pay a smaller amount into the CPP than men, and this means a smaller CPP pension when they retire. Statistics Canada (1996) reports that in 1993 women made only 39 percent of the total contributions to the CPP. Women received only 58 percent of the average CPP benefits received by men in 1995. The gap between CPP payments to men and to women grew from 1977 to 1987. In 1987 most women got less than 60 percent and many got less than 40 percent of the maximum CPP. In that same year most men received between 80 percent and 100 percent of the maximum CPP. Low incomes and short careers at paid labour explain this gap (National Council of Welfare 1989b).

A look at newly retired workers (i.e., those aged 65–69 in June 1989) found that only 57 percent of females in that age group compared with 96 percent of males received CPP benefits. Women in 1993 received only $4618 a year on average in CPP benefits compared with $6983 for men (Statistics Canada 1996). Women on average today earn only 60 to 70 percent of the earnings of men (National Council of Welfare 1990a). This means that even in the future women will have a lower proportion of the maximum CPP than men (National Council of Welfare 1996a).

The National Council of Welfare sums up these findings. Women, the Council says, "become the prime victims of the built-in injustices of our labour market, which excludes women from the best positions, pays them less than they are worth and segregates them into a narrow range of low-wage occupations with few fringe benefits and limited chances for advancement" (National Council of Welfare 1990a, 2).

Widows

Widows make up the largest group among women 65 and over, and, of all women, they benefit least from Canada's pension system. "After fifty years or so of unpaid, faithful service," the National Council of Welfare (1979, 32) says, "a woman's only reward is likely to be poverty." In 1988, 50 percent of women aged 75 and over, most of them widows, lived in poverty. This figure does not include people who live in institutions; if it did, the poverty rate would be higher.

Why do older widows have such low incomes? First, only 51 percent of all workers belong to an occupational pension plan (National Council of Welfare 1990a), and less than half of these occupational pension plans pay survivor benefits to widows. Many of these private-sector plans provided for only five years of survivor payments. "A woman who loses her husband when she is 65," the National Council of Welfare (1989b, 39) says, "and lives until age 85 could be in dire straits for the last 15 years of her life."

Only 69 percent of members of public-sector plans and 27 percent of members of private-sector plans provided a survivor pension if the plan member died before retirement. Even when a survivor plan exists, sometimes a woman gets nothing because her spouse had opted for higher benefits while he was alive. Many plans refund only the worker's contributions with interest if a plan member dies before retirement. Some plans return nothing to the surviving spouse (National Council of Welfare 1989b).

The public pension system also lets widows down. The CPP, for example, sets the benefits for a surviving spouse aged 65 and over at 60 percent of the deceased spouse's pension. The maximum amount payable came to $5235 a year in 1996 (Human Resources Development Canada 1996). The OAS in that year for a single person came to about $4747. Combined, these payments came to only about two-thirds of the poverty line for a single person living in a large Canadian city (National Council of Welfare 1996b). The National Council of Welfare (1984a, 38) says that "a woman with no retirement pension of her own will suffer a drastic reduction in her living standard when her husband dies."

Women coming into old age in the near future will do a little better. More of them work. For example, women between ages 35 and 54 have the highest earnings for women. And women aged 15–24 earned on average 91 percent of men's wages (Ghalam 1995). Many of these women will get CPP pensions in the future. Ghalam (1995) reports that 61 percent of all women aged 18–64 in 1992 paid into the CPP. (At this same time 75 percent of men paid into the CPP.)

Still, many women will get only small pensions. Homemakers will have no occupational pensions; they will get no CPP pension of their own; and if their husband's pension plan pays no survivor benefits, they will get no pension at all. Younger women will do better in the future because more of them work; they have begun to enter male-dominated occupations; and more of them belong to private pension plans (Connelly and MacDonald 1990; Statistics Canada 1996). Also, more women than in the past (21 percent in 1992 compared with only 10 percent in 1982) paid into RRSPs (Ghalam 1995).

Still, the large majority of women have no RRSPs. And those who do, compared with men, pay less into their RRSPs (Ghalam 1995). Lower incomes for women may account for this difference. Also, low wages and part-time work will leave most women without occupational pensions. They will also have small CPP pensions.

The system needs reform: women and men need better occupational pension plans, and women need better survivor and homemaker benefits, and more help from the OAS/GIS/SPA (Dulude 1987). The federal government has proposed some changes to the system. This sparked what some people call "the great pension debate" in the early 1980s. This debate was about whether a public pension plan like the CPP or private pension plans would best serve Canadians. More recent debates have been concerned with universality of the OAS (Myles 1988).

PENSION REFORM

Canada has debated pension reform since the early 1980s. A series of conferences, task forces, and white papers have all proposed changes in the pension system (Government of Canada 1982a; House of Commons Canada 1983). And some change has taken place. For example, by the late 1980s all provinces except British Columbia and Prince Edward Island had some legislation covering occupational pensions. Also, new rules have improved the public pension plan system. What follows are some of the highlights of these reforms.

First, the federal government income security system has made three important improvements over the years: (1) improvements in GIS have led to decreased poverty rates for single older people (National Council of Welfare 1988); (2) as of 1985, all widows and widowers with low incomes would get the SPA; and (3) the federal government continues to index the OAS to the rate of inflation, though it has not increased the OAS to bring it closer to the average industrial wage (AIW).

Second, beginning in June 1984 the CPP also allowed women and men to deduct the years they spent childrearing from their pensionable years. (Until 1984 these years counted as zero income and lowered a person's average lifetime salary.) People who take time off to care for their children can now deduct from their work record the years when their children were under 7 years old. Also, the CPP now provides for **credit splitting** if spouses divorce. Each spouse gets an equal share of the credits accumulated during their time together. This provision, however, includes a hitch: it requires an application for credit splitting. This means that not all eligible people will apply for or arrange credit splitting. Between 1978 and January 1996, for example, only 65 709 people applied for and received approval for credit splitting (National Council of Welfare 1996a).

Third, in May 1985 the federal government announced changes in the Canada Pension Benefits Standards Act. These changes set minimum standards for one million federal government workers and workers in federal government industries such as Crown corporations. The federal government will ask provinces to change their rules to meet these new standards. These changes will affect 3.5 million workers all told. They include:

1. Locked-in vesting mandatory after two years in an occupational plan.

2. Improved portability by transfer of vested pensions to locked-in RRSPs.

3. The right of all full-time workers to join a private plan after two years of work; all part-time workers must have the right to join if they have earned at least 35 percent of the yearly maximum pensionable earnings ($8190 in 1985).

4. Payment of survivor benefits worth at least 60 percent of the amount the couple would have received had the contributor lived. These benefits will continue if the survivor remarries.

5. Division of pension credits and payments 50-50 if a couple divorces, unless the couple or the courts choose a different option.

These changes serve as a model for the private sector as it considers pension reform (National Council of Welfare 1985a).

Fourth, the federal government and the provinces have agreed that all occupational plans shall provide a "joint life/last survivor benefit" (National Council of Welfare 1989b). A spouse will receive at least 60 percent of the occupational pension the couple would have received if both had lived. The pension continues even if the survivor remarries. This provision has one drawback: both spouses must agree to lower pension payments in the present. If the couple chooses a higher pension today, they forego survivor benefits in the future.

These changes balance some of the inequities in the system. The poorest older people on the GIS will benefit from these changes, and so will widows and women who work part-time. But the federal government will still have to tackle some tough issues in the future. These include home-makers' pensions, the rising cost of indexed OAS pensions, and indexation of private pension plans. Women face many disadvantages in old age that current pension reform only partly addresses. Changes in the OAS will help the poorest women. But, "the whole income-security debate," Neysmith (1984, 18–19) writes, "has been defined in terms of pensions that are related to one's track record in the paid-labour force … [and] occupationally based pensions by definition cannot meet the needs of most women" (Neysmith 1984). Canadian society will need to deal with this larger issue through broader reforms. These reforms will have to include increasing opportunities for women in the labour force.

THE COST OF REFORM

Changes in private and public pension plans will mean one thing: pensions will cost more money. CPP rates, for example, will have to rise to about 9 percent of workers' earnings by the year 2030 (from 3.6 percent in 1986) just to keep CPP benefits at 25 percent of the AIW. Better occupational plans will cost more—the federal government estimates a rise in costs to about 11 percent more of a worker's pay. Better survivor benefits will cost about 0.7 percent of a worker's pay (Health and Welfare Canada 1982a). As Canadian society ages, more people will begin to draw pensions. And smaller age cohorts of younger people will have to pay for some of these costs.

How will people feel about these changes? Will younger people revolt at the high cost of pensions for the older generation? The state of Canada's economy will partly determine how younger people will feel about pension costs. A strong economy and low inflation will make it easier to pay more for pensions; increased costs and low wages will make it harder.

Myles (1982) offers two reasons why Canadians will support a stronger pension system in the future. First, he says, without state support, the young would have to help care for their parents themselves, and younger people will prefer to "pool their risks" through a central pension system. Second, he says, middle-aged people, because they will be old soon themselves, have a self-interest in supporting a strong pension and social security system for the elderly.

In the end a strong pension system—given the longer life expectancy today—makes sense for everyone. As long as taxpayers see this they will continue to support improvements in Canada's retirement income system (Myles 1981b).

The Future

Finance Minister Paul Martin proposed a new **Seniors Benefit** in his 1996 budget. This program will replace the OAS and GIS starting in 2001. The current group of older people (people aged 60 and over as of December 31, 1995, and their spouses) will still get OAS and GIS payments. They may choose to move to the new system if it improves their pension. The program proposes to maintain or increase benefits for 75 percent of older people. It expects to improve the pensions of 90 percent of single older women.

The Seniors Benefit promises some improvements over the current system. For example, people who get the GIS (the poorest older people) or the Spouse's Allowance will get $120 more per year. People will get the Seniors Benefit tax free

and the government will index the program to inflation. The government will calculate the Benefit based on a couple's combined income. But each spouse in a couple will get his or her own cheque for half the Benefit. The program plans to slow the growth in public pension costs by targeting help to people with the most need (Government of Canada 1996a). For example, people with incomes up to $40 000 will get the same or higher benefits under the new plan.

About 6 percent of older people in 1991 had incomes over $40 000 a year (Government of Canada 1993). Most of these people will see decreases in their OAS benefits. Single people with incomes over $52 000 and couples with incomes over $78 000 will get no benefits. The government planned public hearings on this proposal and expected to introduce this legislation in 1996.

This program fits a trend in policy (including health care policy) to limit programs to people most in need. Myles and Teichroew in 1991 (91) projected a "withering away" of the OAS and more emphasis on public support through the GIS in the future. They also projected growth in subsidized private savings through RRSPs and workplace pensions. The Seniors Benefit achieves what Myles and Teichroew (1991, 85) call "the main project of both the Liberal and Conservative parties throughout the 1980s—to make the welfare state more efficient by targeting scarce transfer dollars to those most in need." It also supports the trend to shift responsibility for financial well-being in later life from the state to the individual.

CONCLUSION

Myles and Street (1995) sum up current trends in pension policy reform. The government, they say, will reduce its role in pensions and other benefits to middle-income workers. It will cut back on "social insurance" that provides income security in retirement. It will turn to "social assistance" to help needy older people. "Providing income security above poverty levels," Myles and Street (1995, 352) say, "will be up to the private sector, individuals and families." Pension policies over the past 20 years, including the most recent changes in pension laws, have created a dual pension system. The public system in the form of the GIS and now in the form of the Seniors Benefit will give support to the most needy older people. This system Myles and Teichroew (1991, 99) call "a welfare state for women." It serves people who work outside the labour market. The private system in the form of RRSPs and private pensions plans gives state support to pensions for middle- and upper-income earners. This system serves "organized workers and the predominantly male occupations of employed professionals and managers" (Myles and Teichroew 1991, 99).

This may not produce the end product that the government wants. Current and future policies encourage middle-aged, middle- and upper-income earners to save more money in RRSPs. This will cost the government money in lost taxes. And this will counteract some of the savings made by cutting OAS payments to middle- and upper-income retirees (Myles and Street 1995). Myles and Street (1995) conclude that a larger retired population will cost society more money one way or another. Policies simply shift the cost of a retired population from one group to another (from young taxpayers to retirees who have to live on their own resources).

A new view of retirement could help solve this problem. Some studies project a shortage of young workers in Canada in the future (McDonald and Chen 1995). This would create potential jobs for older workers. And this would reduce the cost of retirement pensions to the state. But, so far, older workers have shown little interest in staying at work. Retirement rates have increased and people now leave work earlier than ever before. A change in retirement pensions for middle- and upper-income workers and more job insecurity in mid-life could lead to new patterns of retirement in the future.

SUMMARY

1. Canada's pension system has a sound structure, but the current system "is out of balance" (National Council of Welfare 1984a, 71). Some people—very old women, people from lower-income brackets, people with low levels of education, widows, and homemakers—all run a higher than average risk of poverty in old age.
2. Canada has a three-tiered system: the OAS, GIS, and SPA make up tier one; the CPP/QPP make up tier two; and private pensions and savings make up tier three.
3. The Canadian retirement system has two goals: (1) to keep all older people out of poverty; and (2) to replace pre-retirement income. At present it meets neither goal for many Canadians.
4. Poorer Canadians, the people who need private savings the most in retirement, have the least chance of having any. Private pension plans cover fewer than half of Canadian workers. The CPP at best replaces only 25 percent of a person's income up to the average industrial wage, and the OAS/GIS/SPA leave the poorest older people in poverty.
5. Women, compared with men, face a higher risk of poverty in old age, because unequal coverage by pension plans, lower-paying jobs, and different work patterns due to child-rearing often leave women with lower pensions.
6. Widows run a high risk of poverty in old age. The CPP pays a relatively small survivor pension. Private pension plans offer little help. Many of them have no survivor pension option.
7. The federal government has recently made changes to the system. Reforms include better GIS/SPA payments, better CPP pensions, rules that encourage RRSP contributions, and rules that strengthen private pension plans.
8. Proposed reforms to the CPP and to private plans try to ensure that more Canadians, including homemakers, get pension coverage. Better public and private pensions for these people may reduce the costs of federal government transfers in the future. This will save the government money and give more people a better income in retirement.
9. The government will reduce its role in providing pensions to middle-income workers in the future. Individuals, families, and the private sector will have to provide income for people over the poverty line. The proposed Seniors Benefit will improve pensions for poorer Canadians, but reduce pensions for people with high incomes.
10. Canadians will pay for these reforms as long as they support the notion that everyone—young and old—gains from a strong pension system.

STUDY QUESTIONS

1. Describe the parts of Canada's three-tiered retirement income system.
2. Explain how the Canada Pension Plan funds pensions today.
3. List two strengths and two weaknesses of the private pension system. Why does the private system fail to help most people in retirement?
4. Present the structural causes of financial inequality in old age. What groups face the most financial problems as they age? Why?
5. How has the Canadian government changed the public pension system to provide better coverage for older Canadians?
6. How does the government plan to change the current public pension system to provide better retirement incomes for older people in the future?

KEY TERMS

clawback   required repayment of OAS benefits from wealthier seniors to the government.

credit splitting   each spouse gets an equal share of pension credits accumulated during their time together.

depth of poverty   the distance between a low-income senior's income and the poverty line.

great pension debate   the debate in the 1980s over how to fund public pensions for older Canadians in the future.

income maintenance programs   programs like the Canada and Quebec Pension Plans that help people maintain their pre-retirement income and lifestyle.

income security programs   programs like the Old Age Security and the Guaranteed Income Supplement that help people meet their basic needs in retirement.

indexation   a method of increasing pensions that links them to increases in the cost of living.

portable   this means a pension moves with workers when they change jobs.

registered retirement savings plans (RRSPs) a government plan that allows people to save money for their future pension without paying

income tax on this money. RRSP members pay tax on the money only when they withdraw it in retirement. This defers taxes to a time when the person has a lower income—and so a lower tax rate.

savings plan   each worker pays a percentage of his or her salary into the CPP each month. The payments are credited to individual workers, and, when they retire, their pension will depend on how much they paid into the plan.

Seniors Benefit   this program will replace the OAS and GIS starting in 2001. The program proposes to maintain or increase benefits for 75 percent of older people.

transfer plan   the CPP also works like a transfer plan because the money paid in today does not go into a private account for each person. It goes to pay the pensions of retired plan members today. Pension experts also call this a pay-as-you-go plan.

universality   the idea that everyone in Canada has a right to a public pension regardless of his or her income.

vesting   workers with a fully vested pension have credit for their total pension contributions (their own and their employer's contributions) even if they move from one employer to another.

SELECTED READINGS

Bryden, Kenneth. *Old Age Pensions and Policy-Making in Canada*. Montreal: McGill-Queen's University Press, 1974.

One of the few reports on the history of the pension system. Bryden is a political scientist, so he looks behind the historical events to discover trends in public policy.

Myles, J., and L. Teichroew. "The Politics of Dualism: Pension Policy in Canada." In J. Myles and J. Quadagno, eds. *States, Labor Markets, and the Future of Old-Age Policy*, 84–104. Philadelphia: Temple University Press, 1991.

This article describes the structure of Canada's pension system in terms of government and business interests. The authors show that the mix of public and private pensions in the Canadian system satisfies both groups. They show that the Canadian pension system cares for the poor. But it has begun to shift much of the responsibility for middle-class pensions to the individual (e.g., the support of RRSPs). The authors propose that this shift to individual responsibility will also take place in social and health care policies.

National Council of Welfare. *A Pension Primer*. Ottawa: Minister of Supply and Services, 1996.

This report on Canada's pension system presents facts and information in an interesting, readable style, and includes a glossary of terms. This report argues that the pension system needs improvement. The Council will mail this and other reports on request at no cost. Write to the National Council of Welfare, 2nd floor, 1010 Somerset St. W., Ottawa, ON K1A 0J9.

Women's Bureau, Labour Canada. *Women in the Labour Force*. 1990–91 ed. Cat. No. L016-1728/90E. Ottawa: Minister of Supply and Services, Canada 1990.

Current facts on women and work. The report includes figures on labour force participation, earnings of men and women, and pensions. This source gives up-to-date information that you can interpret for yourself.

Retirement and Work

INTRODUCTION

Claude Rioux retired six months after his sixty-fifth birthday. He had worked as a warehouseman for an electronic supply company. Claude never thought much about retirement in his middle years, but a year or two before he retired he began to feel he had nothing in common with his fellow workers. Most of his friends had retired, and most of his new co-workers had just left high school. They talked about girls and motorcycles and listened to loud music. He had always liked work, but he began to enjoy it less each day. After he turned 65 his boss came by to ask if he had any retirement plans. Once the boss called him into his office and asked him when he planned to leave, "I said I didn't know," Claude says. "Why give him the satisfaction of thinking he could push me out? Hell, I still do a good job. Better than some of the kids who work here now. Oh, I planned to leave in January, but I wouldn't tell him. I thought, 'I'll leave when I'm good and ready.'"

No one forced Claude to retire, but he did. And he left work just about on schedule. He had little reason to keep working past age 65. He had a small pension from work as well as his CPP and OAS pensions, and he planned to open a small electronics repair shop at home. He stayed on until January only to show that no one could push him around.

Statistics Canada reports that a smaller proportion of men and women work past age 65 than ever before. In 1991 only 22 percent of men and 10 percent of women aged 65 to 69 continued to work in the labour force. After age 75 the labour force participation rate falls to only 7 percent of men and 3 percent of women (Norland 1994). Canadians now retire on average at age 62 (Government of Canada 1993). These figures show that retirement has become a normative life event. Some people will spend a quarter or more of their adult life in retirement.

Gerontologists view retirement today from two points of view: first, as a social institution and, second, as a process of personal adjustment. This chapter will look at retirement from each of these perspectives. It will look at (1) the origin and role of retirement in modern society, (2) the forces that lead a person to retire, and (3) how people adjust to retirement.

RETIREMENT AS A SOCIAL INSTITUTION

The Origins of Retirement

Myles (1984) traces old age today to two developments. The first is the **retirement principle**—the idea that at a fixed age, regardless of mental or physical ability, a person leaves work. The second is the retirement wage—a pension paid by the state to support all older people. Myles (1984, 7) says that a new group of people grew out of these two developments: "a population of elders still fit for production who do not engage in economic activity."

Employers and employees both supported the retirement principle in North America. Industry supported it for two reasons: first, retirement allowed companies to retire older, skilled workers and hire younger, less-skilled workers at lower wages; and, second, companies, using a philosophy of "scientific management," sought to speed up production and get more out of their workers. Unions offered to have workers work faster if companies reduced the work day, but a faster pace of work made it hard for older workers to compete with younger workers (Atchley 1985). Retirement gave older workers a graceful way to leave work.

The Canadian government supported the retirement principle for a number of reasons. Canada's first civil service commissioner, Adam Shortt, said in 1922 that retirement relieves the government of the embarrassment and extravagance of retaining the services of officers who have outlived their usefulness; creates a proper flow of promotions; renders the service more mobile; deters efficient workers from leaving the public service for private employment ... [and] in general tends to promote efficiency in every way (quoted in Bolger, 1980, 8, cited in Myles 1984, 13).

Canada introduced the Old Age Pension Act in 1927 to promote the goals outlined above and to solve a social problem created by retired workers. Matthews and Tindale (1987) give three reasons for this act. First, more people lived to old age. Second, many old people lived in poverty. Third, employers needed to reduce unemployment and increase productivity. The Pension Act encouraged retirement and provided a basic income to the poorest older people.

Unions in North America supported retirement for their own reasons. Unions wanted companies to use seniority (first hired, last fired) as a method for deciding layoffs or cutbacks. Seniority gave workers a right to a job, and it gave the oldest workers the most job security. But companies resisted the seniority system because older workers cost them more and seniority rights made it hard for them to fire inefficient older workers. Retirement served both unions and employers. It limited seniority rights to people under the age of retirement and allowed companies to let older workers go. The unions traded the older worker's right to a job for job security in middle age (Haber 1978, cited in Atchley 1985, 54).

Still, few people retired in the past compared with today. First, in Canada many people worked on farms or in small businesses with no retirement age. Second, and most important, a lack of retirement income kept most people working as long as they could. Only with the increase in public pensions and social supports for older people after World War II did retirement spread (Myles 1984).

The U.S. Social Security program led the way for this change. The U.S. designed Social Security as a way to get people to retire (Myles 1984, 16). Until then governments gave social assistance to older people, but this assistance, like Canada's early

Exhibit 10.1

Labour Force Participation Rates by Age and Sex, Canada, 1991

Note that labour force participation rates increase between ages 15 and 24 for both men and women. By age 24 over 90 percent of males and 80 percent of females work in the labour force. For men, high rates of participation hold until around age 55. Then a gradual drop occurs (from 84 percent of 55-year-olds in the labour force to 42 percent of those age 64). A sharp (12 percent) drop occurs at age 65. By age 75 only 10 percent of men remain at work.

The pattern of labour force participation for women mirrors that of men with some differences. First, women have lower rates of participation throughout adulthood. Second, women begin to leave the labour force earlier. Their rates drop from 77 percent at age 47 to 20 percent by age 64. Third, women show a less sharp decline at age 65 and they leave the labour force more slowly in later life.

Source: J.A. Norland, *Profile of Canada's Seniors*, Cat. No. 96–312E (Ottawa: Statistics Canada and Prentice Hall Canada, 1994). Reproduced by authority of the Minister of Industry, 1996, Statistics Canada.

old age assistance program, gave only the poorest older people a small amount of money to help them survive. The government based the program on the English poor law notion of "less eligibility." This rule held that assistance should relieve poverty, but should come to less than the lowest working wage.

Social Security, and later Canada's public pension system, set a new goal for public pensions. These programs promised to make up for a retiree's lost income. "By 1980," Myles (1984, 21) says, "the institution of retirement had been consolidated and old age had become a period in the life cycle defined and sustained by the welfare state."

Government now plays the major role in guaranteeing pensions to older retirees. Public pensions and transfer payments act as a deferred wage because people pay into the program through taxes and CPP/QPP payments while they work. In Canada, though, the amount a person gets does not depend only on how much he or she paid in. People today get "a share of the social product over and above any claims they may have possessed in their capacity as wage earners" (Myles 1984, 29). Myles calls this a citizen's wage. This wage makes retirement a time of economic security and freedom for many older people.

Schulz (1985) estimates that, without government support, workers would have to save 20 percent of their income each year just to get a pension equal to 60 to 65 percent of their earnings during the last five years before retirement. Few people could afford to save this much on their own. With government help, retirement has become an option for many more people than ever before. Statistics Canada reports that in 1971, for example, 15.1 percent of men and women aged 65 and over took part in the labour force. This figure dropped to 10.1 percent in 1981 and 8.7 percent in 1991 (Statistics Canada 1993).

Men aged 65 to 69 showed the greatest decrease in labour force participation during the 1980s. Their participation rate fell by almost 27 percent from 1979 to 1989. Men aged 55 to 64 showed the second-largest drop. Their participation rate fell by 15 percent (Statistics Canada 1990e). During this same time the dollar amount of government income security payments increased and more people received Canada Pension Plan pensions. The retirement trends for the past decade support the idea that people tend

to retire early if they have a good pension. The 1989 General Social Survey (cited in Lowe 1992) found that 43 percent of employed people planned to retire before age 65. Only 1 percent planned to retire after age 65.

A study done by Health and Welfare Canada says that by age 60, 13 percent of men and 50 percent of women who worked sometime between age 45 and 60 had retired. By age 65, about 50 percent of men and 75 percent of women had retired, and by age 70, about 90 percent of both groups had retired (Ciffin and Martin 1977).

At every age after age 61, for example, a higher proportion of men had retired in 1975 than in 1961. Ciffin and Martin (1977, 86) conclude that "there was a major shift towards earlier retirement ages between 1961 and 1975." Men shifted away from retirement at about age 70 to retirement at about age 65. Ciffin and Martin (1977, 87) predict "a further shift towards earlier retirement ages" in the future, if men have enough income. (A higher proportion of women than men had retired at all ages in 1975.)

McDonald and Wanner (1990) support this projection. They report a general trend toward lower labour force participation rates for men aged 65 and over from 1975 to 1986 (17.2 percent and 11.2 percent, respectively). Women in this age group showed much lower rates of labour force participation in both 1975 and 1986 (4.4 percent and 3.6 percent, respectively) and a fairly stable rate over time.

"In 1975," Ciffin and Martin (1977, 85) say, "age 65 clearly was 'institutionalized' with about 25 percent of men retiring at 65 and over 40 percent of the active men expecting to retire at 65. No normal retirement age existed for women." A study by Atchley (1982, 159) supports this difference in patterns of retirement for men and women. He reports that men more often than women planned to retire at a specific age and that women were more likely than men to plan to retire before age 60 or after age 70. Gee and Kimball (1987) report that pension eligibility best predicts when a woman will retire.

In Canada more women, compared with men, retire early. Many women retire because their spouse has retired. And because women often marry older men, they retire at an earlier age on average than men. They also tend to return to work after widowhood (Stryckman 1987). A

Canadian study (Matthews and Tindale 1987) compared the reasons men and women retire. The researchers found that women, more often than men, retire because of the ill health of a spouse or a family member. Atchley (1982) says that these facts should "caution against relying too heavily on very general statements about women's retirement." They should also caution against using data based on male retirement patterns to draw conclusions about retirement for women.

WHY DO PEOPLE RETIRE?

A number of personal conditions lead people to choose retirement. These include health, a spouse's decision to retire, and attitudes toward work. Social forces can also lead a person to choose retirement. These forces include: (1) mandatory retirement rules, (2) better pensions that start at age 65, and (3) a more positive societal attitude toward retirement.

Exhibit 10.2

Functional vs. Formal Criteria for Retirement

Mandatory retirement uses a formal criterion (a specific age) to decide when a person should retire. Critics of this approach say that people should be judged on their functional ability. Shephard (1995), for example, reports that decreases in physical ability do not necessarily lead to a loss of work ability. Salthouse and Maurer (1996, 355) reviewed the literature on age and work ability. They conclude that "there is little or no relation between age and work performance or job proficiency." Gibson, Zerbe, and Franken (1993) studied older and younger workers' views of employees. Both younger and older workers rated older workers as higher on initiative, stability, and experience. And people can overcome many of the changes that come with age. People who can still do their jobs should not be forced to retire. This raises the question of how to evaluate a worker's performance. Some researchers have developed functional measures of workers' abilities that allow an employer to judge a worker's competence.

Koyl (1974) created a test called the "GULHEMP" scale (General physique, Upper extremities, Lower extremities, Hearing, Eyesight, Mentality [Intelligence], and Personality) that does this. The civil service in Canada uses this measure, and so does the de Havilland Aircraft company in Toronto. This scale, however, has its limits. Stagner (1985) says that the GULHEMP measures of intelligence and personality need to be broken down into more precise measures. Also, the GULHEMP puts too much emphasis on physical ability, given the increase in high-technology, white-collar jobs. Still, employers have used the measure with some success to place older employees in new jobs (Meier and Kerr 1976). The GULHEMP and other measures of workers' abilities could help employers find and keep the best workers for the job, regardless of the worker's age. These measures can also help older workers find work that best suits their abilities.

Employers could also use measures of ability to help workers do their jobs. Workplace design often fits a young male in ideal physical condition. Gaullier 1988 (cited in National Advisory Council 1992c) says that about 70 percent of today's workforce do not fit this ideal. Shephard (1995) suggests job redesign and ergonomic supports to help older workers do their work. Some manufacturing companies provide lift supports to aid older workers and nonslip floors to prevent accidents. They also provide fitness classes and space for workers to exercise. These kinds of programs take advantage of older workers' abilities. They allow a company to keep older workers who have a lifetime of experience and skill.

The Debate concerning Mandatory Retirement

No federal law in Canada forces a person to retire at age 65, and no statute requires a worker to leave work at a certain age. The federal public service ended mandatory retirement in 1986 (Guppy 1989).

Still, 80 percent of pension plans, covering 72 percent of all members, used 65 as the normal retirement age (Health and Welfare Canada 1979, 119). One government report concluded that "mandatory retirement at 65 is practised by government and educational institutions, and employers in general follow this policy" (Statistics Canada 1979a, Chart 9).

The debate over mandatory retirement concerns two principles: (1) that of individual equality and justice, and (2) that of group rights (Guppy 1989). The first principle says that society should prohibit discrimination against a person on the basis of race, religion, gender, or age. The Croll Commission report, *Retirement without Tears* (Senate of Canada 1979), used this principle in its argument against mandatory retirement, which, it said, violates the older worker's human rights. "Discriminating against people in employment because they are no longer young," the report says, "[is] clearly objectionable on social grounds. [It is] no more justifiable than discrimination because of religion" (Senate of Canada 1979, 128). The second principle says that groups have the right to a fair share of social opportunities. Affirmative action regulations are based on this principle. The debate often focuses on specific issues like the need for older workers to allow younger workers a chance to work. But beneath this and other issues lurk the conflicting principles of individual versus group rights.

Only about one-third of Canadians aged 15 or over support mandatory retirement (Lowe 1992). The Canadian Charter of Rights and Freedoms appears to outlaw mandatory retirement based on age. The Charter states in Section 15(1) that "every individual is equal before and under the law and has the right to the equal protection and equal benefit of the law without discrimination and, in particular, without discrimination based on race, national or ethnic origin, colour, religion, sex, age or mental or physical ability" (cited in Guppy 1989). But, Guppy says (1989), the Charter contains other sections that make this passage unclear. For example, the charter does not regulate private conduct. So, it may not apply to private-sector retirement agreements. Also, the Charter protects the good of society from individual freedoms. Guppy (1989, 175) concludes that "the Charter does not ... offer a clear formula to follow in deciding the future of mandatory retirement."

On December 7, 1990, the Supreme Court of Canada ruled on a challenge to mandatory retirement brought by seven professors and a librarian in Ontario. The court ruled by a 5-2 vote in favour of mandatory retirement. The decision upheld the "constitutional viability of public service employers, including government, hospitals and universities, requiring employees to retire at age 65." The decision shows the kind of contradictions in the Charter that Guppy (1989) described. The majority position, written by Justice Gérard LaForest, stated that mandatory retirement constitutes age discrimination and that age discrimination violates individual rights. But it allowed mandatory retirement under Section 1 of the Charter as a reasonable limitation and a "minor" infringement that will add to "the greater public good" (Canadian Association of University Teachers 1991).

Employers swayed the Court by claiming that an end to mandatory retirement would lead to problems in the labour force and would limit the opportunities of younger workers. The ruling did not clearly apply to the private sector, but can serve as a precedent for application to the private sector. Also, the ruling will apply in provinces like Ontario that allow mandatory retirement, but not in provinces like Manitoba, Quebec, and New Brunswick that prohibit it.

Justice Claire L'Heureux-Dubé wrote a dissenting opinion that pointed out the negative effect of mandatory retirement on women. Working women often have fewer years in the workforce than men and so, have less pension coverage if they have to retire at age 65. She also pointed out that in places that have ended mandatory retirement, the new policy has had no proven negative effect: universities have kept their tenure systems; retirement plans have stayed in place; and there is no evidence of rising unemployment among young workers (Canadian Association of University Teachers 1991).

The concern in the Supreme Court ruling about opening positions for the young through mandatory retirement curiously comes at a time when universities face a shortage (not an overload) of young scholars. And this shortage of younger, skilled workers will appear throughout Canadian society in the years ahead. Employers may find that they have to entice older workers to stay at work (McDonald and Wanner 1990). Tindale (1991, 19) says that while "mandatory retirement will not disappear with a bang, by means of precedent-setting judicial decisions, it may well disappear with a whimper of attrition as the labour force shortage grows."

Better Pensions

Studies show again and again that most workers retire as soon as they can afford to. For most Canadians this means age 65. Méthot (1987) concludes that if mandatory retirement ceased to exist, this would have little effect on the number of older workers.

At least three economic forces lead workers to retire at age 65 today. First, some workers with good pension plans may earn more money in retirement than if they keep on working. Taxes, the cost of commuting, clothes, lunches, and other work-related expenses may make work an expensive option.

Second, most private pension plans begin to pay full benefits at age 65. Quinn and Burkhauser (1990) report that many occupational pension plans penalize a person for staying on past retirement age. These plans provide a strong incentive to retire. This leads many people to retire at 65 so that they can enjoy retirement while they still have good health.

Third, OAS/GIS payments start at age 65, as do the Canada and Quebec Pension Plan payments. A person who works past age 65 will still get these benefits, but will lose a large portion of them through higher taxes. The GIS program also discourages older people from working. In 1992 the federal government reduced the GIS by $1 for each $2 a person earned; a person who earned a provincial supplement lost the other $1 from his or her supplement benefits. Government policies such as these result in a 100 percent "taxback" on the poorest people, who get nothing for work up to the amount equal to their GIS and provincial supplements. The taxback takes money from the older person's income next year for money earned this year. This means that low-income older people who work risk losing next year's income supplements (as well as their salary) if they get sick or cannot find a job. These rules create a strong incentive for retirement.

Better pensions and decreased incentives to work have increased the trend toward retirement. This and increased leisure and recreational opportunities have also changed social attitudes toward retirement.

New Attitudes toward Retirement

Atchley (1976, 87) says that "everyone seems to know people ... who carefully planned for retirement only to become sick and die within six months after leaving their jobs." He goes on to say that, no matter what their job, he has "yet to encounter an occupational group for which retirement is related to a decline in self-reported health. It is true that many people expect retirement to adversely affect health, but very few realized their expectations."

A Canadian study by Shapiro and Roos (1982) supports this view. They studied retirees' use of health care services in Manitoba and found that retirees and workers visited the doctor for minor and serious problems at about the same rate. They conclude that "there is no evidence that retirement per se is associated with increased utilization of ambulatory physician services or admission to the hospital" (Shapiro and Roos 1982, 192). Other studies show that, in general, Canadians adjust well to retirement (Gee and Kimball 1987; MacBride 1976; McPherson and Guppy 1979). Matthews et al. (1982) found that the effect of retirement ranked 28 on a scale of 34 life events ranked from greatest effect to least effect. This study suggests that retirement has relatively little impact on most people.

Statistics Canada (Gower 1995) reports a fifteen-year trend toward early retirement for workers aged 55 to 64. Labour force figures show that the number of men in this age group who had left the labour force increased by almost 200 percent from 1975 to 1985. During this same period, the total number of men in this age group increased only 23 percent. By 1994 only 60 percent of men aged 55–64 remained in the labour force (Gower 1995).

Two types of workers tend to take early retirement: workers in poor health and those who expect a good income in retirement (McDonald and Wanner 1990; Quinn and Burkhauser 1990). Sammartino (1987), for example, says that poor health for workers aged 60 to 67 lowers a worker's retirement age by one to three years. People also retire early because they want more leisure time and less work, and they have a positive image of retirement (Gower 1995). Neugarten (1980) says that only a small percentage of workers (about 8 to 10 percent) fit the stereotype of the faithful worker who is forced out of work. "The evidence shows that as one gets older, the desire to continue working is clearly not as strong as it was once thought to be by many sociologists" (Schulz 1980, 199).

Some private pension plans encourage people to choose early retirement. Companies in Canada such as MacMillan Bloedel, Metropolitan Life, and General Motors sponsor early retirement plans. Early retirement allows companies to hire less costly young workers or to leave jobs empty after a retiree leaves. Imperial Oil Limited of Toronto says that early retirement saves as much as 30 percent of the cost of keeping an older worker on until age 65. In 1984, 68 percent of their 220 retirees retired early; on average people retired at age 58 (Finlayson 1985). Imperial Oil also brings back retirees on contract in temporary jobs (National Advisory Council 1992c).

Schulz (1991) says that retirement policies in the developed nations serve as a way to adjust the labour supply. Companies use pension plans and early retirement incentives to ease older workers from the labour force. These programs, Schulz (1991, 303) says, "intentionally ... discourage people from working." Companies use retirement as a buffer against economic change. Retirement incentives allow companies to let older, more expensive workers go and to hire younger people for less money.

Canada's Public Service Superannuation Act allows retirement as early as age 55 with thirty years' service (Health and Welfare Canada 1979). In addition to a pension, some plans give workers a large lump-sum payment to encourage early retirement, and workers tend to take these payments when companies offer them (Pesando and Rea 1977). Other pension plans in Canada allow early retirement on a reduced pension. Ninety-seven percent of pension plans covering 95 percent of their members offer this option (Health and

Welfare Canada 1979). Some private plans even include a special rule allowing early retirement on an unreduced pension for a certain number of years of service or age plus service. The Canadian Pension Plan Advisory Commission (1980) reports that 12 percent of public-sector plans covering well over half of their members and 3 percent of private-sector plans covering 28 percent of their members offer this option.

Changes in the CPP in 1987 also encourage a more flexible retirement age. The plan now allows payments to begin as early as age 60 or as late as age 70. People who retire early get decreases in their basic pension equal to 0.5 percent for each month between the date the pension begins and the month after their sixty-fifth birthday. Retirees cannot earn more than the current maximum annual CPP pension at age 65 ($8725 in 1996). Those who retire after age 70 receive an increase of 0.5 percent on their basic pension for every month between the date the pension begins and the month after their sixty-fifth birthday.

Will these changes lead more people to retire early, or will they lead people to stay at work longer? No one can say yet. One thing seems certain: these changes give workers more choice in timing their retirement than ever before.

ALTERNATIVES TO A FIXED RETIREMENT AGE

Early or delayed retirement are two options workers can choose instead of mandatory retirement at age 65. But a number of other options exist. These include **flexible retirement,** part-time work, and **second careers.**

Flexible Retirement

Atchley (1985, 192) predicts that in the future "the small proportion [of people who do] not want to retire can expect to find it increasingly easier to stay on as long as they can still do the job." Some of these workers may choose flexible retirement. This option allows them to slowly cut back the number of hours they work each week.

A study by Health and Welfare Canada (1979) found that 38 percent of retired men and 41 percent of retired women would have preferred a part-time transition to retirement. Thirty-five percent of working men and 47 percent of working women said they preferred this option. The survey asked respondents to give their first choice for a retirement pattern with no change in pay. Forty-three percent of working men and 44 percent of working women chose a gradual shift into retirement (fewer weeks, fewer days, or fewer hours per day for the same pay). "Most of those failing to retire in the way they wanted," the report says, "were those who preferred a part-time pattern but had to work full-time until retirement" (Health and Welfare Canada 1979, 50).

Older Canadians tend to work if they have occupations that allow for choice in their retirement age and if they can work at their own pace. Two-thirds of farm workers, for example, work past age 65 and a fifth work past age 70 (Health and Welfare Canada 1982b, cited in Matthews and Tindale 1987). Snell and Brown (1987) report that people who find meaning in work and consider their work important also tend to work after retirement. This applies best to older men, who work in managerial jobs. McDonald and Wanner (1982) report that the higher a person's education level, the greater the likelihood that a person will work after age 65. Older women who work most often work in service professions. Many older male workers worked in fishing, forestry, and mining (Matthews and Tindale 1987).

In the future more workers may be able to choose flexible retirement options. But today few workers have the option to stay on in their present jobs part-time. Paris (1989) reports that in a Canadian study 19 percent of 375 companies offered formal job sharing programs. Another 10 percent of these companies said they allowed informal job sharing.

Stryckman (1987) also proposes work sharing as an alternative to either retirement or full-time work. Work sharing spreads the available work for a position over a number of workers. This option would allow workers to work part-time in their current positions and might entice some older workers to stay at work after retirement age. This option fits a trend in the labour force toward more temporary jobs. This gives employers more flexibility in responding to labour demands (David 1993). It also opens opportunities for people who want part-time or temporary work.

Part-Time Work

Part-time work offers older workers an alternative to full retirement. Most people who work past age 65 choose to work part-time instead of full-time (Quinn and Burkhauser 1990). Stone (1994) reports that retired men in good health often work. But they do so for fewer hours per day than before retirement. Norland (1994) reports that in 1991 32 percent of employed men and 48 percent of employed women aged 65 and over worked part-time. Méthot (1987) found that most older people who worked (85 percent of men and 79 percent of women) said they did not want full-time work. The figures for part-time older men and women have increased by about 10 percent since 1975.

A report by Health and Welfare Canada (1982b, 3) says that "opportunities to work part-time are very important to the employment of senior citizens." Some people (women without pensions, widows) want to work part-time because they need the money. Others like to work because it gives them a chance to meet new people. Sometimes people who retired because of bad health find that their health improves enough that they can manage a part-time job. A Canadian study (Health and Welfare Canada 1979), for example, found that 35 percent of men and 63 percent of women who retired due to ill health (about 35 percent of all retirees retire for this reason) said their health had improved. Some of these people may want to work part-time.

Older people sometimes have trouble finding work (Canadian Council on Social Development 1976b). Akyeampong (1987) reports that older unemployed workers (aged 55–64) spent an average of 31.3 weeks out of work, nine weeks longer, on average, than younger workers. The older the person, the more difficulty they will have finding work (David 1993). Schellenberg (1994, 1) says that "many Canadians age 45 and over are facing severe economic hardship due to joblessness. Foot and Gibson (1993, 64) say that unemployment among older workers will remain "an important policy issue" in the years ahead.

Gibson, Zerbe, and Franken (1993) studied employers' views of older workers. They found five barriers to older workers' re-employment. Employers felt that older workers lacked the skills to do the job; they cost more to employ; and they had a harder time fitting into the company's culture. Employers also discriminated against older job seekers. These results show that employers' views often act as barriers to older job seekers. The researchers found that older job seekers also lacked job search skills. Schellenberg (1994), for example, compared job search strategies for older (age 45 and over) and younger people. He reports that older unemployed men and women, compared with younger people, tended not to check directly with employers for new jobs.

McDonald and Wanner (1990, 108) report that Canadian workers with a record of unemployment tend to get "discouraged out" of the job market. Other workers who lose their jobs may not find work that suits them, so they give up looking and retire. Tindale (1991) says that the 1990–92 recession led to 82 000 layoffs of workers aged 55 and over. Over 40 percent of these workers stopped looking for work.

The government, foundations, and local agencies funded 12 Seniors Employment Bureaux (SEB) in Canada in 1994. These SEBs help retired workers find part-time work, or other working arrangements that suit their needs. The SEB began by defining an older worker as someone aged 60 and over. They now help people aged 45 and over. Seniors who leave Canada for the winter sometimes want seasonal work (like gardening) or short-term jobs (like office help). Some older people may take part-time work because they cannot find a full-time job. Schellenberg (1994) studied men and women aged 55–64 who worked part-time in 1993. He reports an increase in part-time work for men and women in this age group between 1981 and 1993. He also says that 41 percent of men and 27 percent of women in this age group worked part-time because they could not find full-time work.

Part-time work serves a number of functions for older people. Some people work part-time to stay busy, others because they need the money. Still others work part-time because they cannot find full-time jobs. People from age 45 on face employment problems if they lose their jobs. And with recent economic changes that lead to downsizing, more and more people in late middle age find themselves out of work. Some of these people may report themselves as early retirees. Part-time work helps some of these people stay out of poverty.

Second Careers

Some people retire to a second career. Job bureaus for seniors report, for example, that teachers sometimes want to work as cabinetmakers; accountants want to work as painters; and homemakers want to work in an office or a retail store. Neugarten (1980, 74) says that "many business executives become engaged in community affairs in the last years of their employment and find it relatively easy to move into those areas after they retire." These people work at second careers for more than the money. A second career allows them to develop skills they could not use when they worked full-time.

Tournier (1972, 129) calls a second career a **"free career."** A second career, he says, differs from leisure and from the kind of work a person does in middle age. "It has a goal, a mission, and that implies organization, loyalty, and even priority over other more selfish pleasures—not in the line of duty, since professional obligations are not involved, but for the love of people. It is, therefore, not an escape, but a presence in the world" (1972, 130). A second career, Tournier says, grows out of interests that lay dormant or undeveloped in middle age. A saleswoman at The Bay, for example, spent her weekends cooking traditional Ukrainian food for her family. When she retired from work she began a career as volunteer kitchen director at her local senior centre. The work gave her a sense of purpose and allows her to use her talents in a new way.

Tournier (1972, 136) also calls a second career a "personal career" because "one has to formulate one's own aim, choose one's own method of work, set one's own daily task and assert one's identity in one's work." A bus driver began a second career as an actor when he joined a seniors' theatre group, and an electrician began a second career as a public figure when a seniors' club elected him president. These people became resources in their communities, and their second careers brought meaning and purpose to their retirement.

ADJUSTMENT TO RETIREMENT

Social class and occupational structures determine some of the options a person will have in retirement. But retirement is also a personal choice and a social process. Atchley, for example, describes eight phases of retirement. Atchley modelled his stages of the retirement process on continuity theory. This approach emphasizes the continuity between the person's pre- and post-retirement life. It presents an alternative to the idea that retirement comes as a crisis in later life. Atchley cautions that these phases "represent a device for making it easier to view retirement as a process, not as an inevitable sequence that everyone must go through" (1985, 196). These stages give some idea of the changes a person undergoes when he or she leaves the labour force. They describe the changing relationship between the individual and social structures as well as the methods people use to cope with these changes.

Phase 1: Pre-Retirement   This phase has two stages—a near and a remote stage. The remote stage takes place many years before retirement. A person may start an RRSP in his forties or buy a piece of land in the country for a future retirement home.

In the near stage people get ready to leave their jobs. They check on pension payments, fill out the necessary forms, and train someone to take over their job. They also worry about their future income and their health. Atchley, Kunkel, and Adlon (1978) report that people create detailed fantasies of retirement and that those with unrealistic retirement plans have some of the worst problems when they retire. In one case a man bought some land for his retirement on an island off the coast of British Columbia. He fantasized about his retirement, seeing it as a return to nature and imagined himself roaming around the island bird-watching, taking pictures of animals, and collecting mushrooms. His dream turned into a nightmare when he told his wife about his plans. "I have no intention of leaving my sister and my bridge club and moving into the woods," she said. "You can go yourself if that's what you want. But count me out." This man spent the first two years of his retirement coping with his anger and disappointment.

Phase 2: The Honeymoon   A euphoric time for most people. They do all the things they never had time for. People with enough money often travel during this phase, taking cruises and long winter vacations.

Phase 3: The Retirement Routine   When they get back from their trip to Hawaii people begin to find a stable routine. This might include an exercise program a few times a week, part-time work, volunteer work, or study. People will keep this routine if they find it satisfying. Some people keep as busy a schedule as they had before they retired, often complaining about all their appointments and saying they plan to slow down. These busy people choose the amount of activity they find satisfying. Other retirees like to take things slower; they disengage from social obligations, such as volunteer board memberships, and schedule more time for socializing with friends and leisure.

Phase 4: Rest and Relaxation   Some people cut back their activity at first, then gradually increase it until they find a schedule that suits them. One man withdrew from all his service clubs and board memberships just after he retired. He and his wife travelled and then settled in a new city. There he started a part-time job and got involved in community service again.

Phase 5: Disenchantment   Matthews et al. (1982) say that in a Canadian study retirees did not report retirement as a critical life event compared with others like the death of a spouse. But results differed for men and women. While men said that 73 percent of other events had more of an effect on them than retirement, women said that 85 percent of events were more critical (Matthews and Brown 1987). Still, some people (almost half) said that retirement had a strong effect on them.

McDonald and Wanner (1990, 73) say that "what little research there is suggests that retirement is not a crisis for everyone, but it does affect some people negatively." Atchley (1976) found, in a cross-sectional study, that less than 10 percent of retirees feel this way. A study by Ekerdt, Bossé, and Levkoff (1985) found high life satisfaction among retirees six months after retirement. But they found a decrease in life satisfaction in men between thirteen and eighteen months after retirement. This drop in satisfaction passed after the first year and a half.

A crisis in a person's life at the time of retirement, like the death of a spouse or a sudden drop in income, can lead to disenchantment with retirement. In one case a man retired early so he could open a small art gallery in a resort. He found that after he moved to the resort his pension did not allow him to keep up his pre-retirement lifestyle. He was forced to get a part-time job as the manager of a small restaurant, and felt frustrated and sorry that he retired when he did.

Phase 6: Reorientation People who feel disenchanted need to take stock and pull themselves together. Family and friends can help, and, in time, most people reorient themselves and adjust to retirement.

Phase 7: Routine Many people move into this stable, enjoyable phase right after the honeymoon phase. Sociologists say these people "take up the retirement role." The retirement role specifies the rights and obligations a person has in retirement. A person has the right, for example, to collect a pension, but is also obliged not to work full-time. Atchley (1985, 196) says that people who adjust to this phase "know what is expected of them and they know what they have to work with—what their capabilities and limitations are. They are self-sufficient adults, going their own way, managing their own affairs."

Phase 8: Termination A person needs independence and good health to play the retirement role. This role ends when a person returns to work or when illness or disability takes away their independence.

A number of studies have tested Atchley's stages to see how well they fit the reality of retirement. At least three studies—one in the United States, one in Norway, and one in Canada—suggest the existence of a honeymoon phase and a disenchantment phase in retirement (Haynes, McMichael, and Tyroler 1977; Solem 1976; Adams and Lefebvre 1980). These studies all based their conclusions on mortality rates after retirement. All three report no sudden rise in mortality rates immediately after retirement, but a rise was seen about three years after retirement (the disenchantment phase). Mortality rates serve as a crude measure of response to retirement and probably reflect only the most extreme cases of disenchantment. More subtle measures are needed to determine whether most retirees follow the pattern Atchley describes.

Atchley's model, even if it proves accurate, will likely apply most to one type of worker: the middle-class, Anglo-Saxon male worker who retires at age 65. Roadburg (1985), for example, says that this model does not describe the pattern of someone who retires early. Roadburg found that many early retirees want to go back to work. He also found that, even after age 81, about half his subjects wanted to go back to work. These people missed the social contacts that work provided, and they wanted something to do.

WOMEN AND RETIREMENT

Connidis (1982) found that women follow different career paths than men. Some take up careers after raising a family; others work during their child-rearing years; some never enter the labour force; and many single women show unbroken work records (Keating and Jeffrey 1983). This variety makes it hard to describe a typical pattern of retirement for women. Few studies have looked at how women adjust to retirement or at what retirement means to them. The studies that have focused on women show diverse patterns among women subjects and large differences between women and men. Atchley (1982) says that different factors shape male and female attitudes to retirement, and different factors lead to life satisfaction for each group. He concludes that "women's retirement is indeed a separate issue compared to men's" (1982, 165). In the past, Beeson (1975) says, researchers have treated women's retirement as a nonevent. Szinovacz (1982) says that until 1975 the annual Gerontological Society of America meetings contained almost no discussion of women's retirement. This has begun to change as more women have started working outside the home (Szinovacz 1983). Researchers have begun to study women's transitions to retirement as a normative event.

Szinovacz (1983), for instance, says that changes in the work patterns of women make their retirement experience similar to that of men. Gauthier (1991) reports, for example, that more women today have occupational pensions than in the past. And he expects the proportion of women with occupational pensions to grow in the future. Szinovacz (1983) says that many women now have long, continuous work records (fifteen or more years) and a strong commitment to work, and they may feel a sense of loss when they retire. Retirement for a woman means the loss of work colleagues, the loss of contact with customers and clients, and the loss of social role.

It may also mean a big drop in income, because many women have no pension plan. Women with a strong work commitment, who have many social contacts at work, and who have low incomes, have the most negative views of retirement. They also have the strongest incentive to work (Nishio and Lank 1987). Szinovacz (1983) reports that women have different retirement needs than men. Women need programs that foster social contact and programs that offer leisure activities. McDaniel (1989) and Johnson and Williamson (1987) call for more research on women and retirement.

NEW DIRECTIONS IN RESEARCH

Retirement research has taken some new directions. O'Rand (1990), for example, reports that dual-career couples fall into several categories. In most cases one spouse retires before the other, and only 20 percent of the time do they do so together. Spouses rely on pension eligibility to decide when to retire. Research has also found a return to the labour force for many of these couples. More longitudinal research on two-earner couples should study the retirement decisions couples make in response to pension eligibility, economic conditions, and marital status (e.g., widowhood).

Studies have begun to look at how life changes in other family members (sickness of a spouse or parent, marriage of children, or widowhood) affect women's careers and retirement patterns. The study of retirement will change as retirement itself changes. As more women enter the labour force, as more single women enter old age, and as better pensions make retirement an established part of adult life, social structures and individual responses to retirement will change. This will lead to new research approaches and new ideas about later life.

CRITIQUE OF THE RETIRE-MENT LITERATURE

McDonald and Wanner (1990) review a wide range of theoretical perspectives on retirement. Micro-level theories like disengagement, activity, and continuity theory each prescribe a different model for a good old age: disengage from activity, stay active in new pursuits, or maintain middle-aged activities. But these theories have some common themes. All of them (1) assume that retirement will bring a decrease in social activity; (2) focus on individual responses to retirement; and (3) assume that retirement will cause problems and that people need to adjust to live a happy life. "Most importantly," McDonald and Wanner (1990, 9) say, each of these theories views retirement "as a problem caused and solved by individual behavior."

Macro-level theories like modernization theory (Cowgill 1974) and age stratification theory (Riley, Johnson, and Foner 1972) take social structures into account. Modernization theory explains that retirement arises when a society industrializes and technology puts older people out of work. Older people then have lower incomes and lower social status. Age stratification theory describes retirement as a role that a person plays in later life. This theory assumes that members of each age cohort will enter retirement and play this role. Like the micro theories, these theories take a functionalist view of retirement. They see it as an inevitable part of modern social life. And they assume that the individual must move through this role as a normal part of the life course (McDonald and Wanner 1990).

Both micro- and macro-level theories place responsibility for coping with the retirement role on the individual. They take the social structure as given and unchangeable and expect the person to adapt. A failure to retire well amounts to a personal failure. Programs like pre-retirement education (PRE) can help a person adapt, but PRE programs seldom question the social structures that create or shape retirement. And they do not criticize the social structures that allow some people to retire easily, while others struggle in old age.

Political economy theory, on the other hand, looks at the sociocultural conditions that shape aging. This perspective sees retirement as the outcome of "economic, political, and social structures" that existed before retirement (McDonald and Wanner 1990, 14). These include beliefs about older workers, the kinds of jobs people have, their salaries, and their opportunities to save or take part in a pension plan.

Gee and Kimball (1987) apply this perspective to a review of a study by Kaye and Monk (1984) on male and female university retirees. The study found that women did more volunteer work in retirement; men did more teaching and research. Kaye and Monk (1984) interpreted this finding to mean that men have greater opportunity or interest in continuing to work after retirement. Gee and Kimball (1987) emphasize that personal motivation explains only part of the difference in male and female retirement activities. More of the women in this sample had worked as university administrators, more of the men had been professors. Gee and Kimball (1987) say that the women in this study may have had little opportunity to continue their administrative work except as volunteers, whereas the men could carry on their research and teaching after retirement within the university structure. The difference in male and female retirement activity probably reflects the different structural opportunities open to these two groups.

This interpretation emphasizes the social forces that affect individual behaviour. The political economy perspective offers "a very useful adjunct to individual explanations ... and holds considerable promise for expanding our understanding of retirement" (McDonald and Wanner 1990, 14).

RETIREMENT AND SOCIAL STRUCTURES

Social Class and Retirement Options

Tournier, in his discussion of second careers, says that before some people can take up a second career they will need "sufficient resources ... for them no longer to have to earn their living" (1972, 134). Guillemard (1977) agrees, arguing that second careers and other options like volunteer work, best fit the lifestyles and backgrounds of middle-class workers (executives, technicians, or engineers). These people form a new privileged group in society. They have good pensions, good health, and higher aspirations than working-class retirees. They may also have the verbal or technical skills that volunteer organizations or community groups value and need.

Discussions about retirement preparation obscure the issue of pension adequacy. Studies show again and again that people will retire if they have a good pension. A study in Quebec (Baillargeon 1982), for example, found that men in both the public and private sectors with indexed pensions had a good attitude to retirement.

Baillargeon (1982) reports that half of higher-level workers look forward to retirement.

Studies show that a person with a good income and a middle-class or upper-middle-class occupation stands a good chance of being satisfied with retirement. People with money have more of a chance to take part in leisure activity, while people with poor pensions and no savings may not be able to retire at all. Middle-class and upper-middle-class workers (white-collar workers, managers, professionals) with orderly work careers (few layoffs or job changes) report high satisfaction in retirement (Simpson, Back, and McKinney 1966).

Studies also show that people with the most education and the highest incomes, married men and single women tended to find or keep work after age 65 (McDonald and Wanner 1990). Women, more than men, reported that they worked because of financial need (McDonald and Wanner 1982). Quinn (1981) studied men 58 to 63 years old. He reports that about a third of the men on salary or wages worked part-time, while 60 percent of self-employed men (many of them professionals) worked part-time. Health and Welfare Canada (1982b) reports that older men with university degrees, for example, have four times the labour force participation rate of older men with less than grade 5 education. Older women with university degrees have five times the participation rate of older women with less than grade 5. Professionals such as doctors, lawyers, and professors can work as consultants or work part-time at their careers (Goodwin and Chen 1991; Health and Welfare Canada 1982b; McDonald and Wanner 1990). Norris (1993) studied retired and working professionals. She found that both groups lived meaningful lives and reported high life satisfaction. The working professionals enjoyed the prestige and challenges of their work. They often delegated work to younger colleagues and used their social networks to maintain their status at work.

Sadavoy (1994) says that most physicians prefer to work. They reject the idea of forced retirement and of age-based assessment. A study of fifty-eight older doctors in Quebec found that 93 percent of them still worked in their practices and 65 percent said they had no plans for retirement, even though they averaged 71.54 years of age (Grauer and Campbell 1983). A report by Statistics Canada (1986b) on husbands and wives in the top percentile of families by income showed that at every age more husbands and wives in these families work compared with all families, and that this gap between the top percentile and other families in the proportion of those working grows with age. In 1980, for example, in all families in which both husbands and wives were aged 65 and over, 25 percent of the husbands and 7 percent of the wives worked. In high-income families with both spouses aged 65 and over, 69 percent of the men and 21 percent of the women worked. Statistics Canada (1986b, 104) says that in high-income families people worked "well beyond the normal age of retirement." Even at ages 75 and over almost half of the high-income men and more than 10 percent of the high-income women still work (Statistics Canada 1986b). The fact that they work puts these people in the high-income group, but also the kinds of work they do—running their own companies or working as independent professionals—allow them to ease out of work at their own pace. In sum, good income predicts that a person can and will retire. But independent professionals, even though they have a good income, often choose to continue working.

Exhibit 10.3

Private Pension Plan Coverage of Paid Workers by Industry and Sex, Canada, December 1987

Industry	Pension Plan Members as % of Paid Workers			Women as % of all Pension Plan Members
	Women	Men	Total	
Core				
Mines, quarries, oil wells	51.0	69.6	67.0	11.0
Construction	12.9	35.9	33.3	4.3
Manufacturing	36.7	59.7	53.0	20.0
Transportation and communications	61.2	71.8	69.0	23.6
Finance, insurance/real estate	50.8	53.0	51.6	61.7
Public administration	70.9	83.9	78.9	34.6
Periphery				
Agriculture	*	52.8	47.9	*
Trade	19.6	31.8	26.1	35.4
Community, business, and personal service	38.8	43.4	40.4	61.6

* Sample inadequate for reliable estimate

As a percentage of paid workers, a higher percentage of men compared with women belong to a pension plan (this is true for both sectors). Except for construction and manufacturing, the core industries, compared with the peripheral industries, have higher percentages of the total labour force in pension plans. Women have less chance to get private pensions because more than two-thirds of them work in the peripheral sector. Except in real estate and personal service occupations, women make up fewer than half of all pension plan members.

Source: Adapted with the permission of the Minister of Public Works and Government Services, 1996, Human Resources Development Canada, *Women in the Labour Force, 1990–91*, Cat. No. LO16–1728/90E, Table 9.

SOCIAL STRUCTURES AND RETIREMENT OPTIONS

Dowd (1980) says that social structures and economic conditions, more than personal preferences, explain why people retire when they do. Dowd (1980, 77) divides the economy into two sectors (the **core** and the **periphery**): "one sector [the core] is highly organized and characterized by high wages and pension systems, and the other [the periphery] is marked by low wages and few, if any fringe benefits." Exhibit 10.3 shows the effect of social structure on the chances of getting a private pension. It shows that workers in the core sector stand a better chance of getting a private pension than workers on the periphery (see also McDonald and Wanner 1987). Calasanti (1988) found that, due to this inequity, periphery retirees have a greater concern about satisfaction with finances. This reflects "the monetary struggles they have experienced throughout their lives" (Calasanti 1988, 22).

In Canada women more often than men work in the peripheral sector—45.8 percent of all women workers provide services; 17.9 percent are in trade occupations; and 2.9 percent work in agriculture (Labour Canada 1986). These occupations often have no mandatory retirement rules, and they allow for easy entry, flexible hours, and part-time work (Robinson, Coberly, and Paul 1985). At the same time, these occupations pay less than core occupations, and in general they offer fewer private pensions. This gives women fewer choices than men when it comes time to retire. McDonald and Wanner (1984), for example, found that single women have one of the lowest rates of early retirement in Canada. They say this probably reflects their concentration in occupations with lower incomes and poorer pensions" (1984, 108). They go on to show (1984, 114) that poorer people of either sex tend not to retire early.

Today, not all Canadians have an income or occupation that produces a satisfactory retirement. Greater equality in retirement opportunity will come only with a decrease in the social inequities based on class and gender.

Orbach (1981, 126) sums up the research on retirement today. "One would have to conclude," he says,

that most persons today have a generally positive attitude toward retirement as a future status, and are more likely to strongly exhibit this attitude the higher their expected retirement income, the better their health, the greater their educational and occupational level and attainment, and the less they find work to be the major or only source of intrinsic satisfaction in life.

The variety within the older population based on differences in gender, social class, age, and so on leads to varied responses to work in later life. People can have full- or part-time work, full retirement, second careers, and so on. This variety suggests that retirement needs further study and that "the term 'retirement' may well conceal more than it reveals" (Quinn and Burkhauser 1990, 320).

CONCLUSION

Some people retire today with private pensions, a Canada Pension Plan pension, and RRSP savings. Other people (many of them women and people who have worked at low-wage jobs) will never retire. A comfortable retirement depends on public support and private wealth. Some writers project that changes in the labour force and the economy will make retirement less common in the future. Taylor (1995, 18) says that "retirement as we know it—ten or twenty years of fun, partly at public expense, as a reward for showing up at work during our adult lives—is doomed. The happy coincidence of generous governments and the postwar economic and population boom that made it possible has come undone." He predicts that few Canadians can save enough to fulfil their retirement dream. And government pensions will fail because too few workers will exist in the future to support the baby boom retirees.

Some changes to Canada's pension system and economy suggest that Taylor may have a point. First, the government has already begun to target government pensions to needy older people. A few years ago the government began to tax back OAS payments from wealthier Canadians. New proposals may limit OAS payments to people with low incomes. Second, Canada Pension Plan contribution rates have begun to climb. They will increase more in the future in order to prepare for the baby boom retirees. Workers may balk at these higher rates in the future. Third, the labour force has begun to change. More people work part-time and job share today than ever before. People change employers many times as corporations downsize and new technologies open up new industries. This will mean fewer private pensions even for people with a full work record.

These changes may mean that people in the future will work to a later age, though they may not work in their first career. Part-time work, second careers, and self-employment trends in later life already point in this direction. Schulz (1991), for example, points to a growing tension between older peoples' desire for leisure and the future need for more workers McDonald and Chen (1995) point to a labour shortage in the future. Will this encourage more older people to work? Will this mean an end to retirement? Will future generations forego the life of leisure and recreation that many retirees enjoy today? McDonald and Chen (1995) argue for finding ways to keep older people in the workforce. This could include retraining workers for service-sector jobs, increased education so that older people can take on more administrative jobs, and changes in pension policy that make retirement less attractive.

Myles (1984) notes that retirement as we know it depends on the **citizen's wage,** a government pension tied to age. Limits to this pension and on other government supports (like free prescription drugs) would encourage older people to work. Likewise, flat incomes and many job changes during a work career will make it harder for a person to save for retirement. All of these trends suggest that people may work to later ages in the future.

But not everyone agrees with this prediction. Schulz (1991) warns that fewer younger workers may not produce more jobs for older people. For example, employers may turn to workers in other countries for computer-based tasks. These employers can ship and receive data from these new workers via satellite (Sheppard 1991). Also, employers may still see retirement as a way to decrease the labour force. "Given also the current rigidity of personnel practices, a lack of educational and training opportunities, and assumptions of declining productivity, the future may see these factors combine to create powerful barriers to employment of older workers" (Schulz 1991, 301). Schulz (1991) sees negative attitudes of employers'

and workers' desire for retirement as the greatest barriers to work in later life. McDonald and Chen (1995, 87) see a "seemingly unwilling labour force engaged in a stampede to early retirement." Sheppard (1991, 293) says that early retirement "may increasingly become a valued end in itself, a life goal." The desire to leave work and the existence of public and private pensions make retirement an attractive option for more people than ever before.

SUMMARY

1. Most people want to retire, and they retire as early as they can if they have a good pension.
2. Some people want to continue working, and they have challenged compulsory retirement rules in court. The Supreme Court of Canada has supported compulsory retirement, except in provinces that prohibit it.
3. Arguments over mandatory retirement may suggest that most workers want to work past age 65, but studies show that if their health is poor or a good income awaits them, most people will leave work before age 65. People now accept retirement as a reward they have earned for years of work, and they will want to collect that reward as soon as they can.
4. Canadians now have more choice about when they retire and what pattern of retirement to follow. Some people take full retirement at age 65, others work part-time, and still others start second careers. In the future, older workers may have the option of flexible retirement.
5. A good income gives retirees the most options and the best chance to plan for and enjoy retirement.
6. Some studies of retirement show that retirees adjust to retirement in stages. New theories of retirement and new research approaches may emerge as more women retire from the labour force.
7. Retirement research has focused in the past on how individuals cope with retirement. A sociostructural view of retirement links individual behaviour to social and economic inequities in society. More research needs to be done on the effects of gender, educational background, and socioeconomic status on retirement.

STUDY QUESTIONS

1. List the two perspectives that gerontologists use to study retirement.
2. Explain how the retirement principle and the retirement wage give rise to the social institution called retirement.
3. What conditions lead people to choose retirement?
4. Explain the two principles involved in the debate over mandatory retirement.
5. Why does the practice of mandatory retirement affect only a small number of people?
6. What developments have made early retirement possible for older people today?
7. Describe two alternatives to fixed retirement age.
8. List Atchley's eight stages of the retirement process.
9. How does pre-retirement education help people avoid some of the problems that retirees face?
10. What social groups stand the most chance of being satisfied with retirement? What social groups usually opt to continue working past the normal retirement age?

KEY TERMS

citizen's wage   a government pension tied to age.

core sector   that sector of the economy that includes the most stable, high-paying jobs. Core sector workers often have pensions from their workplace.

flexible retirement   this option allows workers to slowly cut back the number of hours they work each week.

free career   another term for a second career. Tournier (1972) says a free career grows out of interests that lay dormant or undeveloped in middle age.

periphery sector   less stable, low-paying jobs with few, if any, fringe benefits. Periphery sector workers rarely have workplace pensions.

retirement principle   the idea that at a fixed age, regardless of mental or physical ability, a person leaves work.

retirement wage   a pension paid by the state to support all older people.

second career   work that allows people to develop skills they could not use in their pre-retirement career.

SELECTED READINGS

McDonald, P. Lynn, and Richard A. Wanner. *Retirement in Canada*. Toronto: Butterworths, 1990.

A comprehensive review of the Canadian literature on retirement. This book discusses current theories and looks at the social history of retirement as well as how people respond to it. The book presents an excellent discussion of the way social structures influence individual experience.

Myles, John. *Old Age in the Welfare State: The Political Economy of Public Pensions*. Boston: Little, Brown and Company, 1984.

One of the few Canadian studies in the field of aging that takes a political economy perspective. The author presents a sociohistorical view of retirement. He compares retirement in a variety of industrial societies, develops a typology of pension systems, and discusses poverty and social inequality in modern society. A thought-provoking book about how society shapes the experience of aging.

Tindale, Joseph A. *Older Workers in an Aging Work Force*. Prepared for the National Advisory Council on Aging. Ottawa: Minister of Supply and Services Canada, 1991.

This study begins with a look at demography and labour force trends. It then looks at a series of important issues related to retirement. These include the timing of retirement, the relationship of performance to age, and alternatives to a fixed retirement age. The author gives examples of innovative retirement options.

11

Housing and Transportation

INTRODUCTION

Lydia Wosk, 73, lives alone in her own home—a one-and-a-half-storey wood frame house just outside the downtown core. She has only a half-block walk to the bus, and she goes downtown almost every day. Three times a week she rides out to the university for classes. Lydia's husband died seven years ago of a sudden heart attack. The loss left Lydia in shock. One Sunday, about six months after the funeral, her three sons and their wives came over for dinner. "Mom," her oldest son said, "we've been thinking. You don't need a house this big. And you're all alone. Why not move in with us? You could live part of the year with each of us so you wouldn't have to worry about being a burden on anyone."

"I knew what they were planning," Lydia says. "So I was ready. 'This is my house,' I told them, 'I own it. I paid for it. And this is where I'm going to stay.'"

Lydia's house gives her more than just a place to live. It gives meaning to her life. The wall over the TV, for example, holds pictures of her children and grandchildren. The couch and chairs all have hand-crocheted covers she made herself. She says the couch reminds her of the times she and her husband used to watch hockey together on Saturday nights.

A home allows older people like Lydia to feel more independent (Rutman and Freedman 1988). Rutman and Freedman (1988, 24) studied older apartment dwellers and found that home meant "comfort, familiarity, security and independence." It also meant a place where they had control and where they could express their individuality. "I love my home," one woman said simply in a letter to the Ontario Advisory Council on Senior Citizens. "I live alone," another woman said, "but I am never lonely. I like baking, and my door is always open to visitors. I am never too busy to make them a cup of tea with a scone and black currant jelly" (Ontario Advisory Council on Senior Citizens 1978; 1980–81).

Not all older people need or want to live in a single-family house. Some older people live in apartments; others live with their children; still others live in **sheltered housing** (where they get help with meals and cleaning); and some live in rooming houses. The kind of housing that older people need and can afford depends on their health, marital status, income, and ability. A single-family house, for example, presents the most challenges (Kerr and Normand 1992). It demands good health, knowledge about home repairs, and enough income to pay for heat and taxes. An apartment demands less know-how and less worry about heating costs. An apartment with meals served in a common dining room helps people who are too frail to prepare their own meals. A nursing home cares for people too ill to care for themselves. People's housing needs change as they age. Havens (1980, 218–19) found that housing ranked as the second-highest unmet need for women aged 65 to 79, the third-highest unmet need for women aged 80 to 84, and the fourth- or fifth-highest unmet need for women aged 85 and over. Housing declines as an unmet need with age in part because more very old people, compared with younger old people, live in institutions. Filion, Wister and Coblentz (1992) also found that very old people may report less unmet housing need because they give little thought to housing options.

Canada's housing system today allows older people many choices about where to live. Housing options include private houses, apartments, congregate housing, homes for the elderly, and nursing homes. All of these housing options have a place in the housing market.

This chapter will look at (1) the housing options available to older people, (2) the programs and policies that exist in Canada to help older people meet their housing needs, and (3) transportation systems that enable older people to keep in touch with their community and use the resources available to them.

AN ECOLOGICAL MODEL OF HOUSING

Lawton and Nahemow (1973) created an **ecological model** that describes the relationship between the older person and his or her environment. Their model describes the interrelation of two variables: individual capability (competence) and the demands of the environment (**environmental press**). Lawton and Nahemow define capability as the aggregate of a person's abilities, including health, psychological adjustment, and intelligence. They define environmental demand as environmental forces that, combined with need, lead a person to make a response (1973, 659).

People feel the most comfort when their capability matches the demands of the environment and they can fulfil their needs. Too great or too little environmental demand leads to a decreased feeling of well-being and a maladaptive response (see also Schooler 1990). A healthy person in a hospital bed, for example, will feel bored and lethargic because the environment demands too little. A person recovering from a stroke may feel fatigued after a ten-minute conversation because the conversation demands too much from them. The Lawton-Nahemow model says that people try to find a comfortable fit between what they can do and what they need to do to meet their needs (see Exhibit 11.1).

Parmelee and Lawton (1990) propose an updated version of the person–environment fit model. This revised model redefines the competence dimension as "autonomy" and redefines the environmental press dimension as "security." An autonomous person (one with high competence) can pursue his own goals with his own resources. He has freedom of choice of choice and action. A secure environment (one with little press) can help a person to achieve his goals if he has some disability. A secure environment offers dependable physical and social resources. Autonomy and security, Parmelee and Lawton (1990, 466) say, "form a dialectic that lies at the heart of person–environment relations in late life." An increase in security—for example, a move to a nursing home—puts limits on a person's autonomy. Likewise, greater autonomy, like driving a car, entails some risk.

Housing and transportation should maximize but provide enough security for a feeling of comfort. Loss of a spouse, changes in a person's informal supports, and illness may all lead to changes in a person's autonomy. And this may lead to changes in their housing needs. Some people will need help in order to feel secure. Help can include home maintenance, financial aid, and changes that adapt the environment to fit the person's level of autonomy. Housing options offer different balances between autonomy and security. The most suitable choice will depend on the older person's ability, and this will change over time.

The current approach to housing for older people in Canada focuses on **aging in place** (Blackie 1986, 5; Haldemann and Wister 1992).

This policy attempts to provide older people with environmental, social, and economic supports so that they can stay in their own homes. But, as Parmelee and Lawton (1990) point out, a move from one type of housing to another may offer the best autonomy–security balance.

This chapter uses the ecological model to look at the housing and transportation options that exist for older people. An ideal housing system would allow people to match their ability to the environment's demands. It would help them to stay where they are as long as they want to stay there, and it would allow a smooth movement from one setting to another when a change in a person's ability or needs makes a move necessary.

LIVING ARRANGEMENTS

Living arrangements refer to the type of household a person lives in.* This can include living in an institution, living with a spouse, living with grown children, living with relatives or nonrelatives, or living alone. Older Canadians live in all of these types of arrangements. But the figures differ for men and for women. McDaniel (1994b) reports that in 1990, 78 percent of men aged 65 and over lived in family households compared with 47 percent of women in this age group. Of men aged 65 and over in 1990, 16 percent lived alone compared with 42 percent of women in this age group. About 2 percent of men and women in this age group in 1991 lived in institutions (Norland 1994).

One of the most dramatic changes in living arrangements over the past several decades in Canada has been the increase in the proportion of older people, particularly women, who live alone. Wister (1985, 127) calls this an "unprecedented rise in single-person living among seniors." Béland (1987) reports that in Quebec, for example, the number of older people who lived alone more than tripled between 1956 and 1976, going from 5.6 percent to 19.1 percent. This corresponds to a drop in the proportion of older people who lived with family members. Béland says that a decrease in the number of children older people might

---

* Statistics Canada (Norland 1994, 31) defines a household as "a person or persons who occupy the same dwelling and do not have a usual place of residence elsewhere in Canada."

Exhibit 11.1

The Lawton-Nahemow Ecological Model

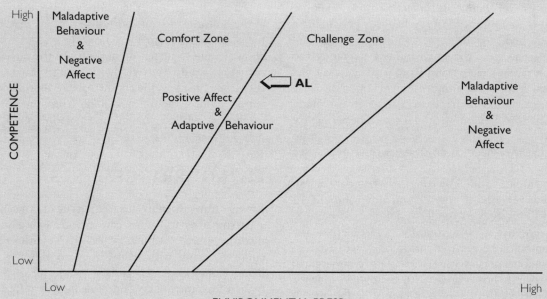

ENVIRONMENTAL PRESS

The ecological model posits that "when a person of a given level of competence behaves in an environment of a given press level" the result could be placed on a chart like the one above (Lawton 1980, 11). The chart shows the results of the fit between a person's competence and environmental press in terms of the person's behaviour and affect (feeling). The model shows that varied combinations of competence and press can lead to adaptive behaviour and positive affect. Likewise the model shows that improvement in person–environment fit can take place on two dimensions: the person can move to or create a less demanding environment; the person can improve her competence; or she can do both.

The chart also illustrates the following points:

1. The mid-point of the chart (AL) represents average press at a given level of competence. To the immediate left of the mid-point is the "comfort zone" where a person feels most at ease.

2. As press increases, adaptation takes place until the press goes beyond the person's ability to adapt (the right diagonal).

3. If a press decreases below the adaptation level, a person will feel bored and anxious (the left diagonal).

4. The "challenge zone" represents the points where press encourages the maximum use of a person's ability.

5. The greater the competence, the greater the adaptive ability; the lower the competence, the lower the adaptive ability.

6. No matter how high a person's competence, at some level of press she will lose the ability to adapt. No matter how low a person's competence, she still has some adaptive ability.

7. A person with low competence can be easily upset by even a small increase in press. But a person with low competence can benefit from even a small improvement in the environment (Lawton 1980).

Source: M.P. Lawton and L. Nahemow, "Ecology and the Aging Process," in C. Eisdorfer and M.P. Lawton, eds., *Psychology of Adult Development and Aging* (Washington: American Psychological Association, 1973). Copyright © 1973 by the American Psychological Association. Reprinted with permission..

move in with may account for this trend. He also links the increase in people living alone to the norms of independence and autonomy. People who live with their children, he says, "are mostly women, very old, widowed, ill, and suffering from some functional incapacities" (Béland 1987, 797; Béland 1984b).

Hamilton and Brehaut (1992, 8–11) studied 75 single older women on Prince Edward Island who lived alone. These women report their desire for independence. "I mean if you're independent," one woman says, "you want to stay independent." Many of the women in this study also report that they rely on family and friends to support them in their independence. "I feel quite independent," one woman says, "and that's due to my own family's care."

A study by Doyle (1994) in British Columbia also found that older women who lived alone enjoyed their freedom. Over 88 percent of these women said that living alone allowed them to do what they want, when they want to do it. Doyle says that these women cared for others throughout their lives. These women enjoyed caring only for themselves and felt "it's my turn now!" (Doyle 1994, 43).

Men and women aged 75 and over, compared with people aged 65 to 74, show even more dramatic differences in the tendency to live alone. Two-thirds (62.3%) of men aged 75 and over lived in families in 1991, either with their wives or with others. Less than a third (27.7%) of women in this age group lived in families in that year. Less than a fifth (17.1%) of men aged 75 and over lived alone in 1991; but more than a third (39.3%) of women in this age group lived alone in that year (up by 4.2% from 1981) (Priest 1994). A report from Statistics Canada (Stone and Frenken 1988) shows a slowdown in the trend toward living alone among elderly women for younger age groups (65–85 years) (Stone and Frenken 1988). This corresponds to a decline in widowhood rates. Still, elderly women make up 77 percent of all older people who live alone (*Canadian Social Trends* 1989).

Three things explain this trend toward women living alone. First, demographic changes and social norms make it more likely that a woman, rather than a man, will live alone in old age. The National Council of Welfare (1990a) reports that in 1979, 74 percent of women could expect to live as widows at some time in their lives. By the late 1980s this figure rose to 84 percent of women compared with only 60 percent of men. In 1991 widows aged 65 and over outnumbered widowers in this age group by more than five to one (Norland 1994). And fewer widowed women remarry than widowed men (Connidis and Rempel 1983; Fletcher and Stone 1980).

Social pressure works against remarriage for women. Also, social norms say that a woman should choose a man her own age or older when she remarries. At the same time, it is more socially acceptable that a man choose to remarry a younger than an older woman (Abu-Laban 1978; Veevers 1987). This leaves older women with a small pool of potential mates. In Canada in 1991 there were only twenty-nine potential grooms for every one hundred unmarried women aged 65, and only twenty-six potential grooms for every one hundred unmarried women aged 75 to 84 (Norland 1994).

Second, better government pension plans and subsidized housing make living alone in a private household a more viable option for more women today (Krivo and Mutchler 1989). In 1990, for example, people aged 65 and over made up 40 percent of people in subsidized housing. Older women who live alone make up the largest group in subsidized housing (Blakeney 1992). Community-based health care supports also make it possible for older women with health problems to stay in their own homes, rather than move to a nursing home.

Third, a change in attitudes and values explains this trend. Connidis (1983a), for example, found that most older people say they would rather not live with their children, and Wister (1985) found that older people prefer the privacy and independence that come with living alone. They prefer what Rosenmayr and Kockeis (1963) call **intimacy at a distance.** (See Exhibit 11.3.)

Wister (1985) predicts that an increasing proportion of older women will live alone in the future. A Statistics Canada report on women aged 55–64 supports this prediction (Burke and Spector 1991). This study found that increases in divorce rates, low remarriage rates, and declines in the mortality rate have led to more women in the 55–64 age group living alone. These women, as they age, will increase the proportion of older women who live alone in the future. Priest (1988) projects a 6 percent per year average increase of women aged 75 and over living alone over the next twenty years. He projects that by the year 2001,

Exhibit 11.2

Percentages of Population in Selected Living Arrangements, by Sex for Selected Age Groups, Canada, 1986

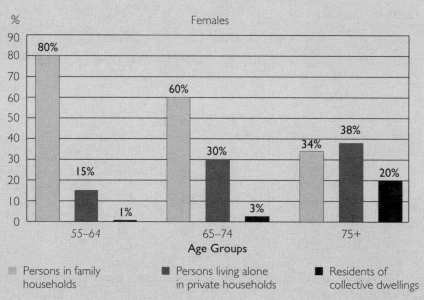

Persons in family households

Persons living alone in private households

Residents of collective dwellings

Source: Adapted from Health and Welfare Canada, *Fact Book on Aging in Canada* (Ottawa: Minister of Supply and Services, 1983), Figure 9.1.2, 69; Statistics Canada, *A Portrait of Seniors in Canada, 1990*, Cat. No. 89-519, Chart 7, 19. Reproduced by authority of the Minister of Industry, 1996, Statistics Canada.

Exhibit 11.3

Intimacy at a Distance

Children and their elderly parents now share what Rosenmayr and Kockeis (1963) call "intimacy at a distance." Young people keep in contact with their parents. Parents and children visit each other, help each other, and keep in touch by phone, but they rarely live with each other.

The National Advisory Council on Aging (1986a) asked seniors living in a seniors' residence why they prefer to live alone. Here are some of their comments:

Albina Tenner: When my doctor advised me that I shouldn't be living alone, my daughter was willing to have me move in with her, but I prefer the independence we have here.

Violet Smith: My son lives in Toronto, and he used to worry about me, but now he knows that someone looks in on me everyday. I looked after my mother-in-law for 14 years, and I decided that no one was going to go through that with me.

Hilda Tickell: My son-in-law and grandsons are very supportive, but they respect my independence. They're only a phonecall away if I need them, but I wouldn't want to be waiting around for them to call, nor would I ever want them to feel that they have to call. I have my own life to live.

Velma Would: I lived with my granddaughter and her husband and that would have worked out except that I began to feel isolated because they were away at work all day. We didn't live close to public transportation, and I began to feel I couldn't get out, especially in winter. I decided to move here because I'm the kind of person who likes to have other people around.

These comments raise some important questions. How much of older people's desire for independence comes from their feeling that they do not want to become a burden on their children? And how much of their desire for independence reflects the fact that in modern society older people have no place in their children's busy lives? Intimacy at a distance helps to solve this cultural dilemma. It allows older people to keep in touch with their children, but without living with them.

Source: Excerpted from National Advisory Council on Aging, *Expression* 3(1), (Ottawa: National Advisory Council on Aging, 1986), 3. Reprinted with the consent of the National Advisory Council on Aging (NACA) and with the permission of the Minister of Public Works and Government Services Canada, 1997.

45 percent of women aged 75 and over will live alone (Priest 1988). This will lead to an explosion of the number of women living alone past age 75.

This trend has policy implications. Unmarried older people have smaller support networks than married people, and they rely more on formal health care services (like home care) than do married couples (Hess and Soldo 1985). They may also neglect their health. Niewind, Krondl, and Lau (1988), for example, report that people who live alone have less varied diets than people who live with others. People with less social contact also showed less use of nutritious foods like vegetables. "The findings on dietary quality come as an additional argument for special attention to dental health and to the housing arrangements for the geriatric population" (Niewind, Krondl, and Lau 1988, 45).

More single older people living alone will increase the demand for suitable apartment housing and better public transportation. Many older women who live alone have low incomes (Silver and Van Diepen 1995). The Canada Mortgage and Housing Corporation estimates that "44 percent of unattached elderly women had **'core' housing need** in 1985" (National Council of Welfare 1990a, 104). This means that their housing "was either inadequate or cost more than 30 percent of their income" (National Council of Welfare 1990a, 104). These women will need housing alternatives like supported housing and homesharing programs.

Exhibit 11.4

Case Study of Reverse Mortgages

Few companies offer reverse mortgages in Canada, and few people know about them. But they may become more common in the future. A company in Vancouver now offers an RAM program that gives some idea of what reverse mortgages can offer homeowners.

James Rogers, the president of a company in Vancouver that offers one of the few programs in Canada, calls it a "reverse insurance policy." People collect the policy's payment in instalments while they live and make one lump-sum payment (their house) when they die. Two examples will show how this plan worked in 1986.

A man, aged 65, who owns a $135 000 house joins the reverse mortgage plan. The plan allows him and his wife to live in the house rent free, and it also pays him $350 a month for life. If he dies before his wife, she continues to receive payments. The company gets the house after they both die.

What about younger people with less equity in their homes? A woman, aged 60, who owns a $100 000 house and joins the program is able to live in her home rent free until she dies. She also gets $260 a month for life. The house goes to the company when she dies. Lower interest rates and rising house prices today make this an attractive plan for mortgage companies.

Source: Author's notes, based on a Canadian Broadcasting Corporation production telecast in 1986.

TYPES OF HOUSING

Single-Family Houses

Most homeowners want to stay in their own homes after they retire. In 1991, 68 percent of households with a head aged 65 and over owned their own home (compared with 61 percent of all households) (Norland 1994). And a large majority (91 percent) of homeowners aged 55 and over live in detached houses (Berger, Godin, and Harvey 1986). Eighty-four percent of seniors in senior households who owned their own homes lived mortgage free (compared with 49 percent for all households) (Norland 1994).

Home ownership differs across the country. The Northwest Territories has the lowest proportion, of all the provinces and territories, of seniors who own homes: 34 percent of those aged 65 to 74, and 42 percent of people aged 75 and over. Newfoundland, compared with the other provinces, has the highest proportion of homeowners among its seniors. Eighty-eight percent of people aged 65 to 74 and 83 percent of people aged 75 and over own their own homes.

Older homeowners tend to have older homes (Berger, Godin, and Harvey 1986) and pay less for rent (including electricity, heating, and services) than younger homeowners and renters at any age (Norland 1994). The large proportion of people who live mortgage free in the oldest age groups probably accounts for this difference (Statistics Canada 1990e).

Most older homeowners take good care of their houses. Only about 10 percent of homeowners 65 and over say their houses need major repairs. About three-quarters of home owners say their houses need only regular maintenance (Almey 1995a). A study of retirees in Canada found that 71 percent of people who owned their own homes said they were satisfied with their housing, compared with two-thirds of all men and women (Health and Welfare Canada 1977b)

Older men, more often than older women, tend to live in single-family houses. Rose and Macdonald (1984) found that in southern Ontario 78 percent of men, compared with 63.3 percent of women, lived in a house (rather than an apartment or collective dwelling). Four-fifths of men who lived in a single-family house, compared with a little more than three-fifths of women, owned their own homes (see also Almey 1995a). Connidis and Rempel (1983) say that fewer women own their own homes because a woman often has to move out of a single-family home as she ages. First, when her husband dies she may have less money to spend on housing. Increased heating costs, maintenance, and taxes can all force a woman to sell her home and move into an apartment. "If I had the money, I would gladly stay here for the rest of my days," a woman in Prince Edward Island says, "but now that he's gone it's going to be a burden" (Hamilton and Brehaut 1992, 19). Another woman told Hamilton and Brehaut (1992, 21): "I don't heat all the house in the winter. I close all but one bedroom in the winter time and the bathroom. And I don't heat my dining room ... Because your oil is so expensive and can't heat it all."

Second, women give up their homes because they know less about how to care for a home. "This is not to say that women are incapable of such tasks but rather that their patterns of socialization have not typically included the knowledge and practice necessary for a comfortable sense of mastery over them" (Connidis and Rempel 1983, 10). Older women say they lack knowledge about repairs, lack experience hiring tradespeople, and can't afford to hire people to do the work (Hamilton and Brehaut 1992). A number of programs in Canada work to help men and women stay in their homes.

Tax and Home Maintenance Programs

Homeowners without mortgages live rent free and have more financial assets than people who rent (Fraser 1982), so they should have the least trouble paying for housing. But many older people have trouble keeping up their homes. They own large, older houses—85 percent of them are single-family, detached—that cost a high proportion of the owner's income to heat and maintain (Statistics Canada 1978a, cited in Health and Welfare Canada 1982b). A study supported by the Canada Mortgage and Housing Corporation (Fraser 1982) found that a third of older homeowners in cities had trouble paying their housing costs, and that half of the money they spent on housing went to pay for utilities. A study in Saskatchewan found that one-third of older homeowners in the province put over 30 percent of their income into

housing costs (Saskatchewan Housing Corporation 1984).

The federal government and the provinces help older homeowners through grants, loans, and tax rebates. In 1988, 630 000 housing units got some financial aid (National Advisory Council on Aging 1991). British Columbia, for example, allows seniors who have lived in the province for at least one year to defer payment of property taxes until they sell their home. At that time they pay the outstanding taxes with interest (at below market rates) out of the money they get for their home. The federal government **Residential Rehabilitation Assistance Program (RRAP)** offers loans of up to $10 000 for city dwellers and $25 000 for rural homeowners to help people improve run-down housing. In 1984, for example, 41 percent of residential rehabilitation grants went to seniors (Government of Canada 1988). The government also grants loans to improve building structures, fire safety, wiring, plumbing, or heating, or to make a house accessible to a wheelchair. By 1991 loans for house repairs in Canada totalled $116 million (Statistics Canada 1993). During the early 1980s the government forgave close to 90 percent of the loans to 3400 older households with low incomes (Health and Welfare Canada 1982b).

Some provinces also sponsor home repair programs that offer low-interest and forgivable loans to low-income older people. Many provinces also offer older people a rebate or tax credit on school property tax. These programs help some older people stay in their own homes. But Blackie (1986) says that they have too many restrictions. They focus on only the most needy cases and on people with health or safety needs. They also focus more on limited home repairs, rather than on maintenance or adaptation of homes to help people stay in their homes.

Home Adaptation

Studies show that the proportion of people with disabilities increases with age. For example, most older people in private households report some mobility (walking and carrying) and agility (bending and stretching) limitations (Statistics Canada 1986, cited in CMHC 1992). Some people close off the upstairs of their home. They live in the downstairs rooms (Hamilton and Brehaut 1992). People who want to age in place may need to adapt their current housing to support independent living. Fox (1995) reviewed findings from the Canadian Health and Disability Survey of people aged 55 and over. She found that about 38 percent of disabled older people needed at least one design change to their homes. But 40 percent of these people did not have the change they needed. People with higher incomes had a greater likelihood of having a needed design change.

The CMHC says that private and nonprofit housing companies have responded to older people's needs. Housing adaptation can take many forms. Universal design, for example, aims to serve people of all ages. Designers use lever door handles, low-threshold tubs, and temperature limits on hot water to improve living for children as well as older people. Trickey et al. (1993) studied the modification needs of a group of older people in Montreal. The researchers found that almost half of the modifications took place in the bathroom. They included grab bars and shower seats. The people in the study tended to use these modifications most.

Life-span housing, begun in Norway, puts all essential rooms (the living room, dining room, kitchen, and bathroom) on the ground floor. This type of housing has no thresholds or steps. Wheelchair housing provides access to all rooms of the house and has design details to meet a wheelchair-bound person's needs. Details include easy-to-reach light switches and sockets, accessible furniture, and space under stoves and sinks so that a person a wheelchair can use them in (CMHC 1992).

Reverse Mortgages

A program known about but almost ignored in Canada could give some older people enough income to stay in their homes. Reverse mortgages allow older people to unfreeze the money tied up in their houses. Statistics Canada reports that between 1969 and 1976 homeowners aged 65 and over had 46 percent of their total wealth invested in their homes (Statistics Canada 1980a, 23). Some homeowners would like to use this money to live on, but as long as they stay in their homes they live asset rich but cash poor. Someone with $150 000 in equity might not have enough cash income to pay the gas or water bill.

Several types of reverse mortgages exist. The most common plan is called the **Reverse Annuity**

Mortgage (RAM) (Bartel and Daly 1981; Canada Mortgage and Housing n.d.). In this plan an older person uses her house to secure a loan from a bank. She then buys a lifetime annuity from an insurance company with the money from the loan. The insurance company pays the bank loan and pays the older person a set amount to live on for life. The older person can stay in her home as long as she wants. The bank takes over the house when the last survivor of a couple dies (Bartel and Daly 1981). This plan has at least one major limitation. The interest payments to the bank will go up if interest rates rise, thus reducing the older person's income.

Interest in reverse mortgages has grown in the past few years. The Retirement Council of Canada says that almost 500 people took out RAMs in Ontario in 1992. These RAMs averaged $60 000. The Ontario Chamber of Commerce sees RAMs as "one of the hottest products around" (Kormos and Horton 1994). But the Canadian Association of Retired Persons (1991, cited in Kormos and Horton 1994, 9) says that "reverse mortgages are not for everyone." And the Credit Union National Association "calls reverse mortgaging 'a costly way to finance retirement'" (C.U.N.A., cited in Kormos and Horton 1994, 9). A reverse mortgage can add interest charges of 25 to 40 percent to the original loan. A $55 000 loan could pay a 70-year-old single man almost $6000 per year as an annuity (a yearly payment for life). This would amount to about $90 000 over fifteen years. But at 11 percent the RAM over fifteen years would produce a debt of $274 117. The loan company would deduct this money from the sale of the house. In other words the RAM would cost $274 117 less $90 000. Or $184 117.

Some people will agree to this cost. They will choose to have more money now. And they have little concern about their finances after they die. Other people will find the cost too high. They may want to leave a larger estate to their children. People need to know the benefits and the costs of RAMs so that they can make informed decisions.

Apartment Living

Statistics Canada (1990e) reports that 38.4 percent of people aged 65 to 74 who live in private households live in apartments (including semidetached houses, row houses, and apartments in duplexes). This figure increases to 48 percent of people aged

75 and over. About 12 percent of people aged 65 to 74 and about 19 percent of people aged 75 and over live in high-rise (i.e., five or more storeys) apartment buildings. The proportion of older people who rent has increased from 23 percent in 1951 to 34 percent in 1991 (Silver and Van Diepen 1995).

Older people often choose to move into an apartment when they can no longer care for a house. A study in British Columbia found that almost one older person in five who moved into a seniors' high-rise did so because they had "difficulty looking after their residence" (Gutman 1983, Table 12). A study (Hodge 1984a) of seniors in eastern Ontario who wanted assisted housing found that about one in six said they could not stay in their home due to age, and about one in ten said they were not well enough to look after their home.

People with good incomes can choose from a wide range of apartments: a high-rise or a low-rise, a two-bedroom suite with a balcony and a view, or an apartment near a bus route and shopping. Other older renters have to settle for less. Many people move to rental housing due to low incomes. Statistics Canada reports that in 1991, 43 percent of older renters had trouble affording their housing (i.e., they spent more than 30 percent of their total income on housing). Only 29 percent of people aged 25–34 reported this problem. A large majority of older renters with problems affording housing (75 percent) lived in apartments. Fifty-one percent lived alone. And 85 percent of older people with affordability problems had government transfers as their main source of income (Lo and Gauthier 1995). These figures show that many older people need rent support to ease the burden of housing costs.

The provincial governments offer several kinds of help to renters: property tax credits, school tax rebates, subsidized low-income housing, and shelter allowances. Tax credits and rebates refund money to renters based on both the amount of rent they pay and their income (Zamprelli 1986). In Quebec, for example, almost 200 000 seniors in 1983 received tax refunds totalling $36 million. This program helped more seniors than any other housing program and accounted for the greatest expenditure on seniors' housing in Quebec (Renaud and Wexler 1986).

Most provinces have built subsidized apartments for low-income seniors. Ontario has taken the lead in supportive housing (sometimes called social housing) for older people in need. The province defines supportive housing as "permanent living arrangements where persons with special needs live as tenants in non-profit settings. Support services are separate from the accommodation, but there is some coordination between the housing operator and the service provider" (MCSS, Health and Citizenship, 1991, 26, cited in Baker 1994). Ontario spent $60 million in 1984 to build or support self-contained apartments for older people (Corke 1986b). In 1993 social housing in Ontario accounted for almost two-fifths (39 percent) of multiple-unit dwellings (like apartment buildings). This came to almost three times the rate in the late 1980s. The other provinces showed much lower rates of social housing, between 3 percent and 7 percent per year from 1986 to 1993 (Lo and Gauthier 1995). Still, most of the other provinces, along with the federal government, offer aid to renters in low-income housing. These programs keep a person's rent at or below 30 percent of their income.

Some provinces offer **shelter allowances** to older people. These allowances subsidize the person, not the housing project (Zamprelli 1985). They allow older people to choose their own apartment from those available in the marketplace. This frees people from having to move into government housing. About 46 percent of rent supplements went to seniors in 1984 (National Advisory Council on Aging 1991). Quebec offers a housing allowance program called Logirente. The program gives rental assistance to seniors who spend more than 30 percent of their income on housing. This helps older people to age in their own place or to choose an alternative to public housing (Renaud and Wexler 1986). The Manitoba SAFER program (Shelter Allowance for Elderly Renters) also gives older renters more choice. The program pays cash rebates (up to a maximum amount) to older tenants who spend more than 25 percent of their income on rent. The rebate depends on the amount by which rental costs exceed 25 percent of the household income.

Zamprelli (1985) compared shelter allowances and low-income housing programs in Canada. He concluded that:

1. Shelter allowances offer an easy-to-use system to support older people. They give people more freedom to choose the housing they want.
2. Low-income housing offers more control of housing quality, and government-subsidized housing can offer health and social services where people live. This can help many older people live in an apartment on their own, even if their health declines.

Zamprelli (1986) reports that in Manitoba 65 to 70 percent of rental households with the head of the household aged 65 or older receive some social housing benefits or shelter allowance. Many of these households contain unattached people with low incomes. Both shelter allowances and subsidized apartments for seniors give low-income older people more opportunity to choose an apartment that meets their needs. These programs

---

Exhibit 11.5

The Canada Mortgage and Housing Corporation (CMHC)

Since the early 1960s CMHC programs have built over 146 000 housing units and established 47 000 hostel beds for older people. Forty thousand more units in Canada, mostly for older people, receive a rent subsidy through CMHC. Older women living on their own make up the largest group that receives rent subsidies. Statistics Canada projects an increase in the need for rent subsidies for older people. Since the mid-1970s more than 174 000 houses (85 percent of which are owned by seniors) have received forgivable loans through the Residential Rehabilitation Assistance Program (RRAP). Gross (1985) says that from 1960 to 1985 the CMHC helped renew, build, or support 16 000 housing units a year for older people. In 1986 the CMHC created a special RRAP program for people with disabilities (CMHC 1992). The CMHC also helps older people buy and sell homes through loan insurance programs.

The CMHC supports nonprofit groups and cooperatives through Section 56.1 of the National Housing Act. These groups build low-income housing for older people. The CMHC will insure up to 100 percent of a loan to one of these groups and will lower interest costs to as low as 2 percent. People who live in these units pay as little as 16 to 25 percent of their income on housing (Nicklin 1985). CMHC policies and programs like these create new rental housing for seniors and give them more choice about where they can live.

Some important CMHC programs include:

1. Public housing. The main form of social housing in Canada from 1948 to 1978. Support for building units and subsidizing rents. Program turned over to provincial housing corporations.
2. Nonprofit and cooperative housing. Replaced Public Housing program in 1978 and ran until 1985. New nonprofit program began in 1985. CMHC backs mortgages and gives subsidy funding. Rent-subsidized housing in up to 50 percent of units. The rest rented at low-end rates.
3. Rent supplement. Covers difference between market rate and tenant's ability to pay based on income. Applies to nonprofit and co-op housing, and also to people on waiting lists for this housing.
4. Rural and Native housing. Covers difference between operation costs and tenants' ability to pay rent in communities of under 2500 people.
5. Project Haven and Project Next Step. Supported the creation of hostel beds for victims of family violence. A program called The Next Step supports housing for people in transition back to the community.
6. Most provinces share the cost of housing developments with the federal government. Quebec's Logirente program takes this approach. It provides a subsidy for rent to help households with heads over age 60.

Source: M. Blakeney, "Canadians in Subsidized Housing," *Canadian Social Trends* (Winter), 24; see also Statistics Canada (1993). Reproduced by authority of the Minister of Industry, 1996, Statistics Canada.

allow low-income seniors to live in affordable, high-quality housing.

Preferences in Apartment Living

Lawton (1982) cautions that no single type of housing fits all older people, but older people do prefer some types of apartments and neighbourhoods over others. Studies have looked at seniors' preferences for age-segregated vs. age-integrated housing, high-rise vs. low-rise housing, and normal vs. special design.

Age-Segregated vs. Age-Integrated Housing

A survey in Ontario (Hough 1981) found that 66 percent of senior respondents wanted neighbours without children, and that more than 64 percent of senior respondents preferred to live in a building among people their own age.

A study by Lawton (1982) of 150 housing sites in the United States found that older people who lived in age-segregated housing showed more feelings of well-being. Hough (1981) reports that seniors accept age-integrated or mixed-age housing if the majority of tenants are seniors and if each age group lives in its own building. This allows the seniors to choose when and how often they want to interact with families (see also Canada Mortgage and Housing 1978).

Kaill (1980) concludes that people prefer building segregation because it gives them more control over their social contacts with other age groups. He adds that "this interpretation does not necessarily imply that older people do not wish to be in contact with younger members of the population, but simply that they wish to retain choice in the matter" (1980, 85).

High-Rise vs. Low-Rise Housing

Studies show that older people prefer single homes and apartments in low-rise rather than high-rise buildings. Lawton (1982, 42) says that, in the United States, "the higher the building, the less satisfied were its tenants with their housing and the less mobile they were in the surrounding community."

Another U.S. study found that people in high-rises showed more boredom, knew fewer people by sight, and engaged in less activity than people in garden apartments. The study also found that smaller numbers of units (under 100) led to a better quality of life (Cranz and Schumacher 1975).

A study of 219 people with middle to low incomes, aged 55 years old and over in Winnipeg (Epstein 1976), found that people in low-rise buildings and in single homes preferred the kinds of settings they already lived in. (Lawton [1982] calls this the principle of people preferring what they have.) Still, 48 percent of people in single detached houses said they preferred medium-rise or row housing to high-rises, and 40 percent of the sample made high-rises their last choice (Epstein 1976).

Other studies in Canada show that older people can and do adapt to high-rise housing. Gutman (1983) reports in one study that 52.8 percent of people living in a high-rise building preferred this type of building. She says that "where a trade-off is required between a high-rise in a 'good' location (i.e., close to public transportation and to community facilities and services) and a low-rise in a 'poor' location, the high-rise should be the structure of choice" (1983, 193).

Normal Design vs. Special Design

Appropriate design can help people stay in their apartments even if they lose some abilities. It also creates a safer, more secure environment. "Design," a CMHC guide says, "can be a positive factor in stimulating effective employment of leisure time, the development of new roles, and a sense of purpose for those of advancing years" (Canada Mortgage and Housing 1978, 2). Gutman (1983, 187) says that "greater compliance with such guidelines would do much to improve the quality of units built for seniors while not substantially increasing construction costs." She found, for example, that older residents liked having easy access to public transportation and downtown services.

A study done by the University of Winnipeg Institute of Urban Studies found that people wanted their own kitchen, a separate bedroom, and a caretaker for the housing block (Epstein 1976). The study also found that older people dislike bachelor apartments (apartments without a bedroom). A study by the Canadian Council on Social Development (1976a) reports this same finding.

Older people also need space for meetings, lounges, coffee shops, chapels, greenhouses, beauty parlours, and exercise rooms. Apartment housing in the past often ignored this need, but some new buildings now include extra public space. They also include recreation and entertainment programs that help people use the space.

Studies show that seniors choose the kind of housing that gives them both security and freedom. Béland (1984a, 184) says that "senior housing represents for [the] elderly a place where some protection is available, while enabling them to preserve personal autonomy."

Enriched Housing

Enriched housing, sometimes called sheltered or congregate housing, builds extra protection for the older person into the housing design. This type of housing gives people more social and health care support than they get in a normal apartment building. Minuk and Davidson (1981, 55) describe enriched housing as "a housing facility where supportive services (meals, housekeeping, medical services) are available on-site on a regular basis for a moderate fee." Baker and Prince (1990), in a review of the literature on enriched housing, concludes that all enriched housing includes a resident warden and an alarm system, and that most also include communal facilities like a dining room and laundry rooms (citing Harper 1984). Heumann and Boldy (1982) estimate that in Great Britain between 5 and 10 percent of older people need this kind of housing.

The term "enriched housing" can apply to any type of housing (Saskatchewan n.d.). Enriched housing in Canada ranges from converted hotels that offer rooms and hot meals for single men, to campus-like settings with high- and low-rise housing and many levels of health care (Byerts 1982). The amount of enrichment differs from setting to setting. Sometimes enrichment means only a lounge with a television set in an apartment building. More elaborate enriched housing includes lounges, shops, and in some cases clinics. Some buildings employ activity workers and program planners who show films and organize exercise programs and field trips for residents (Baumgarten et al. 1988).

Half the people who got government rent support in Manitoba said they would move to this kind of building (Minuk and Davidson 1981). Béland (1984b) found that people chose housing like this because it gave them some protection, but still allowed autonomy. A study in Ontario (United Senior Citizens of Ontario 1985) found that 47 percent of respondents chose supportive housing as a preferred future housing option.

Alberta has a system of 142 lodges run by senior citizen foundations. These lodges house from 15 to 122 people. A person in a lodge has his or her own living space, but shares space for meals and recreation. Residents may also share bathroom space. Lodges do not provide nursing care. They do provide meals and housekeeping to residents. Lodge residents get home care services as they would if they lived in a single-family home or apartment. Nearly half of all lodge residents get home care services (Borden and McGregor 1994). Lodges provide people with the freedom to live on their own and the supports they need to cope with decreased abilities.

The Abbeyfield Society created a model of enriched housing in Great Britain that has spread to Canada (Davis 1991). The Abbeyfield model attempts to combat loneliness and serve people who live at risk in their homes. Most Abbeyfield houses have six to ten residents and a housekeeper. Residents have their own rooms with a bath, but share in chores like cooking. Abbeyfield houses often exist in large older homes in residential neighbourhoods. Several towns in Ontario and British Columbia have Abbeyfield houses. Some Abbeyfield houses provide extra care for people who cannot fully care for themselves. This type of housing appeals to older people who need support, but want to live in a home-like setting.

Critics of enriched housing say that it can lead to early dependency by giving people too many services and that it attracts sick or less able people (Gutman 1978; Lawton 1985), but studies have found more benefits than drawbacks to this kind of housing. Lawton (1976) found that people in enriched housing reported high morale and high life satisfaction. He says that proper planning can discourage dependence. In some cases enriched housing can even foster independence, because it allows individuals to live on their own rather than in institutions. An alarm system for each apartment gives people a sense of security and can save a person's life in an emergency. But something as simple as "I'm okay" signs for door knobs in apart-

Exhibit 11.6

The Svengali of Seniors' Housing

Lions Place opened in August 1983 in Winnipeg. It has eighteen storeys—sixteen for apartments and two for recreation space. When you come into Lions Place from Portage Avenue you enter an open, sunlit two-storey foyer. A hotel-style front desk stands in front of you. Hanging plants filter the light from a glass-enclosed walkway above. On the right, stairs ascend to the second-floor balcony overlooking the entry hall. Behind this lounge stretches over 5000 square feet of lounge space with card tables, soft chairs for reading or relaxing, and more plants. At the back of the lounge stands a two-storey humidified greenhouse where tenants can take classes in gardening and care for their own plants. The second floor includes a coffee shop, an exercise area, a glass-roofed walkway, a carpeted bowling alley, an arts and crafts room, and a billiard room. The exercise area has a whirlpool, sauna, and changing rooms.

The building houses people with a wide range of incomes. No one pays more than 25 percent of his or her monthly income for rent. Provincial rent subsidies help the poorest tenants. Other government subsidies help to run the building.

Lions Place looks and feels like a simple but well-equipped hotel. How do you build this kind of high-rise for older people in a time of government restraint when the Canada Mortgage and Housing Corporation (CMHC) no longer has an interest in senior housing? And when the government only allots 200 new senior suites a year to the entire province of Manitoba?

"You negotiate," Jake Suderman says with a smile.

Jake is Winnipeg's Svengali of senior housing, turning empty lots into comfortable high-rises for older people. Until he retired he managed three buildings for the local Lions Club. And he is a master at outmanoeuvring bureaucrats and goading politicians to take action.

"We started out with $80 000 from the Barbara Bell estate," Jake says. He convinced the Lions Club board of directors to buy an empty downtown lot for $1 million. He then went to the CMHC to arrange a loan. Lloyd Axworthy, federal MP and former provincial MLA from Winnipeg's core area, also supported the project, which became part of Winnipeg's Core Area Initiative. The federal government allowed the Lions Club to build a 287-suite building by giving it suite allotments not used by other provinces.

With the basic plan approved, Jake started a new round of negotiations, this time over the size of the suites and the amount of lounge space. "What you can build," he says, "is dictated by land cost. The CMHC allowed $3500 per suite at that time, and then so many square feet for amenity space. Sometimes you have to embarrass them into changing the rules. I said, 'You're going to build three hundred apartments with *three* lounges? You're kidding? You're going to build a morgue here.'"

In the end Jake got the lounge space he wanted. He also got bigger apartments and twelve empty rooms in the building just for future use as tub rooms. The building includes a geriatric and dental clinic that serves tenants and older people in the community.

Jake also added a staff that runs arts and crafts programs, physical fitness programs, day trips, guest lectures, theatre productions, gardening classes, and discussion groups. These programs keep people physically and psychologically fit. At least one staff member is there to deal with medical and other emergencies twenty-four hours a day.

"Tenants like their suites," Jake says. "But more than anything else they like the staff. In their old apartments they only had a landlord or maybe a family that didn't care much for them. Around here we say, 'We're here just for you.' They know they can approach us. We get them involved—like in the auction or in the annual tea. And we make them feel at home. We let them have something to say."

Exhibit 11.7

Jack's Hotel: A Unique Enriched Housing Option

The term "single-occupant room" (SOR) hotel implies a "low-cost, central city" hotel that serves a "clientele likely to consist of socially marginal people" (Lawton 1985, 466; Ehrlich and Ehrlich 1976). These hotels offer privacy and tolerance for different lifestyles (Eckert 1980; Sokolovsky and Cohen 1981). Only a small number of older people in Canada (less than 0.7 percent of men and 0.4 percent of women 65 and over) live in these hotels. Still, Lawton (1985, 466) says, they meet the needs of a specific group of older people and "an active effort should be made to preserve this resource."

In Winnipeg, Jack's Hotel serves as a model for how a city can maintain this kind of housing. Jack's houses forty-two older men in an enriched setting. The building sits on Winnipeg's Main Street strip in the core of the city. A group of designers, social workers, and architects formed a corporation that arranged to remodel the building. The designers left the foot-thick walls in the building and the old wooden doors on the rooms, but they built a game room, a TV lounge, laundry rooms on each floor, a restaurant, and dining room. They also hired a housekeeper as part of the staff. This person works at the front desk, sets up field trips and billiard tournaments, and helps the men with medical needs. She will call in a nurse if someone needs help, or arrange doctor's appointments for the men.

The men who stay at Jack's say they like it there. Most of them had drifted from hotel to hotel along Main Street before they moved to Jack's. Few of them stayed in one place more than a year. A study by Smith (1979) found that half of Jack's tenants had lived there more than three years, a sign that Jack's meets the needs of these men.

ment buildings encourages neighbourliness. Enriched housing offers an important alternative to people who need support but who do not need the high levels of care given in a nursing home or hospital.

This type of housing can lead to unique problems, however. For example, the average age of residents increases over time as residents age. Some buildings that began with a mixture of age groups among residents ten or fifteen years ago now house a markedly older group, whose average age is 80 or older. This may compromise the self-government that exists in these buildings (Streib, Folts, and LaGreca 1985). Enriched housing complexes could become high-rise nursing homes over time. (See Exhibit 11.7.)

Apartment housing comes in many packages. high-rise, low-rise, public, private, nonprofit, age-segregated, age-integrated, without services, or enriched with services. Older people need this variety because their needs and abilities differ. They also need tax rebates, shelter allowances, and subsidized housing so that they can freely choose the housing that best suits their needs.

Rural seniors have special needs. About 35 percent of older people in Canada live in rural settings and small towns (Hodge 1987). Joseph and Fuller (1991) say that while rural communities often have programs for young and frail older people, they lack a range of options for people who have varied needs for supports. Joseph and Fuller (1991) report that rural communities often lack housing like enriched housing for semi-independent seniors. Zimmer and Chappell (forthcoming) studied urban and rural older people in Manitoba. They found that both groups of older people valued three types of neighbourhood amenities: necessities (e.g., bank or food nearby); social interaction (e.g., friend or senior centre nearby); and life enrichment (e.g., park or library nearby). But rural older people, more often than urban older people, ranked social interaction as very important.

Hodge (1987a) says that where seniors' housing does exist, it often fails to meet design standards. Joseph and Martin-Matthews (1993) say that rural households often lack housing basics like piped water or amenities like freezers and cars.

The poorer the province, the more likely rural older people will live in poor conditions.

Hodge (1987a) studied seniors' housing blocks in nine Ontario rural communities and found that *"only two of the projects have more than 50 percent of the physical and architectural features considered desirable* for senior citizen shelter care facilities" (Hodge 1987a, 149, emphasis in the original). The best project he studied had only 60 percent of the desirable features studied. Projects lacked consistency in design, and many lacked safety features and aids to help people with their daily activities. Hodge (1987a) also found that designers had placed many of the buildings in out-of-the-way locations, making it hard for seniors to use community resources. Some of the criticisms of design and location in this study would apply to urban housing for seniors too.

Keating (1991) reviewed the literature on rural older people in Canada. She found that, compared with all older people, they tend to live in older homes, have fewer services like hot and cold running water and an indoor toilet, and face high maintenance costs. Elders on Aboriginal reserves have some of the poorest facilities. Poor housing leads to poor health and decreased life satisfaction. Keating concludes that "rural elders are ... badly served. By all objective measures, rural elders have fewer amenities in their near environments than do their urban conterparts" (Keating 1991, 47).

NEW IDEAS IN HOUSING

Garden Suites

Granny flats, or **garden suites** (their name in Canada), offer elderly parents a chance to live near, but not with, their children. This arrangement solves one of the dilemmas that some older people face as their physical abilities decline.

Connidis (1983a, 361) asked 400 older people in an Ontario community a simple question: "If circumstances were to change and you had to choose between living with a child or in a facility for seniors, which would you prefer?" She found an "overwhelming tendency to choose a facility for seniors rather than living with children" (1983a, 363). A study in Regina supports Connidis's findings. The Regina study found that "only 8% of the sample indicated that they would move in with a child if they needed 'someone to keep an eye on them' (no health care) suggesting that the majority of seniors 'draw the line' at placing this type of demand on a younger family member" (Senior Citizens' Provincial Council 1981, 47; see also Okraku 1987).

The design of modern houses may have influenced these findings. Most modern houses have only two or three bedrooms and no room for another kitchen, bedroom, or bathroom to house an aging parent. The Australian state, Victoria, started a new kind of housing for older people that overcomes the problems of modern house design. They call this alternative a granny flat. A granny flat consists of a portable modular cottage for a parent. The government arranges to move the cottage onto a son's or daughter's property, then the government connects the flat to the electricity, sewer, water, and telephone services of the house. When the older person dies or moves to a nursing home, or if the family moves, the government takes the cottage away. This allows children to care for their parents as long as they can. The Australian government set up about one thousand granny flats between 1975 and 1982 (Lazarowich and Haley 1982). By 1990 the program had three thousand units in place (Lazarowich 1990). Granny flats cost little (compared with a house), and the older person and the relatives can support one another.

Lazarowich (1986) says that almost all moves to a granny flat start with an invitation from the older person's children. When a family does agree to set up a flat, the family—parents and children—need to talk about what they expect from one another. Most older people do not want to become twenty-four-hour babysitters.

Granny flats (garden suites) may face trouble in Canada from zoning laws and neighbours' attitudes. The suites increase population density in neighbourhoods and neighbours may feel that the units will lower property values.

Corke (1986a) reports one problem with the garden suite concept. A suite in Canada costs about $42 000 installed (almost double the cost of early estimates). She describes this finding as a "price shock." But the price could come down if the idea catches on and factories produce more units.

A program in Vancouver uses duplexes and four-plexes the way garden suites are used. This

---

Exhibit 11.8

Homeless Older People

Some people fall through the cracks of the current housing and social welfare system. They move from place to place, and some of them live on the street or stay in missions or at the Salvation Army. Doolin (1986, 229) says that "the older person on the street is a multiply-disadvantaged individual," often someone who suffers from alcoholism, unemployment, and a broken family.

Men in this category can find a bed at the Salvation Army or the Harbour Light Mission, but homeless women—some of whom carry everything they own in a shopping bag—have few places to go. Almost no research exists on these women in Canada.

Schull (1981) reported on one of these women for *Today Magazine*:

Ruby, an 80 year old woman, lived for 15 years in a culvert in a Montreal park. Lucy Stofle of Auberge Transition, a shelter in Montreal, found her one day in 1976. "It started to rain," she says, "and I ran for cover under some concrete steps. I looked down and there was a dugout hole, a depression in the earth where there were some rags. The rags started to move. I just freaked! I thought, 'Oh, my god, what's that?' I saw it was an old woman. She was just wearing a couple of coats and looked like a part of the earth. She sat up, and I said hello, and she said hello, and I felt embarrassed because I was in her home. She told me she would sleep there and then she'd leave and go down to Ogilvy's department store and use their washroom and sit the rest of the day on the benches of Ste. Catherine and Crescent streets."

Source: Christiane Schull, "Bag Ladies," *Today Magazine*, 15 April 1981, 15–16.

---

program overcomes some of the zoning and building problems in cities. In the Vancouver system, an older person sells her home and uses the money to help buy a duplex that houses her and her child's family. The older person and younger family members share the taxes, repair costs, and any mortgage costs for the new property (Evans and Purdie 1985).

These new housing arrangements will lead to new social interdependencies and new challenges to family relations. What will happen if the older person's child separates from or divorces his or her spouse? Or if the child's family moves to another city? Studies of these options will have to show that they make social as well as financial sense, and trial projects can answer only some of these questions. Only longer-term studies will show whether or not garden suites can work in Canada.

Home Sharing

Blackie (1985) defines home sharing as two people sharing the bathroom, kitchen, and living rooms of a house, but each having his or her own bedroom. Such arrangements make sense because a person with a home may need help with household chores due to poor health, or someone in good health may need companionship and a lower rent. They both gain by living in a shared home. Shared homes (unlike boarding homes) make no profit.

Many models exist for home sharing. People in a shared home can hire a housekeeper and someone to cook, or they can do the housework themselves. One person can move into another's home, or two or more people can move into a new house together. People can decide on their own to move in together, or an agency can arrange a match, set up a trial stay, and then offer counselling after the home gets going (Gutman et al. 1989; Rahder and Farge 1990; Rahder, Farge, and Todres 1992).

A program in Ontario found that people shared their home for three reasons: they wanted to stay in their homes; they needed income from a sharer; or they felt lonely. The program found that people want to move into a shared home for companionship or cheaper housing, or because they have poor health (Rapelje 1985). A study of eighteen Canadian home-sharing agencies found that almost three-fifths (58.5 percent) of people who owned homes wanted to share for companionship. A third (34.5 percent) wanted to share for the income, and a quarter wanted help with maintenance or personal care (Gutman et al. 1989, cited in Rahder and Farge 1990).

Turner and Mangum (1982, cited in Blackie 1985) found that 6 percent of people who own homes and 10 percent of people who rent housing said they had an interest in shared housing, and Rapelje (1985) predicts that as many as 52 000 older people in Ontario might want to share a home.

But shared housing has some problems. First, the Ontario program found more people who want to share their homes than those who want to move into a shared home. Second, Rapelje (1985) says that most matches last less than a year (see also Pritchard 1983). Sharers rarely split over dissatisfaction with the match. They split up for a few reasons: one of the sharers may decide to move into his or her own apartment; one sharer may want to live closer to his or her family; one sharer's health may decline; or one of the pair may remarry.

Rapelje (1985) says that of sixty people in a home-sharing program only three left the program because of a bad match, and most say they would consider sharing a home again. Still, Rapelje's data show that sharers stay together only a short time, and this raises several questions. First, is home sharing worth the trouble and the cost, given the short time that matches last? Second, does the breakup of a match lead to hardship or distress for some sharers? If it does, is this a housing option worth pursuing? More research may be able to answer these questions. In the meantime, shared housing will probably appeal to some people because it will give them a housing option they can afford, the companionship they need, and an alternative to living in an institution (Blackie 1985).

Convertible Housing

Convertible housing refers to single-family housing designed so that an owner can convert the house to include an accessory apartment. An owner can also reconvert the house to single-family design at low cost. The Canada Mortgage and Housing Corporation (CMHC 1988) gives several reasons why older homeowners may choose this type of housing. First, fewer older people live in extended families. An older homeowner may have more room in a single-family house than he or she needs. Second, an accessory apartment can bring in added income at a time when an older homeowner may need the money. Third, the extra income from a renter can help a homeowner stay in his or her family neighbourhood.

The CMHC says that conversion to an accessory apartment will cost between $5000 and $20 000 depending on the home. Deconversion to a single-family home will cost between $2000 and $2500. All of the examples tested by the CMHC would produce rents that would more than cover the cost of conversion. In some cases the homeowner could pay off a conversion loan in five years. The owner would then benefit from the rent at no further cost. An accessory apartment might also make the home more attractive when the homeowner decides to sell. For example, the rent from an accessory apartment would make it easier for a younger family to qualify for a mortgage. This will help first-time home buyers. Convertible housing shows how population aging can create options to improve the lives of younger and older people.

TRANSPORTATION

A home has to suit an older person's abilities and meet his or her needs, but a house or an apartment becomes a prison if the older person cannot get to services, friends, and recreation (Bernardin-Haldemann 1982). The Ontario Advisory Council on the Physically Handicapped goes further. It says that "a community without transportation handicaps its residents. A transportation system which is not accessible or available to all residents handicaps the community" (1987, 1).

Public Transportation

Only a few studies have looked at the transportation needs and use patterns of older people in Canada. Most of these studies report that current systems fail to meet older people's needs (Joseph and Fuller 1991). The National Advisory Council on Aging (1989d) lists transportation and mobility as the third-greatest barrier to seniors' independence. A national study of older people's needs, sponsored by the Canadian Red Cross Society (1983), found that older people need better transport for shopping, making social contacts, and getting medical care. Transportation ranked as one of the top five senior needs in all provinces.

Baker and Thompson (1985) conducted a random sample study of people 55 and older in Victoria, British Columbia. Nearly 20 percent of their respondents reported that transportation was a problem for them. These studies support Havens's earlier research in Manitoba (1980). She found that for older men and women "accessibility of resources" ranked as the highest unmet need for each age cohort in the study (Havens 1980, 218–19). The National Advisory Council on Aging (1985c, 2) says that 11 percent of people aged 55 to 64 are "transportation handicapped"—either they have no public transport or they have trouble using it. This figure jumps to 34 percent for people 80 years old and over.

Rural and urban seniors have different transportation problems. Cities have services, but older people often cannot use them. A survey by the United Senior Citizens of Ontario (1985) found that 9 percent of older people had problems using public transportation. These seniors placed inconvenience first on their list of transportation problems. Rigid routes and schedules make it hard for older people in the suburbs to travel. In the winter long waits for buses, icy sidewalks, or snow mounds at bus stops keep people housebound.

Rural areas often lack public transportation (Health and Welfare Canada 1982b; Hodge 1987). Grant and Rice (1983) describe many rural seniors as "transportation disadvantaged." This group includes (1) people who feel lonely, dissatisfied, and without a confidant, (2) physically frail people over age 74 who never socialize outside their homes, and (3) low-income, widowed women without a car or someone to drive them. A study by the Senior Citizens' Provincial Council (1982) reported that 20 percent of rural seniors could not find transportation to shop in their town and 23 percent said that due to a lack of adequate transportation they had trouble getting to a larger centre once a month.

Hamilton and Brehaut (1992) interviewed women in Prince Edward Island who lived in rural settings. They complained about the lack of public transportation and about their dependence on others. One woman in a small town said, "I don't like the idea that you got to bum somebody to take you uptown now. As long as I had my eyesight I could walk. It's just down and up around the corner. But now I can't walk and in order to go to get your medications, to get your cheques cashed … you got to get somebody to take you." Another woman said, "I got no way of going anywhere. I gotta wait 'til some of the rest of them is ready to come and take me. It's too far off the main highway" (Hamilton and Brehaut (1992, 51–52). The researchers say that people who had their own transportation reported a higher quality of life.

Hodge and McKay (1992) say that very few small towns have public transportation like buses or taxis. But even seniors in towns that have a bus service seldom use it. They asked older people in five small British Columbia towns about their use of the local bus service. They found that only 22 percent of the seniors used the bus regularly and only 37 percent use it once a week or more. People in the study said the bus did not run on weekends or in the evening, it needed advance booking, and they had to wait a long time for the bus. People in these towns said they preferred a fixed bus route or a dial-a-bus option.

People in rural areas need more options. First, designers can place seniors' housing close to the downtown in small towns (Hodge 1987b). Seniors could then walk to the services and shops they need. Second, in small towns transportation programs might include volunteer-run shuttle buses or car pools for seniors. Hodge and McKay (1992) found that about a quarter of older people in towns without buses said they would consider using a taxi voucher system (where a service agency pays the taxi fare for the senior); about a fifth said they preferred a shared taxi ride, or a **mobility club** (a volunteer group where older people provide rides to other seniors). Hodge and McKay (1992) say that rural older people need more options including night and weekend bus services, volunteer drivers, and mobility clubs.

In the cities most older people do not need special transportation services; instead they need to have existing services improved. Only 9 percent of older people in 1981 either used special transportation or said they needed such services but could not get them (National Advisory Council on Aging 1985c). Ninety percent of the transportation disadvantaged said they could use services that already existed if the services changed slightly.

Suggested changes include well-lit subway stations (55 percent of seniors in Montreal say they fear using public transit at night), wider doors, easy-to-read signs, lower steps and rails, and bus stops cleared of snow and ice (National Advisory Council on Aging 1985c). These modifications would help people of all ages.

Private Transportation

Older people, like younger people, prefer auto travel to other forms of transportation (Atkinson 1991; National Advisory Council on Aging 1986b). Sixty percent of Canadians 65 and over own and drive their own cars (Statistics Canada 1984c). Canada now has over 2.5 million drivers over age 55, and the number of older drivers has increased in the past few years. In 1966, 35 percent of older people in Ontario had driver's licences, but by 1982, 50 percent had licences (National Advisory Council on Aging 1986b). In 1986, 87 percent of senior couples said they owned a car or truck. This figure dropped to 63 percent for unattached older men and 33 percent for unattached older women (National Advisory Council on Aging 1991). Still, MacDonald (1989) reports that 70 percent of people aged 55 and over have driver's licences.

A study in Saskatchewan by Grant and Rice (1983) found that 51 percent of rural older people drive themselves, 17 percent ride with another household member, and 33 percent ride with a relative or friend outside the house. A survey by the Senior Citizens' Forum of Montreal found that 33 percent of seniors said they used a car more than any other form of transportation (National Advisory Council on Aging 1985c). More older people will use cars in the future as lifelong drivers reach retirement age (Atkinson 1991).

This increase in senior drivers raises some new transportation issues. First, older people who drive will have to include the rising cost of auto insurance in their budgets. Second, older people in high-rises and downtown apartments will need parking spaces for their cars.

Third, people over age 60 have more accidents and more fatalities per distance driven than middle-aged (40-to-60-year-old) drivers (Evans 1988). Also, older drivers (aged 60+), compared with younger drivers, have more multi-vehicle accidents and stand a greater chance of a serious or fatal injury (MacDonald 1989). This has led the

Canada Safety Council to set up a program called **55 Alive** (Health and Welfare Canada 1989–90). This program helps seniors improve their driving skills and teaches them how aging affects driving. Some people have suggested special driver's licences for daytime-only drivers and non-highway driving. Charness (1993) suggests that smart cars (with automatic guidance systems), head-up instrument displays, and night vision technology make driving easier. Research needs to see whether they also reduce accidents.

The rising number of older people with Alzheimer's disease also poses problems. The Alzheimer Society of Canada (1990, cited in National Advisory Council 1993d) reports that 30 percent of people with Alzheimer's disease still drive. More than three-quarters of these drivers said they had no problem with driving. And over one-quarter of their caregivers thought they had no problem. Still, the Alzheimer Society reports that, over a five-year period, 47 percent of these drivers had an accident.

Some provinces monitor the ability of older drivers. Ontario requires that drivers aged 80 and over take written and road tests each year. Alberta requires drivers aged 75 and over to produce a medical report that says they can drive. Drivers over age 75 have to renew this medical clearance at age 80 and every two years after that. These issues point to the changing transportation needs of an aging population.

New Transportation Needs and Programs

Transportation needs for older people in the future will go beyond current use patterns. New programs may rely on technological change and on "organizational and service-related innovations" (National Advisory Council on Aging 1986b, 3). Older people will run some of these programs themselves. One program in Edmonton, referred to as a **transportation brokerage,** matches passengers with services that meet their needs. Another program described as a "mobility club" in Moncton and the Acadian peninsula helps people in small towns and rural areas. This club formed a nonprofit, self-help transport service. People with cars call in to tell a dispatcher about trips they plan to make in the next week or so. People who need rides call a day before they have to take a trip. A

Exhibit 11.9

A Typology of Transport Lifestyle Groups

A Independent, Own Auto—people with money and physical ability to drive own car and live alone; most mobile seniors. Finances and physical ability impose major limits on car use. This group may switch to other means of transportation as they age.

B Dependent, Access to Auto—people who live with others (mostly for financial reasons) with own car; less mobile.

C Independent, No Auto—have money and independence but may not be able to afford many options like car rental, taxis, or buses.

D Dependent, No Access to Auto—live with others; no auto; much less mobile.

E Sheltered or Group Housing—some phys-ical and economic dependence; can meet trans-portation needs because of group setting.

F Disabled—all income types, but these people have some physical disability and need special transit programs like those used by disabled non-seniors.

G Institutionalized—poor health; others care for needs; have the least unmet mobility needs (because the institution meets their needs).

Individuals vary in their physical ability, their income, and the support they get. Each lifestyle group has its own transportation needs. More transportation options will give all older people more freedom and independence.

Source: Adapted from Ontario Ministry of Municipal Affairs and Housing, Research and Special Projects Branch, *Towards Community Planning for an Aging Society* (Toronto: Queen's Printer for Ontario, 1983), 7. Copyright © Queen's Printer for Ontario, 1983. Reproduced with permission.

dispatcher matches riders with drivers. Drivers also volunteer for up to one emergency trip per month (Grant and Rice 1983).

Joseph and Martin-Matthews (1993) see volunteer programs as a response to decreases in government support. They see more reliance on volunteer transportation programs in the future. Some model programs already exist.

In Ottawa, for example, senior volunteers help run a bus service that takes 25 to 30 seniors grocery shopping each week. Volunteers help people on and off the bus, help them carry packages, and give people rides to other appointments during the week (National Advisory Council on Aging 1986b). Saskatchewan has set up a Rural Transportation Assistance Program (RTAP), which helps small rural communities form a local transit service. The provincial government subsidizes the cost of using a car or van to travel twice a week between these towns and a larger centre (Grant 1983). Grant and Rice (1983) say that rural communities may need to combine a number of options to serve their older people.

THE FUTURE OF HOUSING AND TRANSPORTATION

New technology will improve housing for older people and allow more people to age in place. New technologies include low-tech solutions like countertops that can move up and down to suit the user and barrier-free floor plans. More sophisticated technologies include robotic arms that respond to a user's voice. They can take food out of a cupboard, pour a drink, or put food on the table. Other countries have developed electronic homes with electric door-openers and locks, remote-control window shades, and voice-activated appliances (CMHC 1992). Some of these devices already exist in Canadian homes. They may become standard in the future.

Studies of supports for older people suggest ways to improve housing and transportation. For example, often different providers deliver housing, transportation, and social and health care services to older people. Different policies govern these systems, and they sometimes lack coordination. A number of studies suggest that seniors would benefit from an integration of these systems (Baker 1994; Brink 1994). Blandford, Chappell, and Marshall (1989) describe a program that links seniors' housing to existing community services: in this program tenant resource coordinators (TRCs) were placed in seniors' housing. The TRC provided tenants with information about community services and also coordinated services for tenants (e.g., grocery delivery or friendly visitors). The researchers found that the TRC placements led to improvements in services for seniors and increased dissemination of information about services to tenants. This type of support can help older people get the services they need at a modest cost to owners and managers.

A report titled *Freedom to Move Is Life Itself* presents a variety of proposals that would improve transportation services for older people. The proposals range from changes in technology (easier automobile entry, better bus shelters, special traffic lights) to supportive social arrangements (use of volunteer drivers, developing transportation regions with varied services in each region, conducting research on transportation needs and options) (Ontario Advisory Council on the Physically Handicapped 1987). Joseph and Fuller (1991) call for an integration of housing, service, and transportation policies to meet the needs of seniors (especially those in rural settings). This type of integration would help seniors maintain their autonomy and receive the type of support that best meets their needs.

Haldemann and Wister (1992) reviewed the literature on housing in Canada over the past thirty years. They found that government policies play a large role in creating housing options for older people. Policies range from tax relief, to rent subsidies, to support for reverse mortgages. These policies often provide support that makes it possible for rural older people to stay in "small, difficult-to-service communities" (Joseph and Martin-Matthews 1993). Public policy has tried to provide available, high-quality programs to both rural and urban older people. But cutbacks in funding could change these policies. For example, Joseph and Martin-Matthews (1993) say that cutbacks in services could leave rural older people without the support they need. Research on housing and transportation policy can track the effects of policy

changes on older people. This research would look at ways in which government policy can support housing for different older people. This would include policies targeted to help married and single, middle- and low-income, and urban and rural seniors.

CONCLUSION

People can cope with environmental demands in several ways as they age. They can maintain or improve their abilities (through self-help or rehabilitation). Or they can change their environment (by modifying their homes, moving, or getting help through changes in social policy). Most older people live in a few types of housing. Younger old people, couples, and widows tend to live in their own houses and apartments. As people age, they need more support to maintain their independence. This chapter has focused on the policies and programs in Canada that help older people live in an environment that suits their abilities. This review shows that with some help most older people can live high-quality lives in their own homes and apartments into late old age.

SUMMARY

1. Research on housing and transportation shows that older people enjoy old age most when they feel in control of their environment. People can maintain this control by changing their environment (for example, moving to an apartment from a single-family home or getting help through social policy reform).

2. A good match between a person's ability and environmental demand leads to high life satisfaction. An ideal housing system offers older people a range of housing choices because people's needs differ. People should be able to move from one type of housing to another— from a house, to an apartment, or to enriched housing—as their needs change. Or they should be able to get support to help them stay where they are.

3. Most older people want to stay in the kind of housing they now occupy. Government policies and programs—like rent subsidies, tax rebates, and repair loans—help older people stay where

they are. Other programs—like loan guarantees, new building programs, and shelter allowances—allow older people to move to the kind of housing that suits their needs.

4. Canada offers older people a wide range of housing options. These include single-family homes, apartments, enriched housing, and multi-level enriched housing. New types of housing—garden suites and share-a-home programs—will increase seniors' housing options in the future.

5. More older people than ever before, especially women, live alone. Fewer older people live with family members. People who live alone may need more formal supports to live on their own as they age. This could put more pressure on formal services in the future.

6. Both urban and rural older people value three types of amenities: necessities, social interaction, and life enrichment. Compared with urban older people, rural older people have the poorest facilities and fewest amenities available. Rural older people also ranked social interaction as very important.

7. Good transportation links older people to their community—to services, recreation, and friends. But both urban and rural transportation systems need improvement. Most older people in cities could use the transportation that exists if it were modified to suit their needs. Poor lighting in subways, snow at bus routes, and rigid schedules make urban transportation systems unsuitable for many older people.

8. Rural seniors often have no available transportation, but new programs in rural settings include bus services shared by a number of small towns, volunteer bus services, and people who pool their resources to help one another get around. Older people in rural settings have begun to set up the transportation services they need.

9. Good housing and transportation lead to increased life satisfaction for older people. An environment that fits the person's abilities helps keep older people satisfied, active, and in touch with their community.

STUDY QUESTIONS

1. Describe the ecological model of housing. When does a person feel the most comfortable according to this model?

2. Explain the current government policy regarding housing for older people in Canada. How does the government's policy differ from the ideal housing system?

3. Define the term "living arrangement." What types of living arrangements are available to older Canadians?

4. Why do many older women opt to live alone rather than with other family members? What conditions make this trend possible?

5. Explain the different types of housing that are available to older people today. What kind of people are likely to live in each type of housing?

6. What types of housing designs do seniors prefer? Why? What are the benefits of appropriately designed houses for seniors?

7. List and describe some of the new alternative types of housing that older people can choose today.

8. Describe the major transportation issues raised by an increase in senior drivers.

9. Describe two programs now available to help older people meet their transportation needs.

KEY TERMS

aging in place   the tendency for older people to live into late old age in the same place they lived in their middle years. Many older people desire this.

convertible housing   single-family housing designed so an owner can convert the house to include an accessory apartment. An older person might move into this type of apartment to live close to family members.

core housing need   people with housing that "was either inadequate or cost more than 30 percent of their income" (National Council of Welfare 1990a, 104).

ecological model   the Lawton-Nahemow model of person and environment interaction. It says that a person's ability and the demands of the environment influence the person's life satisfaction and ability to function.

enriched housing housing that provides services like meals and cleaning services to help people live on their own.

environmental press the demands of the environment on a person.

55 Alive a program that helps seniors improve their driving skills and teaches them how aging affects driving.

garden suite Canadian term for granny flat.

granny flat a small portable cottage for an older person placed in the yard of an adult child.

intimacy at a distance the desire of many older people to live near, but not with, their children.

mobility club a volunteer group of older people who provide rides to other seniors.

Residential Rehabilitation Assistance Program RRAP a program whereby the government offers loans of up to $10 000 for city dwellers and $25 000 for rural homeowners to help people improve run-down housing.

Reverse Annuity Mortgage (RAM) A type of reverse mortgage where a person buys a life annuity and gets an income while she lives in her own home. The mortgage company takes over the house when the person dies.

shelter allowances these allowances subsidize the person, not the housing project. They allow older people to choose their own apartment from those available in the marketplace.

sheltered housing a person in this type of housing gets help with meals and cleaning.

transportation brokerage this type of program matches passengers with transportation services that meet their needs.

SELECTED READINGS

Gutman, Gloria, ed. *Shelter and Care of Persons with Dementia*. Vancouver: The Gerontology Research Centre, 1992.

This collection describes a variety of programs and housing designs for people with dementia. Some of the authors describe and evaluate special-care units for dementia patients in institutions. Other authors describe innovative designs—like wandering tracks—that respond to the needs of dementia patients. Finally, a number of authors discuss ways to care for dementia patients in the community. This collection provides insights into the needs of dementia patients and provides many examples of creative responses to their needs.

Gutman, Gloria, and Norman Blackie, eds. *Innovations in Housing and Living Arrangements for Seniors*. Burnaby, B.C.: Gerontology Research Centre, Simon Fraser University, 1985.

A collection of papers presented at a 1984 symposium on housing for older people in Canada. The book includes selections by scholars, private consultants, and government policy-makers. It presents discussions of some of Canada's most creative housing programs for seniors.

Joseph, Alun E., and Anthony M. Fuller. "Towards an Integrative Perspective on the Housing, Services and Transportation Implications of Rural Aging." *Canadian Journal on Aging* 10(1991):127–48.

A review of rural housing needs and options with a focus on Ontario. The researchers present a two-tier model that calls for an integration of housing, services, and transportation. The paper then discusses policy options to meet rural seniors' needs.

Keating, Norah. *Aging in Rural Canada*. Toronto: Butterworths, 1991.

This book looks at a wide range of issues related to aging in rural settings. But it also discusses issues related to independent living as an older person in less populated places. The author takes a fresh look at issues like transportation and isolation. She says that researchers need to understand how older rural seniors view their own situation. Many of them prefer to stay in their homes and feel linked to their communities in spite of objective measures of isolation. This study calls into question negative stereotypes of aging in rural settings.

C H A P T E R

Leisure, Recreation, and Service

INTRODUCTION

Dan Kreske worked as an insurance agent until he retired six years ago. He had a good income from his investments, savings, and Canada Pension Plan. He heard about free university classes and started to attend. Now he goes to class two or three afternoons a week (depending on the courses offered). He has also renewed his interest in athletics. He played golf all through his working years, and he jogged and swam, but in retirement he found he had more time to develop his ability. In the winter of 1986 he competed at Lake Placid, New York, in the Masters Division of the North American Speed Skating Championships. He made two third- and two fourth-place finishes, and won ten points for his team. "I lost to guys twenty-five years younger than I am—it was one of the greatest thrills of my life."

Many older people like Dan Kreske continue to develop established skills and talents in retirement. Other older people discover new interests when they retire, or they discover a talent for poetry, acting, or art. Still others turn to community service, or they may start to do volunteer work in a hospital or senior centre part-time.

Seniors today have more opportunities for self-development and community service than ever before, and many of them have a great desire to develop themselves and give to others as they age. For many older people the years after retirement become a time of search, discovery, and fulfilment. This chapter will review some of the programs and activities that help seniors live a satisfying old age. This chapter will look at: (1) how seniors today spend their time, (2) new personal development programs for seniors (recreation, fitness, and education), and (3) seniors' community involvement.

WHAT DO OLDER PEOPLE DO?

Retired men and women report more free time than any other age group (Harvey, Marshall, and Frederick 1991). Older people use this time to engage in a variety of social activities including participation in political or charitable organizations, or in neighbourhood, community, and school groups. More than two-fifths of older people (over one million seniors) say they attend church weekly (Statistics Canada 1990e). But research shows that compared with younger people, they spend more of their time on solitary activities and at home (Harvey and Singleton 1989; Harvey, Marshall, and Frederick 1991). Statistics Canada's General Social Survey (Statistics Canada 1990e) found that people aged 65 and over spent about 16 percent more time on personal care (including sleep) than people aged 15 to 54.

The General Social Survey (Statistics Canada 1990e) reports that, of people who watched television, men and women aged 65 and over watched more than any other age group (see also Harvey, Marshall, and Frederick 1991). Women, in 1992, watched TV an average of 2.8 hours per day and men watched an average of 3.5 hours per day (Devereaux 1993). Statistics Canada also reports an increase in videocassette recorder ownership. In 1983 2.3 percent of people aged 65 and over owned videocassette recorders. This figure increased to 20.8 percent by 1988.

A study of seniors living in enriched housing in eastern Ontario found that 93 percent of them watched TV every day (Hodge 1984b). Some writers say that people who live alone use TV as a form of social contact (Werner 1976). McPherson (1983) says that TV helps structure time for people who live alone. An older person may watch a morning talk show over breakfast, eat supper with the evening news, and go to sleep after the national news. Some people schedule their days around the afternoon soap operas.

Older people also spend a lot of time reading. Statistics Canada (1989b) reports that over 90 percent of senior couples and about 80 percent of unattached seniors buy reading material. Kinsley and Graves (1983, cited in McPherson and Kozlik 1987) found that people aged 65 and over spent almost an hour and a half per day reading— compared with only 22 minutes for 15-to-17-year-olds and 45 minutes for 25-to-44-year-olds. All studies on leisure activities show the same trend: older people spend most of their time on passive, "receptive," media-related leisure (McPherson and Kozlik 1987; Searle 1987). They spend a lot of this time alone at home, or indoors with friends and relatives (Devereaux 1993). When older people do take part in outdoor activity, the activities usually demand little exertion (like miniature golf and spectator sports) (Strain and Chappell 1982b).

Eight out of ten older people in one study said they had visited friends or relatives in the past week; 40 percent of retired people said they saw friends or relatives more than three times a week; and 20 percent said they saw them daily (Health and Welfare Canada 1983). Chappell (1983a) found that doing something relaxing (like playing cards, walking, or talking) with someone their own age brought older people the greatest pleasure (see also Statistics Canada 1987b).

Other research supports these findings. Tenants in a seniors' housing co-op, for example, ranked talking on the telephone, visiting friends, and visiting relatives, in that order, as their three most important activities (Marmel, Sawyer, and Shell 1983). People look forward to these activities in retirement. A study of working men and women asked them what activities they thought led to a good retirement. Almost three-quarters of them rated seeing relatives and family as an important activity, and more than half rated seeing friends as important. More than three-fifths of these men and women said they expected to have more time to see relatives and friends in retirement (Health and Welfare Canada 1977b).

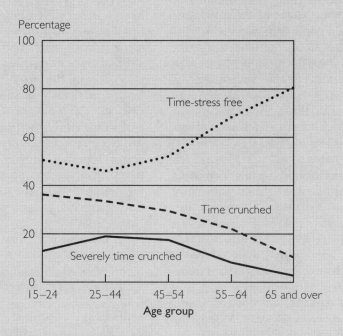

Exhibit 12.1
Percentage of Canadians Affected by Time Stress, 1992

Note that the proportion of people who feel freedom from time stress increases steadily from age 25 on. And older people report the highest rate of people feeling free of time stress. Over 86 percent of retired people report freedom from time stress. They are also the smallest proportion of people who report feeling time crunched (2.7 percent).

Source: J. Frederick, "Are You Time Crunched?" *Canadian Social Trends* (Winter 1993), 8, from Statistics Canada, 1992 General Social Survey. Reproduced by authority of the Minister of Industry, 1996, Statistics Canada.

Older people as a group show some common approaches to the use of their time. They often engage in socially satisfying, nondemanding, nonstrenuous activities. This appears to support the disengagement theory of aging. The Canada Health Survey (cited in Statistics Canada 1983a, 32), for example, said that the low level of seniors' activity was "to be expected in view of the general deterioration which is part of the aging process."

Other research questions this pessimistic conclusion. Studies show different activity preferences among different types of seniors. Income, region, and social status all influence what an older person chooses to do. People with the lowest income and those with the highest show the least interest in spectator sports (McPherson and Kozlik 1980). Those with no income and little education and those with high income and a university degree show the lowest involvement in popular culture activities (like watching TV, listening to music, going to movies, engaging in crafts, and reading newspapers). People with middle incomes and either a high-school diploma or some secondary education show the most involvement in popular culture activities. People with university degrees tend to read more books than other groups (McPherson and Kozlik 1987). "Even within the same age cohort," McPherson and Kozlik (1980, 115) say, "life chances and lifestyles vary because of differences in social status."

Other studies in Canada show that, compared with seniors in eastern Canada, those in the West report more physical activity and more involvement in sports (Curtis and McPherson 1987; McPherson and Kozlik 1987; Statistics Canada 1987b). Also, higher income and more education lead to more active leisure. Roadburg (1985) found that (middle-income) service workers took part in sports, exercise, and dancing, but (lower-income) clerical and sales workers mostly read. Mobily and his colleagues (1995) found that older people's activities varied by season. Not surprisingly, cold weather led to decreases in outdoor activities.

Studies also show that gender influences activity level. Zuzanek and Box (1988) report that women, more than men, say they take part in visiting, religious activities, reading, bingo, sewing, and shopping. Men, more than women, say they take part in sports, outdoor activity, gardening, visiting pubs, do-it-yourself projects, and auto repairs. In general, women spend their free time on expressive social activities, while men spend theirs on passive media consumption and competitive or repair-related activities (Harvey, Marshall, and Frederick 1991; Zuzanek and Box 1988). The researchers say that traditional male and female roles shape leisure activities in later life. Statistics Canada (1990, cited in Cousins and Keating 1995) reports that after age 45 only 10 percent of women compared with 30 percent of men engage in adequate leisure physical activity. "By late life," Cousins and Keating (1995, 340–41) say, "only a small minority of women are active at a health-maintaining level." Cousins (1995a, 74) refers to "the almost universal withdrawal of North American women over their lifecourse" from vigorous, health-promoting activity.

Results from the Canadian General Social Survey support this idea. Corbeil (1995) reports that at all ages men are more active than women in sports. The low participation in sports by women may reflect the fact that fewer women than men have spouses with whom to share sports activity. Studies show that married people living with their spouses have more active lifestyles (Roadburg 1985). Low participation in sports by women may also point up the lack of opportunity women have had to participate in sports in the past. In either case, the difference in activity level between men and women may disappear in the future. Longer life expectancy means that couples will live and stay active together longer. Also, fitness programs (more than sports) appeal to both sexes. Women, for example, show the same amount of participation in exercise programs as men (McPherson and Kozlik 1980).

This research shows that health, education, income, and social status all shape leisure in retirement. Also, McPherson and Kozlik (1987) say that age cohorts may develop leisure subcultures. Older cohorts today may prefer more passive leisure, while younger cohorts may live a more active old age. Each cohort will have its preferred way of spending leisure time, in part based on members' past experience. This means that future cohorts of older people will bring their own interests with them into old age. And they will probably enjoy a wide variety of leisure activities (McPherson and Kozlik 1987).

LEISURE

What theory of aging best describes leisure activity in later life? Most of the research on aging and leisure supports the continuity theory of aging. Cousins (1993) studied older women who take part in exercise programs. She found that they often report that they behaved as "tomboys" as young girls. Cousins (1995a) found that childhood encouragement in sports also led to social support for exercise in later life. Cousins and Keating (1995) show that some women remain active throughout life. They do this by choosing active alternatives at various turning points in their life cycles. McPherson (1985) says that often people keep the leisure preferences in retirement that they had in middle age (see also Searle 1987; Cutler and Hendricks 1990; Singleton et al. 1993; Corbeil 1995). People who enjoyed athletic activity, socializing, or travelling will continue to do these things when they retire (unless something like a sharp drop in health prevents them).

A study by McGuire, Dottavio, and O'Leary (1987), however, suggests that we need at least two theories to account for older people's leisure patterns: continuity theory and the life-span developmental perspective. These researchers looked at data from a nationwide recreation survey in the United States and found two patterns of leisure involvement in older adults. One pattern fits the continuity theory of aging. People who fit this pattern were called **contractors.** This group had stopped at least one outdoor activity in the past year and had not learned any new activity since age 65. A second pattern fits the life-span developmental perspective. The researchers called the people who fit this pattern **expanders.** This group had not stopped any activities in the past year and had added at least one new outdoor activity since age 65.

The study found that contractors had continued the same activities they had learned in childhood. Expanders, on the other hand, continued to add activities throughout life. The researchers could not predict group membership by the use of income, age, race, or gender, and said that leisure service providers should create many options for older adults today. At least one type of older person, the expander, will take advantage of these new opportunities.

Can people learn to make better use of their leisure time? Zuzanek and Box (1988) found that people restructure their time after retirement. They maintain some activities, but they also trade off old activities for new ones. These findings show that people can change and expand their repertoire of activities, and they can develop new interests as they age.

Searle and Mahon (1991; see also Searle et al. 1995) report on a controlled study of a leisure education program in a day hospital. The program included the development of self-awareness, leisure awareness, attitudes, decision-making, social interaction, and leisure skills. The researchers found that **leisure competence** increased with leisure education, and that self-esteem also increased with leisure education. In addition, it was found that leisure education can play a role in rehabilitation settings like day hospitals and can also help healthy people by expanding their knowledge of leisure activity choices (Verduin and McEwen 1984).

NEW ACTIVITIES IN OLD AGE

Outdoor Recreation

Leisure and recreation programs for seniors exist across the country. In Saskatchewan seniors can get free fishing licences and free access to provincial parks. British Columbia gives seniors free camping privileges and reduced rates on fishing licences. Manitoba, Saskatchewan, and Quebec schedule assisted travel tours. Nova Scotia runs fitness and recreation classes. Alberta has a recreation consulting service and promotes senior involvement in theatre. Airlines, buses, theatres, restaurants, and travel agencies across the country offer senior citizens' discounts.

Most of Canada's national parks now have wheelchair facilities, and special picnic tables and parking areas. Also, parks across Canada have programs for seniors. Riding Mountain National Park in Manitoba, for example, has "grandparent hikes" for grandparents and their grandchildren. Prince Albert National Park in Saskatchewan has a yearly seniors' golf tournament and La Mauricie National Park in Quebec has three lakes reserved for seniors. Parks in Cape Breton and Nova Scotia have special films for seniors. Riding Mountain National Park also has a program that gives older people a chance to do something for others. It offers special camping privileges to seniors if they agree to give information and help to other visitors (Hayashida 1983).

Canada's **Participaction** program promotes healthy living and outdoor activities for older people through a program called "Active Age." Active Age encourages older people to adopt healthy, active lifestyles. The program uses many of the principles of successful health promotion activity for older people. For example, it supports community programs that older people already take part in and it builds on older adults' enjoyment of social contacts.

All of these programs and services help older people stay active. Recreation planners need to keep seniors' special needs in mind when they plan programs. For example, older people may lack transportation to get to parks, concerts, or recreation sites. Many cultural events take place in the evening, when older people tend to stay at home. Also, poor design of recreation settings sometimes keeps older people out. One woman noticed that the restrooms at a historical site had been redesigned for wheelchair use, but that a person in a wheelchair would have had to climb twenty steps

Exhibit 12.2

Active Canadians, 1988*

* Participated in physical activity for three or more hours of leisure time per week during at least nine months of the year.

Note that compared with middle-aged people, older people show only a small decline in the proportion who engage in physical activity.

Source: P. Gauthier and A. Haman, "Physical Fitness," *Canadian Social Trends* (Summer 1992), 19, citing Canadian Fitness and Lifestyle Research Institute, *Campbell's Survey on Well-Being in Canada, 1988*. Reproduced by authority of the Minister of Industry, 1996, Statistics Canada.

up the side of a hill to get to them. More awareness of the needs of handicapped people (young and old) will lead to improved facilities, enabling handicapped seniors to enjoy recreational activities.

Fitness

Both the Canada Health Survey (Health and Welfare Canada and Statistics Canada 1981) and the General Social Survey (Statistics Canada 1987b) found that activity declines with age. But a closer look at the findings of the Canada Health Survey shows that decline after age 65 depends more on health than on age. Comparisons of the healthy people in each age group showed that, barring ill health, people stayed active into old age. Of the healthiest 45-to-64-year-olds, 13 percent ranked as "very active," and 18 percent as "sedentary." Of the healthiest people aged 65 and over, the same portion—13 percent—ranked as "very active." Moreover, only 15 percent ranked as "sedentary"—3 percent less than the 45-to-64-year-olds. Finally, the figures for healthy people aged 65 and over do not differ much from the total population (20 percent "very active" and 14 percent "sedentary") (Health and Welfare Canada and Statistics Canada 1981, 79–80). The Canada Health Survey (Health and Welfare Canada and Statistics Canada 1981) says that people in good health and with positive emotional well-being at all ages tend to remain very active and that this is particularly true of older people.

A study of seniors in one housing co-op found that even people with health problems try to stay active. The study found that 49 percent of the tenants had fair-to-poor health; 18 percent had heart or circulation problems; and 45 percent had arthritis and rheumatism. Twenty-eight percent of these people use wheelchairs, walkers, and canes. Still, this study found that 60 percent of these people did full or partial body exercise, and 60 percent of those who exercised did so every day (Marmel, Sawyer, and Shell 1983).

Research shows that, as a group, older people are more active today than in the past. The Canada Fitness Survey (Fitness and Amateur Sport 1982) found that the two oldest groups (55–64 years and 65+) showed the largest increases in fitness activity from 1976 to 1981. The second-oldest age group (55–64 years) doubled its participation in sports from 1976 to 1981, and the oldest group (65+)

reported nearly a three-fold increase in sports activity in those years. The oldest group showed an even more rapid increase in exercise activities. On average, able-bodied people aged 65 and over reported a 13 percent increase in exercise activity between 1976 and 1981, compared with only a 3 percent increase for able-bodied people of all ages.

Statistics Canada's 1985 Health Promotion Survey found that 51 percent of people aged 65 and over engaged in regular exercise (Rootman et al. 1988). These figures do not show whether people have become more active over time or whether newer cohorts of older people bring more active lifestyles into old age. Whatever the reason for the increase, the results are clear: able-bodied older people have a higher rate of exercise participation than all of the other groups in the study, except the 15-to-24-year-olds. (This measure excluded people with disabilities. Older people have lower rates of participation than younger groups, if the figures include people with disabilities.)

Fitness and Health

Some decline in physical function is due to true aging (for example, the slowdown in cell metabolism or decrease in lung elasticity). Research shows, for example, that aerobic capacity and peak performance decline with age even in trained athletes (Stones and Kozma 1980; Ericsson 1990). Researchers still do not know, however, how much of this decline is due to aging and how much is due to past health problems, past habits, and underuse of the body (Stones and Kozma 1982). Studies of fitness training show that exercise can slow and even reverse some of this decline (Cunningham et al. 1987; Goldberg and Hagberg 1990; Shephard 1986).

DeVries (1975), one of the first researchers to study the effects of exercise on older people, says that declines in physical function have more to do with decreased activity than with true aging (see also Goldberg and Hagberg 1990; Ericsson 1990). Kraus and Raab (1961) call this the **hypokinetic disease.** They say that the lack of activity can lead to mental and physical problems, while increases in activity can prevent or reverse these problems.

Other studies find clear signs of improvement in physical and mental well-being as a result of exercise. Spirduso and MacRae (1991) report that aerobic exercise can improve information-processing

Exhibit 12.3

What They're Buying to Get Fit

A Globe and Mail article begins, "Aging boomers are trading in their aerobic equipment for sporting goods that offer a more relaxed route to fitness." Reporter John Heinzl uses the sporting equipment people buy as a guide to their changing lifestyles. He details the trend toward activity that puts less strain on aging muscles and bones.

Getting fit used to mean breaking a sweat. But more and more aging boomers seem to be frowning upon physical exertion.

The fitness movement has shifted into slower gear, largely a reflection of the greying boomer population. And that's dramatically changing how people spend their money on sporting goods, sales figures show.

Golf—roughly equivalent to an intense round of croquet for sheer aerobic benefit—is coming on strong. In the United States, sales of golf clubs and accessories are expected to rise 7 per cent this year to more than $1.4 billion (U.S.), according to the U.S.-based National Sporting Goods Association. While the association tracks sales south of the border only, the trends are similar in Canada, industry experts say.

Camping, another leisure activity masquerading as a sport, is also attracting hordes of aging athletes who are exchanging their Rub A-535 for cans of mosquito repellant. The NSGA is projecting an 8-per-cent jump, to $1.02 billion, in sales of tents, canteens and other camping gear.

If it involves running and jumping, people just aren't doing it as much as before. Sales of aerobic wear and tennis equipment, which have been dropping faster than a topspin lob, are projected to continue their decline in 1995.

More people are gliding instead of running. David Marcus, executive vice-president of sporting retailer Forzani Group Ltd. of Calgary, says in-line skates continue to be the top-selling product across Canada.

Do you think this trend toward more relaxed leisure will continue as the baby boomers age? How would you suggest that the sporting goods and leisure industries respond to an aging population?

Source: John Heinzl, "What We're Buying," *The Globe and Mail* (July 8, 1995), B19.

speed. Aerobics can also lead to improvements in memory, intelligence, and cognitive speed (O'Brien and Vertinsky 1991; Stones and Dawe 1993). Studies by Fischer (1977) and Clarke (1977) show improvements in arterial and muscle flexibility. Cunningham et al. (1987) conducted a controlled study of a clinical training program for retired men. The researchers found significant improvements in the exercise group in maximum volume of oxygen, ventilation, and grip strength.

Shephard (1978) studied thirty-eight people in Toronto over age 65 who took an exercise program four times a week. In seven weeks these people increased aerobic power by 30 percent. After a year they had increased muscle mass and bone density,

and people in the program had lost three-quarters of their excess fat (Edwards 1983). Smith (1982), in a study of older women, found increases in bone mass due to exercise. DeVries (1975, 265) concludes from this literature that "the older organism is definitely trainable. Indeed the percentage of improvement [shown by older people who exercise] is entirely similar to that of the young."

Iso-Ahola (1993) says that an **active leisure lifestyle** does at least two things. It directly benefits health and it helps to buffer the influence of life events and illness. Other studies support this view. Brooks (1994) reports that physical activity reduces the incidence of diabetes and hypertension, and increases bone density (see also Shephard 1990). Caspersen, Powell, and Christenson (1985) note that improved fitness leads to greater endurance, agility, and speed. O'Brien and Vertinsky (1991) found that aerobics improves memory, intelligence, and cognitive speed (see also Arbuckle et al. 1994).

These benefits in turn lead to better functioning in daily life for older people. Active people even in their ninth decade, according to Diamond (1984), stayed interested in their professions and remained physically healthy. Coleman and Iso-Ahola (1993) report that leisure produces self-determination and social support that buffers stress. Iso-Ahola (1993) says that millions of people each year would avoid illness and extend their lives by adopting healthier lifestyles. This in turn might reduce medical costs. He considers prevention of sedentary lifestyles an important social issue.

Fitness and Well-Being

Fitness programs can improve the psychological well-being of older people as well as their health (Caldwell, Smith, and Weissinger 1992; Forgas and Moylan, 1987; O'Brien and Vertinsky 1991). Studies show that exercise reduces depression and at low intensity leads to feelings of exhilaration (Steptoe and Cox, 1988). Eighty percent of individuals in exercise programs report that exercise makes them feel better (Morgan and O'Connor, 1988). Blair et al. (1989) found that moderate exercise can even postpone death. Iso-Ahola (1993) reports on a variety of other psychological benefits of leisure, including happiness, self-actualization, and life satisfaction.

Active leisure also leads to increased social interaction and it allows people to maintain and develop friendships (Coleman and Iso-Ahola, 1993; Iso-Ahola 1989). Many people report that their most enjoyable leisure experiences take place with friends (Larson, Mannell, and Zuzanek, 1986). Social interaction during leisure can serve as an important resource for older people, especially widowed and single seniors. Other fitness programs show similar results. Perri and Templer (1984–85) report that older people in an exercise program improved their self-concept and felt more mastery over their environment.

Mittelman et al. (1989) found similar results in a study of thirty-three seniors who bicycled from Victoria, British Columbia, to St. John's, Newfoundland, in the summer of 1983. The group bicycled six days a week, averaging about 90 km per seven-hour day, and made the trip in one hundred days. The researchers studied the seniors at three points: before they started, at the midpoint of the trip, and two days before the end of the tour. (Eleven seniors dropped out during the tour.) The seniors filled out questionnaires that asked about their background (age, marital status, etc.), health, exercise habits, expectations for the trip, their psychosocial condition, and anxiety. The researchers also gathered data on the seniors' physical condition (weight, height, etc.), strength, heart rate, blood pressure, blood chemistry, and food intake.

The study found that the seniors increased their flexibility during the tour, showed improved cardiovascular response to work, and had blood samples that suggested bone-mineral turnover (a sign of bone mass growth or maintenance). Eighty-five percent of the seniors rated the tour as enjoyable or extremely enjoyable. About a quarter of the group reported that they felt stronger and felt increased well-being. Members also reported increased self-confidence, better fitness, and a sense of accomplishment. The researchers conclude that "bicycle touring has a generally positive effect on the initially fit senior citizen" (Mittelman et al. 1989, 154).

Even in institutions, exercise programs can improve participants' sense of well-being. People in an activity program in a nursing home reported that they felt better, slept better, and did more of their own personal care (LaRocque and Campagna 1983). Studies also show that exercise leads to improved social life and increased happiness (Stacey, Kozma, and Stones 1985; Myers and Hamilton 1985). "This finding alone," Stacey, Kozma, and Stones (1985, 73) say, "provides sufficient justification for enrolling in an exercise program."

The Challenge to Fitness Programs

All fitness programs for older people face two hurdles: getting older people involved and keeping them involved (Myers and Gonda 1986). A Canadian study of physical activity found that the proportion of people who say they never exercise jumps from 19 percent of people under age 55 to

36 percent of people aged 55 and over (Statistics Canada 1987b). The Canada Fitness Survey, for example, found that people aged 65 and over, more than any other group, said they did not want to increase their present level of activity. And, more than any other group, they said that nothing would get them to increase their activity (Fitness and Amateur Sport 1982).

A report by the Red Cross confirms that most seniors today will not join fitness programs. The report also says that seniors avoid fitness classes because they have not done much of this kind of group exercise in the past (Canadian Red Cross Society 1983). The continuity theory of aging supports this view. It says that in old age people will tend to do the things they have always done or try to find substitutes for these activities. This, in part, explains the lower participation rates of women in physical activities. O'Brien and Vertinsky (1991) say that women take part in physical activity to a lesser degree than men from adolescence on (see also Gauthier and Haman 1992). Women also avoid exercise and exertion. The stereotyping that labelled exercise and sport as male activities in the past helps explain this decrease in female physical activity with age. Other factors that lead to decreased activity for women in old age include: arthritis, chronic heart disease, caregiving demands, cost, and fears about injury.

Gutman, Herbert, and Brown (1977) found that half the people in their exercise study had dropped out by the end of the program. Cape (1983) also reported problems with attendance. She ran a fitness program in a nursing home and found that people dropped out, missed classes, or joined in the middle of the program. Mittelman et al. (1989) found that one-third of the seniors in the cross-country bicycle tour already mentioned dropped out before the end. Six of the eleven seniors who left the tour did so because of conflict with the tour leader. Only one senior left the tour because of the workload. Stacey, Kozma, and Stones (1985) report that the people who drop out may need the programs most. They say that older, less happy, and more anxious people tend to drop out of programs.

Leaders also need to choose programs that fit seniors' approach to exercise. Research shows that the best training program consists of high-intensity and high-frequency exercise (Sidney and Shephard 1978). But seniors tend to drop out of this type of program. Myers and Gonda (1986, 177) say that most seniors can improve their physical condition with a less strenuous exercise program. "Walking, dancing or swimming can also be used to enhance aerobic capacity," they say, "and may be more appropriate for older adults than such activities as jogging-running, skating or cross-country skiing." Less strenuous programs fit the needs of more seniors today and they encourage people to attend more often.

Cousins and Burgess (1992) describe a number of ways to attract sedentary seniors to activity programs.

First, they say, program leaders must minimize risk. Shephard (1990) presents a good discussion of the physical risk that exercise poses for people in their 70s and older. This includes injury, extreme fatigue, and in some cases, sudden death. But programs also present a psychological risk. Psychological risk includes fear of embarrassment, ridicule, and failure. People may fail to meet their own or others' expectations. This can even be true of former athletes, who set unrealistic goals for themselves.

A program should allow people to take risk without fear of ridicule or failure. Billie Lucas has worked as an aerobics instructor with seniors for over 20 years. Her program has grown every year and now has over 300 participants. Lucas traces the success of her program to the sense of safety that participants feel. Lucas studies her people carefully. She listens to them, watches how they perform, and builds the program to suit their needs.

Lucas's program has no music, no competition, and no failures. People attend with walkers and canes if they need to. "Each person keeps their own time," she says. "I try out the exercises on me first. Over the years I've learned how fast to go and what's dangerous." "It's amazing," she says, "what people can do if the pace is right for their age."

Second, program leaders must be aware of diversity. Older people vary in their health, ability, and consistency. McPherson and Kozlik (1987) found that seniors' involvement in activities differed by income, education, and region. "Even within the same age cohort," they write (McPherson and Kozlik 1980), "life chances and lifestyles vary because of differences in social status." O'Brien and Vertinsky (1991) say that women take part in physical activity to a lesser degree than men from adolescence on. These researchers and others report that health problems, caregiving demands, fear of too much exertion, and fear of injury also keep women from participation in physical activity (Branigan and Cousins 1995).

Professionals who work with older people need to listen to program members. Good communication between a program leader and participants creates the most successful program. Professionals can then set individual goals for clients, with realistic expectations. Recall that education, income, gender, and personal background influence people's knowledge about exercise and their attitude toward it. Older people need varied types of programs to suit their varied needs. High-intensity and high-frequency exercise, for example, may produce the best training. But many seniors drop out of this kind of program. Myers and Gonda (1986) say that walking or swimming may serve older people better than jogging or running. Programs that allow people to participate at their own pace will fit the needs of more older people and will encourage them to attend more often.

Older people also need to play an active role in planning, assessing, and developing activity programs. This builds commitment to the program and leads to ongoing participation. Waldron and Moore (1991) say that older people often take part in physical activities in order to be with others and for self-actualization. Leaders need to ask seniors about their goals and design programs to meet these goals. Older peoples' goals will often differ from those of younger people in exercise, fitness, or sport programs.

Third, program leaders must make programs enjoyable and rewarding. Bocksnick and Hall (1994) studied recreation programs in six nursing homes. They found that half the residents who took part in the programs felt that they merely filled and killed time. Residents also said they felt pressure to take part in activities. Program leaders had a more positive view of the programs. Leaders need to keep in close touch with what members define as an enjoyable and rewarding program. Shephard (1986), for example, reports that as many as one-half of participants quit exercise classes in the first six months. Older people need to play an active role in planning, assessing, and developing activity programs. This builds commitment to the program and leads to ongoing participation (see Losier, Bourque, and Vallerand 1993).

Waldron and Moore (1991) say that older people often take part in physical activities in order to be with others and for self-actualization. Leaders need to ask seniors about their goals and design programs to meet these goals. Older peoples' goals will often differ from those of younger people in exercise, fitness, or sport programs.

Programs should give people a chance to socialize before and after classes (Stewart 1982; Stirling et al. 1986). Leaders of these programs need to support and encourage participation (O'Brien and Vertinsky 1991; O'Brien 1995). Again, Billie Lucas gives some sage advice. She gives people permission to enjoy themselves during their workout. Her program involves gym exercises followed by a swim in the pool, with lots of time to kibbitz and schmooze. "You want a political discussion," she once told me, "you'll find it in the sauna."

"During the program," she says, "people just talk, and talk, and talk. Sometimes the noise is terrific." "That," she says, "has got a lot to do with the program's success."

SENIOR CENTRES

Most cities and towns across Canada have senior centres. They form the closest thing to a nationwide recreation system for older people. People drop in to their local centre, meet other seniors, play cards, take classes, and in some cases get medical help.

The number of centres in Canada grew considerably from the early 1970s to the 1980s. In Saskatchewan, for example, the number of centres in the province grew from 3 in 1971 to 412 in 1983. Today seniors go to centres to socialize, take part in recreation, or get information (Ouellette 1986). In small communities the centres sometimes offer the only opportunity for social contact. Some centres offer social and health care services as well as recreation. The Regina Native Elders Incorporated runs a centre that offers meals-on-wheels, crafts, and health checkups. Other Aboriginal people's centres offer help with letter writing, filling out forms, and transportation to activities. Almost all activity centres in Saskatchewan belong to the Saskatchewan Seniors Association Incorporated (SSAI). This group promotes new programs and helps centres share

Exhibit 12.4

Charlie Pike

When he was 12 years old, Charlie Pike developed a heart condition that twice nearly killed him. In his early 20s, he tried to buy life insurance but the companies he approached said he was an unacceptable risk. Now, at 79, Pike is a downhill skier and distance swimmer who works out regularly and last summer took up rollerblading to help him stay in shape. He also sells insurance. "Life," says Charle, "is full of surprises."

Pike owns Pike-Vezina Assurance and usually puts in a five-day week at his Boulevard René-Lévesque office in downtown Montreal. Three mornings a week, he alternates gym work with swimming, and most weekends he skis. He has a Montreal Amateur Athletic Association award for swimming 50 miles in the MAA pool during a recent winter. "I used to do 44 to 66 lengths but now I'm doing a little less," says Pike. Last March at B.C.'s Whistler resort, he won a gold medal in a seniors' alpine ski competition, negotiating the 46 gates in a mile-long slalom in 1:25. Then, in November at Alberta's Lake Louise, he finished three seconds behind 38-year-old former Olympic skier Ken Read in a 2000-foot downhill race. "You want to get down there fast enough that all winter no one will beat you in your own age group," says Pike. "That's just sheer ego."

It is also, perhaps more importantly, a reflection of his all-or-nothing challenge to the aging process. "Whenever I feel I've got too much to do, the pressure's too great at the office, I immediately start exercising," says Pike, married with no children. "Your attitude has become old when you say, 'I'm not going to do this or that because it's too much for me.' If you're starting to think that way, then you're really going to age." But fewer over-60s are falling victim to traditional thinking, Pike says. "I do think that a lot of people now believe they are 12 to 15 years younger than their chronological age."

Source: R. Corelli, "Over What Hill?" *Maclean's* (January 10, 1994), 32. Reprinted with permission.

information. The SSAI has over 20 000 members, making it one of the largest organizations of seniors in the country (Senior Citizens' Provincial Council 1983).

In Winnipeg, a nonprofit agency called Age and Opportunity, Inc. (A & O), runs a system of full-service centres. These centres meet the strict standards set by the National Institute of Senior Centres in the United States. A & O centres offer programs like bingo, billiards, and folk dancing, but they also offer members financial and personal counselling and health care. The staff and the members of A & O centres share the work. While the staff ensure that the centres have programs like counselling, education, and health clinics, the members decide on recreation programs, fundraising, and centre maintenance (Age and Opportunity, Inc. 1983). Each centre has a unique program that reflects members' interests and needs. At one centre classes might include English as a second language, at another conversational French. Centres also offer lunch and supper.

In 1990, A & O provided more than 183 000 units of service to older people (Age and Opportunity, Inc. 1990). These units included thousands of meals served at six centres, responses to requests for information, leadership training, and health information (Age and Opportunity, Inc. 1990). Seniors at A & O centres also give to their communities. Members plan programs and help prepare meals, sing in centre choirs, and visit local schools to perform for the students.

Ferraro and Cobb (1987) in the United States found support for two models of senior centre membership: the social agency model and the voluntary organization model. They found that older people in poor health use the centre as a social agency. They attend for lunches and for health

Exhibit 12.5

Hanging around the Mall

Some older people choose not to join a senior centre or other organized group. Researchers Sijpkes, MacLean, and Brown (1983; see also Graham, Graham, and MacLean 1991) of McGill University studied older people who spend their days at the Complexe Desjardins mall in Montreal. They found that many older people use the mall as a drop-in centre. Here they describe a typical case:

An old man who lives in a twenty dollar a week room on Sherbrooke Street in Montreal leaves his room at eleven in the morning of a cold windy day. The streets are treacherously slippery. He carefully negotiates the two blocks to the Jeanne Mance entrance of the subway system. There he takes the escalator down to begin a long subterranean walk, occasionally enlightened by a glimpse of the outdoors, past the metro station, through the Place des Arts complex; he nips under Ste. Catherine Street to finally end up in the main space of Complexe Desjardins. By now he is quite warmed up from his cold outside walk, and he sits down on one of the many benches in the space, talks to some of the older people he knows, reads a newspaper which one of them has bequeathed him, and carefully smokes a cigarette.

Around noon he wanders over to the very centre of the space where he stands for a while watching the daily production of a live TV show for a French local channel. He splurges on a coffee which is available from a variety of little shops in the complex. On his way home he talks to some more people he knows and winds his way back through the underground system.

Source: Excerpted from Peter Sijpkes, Michael MacLean, and David Brown, "Hanging around the Mall," *Recreation Canada*, February 1983, 44–46. Used with the permission of Canadian Parks/Recreation Association.

maintenance services. Married seniors with high life satisfaction and who live with a spouse use the centre as a voluntary organization or social club.

This finding highlights the challenge that neighbourhood centres face from other recreational programs. In 1982 the federal government called senior centres "the most important source of recreation and cultural activity" for older people in Canada (Health and Welfare Canada 1982b). And the Canadian Red Cross Society (1983) found that seniors used senior clubs more than any other recreation service. But today, many young-old seniors see senior centres as one recreational option among many. Figures suggest that the use of senior centres may decrease in the future. Statistics Canada (1987b) reports that only about a quarter of people aged 65 and over said they had attended a senior club or meeting in the past month.

Education programs at universities and colleges, for example, now attract many seniors who might once have been satisfied with the programs at a senior centre. Also, more mobile, younger seniors may prefer to attend an art gallery or fitness program across town that better meets their needs. This will leave less-well, less-mobile older people to use neighbourhood centres. These people take a less active role in leadership and tend to use the centres over a shorter time. A concentration of less healthy seniors in the neighbourhood centre of the future will move centres more toward the social agency model.

Ouellette (1986) studied the recreation preferences of French and English senior citizens' club members in New Brunswick. The findings from this study suggest that Canadian senior centres need to take into account members' sociodemographic and ethnic background. Ouellette (1986) found that marital status, gender, and ethnicity all influence leisure enjoyment and participation. The French-Canadian women in this study, for example, said they enjoyed spiritual activities more than physical ones, while the English-Canadian men said they enjoyed mass media activities more and spiritual activities less. Ouellette (1986) traces the difference in spiritual interest to gender, but also to traditional cultural differences between the French and English. Ouellette says that leisure education and counselling need to take gender and ethnicity into account. He concludes (1986, 226) that "there is some justification to develop and offer programs or services that would differ in orientation and/or content" for particular ethnic groups. Senior centres will need to take ethnicity into account as they alter their programs to fit the needs of a changing older population.

EDUCATION

Most schools today serve the same basic function they did a century and a half ago, when they first began: teaching children to become adults and preparing young people for specific jobs in society (Macleod 1985). This system offers little to the older person, who is already an adult and retired from a job. Statistics Canada says that in 1981 fewer than 1 percent of men and women aged 65 and over enrolled in credit courses. A Statistics Canada (1989b) study found that 9 percent of couples aged 65 and over said they spent some money on education. The study gave no figures for unattached seniors because so few of them reported spending anything on education.

Of seniors who went to school, 70 percent went part-time (Health and Welfare Canada 1983). Devereaux reports that 4 percent of people aged 65 and over take part in formal education (not necessarily for credit). This contrasts with 10 to 29 percent in other age groups (Devereaux 1985). Devereaux (1985) says that, of the people aged 65 and over who enrolled in adult education courses, more than three-quarters of men and over 90 percent of women took hobby courses (e.g., woodworking, painting, cooking) or personal development courses (e.g., history, music appreciation).

More recent results from the Winnipeg Area Study (WAS) support Devereaux's findings. In 1992, the study found that more than half of adults under age 50 had enrolled in classes since 1988, compared with less than one-third of adults aged 50 and over. Of those who took classes, nearly three-quarters of adults under age 50 reported taking classes to improve their careers. But less than 40 percent of adults over age 50 said they took career-related classes. People aged 50 and over showed the greatest tendency of any adult group to enrol in hobby or interest courses (Novak and Percival 1993). People aged 50 and over also showed the greatest tendency to take a course or workshop, rather than a degree or diploma program.

These findings support the theory that older people have less interest in credentials than younger learners. They want shorter, more focused programs. Also, older people most often take education programs for personal growth rather than career development (see also Lansley 1991; Raushi 1989). Chené (1994) studied the meaning of learning in later life through interviews with 55 older people in Quebec. These people came from seven learning contexts including a senior centre, a dance course, and a volunteer training program. Older learners emphasized the family spirit, friendship, and sense of belonging that they got through their learning group. One group member said, "It is a group where one comes regularly. There is a spirit of ... almost a family spirit. You know, we get to know each other, and I like it very much." Another member says that classes give her a purpose in life. "When you wake up in the morning, you say to yourself: 'Oh good, this morning we have a class' ... because our children are all gone, and life is sometimes very empty" (Chené 1994, 770-71). Chené's work shows that older people value the social contacts as well as the knowledge that comes from learning in later life.

The school system, with its emphasis on testing, grading, and credentials, does not appeal to most older learners. Standard theories of aging, like disengagement theory and activity theory, cannot explain older adults' interest in education (Covey 1983). The growth of education programs for seniors today shows that seniors stay engaged. Some older people enrol in formal university and college classes, but many more older people engage in less formal kinds of education, like programs at senior centres and community clubs.

Exhibit 12.6

Illiteracy among the Older Population

Statistics Canada conducted a Survey of Literacy Skills Used in Daily Activities in October 1989. The study included a representative sample of 9500 people aged 16 to 69. The study defined literacy as the skill needed to use print material normally found at work, at home, or in the community. Most Canadian adults, the study found, read well enough to allow them to carry on their daily activities. But nearly 2.7 million adults, or 15 percent of Canadians aged 16 to 69 had trouble reading most of the written material in their environment.

Compared with other age groups, people aged 55 to 69 had the lowest proportion of people with adequate reading skills. Only 36 percent of this older group could meet everyday reading needs. But 63 percent of people aged 35 to 54 could meet these needs, as could 71 percent of people aged 16 to 24 (Statistics Canada 1989c; Normand 1995).

These figures may reflect differences in educational background for the different age groups. The study found, for example, that people with the lowest education had the least reading skills. Other studies (Creative Research Group 1987, cited in One Voice 1989) report that poorer people, francophones, and male seniors all have higher-than-average illiteracy rates. Also, illiteracy varies by region: for example, 28 percent of people 55 and over in British Columbia are illiterate while 50 percent of this age group in the Atlantic provinces are illiterate.

The study showed that a large proportion of seniors today (and in the next few decades) will have problems with everyday reading tasks. Jean Woodsworth, President of One Voice, a seniors' advocacy association, says that people need to be able to "read the directions on a bottle of medicine or tell the difference between a can of cooking oil spray and oven cleaner at the grocery store. People who need community support services have to be able to use a telephone book, at the very least" (One Voice 1990b, 1). An older person may lose social supporters as she ages. If, in the past, friends and relatives did the reading for the older person, the older person may now find herself at risk.

A report of the first national conference on seniors' literacy (One Voice 1990a) says that literacy programs for seniors get low funding priority. The report also calls for more research on the types of literacy programs that work best with seniors. Programs for immigrant seniors, for example, require sensitivity to cultural differences. One Voice used the results of this conference to produce a National Literacy Strategy for Older Canadians (Aitkens 1991). The strategy focuses on public awareness, promoting literacy programs for older people, a commitment to lifelong learning, and improved support systems for older people with low literacy (Aitkens 1990).

Few seniors take up middle-aged types of education that lead to degrees and credentials as activity theory says they should (National Advisory Council on Aging 1990e).

Continuity theory gives one explanation for older people's choice of education; it says that a lifetime of experiences leads a person to certain choices in later life. For example, people with many years of formal schooling will tend to return to school in old age. Also, people who have enjoyed learning as a form of leisure will opt for this type of learning experience. This fits with some of the facts about aging and education today. For example,

older people with higher levels of education tend to return to school. But continuity theory cannot account for the older person who attends university for the first time in retirement, or for the person who takes up a new interest in theatre, film, or music in later life.

The life-span developmental perspective offers another reason older people keep learning. This perspective says that growth and change take place at every stage of life, and that people grow and change in many dimensions. For example, a person may have severe arthritis that keeps him housebound. But he can still learn and grow intellectually. The life-span developmental perspective emphasizes the uniqueness of later adult life stages and the need for a flexible educational system to serve older people. This perspective fits with current theories of lifelong learning. Adult educators (Kidd 1973) say that older learners' needs differ from younger learners. Older learners most often come back to school for personal development and to find meaning in later life. Older learners ask: Is the knowledge useful? Does it help me make better sense of my life and the world around me? Does it help me live more fully and enjoy my life more?

Schools will have to change their ideas about education and educational settings to meet the older student's needs. Myles and Boyd (1982, 271), for example, describe what an older person faces when he or she walks onto a university campus today.

> Mrs. Smith arrives … and finds classes dispersed over a large campus with limited facilities for getting around. The principles of credentialism which lead to the organization of academic activity around exams and the accumulation of credits are of little relevance to her. When she attempts to relax in a recreation area she is subjected to loud music which she finds noxious. … In effect, what Mrs. Smith is encountering is a social institution designed and organized for the young.

To meet the needs of older learners like Mrs. Smith, universities will have to give older students more options about class times, subject choices, and testing methods. They will also have to increase the kinds of social supports—like counselling or pre-registration assistance—that they give to older students. Some of these changes have begun, and others will take place as more older people come back to school.

Universities, for example, have begun to adapt their programs to older learners. Many offer free tuition and special classes for seniors. They give library cards to seniors and involve them in the planning and design of senior education programs. Teachers learn that they need to change their teaching style to fit older students' learning styles. Studies on learning and memory, for example, show that older people take more time to learn something new, and that anxiety, fatigue, and a lack

of practice at school tasks make it harder for older people to succeed. Also, older people will drop out of a program if they cannot link what they learn to what they already know. Instructors need to take more time to present material, allow time for students to ask questions or state their views, and match the pace of their instruction to students' abilities.

The use of appropriate teaching methods along with more flexible schedules and open enrolment will encourage more older students to take secondary or postsecondary courses. A number of universities have started special programs for seniors.

The University of Moncton in New Brunswick and the Université de Sherbrooke in Quebec, for example, each support a program for francophone seniors called **Université du Troisième Age (U3A).** Each U3A group arranges to set up its own programs with the help of a university. Programs often include access to normal university classes, study groups, study trips, and fitness programs. Courses most often focus on the arts, social issues, and the humanities (Radcliffe 1982). A group at Glendon College in Toronto, called Third Age Learning Associates, helps older people across the country set up third-age learning groups (National Advisory Council on Aging 1989b; see also Chené and Fleury 1992).

Distance education methods also open education to older people. Ryerson Polytechnical University offers courses by radio through its Open College. The director of the program says that people aged 65 and over make up between 10 and 20 percent of students in the courses (National Advisory Council on Aging 1989b). Other innovative delivery methods, like homebound learning, will increase educational opportunities for older people.

In the future more older people will probably return to school, and lifelong learning will become a part of Canadian society. Moody (1988a) gives several reasons for this increase in lifelong learning. First, schools show a greater concern for the older student today. They offer more flexible schedules, advice on courses, and in some cases special orientation programs for mature students (Thacker and Novak 1991). Second, career changes and new demands at work lead people to return to school. Almost three-quarters of men and half of women (of all ages) in the labour force take

Exhibit 12.7

Homebound Learning

Education programs have begun to attract more older people. Most take place in schools or in other community centres. But what about the homebound senior? Frail older people, people with disabilities, or people who must stay in because of bad weather—all of these people miss the chance to take part in community-based education programs.

A program in Winnipeg called Homebound Learning Opportunities (HLO), sponsored by Creative Retirement Manitoba, meets the needs of homebound seniors. The program serves people aged 50 and over. Participants range in age from 50 to 94. People have a variety of educational backgrounds and health problems. A facilitator visits a senior at home to offer a course once a week for four to eight weeks. The program also serves groups in hospitals and personal care homes (Penning and Wasyliw 1992).

In one case, for example, a woman had always wanted to learn to paint. But she had a continuous oxygen feed, and others told her that paint fumes would interfere with her breathing. A Homebound Learning consultant suggested the use of acrylic paints and then arranged for her to take a painting course (Kelly 1987). In another case, a woman said she'd always wanted to learn to tap dance. But she now had arthritis in her legs and could barely stand. Could Homebound Learning help? The program arranged for another senior, a dance instructor, to visit this woman. The instructor arranged for the woman to learn tap dancing while sitting on a kitchen stool.

The program began in 1988 with $35 000 from a local foundation. Creative Retirement Manitoba, a nonprofit seniors learning organization started the program. By 1989 a program review found that 232 people took part in 151 individual or group courses for a total of 1334 class hours. In addition, 27 people subscribed to an audio-visual lending library and 70 people took part in an eight-part educational sampler series. By 1992 the program offered a schedule of 125 topics for one-to-one or group learning. Nearly 600 people took advantage of this program.

The program also expanded to include an audio and video library, peer counselling, and televised classes through a local public access station. The most popular individual courses included portable computer operation, a distinguished lecturer series, and armchair fitness exercise. The most popular group topics included armchair fitness, Tai Chi, and acrylic painting (Penning and Wasyliw 1992). In 1992, Creative Retirement offered its "first computer programming course to an 80 year old post-stroke shut-in" (Creative Retirement 1992, 5). The oldest computer student that year was 84 years old. In 1994 the program offered its first course on how to use the Internet. "Shut-ins," a flyer for the program says, "can use their computer or ours to learn how to access a local, national, or international computer 'community' from the comfort of their own home." The program opens a window on the world to people otherwise cut off from their community.

Do people enjoy the program? Reports from students show that they do (Homebound 1989). A husband and wife, for example, began guitar lessons through the HLO program. "We played our first duet the other day," they say. "We hugged each other and laughed, feeling grateful for the opportunity to learn to play guitar at our age. [I have] even practised as much as 3 hours a day on my guitar since starting this course."

Another participant says that he's gained benefits from his relaxation training course. "My wife even listens in on my course and has learned from it. It's doing me good. I think it's a great thing for homebound seniors. It was a God-send for me because I can't get out much anymore. I hope this program stays around."

A guest-home owner says that "the frail residents in our facility definitely show a difference as a result of participation in armchair fitness classes … Residents are clearly more talkative and cheerful both during and after these classes. Residents in particular appreciate being led by a facilitator who is an older adult herself. If she can do it, they feel they should be able to."

(continued)

Exhibit 12.7 (cont.)

Homebound Learning

This program shows that people want to learn throughout life, even if they have a physical problem. It also shows that in an aging society educational programs need greater flexibility than ever before. Kelly, Steinkamp, and Kelly (1987) say that the types of leisure activities people need will change with age. They found that as people age, many social and leisure activities decline. But social and home-based activities show little decline and in some cases an increase. These activities lead to the highest subjective well-being. A homebound learning program fits the social and home-based preferences of many older people. As the older population ages, this type of program will grow in importance.

job-related or academic education programs (Devereaux 1985). Third, studies show that people with more education tend to keep taking classes (both academic and recreational) as they age (Vigoda, Crawford, and Hirdes 1985; Denton, Pineo, and Spencer 1988).

Already, more people go to school for more years than ever before. Statistics Canada says that in 1991 26 percent of people aged 65 and over had some education beyond high school. Five percent of this group have a B.A. or more. But younger age groups have more education. For example, 51 percent of people age 15 to 64 reported schooling beyond a high-school diploma (Norland 1994). And 12 percent of this group have a B.A. or more. Cyr and Schnore (1982) project a 15 percent increase between 1971 and 2011 in young-old men (65–74 years) with postsecondary education and an 8 percent increase in young-old women with post-secondary education. Denton, Pineo, and Spencer (1988) make a similar projection. They estimate that the increase in the number of older Canadians, along with an increase in educational level for older people, will lead to over 200 000 older people enrolled in courses in the year 2010. This will mean a 141 percent increase over 1985 course enrolments. This increase in older students will reshape the philosophies and structures of our educational institutions.

Educational Alte rnatives
Elderhostel

As more older people continue their education, new educational programs will emerge to meet their needs. The **Elderhostel** program serves as an example of educational innovation for seniors (see Exhibit 12.8). About three hundred universities, colleges, conference centres, and research institutes in Canada (at least one in each province, Yukon, and the Northwest Territories) will sponsor Elderhostel programs on their campuses for about 20 000 people in 1996 (Elderhostel 1996). Elderhostel combines university campus life with the European concept of hostelling (travelling from place to place and staying in inexpensive, safe lodgings). Elderhostel students live on a university campus while they take courses. The program also offers "homestay programs," in which students live with a host family. These programs give hostellers a chance to travel, meet new people, and learn things in a variety of settings they might not otherwise see.

The Elderhostel program in Canada accepts students "who have retired or are planning retirement. Participants are normally in their mid-fifties and beyond" (Elderhostel 1996, 2). It does not matter how much education a person has had in the past. Most programs last one week—from Sunday afternoon until the following Saturday morning. A one-week program typically includes three courses. Elderhostel tries to keep the class size small: most programs enrol from thirty-five to forty-five students at a time. In 1996 the typical total fee for the week—including food, rooms, course fees, and fees for extracurricular tours and activities—was $400 in Canada. Fourteen percent of every course fee goes toward administration of the Elderhostel program and toward "Hostelships" (or bursaries) to assist people who cannot afford the program fee.

Exhibit 12.8

Elderhostel

A few excerpts from the Spring 1996 Canadian Elderhostel Catalogue (Elderhostel 1996) will give you some idea why this program has grown so fast:

- The Black Cat Guest Ranch in the Canadian Rockies offers home cooked meals, hiking trails, and hot tubs. The program offers three courses: Natural History of Maligne Canyon (a hike along the canyon ridge with a guide will explore the geology and ecology of the canyon); Raku—Traditional Japanese Pottery (a chance to work in clay and use the ancient raku technique of outdoor firing); Water-Works (a water colour painting course on location in the Rocky Mountains).

- St. Paul's United College at the University of Waterloo sits in the heart of the Amish country of Ontario. The program includes three courses: Experiencing Total Wellness of Mind, Spirit and Body (a course that teaches techniques of spiritual, emotional, mental and physical health); Writing Your Story: Self-Discovery and Legacy (learn to discover and write your own story through journaling); Images of the Holy (a look at how great art, music, and religion has expressed the concept of the Holy).

- The Missisquoi Centre for the Arts is in the village of Glen Sutton, Quebec. Elderhostellers stay in restored 19th-century homes with fireplaces, antiques, and gourmet cuisine. The Centre offers several programs in the Spring of 1996. Courses include: The Great Chefs of Sutton (professional chefs prepare and give the secrets of a special meal that they prepare each day); Run Away to the Circus (learn clowning, tight-rope walking, juggling, and magic); Short Takes on Quebec (a series of discussions on Quebec culture, politics, history, and architecture).

- Mount Saint Vincent University overlooks Halifax's inner harbor. The University has a fitness trail and 75 wooded acres. Courses include: Five Days Before the Mast (a history of sailing ships and personal experience on varied ships from a square-rigger to a modern container ship); Nova Scotia Music (local legends in music presented by a master folklorist); Researching Herman Melville (two professors describe their research into the life of *Moby Dick*'s author).

This selection of programs from across the country gives a glimpse of the options Elderhostellers can choose. Each institution has its own character and history. Elderhostel also offers international programs to England, Indonesia, Hungary, and many other countries. These programs cost more than those in Canada and often require good physical condition. Elderhostel students can choose the courses and the ambiance that suit their interests.

Source: Adapted with the permission of Elderhostel Canada, 1996.

Elderhostel began in 1975 and now offers courses worldwide to over 350 000 people at 2500 institutions in over 60 countries, including Mexico, Bermuda, England, France, the Netherlands, the United States, and Canada (Elderhostel 1996). The University of New Brunswick offered the first course in 1980, and Canadian programs have expanded quickly. From 1980 to 1981 the number of participants in Ontario more than doubled, and in the Maritimes the number of programs grew from one program in 1980 to programs in all four provinces by 1981 (Elderhostel 1981). In 1987, Elderhostel sponsored programs at twenty-one sites in the Maritime provinces (Elderhostel 1987).

Exhibit 12.9

Profile

Older people can provide valuable resources to their community when the community finds ways to use seniors' talents. The example below shows one potential use for senior volunteers.

Every Monday and Wednesday after school, 10-year-old Kenny arrives at the apartment of Alexander Goldring, 86, for five or six cookies, a glass of milk and an hour's reading aloud followed by a spelling test. His tutor is a retired chartered accountant who speaks with a broad New York accent … Kenny says proudly that because of Mr. Goldring's tutoring, his marks in reading have risen from mostly Cs to As and Bs.

A love of books and children and the simple conviction that "if I want to be happy I should make others happy" led Mr. Goldring to join a group of volunteers in Manhattan who worked as tutors.

When he moved to Toronto with his wife seven years ago from New York, he discovered that volunteer tutoring in the public schools was virtually non-existent. Fortunately, he found Clinton Street Public School receptive to the idea, and he now holds weekly readings of poetry and stories for three classes and assigns them compositions and spelling tests. "There's always a glass of water and a nice chair waiting for me. The other day, a grade six class give me a tearful ovation after I read a very sad story about two boys raising money to support their sick sister's stay in the hospital."

Source: Excerpted from Penelope Jahn, "Good Old," *Today Magazine*, January 9, 1982, 11–14, 16.

In addition, French programs now exist in six provinces. The Canadian Elderhostel program produces a bilingual catalogue three times a year that goes to 60 000 Canadians. Programs like Elderhostel will attract more and more people in the future

Institutes for Learning in Retirement

Institutes for Learning in Retirement (ILRs) have met with success at a number of Canadian universities. These programs offer a variety of formats from lectures, to seminars, to travel courses. In most cases older people decide together on the topics they will study. But "central to the ILR philosophy are 'peer-teaching' and 'self-governance'" (Meyers, 1987 cited in Swedburg 1993).

These programs have grown rapidly in number throughout North America over the past few years. The New School for Social Research in New York started the first ILR in 1962 (Beck et al.

1991). Elderhostel has set up an Institute Network throughout North America. Network affiliates grew from 32 in 1989 to 81 in 1991 (*Network News* 1992). And the network continues to expand. Elderhostel has published a newsletter since 1988, titled *Network News*. The newsletter includes examples of institutes' activities, reports on new institutes, and examples of successful courses. Most ILRs work through a local university.

ILR courses have no grades or tests. They often take the form of study groups where students teach one another. Students in the ILRs, some of them retired professionals, often lead the classes. But they may teach subjects far from their specialties. A retired engineer might lead a course in Shakespeare. A professor of adult education might teach a course on French cuisine.

Unique Canadian institutes have developed across the country. Grant McEwan Community College in Alberta, for example, developed a "Senior Studies Institute." The program was established in 1988 "to provide those who have retired with life enriching experiences without the constraints of entrance requirements or exams" (Grant McEwan n.d.). The Institute offers a retirement planning program called "Prime Time"; a variety of eight-week courses on topics like history, geography, and computing; and travel exchanges. The program has an advisory committee of seniors and other community representatives, an advisory board, and a fundraising committee. The program expected 500 students in the fall of 1988.

McGill University has one of the largest and most active Institutes in the country. It began with 197 people registering for courses in 1989. The McGill Institute for Learning in Retirement (MILR) uses peer learning in small groups. Member volunteers act as moderators to plan about thirty nine-week courses on academic topics that interest group members. Courses include "A Comparative Study of a Rumanian Shtetl and a French-Canadian Parish in the 1930s," "Poetry: The Voice of Love," and a current events course in French. A seniors council coordinates the program with the support of the McGill University Centre for Continuing Education.

Some people say that programs like Elderhostel or ILRs segregate older people. They may offer less challenging, low-quality programs. Van der Veen (1990), for example, calls for "inter-age universities" that serve mixed age groups. These universities would take into account the special needs of older adults, but would mix older people with younger people in classes. Some older people might prefer this kind of education. In either case (age-mixed or age-segregated programs), older people enrich campus life. They challenge faculty in new ways, bring fresh interest and ideas to the classroom, and create role models for younger students. Schools that offer the programs mentioned above have found that they benefit when they include older people in their vision of the campus (Scholz 1993).

Older people will want more education because of their higher education level, curiosity, and as a way to keep up with the world around them. Computer technology, something new for all of us, has attracted the interest of many seniors. Normand (1995) reports that in 1993 7.2 percent of women and 12.8 percent of men aged 65 and over said they had taken a computer course. A slightly higher proportion of older men and women say they use a computer. The Internet opens up worlds of information to active and housebound older people. The growth of the Internet into a worldwide information and communication tool happened almost overnight. It has begun to change the way all of us, including older people, keep up with new ideas.

Education institutions have begun to offer courses on the Internet. The government offers information to seniors on the 'Net. And older people use the 'Net to keep in touch with one another. A program sponsored by Creative Retirement Manitoba teaches older people to use the Internet and provides them access to Internet services (see Exhibit 12.11).

COMMUNITY SERVICE THROUGH VOLUNTEER WORK

Exercise, recreation, and education lead to increased life satisfaction for older people. So does community service work or volunteer work—through the chance to give to others. O'Brien and Conger (1991) report that active older people take great satisfaction in their ability to help others. "It is possible," these researchers say, "that the giving of social support may be as important to the integrity of today's aging women as is the taking (O'Brien and Conger 1991, 86).

Stone (1988) reports that seniors gave at least seven types of assistance to others: donations of money, transportation help, personal care, babysitting, housework, yardwork, and volunteer work. Rates of giving differed for each activity. Less than 10 percent of people aged 55 and over engaged in personal care. But more than half of people aged 55 and over donated money to an organization or to other people outside their household. And over 15 percent of people aged 55 and over reported doing volunteer work (Stone 1988).

Statistics Canada (1989a) reports that in 1987 Canada had 50 000 agencies registered as charitable organizations. Twenty-seven percent of adults in a 1987 survey reported that they do volunteer work often in health and welfare field services, administration and client supports, and transportation. Stone (1988) reports that almost one person in four between the ages of 55 and 70 gave transportation help to others. Most of this help (60 percent) went to friends and neighbours.

Exhibit 12.10

A Personal Odyssey: An Educational Adventure

Education for older people can take place outside the classroom. More older people than ever before now take adventure travel holidays. These programs combine travel, learning new skills or information, and some physical challenge. Adventure travel programs range from whitewater raft expeditions, to mountain climbing treks. Rod Dawson describes an educational program that challenged him physically and emotionally.

Once more to dip my paddle and spin the world beneath my keel. A nine day Canadian Outward Bound Wilderness School canoe trip, 100 miles north east of Thunder Bay. Be there such a thing as heaven, it will surely include lakes, rivers, forest trails and campfires from northern Ontario.

A million reasons not to go.

At age 66 would I be able to keep up? I didn't feel old—on the other hand—neither did I feel young. Three major surgeries for cancer had taken a lot of the zip and vinegar out of me. I feared walking that lonesome road to another year—a year that might not be there for me. Maybe I can do it? Maybe I can't?

In the end I went because in my heart I really wanted at least one more trip.

We were all to meet at the airport in Thunder Bay. I opted to travel by bus from Belleville. When two other Outward Bounders boarded the bus in Toronto I knew I wasn't the only economy traveller. We shared a taxi from the bus depot to the airport.

Outward Bound policy states: "It is best that no one in your group has any preconceived ideas about your capabilities, therefore we do not allow spouses or partners to be in the same brigade." There are a few rules with Outward Bound. No alcohol, no smoking and no exclusive relationships. The expectation is that members will come with an open mind. The goal is to build confidence and self esteem. A self affirming experience, not a survival school. ...

Monday morning. We were scheduled for cold water immersion experience and this was September. We were taught canoe strokes and canoe over canoe rescue.

Then off to the Upper Kopka River, our first portage and my moment of truth. I asked to carry the first portage. If I could do this I could handle my share of the trip. When I put the canoe down at the water's edge I knew I had crossed my Rubicon.

Our canoe expedition had begun. Thirteen people, six canoes, five tents and all of our equipment. We travelled and worked together as a group, yet I think for everyone it was a very unique personal experience.

Wednesday. Just before dinner, we were dropped off for our "solo." Each participant was given a plastic tarp, rope, food, matches, sleeping bag and mattress to spend 24 hours alone on an isolated piece of shore. A steady drizzle kept me close to shelter and fire. Without watch or sun to mark the time the solitude was magnificent. Wrapped in a garment of morning mist, time marched forward with an immeasurable cadence and before I was ready 24 hours had passed.

It is said that adult participants in Outward Bound are often at a transition point in their life, reaching an age plateau, leaving an old job, ending a relationship or wondering about the wheres and whys of life. I had no grand expectations, I went only to canoe. But something happened.

On the solo and while paddling the next day, I met myself, my regrets, my hopes, my fears. It was Friday afternoon, paddling bow in the lead canoe I dipped my cup into the lake, drank, looked around and breathed deeply. One year ago this very day I lay in a hospital bed, alive because of surgeons' skills and a frightening array of painful medical technology. The contrast between then and now was so overwhelming that tears ran down my cheeks.

Source: Rod Dawson, "A Personal Odyssey," *Maturity*, January/February, 26–27. Reprinted with permission. Publisher: Maturity Magazine, CYN Investments Ltd.

Statistics Canada (1990e) reports that 19 percent of men and 22 percent of women aged 65 and over work in charitable or service organizations as volunteers (see also Searle 1987). The higher a person's education level the greater the chance that they do volunteer work for an organization. In general, compared with people who live alone, those who lived with a spouse also tended to volunteer more (Stone 1988). Prince and Chappell (1994, 1) report that volunteers have "slightly higher household incomes, and better self-assessed health than non-volunteer seniors."

Research suggests that more older people would work as volunteers if they had the opportunity. A study of people aged 60 and over in Northumberland and Newcastle, Ontario, for example, found that many older people would like to work as volunteers in schools (Hawkins 1980).

Exhibit 12.11

SeniorNet — http://www.crm.mb.ca/scip/

Creative Retirement Manitoba (CRM), an education program run by and for seniors, offers 132 courses to almost 2000 older people each year. The most popular courses include a distinguished-lecturer series, line dancing, and a program on computers that teaches older people to surf the Internet.

The computer program began in 1993 when CRM placed computers in six senior centres throughout Manitoba. Seniors can use the computers for free. CRM has trained coaches to help beginners. The SCIP system (Seniors Communication/Information Project) has a site on the World Wide Web. The SCIP site has information for seniors on varied topics including health, housing, law and consumer issues, and lifestyles.

A report on the program says that almost one-third of the people in the program had no prior experience with computers. Another 41 percent had only "some experience." Only half the program users had computers. The report goes on to say that a large majority of people "found computers exciting, became more interested in them with use, wanted to learn more about them and would use them in the future" (Trombo 1995, 2).

Seniors from around the world, including Europe, Australia, and New Zealand (as well as Canada), have logged onto the SCIP site. On March 6, 1995, the National Center for Supercomputing Applications (NCSA), one of the best-known Internet groups, named the SCIP system their "Pick of the Week." SCIP also features a newsgroup (soc.retirement) where seniors can discuss topics of interest. It has a CyberPals (e-mail penPals) option. It has an option called "Ask a Great-Granny," where grandparents and parents go for advice on family problems. And it includes the full text of the Manitoba Seniors Handbook, the Elderhostel catalogue, and links to other sites on the Internet.

The government hopes that SCIP will lower health care costs. Jon Gerrard, federal secretary of State for Science, Research and Development, said that SCIP "is empowering the people to look after their health better, at a lower cost" (Pihlchyn 1995). He looks forward to lower national health care costs as people have access to more information about self-care.

CRM has already expanded its use of the Internet for senior education. Recently CRM partnered with Elderhostel Canada to offer an electronic dialogue on-line titled "Across Age Learning: Families Today and Tomorrow." This e-mail discussion group brought together people aged 55 and over and college students aged 17 and over to discuss questions like how to maintain links between the generations in a family. Anyone could join the discussion after registering for the program. CRM and Elderhostel also invited response from a panel of researchers interested in family and intergenerational issues.

SCIP has only begun to explore seniors' use of computer technology. This program shows that seniors themselves can lead the way in the development of new computer uses.

For more information about SCIP, log on yourself at the address above. See how seniors make use of this new resource. Or join a discussion group and talk to seniors themselves about issues of interest to you.

Many of the subjects in this study said they would start work right away, if they had the chance. Seventeen percent said they would work in a library; 14 percent said they would listen to a child read; and 14 percent said they would teach students about seniors' hobbies and skills. Prince and Chappell (1994) say that over 80 percent of people in the 1987 National Survey on Volunteer Activity said they would give more time to volunteer work.

Some programs already use older people's talents in the schools. Studio Two, a seniors' drama group, presents plays and skits for students. Creative Retirement Manitoba (a learning centre for seniors) arranges for older people to visit schools and speak about Manitoba history. A similar program was started in Montreal to enrich the school curriculum and to bridge the generation gap. In this program, a worker from the Centre local de services communautaires arranged for a group of seven older people in the downtown core to work with children in a local school. The seniors, who ranged from 55 to 90 years of age, worked with a class of twenty-seven students for ten weeks. Classes included attending a performance of the Montreal Symphony, a slide show on Venice organized by the seniors, and a play put on for the seniors by the students. The classes ended with a bus trip to Canadiana Village and a picnic lunch (Nahmiash 1985).

Volunteer programs can benefit seniors and their communities, but they require coordination. A program in Niagara, Ontario, called Senior Volunteers in Service links volunteers with community needs. The program uses the services of volunteers aged 55 or older. In 1986, 250 people volunteered for more than 3000 hours a month as friendly visitors, meals-on-wheels helpers, and foster grandparents. Some volunteers helped older people with transportation, shopping, or household chores (Rapelje, Goodman, and Swick 1986). Another program called Family Friends linked older people with children who had chronic illnesses or disabilities. The older people visited the children at home and provided support to the families (Kuehne and Sears 1993).

Burden and Lee (1992) studied 141 agencies in Victoria, B.C., that use older volunteers. Nearly all of the agencies said they would like more older volunteers. About a third of the agencies found that office work suited older volunteers. About one-quarter of the agencies said that older people did well in one-to-one relationships. Agencies found older people patient, available, and committed to their volunteer role. Agencies agreed that they enhance volunteering by providing flexible hours, job sharing, and vacations.

Senior volunteers can have a global as well as a local impact. The federal government sponsors a program called **Canadian Executive Service Overseas (CESO).** The program recruits senior volunteers and assigns them to work in underdeveloped countries or with Native groups in Canada. Volunteers, who are mostly retired people between the ages of 60 and 70, give technical and management advice to businesses, do feasibility studies, and help train workers and managers. The program pays travel and maintenance expenses.

From 1969 to 1982 the program sent about 3000 volunteers to work with Native groups, and it has about 750 volunteers on its active list. From 1967 to 1982 CESO had finished about 3000 overseas projects, and it had about 2700 people ready to take on new projects (Health and Welfare Canada 1982b).

Volunteering, whether at a local school or in a foreign country, can give an older person a sense of purpose in life. Bond (1982) studied 323 older volunteers and found that people who volunteer their services have higher life satisfaction than people who do not. He suggests that counsellors prescribe volunteer work for clients who feel dissatisfied with their lives.

CONCLUSION

Older people engage in a wide range of leisure, educational, and community service activities. Government, nonprofit, and for-profit organizations have developed new programs and activities to engage and challenge older people. Future cohorts of older people will have more education than older people in the past. They will bring new interests in education, travel, and service. These people will help define old age as a time of personal growth and community enrichment.

SUMMARY

1. Older people spend a great deal of their time on passive media-related activities like reading the newspaper and watching television. Older

people often spend their time alone, but they also enjoy spending time with others.

2. Income, lifestyle, gender, and health influence what people do and how active they remain in old age. Older people in good health have shown one of the highest rates of increase in sports and exercise activities in the past few years.

3. Physical functions do decline with age, but fitness training can reverse some physical decline. Fitness training can also lead to better sleep patterns, a better self-image, more social contacts, and increased happiness. Even in institutions fitness programs can improve residents' health and well-being.

4. Older people will join and stay in fitness programs if they have control over program content and feel relaxed and unthreatened by competition. More and more older people now value fitness and exercise.

5. An active leisure lifestyle provides physical, psychological, and social benefits in later life. This leads to better functioning and greater life satisfaction.

6. Senior centres across the country offer education, counselling, and recreation for older people. They form the closest thing to a network of recreational programs in Canada. Centre activities will need to change in the future to meet the needs of younger, more active seniors.

7. People with many years of schooling will keep on learning as they age. Universities often sponsor special programs for seniors. Programs like Elderhostel, Creative Retirement Manitoba, and the University of the Third Age offer alternatives to traditional schooling. These programs are designed to fit the older person's interests and learning styles.

8. Computer technology has attracted the interest of many older people. The Internet, for example, has provided new sources of information to both active and housebound older people. It has begun to change the way in which older people have access to news ideas, information, and people.

9. Many older people volunteer to help others. More older people might offer their skills and services to the community if they had the opportunity. New programs help older people find ways to use their skills. Studies show that volunteers report an increase in life satisfaction.

STUDY QUESTIONS

1. How do most older people spend their time in retirement, according to studies on leisure activities? What activities do retired people enjoy most?
2. How and why do the lifestyles of older people vary in retirement? What conditions influence how active a person remains in old age?
3. Research suggests that two theories account for older people's leisure patterns. Name these theories and describe how they account for leisure choices in retirement.
4. Describe some of the programs and services available that can help older people stay active. What special needs must recreational planners consider when they design programs for older people?
5. List some of the physical and psychological benefits of regular exercise and fitness programs for seniors.
6. How can recreational planners attract sedentary seniors to activity programs?
7. What services do senior centres provide for older people? What other types of programs compete with senior centres for older people's participation?
8. Why do older people attend educational programs? What types of courses do they prefer when they go back to school?
9. How will universities and colleges have to modify their programs if they want to attract older students?
10. List and describe the major educational alternatives that are available to older people today. How has home computer use benefited older people?
11. Summarize the major types of activities that lead to increased life satisfaction in later life. Why does volunteer work, in particular, lead to high life satisfaction?

KEY TERMS

active leisure lifestyle this type of lifestyle does at least two things: it directly benefits health and it helps to buffer the influence of life events and illness.

Canadian Executive Service Overseas (CESO) a federal government program that recruits senior volunteers and assigns them to work in under-developed countries or with Aboriginal groups in Canada.

contractors an activity pattern that fits the continuity theory of aging. People who fit this pattern had stopped at least one outdoor activity in the past year and had not learned any new activity since age 65.

Elderhostel a program that combines university campus life with the European concept of hostelling (travelling from place to place and stay-ing in inexpensive, safe lodgings). Elderhostel students live on a university campus while they take courses.

expanders this pattern fits the life-span develop-mental perspective. People who fit this pattern had not stopped any activities in the past year and had added at least one new outdoor activity since age 65.

hypokinetic disease the idea that the lack of activity can lead to mental and physical problems, while increases in activity can prevent or reverse these problems.

Institutes for Learning in Retirement (ILRs) programs that offer a variety of educational formats from lectures, to seminars, to travel courses. In most cases older people decide together on the topics they will study.

leisure competence the ability to make use of leisure time for life satisfaction. Older people can improve this ability.

Participaction a federal government program that promotes healthy living and outdoor activities for people of all ages.

Université du Troisième Age (U3A) a fran-cophone education program that helps groups of older people set up their own programs with the help of a university. Programs often include access to normal university classes, study groups, study trips, and fitness programs.

SELECTED READINGS

Health and Welfare Canada. *Ageing and Independence: Overview of a National Survey.* Cat. No. H88-3/13-1993E. Ottawa: Minister of Supply and Services Canada, 1993.

A national survey that studied people aged 45 and over. This report presents people's assess-ment of their physical activity and satisfaction with activity. The report presents some opti-mistic findings about older people's attitudes toward physical activity. The results on middle-aged people suggest that these people will bring positive attitudes toward activity into old age.

McPherson, Barry D., and Carol Kozlik. "Age Patterns in Leisure Participation: The Canadian Case." In Victor W. Marshall, ed. *Aging in Canada.* 2d ed. Toronto: Fitzhenry and Whiteside, 1987.

A sociological study of differences in leisure patterns by age, occupation, and income. The study shows a continuity of individual leisure patterns from mid-life to old age. It also shows that age, period, and cohort effects all influence leisure activities.

Family Life and Social Relations

INTRODUCTION

Rising divorce rates, the generation gap, and high residential mobility all point to major changes in the modern family (Nett 1988). Add to this the fact that more older people live alone than ever before, and it seems as though families have abandoned their aging members. Shanas (1979) calls this the "hydraheaded myth" of family breakdown. People continue to believe it, even though studies show over and over again that it is not true. Research shows that older people keep in contact with their families, that they rely on family members for help when they need it, and that middle-aged children feel responsible for their aging parents (Bond, Harvey, and Hildebrand 1987; Brody 1990; Campbell and Brody 1985; Paletta 1992). A Canadian survey found that 92 percent of older people feel emotionally close to their families (Synergistics 1993). Studies also show that (not including spouses) children supply most of the help older people need (Morris and Sherwood 1983–84). Brody (1983, 597) concludes, in a study of three generations, that "values about family care of elderly adults have not eroded despite demographic and socioeconomic changes."

Today, most older people, even widowed older women, prefer to see their children, but not to live with them. Better incomes, government rent supports, and health services allow more people to choose this option than ever before. This chapter will look at three influences on family life and social supports: (1) normative age-graded changes (like marriage and widowhood), (2) informal social supports (like help with activities of daily living), and (3) new roles that people take on as they age (such as becoming a grandparent).

NORMATIVE AGE-GRADED LIFE EVENTS

Normative age-graded life events are expected changes in life that correlate with chronological age. They include high-school graduation, retirement, and marriage. Some gerontologists now also define widowhood as a normative life event for older women. Normative age-graded events define a person's status in society, the person's roles, and the person's relationships. When an event takes place, it signals a change in a person's social status

and often also a change in their social network. The following sections will focus on two normative events: marriage (including divorce and sexuality) and widowhood.

Marriage

Nearly all Canadians get married. Gee (1987) reports that in Canada by ages 45 to 49, 92.5 percent of men and 94.2 percent of women have married. This figure increases to 95 percent by ages 50–64 (McDaniel 1994a). About half of Canadians who marry stay married to the same person until their spouse's death (National Advisory Council 1993c).

Norland (1994) reports that 88 percent of senior families contained a married couple (a senior family has at least two people in it and at least one senior). Most of these families (59 percent) had two senior spouses and contained only two people.

Married seniors have some advantages over their unmarried age mates. First, married couples tend to have more financial resources than unmarried people aged 65 and over. Couples tend to be younger than unmarried older people, and often one or both members of the couple work. Even among people the same age, married couples have more money. This may be because they had a higher lifetime income than unmarried people, more savings, and a family home.

Second, the large majority of older people report marital satisfaction, and they say they enjoy their marriage now more than ever (Connidis 1989a). Almost three-quarters of married couples aged 65 and over say they are "very satisfied" with their romantic relationship, and these people report higher satisfaction with their romantic relationship than any other age group (Statistics Canada 1980b; Connidis 1989a). Hess and Soldo (1985) say that older couples report high life satisfaction because these people (and their marriages) have survived economic hard times and the stress of raising children, and have overcome any irritation with their partner's quirks and habits. Couples with children also enjoy a new freedom in old age. They live adult-centred lives that allow them to travel, visit with friends, share work at home, and do things together (Abu-Laban 1978).

Third, research shows that married people adjust better than nonmarried people to aging

(Bengtson, Rosenthal, and Burton 1990). A good marriage gives the couple intimacy, mutual support, and high life satisfaction (Connidis 1989a; Strain and Chappell 1982a). Married older people have more daily contact with others and they have more people in their social networks (Chappell and Prince 1994). Marriage also leads to longer life (especially for men) and better health (Connidis 1989a). Married older people, compared with nonmarrieds, have fewer acute and chronic illnesses, fewer limits on their activities, and shorter hospital stays (Hess and Soldo, 1985). They also stand the best chance of staying out of nursing homes if they get sick, because they have someone to care for them. Marriage gives a person a live-in support system (Chappell and Blandford 1987b). Wister (1986), for example, found that married seniors feel less need for outside social

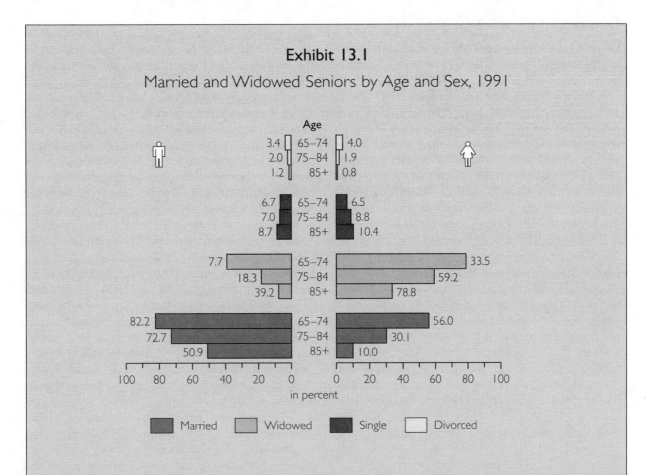

Exhibit 13.1

Married and Widowed Seniors by Age and Sex, 1991

Age

	Men	Age	Women	
	3.4	65–74	4.0	
	2.0	75–84	1.9	
	1.2	85+	0.8	
	6.7	65–74	6.5	
	7.0	75–84	8.8	
	8.7	85+	10.4	
	7.7	65–74	33.5	
	18.3	75–84	59.2	
	39.2	85+	78.8	
	82.2	65–74	56.0	
	72.7	75–84	30.1	
	50.9	85+	10.0	

in percent

■ Married   ■ Widowed   ■ Single   □ Divorced

Note that more men than women are married at every age presented here. Note also that the difference in rates of marriages between men and women increases with age. More than half of men age 85 and over are married compared with only 10 percent of the oldest women. Widowhood rates for men and women differ as well. Very few men compared with about a third of women are widowed at ages 65–74. By age 85 and over women have double the proportion of widows compared with men. These figures point to the different life experiences of men and women in later life due to mortality and the tendencies of each sex to remarry.

Source: Adapted from J.A. Norland. *Profile of Canada's Seniors,* Cat. No. 96-312E, Table 4.1, 22 (Ottawa: Statistics Canada and Prentice Hall Canada, 1994). Reproduced with the permission of the Minister of Industry, 1996, Statistics Canada.

relations. They also report a greater likelihood than nonmarried seniors of having sexual relations. Connidis (1989a) cautions that these findings apply only to good marriages. Constant bickering and dissatisfaction in a marriage can lead to depression and illness. Connidis (1989a) says that researchers need to look at the quality of a marriage as well as a person's marital status to understand the impact of marriage on well-being.

Divorce

Divorce is not a normative life event, but because it relates to marriage and may become more common in the future, it deserves some mention here.

About 4 percent of people aged 65 to 74 in 1991 report that they have divorced. This rate more than doubled from 1976 to 1991 and represents a shift toward greater acceptability of divorce among older people (Norland 1994; Statistics Canada 1990e). Bengtson, Rosenthal, and Burton (1990) say that money, education, and strong social networks lead to good adjustment after divorce. But little research exists on divorced older people.

Payne (1994) studied divorce and separation in later life (she combined these two groups). She found that almost one-third of separated and divorced older people had incomes below $10 000 per year. This proportion rises to 40.8 percent of separated and divorced women. Only 5.6 percent of all married people and 7.7 percent of married women had incomes this low. The National Advisory Council on Aging (1993c) says that divorced women rarely regain their lost income due to divorce unless they remarry. Older women show less likelihood of remarriage and so feel the economic effects of divorce for many years. Separated and divorced older people in general, like people in other marital groups, report good health and low stress. But they have smaller social networks than married or widowed older people (Strain and Payne 1992).

Divorced older men have the smallest social networks, the weakest ties to their families, and the lowest life satisfaction of any marital group. Payne (1994) says that researchers need to look at family relationships of divorced older people. Also, researchers should study cultural variations in how people adapt to divorce. Longer life expectancies in the future could produce marriages that would last 50 years or more. But the increased rate of divorce means that marriages now last on average less than 32 years (National Advisory Council 1993c). Payne (1994) predicts a higher divorce rate and more divorced older people in the future. The National Advisory Council on Aging (1993c) says that in the future 40 percent of new marriages could end in divorce. This will make the economic well-being, mental health, and family life of divorced older people more important in the future.

Sexuality

Studies show that most older people have an interest in sex throughout life and that, given good health and a partner, older people can (and do) have sexual relations into late old age. Pfeiffer, Verwoerdt, and Wang (1968; also Verwoerdt, Pfeiffer, and Wang 1969) report on findings from one of the first studies of sexuality that included a large number of older people, the Duke Longitudinal Study of Aging. This study included data on 254 people between the ages of 60 and 94. Cross-sectional analysis showed a drop in sexual interest and activity with age, but longitudinal data showed many patterns of sexual change. About 20 percent of the men, for example, showed an increase in sexual interest and activity with age. The researchers found that on average men stopped having intercourse at age 68, but the age when men stopped ranged from 49 to 90. Masters and Johnson (1970) report that men stop having sex because of boredom, interest in outside activities, fatigue, eating or drinking too much, illness, or fear of failure.

Women stop having sexual relations earlier than men—on average at age 60. This reflects the higher rates of widowhood for women in old age. Research shows that whether a woman maintains an active sex life or not depends on the presence of an active sexual partner. Widowhood or a husband's decision to stop having sex often put an end to a woman's sexual activity.

The Duke University research found that sexual activity in old age depends most on a person's pattern of sexual activity in the past. Men and women who have a partner and who enjoyed sex in the past will continue to enjoy it as they age (Palmore 1981). The Duke study also found that sexual activity leads to high life satisfaction and good health for people between ages 45 and 70.

Exhibit 13.2

Seniors Show a Strong Interest in Sex

Starr and Weiner (1981) studied a convenience sample of 800 people between the ages of 60 and 91 from across the United States. Two-thirds of the sample were women. All of them lived in the community and reported good health. Starr and Weiner found that older people report a strong interest in sex. "They think about it, desire it, and engage in it when they can, with the same average frequency that Kinsey reported for his 40-year-olds" (Starr and Weiner 1981, 35). Nearly all of these people (97 percent) said they like sex, and the majority (75 percent) said they enjoy it as much or more now as in their youth. A 72-year-old woman said that now she had "no concern about pregnancy, [and] therefore an increase in pleasure" (Starr and Weiner 1981, 88). A 74-year-old widower said that lovemaking now was "Great. Now you can do things that you could not do before" (Starr and Weiner 1981, 194). Eighty percent of the sample thought sex had a good effect on an older person's health. About two-thirds (66.5 percent) of the sample considered orgasm very important to their sexual experience. Half of the sample (51.6 percent) thought that intercourse was the most important part of sex. Over seventy percent (71.7 percent) said that their sexual experiences left them satisfied.

The findings also show that people adjust their expectations and their activities to meet their needs.

For example, nearly half the men (43.6 percent) and women (47.0 percent) said that they masturbate. This proportion increased among the widowed, divorced, and single people in the sample. About a fifth of the sample (19.9 percent) said that they masturbate if a sexual experience leaves them unsatisfied. Almost another fifth (17.8 percent) said they keep on trying. About two-thirds (62.2 percent) of the sample said that "sexy pictures, books, or movies" got them excited. One 72-year-old man said that he "often read sexy books as an aphrodisiac" (Starr and Weiner 1981, 50). These findings show that while their bodies change with age, people can maintain a good attitude toward sex and live active, enjoyable sex lives into their ninth decade.

This study gives an insight into sexuality in old age, but it has a built-in bias. The people who filled out the Starr and Weiner questionnaire may differ in some important ways from those who did not. People who answer questions about their sex lives, for example, may have more active sex lives than those who won't answer these questions. This makes it hard to generalize from these findings. Future studies will need to use random samples of seniors to see whether these findings fit the general population.

Palmore sums up the Duke findings: "These statistics," he writes, "show that most older married persons are not asexual; on the contrary, substantial proportions remain sexually active until at least their 80s. They also show that impotence and sexual problems in old age are reversible, and that substantial proportions at all ages report increasing sexual activity" (1981, 89).

Adaptations in Sexuality Due to Age

Sexually active older people have to adjust to changes in their bodies as they age. A man, as he ages, takes longer to get an erection, takes longer to feel ready for intercourse again, and may have

shorter, less intense orgasms. A woman, as she ages, may find that her vagina loses elasticity and opens less fully, and that she may have shorter orgasms. Older couples may need to use vaginal lubrication.

Weg (1983) says that people can accept many changes as they get older—changes in strength, the senses, and athletic ability. But, she says, a change in sexual function can visit "painful damage upon self-concept, motivation, and the zest for life. Culture still equates sexual performance with manliness or womanliness" (Weg 1983, 46; see also Turner and Adams 1983). Butler and Lewis (1976) describe a **second language of sex** that can overcome the feelings Weg describes. This language focuses on responsiveness, caring, and affection.

Sometimes a couple will need medical help or counselling to cope with changes in sexual performance (Szasz 1980). This can take the form of a medical checkup, information about changes in the body with age, or sex therapy (Corby and Zarit 1983; Weg 1983). Studies show that older people can (and many do) make these adjustments as they age.

Changing Attitudes to Sex in Old Age

Many researchers say that negative individual and societal attitudes toward sexuality may inhibit sexual activity in later life (Schlesinger 1983; Weg 1983). Schlesinger (1983), for example, says that virility gets labelled as lechery in an old man. Older people in institutions face special problems because they have less control over their lives (Kassel 1983). The views of the staff and the policies in some institutions can limit a person's sexual activity.

Mullens (1983) studied the sexual activity of older people in seniors' housing and in nursing homes. He found that people in nursing homes, compared with people in seniors' housing, had less privacy and freedom. Only 28 percent of the homes gave staff training in sexuality and aging. "With a few exceptions," Mullens (1983, 5) says, "sexual relations among residents were either not allowed or not encouraged except for married couples." Mullens found that older people themselves took a restrictive view of sex and he concludes that seniors "adhere to their Victorian upbringing" (1983, 7).

These attitudes of staff and older people toward sexuality will change for several reasons as new cohorts of people enter old age. First, gerontology courses teach younger people and professionals the facts about sex in old age. This can change the attitudes of those who work with older people (Damrosch 1984). Second, books that give advice to older people now, more than in the past, encourage sexual activity. In the past these books typically spoke to middle-aged children about caring for their aging parents, but a more recent study of these books found that they now give advice directly to older people (Arluke, Levin, and Suchwalko 1984). Third, cohorts differ in their views on sexual relations. Older cohorts have a

more conservative view of sex, and most older people today do not favour sex outside of marriage.

Poulin and Mishara (1994), for example, studied adult children's and their parents' attitudes toward sex. The researchers conducted their study in Quebec and found that both groups had positive attitudes toward sexuality. But people with more religious belief showed more negative attitudes toward sex. And the young adults, compared with their parents, showed more positive attitudes toward physical sexuality. The researchers say that generational differences may account for the less positive view of physical sex among older people.

Older people in the future may take a more positive attitude toward sex. Younger cohorts have more open attitudes to sex, and if they bring these attitudes with them into old age, there will be a more positive view of sex and more sexual activity among older people. Weg (1983), however, warns against any new vision of sexuality in old age, saying that older people will only face a new stereotype if they feel they must have a partner and stay sexually active as they age. "There is no one way to love or to be loved," Weg says (1983, 76), "there is no one liaison that is superior to another. No one life-style in singlehood or marriage, heterosexual or homosexual, will suit all persons. Self-pleasuring, homosexuality, bisexuality, celibacy, and heterosexuality are all in the human sexual repertoire."

Homosexuality in Later Life

Most studies of sexuality in later life have focused on married or single heterosexuals. Few studies report on male and female homosexual seniors (Lee 1987). Do they face unique problems as they age? Do male and female homosexuals adapt better or less well than heterosexuals to sexual changes with age? Like heterosexuals, gays and lesbians decrease their sexual activity with age. Weinberg (1969) says that the gay and lesbian culture values youth more than the straight culture, and this may cause problems for male and female homosexuals as they age. But this may differ for men and women. Laner (1979) reports that, compared with men, lesbians have a less negative view of the physical changes that come with age. A collection of autobiographical writings (Adelman 1987) suggests that the women's movement has reduced the generation gap between young and old lesbians.

Lee (1987) conducted the first study of gay aging men in Canada. He studied 47 English-speaking men aged 50 to 80 years of age and interviewed them once a year for four years. Lee found that men who had partners in the past—a wife, lovers, or a combination of both—reported life satisfaction even if they now lived alone. Lee found that homosexual men with lovers tend to report high life satisfaction, but he also says that having a lover in later life "is not easy to achieve" (Lee 1987, 147). Only two men, out of the eight who lived with lovers, had found their lovers during the four years of his study.

Lee also found that men who preferred other gays as friends and those who knew an older gay man as a role model showed higher life satisfaction. This supports another finding from this study. Lee found that gay men involved in gay social life reported high life satisfaction.

Lee's findings show that older gay men get life satisfaction from many of the same things as heterosexual men—companionship, sexual fulfilment, and friendship. They also have unique sources of satisfaction and face unique challenges as they age. Lee's study shows that gay men can adapt to the changes that come with age and that "it is possible to achieve … happiness alone or by sharing life with a lover, even one found late in life" (Lee 1987, 151).

One theme appears in nearly all the studies of homosexuality in later life. Societal attitudes toward homosexuality have shaped and continue to shape the lives of gay and lesbian older people. Many older gay and lesbian people have had to adapt their lives in order to live in a heterosexual world. Societal homophobia led many gay and lesbian older people to hide their homosexual relationships (Kehoe 1989). They feared that exposure might cost them their jobs.

Friend (1991) says that gay and lesbian adaptations to a hostile society may lead to successful aging. First, he says that gays and lesbians have experience in constructing a positive image of themselves in spite of social definitions. This may help them construct a positive image of themselves as they age. Second, gays and lesbians have experience in creating supportive relationships. This may help them create the support networks they need as they age. Third, many gays and lesbians have experience with political advocacy. These people

will be better able to defend their rights as they age.

Research on homosexuality in later life has only begun. Lee (1991) proposes some research questions that need study. These include the longitudinal study of aging gay and lesbian couples, gay widowhood, and aged gays and lesbians in the homosexual community (see Grube 1991). Studies of gay and lesbian aging show that societal influences and past experiences shape a person's life in old age. They also show that sexuality plays an important part in homosexual as well as heterosexual aging.

Widowhood

Nagnur and Adams (1989) report that, in Canada, the large majority of older couples (70 percent) remain married until widowhood. The proportion of married people drops (largely due to mortality) from about age 40 onward. For people aged 65 to 74, 82 percent of men and 56 percent of women are married. For people aged 85 and over, 51 percent of men and only 10 percent of women are married (Norland 1994). After 30 years of marriage a woman, compared with a man, runs three times the risk of widowhood.

She also has less likelihood of remarriage. These figures show that women face a greater chance of widowhood than men and a greater chance of living alone in old age. But men and women differ in their tendency to remarry after the loss of a spouse. Nagnur and Adams (1987) report that men aged 55 and over have a marriage rate (3.3 per 1000) twice that of women the same age (1.7 per 1000). Among people aged 70 and over, for example, men, compared with women, have nine times the remarriage rate (National Advisory Council 1993c). This meant that in 1991 almost half (47 percent) of women aged 65 and over were widowed (and remained unmarried) compared with 13 percent of men in that age group (Norland 1994).

Widows outnumber widowers for three reasons: (1) women live longer than men; (2) women marry older men; and (3) men, more than women, tend to remarry after widowhood. Exhibit 13.3 shows the outcome of these three trends.

Today almost 70 percent of widows are over age 65. Statistics Canada says that a widow at age 65 can expect to live almost nineteen more years. A

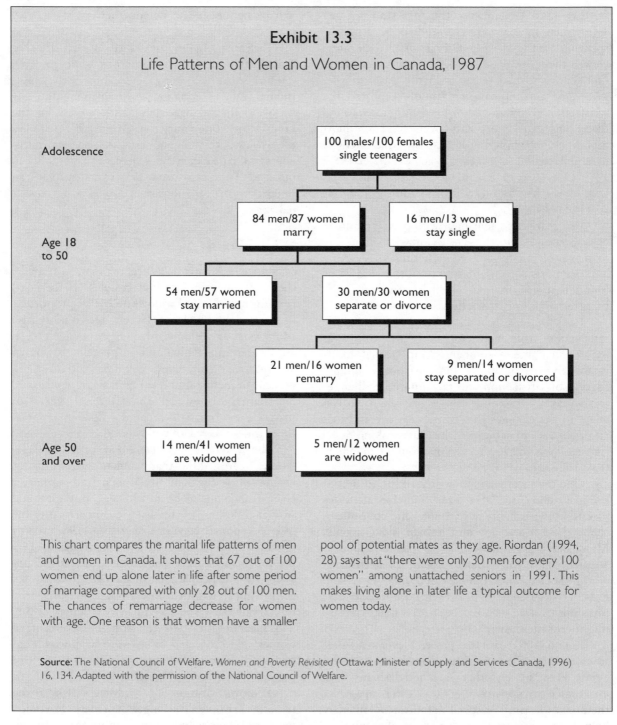

Exhibit 13.3

Life Patterns of Men and Women in Canada, 1987

Adolescence — 100 males/100 females single teenagers

Age 18 to 50 — 84 men/87 women marry / 16 men/13 women stay single

54 men/57 women stay married / 30 men/30 women separate or divorce

21 men/16 women remarry / 9 men/14 women stay separated or divorced

Age 50 and over — 14 men/41 women are widowed / 5 men/12 women are widowed

This chart compares the marital life patterns of men and women in Canada. It shows that 67 out of 100 women end up alone later in life after some period of marriage compared with only 28 out of 100 men. The chances of remarriage decrease for women with age. One reason is that women have a smaller pool of potential mates as they age. Riordan (1994, 28) says that "there were only 30 men for every 100 women" among unattached seniors in 1991. This makes living alone in later life a typical outcome for women today.

Source: The National Council of Welfare, *Women and Poverty Revisited* (Ottawa: Minister of Supply and Services Canada, 1996) 16, 134. Adapted with the permission of the National Council of Welfare.

woman widowed at age 80 can expect to live almost nine years after her spouse dies (Statistics Canada 1984d, cited in Matthews 1985). Matthews (1987) calls widowhood an "expectable life event," one that creates a great deal of stress (Holmes and Rahe 1967; Matthews 1982; Matthews et al. 1982). This means that many men and most women will go through the pain of widowhood (Gee 1986). Studies of widowhood have focused on two themes: the social supports that buffer widows' and widowers' stress and the differences between widows' and widowers' responses to widowhood.

Exhibit 13.4

Late-Blooming Love

Al Bennett, a retired Toronto accountant, knows firsthand about late-blooming love. A widower, he met his match through an introduction agency. "I was just looking for companionship," says Bennett, 66. "But then the lights went on and the whistles blew." He and Margaret, a 59-year-old widow, plan to marry next year. "There's a whole new world in front of us," he says, adding that their families—seven children and eight grandchildren between them—have been supportive. "But I think some chil-dren throw roadblocks," he says. "They think some-one else will get the inheritance, or they think daddy or mommy shouldn't be doing these things."

As for sex, Bennett allows that some seniors may not require it. "But it shouldn't be taken for granted that because you're 65, you're dead from the waist down." While sex "may not be as frequent in many cases," he says, "it is far more satisfying. We are who we are, we're not trying to demonstrate that we are Michelle Pfeiffer or whoever."

Source: M. Nemeth, "Amazing Greys," *Maclean's*, January 10, 28.

Widowers

Most studies of widowhood contain too few men to compare with women, but a few studies show how the loss of a spouse affects each gender. First, stud-ies of family supports, friendship, and **confidants** (someone in whom one confides) show that women have more social supports than men (Connidis and Davies 1992; McDaniel and McKinnon 1993). Most older men today have spent their lives focused on their careers, while older women today have spent their lives focused on people. This gives older women more close relationships than men in old age. It also makes men more vulnerable when illness and the death of a spouse occur. "Widowed men," Hess and Soldo (1985, 75) say, "are doubly bereft—they have lost both a helpmate and confi-dante. ... Conversely, the widowed woman is unlikely to be entirely devoid of close friends."

Second, wives link men to wider social networks. Women more often than men say they have close relationships with family and friends besides their husband. They often name these friends, relatives, and children as their confidants, and they keep up these relationships when their husband dies (Connidis and Davies 1990; Powers and Bultena 1980; Strain and Chappell 1982a). A man whose wife dies loses a wife, a companion, and a social secretary (Antonucci 1990; McDaniel and McKinnon 1993). This may explain why many men rush into another marriage after they lose a spouse. Wu (1995), for example, found that widowed men remarry sooner than widowed women. After five years, for example, less than 6 percent of widows have remarried. But over 22 percent of widowers have remarried. Within 10 years 35 percent of men have remarried (compared with only 11 percent of women).

Third, men find it harder to make new friends or to join groups for help. Dr. Alan Lyall, who directed a program for widowers at the Clarke Institute of Psychiatry in Toronto, says that "men are not apt to use talking as a source of support. The women come to the Clarke and the men go across the street to the Silver Dollar tavern" (Wylie 1981, 34–38). Studies show that widowers suffer from isolation and loneliness (Pihlblad, Adams, and Rosencranz 1972). Compared with women, they also run a higher risk of suicide (Resnick and Cantor 1970; Rushing 1968; Maris 1969). This literature suggests that men suffer more than women when they lose a spouse because they have fewer social contacts than women.

Wister and Strain (1986) used a large Canadian random sample to compare widows and widowers. Unlike previous studies, this study found no difference between the well-being of men and women, even though women had more friends and confidants than men (see also Matthews 1987).

They say that widowers may need less social support than widows to feel satisfied. Also, men may enjoy comradeship and sharing interests with others rather than the closeness of a confidant relationship. Wister and Strain (1986) conclude that older men may not want or need the same kinds of social relations as older women:

> Overall, it is clear from the results that there is little support for the view expressed in the literature that older widowers suffer from greater social and psychological disadvantages than widows. It would appear that this myth has developed out of an inherent bias among some researchers to assume similar social-psychological needs across genders. (1986, 18)

This study suggests that men and women have different friendship and confidant needs, possibly due to the kinds of relationships men and women learn to form earlier in life. More research on the social lives of widowers will show how their needs differ (if they do) from those of widows.

Widows

Social supports and family roles buffer the stress of widowhood for women. Norris (1980) found that women stayed socially active in mother and grandmother roles after their husbands died, and that they also held onto their wife role. These women had lost their husbands on average ten years before, but when Norris (1980, 142) asked them if being married made their ""daily activities more satisfying and easy to deal with," many of these widows agreed. She found that these widows "remained emotionally committed to being wives" even many years after their husbands died.

Studies of widowhood find that people go through stages in response to widowhood. First many widows (and widowers) report intense grief, meaninglessness, and loss of identity. Over time grief decreases and the person builds new relationships (Rosenthal and Gladstone 1993). Studies show that a woman's age predicts how much grief she will feel when her husband dies. Younger widows, whose husbands die suddenly, feel more intense grief than older widows (Vachon et al. 1976; Vachon 1981). A woman who loses a spouse "on time" (for example, in her late sixties) tends to expect her husband's death. She has made this a part of her life plan (Matthews 1987), and, more often than a widower, she will have widowed

friends, as well as siblings, to give her support (Connidis 1994).

Strain and Chappell (1982a) asked 400 older people whether they had any confidants. They found that 77 percent of the people in their sample had at least one confidant, and 51 percent had two or more. More women than men had confidants, and men more often than women named their spouse as their confidant (Chappell 1990; Keith et al. 1984). Studies show that confidants contribute to good morale (Chappell and Badger 1989). They also buffer people from anxiety and tension. Lowenthal and Haven (1968) studied role loss in old age (not just widowhood) and found that people with no confidants felt more depressed than those who had one. This finding held even if the person with no confidant increased their interactions and the person who had one decreased theirs. Strain and Chappell (1982a, 496) say that

> the existence of at least one confidant relationship, irrespective of the number of times one might have contact with that confidant, emerges as a significant predictor of life satisfaction. This lends support to the argument ... that it may not be the usually reported frequency of interaction that is important to the quality of life, but rather the quality of that interaction.

Strain and Chappell (1982a) found that widows often chose a sister or brother or a friend their age as a confidant. Matthews (1985) found that many widowed women get support from their sisters. She says that more than half the widows in her study saw at least one of their sisters or brothers several times a month and that more than half of them listed a sibling, often a sister, as someone who gives them social support (see also Bengtson, Rosenthal, and Burton 1990; Canada 1993; and Connidis 1989c). Rosenthal and Gladstone (1993) say that siblings connect a person to the past and provide an anchor for a person's identity. Harvey (1984, cited in Matthews 1985) found that 25 percent of the widows in her sample had contact with a sibling at least once a week, and 10 percent had contact more than once a week.

Relatively few widows remarry. This, in part, reflects the larger number of eligible women compared with older men. Those who do remarry say they want companionship and the feeling that they add to another person's happiness. Many widows enjoy the freedom of unmarried life. And they may want to avoid the role of caregiver in a new marriage (Rosenthal and Gladstone 1993). McDaniel (1989) says that older women's greater life expectancy and their tendency to remain widowed leads to many of the problems that older women face. Inflation, for example, will eat away at a survivor's pension, if the widow has one. She will face a decreasing ability to look after herself in her own home. And she runs a greater risk of institutionalization than a married person because she will lack spousal supports if she gets sick (Dulude 1987; Matthews 1982). Widowhood, in spite of good social supports, may put a woman at greater risk as she ages.

INFORMAL SUPPORTS FOR OLDER PEOPLE

Normative events and sociocultural conditions influence the quality of life in old age, but they do not determine it. Older people can and do respond actively to the changes that aging brings. Their response depends on their personality, past experience, and social resources. This section will look at the methods older people use to cope with aging.

Chappell and Prince (1994, 1) say that the 1990s mark the "rediscovery of informal care." Through the 1970s social policy focused on how the welfare state could help older people meet their needs. This model saw the family at risk due to rapid social change. The state attempted to create a safety net of formal supports for older people. Writers during the 1980s began a critique of this system. Critics of the state saw state support as wasteful, costly, and intrusive. Some critics claimed that the state undermined family life and supported negative views of older people as weak and needy. Binstock (1983) calls this a **compassionate stereotype.** A concern in the 1990s for the high cost of state services also drives this new interest in **informal support.** These trends have created a renewed focus on the family and community supports. Policy in the 1990s often speaks of partnerships between state programs and informal supports (Chappell and Prince 1994).

The term **formal support** refers to professional caregivers such as doctors, nurses, and social workers. People pay for formal supports either from their own resources or through their taxes. The term informal supports refers to the unpaid help given by friends, neighbours, and family. Informal supports include everyday help such as rides to the doctor or to a shopping centre, help with yardwork, or just a visit from a neighbour. Informal supporters can also help an older person cope with a personal crisis, adjust to a change in health, or locate a formal service (Snider 1981). The National Advisory Council on Aging (1990d) estimates that 270 000 seniors in the community need informal support.

Studies find, for example, that few older people who need help with daily chores or health care use only formal care. More often people use both the formal and informal support systems. Béland (1989) found that, in a random sample of 538 older people in Quebec, high users of formal services also used informal services a great deal (see also Chipperfield 1994). Studies show that people usually turn to the formal system only after the informal system breaks down (Chappell and Havens 1985; Brody 1981; O'Brien and Wagner 1980).

Snell (1990) studied the legal history of family support in Canada in the 1920s and 1930s and found that these laws expected families to care for their older members. The federal Criminal Code still requires children to provide parents with the basic necessities of life if the parents cannot provide for themselves. All provinces have legislation that requires a child to support needy parents if the parents support themselves (McDonald et al. 1991).

Today, most older people get voluntary informal support from their families. Stone (1988) says that informal caregivers (family and friends) provide 75 to 85 percent of health care to older people (see also Kane, Evans, and McFadyen 1990). People continue to get support, especially from the nuclear family, even after they face a health care crisis (Stolar, Hill, and Tomblin 1986). Informal supports can also buffer stress from life events like widowhood or illness (Rosenthal 1987a). A greater proportion of older women, compared with older men, got emotional support from children or friends (McDaniel 1993). A study in Quebec found that older men, compared with older women, had smaller support networks. Men, more often than women, had no family members in their networks (Corin, Sherif, and Bergeron 1983 cited in Woodward 1994).

Stone (1988, 14) found that the availability of **primary potential support groups** changed as people aged. He defines this type of group as family and close friends who give help to the older person and who can expect help from the older person. Stone (1988) reports that about a third of people aged 65 to 79 lived with a spouse and had family and friendship ties. Men more often than women had this kind of support group structure. Past the age of 80, community-dwelling seniors tended to live alone, but they still had links outside their household to children, close friends, and other relatives (McDaniel 1994a; Stone 1988). Women more often than men had this kind of support group structure. Very old people in institutions probably have smaller support structures or none at all.

Stone's research describes the "potential" support group available to older people. Other studies have looked at how older people choose their informal supporters out of this potential group. Studies have also looked at what tasks informal supporters do. Two models describe the way people use informal supports: (1) the **task specificity model** says that different groups (family, friends, neighbours) have different abilities and offer different types of support (Litwak 1985). Each group plays a specific role in supporting the older person; (2) the **hierarchical compensatory model** of support states that people choose their supports first from their inner family circle. They then move outward to get support from less intimate people as they need more help (Cantor and Little 1985). This model, for example, says that a married older person will get help first from a spouse, and a widow or widower will get help from a child (most often a daughter) (Chappell 1991; Walker 1991). The older person will then turn to friends, neighbours, and formal supports in that order.

Penning (1990) compared the ability of these two models to explain older people's use of informal supports. She found only limited support for each model. Older people tended to use a variety of formal and informal supports at the same time and not in a specific hierarchical order. She also found that groups did a variety of tasks that overlapped. For example, relatives and neighbours may both help with household tasks. Penning (1990, 227) says that "it is unlikely that assistance is provided routinely and uniformly on the basis of a set order

of preference." Penning (1990, 227; see also Corin 1987) concludes that "the issue of who provides assistance to whom, of what type, and under what conditions is complex."

Stolar and her colleagues (1993) support this conclusion. She studied older people who lived in the community. She found that people chose a supporter according to their specific need. This seems to support the task specificity model. But she also found that gender and marital status led people to make different choices of supporters. The availability of support for married people, for example, led them to turn to their spouse for support. Men more often had this option than women (due to widowhood). Widows most often said children served as their main source of support. Neither model alone explains the supports that older people use.

Chappell (1991) adds another dimension to this complexity. Her research suggests that whether or not an older person lives with someone strongly influences the type of support they get. If an older person lives with another person, the person they live with will likely give them support for the activities necessary to daily living. Litwak (1985) found that this held true for spouses, but Chappell found that it was the case regardless of the relation of the housemate to the older person. This means that shared living arrangements (between siblings or friends) may help widowed or childless older people live in the community. A later study by Chappell and Blandford (1991) found that two conditions led to the use of formal supports along with informal supports. First, some older people have incomplete informal networks and need specific kinds of help (like someone to shop for them). Second, some older people who have intact networks have high health care needs. The informal and formal systems work together in these cases to share the overall load.

Chappell (1989a) found that men get less informal support than women from nonspousal supporters. This showed up most clearly for less serious illnesses. Chappell (1989a) concludes that women's stronger emotional bonds with friends and family lead to greater support. Chappell, Segall, and Lewis (1990) found the same trend toward greater support for women regardless of the type of illness (common ailments, health emergencies, or functional disability). Compared with men, women tended to consult more family and friends regarding common ailments. Women, more often than men, said they would consult a relative outside the house for a health emergency. And women, compared with men, reported support from more helpers and more help from daughters and relatives for functional disabilities.

Rosenthal (National Advisory Council on Aging 1986a, 4), estimates that 70 to 80 percent of the health care that allows people to stay in their home comes from informal supports—a spouse or child (though the type of support available and used may differ by gender). Chappell and Segall (1989) report that when older people have a helping network, they feel greater subjective well-being. The researchers found that older people who had children to help during an emergency felt more secure and those who had spouses to help with everyday ailments felt that they had good consultation and advice.

Chappell and Havens (1985) studied 800 older people in Winnipeg. Four hundred of these people used formal home care services; the other 400 came from a random sample of the population not using these services. They found that more than half of their total sample (58 percent) received help of some kind. Ninety-four percent of those who received help got it from informal sources. Also, of the 15 percent who got formal care, 80 percent also got informal care. Chappell and Havens found that people who got help with everyday activities— dressing, shopping, telephoning—were more likely to get help from informal than formal supports. The researchers conclude that "most elderly persons cope well within the community without an inordinate amount of assistance. Further … [these findings] also support the claims that informal care to aging members is alive and well. This is true even when the elderly individuals are recipients of formal care such as that provided by [home care programs]" (Chappell and Havens 1985, 227).

Children as a Source of Informal Support

Adult children provide much of the support needed by their adult parents. Crawford, Bond, and Balshaw (1994) found that strong feelings of attachment to a parent lead to caregiving. Also, feelings of closeness between children and parents lead to high life satisfaction and happiness (Connidis and McMullin 1992). They also found

that daughters, compared with sons, provide more care to parents. Aronson (1990a) traces this difference to cultural pressures on women to give care. One woman put this simply: "Who else is going to do it?" (Aronson 1992).

Wolfson and her colleagues (1993) studied adult children's attitudes toward care for their parents. The children in this study felt strongly that children should give emotional, physical, and financial support to their parents. The adult children felt less certain that they could give all three kinds of support. Children felt most able to give parents emotional support. They felt less able to give parents physical and financial support. The researchers conclude that children want to help their parents. But they lack some of the resources (time to give physical care and money) to give all the support their parents may need.

Still, even with limited time and energy, children support their elderly parents. Hall (1989) found that even hospitalized older people receive informal help from their children. He studied twenty-seven adult children who care for hospitalized, chronically ill parents. The adult children reported that their parents depended on them a lot and they predicted a high future dependence. They also reported that they gave their parents a lot of psychological support, got involved in bureaucratic mediation in the hospital, and gave their parents personal care. Hall (1989) found that caregiving created stress for the children, but they continued to help their parents.

Studies show that adult children and their parents see the amount of support provided by the children differently. Many studies report that older people feel they receive less support than their children say they give (Bond and Harvey 1991). Bengtson and Kuypers (1971) refer to this as differences in the **developmental stake.** Older people have a greater stake in the relationship with their children and, so, tend to emphasize the existence of family harmony and solidarity. They may de-emphasize the amount of support they receive in order not to see themselves as a burden on their children. This difference in perception can create tensions in the family. Adult children may feel that their parents do not appreciate how much they do for them, even though the children may feel they do as much as they can.

Gatz, Bengtson, and Blum (1990) say that intergenerational interaction may have grown in intensity in recent years. Older people and their children live longer lives and spend more years interacting with one another. Gee (1988) reports that in Canada from the 1830s to the 1950s the number of years spent parenting declined for women. But the time spent as an adult child increased. Today, people spend more years as an adult child of living parents than as parents of young children (Bengtson, Rosenthal, and Burton 1990; Gee 1988). This trend will continue in the future. In some cases child caregivers will also need support as they grow older. Stolar, Hill, and Tomblin (1986) say that many nuclear families need more support and should get more from the formal care system.

Jutras (1988) says that changes in the family may limit informal caregiving in the future (see also Marshall 1987). She says that geographic mobility, immigration, greater numbers of 18-to-25-year-olds at home, smaller modern homes, multi-generational help needs, more pressure on fewer children, women in the workforce, caregiver burnout, and conflicting demands on caregivers may all put pressure on the informal care system. A lower birthrate and smaller numbers of children per family, for example, mean that middle-aged children will have fewer siblings to help support their aging parents (Gatz, Bengtson, and Blum 1990, citing Hagestad 1986).

Friends as a Source of Informal Support

Blau (1973) says that people enjoy friends most in youth and in old age. For example, the group aged 65 and over reported the highest proportion of people (30 percent) with ten or more friends (McDaniel 1994a). High-quality friendships in later life lead to high life satisfaction (O'Connor 1995). Synge and Luxton (1984) found that 20 percent of women aged 74 and over received visits from nonrelatives every day or two. Almost 30 percent said they received visits once or twice a week. Studies also show that older people get more enjoyment out of visits with friends than with family. Researchers say that people in a family may visit one another as a matter of routine or because they feel obliged to see one another. But when older people see their friends, they do so out of choice (Antonucci 1990). Older people also may have more in common with their friends than with

younger family members, and this leads to greater warmth and good feeling (Chappell 1980).

Most older people choose friends from their own age group. Chappell (1983a) studied 400 noninstitutionalized older people living in Winnipeg. Eighty-three percent of the people in this sample said that their close friends were also older people. On average these older people had less than one friend under the age of 60. These people reported more contact with friends than with relatives (who lived outside their home) or with neighbours, and they felt more satisfied with their friendships than with other relationships outside the home.

Rempel (1985) found that childless older people create a network of supportive friends, and they report as much life satisfaction as older people who have children. Connidis and McMullin (1992; 1994) report that childless older people (aged 55 and over) develop unique social networks with friends and relatives. Connidis (1994; also Connidis and Davies 1992; Strain and Payne 1992) found, for example, that childless older people, compared with people with children, set up more supportive ties with their siblings. They tend to get more support from siblings when they get ill. Childless siblings also tend to give support to their brothers and sisters.

Childless older people also create active social lives for themselves (Marcil-Gratton and Légaré 1992). They arrange outings with relatives and friends and often do things outside their homes. Those who have chosen to have no children report high life satisfaction and happiness. They have about the same satisfaction with life as married older people who have close relations with their children. Rempel (1985) found that compared with people with children, childless older people feel more satisfied with their health, housing, and income. Rempel concludes that "family is not necessarily the crucial element in determining high life quality in old age" (1985, 347). Still, the social networks of older childless people offer less support when the older person becomes sick. These networks also provide less support for activities of daily living (Bengtson, Rosenthal, and Burton 1990). For this reason, childless older people need more formal supports than do older parents. They also face a greater risk of institutionalization than do people with children.

Researchers say that friendships can help older people overcome problems caused by lost work roles and the lost spouse role in old age. Norris and her colleagues (1983) say that older people use friends and family their own age as role models and for emotional support. "Since friendship rests on mutual choice and mutual need and involves a voluntary exchange of sociability between equals, it sustains a person's sense of usefulness and self-esteem more effectively than filial relationships" (Chappell 1980, 173). Friends who are the same age often share the same physical limits, the same interests, and the same historical background. Studies of family supporters (who live outside the older person's home) and friendships show that older people often rely on friends their own age for social and emotional support. This research suggests that different people in the older person's social network (children, neighbours, friends) serve different functions in the older person's support system. A child may help a parent with activities of daily living like banking, transportation, or house-keeping. Neighbours and friends can serve as confidants and social partners. A variety of relationships creates a full and satisfying support network.

Informal Support and Caregiver Burden

Research shows that older people often use informal supports (Chappell and Havens 1985; Thompson 1989) and that these supports succeed in keeping people out of institutions (Hess and Soldo 1985). Married people, for example, have a built-in caregiving system. Most older Canadians reported their spouse as their main source of support (McDaniel 1994a). Pruchno (1990) found that even old and frail people continued to give care to their cognitively impaired spouses. Hess and Soldo (1985, 78) report that "75 percent more married than unmarried elderly with functional health limitations rely exclusively on care services produced within their own households." One study reports that this can lead to an average of 75 hours a week of caregiving work (Pruchno and Resch 1989). Even in late old age, when people have serious functional disabilities, married people have half the institutionalization rate of unmarried older people (Hess and Soldo 1985).

Many studies report that giving care to a physically disabled or cognitively impaired older person can lead to feelings of **caregiver burden.** This refers to problems and stress due to caregiving. Some research (Horowitz and Shindelman 1981) suggests that spouses of those receiving care suffer a greater burden from caregiving than do adult children. They may feel the strain more as they see their partner decline (especially if the person shows mental as well as physical decline). Hadjistav-ropoulos and his colleagues (1994), for example, found that caregivers felt the most burden when they perceived a decline in a patient's mood and memory. The researchers (Hadjistavropoulos et al. 1994, 312) say that "actual deficits are relatively unimportant in the determination of caregiver burden. More important is the caregivers' appraisal of the severity of these deficits."

Spouses may have health problems themselves that make caregiving difficult and add to the feeling of burden. They may also have fewer resources (financial and social) to call on than would a middle-aged child. Pruchno (1990) found that spouses got little support from others and that even task support and social support failed to reduce spouses' feelings of burden. Jutras and Lavoie (1995) report that people who lived with an impaired older person (many of them spouses), compared with those who did not, felt stress and reported poor psychological well-being. Neysmith and Nichols (1994) report that family caregivers feel a loss of control and autonomy. Kin caregivers also report problems doing tasks like cleaning and shopping.

Even after a spouse enters an institution a caregiver spouse feels caregiver burden. Novak and Guest (1992) found that spouses of institutionalized older people, compared with adult children, felt more physical and developmental burden. Physical burden referred to the strain of long visits and travel to the institution. Developmental burden referred to spouses' feelings of being unable to get on with life. Rosenthal and her colleagues (1993) found that long distances to travel for visits led to feelings of depression. MacKenzie and MacLean (1992) report similar findings. They also report that some spouses feel lonely and believe that friends and family do not understand their condition (see also Gladstone 1995). One wife told Gladstone (1995, 56), "When you're apart after never being apart it has an effect on you. You seem to be in a turmoil. We'd known each other since we were 14 years old so we were together a long, long time."

Rosenthal and Dawson (1991) refer to **quasi-widowhood.** Ross, Rosenthal, and Dawson (1994, 26) studied 40 wives who had placed their husbands in nursing homes. These women say that they felt relief after placement. But they also felt failure, "anger, guilt, sadness, depression and grief." Most women over time adapt to living with a spouse in an institution. Some women accept the loss of their spouse as a friend and companion. They restructure their lives outside the institution (Rosenthal and Dawson 1992).

Other spouses keep close ties to the institution. About a third of them visited their husbands often, nine months after placement. This group, the researchers said, were "holding on to the past." They often had husbands with physical impairments. Overall they felt more depressed at the end of nine months and felt dissatisfied with their husband's care. This study suggests that wives who begin to give up the caregiver role do better after institutionalization. The researchers found that about two-thirds of spouses gave up some of their caregiving responsibility. These wives had cognitively impaired spouses. They visited less and allowed staff to take on the job of caring. This group began a process called "embracing new realities." They felt less depressed and said they felt "sort of like a widow" (Ross, Rosenthal, and Dawson 1994, 29). Healing began to take place as wives gained distance from the caregiver role.

Some caregivers report feelings of satisfaction and accomplishment (Colerick and George 1986). Cohen et al. (1994) found that 55 percent of caregivers spontaneously mentioned something positive about caregiving. They often mentioned that they enjoyed helping their care receiver feel better. They also felt duty and love toward their care receiver. Fitting et al. (1986) found that one-quarter of husbands reported improved relationships with their wives after they began caregiving. In another study, a majority of daughters, who had completed their caregiving work, said that they felt glad that they helped when they did (Lewis and Meredith 1988). One caregiver, for example, reports that care for his aunt in his home improved family life. He says she brought a "sort of wisdom" to the family (Nemeth and Howse 1994, 35). "Both my parents," he says, "have instilled in me the pride in family and the responsibility to look after your own. ... It's hard to put into words. You do something because it's the right thing to do" (Nemeth and Howse 1994, 35).

But most families pay an emotional and psychological price when they take on informal caregiving (Bond, Harvey, and Hildebrand 1987). And caregivers of cognitively impaired older people, many of them spouses, feel the most stress (Canadian Study 1994). When policy-makers talk about "shifting care to the community," this usually means shifting the job to a daughter or wife (Aronson 1985; Chappell 1982a; Hooyman 1990; Matthews and Campbell 1995). The Canadian Study of Health and Aging (1994), a nationwide random sample study, found that women made up 75 percent of informal caregivers. This study and others find that caregivers often feel isolated, fatigued, and overwhelmed by the strain of care (Canadian Study 1994; Novak and Guest 1989; Zarit, Reever, and Bach-Peterson 1980).

A respondent in one study of middle-aged children said, "I have looked after both parents for twenty-seven years and they have become very dependent on me. We are very tied down and I don't know how much more my nerves and health can stand" (Marshall, Rosenthal, and Synge 1983). In another study a woman said, "[Mother] has been getting more and more forgetful and confused and can't be alone at all. I'm depressed, and I don't sleep well. How can I go to work when she needs constant supervision?" (Brody 1990, ix).

Caregiving leads to a variety of tensions for middle-aged children. They often feel both intense pressure in trying to meet the demands on their time made by work, their children, and caregiving, and emotional upset at having to deal with an ill parent (Gee and Kimball 1987; Bond et al. 1990). Gatz, Bengtson, and Blum (1990) say that caregiving brings up the inherent tension between the adult child's personal autonomy and his or her interdependence within a family. A daughter in a Toronto study says, "We were living in the present, for my mother, without being able to make definite vacation plans, or whatever, or take subscriptions to anything. We were living in the present in such a way that [it] was living in her present, in that hell" (Globerman 1994, 217–18). These feelings can lead to resentment and frustration.

Even adult children who do not consider themselves caregivers may feel concern about their parents. A child with a parent in an institution says, "Our whole lives are caught up with my mother in her disease [Alzheimer's]. It's with us 24 hours a day. We're constantly a victim of, or reminded of it all the time." A study by Marshall et al. (1983)

found that about a third of adult children reported worry about the future health of their parents. The closer the feelings between children and parents and the more frequent the contact between them, the more the children worried (Marshall 1987).

In the case of widowed or divorced older people with children, middle-aged daughters most often take on the job of caregiving. Kaden and McDaniel (1990) found that daughters provided 87 percent of daily and weekly assistance to their parents (compared with 13 percent for sons). Mothers receive 70 percent of this care. Horowitz (1985; see also Canadian Study 1994) found that sons take on the job of caregiver only when the parents have no daughter to help. She found that sons called and visited parents less often than daughters and also that they prepared meals, cleaned house, or gave personal care to their parents less often.

Jutras and Veilleux (1991) report no difference in caregiver burden between men and women. But most studies show that females report more strain from caregiving than males (Marcus and Jaeger, 1984). These women suffer physical strain, lower morale, and greater psychological burden than men (Marcus and Jaeger 1984; Zarit, Reever, and Bach-Peterson 1980). Brody (1981; see also Schlesinger and Raphael 1992) proposed that women can get caught in the middle—sandwiched between care for their children and care for their parents. "Such women are in middle age, in the middle from a generational standpoint, and in the middle in that the demands of their various roles compete for their time and energy" (1981, 471). But recent studies question this view of middle-age. They find that relatively few women get caught in the middle like this.

Statistics Canada (Smith and Dumas 1994, 115) defines the **sandwich generation** as "people aged 35 to 64 who have at least one child at home and at least one parent aged 65 or over." Smith and Dumas (1994) report that 37 percent of 35-to-64-year-olds fall into this group. But they go on to say that "the common view that membership in this generation brings with it a high risk of having to support a heavy burden of dependence seems … not to have a demographic foundation. Two members out of three of this group do not have children or parents in the age groups most associated with dependence: children under 5 and parents aged 85 or older" (Smith and Dumas 1994, 124). Also, data show that sandwich generation children provide few services (like transportation or personal care) to their parents.

Research by Rosenthal, Matthews, and Marshall (1989) support this finding. They studied a random sample of middle-aged women. They found that less than half these women risked having children and a parent to care for. Many of the parents of the older women in the group had died. And few of those with living older parents had children to care for. The younger women in the group with children had younger parents in relatively good health.

Does this mean that middle-aged children feel little caregiver burden? First, a large minority (about one-third) of sandwich generation members do face demands from children and very old parents. Hirdes and Strain (1995) looked at the balance of exchange in support (like housework and personal care) between young, middle-aged, and older people in Canada. They found that children and older people tend to get more support than they give. But middle-aged people tend to provide more support than they get. Second, the need to give care to an older parent alone may create tensions for middle-aged children. Third, middle-aged women do more caregiving than men. Many of these women work outside the home and face demands at work that making caregiving for a parent more stressful.

For example, the trend toward women working outside the home has created a "care-giving crunch" that places heavy burdens on women (Myles 1991, 83). This crunch exists because society expects women to serve as caregivers. Neal et al. (1990) found that employed caregivers, compared with employed non-caregivers, experience more stress and greater absenteeism from work. The researchers say that caregivers need family strategies to cope with stress. They also need job flexibility and community supports to help them stay at work.

Gottlieb (1989) says that four conditions influence feelings of burden: past and present relationships with the care receiver, the support a caregiver can draw on, psychological coping methods, and the impact of caregiving on other spheres of life (see also Chiriboga, Weiler, and Nielsen 1990; Ducharme 1994). He emphasizes that caregiving takes place in the context of an ongoing relationship. He warns against simply counting the amount of burden or satisfaction a caregiver feels.

Aronson (1985) says that the government should pay for care given by family members. She also says that because the Canada Pension Plan pays benefits based on average yearly earnings over a lifetime, Canada society should allow caregivers to drop out the years they spend caregiving when they add up their pensionable years of work instead of counting them as years of zero income. Aronson admits that these reforms will cost the government more money and that the government will probably resist funding them. Unless some reform takes place, however, women will continue to absorb the cost of caregiving in the community. Myles says that changed workplace norms and more sympathetic personnel practices can help ease this crunch. But he also calls for more radical reform, saying that "nothing short of a revolution in gender relations and in the sexual division of care-giving work is required to solve the problem" (Myles 1991, 84).

Care for the Caregiver

A number of researchers (Chappell 1989b; Gatz, Bengtson, and Blum 1990; National Advisory Council on Aging 1990d) have proposed ways to ease caregiver burden. Some of these proposals are listed below.

1. Family counselling can help ease the burden of caregiving. This works best when it takes into account the entire family system—the caregiver's spouse, children, and siblings as well as the older person. Counselling can help caregivers deal with moral conflicts about how much protection to give a care receiver. Counselling or psychotherapy can help a caregiver deal with stress and depression.

2. **Support groups** give caregivers information about how to cope with caregiving demands. They also give caregivers emotional support. The Alzheimer's Society, hospitals, and churches offer support groups. Some groups offer support based on a specific disease (e.g., dementia or cancer). Some of these groups have a professional leader; others work as self-help groups. People in these groups often report feelings of relief and greater ability to manage as caregivers (Toseland et al., 1992). Demers and Lavoie (1996) found mixed results in a study of support groups. They found that caregiver burden increased among support group members. But they found that depressive symptoms remained stable.

3. Community services include **respite services.** These range from friendly visitors, who stay with the care receiver for a few hours, to full-day adult day care, to longer institutional respite. All of these programs give caregivers a break from the demands of caregiving. Institutional respite programs can last from several days to several weeks, allowing caregivers to take vacations, deal with personal needs like medical treatment, or simply rest. Rapelje (1992, 243) calls respite programs "the best kept secret in the Canadian health care field." Burdz, Eaton, and Bond (1988) found that behaviour problems decreased after respite. But caregivers still felt some burden. Other studies of respite have also found mixed results. Lawton, Brody, and Saperstein (1989) report little measurable benefit from respite care beyond the feeling of caregiver satisfaction. Still, Neysmith and Nichols (1994) say, family caregivers value and want respite.

4. **Eldercare** programs at work can help family caregivers cope. Brody and Schoonover (1986) say that 28 percent of nonworking, middle-aged caregiving daughters in their study quit their jobs to take care of their mothers. Other women reduced their work hours, and some had thought about quitting. Brody and Schoonover found that the mothers of working women got the same number of hours of care (formal and informal) as the mothers of nonworking women, but the working women often had to pay for personal care and meal services. These paid services filled in for them while they worked.

A study done by Canadian Aging Research Network (CARNET) asked over 5000 employees in eight organizations about their caregiving responsibilities (Gottlieb and Kelloway 1993). The researchers found that 46 percent of workers give some care to an older person. Types of care fell into three groups: ADL care (help with bathing, grooming); IADL care (help with shopping, transportation); management help (money management, arranging for help). Management help created some of the greatest stress on workers. Twenty-six percent of the people who give eldercare also care for a child under age 19. Gottlieb and his colleagues (1994; also Matthews and Campbell 1995) found that women with young children at home and who give eldercare face a high risk of personal and job costs. One-quarter of workers who give eldercare average 9 hours per week helping with activities of daily living as well as general care. The rest averaged 3 hours per week of general help like household chores (Gottlieb and Kelloway 1993; see also Gottlieb, Kelloway, and Fraboni 1994).

Eldercare for many workers leads to stress and time away from the job. About one-third of working caregivers said the caregiving disturbed their work (Canadian Study 1994). Barling, MacEwen, and Kelloway (1994; see also Matthews and Rosenthal 1993) found that eldercare led to absenteeism from work and psychological strain. People who cared for young children and an elder, compared with other workers, had four times the proportion of absences from work. A study of eldercare in Alberta (McKinnon 1991, cited in Rosenthal and Gladstone 1993) found that 5 percent of working women said they had quit work in the past to care for an older person. Caregiving also leads to fewer special projects at work, less business travel, and fewer promotions (Canadian Press 1993). Caregivers also had to cut back on leisure, education, and volunteer activities.

Some companies have responded to this problem. The Royal Bank began an eldercare program in 1992. This program offers counselling and refers workers to community supports (Nemeth and Howse 1994). Gottlieb and Kelloway (1993) found that flexible work schedules for caregivers led to less stress and more job satisfaction. Dual caregivers (who care for children and elders) made the most use of Employee Assistance Programs and part-time employment. Still, companies could do more to inform workers about eldercare options. Gottlieb and Kelloway found 46 percent of workers give eldercare, but only 8 percent of them had information on eldercare programs. Companies could make eldercare information and programs more available to workers.

Mohide et al. (1990) conducted a controlled study of the combined effects of a variety of intervention methods. The study offered caregivers health care for themselves, an education program on caregiving, help with problem solving, in-home respite, and a self-help support group. The control group received normal community nursing care. The researchers found mixed results. Neither the intervention nor the control group felt less depressed or anxious after the six-month study. But the experimental group did show some improvement. Their quality of life was better; they kept their care receivers in the community longer; they found caregiving less trouble; and they felt more satisfied with nursing support. This study shows that intervention can relieve some degree of caregiver burden. But researchers need to use a variety of approaches to measure the benefits of support. Also, George (1990, 581) says, "given that we know little about the caregiver stress process, perhaps we should not be surprised if it is difficult to document that our interventions have strong positive effects."

Chappell (1989b) reports on a number of programs that might relieve caregiver burden. These include pay for caregivers, employers' support of caregivers through family leave programs, and a program by IBM that offers an Elder Care Referral System to help caregivers cope with the social service system. Marshall (1989) projects a rapid growth in employee assistance programs for caregivers. But little evidence suggests that payment will lead people to take on the caregiver role, or that money alone will relieve burden (Arling and McAuley 1983; Noelker and Poulshock 1982). Chappell (1989b) recommends careful research on the value of paying caregivers and on the effectiveness of corporate support programs.

Interventions cannot completely do away with all feelings of burden. Nor should they. Spouses and children will feel loss, anger, and frustration as they see a person close to them suffer through an illness. These feelings reflect a legitimate response to a parent's or spouse's suffering. But interventions can help caregivers understand caregiving; they can help caregivers cope with the everyday demands of care; and they can give caregivers emotional support.

Exhibit 13.5

Feelings of Caregiver Burden

A report published by the Canada Mortgage and Housing Corporation (Gnaedinger 1989) includes comments by caregivers about their experiences. These comments reveal the stresses that caregivers face.

- I was out of energy, out of patience … and I was afraid I was out of love, because I was starting to scream at him … and he hit me one time. Every day he is slowly dying and part of me is dying with him, and our marriage is dying with him … I am not widowed, not married … what am I?

- How many sleepless nights I had, I can't tell you. I looked like the wrath of God. Eventually my kids said to me, "C'mon Dad, we're losing Mother, we don't want to lose you too!"

- He destroyed my personality … I didn't realize what an impact it had on me.

- My mother is like a baby that we care for … our life has been shattered by this disease and it continues to shape our habits, but we wish to continue this experience to the end … our mother became ill when she was 72 years old, she is now 81 years old. She continues to be our mother in spite of her soul being gone.

- I don't think I would survive if I had to go through it again today. One has to have lived it in order to understand. I am still not able to remember the whole experience unemotionally, although it has been 8 years since he passed away.

- As I am printing this I have started to cry. God help other caregivers who have to go through all the stages of this horrendous disease.

Source: Nancy Gnaedinger, *Housing Alzheimer's Disease at Home* (Ottawa: Canada Mortgage and Housing Corporation, 1989). Reproduced with the permission of the Minister of Public Works and Government Services Canada, 1996.

Few of the proposals to ease caregiver burden address the large-scale issues of gender inequality or the changing role of women in the labour force. But Myles (1991, cited in McDaniel and Gee 1993) says that these and other large-scale social issues may create a new crisis for the welfare state. For example, current programs and policies to help caregivers take family caregiving for granted. This puts the burden on female family members. Help for caregivers comes into play only when family care breaks down. And the current rhetoric about family care suggests that the state will try to shift more caregiving to family members (McDaniel and Gee 1993). McDaniel and Gee (1993) say that caregiving demands will increase in the future. They propose more studies of caregiving policies.

The Future of Informal Support

Informal supports play a vital role in the well-being of older people. But the availability of informal supports may decrease in the years ahead. At least three changes in Canadian society point to this likelihood.

First, changes in demography may decrease the amount of informal support older people will get in the future. Family size has shrunk, so older people in the future will have fewer children to call on for help (Crimmins and Ingegneri 1990). Stolar, Hill, and Tomblin (1986) note that a decrease in the availability of nuclear family supports increases the risk of institutionalization.

Also, the number of children over the age of 65 who care for their parents will increase in the future as more people live longer (Bengtson, Rosenthal, and Burton 1990). Some of these children will be unable to care for their parents, and some may need health care help themselves.

Second, as people live longer, their support groups suffer from cohort attrition (Stone 1987). Peers die off over time, leaving members of some support networks without help. This makes children a vital source of support for most older people as they age (Marshall, Rosenthal, and Synge 1981). Synge (no date), in a study of social supports, found that the older the woman the more often she turned to a child for emotional support. Thirty-one percent of women aged 40 to 54 said they turned first to a child, compared with 63 percent of women aged 70 or over.

Because women outlive men more often than men outlive women, they have to turn to children for support. Few studies have looked at how older women feel about relying on their children. Aronson (1990b) found that older women feel ambivalent about depending on their children. Her qualitative study contained 14 women aged 59 to 85. Women in this study said they could depend on their daughters for help, but they wanted to be independent and self-reliant. They felt torn by the need for support and the feeling that they might burden their children. To deal with this, these older women set limits on the amount and kind of help they would accept. But they could not deal openly with the sense that they lived marginal lives in their families. Aronson (1990b) says that research needs to look more closely at older women who receive care. This will give family members and policy-makers a better idea of what kind of support the older person wants.

Very old people will even lose their children. Shanas and her colleagues (1968, cited in Abu-Laban 1980a) found that in Britain, Denmark, and the United States between 20 and 25 percent of all older people have no children. Similar trends will show up in Canada in the years ahead. Very old people (many of them women) will need more formal supports as they age.

Third, expressive ties for older people tend to decline because of widowhood and cohort attrition. This leads older people to use their remaining ties to meet expressive needs. This may cause problems for the baby boom generation in the future. They have had fewer children of their own than older people today. In the second or third decade of the next century, the middle-aged children of baby boom parents may find themselves swamped by their parents' care needs.

These trends suggest potential problems with the availability of informal supports in the future. But other trends might lead to stronger informal supports. First, longer life expectancy means that spouses will live together longer than ever before. This will give married couples more informal support as they age.

Second, current trends in health promotion (better diet, exercise, and a decrease in smoking) may lead to better health in old age (Stone and Fletcher 1986). If these trends continue, older people in the future may need less long-term health care support.

Third, new types of groups based on the mutual needs of older people may develop. Novak and Stone (1985) call these **semiformal structures** because they fall between the informal (voluntary) support structures of the family and the formal (professionalized) structures of the health and social service systems. Semiformal structures include car pools, groups of people in the same building who shop together, friendly visitors, or "daily hello" phone callers. These groups and relationships do not rely on informal kinship, friendship bonds, or on the fee-for-service bond of formal supports. Instead, they are based on a bond of reciprocity and on the fact that they bring mutual benefit to users. More of these groups in the future could make up for losses in older people's networks.

Both trends—the decrease in informal supports and the increase in alternative forms of support (including home care and semiformal structures)—could get stronger in the future. The well-being of older people in the future will depend on how well alternatives to traditional supports meet their needs.

Rosenthal (1994) cautions that current trends in policy may lead to future problems in long-term care. Current policy supports a shift in responsibility for elder care from institutions and professionals to "the community." This often means a shift to the family. And this often means a shift to the middle-aged or older woman. Government policy has begun to view formal support as an aid to family support. Guberman and her colleagues (1992) say that the health system has begun to use women in the family as a substitute for institutional care. Rosenthal worries that the government will not provide enough community services to meet the needs of these caregivers. Women who choose to care for older family members need support at work, good community supports, and institutional care when their care receiver needs it (Rosenthal 1994). She also worries that fewer institutional beds will leave families without this option when they need it.

Rosenthal (1994) says that formal support should play the central part in social support. Families (middle-aged women) can then decide how much or how little of this support they need. "We should not overestimate the availability or quality of family care," Rosenthal (1994, 421) says. "Some older people do not have family members who are able to provide care." Others may have family members who do not have the time or energy to give more than emotional support. Still others may prefer professional help to family care (Connidis and McMullin 1994). Guberman and her colleagues (1992, 616) say that when policies assume that women will "provide unpaid labor in the home, questions of choice become moot." The movement toward community should not force middle-aged women into a caregiving role.

ELDER ABUSE

Most older people get support and comfort from their families, but some people face exploitation and abuse. No single definition of elder abuse exists (McDonald et al. 1991; Stones 1994). But one of the broadest definitions refers to "harm to an older person caused by someone in a position of trust, who may have control over the victim" (Government 1992, 1). Elder abuse includes physical abuse, psychosocial abuse, financial abuse, and neglect (active or passive) (National Clearinghouse on Family Violence 1990, cited in Wigdor 1991). Research shows that most elder abuse comes from family members. This leads many abused older people to suffer in silence, and makes elder abuse hard to estimate and harder to eliminate. A number of new studies of elder abuse in Canada discuss recent research findings, policy issues, and best practice.

Recent Research Findings

Most Canadian research on elder abuse has used convenience samples, sometimes with low response rates. This makes generalization from these findings uncertain. Podnieks et al. (1990) conducted Canada's first random-sample survey on elder abuse. The researchers conducted telephone interviews with a sample of 2008 people aged 65

plus who lived in private households. These people present a statistically reliable picture of the 91 percent of seniors who live on their own in the community. The survey asked about abuse carried out by family members and other intimates.

The sample contained about two-thirds women; 73 percent of respondents owned their own homes; and 52 percent were married. About a third of the respondents received the Guaranteed Income Supplement (the federal government pension that goes to the poorest seniors); 63 percent reported good or excellent health; and the large majority shopped, cooked, and cleaned for themselves. Relatively few respondents reported feeling lonely, bored or downhearted. The majority by far (92 percent) said they felt fairly happy or very happy.

The researchers defined four categories of abuse: material abuse, chronic verbal aggression, physical violence, and neglect (Podnieks et al. 1990). The study counted only the most serious and obvious cases. Because of this, the researchers caution that their findings probably underestimate the number of abused older people.

The study estimates that about 4 percent of all older people (about 98 000 people) in private dwellings in Canada have experienced abuse since turning age 65. This is similar to the rate (3.2 percent) that Pillemer and Finkelhor (1988) report for a random sample study in the United States Most of these cases involve passive, verbal, emotional, and financial abuse, rather than physical violence or neglect. This fits with the findings of other U.S. and Canadian studies (Belanger 1981; Hickey and Douglass 1981; Stevenson 1985).

Podnieks and her colleagues (1990) found that about 2.5 percent of seniors in the Canadian study have experienced material abuse (potentially 60 000 people nation-wide); about 1.4 percent of seniors experienced chronic verbal aggression (potentially 34 000 people nation-wide); about 0.5 percent of seniors experienced physical violence (potentially 12 000 people nation-wide); and about 0.4 percent of seniors experienced neglect (potentially 10 000 people nation-wide). The study also found a fifth common form of abuse: denial of access to grandchildren. About 4 percent of seniors (98 000 people) report denial of access at least once since they turned age 65. If the researchers had included this category at the start of their study, the overall prevalence rate of abuse would nearly

Exhibit 13.6

Senior Suffers Abuse of Trust

Dr. Peter Ingram, a psychogeriatric specialist in Winnipeg, describes a case of material abuse. He goes on to explain the options open to him and his patient once he detects the abuse.

Anastasia Kowalchuk (not her real name) is angry. She can't understand why the bank took $12,000 of her money, more than half the 87-year-old woman's savings.

Her niece, who had been visiting from Toronto, took her to the bank where Anastasia hoped to withdraw some money to donate to her community's nursing home, where she plans to move this year. She was shocked to see how little money she had left. With the help of her niece, she asked the bank to find out what had happened.

On a return visit, the bank manager showed her the transaction slip with her signature, authorizing the withdrawal. Although Anastasia's vision is dim from cataracts, she had to agree the signature looked like her own.

Anastasia has had trouble remembering things for some time. She forgets to pay her bills and deposit her pension cheques. When her friend Mary offered to help her with cooking meals and housekeeping two years ago for a small salary, it seemed like a good way to stay out of the nursing home.

When Mary more recently suggested she also help with the banking, Anastasia agreed. Now Mary is acting strangely, she has been shouting at her and told her not to talk to Sophia or Kateryna, her neighbors. As Anastasia speaks only a little English, she feels isolated without her daily chats in Ukrainian with her two elderly friends. She wishes her husband were alive to explain things.

Anastasia's family doctor asked Dr. Ingram and his staff to assess her and look into the situation. A community nurse interviewed Anastasia's niece, neighbours, and someone from the bank. Dr. Ingram concludes that Anastasia may suffer from dementia and material abuse. Dr. Ingram will decide whether Anastasia can manage her finances or whether he should apply for an Order of Supervision. This order allows the Public Trustee to take over Anastasia's finances and ensures the safety of her savings.

Dr. Ingram may find that Anastasia has enough cognitive ability to look after her own affairs. In this case he can only warn her to take more care in managing her finances. If the abuser comes from Anastasia's family, Dr. Ingram says, "often nothing changes."

"This is very frustrating," he says, "and I find it hard to walk away from these people without helping them."

Source: P. Ingram, "Senior Suffers Abuse of Trust," *Winnipeg Free Press*, January 11, 1996, A6.

have doubled to 7 percent of seniors (172 000 people) (Podnieks et al. 1989). Nearly 0.8 percent of seniors suffer from more than one form of abuse (potentially 190 00 people nation-wide).

The Prairies had the lowest rate of abuse (30 per 1000). British Columbia had the highest rate of abuse (53 per 1000). Female victims of abuse outnumbered male victims by almost two to one. The study found that some types of people faced a higher risk for some types of abuse than for others. For example, people who reported material abuse tended to live more isolated lives and to have poor health. These people faced abuse from varied sources including spouses, friends, children, and distant relatives. People who reported neglect were most often women with poor health, low morale, and a dependence on others for functional help. These people faced abuse from spouses, children,

Exhibit 13.7

What Are Your Attitudes and Beliefs about Elder Abuse?

Researcher Michael J. Stones has created a research tool, the Elder Abuse Aptitude Test (EAAT), to study attitudes and beliefs about elder abuse. Fill out the EAAT below and total your score to assess your attitudes and beliefs. The EAAT will also sensitize you to the many types of abuse that older people can face.

The following statements refer to how people sometimes act towards seniors. They only refer to behaviour by someone a senior has reason to trust. That person could be a relative or someone who takes care of the senior. That person could also be someone paid to help or look after the senior's affairs, such as a doctor, a nurse, or homemaker, or lawyer. The questions do not refer to how strangers treat seniors. Do you understand the kinds of people the questions refer to?

Please indicate whether the action below are (1) not abusive, (2), possibly abusive, (3) abusive, (4) severely abusive, or (5) very severely abusive towards a senior if done by someone a senior has reason to trust. Remember that the questions don't apply to act by a stranger. Circle a number next to each statement, such that:

1. means Not Abusive
2. means Possibly Abusive
3. means Abusive
4. means Severely Abusive
5. means Very Severely Abusive

A person a senior has reason to trust who

1. Steals something a senior values	[1]	[2]	[3]	[4]	[5]
2. Makes a senior pay too much for things like house repairs or medical aids	[1]	[2]	[3]	[4]	[5]
3. Pushes or shoves a senior	[1]	[2]	[3]	[4]	[5]
4. Lies to a senior in a harmful way	[1]	[2]	[3]	[4]	[5]
5. Opens a senior's mail without permission	[1]	[2]	[3]	[4]	[5]
6. Pressures a senior to do paid work when that senior doesn't want to	[1]	[2]	[3]	[4]	[5]
7. Doesn't take a senior places that senior has to go (like a doctor's appointment)	[1]	[2]	[3]	[4]	[5]
8. Withholds information that may be important to a senior	[1]	[2]	[3]	[4]	[5]
9. Unreasonably orders a senior around	[1]	[2]	[3]	[4]	[5]
10. Doesn't provide a senior with proper clothing when needed	[1]	[2]	[3]	[4]	[5]
11. Tells a senior that he or she is "too much trouble"	[1]	[2]	[3]	[4]	[5]
12. Fails to provide proper nutrition for a senior	[1]	[2]	[3]	[4]	[5]
13. Disbelieves a senior who claims to be abused without checking that claim	[1]	[2]	[3]	[4]	[5]

How did you score? How did your classmates score? Stones reports average scores of 4.07 for 22–40-year-olds; 3.83 for 41–64-year-olds; and 3.50 for 65–93-year-olds. How do you think people from other backgrounds or with little knowledge of elder abuse would score?

Source: M.J. Stones, *Rules and Tools: The Meaning and Measurement of Elder Abuse: A Manual for Milestones* (Newfoundland, 1994). Reprinted with permission, M.J. Stones and D. Pittman, "Individual Differences in Attitudes about Elder Abuse: The Elder Abuse Attitude Test (EAAT)," *Canadian Journal on Aging*, 14 (Supp. 2) (1995), 61–71.

and nonfamily caregivers. Research has often focused on cases where a child caregiver abuses an older person they care for. But recent studies show that often the abusing child relies on the abused person for support. And financial dependence can lead to resentment, anger, and abuse. Pittaway and Gallagher (1995) found that in 56.4 percent of cases of abused older people (aged 55 and over in their study) the abuser partly or wholly depended on the abused person.

People who reported chronic verbal abuse and physical violence had some things in common. They tended to be married, and they reported that most of the abuse came from their spouse. Both men and women report abuse. Men reported a higher incidence of physical abuse (see also McDonald et al. 1991). Victims of verbal abuse (mostly women) reported that stress and emotional problems led to abuse, while victims of physical violence reported that alcohol led to abuse and that in more than half of the cases physical violence led to injury. More than one-quarter of these cases required medical attention. "In nearly two-thirds of the cases [of physical violence]," Podnieks et al. (1989, 9) write, "victims had been slapped or hit with an object. In more than one-third of the cases, victims had been threatened with a knife or gun during the past year."

Aronson, Thornewell, and Williams (1995; see also Neysmith 1995) take a feminist approach to the study of elder abuse. They say that the term elder abuse masks the link between abuse against older women and the relative powerlessness of women throughout life. They prefer the term "wife assault in old age" to describe the physical abuse of older women. Aronson and her colleagues say that studies of elder abuse must link current abuse to structured social inequalities. Pittaway, Westhues, and Peressini (1995) say that Western society has undervalued women's work as caregivers in the family. This made most older women dependent on men for financial support throughout their lives. "From a feminist perspective," Pittaway and her colleagues (1995, 42) say, "the societal inequities which exist for women may just continue into old age unless these issues are addressed."

Policy Issues

Policy refers to regulations and guidelines on how to deal with elder abuse (MacLean and Williams 1995). Elder abuse policies attempt to help the older abused person. Policies can include criminal court action, mandatory reporting, guardianship and power of attorney, and mediation to resolve disputes. But these methods use public means (by a social worker or police) to improve a family relationship. And this often fails. The law, for example, assumes that two people in a dispute have only a limited relation to each other. But an abused spouse or parent often has a long-term relationship with his abuser. And he may want to maintain this relationship (sometimes at risk to himself). For example, a study of the effectiveness of adult protective legislation (Bond, Penner, and Yellen 1995) found "an atmosphere of non-cooperation by both the alleged abuser and the victim during investigations ... and a reluctance to report cases." The researchers found that few cases get to court.

Legal action may do little to improve the abused person's life. A legal outcome, like removing the abused person from a setting, may cause more stress to the abused person. Likewise, the abused person may reject legal remedies like jailing an abusing child or spouse whom they depend on for help. Pittaway and Gallagher (1995) found that nearly a fifth (18.1 percent) of abused older people in their study said they feared reprisal. Bond, Penner, and Yellen (1992, 14) say that "funding and provision of staff and services are far more important in the effective amelioration of elder abuse than any particular legislative approach."

Future Issues in Elder Abuse

Wolf and Pillemer (1989) note that elder abuse and neglect have existed throughout history (see also Stearns 1986). What, they ask, accounts for the sudden interest in abuse and neglect? They trace this interest to four social changes: (1) the growth of the older population; (2) the increased political power of older people; (3) the women's movement and a critical analysis of the family; and (4) the state's willingness to intervene in family life.

Some authors (Callahan 1986; Crystal 1986) argue that formal service agencies have adopted the cause of elder abuse in order to expand their influence and get more funding. These authors link the sudden interest in elder abuse to the expansion of the welfare state. Crystal (1986) argues that some approaches, like mandatory reporting of abuse, will do little to help abused older people. He says that special programs aimed at reducing elder abuse reinforce negative stereotypes of older people as feeble and helpless. Wolf and Pillemer (1989) take a different view. They see health and social service professionals' intervention in child abuse and in elder abuse as parallel. In both cases professionals, on behalf of the state, set out to protect a vulnerable minority. Through this process elder abuse has become a legitimate social problem. They see this as a first step in creating social policies to protect abused older people.

The research on elder abuse supports the idea that older people suffer from varied forms of mistreatment. Some subgroups may have a higher-than-average risk of abuse. Pittaway and Westhues (1993), for example, studied 605 older people who used health care and social services in London, Ontario. They found physical abuse rates of over 14 percent among this group (compared with only 0.5 percent in Podnieks's [1990] study). Most of these people reported abuse from their spouse. They also reported high rates of other forms of abuse. Fourteen percent reported chronic verbal aggression and about the same percent reported neglect.

Research supports the idea that many abused older people need help. Some groups—those who go for health or social service help—may face more risk and need extra attention. Still, the research shows that the vast majority of older people do not experience abuse. These figures should make us more aware of abuse and also help keep the issue of abuse in perspective.

Canadian researchers have explored the causes, theories, and responses to elder abuse. This research has mushroomed in the past few years. Future studies will propose policies and practices to help ensure the safety of a growing and diverse older population.

OLDER PEOPLE AS SUPPORTERS

Most of the writing on older people in families focuses on their needs and on what other people do for them, but older people also give help to their families. Shanas (1967) says that "far from being the passive recipients of their adult children's bounty, reciprocal help is given in the form of home services, monetary assistance, assistance in time of illness and other crisis situations and, in addition, older parents often provide child care services." Chappell (1992) says that reciprocity leads to well-being and that the give and take of relationships leads to higher morale.

Older people give at least three kinds of support: first, they help their spouses and children with health care and daily chores; second, they give their children financial support; and third, they give emotional support to and serve as role models for younger family members.

Daily Help by Older People

Neysmith (1982) says that society does not see the daily help older people give to their families, because it goes on in private. She studied 200 older men and women in Ontario and found that over 80 percent of these people said they helped their family and friends. Chappell (1983a) found that spouses and peers (many of them over age 65) provide most of the social and health care support needed by their family and friends. Chappell and Havens (1985) found that in a sample of elderly home care support users and nonusers, 55 percent of users and nonusers provided support to others. Most of them gave support through an informal network.

McDaniel (1994a) reports that 28 percent of older people give transportation help to others outside their household; 19 percent help with child care; and 24 percent give financial support to someone outside their household. Older people also help others with housework and household maintenance. Connidis (1989b) found that most people who volunteer do so for an organization and that those who help with transportation most often do so for a friend, neighbour, or relative (not living with them). Older people who help with housework or yardwork do so most often for their children, or for a friend or neighbour. And older people who help with personal care most often help a friend, neighbour, or relative (not living with them).

The types of help people provide differ by gender. More men than women give transportation help, help with yardwork, and help with home maintenance. More women than men give help as volunteers, help with housework, personal care, and babysitting (McDaniel 1994a). The tendency to help differs with subjective health, age, gender, education, and marital status. Connidis (1989b) found that younger old people (aged 65–69) who are in excellent health, have some postsecondary education, live with a spouse, and live on the Prairies tend to give the most help.

These findings show that most older people live interdependently with family, neighbours, and friends. They give and receive help with practical activities, finances, and advice throughout their lives (see also Antonucci 1990; Antonucci and Akiyama 1987).

Financial Support

Older people give younger members of their families financial support. The amount and kind of support given differs by social class and ethnic group, but studies show that even middle-aged people think of their parents as givers (Baruch and Barnet 1983). Other studies show that the elderly give more money to their children than they get from them (Cheal 1983, 1989–90; 1985b; 1986; Schorr 1980).

Emotional Supporters and Role Models

Research shows that adult children rely on their parents as role models throughout their lives and turn first to their parents for support and help if they lose a spouse (Bankoff 1983; Schwartz 1979). Older family members derive great satisfaction from the help they give to their children and to other younger family members. Neysmith (1982) asked 200 older people in Ontario about the roles they play in their families. About half the people in the study reported the role of keeping their families together—they told family members about one another and organized family events. All of the people in this study saw this as an important job. Neysmith found that people who played this role had higher morale than people who did not.

Rosenthal, Marshall, and Synge (1980) found that older people play many roles in their families. These include the "occupational sponsor" (the person who helps others find jobs or get started in business), the "comforter" (the person people turn to for personal advice and support) (Rosenthal 1987b), the "ambassador" (the person who represents the family at ceremonies), the "head of the family" (the person who makes choices that others go along with), and the "kinkeeper" (the person who keeps people in touch with one another).

Rosenthal (1985) found that women generally occupy the kinkeeper role. Families with kinkeepers tend to get together more often. Men in families with kinkeepers benefit by having stronger ties to their siblings.

Connidis (1989a) reports that older parents least enjoy helping their children with chores like cooking or shopping. But they most enjoy visiting and socializing with their children and grandchildren. Older parents bring their families together on special occasions, fostering increased contact among family members. Older women often serve as advisers and confidants to their widowed daughters.

Family roles can give meaning and purpose to an older person's life. Black (1985) found that older people had the best emotional well-being when they gave as well as received support. Reciprocity made older people feel useful, independent, and worthwhile. Black says that professionals should help older people find ways to give to their supporters, since this will create more fulfilling relationships between parents and their children.

GRANDPARENTING

More people will enter the grandparent role today than ever before and many of them will enter this role in midlife. McDaniel (1994a) reports that 76 percent of older people have at least one grandchild and most older people have four or more. McDaniel (1993; 1994a) says that 40 percent of people with a grandparent report seeing their grandparent at least once a month. People aged 15–24 reported the most frequent contact with their grandparents.

Hagestad (1985, 48) calls today's grandparents "demographic pioneers." Bengtson (1985) says that grandparents differ in how they play this role. Some grandparents feel that they do enough by simply being present; others play a more active role as family arbitrators, watchdogs, or family historians. Grandparents often look out for the well-being of younger relatives, help them when they can, and create links between family members. The grandparent role offers older people one of the most satisfying and enjoyable ways to give to other family members.

A study of grandmothers (Robertson 1977) found that 80 percent felt proud and happy about

Exhibit 13.8

Volunteer Grandmother: An Answer to the Loss of Family with Age

In a surrogate family, an older person and a younger family adopt one another. Over time they may build up the kind of feeling for one another that natural families share.

At 51, Marion is a volunteer grandmother.

Besides liking small children, Marion says she became a "granny," because her own children were taking her for granted.

"They have their own lives. I was active in the sorority for two years, but now I need to fill the void."

For Brenda Wylie [the mother of Marion's surrogate grandchildren] ... Winnipeg's Grandparenting Program has lessened the isolation of being in a city 2,218 km from her own parents.

"They (her parents) are in Ottawa. They're wonderful grandparents, that's why we wanted someone here. We knew what we were missing."

Brenda adds that although she was thinking of the children when she asked for a grandparent, Marion has become a friend to the entire family.

"It's nice to have someone else to spend time with. We often chat on the phone."

Marion says she is pleased with how things have turned out since being matched four months ago.

"I think I've got the best family. We fit together so beautifully. It's hard to believe we're not a natural family."

Source: "Volunteer Granny Becomes 'Friend' to All of the Family," *Winnipeg Sun*, December 22, 1985, 53. Reproduced with permission.

grandmotherhood. The younger grandmothers in the study felt they should be role models for grandchildren and teach them to work hard and be good. These younger grandmothers often had husbands and jobs, and, as a result, had less time for grandchildren than the older grandmothers. Older grandmothers—most of them widows and women without jobs—took a personal view of grandparenting. They enjoyed their role because it increased their life satisfaction. These women spent the most time with their grandchildren, and the grandparent role meant more to them than to younger grandmothers.

Research shows that grandchildren value their grandparents. Younger grandchildren say they like grandparents for the presents they bring them, and older children like what they do with their grandparents (Kahana and Kahana 1970). Studies show that children's feelings about their grandparents depend on the relationship between the grandparents and the parents. Robertson (1977) found that only when parents approve do grandmothers get involved in activities with grandchildren.

What a grandparent makes of the grandparent role depends on the older person's gender, age, marital status, and relationship with his or her adult children (Bengtson 1985). Neugarten and Weinstein (1964) studied styles of grandparenting. They describe five styles: a formal style, a fun-seeker style, a surrogate-parent style, a reservoir-of-family-wisdom style, and a distant-figure style. Only a few of the grandparents (most of them grandfathers) showed a reservoir-of-family-wisdom style; this type of person had special skills or resources to give.

Only a few of the people in this study (all of them grandmothers) showed a surrogate-parent style; this type of person looked after grandchildren while parents worked. About one-third of the grandfathers and one-fifth of the grandmothers showed a distant-figure style; this type of person had friendly feelings for their grandchildren, but did not see them very often. About a quarter of the grandfathers and a third of the grandmothers showed a fun-seeker style; this type of person spent leisure time with their grandchildren and had fun with them. About a third of both grandmothers and grandfathers showed a formal style; this type of person left parenting to the parents and did not offer advice on child rearing. The researchers found that older grandparents (aged 65 or over) more often took on a formal style, while younger grandparents tended to take on a fun-seeker style. This research shows that the grandparent role allows room for personal expression and that older people can use it as a source of emotional satisfaction.

A more recent study by Cherlin and Furstenberg (1985) looked at the grandparenting styles of 510 U.S. grandparents with teenaged grandchildren. They report five styles of grandparenting: detached, passive, supportive, authoritative, and influential. Detached and passive grandparents were usually older than grandparents in the other groups and tended to take a more hands-off relationship to grandparenting. One woman summarized this attitude simply: "I don't think the grandparents should interfere with the parents" (Cherlin and Furstenberg 1985, 107). Detached grandparents also tended to see their grandchildren less often and to live further from them than did grandparents in other groups.

Influential grandparents tended to be younger. They were apt to get more involved in their grandchildren's lives. One grandfather said, "if he has some problem, he'll come over to see me. ... And if I need some help, like getting some screens down ... for the summer, I'll get him to help me bring those down" (Cherlin and Furstenberg 1985, 108). The influential grandparents lived closer and saw their grandchildren more often than grandparents in other groups. These findings suggest that aging and decreased activity level may lead to decreases in grandparents' influence on their grandchildren. Some of the grandparents in this study used "selective investment" to focus their energy on some of their closer or more personable grandchildren.

Hagestad (1985) conducted a study of grandmothers and grandfathers in Chicago. She found that both men and women talked with their grandchildren about practical life in adult society. The grandfathers took an instrumental or practical view of their role. They gave advice on job hunting, education, and managing money. The grandmothers more often dealt with family life and relationships. Hagestad (1985) reports that grandmothers more often than grandfathers changed their own view on social issues, dress, and education due to

their grandchildren's opinions on them. Hagestad (1985, 41) calls this "reversed socialization." Hagestad's work shows that grandchildren and grandparents have an influence on one another.

Gladstone (1988, 1989, 1991) found that the grandparent's relationship to the grandchild relies in part on the mediation of their children and children-in-law. Gladstone (1989) studied 110 grandparents in nonintact families (in which parents have split up). He found that adult children and children-in-law act as mediators between grandchildren and grandparents. They can obstruct or arrange visits. Children-in-law, for example, could inhibit contact by keeping the former spouse from seeing children and this would, in turn, keep the grandparent from seeing the children. Contact with grandchildren of divorced or separated children depended on the grandparent's relationship to the former child-in-law, whether the child or the child-in-law had custody of the grandchild, and geographical closeness (Gladstone 1987; Johnson 1985). Kruk (1995) found that denial of access by a child-in-law (often in the case of divorce) accounted for most cases of contact loss.

Gladstone (1989) concludes that grandparents can negotiate relationships with their children and children-in-law in broken marriages to enhance contact with their grandchildren. This can present a challenge to the grandparent when emotions erupt during separations and divorces. Family practitioners can help to enhance grandparent–grandchild relationships during these times. Kruk (1995) says that family therapists should include grandparents in their work with post-divorce couples. This recognizes the grandparents' role in the post-divorce family. It also allows them to support their grandchildren during this stressful time.

A self-help group with chapters across the country called **GRAND (Grandparents Requesting Access aNd Dignity)** helps grandparents who cannot get access to their grandchildren. The group started in 1983. It provides education and support, and lobbies for changes in laws to protect grandparents' access to their grandchildren (National Advisory Council 1990a; 1994a). GRAND collected 10 000 names on a petition to change the Divorce Act. They presented the petition to the House of Commons. The petition asks that the Divorce Act include a statement like the one in the Quebec Civil Code that says "In no case may a father or mother, without serious cause, place obstacles between the child and grandparents" (Health Canada 1993–94, 11).

Kruk (1995) reports that grandparents who used legal means to get access to grandchildren had some success. One Toronto lawyer reports that he handled 40 cases for grandparents between 1992 and 1995. He won every case and got the grandparents custody or access (Davis 1996). But grandparents who go to court risk increasing the tension with the child-in-law. Kruk (1995) says that legislative support for grandparent rights would decrease the need for legal action. Today, grandparents have to show the courts why they should have access to their grandchildren. A change in the law would guarantee grandparents' rights of access.

FUTURE RESEARCH

Research on the family and social supports in later life focuses on what Abu-Laban (1980b, 196) calls the "the 'normal' (or at least the research worthy) aged … [the] gray-haired, Anglo-Celtic, heterosexual, life-long marrieds, who have produced children and grandchildren." Studies report how this ideal family copes with the normal crises of growing older. These studies then turn to "the support ties of the white-haired, Anglo-Celtic, widowed mother and grandmother" (Abu-Laban 1980b, 196).

Abu-Laban (1980a) and others (Hess and Soldo 1985) criticize this narrow view of family life. First, the literature idealizes marriage and the caregiving spouse, but it says little about the dysfunctions that marriage and the use of informal supports can create. Hess and Soldo (1985, 83) say that "under some circumstances, for some couples, there are clear drawbacks to having a spouse." Married couples, for example, make less use of formal services. The caregiver spouse may see the use of formal supports as an admission of defeat. The failure to use available supports can make life harder for both spouses. Also, when spouses rely on each other for support, they can lose contact with friends and relatives. This can lead to feelings of burden, isolation, and depression for both spouses. More research on marriage in later life should focus on both the benefits and the problems that marriage can bring.

Second, the structure of the family has changed. McDaniel (1994a, 116) says that the "family for today's seniors is complex and multi-generational." Many older people today have living siblings, adult children, and grandchildren. Families will have more generations alive at one time than ever before. This means that older people today have large reservoirs of potential informal support. "Canadians over the age of 65 are in touch with both the past—their large families of origin—and the future, their children's children" (McDaniel 1994a, 117). We know little about the lives of older people in these family structures.

Older people in the future (around the year 2025), compared with older people today, will have fewer children and fewer siblings. This will give them a smaller pool of close relatives to call on for support. This could lead to increased reliance on **fictive kin.** This refers to close relationships with nonrelatives like neighbours, home care workers, and friends (Rosenthal and Gladstone 1993).

Third, research on older people's family life has almost ignored the lives of certain types of people. Little research has been done on never-married older people (in 1994, 6.5 percent of men and 7.2 percent of women aged 65 and over had never married) or divorced older people (in 1994, 3.4 percent of men and 3.7 percent of women aged 65 and over were divorced) (Statistics Canada 1990e; Abu-Laban 1978).

Stull and Scarisbrick-Hauser (1989) conducted one of the few studies of never-married older people in the United States They found that these people have generally good health, satisfaction with their standard of living, active lives, and happiness. They appear to be similar to married, divorced or separated, and widowed older people in these dimensions. A higher proportion of the never-married people in this study, compared with the widowed and divorced or separated, live with someone else (siblings, other relatives, or nonrelatives).

Never-married older people also tend to rely more on siblings and friends than do married or widowed people (Connidis 1989c; Connidis and McMullin 1994). They tend to have strong relationships with parents, aunts, uncles, nieces, and nephews. They tend to have both good emotional support and good help in everyday life (Connidis and McMullin 1994). This may apply most to never-married women.

Never-married men tend to have weaker family relations (Rosenthal and Gladstone 1993). These findings suggest that most never-married people have good support networks and do not necessarily face a high risk of institutionalization. The researchers say that future research should look at the coping strategies that never-married people use to maintain their high quality of life.

Fourth, few studies have compared the family life of older people from different ethnic backgrounds. More research on ethnicity in old age should look at family relations, informal supports, and the use of social services by different ethnic groups (Driedger and Chappell 1987).

Fifth, though research during the 1970s and 1980s focused mostly on older women, making up for the absence of research on women in other parts of the social science literature, few studies have looked at older men. Researchers need to look at male friendships, widowers, grandfathering, gay men as they age, and male remarriage. Studies that have described men show that they face special challenges in old age.

Sixth, Oderkirk (1994, 7) says that marriage "seems increasingly fragile, as marriage breakdown occurs more frequently and with increasing ease. ... More and more adults alternate between conjugal and solo-living periods." Current low marriage rates among younger people, increases in common-law relationships, high divorce rates, and fewer remarriages in middle and later life will lead to new patterns of family life for older people. These trends may produce more unmarried older people, both men and women. They may also lead to more older people with children from several marriages.

An older person in the future may have several sets of children and grandchildren from several marriages. Their children too may have children from several marriages. The study of these family structures in the future will give a more complete picture of family life in old age.

CONCLUSION

Older people live rich social lives. They interact with family members, friends, and neighbours as well as with their spouses. Most older people rely on these networks of family and friends for social, emotional, and health care support. Older people also give to their families and serve as role models for the young. Old age is a time of change—the death of a spouse, for example, creates one of life's greatest stresses. But research shows that most older people cope with the challenges of aging and manage to live satisfying social lives.

SUMMARY

1. The myth persists that middle-aged children abandon their elderly parents, but studies show again and again that children maintain contact with their parents, provide them with help, and get help from them when they need it.

2. A good marriage provides support for both partners as they age. Married older people use less formal care, rely less on children and friends for support, and have a lower institutionalization rate than unmarried older people. Older women run a higher risk than older men of losing this support due to widowhood.

3. Older people have an interest in sex throughout life. Most people will need to adjust their expectations about sexual performance in later life. But, given good health and a willing partner, older people can enjoy sexual relations into late old age. New attitudes toward sexuality may encourage more sexual activity in later life. Studies of homosexuality in later life report that gay and lesbian older people can stay sexually and socially satisfied as they age.

4. Widowhood has become an expected life event for women in Canada, though it still creates stress in a woman's life. Researchers disagree about the impact of widowhood on men. Some studies show that men have fewer social supports and that they suffer from isolation, loneliness, and a high risk of suicide. More recent studies suggest that men may need less social support than women and that they adapt in different ways to widowhood.

5. More older women than ever before choose to live alone, rather than with their children. Better pensions, subsidized housing, and enriched housing will make this an option for more older women in the future.

6. Most older people keep up social contacts with relatives and friends as they age. Through visits or by using the telephone, older people (mostly women) give one another emotional support. Confidants help older people cope with anxiety and tension.

7. Older people often depend on informal support networks for emotional and health care support, but informal support can place a burden on family members (most often a wife or daughter). These burdened caregivers may lose their income from work, their pensions, and even their health due to caregiving demands. Government financial support for caregivers would make caregiving a less burdensome option for many people and would recognize their valuable service to the community.

8. Adult children provide most of the informal support needed by their adult parents. Research shows that strong feelings of attachment to a parent leads to caregiving. Also feelings of closeness between parents and children lead to satisfaction and happiness.

9. Some trends, such as cohort attrition for very old people and smaller families for baby boomers, suggest that informal supports will decline in the future. Other trends, like longer life expectancy for spouses and the development of semiformal structures, suggest that older people will still rely on informal supports in the years ahead. These two trends may counterbalance each other, and older people in the future may develop new types of social supports.

10. Elder abuse may affect as many as 4 percent of older Canadians (98 000 people). Most abuse takes the form of material abuse and chronic verbal aggression. A smaller proportion of older people face physical aggression and neglect. Education for police, counsellors, and seniors themselves may help reduce the incidence of abuse. Legal services, mental health services, and shelters could help older people to cope with the aftermath of abuse.

11. Older people give support as well as receive it. They help their children socially, financially, and emotionally. They help their peers by acting as confidants. Older people, like younger people, get esteem and a sense of purpose from helping others.

12. Grandparenting offers older people one of the most enjoyable roles in old age. It has few responsibilities attached to it, so older people can shape the role to suit their personality, lifestyle, and interests.

13. Many gaps still exist in the literature on family life in old age. Research on atypical groups of older people—for example, gay older people, never-married people, and widowers—will increase our understanding of family and intimate relations in later life.

STUDY QUESTIONS

1. Define the term "normative age-graded life events" and give some examples. What does this type of event signal in a person's life?

2. What are the benefits of marriage in old age? How does divorce affect people in old age?

3. Explain why widows outnumber widowers in the aging population. Why do men seem to suffer more than women socially and psychologically when they lose a spouse?

4. Explain the difference between formal and informal support. What kind of support do most older people get? Describe the benefits of this type of support. How do older people choose their potential support groups?

5. In addition to family, where else may older people look for informal support?

6. Define the term "sandwich generation." What are the major difficulties that arise when people take on the role of caregiver to their aged parents?

7. Discuss several things that may ease the burden of caregiving on spouses or adult children.

8. Why do demographers project that the availability of informal supports may decrease in the future? In the absence of informal support, what other types of support should be available to the older population?

9. What are the four types of elder abuse? How common is elder abuse and who is often responsible for abusing an older person? Suggest some ways in which elder abuse can be prevented, both in the community and in institutions.

10. In what ways do older people provide reciprocal help to their families and their communities?

11. Explain the five major styles of grandparenting.

12. Why do some gerontologists believe that researchers could expand the scope of studies

in aging and the family? What types of issues and trends should this research address?

KEY TERMS

caregiver burden   refers to problems and stress due to caregiving.

compassionate stereotype   the idea that older people all need help and public support.

confidant   someone in whom one confides.

developmental stake   the idea that, compared with their children, older people have a greater stake in the relationship with their children. This leads older people to emphasize the existence of family harmony and solidarity.

eldercare   programs at a workplace that can help family caregivers cope with care for an older family member.

fictive kin   refers to close relationships an older person develops with nonrelatives like neighbours, home care workers, and friends.

formal support   professional caregivers such as doctors, nurses, and social workers. People pay for formal supports either from their own resources or through their taxes.

GRAND (Grandparents Requesting Access aNd Dignity)   a group that helps grandparents who cannot get access to their grandchildren.

hierarchical compensatory model   people choose their supports first from their inner family circle. They then move outward to get support from less intimate people as they need more help.

informal support   family and community supports.

normative age-graded life events   expected changes in life that correlate with chronological age. They include high-school graduation, retirement, and marriage.

primary potential support groups   family and close friends who give help to the older person and who can expect help from the older person.

quasi-widowhood   the idea that people feel grief and depression after placing a spouse in a nursing home.

respite services   range from friendly visitors, who stay with the care receiver for a few hours, to full-day adult day care, to longer institutional respite.

sandwich generation   people aged 35 to 64 with at least one child at home and at least one parent aged 65 or over.

second language of sex   focuses on responsiveness, caring, and affection.

semiformal structures   includes car pools, groups of people in the same building who shop together, friendly visitors, or "daily hello" phone callers.

support groups   groups that give caregivers information about how to cope with caregiving demands. They also give caregivers emotional support.

task specificity model   different groups (family, friends, neighbours) have different abilities and offer different types of support. Each group plays a specific role in supporting the older person.

SELECTED READINGS

Chappell, N.L. *Social Support and Aging.* Toronto: Butterworths, 1992.

This book focuses on informal supports in later life. The author reviews theories, research, and policies that show the importance of informal supports for the well-being of older people. Supports include friendship, confidant relationships, supports for activities of daily living, and emotional support. The book also contains discussions of support for frail older people and the effects of caregiving on caregivers. An excellent review of the literature and a good discussion of the issues.

MacLean, M.J., ed. *Abuse and Neglect of Older Canadians: Strategies for Change.* Toronto: Thompson Educational Publishing, 1995.

An up-to-date review of issues in elder abuse and neglect. The book covers four themes: practice, policy, education, and research. It contains writings by some of the most active researchers and practitioners in the field.

National Advisory Council on Aging. *Marital Disruption in Later Life.* Cat. No. H71-3/17-1994E, 47–63. Ottawa: Minister of Supply and Services Canada, 1994.

A collection of papers on the stresses that marriage can bring in later life. The papers range from a personal account of caregiving for a husband with Alzheimer's disease to more academic studies of caregiving for an institutionalized spouse. Articles also deal with widowhood, separation, and divorce. The papers show the range of problems that come with marriage in later life. They also show the ways in which people (many of them women) cope with these stresses. Readable and with many examples to bring these issues to life.

CHAPTER 14

Death and Dying

INTRODUCTION

Draw a line across a piece of paper. Put the word "birth" at the left-hand end of the line. Put the word "death" at the right-hand end of the line. Now put a dot for today's date. Put the date of your birth under the "birth" dot. Now put the date you project for your death under the dot that says "death."

How did you feel about fixing a date for your death? How did you come up with a date? Do people of different ages think the same way about death? Do you look forward to your next birthday? Or do you think about how few years you have left to do the things you want to do? How do older people think and feel about death?

This chapter will look at death in old age. It will focus on (1) attitudes toward death and on where death takes place, (2) ethical questions about death and dying, and (3) mourning and grief.

DEATH IN OLD AGE

In the past, high infant mortality rates, childhood diseases, and high female death rates during child-bearing years made death among all age groups a common event. Gee (1985, 2) says that "of 1,000 females born in Canada in 1831, approximately two-thirds would survive to age 20, less than one-half to age 44, and substantially less than one-third to age 65." Today, she says, "the vast majority of women survive to ages 20 and 45 and a large percentage (approximately 86 percent) are alive at age 65" (1985, 3). Longer life expectancy today means that death often takes place in old age (Marshall and Levy 1990). Today people aged 65 or over make up 80 percent of all dying patients (Fisher, Nadon, and Shedletsky 1983).

Only a small number of studies have looked at how older people feel about death. Marshall (1975) says that the major theories of aging avoid the subject. According to activity theory, for example, people want to stay active throughout their lives. They substitute new roles and activities for ones that they lose as they age. When people retire, activity theory says that they will have the highest life satisfaction if they find new things to do. This theory says nothing about death (Marshall 1980b).

Disengagement theory says that people want to disengage from social roles as they age. This theory also says that retirement and withdrawal from social responsibilities leads to high life satisfaction. According to this theory an awareness of impending death starts the process of disengagement. People know that they will die soon, so they ease their way out of social life. Disengagement produces a smooth transition of power from one generation to the next. Death has a less disruptive effect on society if older people disengage from social roles as they age. This theory focuses on the social effects of dying, but it says little about death as a personal experience or about how older people feel about death.

Erikson's (1963) theory of ego development says that the last stage of life leads to a life review. A person looks over his or her life, ties up loose ends, and prepares for death. Erikson describes this as **ego integrity.** "It is the acceptance of one's one and only life cycle as something that had to be and that, by necessity, permitted of no substitutions" (1963, 268). The integrated person accepts his or her biography and culture. And with this acceptance "death loses its sting" (1963, 268). Robert Peck ([1955] 1968) says that in the last part of this last stage a person can achieve **ego transcendence.** People in this stage feel a deep concern for others and for the culture they will leave when they die.

These theories say that older people respond to death in more than one way: some people deny it; some accept it; and some embrace it. The few studies that have tested these theories have found complex combinations of acceptance and rejection of death.

Marshall (1974) found an ambivalence toward death among older people in a retirement community and in a nursing home. All of his subjects had disengaged from the middle-aged roles of work and parenthood; most of them said they accepted death; and some of them said they desired it. But Marshall found that these people also wanted to keep on living. Many of them said they wanted to live because their lives had meaning for others. Some of them worked for their retirement community; others said that someone depended on them, and they wanted to live to care for this person.

Chappell (1975) found that relationships with others give older people a more positive view of the future. She asked forty elderly people in a hospital how long they had to live and how they thought about the time they had left. She found

Exhibit 14.1

Death and Dying among the Hutterites

In an article on aging and death, Professor Joseph W. Eaton reprinted the following letter from a Hutterite farmer to his sister. The letter describes the death of their younger brother.

Dear sister, our dear brother came home on September 8, on a Wednesday morning about 5 o'clock. He said that he had a fairly nice trip. He cried a great deal because of pains. He stated that distress teaches one to pray. I went immediately the following day to visit with him. I could hardly look at him, it was so painful to me; he looked so terrible that it made my heart almost break. However, I remained with him until he died, and until the funeral was over.

Two evenings before his death, his home was full of people, approximately 25 were there. He expressed a heavenly pleasure when he saw them all and said he could not express his pleasure in seeing them. It struck me almost as a miracle when I saw this starved and weak body lying there, telling us such a strong story. We listened to him, warned him not to talk so much because it may do him harm. However, he stated, "While I am still alive, I can speak. When I will be dead, then, of course, I won't be able to tell you what I have to say." …

He stated that dying does not cause him any difficulty; he said that he had a clear conscience and is in peace with God and all people. He asked many people in my presence whether they had something against him. However, everybody replied in the negative. They said to him that they themselves were in peace with him …

[Just before his death] his children stood around him with a sad heart, and all realized that his departure will be soon. He called his oldest son, gave him his hand and pressed a kiss on his forehead, and advised him how he should behave in the future. Among other words he told him he should obey his preacher, the boss and the field boss, and if the community entrusted a position to him, he should execute same as well as he could, and not only superficially …

[He then calls to his side his daughter, the colony business manager, his wife and his brother]. He said, "I am at peace with God and with all people. I have a clear and good conscience. I am ready to depart, but now everything goes so slow. I have only one desire and that is to go to my Lord." He said quite frequently how good it is to have a clear and peaceful conscience. He advised us also that we should prepare ourselves, because the pleasure was inexpressible.

So I have described to you the events and experiences which I have seen with my own eyes, and it is my request and my wish that we all should prepare ourselves. Blessed by God.

Source: Joseph W. Eaton, "The Art of Aging and Dying," *The Gerontologist* 4 (1964): 94–112. Reproduced with permission of *The Gerontologist*.

that all of these people knew that they would die soon and they all said they felt ready to die. But only half the people in this study said they saw their future as a time of waiting for death. The other half saw the future as a time to keep on living. Chappell found that people looked forward to activities if they had social contacts outside the hospital. These contacts gave them continuity with the past and allowed them to extend their lives into the future.

Studies that compare older and younger people find that older people think about death more, but feel less afraid of death than the young. Lavigne and Lévesque (1992) studied older people in long-term care centres in Montreal. They found that about a third of the people in the study thought of their own death when they heard of the death of a peer. A Canadian study by Gesser, Wong, and Reker (1986) studied the fear of death and three kinds of death acceptance among old and young people. They found that older people showed less fear and more acceptance of death than younger people. They also found that as fear of death decreased, hopelessness decreased and happiness increased. They say that people who get over the fear of death feel satisfied with life. These people find meaning and purpose in the time they have left, and they feel in control of their lives.

People with different religious beliefs differ in their attitudes to death. Gesser, Wong, and Reker (1986) found that older people more than younger people accepted life after death. "It may be," they say (1986, 20), "that belief in the afterlife helps the elderly to find meaning and purpose in life, as well as in death … Older people overcome their fear of death because they feel that life after death goes on." Most religions teach that people get the kind of afterlife they deserve. Studies show that people with mild or uncertain religious belief fear death most, while those with strong religious beliefs or no belief at all deal with death best (Gorer 1967; Kalish 1963). People with a mild belief may accept enough of religion to believe in an afterlife, but not enough to feel they will have a good one.

INSTITUTIONAL DEATH

Religious belief and a sense of purpose can help buffer the fear of death, but how and where a person expects to die also affects how he or she feels about death. In the past most people died at home, surrounded by family, friends, and neighbours. Some cultures still ensure this kind of death (see Exhibit 14.1). But in Canada a large majority of deaths (for people of all ages) take place in hospitals.

A study at the Baycrest Centre for Geriatric Care in Toronto compared the death rate in the centre's hospital, nursing home, and apartment complex. The study found that the hospital had a death rate more than 20 times greater than that of the nursing home and more than 130 times greater than that of the apartment complex. Shapiro (1983) studied hospital use by a group of more than 3000 patients aged 68 and over and found that about two-thirds of the sample entered the hospital in the year they died.

Hospitals will take in more and more dying patients as the population ages, but studies show that many doctors and nurses in hospitals feel uncomfortable with dying patients. A U.S. study found that 76 percent of doctors in hospitals felt uncomfortable dealing with their dying patients. Sixty percent said they needed some kind of educational counselling (Zorza and Zorza 1979). A study of U.S. medical schools (Dickinson 1976) found that only 7 out of 107 had taken a full course on how to relate to dying patients and their families. Dickinson and Pearson (1980–81) found that physicians who had taken such courses related more easily to dying patients. Eakes (1985) found that nursing home workers who felt more comfortable with death placed a higher value on older patients.

A study at Royal Victoria Hospital in Montreal found that patients wanted to know their diagnoses and their chance of recovery, but doctors did not want to speak openly about death and had little interest in patients' emotions. Social workers also tended to play down patients' problems (Mount, Jones, and Patterson 1974). Shedletsky and Fisher (1986) replicated this study twelve years later. They found that almost all staff (97 percent) felt that patients should be told about their terminal illness, but only 80 percent said that patients on their units were told, and 70 percent of staff members said that discussions of death and dying never or infrequently took place. Nearly all staff members (97.6 percent) felt that hospitals should meet patients' emotional needs, but 41 percent felt that these needs are never or infrequently met.

Skelton (1982) reports that medical staff sometimes feel guilty or angry about dying patients. Because they have spent all of their professional lives learning to keep people alive, they think of death as a failure and avoid dying patients or respond less quickly to their needs (Sudnow 1967). Health and Welfare Canada (1982d, 4) says that the dying patient does not fit the model of health care of the acute hospital. "Skills of investigating, diagnosing, curing and prolonging life [the goals of an acute care hospital where people have short-term, curable illnesses] are not relevant to the care of the dying."

CHANGES IN THE TREATMENT OF THE DYING

The health care system has begun to change its approach to dying patients of all ages. Two doctors more than any others—Elisabeth Kübler-Ross in the United States and Dame Cicely Saunders in England—started this reform.

Kübler-Ross wrote a series of books that described death and dying from the patient's point of view. A study of death and dying courses in Canada found that 55 percent of the courses used her books and that over 20 percent of the departments that taught these courses cited her work as one of the most important reasons for the growth of interest in death and dying (Klug and Waugh 1982).

Saunders created a new institution for caring for the dying—the hospice. Her work has led to a worldwide hospice movement and to the growth of treatment centres for the dying across Canada.

Stages of Death and Dying

Kübler-Ross (1969) described five stages that her patients went through before they died. First, she says, people deny that they are dying. They say, "Not me." They may believe that the doctor has the wrong X-rays or someone else's tests. They may go from specialist to specialist looking for a new diagnosis. They may not even hear the doctor tell them they have a fatal illness.

Second, she says, people feel angry. They begin to believe that they will die. "Why me?" they ask. At this point the person blames the doctor or their spouse or God for their illness.

Third, they begin to bargain. The person says, "Yes, me, but ..." A person may try to make deals with the hospital staff: they may promise to be a good patient and to follow doctor's orders, if only they will get better. They may bargain with God: promising to go to church or to live a more pious life. They may bargain with God for one more summer at the cottage, or for enough time to see a son married, a grandchild born, or their next birthday.

Fourth, the person feels depressed. Their illness gets worse, and they know they will die. The person says, "Yes, me," and they feel a great sadness. Kübler-Ross says that depression has two stages. In the first stage the person mourns present losses—the loss of family, career, and the things they love, like a home, car, or cottage. In the second stage the person mourns future losses—the loss of good times to come, the chance to see children or grandchildren grow up, and other future events. The person begins to say goodbye in this stage.

Fifth, the person accepts death. He or she says, "My time is close now ... it's OK." The person accepts that they will die, and they say goodbye to family and friends and die in peace.

Kübler-Ross says that at every stage a patient holds on to hope. At first a person may hope the doctor made a mistake, later they may hope for a remission if they have cancer, and later still they may hope for a painless death.

Some writers question the number of Kübler-Ross's stages or their order. Metzger (1979–80) studied two patient-spouse couples in which the patients had terminal illnesses. She interviewed each couple three times and found that in both cases patients described "hope" as their main experience along with some anger. She did not find that these subjects went through a series of stages. Shneidman (1984, 199) rejects Kübler-Ross's stage theory—"the notion that human beings, as they die, are somehow marched in lock step through a series of stages of the dying process"—on clinical grounds. He reports a wide range of emotions, needs, and coping methods that dying people use. "A few of these in some people, dozens in others—experienced in an impressive variety of ways" (1984, 199). Feigenberg (1980) criticizes Kübler-Ross's impressionistic methods and the unscientific presentation of her results. Butler (1968) says, moreover, that people have as much right to anger or denial as they do to acceptance and that they have a right to these feelings when they have them, not when a stage theory allows them. Feigenberg points out the danger of accepting these stages as a pattern that everyone must follow: "The stages of Kübler-Ross have come to be regarded as a checklist for the process of dying ... And if a patient clearly deviates from this pattern, one is now liable to hear from the hospital staff that his dying is 'wrong'" (Feigenberg 1980, cited in Shneidman 1984, 199).

Kübler-Ross (1969) herself says that patients can skip stages; stages can overlap; and people can go back over the same stage many times. Some responses, like anger, come up again and again. Also, different illnesses create different trajectories of death or different patterns of response. Kübler-Ross based her model on cancer patients in a hospital, but cancer patients who have remissions may go through these stages more than once.

People with other illnesses show other trajectories. Sometimes, a person can have long plateaus between times of decline. On the other hand, someone who dies shortly after an auto accident may not go through any of these stages.

Shneidman (1984, 200) says that people respond to dying in the same way they respond to other major stresses in their lives: "One dies as one has lived in the terrible moments of one's life." However, Shneidman presents little research to support this view. He may exaggerate the individual differences among dying patients in the same way that Kübler-Ross exaggerates the commonality.

All sides of this debate share one thing: they have brought discussion and thinking about death into public life. People who have to cope with death and dying—patients, their families, and medical staff—now have a number of ways to think, and talk, about death (Novak and Axelrod 1979). This has freed many people from the fear and silence that surrounded death and dying only a few years ago.

The Hospice Movement

The idea of a **hospice** dates back to at least the Middle Ages in Europe. Hospices at that time took in travellers who needed food, shelter, and care. Hospices today meet the special needs of dying patients. Dame Cicely Saunders opened the first modern hospice, St. Christopher's, in London in 1967.

St. Christopher's has sixty-two beds, in-patient and out-patient services, a home visiting program, a day-care centre for the children of staff, and private rooms for older people. The hospice welcomes visitors, including children, and allows families to cook for their dying relatives if they want to. There are also rooms for relatives who want to stay overnight. St. Christopher's does not use methods to extend life; it tries to relieve symptoms and to help the patients enjoy their last days.

Hospice Program Goals

Saunders says that a "hospice is a program, not a place" (cited in Canadian Medical Association 1987, 34). First, a hospice controls pain. People fear death for many reasons, but often people fear the pain that may accompany death more than death itself. Pain relief ensures that the person will die in comfort, and this relieves much of the patient's fear and anxiety. St. Christopher's pioneered the pain relief techniques now used by hospices around the world.

St. Christopher's created the Brompton mix—a mixture of heroin or morphine, cocaine, Stemetil syrup, and chloroform water—to relieve chronic pain. Medical staff base pain control on two techniques: first, they adjust drug dosage until it relieves a patient's pain. "The aim," Saunders (1984, 268) says, "is to titrate the level of analgesia against the patient's pain, gradually increasing the dose until the patient is pain free." Then, the nurses give the next dose before the previous one has worn off. Hospitals often wait until a person shows signs of pain before they give the next dose of pain reliever. By giving the analgesic "before the patient may think it necessary [usually every four hours] … It is possible to erase the memory and fear of pain" (Saunders 1984, 268). Patients cared for by this method need lower dosages to maintain a pain-free state because the drug does not have to overcome the pain that has begun. Lower dosages mean that patients stay more alert. Skelton (1982) says that 90 percent of people can get complete pain relief in a hospice setting, and all but 1 to 2 percent can get some help.

Second, a hospice allows a person to die a simple death. The hospice does not use respirators or resuscitators to keep someone alive. Staff make dying a part of life in the hospice. They leave the curtains open around a dying person's bed so that patients can see that their roommates have died. Patients also know they have a say in their treatment; they can ask for medication when they feel they need it; and they can ask to die at home. Saunders (1984) reports that people who die at home often feel more pain than people who die in the hospice. And caregivers often feel burdened by the demands of care. St. Christopher's (and other hospices) agree to readmit patients whenever the patient or the family needs more support.

Third, a hospice gives people love and care. Staff members focus on the comfort of the patient, taking the time to touch patients and hold them. The hospice will serve special foods that patients like or give them soothing scented baths. The hospice also helps patients do as much for themselves as they can; this increases patients' well-being by giving them a sense of control over their treatment. The family of dying patients also receive care. A Family Service Project at St.

Christopher's offers help to families who find it hard to cope with their grief (see also Levy 1987). Saunders (1984, 269) says that "staff and volunteers visit to assess the need and to offer support, and if more specialized help is indicated, this can be arranged."

Hospices spread to North America during the 1970s and early 1980s. More than 1000 hospices opened in the United States between 1974 and 1984. In Canada hospice organizations exist in Quebec, Ontario, British Columbia, and Manitoba (Manitoba Health Organizations n.d.). Most provinces also have palliative (terminal) care units, palliative care teams, or a palliative care expert on staff in hospitals (Health and Welfare Canada 1982d).

Palliative Care

The **palliative care** services guidelines define palliative care as "a program of active compassionate care primarily directed towards improving the quality of life for the dying." A complete program of palliative care includes symptom control and spiritual support as well as bereavement support and education (Subcommittee on Institutional Program Guidelines 1989, 1). Palliative care units do the same work as hospices, but they most often exist within a large acute-care hospital. Mori (1991, 10) says that the Canadian health care system prefers the term palliative care to the term hospice "because of the negative connotations associated with the word *hospice* in French and Spanish."

The Canadian Palliative Care Foundation began in 1991. It found 116 palliative care programs operating in Canada in 1983 (up from 2 in 1975) (Southall 1982). These programs had 266 available beds, 63 percent of them in large general or teaching hospitals and 32 percent in chronic and extended care hospitals (Canadian Medical Association 1987). The 1994 *Canadian Directory of Services Palliative Care and HIV/AIDS* reports that the number of palliative care programs in Canada had grown to 415 from 118 in 1981 (Senate of Canada 1995). But little reliable information on palliative care programs across Canada exists. Mori (1991, 11) reports that many settings offer palliative care services including "free-standing hospices, home-based palliative care, hospital-based palliative care, and nursing-home–based

palliative care." Workers in palliative care programs include nurses, physiotherapists, psychologists, and volunteers.

Some provincial home care programs also offer palliative care. Ninety-five percent of the people who used these programs had terminal cancer. The Palliative Care Foundation estimates that 200 community-based palliative care programs (programs to help people stay in their homes) existed in Canada by the end of 1984 (Ley 1985).

The Canadian Medical Association (1987) estimates that people aged 65 and over make up about 70 percent of palliative care patients in Canada. Older people have some special needs that palliative care programs need to take into account. Many older people will have no one at home to provide palliative care outside the institution. Multiple pathologies may make pain control more complex. Frail older people on palliative home care may also need the use of respite beds and a day hospital (Canadian Medical Association 1987).

Ross and McDonald (1994) talked with forty nurses who provide palliative home care. These nurses reported that the health care system often made it hard for them to deliver palliative care at home. They blamed bureaucracy, fragmented services, and too much focus on efficiency. These forces interfered with the quality care they wanted to provide. It kept them from giving patients the emotional support they wanted to give. These nurses point to the tension between the values of palliative care and the structure of the current health care system.

The Royal Victoria Hospital in Montreal opened a twelve-bed, in-patient palliative care unit in 1975 and expanded the unit to eighteen beds by 1982. The unit offers music therapy, counselling, and physiotherapy as well as care by doctors and nurses. The unit's staff works as a team and practices "whole person medicine" (Doutre, Stillwell, and Ajemian 1979). This means that they care for the spiritual, emotional, psychological, and physical needs of the patient. The program also offers a seven-day-a-week, twenty-four-hour home care service. The unit's staff keeps patients pain-free in their homes through drug therapy and gives family members advice and support in caring for the dying person. The unit ensures that a patient can come back to the hospital at any time. This allows dying patients to leave the hospital and in some cases to die at home. The unit also has a bereavement follow-up team that visits and supports families after the patient dies.

The Royal Victoria unit admits people of all ages. A five-year study of the unit from January 1975 to April 1980 found that about a third of the people admitted had lung, breast, or bowel cancer. Patients stayed on the unit an average of twenty-four days, about half stayed a week or less, and 78 percent stayed less than four weeks. The large majority of patients (86 percent) admitted to the unit died there. About 13 percent of patients in the home care program died at home; the rest came back to the hospital to die (Ajemian and Mount 1981).

One study at the Royal Victoria Hospital compared the palliative care unit with a surgical ward. Buckingham (Buckingham et al. 1976) had himself admitted as a cancer patient to both types of units. He dieted for six months and lost twenty-two pounds, exposed his skin to ultraviolet rays to make it look as if he had received radiation treatment, stuck himself with needles, and had a doctor do minor surgery to make it look as if he had had intravenous injections and a biopsy. He learned how patients with cancer of the pancreas behaved, and he imitated their behaviour. He also grew a stubbly beard and failed to bathe for several days.

Buckingham reports that he got more personal attention and kinder treatment on the palliative care ward. On the surgical ward, he found, doctors spent less than ten minutes per day with him and less than five minutes per visit. Also, doctors travelled in groups, and this discouraged patients from talking to their doctors about their feelings. Buckingham reports that staff on the surgical ward avoided eye contact with patients, called patients by their disease, not their name, dwelt on the worst things about a patient's illness, and showed little good feeling toward dying patients. His staff contacts lasted on average less than six minutes per visit.

The palliative care unit showed more interest in him as a person. The nurses looked him in the eye when they talked to him and asked him personal, friendly questions, such as what food he enjoyed eating. Buckingham reports that when families wanted to talk to their doctor the staff got the doctor on the phone as soon as possible. Families also spent a lot of time helping to care for patients: they fed patients, brought urinals, and fixed patients' pillows. The staff supported family members as they helped care for their dying relatives. Buckingham's staff contacts averaged nineteen minutes on the palliative care unit. Compared with the surgical ward, on the palliative care unit he spent almost 400 percent more time talking to staff, patients, and their families.

A study by Thompson (1985–86) supports Buckingham's findings. Thompson compared palliative care, surgical, and pediatric nurses' attitudes to death. He found that palliative care nurses "approach their work with the dying with greater ease, may enter into more personal relationships with dying patients … and come away from their work with the feelings that the work itself is rewarding and that they have been useful" (1985–86, 240). Thompson concludes that the values of the palliative care setting (more than nurses' past experiences) explain this positive attitude to dying patients and their needs.

Buckingham also reports that patients supported and comforted one another on the palliative care unit. "The palliative care unit facilitated this powerful support system by allowing more patient-family freedom and mobility, with open visiting and encouragement of family participation in the care of the patient" (Buckingham et al. 1976, 1214). A study by Kane and others (1984) found that, compared with conventional care, palliative care created more family and patient satisfaction and less family anxiety. Buckingham concluded that palliative care units meet the dying person's special need for emotional and social support as well as physical care (see also Mount and Scott 1983).

Palliative Care for the Elderly

Palliative care units take in patients of all ages. Patients at Royal Victoria Hospital, for example, ranged from 20 years old to over 90. Studies show that palliative care can help most older people as well as younger people, but some older patients have unique needs. Shedletsky, Fisher, and Nadon (1982) studied the records of forty older patients (average age 80.6 years) who had died in the extended care wing of a hospital. Extended care hospital settings take in many older people with long-term illnesses who need constant medical care. These units often have a palliative care treatment philosophy. The researchers found that older extended care patients differed from younger

Exhibit 14.2

The Benefits of Palliative Care

Margaret Murray describes the difference between dying on an acute care hospital ward and on a palliative care ward. She shows the benefits of palliative care to the patient and to the patient's family.

My Aunt Harriet was an attractive, intelligent businesswoman who lost a four-year battle with cancer when she was in her mid-sixties. The initial surgery and radiotherapy gave her a few more years to play tennis and pursue her other interests, but the final year with more surgery and various experiments with chemotherapy was almost straight downhill for her.

About five weeks before she died, Harriet was admitted to a large downtown hospital after her bowel and bladder function failed. Up until her admission, she had been living with my parents, spending her days in the living room with her family, and getting about the house in a wheelchair. After less than two weeks of hospitalization, her change was startling.

One Sunday afternoon, we visited her in hospital and found her slumped in a large chair, her drooping head almost touching the bare overbed table apparently to prevent her from falling. With some difficulty we roused her, and she began to report a conversation with her husband who had been dead for 30 years. We tried to make her as comfortable as possible and to bring her back to the present with quiet conversation. This was only moderately successful. She continued to doze and awaken only enough to plead with us to put her back to bed. Eventually, I approached her nurse for help, and was told that my aunt should stay up because she "needed the stimulation"! Since she had been alone before our arrival, without company and in no position to look out a window or watch television, this was a remarkable concept.

Although the nurse was never impolite, she left me with the feeling that her care was given with gritted teeth—she did not know how to care for the "difficult" patient, who did not know what was good for her. I wanted to say "She's dying! The complications of immobility are not as important as her need for comfort, dignity and peace." But I felt she wouldn't understand. …

A few days later, "Auntie Harry" was transferred to the Palliative Care Unit at the [Salvation Army'] Grace Hospital [in Toronto]. On my first visit I found her in a sunny four-bed room, sitting up and brightly awaiting the arrival of her dinner. She had been up once that day, gently lifted into a wheelchair and taken to the lounge where she was introduced to some of the other patients. She enjoyed the brief social interaction, and was returned to bed before she became too tired. Now, she was looking forward to another excursion after supper. Her conversation was relevant and lucid; she was appreciative of her surroundings and had many compliments for the staff. That day I left with the feeling that an enormous burden had been lifted from my shoulders—my aunt was still dying, but somehow it was alright now, for her and for the rest of the family.

Source: M.E. Murray, "Palliative Care," *Canadian Nurse* 77(5)(1981), 16–17. Reproduced with permission from *The Canadian Nurse/L'infirmière canadienne*, vol. 77, no. 5.

palliative care patients. First, older patients averaged more diagnoses than the younger patients. Second, the younger patients typically had cancer; while the older patients typically suffered from circulatory and respiratory diseases (Shedletsky, Fisher, and Nadon 1982). Third, relatively few younger patients died from respiratory failure, while respiratory failure caused about 50 percent of all deaths in the older group.

Shedletsky, Fisher, and Nadon (1982) found that drug treatment helped about 80 percent of the people with pain and skin problems. The staff reported that just before death 75 percent of the patients felt no pain or distress and 75 percent were conscious or semi-conscious. The staff found, however, that patients with respiratory problems got the least benefit from drug treatment, and this group made up the largest portion of people with discomfort before death. The researchers concluded that some groups of older extended care patients may have special palliative care needs.

Mori (1991) describes a number of challenges that face palliative care programs. First, health care system funding limits some palliative care services. For example, hospitals cannot claim reimbursement for non–patient-related services. So, only two-thirds of palliative programs cover bereavement counselling. Also, physicians get low pay for home visits. This limits their interest in palliative home care. Second, health care workers and the public need more knowledge about palliative care. The public needs to know what this option offers. Professionals need to know how to work effectively on a palliative care team. They need better primary training and more frequent continuing education (Senate of Canada 1995). Third, palliative care programs favour people with a primary caregiver. One study (Levy 1987, cited in Mori 1991) found that most palliative care programs served married women with husbands. Older women, many of them widowed, often lack a primary caregiver. This makes them ineligible for palliative care.

Mori (1991) says that palliative care turns some assumptions of the health care system on their head. First, palliative care acknowledges the limits of curative medicine. It accepts death as part of life. Second, palliative care takes time. It follows the natural course of an individual's death. Health care services adjust to suit each person's needs. It puts the individual's need for comfort first. Third, palliative care treats the whole person. This includes the person's caregivers and social support system. Palliative care calls for a different kind of health care practice, one that broadens the health care options for dying patients.

ETHICAL ISSUES

Palliative care and other approaches to the treatment of dying patients raise a variety of ethical questions. Is it ethical, for example, to stop actively treating a person's illness? Does the decision not to put someone on a respirator or not to use a heroic life-saving measure contribute to the person's death? Philosophers, physicians, and legal experts have looked at these and other issues related to dying today.

Two ethical questions come up again and again in the writing on death and dying. First, should patients be told that they have a terminal illness? Second, when should a doctor allow a person to die?

To Tell or Not to Tell

Somerville (1989), in a discussion of informed consent in the case of surgery, says that telling patients about their condition and about the course of treatment can reduce their suffering. This information gives patients a sense of control over the process and promotes trust in the physician. She notes (1989, 130) that in some cases keeping information from the patient may lead to a "substantial benefit." But this benefit must clearly outweigh any harm that information might do to the patient. Also patients have a right to know about the choice of treatment the physician has made and about alternative treatments, including the choice of no treatment (see also Saint-Arnaud 1993).

Somerville (1989) says that physicians involved in active treatment (e.g., surgeons) should continue to communicate with dying patients. They can discuss the patient's "condition, prognosis and feelings" (Somerville 1989, 139). Failure to communicate with a terminally ill patient can lead to "a state of 'pre-mortem' loneliness" that patients can fear more than death (Somerville 1989, 139).

Glaser and Strauss (1977) describe two "awareness contexts" for dying: an **open awareness context** and a **closed awareness context.** In a closed awareness context, everyone (including the patient) knows the patient is dying, but no one speaks about it. Glaser and Strauss say this leads to a "ritual drama of mutual pretense" (1977, 271). Family members will talk to a patient about next summer at the cottage or Christmas in Hawaii, even though they all know the patient has only a few days to live. Glaser and Strauss say that this approach has some advantages over more open approaches. It protects the staff, family, and patient from exposing their feelings, and some patients may prefer to die this way. Glaser and Strauss go on to say that a closed awareness context can also cause problems: it can lead to loneliness and isolation for the patient.

Most dying patients today prefer an open awareness context, where the staff, the patient, and the family all know and share the knowledge that the patient is dying. This allows the physician to communicate clearly the degree of risk a patient faces. The physician may say, "You have a terminal illness, but you may still live several years." An open awareness context also allows the patient to speak openly about death and to share his or her feelings about dying. In addition, it gives the dying person a chance to make decisions about treatment, last-minute financial decisions, settlement of family affairs, and the opportunity to arrange the religious support he or she prefers. Some people will not want an open awareness context, and health workers should respect this right. Skelton (1982, 557) says "we should tell everyone as much as they wish to know."

A study at Royal Victoria Hospital in Montreal found that most patients want open and honest answers from their doctors (Mount, Jones, and Patterson 1974). The study also found that whether doctors felt they should tell their patients depended on whether they themselves would want to be told. Eighty-four percent of doctors who would have wanted to know their prognoses also felt their patients would want to know. But only 45 percent of doctors who would not have wanted to know their own condition felt their patients would want to know. These findings suggest that doctors may be protecting themselves from their discomfort with death when they withhold a diagnosis from a patient, and that they need more education about patients' feelings and needs. They may also need a chance to talk about and reflect on their own feelings about death and dying.

Euthanasia

Doctors sometimes face ethical conflicts when they treat dying patients. Medical ethics says that a doctor should heal and cure patients, but the Hippocratic oath also says that a doctor should first "do no harm." What should a doctor do when machines, surgery, or drugs that extend a person's life also prolong their suffering? What should a doctor do when a patient asks to die? And what does the law in Canada say about **euthanasia** (helping someone achieve a painless death)?

First, when is a person dead? When they stop breathing? When their heart stops beating? Or when their brain waves stop? Harvard Medical School (1968) gives four criteria for death: the person (1) no longer makes a response; (2) no

longer breathes or moves; (3) has no reflexes; and (4) has no sign of brain activity on two EEGs taken twenty-four hours apart. But what if a machine keeps someone breathing, or a heart pump keeps someone's heart beating? Are these people alive or dead? When does a family or a doctor have the right to take someone off these machines?

At present a person who lacks the mental competence to refuse treatment must rely on someone else to act for them. Family members, a friend, or a medical doctor often make this decision. Even if a person has told someone their wishes or has written a statement of their wish to end treatment at a certain point, these have no binding effect in Canada.

The Law Reform Commission of Canada (1982) reviewed the question of mercy killing in a study called *Euthanasia, Aiding Suicide and Cessation of Treatment*. The Commission found that the Canadian courts have never convicted a doctor in Canada for giving a patient large doses of pain-killing drugs, for stopping useless treatment, or for deciding not to treat a secondary illness (like pneumonia in a terminal cancer patient). The courts, however, could try doctors on these grounds. This means that every doctor who decides to stop treatment risks becoming a test case in the courts. The Commission feels that the Criminal Code of Canada should give doctors clearer guidance.

The Commission reviewed ways to relieve doctors of criminal liability. citing the example of California, which in 1976 passed Bill 3060, called the Natural Death Act. This bill allows a person to write a living will that authorizes relatives or doctors to withdraw or withhold artificial methods of life support in cases of terminal illness. It also attempts to relieve doctors of responsibility for stopping treatment. Forty U.S. states recognize living wills.

Kelly et al. (1989) studied physicians in nine countries and found that doctors would value having specific directions on the type of care a patient wants. Using the results of the study, the researchers produced a booklet called *Let Me Decide* that offers a model of a living will and of a **"health care directive."** The directive gives specific information to family members and doctors about the amount of treatment the person prefers under different conditions. The person also writes out a personal statement about preferences for care as part of the directive (Kelly et al. 1989).

Exhibit 14.3

Euthanasia and Assisted Suicide: What They Mean

Euthanasia, sometimes referred to as mercy killing, comes from Greek; its literal meaning is "good death." A distinction is often drawn between "passive" and "active" euthanasia.

Passive euthanasia means withholding or ceasing treatment of someone who is ill or injured and not expected to recover—e.g., turning off life support systems and allowing a person to die "naturally."

Active euthanasia means intervening actively to end a person's life—e.g., administering a lethal dose of sedatives to someone with a terminal illness. If performed with the consent of the person concerned, this is called "voluntary euthanasia."

Assisted suicide involves providing the means for someone to commit suicide (e.g., prescription drugs) with or without direct participation in the event.

Source: National Advisory Council on Aging, "Euthanasia and Assisted Suicide: What They Mean," Expressions 10(1) (1994), 2. Reproduced with the consent of the National Advisory Council on Aging (NACA) and with the permission of the Minister of Public Works and Government Affairs, 1997.

The Manitoba Law Reform Commission (1990) reviewed two types of advance directives for the termination of health care treatment—the **living will** and **durable power of attorney,** which gives an attorney the right to make decisions on behalf of the ill person. None of Canada's provinces recognized the living will as of 1993. But, Saint-Arnaud (1993) says, courts will take the living will into account if a family member challenges a health professional's actions. Only Nova Scotia and Quebec recognize the durable power of attorney. Outside these two provinces, a doctor is not legally bound by either of these documents.

Manitoba recently passed a Health Care Directives Act. This act allows people to appoint someone to make medical decisions for them if they become disabled. The **advance directive** differs from a living will. It states precisely the treatment and care desired (Saint-Arnaud 1993). Directives state what medical actions a person wants under what conditions. Directives also state who has the right to make the decisions. The courts will honour advance directives. But a person's relatives or friends need to make health care professionals aware of the directive and what it says.

Advance directives pose problems that need public discussion. First, in some cases people may change their minds as they near death, but they will not get a chance to change their living will.

Second, the Law Reform Commission of Canada (1982, 10) says that "a terminally ill patient has a right, not a secondary or subordinate right but a primary right, to die with dignity and not to fall victim to heroic measures." People should not need advanced directives to protect themselves from heroic treatment. Third, subtle forms of coercion may influence an older person's instructions in an advance directive. Older people may propose an end to treatment because they feel that they will burden others with their care.

Durable power of attorney for health care poses other problems. First, an attorney may refuse to decide or might not be available to make a decision. Second, the attorney may make an improper decision. And third, a physician may ask the attorney's permission to act too early in order to override a patient's refusal to allow treatment (Manitoba Law Reform Commission 1990). These issues and others need to be resolved.

The Law Reform Commission of Canada (1982) says that in Canada today doctors should not feel compelled to take heroic measures to keep someone alive and patients should not have to write advance directives to protect themselves from a doctor's fear of prosecution. The Commission says that the law and medical ethics distinguish between killing someone and allowing someone to die. Walton and Fleming (1980, 58) say that a doctor who sets out to kill a patient—for

Exhibit 14.4

A Living Will

The living will format below appears in the California Natural Death Act. The "Directive" below gives an idea of what such a will should contain. Read it over and consider the pros and cons of living wills. Would you fill one out? Would you witness a friend's? Do you think Canada should allow the use of living wills?

Directive to Physician

Directive made this _____ day of _____ (month, year). I _____ , being of sound mind, wilfully and voluntarily make known my desire that my life shall not be artificially prolonged under the circumstances set forth below, and do hereby declare:

1. If at any time I should have an incurable injury, disease, or illness certified to be a terminal condition by two physicians, and where the application of life-sustaining procedures would serve only to artificially prolong the moment of my death and where my physician determines that my death is imminent whether or not life-sustaining procedures are utilized, I direct that such procedures be withheld or withdrawn and that I be permitted to die naturally.

2. In the absence of my ability to give directions regarding the use of such life-sustaining procedures, it is my intention that this directive shall be honoured by my family and physician(s) as the final expression of my legal right to refuse medical or surgical treatment and accept the consequences from such refusal.

3. If I have been diagnosed as pregnant and that diagnosis is known to my physician, this directive shall have no force or effect during the course of my pregnancy.

4. I have been diagnosed and notified at least 14 days ago as having a terminal condition by _____ , M.D., whose address is _____ , and whose telephone number is _____ . I understand that if I have not filled in the physician's name and address, it shall be presumed that I did not have a terminal condition when I made out this directive.

5. This directive shall have no force or effect five years from the date filled in above.

6. I understand the full import of this directive and I am emotionally and mentally competent to make this directive.

Signed _____

City, County and State of Residence _____

The declarant has been personally known to me and I believe him or her to be of sound mind.

Witness _____

Source: California Natural Death Act. The contents of this document are in the public domain.

example, by giving the patient a drug overdose—"has committed himself more firmly. He is therefore more directly accountable for the outcome." A doctor who allows death to happen—for example, by not putting a person on a respirator or by taking someone off a respirator—may or may not cause a person's death. The person may live even without the treatment. Walton and Fleming (1980) say that ethical treatment should offer the most options for the patient. "A passive course of action," they say, "... provides a sensible alternative to aggressive treatment and, at the same time, allows for unexplainable and unforeseen events which may be of great benefit to the patient" (Walton and Fleming 1980, 60).

The current law leaves many questions open. Once treatment has begun, for instance, the law inhibits a doctor from discontinuing treatment. The doctor may know, through an advance directive, that after some time the patient would want treatment discontinued. But, by discontinuance the doctor risks legal action. The absence of support in the law for advance directives leaves the doctor open to civil action, criminal liability, and charges of misconduct from the medical profession (Manitoba Law Reform Commission 1990).

Both the law and medical ethics reject **active euthanasia**—killing someone either because they ask for death or to relieve their suffering. The Law Reform Commission of Canada (1982) says that a law to support active euthanasia would create more risks than benefits and might lead to new methods of euthanasia. Skelton (1982), a pioneer in palliative care in Canada, states the experts' case simply, saying that requests for active euthanasia often

hide a request for better care. "I believe most sincerely," he says, "that if adequate care is given to dying patients the question of responding to requests for active euthanasia is eliminated" (1982, 558; see also Maté 1993, cited in National Advisory Council 1994d).

Henteleff (1978) puts the ethical question in the context of professional responsibility. The patient, he says, has two needs: biological and moral. The doctor can help dying patients meet both these needs: he or she can relieve a person's physical distress and avoid treatment that will keep a person from finding meaning in his or her last days. Weisman (1972) says that medicine can and should help people die in the way they want to die. He calls this an "appropriate death."

Recent cases in the United States raise the issue of the legality of physician-assisted suicide. This refers to cases where a doctor gives a person the means to commit suicide or advises them on

---

Exhibit 14.5

Cessation of Treatment in Canada

Section 198 of the Criminal Code of Canada says that a person who gives medical or surgical treatment should act with reasonable skill and care. Section 199 says that a person has to continue an act once he or she begins, if by stopping the act he or she endangers someone's life. These sections seem to make a doctor criminally liable for stopping useless treatment. The Law Reform Commission of Canada says that these sections do not apply to a doctor who stops treatment after careful review of a case. The Commission gives an example to show why:

A doctor turns off a respirator, knowing, as he does so, that the patient will no longer be ventilated and thus will probably die. Let us suppose, in one instance, that before doing so he has assured himself, using standard medical procedures and tests, that the patient is already in a state of irreversible coma. Here the act of turning off the respirator, while technically constituting a positive act of cessation of treatment within the meaning of section 199, could not serve as a valid basis for criminal liability, and for two reasons. Firstly, the continuation of treatment is not reasonable in this case

given the condition of the patient and, secondly, the cessation of treatment does not reflect wanton or reckless disregard for life on the part of the physician. But on the other hand, let us assume that this doctor performs the same act without first assuring himself of the patient's condition. There would probably then be grounds for applying these provisions, since by ceasing treatment without taking the precaution of assuring himself that such cessation will not endanger the patient, he would be showing wanton or reckless disregard for the patient's life or safety.

Source: Law Reform Commission of Canada, *Euthanasia, Aiding Suicide and Cessation of Treatment*, Working Paper 28 (Ottawa: Minister of Supply and Services, 1982), 17–18. Reproduced with the permission of the Minister of Public Works and Government Services Canada, 1996.

Exhibit 14.6

Proposed Changes in Canadian Law

The Law Reform Commission proposes that the Criminal Code of Canada include the following statements.

1. Nothing in sections 14, 45, 198, 199 of the Criminal Code shall be interpreted as requiring a physician

   (a) to continue to administer or to undertake medical treatment against the clearly expressed wishes of the person for whom such treatment is intended;

   (b) to continue to administer or to undertake medical treatment, when such treatment is medically useless and is not in the best interests of the person for whom it is intended, except in accordance with the clearly expressed wishes of this person.

2. Nothing in sections 14, 45, 198, 199 of the Criminal Code shall be interpreted as preventing a physician from undertaking or ceasing to administer palliative care and measures intended to eliminate or to relieve the suffering of a person for the sole reason that such care or measures are likely to shorten the life expectancy of this person.

Source: Law Reform Commission of Canada, *Euthanasia, Aiding Suicide and Cessation of Treatment,* Working Paper 28 (Ottawa: Minister of Supply and Services, 1982), 70–71. Reproduced with the permission of the Minister of Public Works and Government Services Canada, 1996.

how to commit suicide. In these cases patients take the action themselves. The Second Circuit of Appeals in the United States in 1966 struck down a New York State law that forbade physicians to help patients die. This followed a similar ruling in California. A doctor in the United States can now follow a patient's request to withhold or withdraw treatment (Mattos and Sachs 1996). A doctor can also prescribe a lethal dose of drugs to patients with a terminal disease who ask for help to end their lives. Controversy exists over this practice. But Michigan courts have acquitted Dr. Jack Kevorkian of murder three times (as of 1996) in cases where he has helped patients commit suicide.

Supporters and critics of these decisions often argue about the issue of consent. Supporters of assisted suicide say that the patient's right to accept or refuse treatment will protect people from abuse of assisted suicide. Critics of assisted suicide fear that this will lead to mercy killing without patients' consent. Krauthammer (1996) reports that in the Netherlands this has occurred (see also Senate of Canada 1995). Also, some doctors may consent to patient requests too quickly. Few guidelines exist today for doctors to follow. Medical associations have begun to review their standards in light of recent court actions and social changes.

Canadian law prohibits a doctor from helping patients end their lives. A recent case in Canada (*Rodriguez vs. British Columbia*) in 1993 supported the Criminal Code's provisions against physician-assisted suicide (Health Canada 1994). Sue Rodriguez, a 42-year-old mother, had amyotrophic lateral sclerosis (Lou Gehrig's disease). Her health decreased and she would soon lose the ability to speak, swallow, or move. She had between two and fourteen months to live. She requested a court order from the Supreme Court of British Columbia to allow her to have a physician help her end her life when she chose. She asked the court to declare the Criminal Code statute (s. 241[b]) invalid. This statue prohibits assisted suicide.

The court held that Rodriguez did not have the right to have a doctor help her end her life. The court split 5-4 against her request. Some of the dissenting justices proposed procedural guidelines that could allow physician-assisted suicide. A court of appeal supported the majority opinion against Rodriguez's request. The outcome reflects "social divisions about how to reconcile the strongly held values of self-determination and the sanctity of life (National Advisory Council 1994d, 5).

Public debate on this issue will grow. Medicine now has the ability to prolong life through technology. This will mean more years of pain and suffering for some patients. Also, the cost of keeping people alive on machines and with expensive medications will also increase. Some people will support active euthanasia on economic grounds. Also, religion has less influence on issues like this today. And many people see the choice of active euthanasia as a right in modern society (National Advisory Council 1994d).

The National Advisory Council on Aging (1994d) reports that in 1968, 45 percent of Canadians approved of legalized mercy killing. This figure increased, by 1992, to 77 percent of Canadians. The Canadian Medical Association (CMA) conducted a study of physicians' views of physician-assisted suicide. The study found that over 60 percent of doctors wanted to change the Criminal Code. They wanted to do away with the laws that prohibit physician-assisted suicide (cited in National Advisory Council 1994d). In 1994, the ethics committee of the CMA supported doctors' right to assist in suicide. The committee also proposed that the CMA set up guidelines for physicians who choose to assist a patient in suicide. But CMA members voted against the committee's recommendation. They voted to ban doctors from engaging in physician-assisted suicide. Disagreement exists, even within the medical profession, over the practice of physician-assisted suicide. This debate will continue as Canadians sort out the implications of changing the law.

MOURNING AND GRIEF

When an older person dies he or she often leaves behind children and sometimes a spouse. These survivors need to adjust to the loss, and society can help with this adjustment. Funeral practices and rituals structure the grieving process. They prescribe what mourners should say, what they should wear, and in some cultures how they should sit. Mourners in Christian cultures wear black; mourners in some Oriental cultures wear white. North American society values silent, unemotional grieving; Chinese families hire professional mourners to make loud wailing noises at the funeral. Jewish tradition requires that the family "sit shiva" for seven days after a funeral. According to this custom, mourners tear their clothes, sit on low chairs to deny themselves physical comfort,

cover the mirrors in their home, and light a candle that burns for one week. The mourning family accepts visitors throughout the week, and ten men gather at the house each day for prayer. Mourning continues in less intense stages for a year until the unveiling of a commemorative stone on the grave of the deceased (Goldberg 1981–82).

Each culture has its own funeral rituals and mourning practices, but all of them have a common purpose: to help the bereaved family cope with grief and re-establish community bonds after the loss of a community member.

Regardless of the culture a person belongs to or the type of funeral he or she attends, each bereaved person has to work through personal feelings of grief. Some research in North America shows that mourners go through stages of grief. Lindemann (1944) describes three such stages: an initial response phase, an intermediate phase, and a recovery phase.

First, the bereaved person feels shock and disbelief. They may report feeling cold and numb, and some people say they feel dazed, empty, and confused. These feelings protect a person from feelings of sorrow. People in this phase often fear that they will break down in public. This phase can last for several weeks.

Second, the person will begin to review what has happened. This takes three forms: (a) The bereaved person obsessively reviews one or two scenes related to the death, or she may berate herself for something she should have said or done. (b) The bereaved person searches for a meaning for the death. Religious people may find solace in knowing that God willed this death. (c) The bereaved person searches for the deceased. This may mean that a widow goes to places where she expects to see her spouse. She may also feel his presence while watching TV, eating dinner, or lying in bed. Some people even call out to their spouses and expect an answer. This phase lasts about a year.

Third, the bereaved person begins to recover. Survivors look for social contacts: they may join a club or go on a cruise. They feel that they have come through an ordeal, and say they feel stronger and more competent than before. This stage begins around the second year after the death.

Gorer (1965) says that successful **grief work** includes: (1) breaking bonds to the deceased, (2) readjustment to the environment without the

Exhibit 14.7

A Family's Response to Death and Dying

The academic discussions of the right to decide on prolonging life often focus on medical and legal issues. But every day in Canada people, along with their physicians and nursing staff, make decisions about their older family members. These decisions, at their best, take place within a context of openness and trust between families and health care professionals. The following case shows how one family decided against aggressive treatment:

Mrs. Walker, 78, moved into an apartment in the Beth Sharon Senior Complex in early December. The complex offered her a supportive environment. It had a security system, access for a wheelchair, and a chance to socialize with other residents.

Mrs. Walker had played an active part in her community for many years as a hospital volunteer and businessperson. So, when she moved into her apartment complex, she joined the Beth Sharon Seniors Group and regularly attended their afternoon teas in a nearby centre. On January 10, as she left for the tea, she lost her balance, fell down a flight of stairs, and severely injured her head. When an ambulance arrived she was found unconscious and was taken to a nearby hospital for emergency treatment.

Mrs. Walker's daughter, Phyllis, a nurse, rushed to the hospital when she was called. The neurosurgeon on staff had already completed a CAT scan and showed it to Phyllis. "I don't like the look of this," he said, "there appears to be severe bleeding at the base of the brain stem. She's not likely to be well again, or indeed function on her own."

Phyllis left the ward to talk with her sister and other family members. They agreed that they would not press for an operation to remove the blood clot. Surgery would almost certainly lead to the necessity of a respirator and other artificial means of life support. Over the next few days, as the family waited for some change in their mother's condition, Phyllis would suggest various actions or ask for another test. Each time the surgeon in charge would ask a simple question, "Would your mother like us to do that?" And each time Phyllis agreed that her mother would not want aggressive treatment to prolong her life. The decision to wait became harder to sustain as Mrs. Walker's breathing faltered. But the family stayed with its decision, based on Mrs. Walker's many discussions with them. Family members and close friends supported the family's decision to follow their mother's wishes.

Sixteen days after entering the hospital, and without regaining consciousness, Mrs. Walker died. She was cremated, in accordance with her request, and her family held a memorial service to celebrate her life.

deceased, and (3) forming new relationships. Not everyone makes a smooth trip through these stages. Sometimes a person can show a delayed emotional response to a parent's or a spouse's death. The person seems to cope well, displaying lots of zest and energy, but he may have internalized his grief. This can lead to emotional upset and physical illness later.

The case of Joanna will show the cost of morbid grieving. While her husband was in the hospital dying of brain cancer, she visited him every day. At the same time she carried on a career in real estate and worked on a master's degree. For two years she ran herself into the ground. She went to the hospital twice a day, at noon and at supper time, to feed her husband his meals; then she would jump in her car and show another house or run home to work on a paper.

When her husband died, she was determined that nothing was going to stop her. "I didn't allow myself time to grieve," she says. "After his death, I travelled. At Christmas I went to Spain, Hawaii, or wherever. At Easter I went somewhere. I went to Europe. There was never a day—I didn't allow myself any time at all. Do you get the picture? No time to breathe."

To keep going she used pills and alcohol. Then she started collecting pills and drinking more.

Exhibit 14.8

Controversy: Setting Limits

Daniel Callahan, in his book *Setting Limits*, suggests one way to deal with the rising costs of health care: ration health care for the elderly. He cites three reasons for this proposal. First, compared with the health care used by children, older people as a group use a large amount of health care. Second, a large and growing portion of research and technology goes to reverse the health conditions of the elderly. Third, more than a fair share of money for health care to the elderly goes to care for dying people.

Today people can expect to receive health care treatment if they need it and have some hope of recovery. But some evidence suggests that rationing of health care by age may already be taking place. Kjellstrand and Moody (1994), for example, studied the acceptance rate of older people into dialysis programs in Canada. They found that Canada has a much lower acceptance rate for older people than the United States. The authors say that physicians ration access to dialysis and use age as a criterion. They go on to say that physicians may use age to decide how aggressively to pursue treatment.

Callahan (1987) wants to make rationing by age an accepted part of medical practice. He argues against the use of medical need as a criterion for treating older people. Instead he proposes that we base the decision to treat an illness on age or on the concept of the "natural life span" (1987, 137), which Callahan defines as 70 to 80 years. He argues that society should commit itself to high-quality care for people throughout this span. But, beyond this point, medicine and government support of health care should focus on the relief of suffering, not the extension of life. This policy, he says, would remove the burden of high health care costs for the very old. He presents the following three principles for the use of age as a way to decide on treatment:

1. Medical care should not resist death after patients have lived out their natural life span.
2. Medical care should only relieve suffering for those who have lived their natural life span.
3. Medical technologies that can extend life beyond the natural life span should not have to be used for this purpose.

These policies, Callahan argues, would remove the uncertainty older people and their children face about the high cost of treatment; it would lead to a high quality of life until late old age; and it would remove the social threat posed by the rising cost of health care for the elderly.

Binstock and Kahana (1988) find that Callahan's argument lacks consistency. Callahan, for example, would make an exception for physically strong and mentally alert people who came down with a sudden illness. Also, he would apply his plan only to physically frail people or to those in need of long-term care. Binstock and Kahana (1988) say that this leaves open the question of who will decide who should get care. Will a second illness lead to the withdrawal of care? A third? And what about the mentally alert, frail person who could live a satisfying life with medical support? Why deny this person treatment? Binstock and Kahana (1988, 426) say that Callahan "does not hesitate to undertake sweeping moral judgments … [but] does not develop the moral basis for his own proposal." Why, for example, does he support the use of age as a criterion, over all others, for deciding on medical treatment?

Glass (1993) notes that age serves as a weak basis for making decisions about life and death issues. For example, gerontologists show that older people of the same age vary in their health and need for health care. Also, Callahan assumes that an older frail person has less social worth than a younger healthy person. "The criterion of social worth values the individual only as an instrument of society and not as a person deserving of respect simply because he or she is a human being" (Glass 1993, 75). Glass (1993, 80) argues that each person (whatever his or her age) deserves treatments that "best serve their interest or their wishes *as they have defined them.*"

Callahan only vaguely refers to the kinds of social, moral, and ethical changes that would have to come about for his proposal to work. And he makes little reference to how this kind of social change would occur. Still, Binstock and Kahana (1988, 426) concede that this book "is likely to be a point of reference in such discussions for some time to come."

"That was my way of coping, my way of standing the pain. I needed some kind of anesthetic," she says. At the end of this downward spiral Joanna drove the front of her car through a restaurant window. She got out of her car, walked through the windowframe, sat down at a booth in the restaurant, and waited for the police to take her away (Novak 1985).

Only about 25 percent of bereaved people go through morbid grieving (and few people show Joanna's extreme denial) (Schulz 1978). But many people deviate from the pattern of bereavement that stage models of grieving describe (Wortman and Silver 1990). Older people, for example, tend to show a delayed and more extreme grief reaction than younger people. Sanders (1980–81) compared the scores on a "grief experience inventory" of forty-five bereaved spouses in two age groups (people over age 65 and under 63). She found that older spouses showed less grief than younger spouses at the time of a first interview (shortly after their spouse's death). At the second interview older spouses showed higher scores than younger spouses on scales of denial and physical symptoms, and increases in ten other scales compared with younger spouses. Barrett and Schneweis (1980–81, 102) also report that life after a spouse's death "persists in being stressful for years." These results show that an older person may need help long after his or her spouse's death.

Baker (1991) reports that spouses who have died continue to influence the living in many ways. People sometimes talk to a dead spouse, ask them for advice, or try to imagine what they would do in a situation the surviving spouse is facing. One woman said she felt her husband lie down next to her in bed some months after his funeral. Widows or widowers will sometimes decide against remarriage because of the close tie that still exists with their dead spouse. Moss and Moss (1984–85) consider this a normal response to widowhood in old age and "a nourishing link to the past" (1984–85, 204). More research on bereavement in old age will show how this experience differs from bereavement in younger people (Wortman and Silver 1990).

CONCLUSION

This chapter has touched on some of the complex issues related to death and dying. Each religion has its own views on issues like euthanasia, funeral practices, and mourning. Each culture shapes its members' beliefs about the meaning of death, about life after death, and about care for the sick and dying. People will respond in unique ways to their own death and to the deaths of people they know and love. Today, changes in technology, the management of terminal illness, and the meaning of death raise new questions about death and dying. The study of death and dying can help people to understand these issues and make better choices for themselves.

SUMMARY

1. Attitudes to death vary by age, religion, and culture. Older people generally accept death more than younger people. Like younger people, older people say they want to continue living, if they feel their life has meaning.
2. People with either no religious belief or a very strong one seem to cope with death best.
3. Death occurs more often in old age today than in the past, and it also occurs more often in an institution. These trends will increase as the population ages.
4. Elisabeth Kübler-Ross reports five stages of dying. Not everyone goes through all of these stages in the order Kübler-Ross describes, but her writings encouraged a more open discussion of death and dying when they first appeared.
5. Cicely Saunders opened the first modern hospice in England in 1967. St. Christopher's Hospice offers an alternative to hospital care for the dying. Hospices offer pain control and a home-like setting for death.
6. Palliative care units in hospitals offer the same comfort and care as a hospice. Some of these units will help patients die in their own homes. They also assure patients that they can return to the hospital at any time.
7. Most experts and patients prefer an open awareness context for dying. A closed awareness context can lead to isolation and loneliness for the patient (though some people may prefer not to speak openly about death). Doctors today need to understand their own feelings about death and dying, so they can give their patients the kind of care that their patients prefer.

8. Doctors say that proper pain control would end the fear that leads people to ask for euthanasia. The law in Canada today does not require doctors to take heroic measures to keep a terminally ill patient alive. Canada needs clearer guidelines to help doctors decide about stopping treatment for people in comas. Canadian law does prohibit active euthanasia. Judicial review of cases would lead to more rational decisions about termination of life.

9. Health care directives relieve doctors of criminal liability. They give family members and doctors specific information about the amount of treatment a person prefers. They also state who has the right to make decisions on behalf of the patient.

10. Death leads to grief and mourning for survivors. Culture and religion help people cope with feelings of grief. Funerals, for example, bring the community together and give mourners support. Still, each person has to work through feelings of grief in his or her own way. Researchers say that mourners go through stages of grief and that if all goes well they will emerge from grieving to carry on their life.

STUDY QUESTIONS

1. Researchers have proposed three theories that describe how older people respond to death. List and explain each of these theories.

2. Describe the means that older people use to buffer their fear of death.

3. How has population aging changed the context of dying?

4. Describe how Elizabeth Kübler-Ross and Cicely Saunders each influenced thinking about death and dying.

5. Explain the main function of a hospice. What methods do hospices use to help people enjoy their last days?

6. Compare and contrast palliative care units and hospices. Why do researchers think that, compared with a normal hospital, palliative care units cost less money to care for dying patients?

7. What moral issues did the Sue Rodriguez case raise? What conflict did this case raise between the medical profession and the Canadian legal system? How can Canadian society resolve this conflict for the future?

8. Describe the three stages of grief. Describe successful grief work. How do older and younger people differ in their grieving patterns?

KEY TERMS

active euthanasia   intervening actively to end a person's life.

advance directive   states precisely the treatment and care desired (Saint-Arnaud 1993). Directives state what medical actions a person wants under what conditions. They also state who has the right to make the decisions.

closed awareness context   everyone (including the patient) knows the patient is dying, but no one speaks about it.

durable power of attorney   gives an attorney the right to make decisions on behalf of the ill person.

ego integrity   "It is the acceptance of one's one and only life cycle as something that had to be and that, by necessity, permitted of no substitutions" (Erikson 1963, 268).

ego transcendence   a late stage of psychosocial development. People in this stage feel a deep concern for others and for the culture they will leave when they die.

euthanasia   helping someone achieve a painless death.

grief work   includes: (1) breaking bonds to the deceased, (2) readjustment to the environment without the deceased, and (3) forming new relationships.

health care directive   gives specific information to family members and doctors about the amount of treatment the person prefers under different conditions.

hospice   hospices today meet the special needs of dying patients. Dame Cecily Saunders opened the first modern hospice, St. Christopher's, in London in 1967.

living will   specifies the limits of health care treatment desired in case of a terminal illness. None of Canada's provinces recognized the living will as of 1993. But, Saint-Arnaud (1993) says, courts will take the living will into account if a family member challenges a health professional.

open awareness context everyone including the patient knows and acknowledges that the patient is dying.

palliative care "a program of active compassionate care primarily directed towards improving the quality of life for the dying." A complete program of palliative care includes symptom control and spiritual support as well as bereavement support and education (Subcommittee on Institutional Program Guidelines 1989, 1).

SELECTED READINGS

Bolton, Anne M. "Who Can Let You Die?" *Canadian Journal on Aging* 8 (1989): 238–43.

A brief, informative discussion of the legal issues regarding cessation of treatment. Clearly written, understandable to nonlawyers.

National Advisory Council on Aging, *Ethics and Aging* (Ottawa: Minister of Supply and Services Canada, 1993).

A collection of articles on issues related to death and dying. The collection includes a discussion of decision-making with respect to end-of-life treatment. It also includes a discussion of health care rationing. These essays present clear and orderly discussions of many complex issues that we read about in the newspapers. Well-written and thoughtful essays.

Senate of Canada, *Of Life and Death*, Report of the Special Senate Committee on Euthanasia and Assisted Suicide (Ottawa: Queens Printer of Canada, 1995).

An overview of the issues related to euthanasia and assisted suicide. The report presents testimony from experts across Canada. It reviews important court cases and summarizes the laws on these issues in other countries. An excellent current review of the issues.

Societal Change

Politics and Policy

INTRODUCTION

Researcher Monica Townson (1994, 7) asked a question that underlies much of the public's interest in aging: "Can Canada afford its ageing population?" The question suggests that an older population will break the national bank. That may lead to social and economic crisis. An aging society will need more of everything: health care, income support, social services, housing, and transportation. An aging society will also put new demands on family and community life. It may lead to more caregiver burden and stress for middle-aged workers. The government will have to respond to these needs. And it will have to do so in a time of economic restraint. What role will politics and policy play in an aging society?

Studies of aging and politics in Canada attempt to understand the relationship between an aging society and governmental policy. These studies have only just begun. Pratt (1984) says that before 1980 political scientists saw little reason to study aging. First, in the 1950s and 1960s scholars concerned themselves mostly with voting behaviour and political opinions. They found that the largest changes in opinion took place as people moved from adolescence to adulthood. The opinions of adult voters were stable, for the most part, from middle age on. As a result, political scientists tended to ignore the study of older age groups.

Second, with this focus on voting behaviour, political scientists showed little concern for policy issues such as health care, housing, or pension issues (one exception is Bryden's [1974] study of pension policy). Third, until the 1980s gerontology sat near the bottom of the disciplinary hierarchy in Canada. Pratt (1984) says that researchers in all disciplines found it hard to get funds for aging research. Under such conditions, political scientists were not inclined to study aging.

The start of a Strategic Grants program for Population Aging in 1979 increased interest in the study of aging and politics. But this interest has grown slowly: Pratt (1984) reported fewer than ten gerontological studies by Canadian political scientists. These studies, at best, give a hint of the issues that concern gerontologists when they study politics.

Pratt's (1984) review shows that gerontologists study aging and politics from at least three points of view. First, they study political participation, including seniors' voting patterns and political attitudes, and the number of seniors who hold public office. Second, gerontologists examine senior activism and group conflict. This includes the study of senior pressure groups and public protests. Third, they look at the context of political action—the policies and structures of the government.

This chapter will look at each of these topics. It will (1) describe the range of seniors' political activity in Canada, (2) describe the government agencies that translate seniors' needs into policy, and (3) consider seniors' political participation in the future.

POLITICAL PARTICIPATION

Sociologists define political participation as behaviour that leads to the selection of leaders and the choice of public policy. Seniors take part in politics in a number of ways. They read about political issues, and listen to and watch public affairs radio and TV shows. They also vote, hold political office, and sometimes protest government decisions.

Voting

Studies done on voting patterns during the 1960s in the United States (Milbrath 1965) and in other countries supported the disengagement theory of aging. They found that young adults had lower voter turnout than middle-aged people; middle-aged people (in their forties and fifties) showed the highest voter turnout; and older people showed less voter turnout than middle-aged people, though more than young adults. Regenstreif (1965, 88) concluded from Canadian data that "there is strong evidence that people past the age of 65 suffer a diminution of interest in politics for a variety of reasons. Turn-out and general participation follow these patterns."

Later Canadian studies questioned these findings. Van Loon (1970), in a study of 1965 Canadian election figures, found only a slight peak in middle age. Laskin and Baird (1970) studied Saskatchewan local, provincial, and federal voting records in a small town and found similar voter turnout among younger and older age groups.

Other studies in the United States and Canada also question the conclusion that older people participate less than younger people in political activity. These studies control for socioeconomic status, health, and physical mobility. They show that given the same background, health, and mobility, younger and older people show similar levels of political activity (Hudson and Strate 1985; Jacobs 1990; Verba and Nie 1972). Yelaja (1981, 14) reports that in a study of eighty-two Canadians aged 50 and over, "in terms of political attention ... political participation and activity, the older, retired persons tended to exhibit a higher level of participation and activity than the younger and employed respondents." Kernaghan (1982) found that in the 1974 Canadian federal election the figures for voter turnout declined only after age 85.

Curtis and Lambert (1976) found similar results for the 1965 and 1968 Canadian federal elections. In one report they reviewed the voting and political interest patterns for a sample of 2767 Canadians aged 21 years and older during the 1968 election. When they looked at their total sample, they found that, compared with younger people, older people showed less voting and election interest. This supported the findings of earlier studies that showed a decrease in voting and political interest among older age groups. Curtis and Lambert then looked at groups of people with the same income, education, occupation, region, community size, marital status, sex, and language. They found that older people with different backgrounds voted at different rates. They found that English-Canadian males, for example, have a greater tendency to vote in later life than English-Canadian women, but both groups show about the same interest in election issues. They also found that French-Canadian males and females show little difference in voting patterns with age, but French-Canadian males show a greater political interest than French-Canadian females. They also found differences between the two language groups. They found that older (over age 50) English-Canadian males and females are more likely to vote than their French-Canadian counterparts.

When they looked at people within each group (French-Canadian male, French-Canadian female, English-Canadian female, English-Canadian male), they found no difference in voting or political interest with age. They say that "there is little or no evidence suggesting a decline in either voting or electoral interest as a function of age" (Curtis and Lambert 1976, 302). They found, instead, that even past the age of 70 people

remained active in voting and in their affiliations with political groups. When older people did not vote, they gave frailty or illness as a reason, not lack of interest.

The researchers say they were "struck with [their] failure to detect any clear evidence for a reduction in reported organizational involvement or affiliation with age once controls are made ... So far as voting and political interest are concerned, there is either no drop-off with age or even some modest increases" (1976, 305–6).

Most of the reported Canadian research on voting patterns relies on cross-sectional data. These data allow researchers to compare the voting behaviour of different age groups at one point in time. But they do not allow researchers to draw conclusions about changes in voting behaviour with age. Researchers need to use longitudinal methods to study the effects of age on voting behaviour.

Still, the research on voting behaviour reports that seniors take an active interest in politics. Combined with their growing numbers, this interest may give older people more political power in the future. Gifford (1982) says that the median age for voters has risen in Canada from 30 years in 1881 to 42 years in 1981. He says that the median age will rise to 48 by 2031. At that time, he says, voters aged 65 and over will make up 26 percent of the voting public, compared with only 13.3 percent in 1981 (Gifford 1983). The large numbers of future seniors and their high voter participation rate could lead them to form a **voting bloc.** This bloc could sway government policy through the electoral process.

Will seniors use their voting strength to shape Canadian policy and achieve specific goals? They have on one or two occasions in the past. Gifford (1982) points to "the Diefenbaker 'pension increase' landslide of 1958" as one. Kernaghan (1982) points to the National Pensioners and Senior Citizens Federation campaign to create the Canada Pension Plan between 1963 and 1965 as another (citing Bryden 1974, 194–97). Kernaghan and Kuper (1983) say that seniors groups have begun to play a more important role in policy-making. But most experts do not think that seniors will form a permanent voting bloc (Binstock 1986; Heclo 1988).

First, studies in Canada show that many people keep the same political stance throughout

Exhibit 15.1

Age Distribution of Canada's Population: % of Population 65 Years and Over, Median Age of Voters, and Percent of Voters 65 and Over, 1881–2031

Year	65+ as % of Pop.	Median Age of Voters	65+ % of Voters
1881	4.1	30	8.5
1931	5.6	40	9.9
1961	7.6	41	12.9
1981	9.7	42	13.3
2001	12.3	45	16.2
2021	16.6	47	20.9
2031	20.9	48	26.0

Source: Adapted from C.G. Gifford, "Senior Politics," *Policy Options*, September 1983, 14. Reproduced with the permission of the Institute for Research on Public Policy.

their lives. Conservatives tend to stay that way; so do Liberals and New Democrats. Regenstreif (1965) found, in an analysis of the 1962 Canadian federal election, that the New Democratic Party got the strongest support from voters who at that time were 40 to 49 years old. These voters voted for the first time during the 1940s, when the CCF (forerunner of the NDP) led the Liberals in popular support. This historical period shaped their voting patterns, so that "the political atmosphere of the early and middle 1940s continues to cast its spell on political life" (1965, 87). Likewise, people who came of age during the Depression of the 1930s or who served in World War II will have their own view of Canadian political life and their own party affiliations.

Second, older people differ in social class, ethnic background, and in what part of the country they live. They have varying needs and define issues differently. Wealthy seniors, for example, may have little interest in the continued indexation of the Guaranteed Income Supplement, while a poor older widow may listen carefully to what a politician says about public pension policy. Voters in the Maritimes tend to favour the Liberal and Progressive Conservative parties, while Ontario and the Prairie provinces show the greatest support for the NDP (Clarke et al. 1980). These and other differences lead older people to vote for one party over the others and to favour certain policies and reject others. Clarke and his

colleagues reviewed voting patterns by age for three federal elections (1965, 1968, 1974). They did find (for all three elections) that a larger portion of voters in older age groups (26 percent of those 21–29 voted PC, compared with 35 percent of respondents aged 60 and over) favoured the Progressive Conservative Party. But they conclude that this relatively small difference provides "no evidence of pronounced differences in voting behaviour of different age groups in Canadian federal elections" (1980, 87).

Third, seniors take into account other needs than their own when they vote (Powell 1987). Most older people, for example, have children and grandchildren. A senior may vote for a politician because that person's party promises to provide jobs for the young or day care for mothers. Senior voters will vote as a bloc if a policy or party threatens to cut pensions or increase the costs of services, but most of the time senior issues play only a small part in determining seniors' voting behaviours.

Even if they do not form a voting bloc, seniors can use other methods to shape government policy. Frank (1992) reports that older people, more than younger people, use their finances to influence politics. Older people have the highest rate of federal political contributions. Older people also engage in activities that shape social policy. Verba, Nie, and Kim (1971, 10) say that elections set the pattern of government policy, but "the most important set of political activities may be the myriad attempts to influence governmental decisions … between elections." A study by Kernaghan and Kuper (1983) shows that almost all provincial and federal government agencies make policies that affect seniors. Some agencies, like federal and provincial departments of health, play a central role in policy-making for seniors, while others, like transportation or consumer affairs, play a smaller role. Pross (1975) says that seniors will have an impact on policy only if federal and provincial public servants recognize their right to participate in policy-making.

Seniors can take an active part in Canadian policy making in at least three ways:

1. Governments have set up seniors' councils, advisory groups, and committees to shape policies for seniors. Seniors can work with these councils to create change from within the system.

2. Seniors can form **advocacy groups** that lobby the government for policy change. These groups would pass resolutions, write reports, and meet with government officials to discuss seniors' issues. These groups may have the greatest impact on policies for seniors. If they achieve legitimacy, advocacy groups can play an ongoing part in policy formation.

3. Seniors can form **protest groups.** Ongoing advocacy groups (like provincial senior societies) can protest government policies, and so can special groups that emerge to protest a specific issue. The Senate of Canada's report (Senate of Canada 1979) on retirement age policies supports this approach. It says, "the retired elderly should organize, protest and show militancy in order to improve their chances of achieving dignity, obtaining higher incomes as well as medical and other services and finding useful work" (Senate of Canada 1979, 115).

Seniors have started to work in all of these directions in the past few years. The following sections review some recent senior political activities.

Senior Advocacy Groups

Sociologists define political power as the ability of one group to achieve its interests over those of others. A group can gain power by having its members elected to office, by violently overthrowing the government, or by putting pressure on government officials. Advocacy groups take this last approach. One of the first advocacy groups for seniors in history, the Old Age Pensioners' Organization, was formed in British Columbia in 1932 to protest the rigid use of a means test for pensioners. Later, in the 1940s and 1950s, provincial senior organizations were formed on the Prairies and in Ontario. In 1954 these provincial groups united to become the National Pensioners and Senior Citizens Federation. Senior organizations formed in the Maritime provinces during the 1960s and 1970s. These provincial organizations and national federations now meet each year to pass resolutions on seniors issues, like the cost of insurance, the quality of nursing home care, and the price of drugs. They then send these resolutions to the appropriate provincial or federal agencies. These groups also lobby government leaders between yearly meetings (Bryden 1974, 195).

Statistics Canada (1990e) found that half of all seniors report involvement in a political organization, about double the rate of their involvement in any other type of group. Many of these people belong to one or more of the 3700 social clubs or senior centres in Canada. Few of these local clubs do direct advocacy work, but often a club belongs to a provincial or national federation.

The National Advisory Council on Aging (1989, cited in Pratt 1993) reported that eight national senior organizations existed in Canada in the late 1980s. Seven provinces have over forty special advocacy groups. These groups respond to specific issues by presenting briefs to government committees or to cabinet ministers. They include Canadian Pensioners Concerned (twenty local branches in Ontario, Nova Scotia, and Alberta), the United Senior Citizens of Ontario (with over 1300 member clubs and between 350 000 and 400 000 members), Seniors Action Now (branches in Saskatchewan and British Columbia), and L'Association Québécoise pour la Défense des Droits des Retraites et Préretraites (fifteen branches in Quebec) (Gifford 1982; Yelaja 1989). Yelaja (1989) also reports on the rise of advocacy groups based on ethnic identity like the Association of Jewish Seniors in Toronto.

Hundreds of special-needs groups also exist throughout the country. These include teachers' groups, government employee groups, and groups related to a single corporation. These groups work to protect pension plans and benefits of former employees. Other organizations like the Royal Canadian Legion have many older members and a well-developed program to help seniors.

Pratt (1993) reports that senior advocacy has grown in Canada. More groups and more types of groups exist than ever before. Volunteers run most advocacy groups in Canada. Few of them lobby the bureaucracy for change. The groups lack funds to keep up a lobby campaign and their distance from Ottawa makes lobbying impractical. Instead, these groups focus their efforts on elected officials. Many of these groups hold annual meetings, pass resolutions, and present these to the appropriate cabinet ministers. These groups' effect on policy-makers has grown in recent years. Pratt sums up his research on **interest group** power in Canada. "While interest groups must compete with other political actors in seeking to influence the scope and content of political agendas," he says, "their influence nevertheless has been (and remains) fairly considerable" (Pratt 1987, 75, cited in Pratt 1993).

These groups carry on work similar to the influential American Association of Retired Persons (AARP) in the United States. AARP has about 25 million members and is the "largest organized interest group in America" (Jacobs 1990, 353). Its permanent headquarters are in Washington, D.C., and it employs full-time

---

Exhibit 15.2

A Profile of Some Seniors Groups and What They Do

Quebec

The Federation de l'Âge d'Or du Québec (FADOQ) started in 1973. It is the most highly organized and financially secure of the provincial federations, and has twenty-six full-time paid staff members and maintains active contact with over a dozen departments in the Quebec government. The federation lobbies for change, publishes a newspaper, and writes briefs to the government on seniors' issues. The federation had about 200 000 individual members and 1200 institutional members in 1991. The federation has refused affiliation with the National Pensioners and Senior Citizens Federation. The FADOQ has no national base of support, but it has considerable influence on policy within the province of Quebec.

Ontario

The United Senior Citizens of Ontario now has over 1000 affiliated clubs and over 260 000 members. Members also automatically belong to the National Pensioners and Senior Citizens Federation. The association works for pension increases, tax relief, and medicare benefits. It also presents briefs to the provincial government on health care, housing, and recreation issues, and publishes a monthly newsletter. It takes credit for better government pensions, increases in seniors' housing, and provincial tax credits for seniors.

Alberta

The Alberta Council on Aging represents 40 000 seniors in Alberta. It has two goals: to identify seniors' needs and get senior (65+) leaders to take action. In 1979 the Council conducted a study of consumer concerns; in 1980 it studied the participation of older people in the performing arts; and in 1982 it set up a community improvement program called Project Involvement. The council publishes *Foresight*, a magazine for retirement planning that forty-five companies now use in their pre-retirement education programs. The Council also writes briefs and letters to tell the provincial government about seniors' needs. In 1983 it opposed user fees for health care services, filed a report to the Task Force on Older Women, and expressed concern over crime and the elderly.

These groups keep the channels of communication with government open. Both seniors and the government gain from this relationship. Seniors can use these channels to stimulate policies that meet their needs, and government can learn about seniors' responses to ongoing policies and programs.

researchers and lobbyists to lobby the government on senior issues. AARP also publishes a national magazine, *Modern Maturity*, and offers services like life insurance, wholesale drugs, and travel discounts.

The United States has a number of other large groups that speak out on senior issues. These include the National Association of Retired Federal Employees, with more than 180 000 members; the National Council of Senior Citizens, which has about 3 million members; and the National Council on the Aging, a federation of more than 1000 agencies that works for and with older people (Atchley 1985; Hendricks and Hendricks 1986). These groups have large budgets and bureaucratic structures that give them legitimacy in the eyes of government officials.

The United States also has a multi-age activist group called the Gray Panthers. This group began as a coalition of older people and students in the late 1960s, and today maintains a commitment to multi-age membership. But most new members are older people. The group's founder, Maggie Kuhn, appeared on U.S. television talk shows and was written about in the press. The Gray Panthers attract media attention because the group portrays older people as militant activists who will use street theatre or sit-ins to draw attention to their needs. The Gray Panthers have organized tenants (of all ages) in Washington, D.C., set up a multi-age living project in Boston, and helped fight for better food in school cafeterias in San Diego, California (Jacobs and Hess 1980). Jacobs and Hess say that the Panthers will probably never attract large numbers of seniors, but the group does serve a purpose. It casts older people in a new and dramatic role as social critics and activists who fight to improve life for young and old.

Some national seniors advocacy associations have recently emerged in Canada. One group, the **Canadian Association of Retired Persons (CARP)** is "a non-profit organization dedicated to improving the quality of life for Canadians 50 or over, retired or not" (Canadian Association of Retired Persons 1991, 1). CARP began in 1986 and claims it had 65 000 members nation-wide in 1991. The organization produces a quarterly newsletter, provides information on hotel, motel, and car rental savings, and makes presentations to governments on behalf of seniors.

One Voice—The Canadian Seniors Network, a nonprofit organization, also advocates on behalf of older people. One Voice began in 1987 with funding from the Samuel and Saidye Bronfman Family Foundation. Members of One Voice work to improve "the condition and independence of older Canadians. They endorse the adoption of programs and policies that promote their well-being and continued development. They encourage full and active participation of older adults in making decisions that affect their lives" (Geoffroy 1994, 5). Projects include the creation of a Canadian Seniors Packaging Advisory Council to advocate safer package design; the sponsorship of cross-Canada housing workshops, and the publication of a "Seniors Election Guide" to help seniors understand national issues. One Voice has a national focus and has won the support of many seniors groups across the country. One Voice also works to influence the federal bureaucracy through professional lobbying (Pratt 1993).

Still, Canadian seniors groups lack the national impact of either the AARP or the Gray Panthers for at least two reasons. First, in Canada, the provinces set policies for health care, housing, and social services. This gives lobbying a provincial focus and makes the provincial federations as important as the national federations as advocates of seniors' needs (Gifford 1990).

Second, pressure group activity in Canada is "more limited, more secretive and more focused on the bureaucracy than in the United States" (Kernaghan and Kuper 1983, 30). The policy system in Canada "tends to be characterized by superficial public deliberations and by the assignment of major responsibility for policy development to the political executive, the administrative arena, and recognized pressure groups" (Pross 1975). This makes it harder in Canada than in the United States for seniors to influence policymakers.

Senior Activism

A social movement forms when a group (1) coalesces around a set of issues, (2) creates an image of itself in the media as concerned and important, (3) exerts pressure on government agencies, public policies, and people who make decisions, and (4) has expertise and can raise money or votes on behalf of the issues it represents (Hendricks and Hendricks 1986). Binstock (1972; see also Gifford 1985) says that age alone cannot form the basis of a cohesive social movement because seniors' groups lack the financial stability, the organizational rigour, and the large numbers of supporters needed to form a movement. Pratt (1983) disagrees. He sees a growing class consciousness among seniors in North America today and predicts that this will form the basis for a social movement. Yelaja (1981) found that a working younger group of older people (aged 50–64) reported more political activity than older groups (aged 65–74 and 75+). The youngest group reported that they took part in lobby and advocacy activities related to older people's well-being. Yelaja (1989) says that this younger group in Canada will create a more politically active senior population in the future.

Seniors in Canada have on occasion joined together in a national social movement. This has happened three times in the recent past; each time seniors felt threatened by cutbacks in government programs (Gifford 1983). Seniors acted as a movement in 1972 during the federal election campaign, when they protested low Old Age Security payments. Protests included mass meetings in Vancouver and a demonstration at Toronto's City Hall (Gifford 1983). They acted as a movement again in 1980, in British Columbia, when the Social Credit government threatened to postpone a denti-care program and to raise automobile insurance rates. Again, in 1985 seniors protested government policy, this time the federal government's plan to limit indexation of the Old Age Security and Guaranteed Income Supplement programs. This last case shows that seniors can wield power on specific occasions when they organize.

De-Indexing the Old Age Security Program: A Case Study of Senior Protest and Government Response

In the winter of 1985 the Progressive Conservative government, led by Prime Minister Brian Mulroney, faced a dilemma. On the one hand, the business community demanded that the government cut spending and reduce the national debt. On the other hand, the government was obliged, in 1985, to pay out over $11 billion in OAS and GIS pensions. This amount increases each year because the government indexes the OAS and GIS programs to the consumer price index (CPI) (a measure of the cost of living). The government wanted to cut these payments to appease the busi-

ness community, but was unable to because the prime minister had committed the government to retain these universal programs.

On May 23, 1985, Finance Minister Michael Wilson tried to resolve the dilemma in his budget by introducing a measure by which the government would only increase the pension payments if the CPI rose by more than 3 percent. Increases would only cover the difference between the first 3 percent rise and the actual CPI increase. (If the CPI rose 5 percent, pensioners would get only a 2 percent raise. If it rose 2.5 percent, pensioners would get no increase in their pensions.) The government projected that this change would save $1.6 billion by 1990–91. Wilson scheduled the change for January 1, 1986.

The plan brought a howl of protest from older people, interest groups, and politicians across the country. First, the change would cut the income of all older people, rich and poor. The poorest people, many of whom were living below the poverty line already, would fall deeper into poverty. Second, many older people had voted PC and expected the prime minister to honour his promise to leave the government pension program alone. This budget reversed his promise to treat universal programs as a "sacred trust," and many older people felt betrayed.

Seniors across the country joined together for the largest senior protest in Canadian history. They signed petitions, held news conferences, and sent letters to Parliament. Seniors also confronted politicians face to face. On June 18, 1985, seniors in Halifax confronted Finance Minister Wilson in a closed meeting and argued against de-indexation (*Globe and Mail* 1985). In the third week of June, seniors marched on Parliament Hill.

Other groups joined seniors in their protests. NDP and Liberal MPs attacked the government in Parliament daily, and some Tory MPs said that they, too, supported fully indexed pensions. The Council of Maritime Premiers united in opposition to de-indexing. Business groups and leaders also supported the seniors: The Canadian Chamber of Commerce, the Business Council on National Issues, and the Canadian Organization of Small Business stated that the government should fully protect old age pensions and find other ways to cut spending and reduce the deficit.

Interest groups like the Advisory Council on the Status of Women and the Canadian Council of

Social Development (CCSD) also protested the proposed budget changes. The CCSD predicted that the government's plan would force as many as 200 000 more older people into poverty by 1990 (Cernetig 1985).

The **de-indexation protest** made front-page news across the country. By mid-June, after reading a post-budget poll indicating a lack of confidence in the government, the prime minister promised to re-evaluate the de-indexation plan. On June 27, after five weeks of pressure, the government gave in and agreed to continue indexing pensions to the rate of inflation. Finance Minister Wilson said the government rescinded the plan because the government "recognized the anxieties of senior citizens" (Montgomery 1985).

This nation-wide protest teaches us some lessons about senior politics in Canada. First, seniors can act as a group to change federal policy, but only if they speak with a single voice. Second, seniors can use opinion polls, the media, and direct confrontation to pressure the government. Third, seniors need to ally themselves with other power blocs in society, such as political parties, and business and service groups.

Studies show that senior interest groups cannot succeed by themselves, because they lack sufficient power (Trela 1976). But they can make an issue visible and get other groups to support their cause (Neysmith 1987). Middle-aged people, for example, will often support health care and income policies for older people because middle-aged people are aware that they will be old someday themselves. Also, middle-aged children prefer to pay for services their elderly parents need through their taxes, rather than support their parents directly. Anti-poverty and women's groups will also support seniors' needs. If seniors can link their concerns with those of other groups, they will increase their political power. Gifford (1990) recommends an important future role for seniors in politics. He says that they can "set an example of global citizenship, for the survival of the planet" (Gifford 1990, 133).

GOVERNMENT AND AGING POLICY

Political participation and power both shape public policy. But political action takes place in a social and historical context. Myles (1984) says that gerontologists need to understand the history and structure of the welfare state to understand old age (see Exhibit 15.3). "This is simply because the contemporary welfare state in the capitalist democracies is largely a welfare state for the elderly" (1984, 2). Programs for older people now make up the biggest part of the welfare state's budget, and attempts to cut this share, like the move to de-index OAS payments, will meet with protests from all parts of society (Myles 1988). "The majority of the elderly," Myles says (1984, 6), "now depend on such benefits for most of their income. The widespread reaction against benefit cuts by both young and old reflected this fact."

Myles (1984) and others (Neugarten and Havighurst 1979) predict that the state will play an even more important role in older people's lives in the future mainly for three reasons. First, the state's budget will increase as the population ages. An aging population, for example, will require a redistribution of resources from younger to older people. The state will manage this transfer through taxation and government programs. The national health care system already does this, and so does the Old Age Security and Guaranteed Income Supplement program.

Second, the state has begun to redefine its role in providing income support to older people. Recent changes to Canada's pension policies, for example, point the way to a withdrawal of support for middle-income earners through government pension plans (the OAS/GIS/SPA). Instead, middle-class people have been encouraged to save for retirement by the raised limit on RRSP contributions and the concomitant increases in tax deductions. These policy changes leave income security programs to the poorest Canadians. At the same time they create a "new 'welfare state'" for middle-income seniors, who already have private pension plans (Myles 1988, 52).

Third, the redistribution of wealth from young people to older people, and from state support to private support for middle- and upper-class seniors will require more government planning. The government has already proposed a Seniors Benefit to replace the OAS and GIS. It also had to raise Canada Pension Plan payments to meet the needs of older people today. The government will have to plan for rate increases in the future to meet the needs of a growing older population.

Exhibit 15.3

Major Federal Social Security Legislation Related to Aging

All levels of government provide programs to help older people meet their basic needs. This table gives a summary of the major federal government social security legislation since 1918.

1918	Pension Act
1927	Old Age Pension Act
1944	National Housing Act
1948	National Health Grants Program
1951	Old Age Security Act (OAS)
1951	Old Age Assistance Act
1954	Federal Disabled Persons Act
1957	Hospital Insurance and Diagnostics Services Act
1966	Canada Pension Plan (CPP)
1966	Medical Care Act
1967	Guaranteed Income Supplement (GIS)
1968	Medical Care Act

1975	Spouse's Allowance Act (SPA)
1977	Federal Extended Health Care Services Program (Implemented in Federal-Provincial Fiscal Arrangements and Established Program Financing Act)
1979	Extended SPA
1984	Canada Health Act
1985	Pension Benefits Standards Act

In addition to these programs, each province offers programs that include support for housing, income supplement, and health care benefits (like pharmacare).

Source: Adapted from Statistics Canada, *Canada Year Book*, 1990a and 1993 (Ottawa: Minister of Supply and Services Canada and Minister of Industry, Science and Technology). Reproduced by authority of the Minister of Industry, 1996, Statistics Canada..

A number of government agencies have been set up to develop policies for the transfer of resources to older people. These include the ministries responsible for pensions, health, and housing. In addition, some agencies advise the government on policies and programs.

- The federal Office on Aging exists within the Department of Health and Welfare. It gathers facts and information about aging in Canada and advises the government on policy issues. The office also helped produce *The Fact Book on Aging in Canada* (Health and Welfare Canada 1983) and The Seniors Boom (Stone and Fletcher 1986)—two summaries of data on older people in Canada.
- The Minister of State for Seniors acts as spokesperson for seniors and represents their views in cabinet. The minister consults with seniors and groups throughout the country (Government of Canada 1988).
- Health Canada set up a Seniors Directorate on April 1, 1994. This organization brings together the Seniors Secretariat, the Seniors Community

Programs, the Seniors Independence Research Program, and the Secretariat to the National Advisory Council on Aging. The Directorate will provide support to the Minister of Health and the National Advisory Council on Aging. It advises government on strategies related to older people, consults with community groups, and coordinates and manages the federal seniors strategy.

- The National Advisory Council on Aging, which began its work on May 1, 1980, has eighteen members. It meets twice a year to counsel the Minister of Health and Welfare on issues related to seniors' quality of life. It also promotes a positive image of older people and encourages seniors to take political action. Members of the council include researchers, members of national and provincial organizations, medical experts, seniors, and the general public (National Advisory Council 1989a). The council publishes an annual report and makes recommendations to the Minister of National Health and Welfare. The council also publishes a quarterly newsletter called *Expression*. Each issue presents a readable review of the latest facts on aging, comments from seniors, and reports on research. It also publishes a series of scholarly reports titled "Writings in Gerontology" and a statistical bulletin called *Info-Age*.

- Provincial Advisory Councils present seniors' views to provincial governments. They also assess policies and work to coordinate provincial programs and services for seniors. Between 1970 and 1980 five provinces—Alberta, Saskatchewan, Manitoba, Ontario, and Nova Scotia—set up advisory councils. The councils write newsletters, and produce information packages and directories of services for seniors (Long and Shelton 1982). Provincial governments also learn about seniors' needs from departments set up to coordinate seniors' programs and from senior citizens' secretariats. These agencies sometimes act as advocates for seniors in their provinces.

THE ROLE OF GOVERNMENT IN IMPROVING LIFE FOR OLDER PEOPLE

A large government deficit and a slow economy will put limits on what older people can achieve through protest and pressure groups. A policy that cuts the federal deficit, for example, will probably also cut social support programs for seniors (Neysmith 1986).

What can seniors do to improve programs and services under these conditions? They can make some gains by lobbying for programs that meet their needs and save the government money. For example, seniors can support the coordination of government departments (Kernaghan 1982). They can also support housing programs that include recreation and health care services that work to keep older people out of institutions. Chappell and Penning (1979) say that programs like home care could save money and at the same time provide more humane treatment for older people. "The current trend [away from institutionalization]," they say, "seems to reflect one situation in which economic efficiency and humanism are not contradictory" (1979, 380). Seniors can look for and promote other programs and policies like health

promotion and education programs that will improve seniors' quality of life.

Seniors who take an active part in lobbying or who write briefs and letters to the government are also helping to create better policies for the future and getting the government used to consulting with seniors on seniors' issues. The trend today points to more senior activism in the future. Agencies within the government, like the National Advisory Council on Aging, support and promote this new activist stance. There are also trends in some countries toward proportional representation (a system that gives minority groups more influence in government). Gifford (1987) says that in four European countries pensioners sought to form political parties. Each of these countries had proportional representation systems. And referenda (votes on specific political issues) could also give more power to older people if this trend catches on in Canada.

Gifford (1987) reports on two other trends that may affect seniors politically in the future. First, seniors may set up their own sections within the national political parties (similar to youth sections that already exist). Seniors in the Nova Scotia New Democratic Party have already done this. Second, seniors may spend more time advocating social causes. Canadian seniors have already set up groups like Veterans Against Nuclear Arms and Pensions for Peace. They also work for groups like Amnesty International, Oxfam, and groups with environmental concerns. Curtis and Lambert (1976) say that higher levels of education, better health, the existence of organizations that support activism, more free time, and the larger number of older people in the future will all lead to more political activism by seniors.

The study of aging and politics in Canada has just begun, and, as Pratt (1979, 186) says, "there would appear to be challenge enough here for several scholars." Current trends toward senior activism, for example, raise new questions for political scientists and gerontologists. Will new generations of seniors show the same consistency in voting patterns as seniors in the past? Or will they shift their votes depending on the issues? Only longitudinal studies of voting can answer these questions (Braungart and Braungart 1986). Will seniors become more vocal, organized, and effective in their lobbying efforts? Will they form a social movement? To answer these questions gerontologists need to know more about the structure of and decision-making processes in seniors' political groups. Will more and more seniors turn their attention to larger social issues like environmental protection, peace, and anti-poverty campaigns? Before answering this, researchers will need to study the values and commitments of new generations of seniors.

The study of politics and aging in Canada has already moved beyond the study of voting patterns. In the future, political scientists will find many new questions to ask about the political behaviour of Canada's growing and changing senior population.

FUTURE TRENDS IN POLITICS

Jacobs (1990) says that discussions of politics and aging often come down to the issue of the fair distribution of resources to the older and younger generations. Rosenzweig (1991) dealt with this topic in an address given at the annual meeting of the Gerontological Society of America. He said that unless older people willingly give up some of their current benefits in a time of scarcity, they will create a "disastrous'" effect on society. "Of every nondefense, noninterest dollar in the federal budget [in the United States]," he said, "47 cents is spent on programs for people age 65 and over." He added that this "will grow to more than 50 cents by 1995 and 57 cents by 2000" (Rosenzweig 1991, 2). He projects that these costs will lead to a conflict between retirees and the rest of society, including future retirees. And he says that leaders of interest groups ought to help their members "shape a conception of their interests that fits their own immediate needs into the needs of the larger community on whose overall well-being their own ultimately depends" (Rosenzweig 1991, 2).

Rosenzweig spoke out of his experience in the United States. The issue of **generational equity** has sparked debate and controversy there. It has led to the creation of a group called **Americans for Generational Equity (AGE)** that promotes this idea. This group grew from fewer than 100 members in 1985 to over 1000 members in 1990 (Wisensale 1993). AGE believes that young and middle-aged people cannot pay the high costs for services to older and younger people. AGE

proposes cuts to programs for older people to free up money for the young. For example, it proposes to replace Social Security with a system of welfare for the poorest older people (Quadagno 1991).

One member of AGE proposed that health care providers should deny some treatments to older people (Binstock 1992). This group has now joined with the Association of Baby Boomers (ABB) to promote these views. Other U.S. groups like the **Concord Coalition** propose a means test for Social Security and Medicare. The Coalition says that only people who earn under $40 000 per year should get Social Security and Medicare. These groups gather support by pitting the interests of older people against those of the young. They argue that programs for older people take money from programs for poor children. Townson (1994, 14) says that in the United States the media have taken up the cause of "kids versus canes." The United States, Clark (1993) says, tends to target policies to meet specific age-based needs. For example, Medicare serves only older people. This approach to policy creates the context for a conflict between the old (who can get these services) and the young (who cannot).

Canadian policies tend to unify, rather than divide, the interests of the young and old. For example, Canada shows the same trend toward decreased poverty for older people and increased poverty for children (Ng 1992). But Canadians, unlike Americans, have not tried to blame older people for the increased poverty of the young. Myles and Teichroew (1991, 85) say that the generational equity controversy has "had little impact in Canada. The prospect of the fiscal burden expected as a result of a long-term process of population aging has been received with relative equanimity by public, corporate, and policy elites ... Nor has the debate over intergenerational equity ... had any success north of the U.S. border." Canadians have generally talked about "continued sharing and cooperation among generations" (Ng 1992, 15). Clark (1993) says that broader-based social programs create a sense of common interest. For example, Canada's national health care system serves people of all ages. For this reason it tends to unify national concerns around good health regardless of age. Clark (1993, 498) says that "what is interpreted in the U.S. as a crisis is simply seen in Canada as a challenge to good government."

Still, some rumblings in the Canadian press and some changes in public pension policies suggest this complacency may change (See Exhibit 15.4). Loveland (1994, A21), for example, in a submission to the House of Commons, says that "it is abundantly clear that this huge government debt 'belongs' to older Canadians, as opposed to younger Canadians." He goes on to ask for greater equity between young and old and for reduced benefits for older people.

Townson (1994), in a review of the intergenerational equity debate, asks, "Do we need to change the social contract with seniors?" She answers that this debate often exaggerates the cost of programs for older people and plays down the economy's ability to meet these costs. This view assumes that nothing will change either in the economy or in public policy in the future.

Northcott (1994) studied public perceptions of an economic crisis due to population aging in Canada. He found that people tend to see population aging as a problem with broad impact. He reports that this view could lead to undesirable public policies. Gee and McDaniel (1995) say that population aging "has become, in many ways, the paradigm by which social policy is driven. If welfare, health and/or public pensions costs are increasing, population aging is seen as the culprit." They go on to say that this creates the image of a society without the resources to help its older people. This paradigm views older people as a burden on young people who cannot afford the cost.

But this view supports **demographic determinism**—the idea that population dictates what government must do. But, how the public defines a policy plays a large role in what responses appear to make sense. For example, if the public sees population aging as an economic crisis it will accept cuts in social programs to avoid the crisis. On the other hand, the public could see population aging as the outcome of successful past social policies (Gee and McDaniel 1995). Then the public might give more support for existing social programs.

Also, demographic determinism sees society as doomed to face a crisis. This leads to proposed cuts in programs, rather than creative solutions to broad issues. For example, a stronger economy would make programs for older people more affordable. Even a 2 percent rise in economic growth would allow Canadian society to serve both young and old. Likewise, containment of health care costs (the cause of much of the rise in program costs for older people) would make programs for older people less expensive.

Marmor and his colleagues (1990) propose two responses to the challenge of a larger older population: first, sound management of economic policies to maintain growth, and second, "a willingness to adjust benefit levels, the retirement age, and fiscal policies" in response to economic conditions. Some of these changes have begun to take place as the federal government changes OAS and GIS policies, and as the government adjusts the rate of payments into the CPP. The intergenerational equity debate underscores the need for cooperation between the generations in politics.

Canadian society has not accepted the U.S. version of conflict between the young and the old. In part, Canadian social policies may account for this. Many policies, like the Canadian pension system, expect older people to fund much of their retirement with their own resources. Canadians, compared with Americans, for example, "rely more heavily on occupational pensions or private savings to maintain living standards in old age" (Townson 1994, 24). Public pensions have mostly supported the poor (through the Guaranteed Income Supplement). The middle class has had to rely on private pensions, savings, and CPP payments to maintain their living standard. This means that older Canadians, compared with Americans, make less demand on public funds (Myles and Teichroew 1991). Also, their retirement savings serve as capital for business and industry. These groups have little reason to attack this system. Myles and Teichroew (1991) say that this explains the lack of interest in intergenerational equity issues.

Still, older Canadians must keep in mind the needs of the young and middle-aged or they will lose support. And this support will make the difference between success and failure in seniors' political efforts. Bengtson (1991, 2) warns that "if inflation continues to rise, the elderly are more likely to be perceived as 'Greedy Geezers' in their mortgage-free houses." Senior groups need to show their concern for wider social and economic conditions and will have to balance their own needs with those of others and with those of future generations.

Exhibit 15.4

Pensions and Generational Equity

Canadians have not engaged in a formal debate over generational equity as in the United States. But the issue has emerged in the popular press in a number of articles. Reporter Peter Shawn Taylor looks at generational equity and the retirement income system.

While most Canadians worry about how to hold the retirement dream together, few consider whether it *should* be sustained. It shouldn't. ... It was never meant to be what it has become, and the sooner Canadians turn to the question of how best to end it, the better. Funding for leisure in later life must become a personal responsibility, not a social obligation. Retirees must stop insisting they have a right to siphon money from their kids to help make their golden years enjoyable. Government programmes must be directed only to those in dire need. The rest of us will have to accept that a long and relaxing retirement will be affordable only for the wealthy, and that, if we are physically able, we will have to work until we are at least seventy years old. Retirement was fun while it lasted, but it's over. ...

Consider the Canada Pension Plan. Unlike contributions to a conventional pension, your contributions do not go into your own account but fund the CPP payments of today's pensioners. When you retire, your CPP benefits will be paid by people working at that time—today's children. It's really an elaborate, government-sponsored pyramid scheme, as are the OAS and GIS. Which is why those vociferous seniors who storm Parliament Hill haven't earned their retirement. No-one ever earns the full cost of retirement benefits. Government programmes pay retirees as much as five dollars from the taxes of working Canadians for every dollar the retiree has contributed. Like all pyramid schemes, the CPP worked fine as long as the baby boom kept supplying more and more young workers to fund it. In its early years, there were six workers for every eligible recipient. But just as the programme was born, the baby boom ended. Between 1982 and 1992, the number of CPP recipients more than doubled, while the number of contributors increased by only eleven per cent. By 2031, when the boomers will be retired, there will be just 2.6 workers per recipient. ...

It's not that Canadians don't sense what is going on. In a Gallup poll commissioned last fall by four consulting firms fighting the possible taxation of RRSPs, almost seventy per cent of respondents aged thirty to forty-nine did not believe the government programmes would be able to support them when they retired. Sixty-one per cent of all respondents said they did not think they were saving enough for retirement. But still Canadians cling to their dreams of a long and prosperous retirement, and to their notions of retirement benefits as entitlements.

... at every suggestion of reductions in the retirement wage, the seniors militia inundates newspapers with letters to the editors defending their inviolable rights to their programmes and demanding that they be left alone. Working Canadians, they seem to think, owe them the massive taxes that will be needed to keep funding the retirement wage.

Taylor makes several telling points. First, the cost of public pensions will rise and may seem burdensome to younger people in the future. Second, current baby boomers have an interest in keeping these pensions in place for their own future well-being. Third, older people form a strong and vocal lobby group that will fight for current programs. This mix of interests may lead to intergenerational tensions in the future.

Do you think Canada will see conflict between the young and the old over pension costs?

Source: P.S. Taylor, "Grandma! Grandpa! Back to Work," *Saturday Night*, June 1995, 18+. Reprinted with permission.

CONCLUSION

Many Canadians already suspect that their retirement dream will remain unfulfilled. A 1994 Gallup poll found that 70 percent of people aged 30 to 49 did not believe that government programs would support them in old age. And 61 percent thought they did not save enough for retirement (cited in Taylor 1995). Current trends in public policy support these doubts. Townson (1994, 25) notes the loss of universal benefits "through income tests (of the age credit in the income tax) and claw-back (of OAS)." She also points to increased private arrangements for long-term care and more care expected from families, without an increase in community support. Townson (1994, 25) goes on to say that "seniors themselves are being asked to bear more of the cost of their care. And there is undoubtedly more to come." These changes show a trend away from support for all older people toward a focus of Canadian programs on the poor. These changes could erode widespread support for many of these programs. And this would change the long-term commitment Canadian society has made toward support of older people.

Current concern about the cost of programs for older people drive the interest in reform. But Townson (1994, 7–8) says that these changes "are political, not economic choices. They are questions of political priorities, not economic imperatives." The debate over these priorities will increase in the years ahead. The outcome for older people will depend on how well they make the case for their needs.

SUMMARY

1. Recent studies of political activity by seniors show that people stay politically active as long as they have good health and mobility.
2. The increase in the median age of voters will likely continue in the near future and may give older voters more political power.
3. Long-standing commitments to political parties, as well as regional, cultural, and social class differences, will keep seniors from forming a single voting bloc.
4. Advocacy or pressure groups can have a strong effect on government policy-making, and older people have begun to organize for action.
5. Seniors' clubs throughout the country are affiliated with provincial and national associations. These groups act as advocates for older people.
6. Because the provinces take most of the responsibility for housing, health, and social service policies, senior advocacy has a provincial focus. This partly explains why seniors in Canada have never formed a powerful national lobby and why they have directed their lobbying efforts at provincial governments.
7. Seniors have joined together to protest government policy at least three times in the recent past. The most recent protest led the federal government to reverse its decision to de-index pensions. A united front, media coverage, plus the support of other influential groups helped seniors confront the government and win.
8. Seniors can influence government policies through the offices of provincial gerontologists, seniors' councils, and the National Advisory Council on Aging. They can also advocate programs that both meet seniors' needs and save the government money.
9. The discussion of politics and aging often involves the issue of fair distribution of resources to the older and younger generations. Older Canadians must keep in mind the needs of young and middle-aged people or they will lose support. Senior groups will need to balance their own needs with the needs of others and those of future generations.
10. Seniors will probably stay politically active in the future. They will also work for social causes that help all age groups.

STUDY QUESTIONS

1. Define the term "political participation." In what ways do older people take part in politics?
2. Describe the voting behaviour of senior citizens. Why don't older people tend to vote as a bloc?
3. How can seniors take an active part in Canadian policy-making?
4. What are the two major senior advocacy groups in Canada? What types of issues do these groups address? Why do Canadian seniors groups lack the national impact of the U.S. advocacy groups?

5. When do senior groups usually form social movements? Describe the issue that led to the de-indexation protest.

6. What are the major government agencies that develop policies for the transfer of resources to older people? How do each of these agencies function?

7. What factors will enable older people to become more politically active in the future?

8. Explain the concept of demographic determinism. How can the government successfully respond to the challenge of an older population?

KEY TERMS

advocacy groups   groups that lobby the government for policy change.

Americans for Generational Equity (AGE) AGE believes that young and middle-aged people cannot pay the high costs for services to older and younger people. AGE proposes cuts to programs for older people to free up money for the young.

Canadian Association of Retired Persons (CARP)   a nonprofit organization that seeks to improve the quality of life for all Canadians 50 or over.

Concord Coalition   a U.S. group that proposes a means test for Social Security and Medicare.

de-indexation protest   a national protest by older people against the federal government's attempt to de-index Old Age Security payments.

demographic determinism   the idea that population structure and change dictate what the government must do.

generational equity   the call for a smaller proportion of public support for older people. Based on the belief that older people use a disproportionate share of public resources.

interest group   a group that seeks to influence political actors and political agendas.

One Voice—The Canadian Seniors Network a nonprofit organization that works on behalf of older people. One Voice began in 1987.

protest groups   some groups (like provincial senior societies) that criticize government policies.

voting bloc   a group that votes as a unit based on an issue about which group members feel strongly.

SELECTED READINGS

Myles, John. "Social Policy in Canada." In Eloise Rathbone-McEwan and Betty Havens, eds. *North American Elders: United States and Canadian Perspectives.* New York: Greenwood, 1988.

   A review of Canada's pension policy that focuses on the pension debates of the past twenty-five years. Myles shows how tensions between social classes and interest groups shape social policy.

Pratt, Henry J. *Gray Agendas: Interest Groups and Public Pensions in Canada, Britain, and the United States.* Ann Arbor: The University of Michigan Press, 1993.

   A comparison of the politics behind public pensions in these three countries. Pratt devotes a separate chapter to the development of pensions in Canada. He describes the role that senior groups have played in creating and maintaining Canada's public pension system. He also describes the wider political and economic forces that shaped programs like the the Canada Pension Plan.

Townson, M. *The Social Contract and Seniors: Preparing for the 21st Century.* Ottawa: National Advisory Council on Aging, 1994.

   The author addresses an issue that has shaped debate over aging policy in the United States: the cost of an aging society. This debate focuses on generational equity and asks what each generation owes the other. It proposes a conflict between the old and the young. Townson offers a number of responses to population aging in Canada that can avoid this conflict in the future.

The Future of Aging in Canada

INTRODUCTION

This book began by saying that gerontology has two goals: to learn about aging and to use that knowledge to improve life for older people. Students who have read this far already know a lot more about aging than they did when they began their study of gerontology. But they may want to know about future directions in education and practice. This chapter will look at (1) issues that will challenge an aging society, (2) gerontology education in Canada, and (3) careers in gerontology.

ISSUES THAT WILL CHALLENGE CANADIAN SOCIETY

What do all of the findings in this and the previous chapters have in common? What message can a person draw from this mass of research?

The research shows that individual and population aging will bring social change. It will even lead to changes in our concept of old age and changes in how individuals and society can respond to aging.

In 1989 the National Advisory Council on Aging published *1989 and Beyond: Challenges of an Aging Society*. This book (National Advisory Council 1989a, 3) lists "the kinds of issues that will become more important or that will emerge in the years ahead as a result of the aging of the population and the changing characteristics of older people." *1989 and Beyond* covers six themes: (1) health and social care, (2) income, (3) environment, (4) information and technology, (5) activities, and (6) ethnic and Native groups. Under each theme the council lists challenges that Canada will have to face in the years ahead. These include the reallocation of resources toward long-term health care, pay equity for women, the development of new ways to adapt housing, the reduction of illiteracy among seniors, an increased flexibility of timing for retirement, and greater participation by members of ethnic groups in planning services. These challenges and the other challenges outlined in the report, present a program for social reform and research in the years ahead. Social planners will need more knowledge about aging and older people to carry out these reforms.

GERONTOLOGICAL EDUCATION

Students take gerontology courses for many reasons. The Carnegie Foundation in the United States lists three educational philosophies that guide gerontology courses: scientific, professional, and liberal. The **scientific approach** focuses on research and data collection using the scientific method. The **professional approach** focuses on improving services to older people and solving social problems. The **liberal approach** focuses on teaching everyone about the process of aging and about normal human development. Courses often combine one or more of these approaches.

A gerontology course for nurses, for example, might teach students about human development and also involve them in a research project. A course for undergraduates might include a discussion of sociological methods and a study of normal aging. Peterson and his colleagues (1987) found that most gerontology programs include a course on social gerontology and the psychology of aging. A large proportion of programs require courses in the biology/physiology of aging and the sociology of aging. Canadians will need all three types of gerontology education in the years ahead.

Thornton (1992) reports that most universities have undergraduate courses in the psychology of aging, the sociology of aging, or human development. These courses cover factual and theoretical knowledge about aging and social issues. Most courses include a study of attitudes toward older people, retirement, family life, and demography. A study of nursing curricula (Earthy 1993) in Canada found that most schools taught about "the developmental tasks in later life, successful social and psychologic adaptation to aging, and normal physical changes." Earthy (1993) proposes more gerontology education for nurses in the classroom and in clinical settings.

But no program can train nursing (or other) professionals once and for all. Beckingham (1995) calls for continuing education throughout a nurse's career. She and her colleagues developed a "train the trainer" series for nurse educators. And they have developed outreach materials to teach how to assess the health needs of older clients.

McMaster University has the largest educational centre in Canada devoted to academic gerontology, the Educational Centre for Aging and Health (ECAH) (Thornton 1992). The ECAH offers faculty support and sponsors educational activities. The Ontario government funds this program. ECAH works with the five health science centres in Ontario to develop core curricula in aging (Macpherson and Blumberg 1992; Macpherson 1995; Puxty 1995). McMaster also offers a three-year bachelor's degree and a four-year honours bachelor's degree in "gerontology and another subject." The ECAH supports new curriculum development in gerontology. For example, the ECAH funded the development of new gerontology content for three existing social work programs (Watt and Meredith 1995).

The University of Manitoba offers an interdisciplinary "option in aging." This program enrols students from the faculties of Physical Education and Recreation Studies, Architecture, Arts, Nursing, Social Work, and Human Ecology. Students take eighteen hours of study in gerontology. All students in the option must take two interdisciplinary courses: Health and Physical Aspects of Aging and The Social Aspects of Aging. Students then take twelve hours of courses, at least three from their own discipline. Many other schools offer similar gerontology diplomas or specializations within degree programs.

Most gerontology instructors have degrees in established academic disciplines. Marcus (1980; 1978) asked thirty-seven gerontology teachers in Canada about the courses they teach. Twenty-two of her thirty respondents taught in departments of social work, psychology, or sociology. She says that this "is probably a correct indication of academic interest in gerontology. Only one instructor classified himself as a gerontologist" (1980, 8).

People who work in institutions need ongoing training. Many workers—registered nurses, licensed practical nurses, and nurse's aides—got little or no training in gerontology in the past. Other workers need to update their knowledge of older people. Universities and community colleges offer some of this training. Large institutions like hospitals offer practical training in aging; these programs range from lectures to in-service seminars to on-site training courses.

Alberta, for example, has created Long Term Care Inservice Resource Centres to help professionals keep up-to-date with knowledge about aging. The centres serve 91 nursing homes, 69 auxiliary hospitals, and 27 home care offices across the province. The centres provide materials for education and training to professionals at these

Exhibit 16.1

Educating the Next Generation about Older People

"Bridging the Generation Gap," a program for students at Elbow Valley Elementary School in Calgary, has created a new role for seniors in the schools. The program uses computers to link twenty-seven 8- and 9-year-old students with ten seniors in Calgary and seven in Santa Cruz, California. The seniors and the students correspond regularly on the SeniorNet computer network. Students get paired with a senior and use the bulletin board to share information and ideas.

Brant Parker, the teacher at Elbow Valley Elementary School in Calgary who organized this program, says that students usually ask about "the 'olden days,' accounts of [the senior's] childhood, significant events of the past, or thoughts on the present and future" (Parker 1991). Students also tell the seniors things about their background, experiences, and achievements.

Marsha Quarter, a Grade 3 student, says, "I really look forward to the letters." Grace James, one of the Calgary seniors, says that the program "widens your scope. [The students] ask the questions and sometimes you have to go and do some research at the library" (Ross 1990). Seniors can also use the SeniorNet network to correspond with seniors all over North America.

The students have held a tea for their computer pals each year during Senior Citizen Awareness Week. Parker (1991) says that students have gained a new awareness of how much seniors have to offer and now have greater respect for them.

sites. The centres work to improve care and raise staff morale. The centres loan books, audio-visual resources, and computer-aided instructional packages to workers. The centres also sponsor teleconference presentations and day-long seminars. People in the field make active use of the centre and in 1991 the Alberta Government approved the continuation of support for the program (Church 1991).

Skinkle and Grant (1988) report on the value of in-service training. They conducted a random sample study of eighty-six nursing home aides in Saskatchewan. The study compared aides who had taken an in-service training program and those who had not. Graduates of the program, compared with nongraduates, knew more about nursing skills, more about aging, and more about the philosophy of long-term care. They also felt, more than the nongraduates, that their health team functioned effectively. Both groups showed similar positive views of older people. "The results are sufficiently positive for us to recommend the further development and evaluation of such training programs across Canada" (Skinkle and Grant 1988, 56).

Certificate and diploma programs also exist in universities and community colleges to upgrade workers' knowledge. The Association for Gerontology in Higher Education (1990) compiled a list of the 195 certificate programs offered in North American universities and colleges in 1987. Universities offer these programs at the graduate and undergraduate levels. They generally include a series of courses as well as a practicum.

Some institutions offer continuing education certificates. These vary in both length and rigour. The University of Alberta Faculty of Extension, for example, offers a certificate program for professionals in the field of aging. The program requires that students have a university degree, a two-year diploma, or that they be RNs with field experience. The program includes 251 credit hours of courses. This includes two core courses (an introduction to gerontology and the psychology of aging) along with electives.

Some employers subsidize employees' tuition for certificate and diploma programs, while others offer pay raises to employees who complete certificate or diploma programs. The Department of Veterans Affairs, for example, asked its para-professional counselling staff if they wanted more training in gerontology. More than 89 percent of those who answered said they did, and the same portion wanted a diploma program. The department then arranged with institutions that offered certificate and diploma programs across the country to schedule their programs at times convenient to Veterans Affairs staff (Boyce and Morgan 1982). The department offered the program for three weeks in 1981–82, and more training programs for middle and senior management and health care workers were planned as a result.

Cohen (1990), Coordinator of the Gerontology Certificate Programme at Ryerson Polytechnic University in Toronto, notes the importance of training the next generation of gerontology workers. She says that students should come to view themselves as advocates and facilitators who can empower older men and women. Many women who take gerontology courses do so after serving as caregivers to older family members. A survey done at Ryerson in the fall of 1989 found that 87 percent of respondents were women whose average age was 43. New issues raised by these women show their orientation to the field. They emphasized their need to understand aging within a broader societal context. They wanted to know about economics, law, advocacy, ethnicity, health care, and the role of women. Cohen (1990) argues for a multidisciplinary approach that would include political science, economics, women's studies, and public administration.

Medical doctors also need more gerontology education (Canadian Medical Association 1987). Family doctors and internists see many older people now. The Canadian Medical Association (CMA) (citing Woods Gordon 1984) says that more than 20 percent of physician services go to people aged 65 and over. Robertson (1981) projects that in the future older people will make up more than half the patients that family doctors and internists see. But the Medical Council of Canada qualifying exams pay little attention to geriatric medicine. Less than 2 percent of the questions on the exam (between 1982 and 1987) dealt with geriatric medicine, while 20 percent of them dealt with pediatrics. A Canadian report done as long ago as 1977 suggested that medical training focus more on aging. It suggested that medical students study gerontology and geriatric medicine each year in school. The report suggested providing 100 hours of instruction over four years (Health and Welfare Canada 1977a). The CMA (1987) says that medical school students should spend some time working in parts of the community where older people live. Students should meet older patients in outpatient clinics, rehabilitation hospitals, and nursing homes.

The CMA also says that training in geriatrics has improved in the past few years. In 1987 fifteen of the sixteen medical schools had some geriatric medicine in their curricula. And most schools now offer students clinical rotations in geriatric medicine. Still, both Robertson (1981) and the CMA (1987) found that only one university required that medical students do clinical work in geriatric medicine in their third and fourth years. A survey of physicians who practise geriatric medicine (Skelton 1986) found that only 13 percent had had undergraduate training in geriatric medicine. Twenty percent of these physicians had only had lectures on the subject. Only 69 percent had formal postgraduate training in geriatric medicine. The CMA concludes that little postgraduate training exists for physicians outside specialist training programs. Where training does exist, it gives physicians a better understanding of older people (Herrmann, Shulman, and Silver 1992).

Canada needs to train more researchers, academics, and health care workers in gerontology (Blumberg and Macpherson 1993; Matthews and Stryckman 1988). Research (Hirst, Miller, and Wenger 1992) suggests that health care workers need a range of programs to choose from. Some people will choose a college program, others will want a university program. Still others may prefer in-service education. Right now, most gerontology education takes place on the job or in postgraduate certificate and diploma programs. Rarely does gerontology education lead to more pay or to a higher-status job. Most people take these programs out of personal interest and often at their own expense. People who work as nurse's aides, orderlies, and paid homemakers receive low salaries and have the least formal gerontological education. These workers need encouragement and in some cases financial support before they will attend gerontology programs. Employers and the government should support gerontology education so that workers in the field get the knowledge they need.

OCCUPATIONS AND CAREERS IN GERONTOLOGY

"Are you looking for a job in an area that is growing rapidly, that needs people with a broad range of skills, that will improve people's lives, and that will be exciting, challenging, and rewarding? Consider a career in the field of aging!" (Heinemann, Douglass, and Lobenstine 1995, 1). This invitation appears in a booklet titled *Careers in Aging*. The authors go on to promote gerontology as a field with many career options. These range from front-line work with older people to research and teaching.

Other sources also suggest the need for more direct service, administrative, and para-professional workers in the future. Health and Welfare Canada (1985) reports that the number of registered nurses and orderlies in Canada increased by 50 percent from 1974 to 1984; the number of occupational therapists and physiotherapists increased by over 70 percent; and the number of physicians increased by 33 percent in that same time. Not all of these health care professionals work only with older people, but many of them do. Peterson (1987), for example, estimates that nurses occupy three out of every five jobs in nursing homes. And more nurses will be needed to work with older people in the future. A U.S. study predicts that the number of nurses who work in nursing homes will increase by two and a half times between the mid-1980s and the year 2000; the number of physical therapists will triple; and the number of occupational therapists will increase by 900 percent (National Institute on Aging 1987). Canada will need to train more of these professionals as well as social workers, nurse's aides, physicians, and counsellors in the years ahead.

Students with a bachelor of arts degree and a course or two in aging will have a difficult time finding work in gerontology. However, those with graduate training in an established discipline like psychology, sociology, or social work will find more opportunities. Social work and the health care professions (nursing, physiotherapy) offer the easiest access to working with older people. A master's degree in social work or a bachelor's degree in nursing open many jobs (Peterson 1987). A graduate degree in public health or administrative studies can lead to government work designing or administering programs for older people. Graduates with entrepreneurial drive may start

Exhibit 16.2

What Kind of Work Can You Do in the Field of Aging?

Peterson, Douglass, and Lobenstine (1996, 6) define professionals who understand aging and work with older people as "gerontological specialists." These writers list seven roles that gerontological specialists can play:

1. **Direct Service Providers.** These people work with individual older people or small groups. They assess an older person's needs and help find or provide services to meet those needs. Counsellors, therapists, and nurses do this kind of work.

2. **Program Planners and Evaluators.** These people develop programs to meet older people's needs. They often look at the needs of an entire community or groups within the community. Social workers and community service agency workers do this kind of work.

3. **Managers and Administrators.** They oversee the organizations that serve older people. Hospital and nursing home administrators as well as government agency directors do this kind of work.

4. **Marketers and Product Developers.** Corporations or organizations hire these people to market new products and services for older people. They look for unfilled needs and let people know about new products.

Marketing and advertising specialists do this kind of work.

5. **Advocates.** These people encourage government and the private sector to serve older people. They often work for a nonprofit organization and support specific programs. Executive directors of groups like the Alzheimer's Society do this kind of work.

6. **Educators and Trainers.** These people run workshops and teach courses on aging. Programs range from in-service workshops to graduate courses in universities.

7. **Researchers.** These people design and conduct studies to answer theoretical and practical questions about aging. They publish reports in professional journals, present at conferences, and write books that describe their findings. Some researchers conduct program evaluations to help improve services to older people.

Peterson and his colleagues say that in most cases more education translates into a higher salary. Someone with a master's degree will most often earn more than someone with a bachelor's degree. In general, they say, gerontology specialists get about the same pay as other people in established fields.

Source: D.A. Peterson, E.B. Douglass, and J.C. Lobenstine, *Careers in Aging: Opportunities and Options* (Washington, D.C.: The Association for Gerontology in Higher Education, 1996). Reprinted with permission.

businesses that serve older people. A student with a graduate degree, for example, could consult with major corporations on retirement education or staff training.

The Standards Committee of the Association for Gerontology in Higher Education (Standards Committee 1990) recommends the expansion of courses and programs in gerontology to include more courses, minors, majors, and specializations in gerontology at the graduate and undergraduate level. New developments will also include specialized programs in long-term care administration,

public policy, and research. As education programs develop within professional faculties, these faculties will produce a statement of competencies for gerontology programs in their professions. All of these changes will improve the educational opportunities for students who want to work with the elderly.

CONCLUSION

Gerontologists in the future will learn more about aging, and their research will shape social policy.

Their research will also help with "the most difficult challenge of all: re-connecting with aging and re-inserting seniors in all dimensions of community life" (Bégin 1985, 196). Gerontology can change people's attitudes to aging and give people more knowledge about their families, their friends, and themselves.

An incident in my own life made this clear to me. After my father's funeral, my mother, my sister, my father's brothers, and I got into a rented limousine and drove to the cemetery. The funeral director stopped the cars in the funeral procession at the cemetery gate. We saw the hearse pull ahead and stop a hundred yards away. I turned around to talk to one of my uncles in our car. A few minutes later the director waved all the cars on. We stopped behind the hearse and got out. It was empty. The director led us to the graveside. We stood close to the grave, but we could not see the coffin or any earth. A blanket of fake grass covered the earth that had come from the grave. Another blanket covered the coffin. Relatives and friends gathered to the side and behind us. The director said some prayers and a few kind words. My mother, my sister, and I stood and stared at the fake grass. I think we were supposed to leave. But I motioned to the director to pull the grass back. He looked surprised. I told him to pull the grass back. He did. We saw the corner of the coffin and the corner of the grave, and we started to cry.

I tell this story because my knowledge of aging and death and dying gave me the confidence to act. I felt I should do something, and I knew what I had to do. I find that I use my knowledge of aging in dozens of ways each day. I use it to understand my family and friends better and to understand the kinds of changes we go through as we age. Knowledge about aging allows me to plan for my own future with less fear and denial. The study of aging can make old age a better time of life for each of us and for the people we love.

SUMMARY

1. The National Advisory Council on Aging lists a variety of themes that will challenge gerontology in the years ahead. These include health and social care, information and technology, and ethnic diversity.

2. Most universities in Canada offer one or more courses related to gerontology. Some schools offer postgraduate certificate or diploma programs. Professionals who work with older people also need ongoing training. Gerontology programs and training programs should give professionals a broad interdisciplinary view of later life.

3. Medical doctors and medical students need more knowledge of gerontology and geriatric medicine, because they will see more older patients in the coming years. Health care workers, like nurses and activity workers, also need more training because they have the most contact with older patients. They often have no incentive, other than personal interest, to get training in gerontology. Pay raises linked to continuing education and tuition support for continuing education programs would encourage professionals to learn more about aging.

4. In the future, Canada will need more personnel to work with older people. People in the health care and social service professions will have the best chance to work with seniors.

5. Knowledge of aging will help you, your friends, and your family to live a good old age.

STUDY QUESTIONS

1. What kinds of issues will emerge in the years ahead as a result of the aging of the population?
2. List and explain the three educational philosophies that shape the structure of gerontology courses.
3. Who needs ongoing training in gerontology? Why do people need continuing education in these fields? What types of gerontology programs should colleges and universities offer people who work in the health care professions?
4. Why will people who work in the medical profession need more gerontology education in the future?
5. What types of things can students do to improve their chances of finding jobs in the field of aging?

KEY TERMS

liberal approach   an approach to the study of aging that focuses on teaching everyone about the process of aging.

professional approach   an approach to the study of aging that focuses on improving services to older people and solving social problems.

scientific approach   an approach to the study of aging that focuses on research and data collection using the scientific method.

SELECTED READINGS

Baines, Carol, P. Evans, and Sheila Neysmith, eds. *Women's Caring. Feminist Perspectives on Welfare.* Toronto: McClelland and Stewart, 1991.

This book looks at caring from a feminist perspective. The authors look at the caring roles that women play and the economic consequences of these roles. The analysis shows that women shoulder the burden of family care for older people in Canada today. The authors call for more sharing of caregiving responsibilities. This book points to an important issue in a time when governments call for more community care. The shift to community or home care will place more burden on women in society. This book serves as a good source for judging the costs of this policy shift to women.

Peterson, David A. *Career Paths in the Field of Aging: Professional Gerontology.* Lexington, MA: Lexington Books, 1987.

A good overview of gerontology education and job opportunities in the field of aging. A heavy U.S. orientation, but information about degree programs and proposals for continuing professional education will be of interest to Canadian students.

References

1,10* Abercrombie, Nicholas, Stephen Hill, and Bryan S. Turner. 1984. *The Penguin Dictionary of Sociology*. Harmondsworth, England: Penguin.

7 Abrahams, R. 1972. "Mutual Help for the Widowed." *Social Work* 19:54–61.

11,13 Abu-Laban, Sharon McIrvin. 1978. "The Family Life of Older Canadians." *Canadian Home Economics Journal* 28:16–25.

13 Abu-Laban, Sharon McIrvin. 1980a. "The Family Life of Older Canadians." In Victor W. Marshall, ed. *Aging in Canada*. Toronto: Fitzhenry and Whiteside.

13 Abu-Laban, Sharon McIrvin. 1980b. "Social Supports in Older Age: The Need for New Research Directions." *Essence* 4:195–209.

2 Achenbaum, W.A. 1993. "One Way to Bridge the Two Cultures: Advancing Qualitative Gerontology through Professional Autobiographies." *Canadian Journal on Aging* 12(2): 143–56.

3 Achenbaum, A., and P.N. Stearns. 1978. "Old Age and Modernization." *The Gerontologist* 18: 307–12.

10 Adams, O.B., and D.L.A. Lefebvre. 1980. *Retirement and Mortality: An Examination of Mortality in a Group of Retired Canadians*. Cat. No. 83-521E. Ottawa: Minister of Supply and Services.

13 Adelman, M. 1987. *Long Time Passing: Lives of Older Lesbians*. Boston: Alyson.

8 Agbayewa, M.O. 1990. "A Psychiatric Clinic within a Geriatric Medical Day Hospital: Descriptive Study." *Canadian Journal on Aging* 9:5–12.

12 Age and Opportunity, Inc. 1983. *Working Arrangements between Staff and Senior Centre Membership Organizations*. Winnipeg: Age and Opportunity, Inc.

12 Age and Opportunity, Inc. 1990. *Working Arrangements between Staff and Senior Centre Membership Organizations*. Winnipeg: Age and Opportunity, Inc.

1 *Aging Today*. 1994. "Unreported Crime: The Secret Shame of the Very Old." *Aging Today* (July/August):4.

12 Aitkens, Andrew. 1990. "Literacy and Older Canadians: A New Imperative." Press release.

Ottawa: One Voice, the Canadian Seniors Network.

12 Aitkens, Andrew. 1991. *A National Literacy Strategy for Older Canadians*. Ottawa: One Voice, the Canadian Seniors Network.

14 Ajemian, Ina, and Balfour M. Mount, eds. 1981. *The R.V.H. Manual on Palliative/Hospice Care*. New York: Arno Press.

10 Akyeampong, E. 1987. "Older Workers in the Canadian Labour Market." *The Labour Force* 43:85–120.

11 Almey, M. 1995a. "Housing and Household Facilities." In Statistics Canada, *Women in Canada: A Statistical Report*, 3d ed., 28–31. Ottawa: Minister of Supply and Services Canada.

9 Almey, M. 1995b. "Labour Force Characteristics." In Statistics Canada, *Women In Canada: A Statistical Report*, 3d ed., 64–83. Cat. No. 89-503E. Ottawa: Minister of Supply and Services.

6 Alpaugh, Patricia K., and J.E. Birren. 1977. "Variables Affecting Creative Contributions across the Adult Life Span." *Human Development* 20:240–48.

8 American Association of Retired Persons. 1984. *Prescription Drugs: A Survey of Consumer Use, Attitudes and Behavior*. Washington, DC: American Association of Retired Persons.

6 American Psychiatric Association. 1980. *Diagnostic and Statistical Manual of Mental Disorders*. 3d ed. Washington, DC: American Psychiatric Association.

3 Amoss, P.T., and S. Harrell. 1981. "Introduction: An Anthropological Perspective on Aging." In P.T. Amoss and S. Harrell, eds. *Other Ways of Growing Old: Anthropological Perspectives*. Stanford, CA: Stanford University Press.

8 Anderson, G.M., K.J. Kerluke, I.R. Pulcins, C. Hertzman, and M.L. Barer. 1993. "Trends and Determinants of Prescription Drug Expenditures in the Elderly: Data from the British Columbia Pharmacare Program." *Inquiry Chicago* 30(2):199–207.

10 Anderson, Kathryn, Robert L. Clark, and Thomas Johnson. 1980. "Retirement in Dual-Career Families." In Robert L. Clark, ed.

* Numbers indicate the chapters in which the source is cited.

Retirement Policy in an Aging Society. Durham N.C.: Duke University Press.

6 Annon, T.A.K., and D.W. Lee. 1994. "Reading Speed and Prose Memory in Older and Younger Adults." *Psychology and Aging* 9(2):216–23.

13 Antonucci, Toni C. 1990. "Social Supports and Social Relationships." In Robert H. Binstock and Linda K. George, eds. *Handbook of Aging and the Social Sciences*. 3d ed. San Diego: Academic Press.

13 Antonucci, Toni C., and Hiroko Akiyama. 1987. "Social Networks in Adult Life and a Preliminary Examination of the Convoy Model." *Journal of Gerontology* 42:519–27.

3 Araba, Nana. 1988. "Social Change: Family Role and Responsibilities of the Elderly in Africa." In *Aging around the World: A Report on the President's Symposium, "Aging in Tomorrow's World: An International Perspective."* The Gerontological Society of America.

3 Arai, K. 1994. "Paving the Way for an Aged Society." *Pacific Friend* 22(2):5–8.

12 Arbuckle, T.Y., D.P. Gold, J.S. Chaikelson, and S. Lapidus. 1994. "Measurement of Activity in the Elderly: The Activities Checklist." *Canadian Journal on Aging* 13(4):550–65.

6 Arenberg, D. 1977. "Memory and Learning Do Decline Late in Life." Paper presented at a Conference on Aging and Social Policy. Vichy, France.

2 Ariès, Phillipe. 1962. *Centuries of Childhood: A Social History of Family Life*. Trans. Robert Baldick, New York: Alfred A. Knopf.

13 Arling, G., and W. McAuley. 1983. "The Feasibility of Public Payments for Family Caregivers." *The Gerontologist* 23:300–306.

13 Arluke, Arnold, Jack Levin, and John Suchwalko. 1984. "Sexuality and Romance in Advice Books for the Elderly." *The Gerontologist* 24:415–19.

9 Armstrong, Pat, and Hugh Armstrong. 1981. *Women and Jobs: The Canadian Case*. Ottawa: Canadian Centre for Policy Alternatives.

9 Armstrong, Pat, and Hugh Armstrong. 1984. *The Double Ghetto: Canadian Women and Their Segregated Work*. Rev. ed. Toronto: McClelland and Stewart.

7 Armstrong-Esther, C.A. 1994. "Health and Social Needs of Native Seniors." In National Advisory Council on Aging, *Aboriginal Seniors' Issues*, 39–48. Cat. No. H71-2/1-15-1994E. Ottawa: Minister of Supply and Services Canada.

13 Aronson, J. 1990b. "Women's Perspectives on Informal Care of the Elderly: Public Ideology and Personal Experience of Giving and Receiving Care." *Aging and Society* 10, 61–84.

13 Aronson, J. 1992. "Women's Sense of Responsibility for the Care of Old People: 'But Who Else Is Going to Do It?'" *Gender and Society* 6(1):8–29.

8 Aronson, Jane, Victor W. Marshall, and Joanne Sulman. 1987. "Patients Awaiting Discharge from Hospital." In Victor W. Marshall, ed. *Aging in Canada: Social Perspectives*. Toronto: Fitzhenry and Whiteside.

13 Aronson, J., C. Thornewell, and K. Williams. 1995. "Wife Assault in Old Age: Coming Out of Obscurity." *Canadian Journal on Aging* 14(Supp. 2):72–88.

13 Aronson, Jane. 1985. "Family Care of the Elderly: Underlying Assumptions and Their Consequences." *Canadian Journal on Aging* 4:115–25.

13 Aronson, Jane. 1990a. "Older Women's Experiences of Needing Care: Choice or Compulsion." *Canadian Journal on Aging* 9:234–47.

4 Artibise, A. 1977. *Winnipeg: An Illustrated History*. Toronto: Lorimer.

16 Association for Gerontology in Higher Education Standards Committee. 1990. In T.A. Rich, J.R. Connelly, and E.B. Douglas, eds., *Standards and Guidelines for Gerontology Programs*. 2d ed. Washington, DC: AGHE.

7 Atchley, Robert C. 1971. "Disengagement among Professors." *Journal of Gerontology* 26:476–80.

10 Atchley, Robert C. 1976. *The Sociology of Retirement*. Cambridge, MA: Schenkman.

3 Atchley, Robert C. 1980. *The Social Forces in Later Life*. 3d ed. Belmont, CA: Wadsworth.

7,10 Atchley, Robert C. 1982. "The Process of Retirement: Comparing Women and Men." In Maximiliane Szinovacz, ed. *Women's Retirement*. Beverly Hills, CA: Sage.

1,10,15 Atchley, Robert C. 1985. *Social Forces and Aging*. 4th ed. Belmont, CA: Wadsworth.

10 Atchley, Robert C., Suzanne R. Kunkell, and Carl Adlon. 1978. *An Evaluation of Preretirement Programs: Results from an Experimental Study*. Oxford, OH: Scripps Foundation Gerontology Center, Miami University.

1,11 Atkinson, Wally. 1991. "Improving Transportation Systems for Seniors Benefits All." Paper presented at the FCM National Forum on Seniors Transportation, titled Freedom to Move Is Life Itself, Winnipeg.

8 Auer, Ludwig. 1987. *Canadian Hospital Costs and Productivity: A Study Prepared for the Economic*

Council of Canada. Ottawa: Minister of Supply and Services.

4 Auerbach, Lewis, and A. Gerber. 1976. *Perceptions 2: Implications of the Changing Age Structure of the Canadian Population*. Ottawa: Supply and Services Canada for the Science Council of Canada.

5 Aussman, L.M, and R.M. Russell. 1990. "Nutrition and Aging." In E.L. Schneider and J.W. Rowe, eds., *Handbook of the Biology of Aging*. 3d ed. San Diego: Academic Press.

6 Backman, L. 1985. "Further Evidence for the Lack of Adult Age Differences on Free Recall of Subject-Performed Tasks: The Importance of Motor Action." *Human Learning* 4:79–87.

7 Bagley, C.R. 1993. "Mental Health and Social Adjustment of Elderly Chinese Immigrants in Canada." *Canada's Mental Health* 41(3):6–10.

10 Baillargeon, Richard. 1982. "Determinants of Early Retirement." *Canada's Mental Health* 30:20–22.

11 Baker, J.G. 1994. "Supportive Housing for Elderly Persons in Ontario." In G. Gutman and A.V. Wister, eds. *Progressive Accommodation for Seniors: Interfacing Shelter and Services*, 85–99. Vancouver, BC: Gerontology Research Centre.

3 Baker, Paul M. 1983a. "Ageism, Sex, and Age: A Factorial Survey Approach." *Canadian Journal on Aging* 2:177–84.

1 Baker, Paul M. 1983b. "Old before My Time." Videotape. Victoria, BC: Centre on Aging, University of Victoria.

3 Baker, Paul M. 1987. "The Dega and the Nacirema." In B. Hess and E. Markson, eds. *Growing Old in America*. 3d ed. New Brunswick, NJ: Transaction Books.

14 Baker, Paul M. 1991. "Socialization after Death: The Might of the Living Dead." In B. Hess and E. Markson, eds. *Growing Old in America*. 4th ed. New York: Transaction Books.

11 Baker, P.M., and M. Prince. 1990. "Supportive Housing Preferences among the Elderly." *Journal of Housing for the Elderly* 7:5–24.

11 Baker, P.M., and Victor Thompson. 1985. "Victoria Seniors Survey 1: Needs and Utilization of Services." Paper presented at the 14th Annual Scientific and Educational Meeting of the Canadian Association on Gerontology.

14 Baltes, M.M. 1977–78. "On the Relationship of Significant Yearly Events and Time of Death: Random or Systematic Distribution?" *Omega* 8:165–72.

6 Baltes, P.B. 1987. "Developmental Psychology." In G.L. Maddox, ed. The *Encyclopedia of Aging*. New York: Springer.

6 Baltes, P.B. 1992. "Wise, and Otherwise." *Natural History* (February):50–51.

6 Baltes, P.B. 1993. "Aging Mind: Potential and Limits." *The Gerontologist* 33(5):580–94.

6 Baltes, P.B., and M.M. Baltes. 1990. "Psychological Perspectives on Successful Aging: The Model of Selective Optimization with Compensation." In P.B. Baltes and M.M. Baltes, eds. *Successful Aging: Perspectives from the Behavioral Sciences*, 1–34. Cambridge: Cambridge University Press.

7 Baltes, Paul B., Steven W. Cornelius, and John R. Nesselroade. 1979. "Cohort Effects in *Developmental Psychology*." In John R. Nesselroade and Paul B. Baltes, eds. *Longitudinal Research in the Study of Behavior and Development*. New York: Academic Press.

7 Baltes, P.B., and L.R. Goulet. 1970. "Status and Issues of a Life-Span *Developmental Psychology*." In L.R. Goulet and Paul B. Baltes, eds. *Life-Span Developmental Psychology: Research and Theory*. New York: Academic Press.

2 Baltes, P.B., H.W. Reese, and J.R. Nesselroade. 1977. *Life-Span Developmental Psychology: Introduction to Research Methods*. Monterey, CA: Brooks/Cole.

2 Baltes, P. B., and K.W. Schaie. 1982. "The Myth of the Twilight Years." In Steven H. Zarit, ed. *Readings in Aging and Death: Contemporary Perspectives*. 2d ed. New York: Harper and Row.

6 Baltes, P.B., J. Smith, U.M. Staudinger, and D. Sowarka. 1990. "Wisdom: One Facet of Successful Aging?" In M. Perlmutter, ed. *Late Life Potential*. Washington, DC: The Gerontological Society of America.

6 Baltes, P.B., and S.L. Willis. 1981. "Enhancement (Plasticity) of Intellectual Functioning: Penn State's Adult Development and Enrichment Project (ADEPT)." In F.I.M. Craik and S.E. Trehub, eds. *Aging and Cognitive Processes*. New York: Plenum.

6 Baltes, P.B., and S.L. Willis. 1982. "Toward Psychological Theories of Aging and Development." In J.E. Birren and K.W. Schaie, eds. *Handbook of the Psychology of Aging*. New York: Van Nostrand Reinhold.

13 Bankoff, Elizabeth A. 1983. "Aged Parents and Their Widowed Daughters: A Support Relationship." *Journal of Gerontology* 38:226–30.

8 Barer, Morris L., and Robert G. Evans. 1989. "Riding North on a South-Bound Horse? Expenditures, Prices, Utilization and Incomes in the Canadian Health Care System." In Robert G. Evans and Greg L. Stoddart, eds. *Medicare at*

Maturity: Achievements, Lessons and Challenges. Calgary: University of Calgary Press.

5,8   Barer, M.L., R.G. Evans, and C. Hertzman. 1995. "Avalanche or Glacier?: Health Care and the Demographic Rhetoric." *Canadian Journal on Aging* 14(2):193–224.

8   Barer, Morris L., Robert B. Evans, Clyde Hertzman, and Jonathan Lomas. 1986. "Toward Efficient Aging: Rhetoric and Evidence." Paper prepared for presentation at Third Canadian Conference on Health Economics, Winnipeg.

8   Barer, M.L., C. Hertzman, R. Miller, and M.V. Pascali. 1992. "On Being Old and Sick: The Burden of Health Care for the Elderly in Canada and the United States." *Journal of Health Politics, Policy and Law* 17(4):763–82.

7   Baril, G., and G. Mori. 1991. "Leaving the Fold: Declining Church Attendance." *Canadian Social Trends* (Autumn):21–24.

13   Barling, J., MacEwen, K.E., and Kelloway, E.K. 1994. "Predictors and Outcomes of Elder-Care-Based Interrole Conflict." *Psychology and Aging* 9(3):391–97.

12,14   Barrett, Carol J., and Karen M. Schneweis. 1980–81. "An Empirical Search for Stages of Widowhood." *Omega* 11:97–104.

6   Barrett, J.R., and M. Wright. 1981. "Age-Related Facilitation in Recall Following Semantic Processing." *Journal of Gerontology* 2:194–99.

11   Bartel, Henry, and Michael J. Daly. 1981. *Reverse Mortgages: A New Class of Financial Instruments for the Elderly.* Discussion Paper No. 188. Ottawa: Economic Council of Canada.

5   Bartoshuk, Linda M., and James M. Weiffenbach. 1990. "Chemical Senses and Aging." In Edward L. Schneider and John W. Rowe, eds. *Handbook of the Biology of Aging.* 3d ed. San Diego: Academic Press.

13   Baruch, G., and R.C. Barnet. 1983. "Adult Daughters' Relationships with Their Mothers." *Journal of Marriage and the Family* 45:601–6.

8   Battista, Renaldo N., Robert A. Spasoff, and Walter O. Spitzer. 1989. "Choice of Technique: Patterns of Medical Practices." In Robert G. Evans and Greg L. Stoddart, eds. *Medicare at Maturity: Achievements, Lessons and Challenges.* Calgary: University of Calgary Press.

2   Baum, Martha, and Rainer C. Baum. 1980. *Growing Old: A Societal Perspective.* Englewood Cliffs, NJ: Prentice-Hall.

11   Baumgarten, Mona, Daniel Thomas, Louise Poulin de Courval, and Claire Infante-Rivard. 1988. "Evaluation of a Mutual Help Network for the Elderly Residents of Planned Housing." *Psychology and Aging* 3:393–98.

4   Beaujot, R., and K. McQuillan. 1982. *Growth and Dualism: The Demographic Development of Canadian Society.* Toronto: Gage.

12   Beck, M., D. Glick, J. Gordon, and L. Picker. 1991. *Newsweek*, November 11, 60–63.

16   Beckingham, A.C. 1995. "Models for Continuing Nursing Education in Gerontology." *Educational Gerontology* 21:35–53.

10   Beeson, D. 1975. "Women in Studies of Aging: A Critique and Suggestion." *Social Problems* 23:52–59.

16   Bégin, Monique. 1985. "The New Society: On Aging and Seniors as an Enrichment to Civilization." In Ellen M. Gee and Gloria M. Gutman, eds. *Canadian Gerontological Collection V.* Winnipeg: Canadian Association on Gerontology.

11   Béland, François. 1984a. "The Decision of Elderly Persons to Leave Their Homes." *The Gerontologist* 24:179–85.

11   Béland, François. 1984b. "The Family and Adults 65 Years and Over: Co-Residency and Availability of Help." *Canadian Review of Sociology and Anthropology* 21:302–17.

11   Béland, François. 1987. "Living Arrangement Preferences among Elderly People." *The Gerontologist* 27:797–803.

1,11   Béland, François. 1988. "Research in Social Gerontology in Québec: An Obscure Originality or a Deserved Obscurity?" *Canadian Journal on Aging* 7:293–310.

13   Béland, François. 1989. "Patterns of Health and Social Services Utilization." *Canadian Journal on Aging* 8:19–33.

8   Béland, F. 1995. "Costs of Ambulatory Medical Care over the Long Term in the Quebec Medicare System." *Canadian Journal on Aging* 14(2):391–413.

8   Béland, F., and E. Shapiro. 1994. "Ten Provinces in Search of a Long Term Care Policy." In V. Marshall and B. McPherson, eds. *Aging: Canadian Perspectives*, 245–67. Peterborough, ON: Broadview Press/*Journal of Canadian Studies.*

13   Belanger, L. 1981. "The Types of Violence the Elderly Are Victims Of: Results of a Survey Done with Personnel Working with the Elderly." Paper presented to the Gerontological Society of America 34th Annual Scientific Meeting.

1   Bell, J. 1992. "In Search of a Discourse on Aging: The Elderly on Television." *The Gerontologist* 32:305–11.

5   Benet, S. 1976. *How to Live to Be 100*. New York: Dial.

7   Beneteau, R. 1988. "Trends in Suicide." *Canadian Social Trends* (Winter): 22–24.

13   Bengtson, Vern L. 1985. "Diversity and Symbolism in Grandparental Roles." In Vern L. Bengtson and Joan F. Robertson, eds. *Grandparenthood*. Beverly Hills, CA: Sage.

15   Bengtson, V.L. 1991. "Age-Group Relations May Worsen, Says GSA President." *Gerontology News* (January):2.

3   Bengtson, V. L., J.J. Dowd, D.H. Smith, and A. Inkeles. 1975. "Modernization, Modernity and Perceptions of Aging: A Cross-Cultural Study." *Journal of Gerontology* 30:688–95.

13   Bengtson, Vern L., and Joseph A. Kuypers. 1971. "Generational Differences and the Developmental Stake." *International Journal of Aging and Human Development* 2:249–60.

13   Bengtson, Vern, Carolyn Rosenthal, and Linda Burton. 1990. "Families and Aging: Diversity and Heterogeneity." In Robert H. Binstock and Linda K. George, eds. *Handbook of Aging and the Social Sciences*. San Diego: Academic Press.

5   Bennett, Neil G., and Lea Keil Garson. 1986. "Extraordinary Longevity in the Soviet Union: Fact or Artifact?" *The Gerontologist* 26:358–61.

11   Berger, Earl, Richard Godin, and Alan C. Harvey. 1986. "Older Canadians: Housing Market Characteristics and Demand." In Gloria Gutman and Norman Blackie, eds. *Aging in Place: Housing Adaptations and Options for Remaining in the Community*. Burnaby, BC: The Gerontology Research Centre, Simon Fraser University.

2   Berger, P.L., and T. Luckman. 1967. *The Social Construction of Reality*. Garden City, NY: Doubleday.

3   Berkner, Lutz. 1972. "The Stem Family and the Development Cycle of the Peasant Household: An Eighteenth-Century Austrian Example." *American Historical Review* 77:398–418.

2   Berman, L., and I. Sobkowska-Ashcroft. 1985. "Views of Sex in Old Age in the Great Literature of the Western World." Paper presented at the Canadian Association of Gerontology 14th Annual Scientific and Educational Meeting, Hamilton.

1,2   Berman, L., and I. Sobkowska-Ashcroft. 1986. "The Old in Language and Literature." *Language and Communication* 6:139–45.

1,2   Berman, Lorna, and Irina Sobkowska-Ashcroft. 1987. *Images and Impressions of Old Age in the Great Works of Western Literature (700 B.C.– 1900 A.D.)*. Lewiston, NY: The Edwin Mellen Press.

11   Bernardin-Haldemann, Verena. 1982. "Housing Satisfaction—Life Satisfaction." Paper presented at the Annual Scientific and Educational Meeting of the Canadian Association on Gerontology. Winnipeg.

1   Bernardin-Haldemann, Verena. 1988. "Research in Social Gerontology: Observe, Understand or Explain?" *Canadian Journal on Aging* 7:327–32.

9   Best, P. 1995. "Women, Men and Work." *Canadian Social Trends* (Spring):30–33.

7   Bienvenue, R., and B. Havens. 1986. "Structural Inequalities, Informal Networks: A Comparison of Native and Non-Native Elderly." *Canadian Journal on Aging* 5:241–48.

3   Biesele, M., and N. Howell. 1981. "'The Old Give You Life': Aging Among Kung Hunter-Gatherers." In P.T. Amoss and S. Harrell, eds. *Other Ways of Growing Old: Anthropological Perspectives*. Stanford, CA: Stanford University Press.

3   Biggs, B., and R. Bollman. 1991. "Urbanization in Canada." *Canadian Social Trends* (Summer): 22–27.

15   Binstock, Robert H. 1972. "Interest-Group Liberalism and the Politics of Aging." *The Gerontologist* 12:265–80.

13   Binstock, R.H. 1983. "The Aged as Scapegoats." *The Gerontologist* 23:136–43.

15   Binstock, Robert H. 1986. "Public Policy and the Elderly." *Journal of Geriatric Psychiatry* 19:115–43.

15   Binstock, R.H. 1992. "The Oldest Old and 'Intergenerational Equity.'" In R.M. Suzman, D.P. Willis, and K.G. Manton, eds. *The Oldest Old*, 394–417. New York: Oxford University Press.

8   Binstock, R.H. 1993. "Healthcare Costs around the World: Is Aging a Fiscal 'Black Hole'?" *Generations* (Winter):37–42.

2   Binstock, R.H., and L.K. George, eds. 1990. *Handbook of Aging and the Social Sciences*, 3d ed. San Diego: Academic Press.

14   Binstock, Robert H., and Jeff Kahana. 1988. "An Essay on Setting Limits: Medical Goals in an Aging Society." *The Gerontologist* 28:424–26.

2   Birren, James E. 1968. "Principles of Research on Aging." In Bernice L. Neugarten, ed. *Middle Age and Aging*. Chicago: University of Chicago Press.

2   Birren, James E., and V.L. Bengtson, eds. 1988. *Emergent Theories in Aging*. New York: Springer.

1   Birren, J.E., and V. Clayton. 1975. "History of Gerontology." In D.S. Woodruff and J.E.

Birren, eds. *Aging: Scientific Perspectives and Social Issues*. New York: D. Van Nostrand.

6   Birren, J.E., and J.F. Schroots. 1996. "History, Concepts, and Theory in the Psychology of Aging." In J.E. Birren and K.W. Schaie, eds. *Handbook of the Psychology of Aging*, 4th ed., 3–23. San Diego: Academic Press.

2   Black, C. 1995. "Using Existing Data Sets to Study Aging and the Elderly: An Introduction." *Canadian Journal on Aging* 14(supp. 1.):135–50.

5,8 Black, C., N.P. Roos, B. Havens, and L. MacWilliam. 1995. "Rising Use of Physician Services by the Elderly: The Contribution of Morbidity." *Canadian Journal on Aging* 14(2): 225–44.

13   Black, M. 1985. "Health and Social Support of Older Adults in the Community." *Canadian Journal on Aging* 4:213–26.

11   Blackie, Norman. 1985. "Shared Housing: Principles and Practices." In Gloria Gutman and Norman Blackie, eds. *Innovations in Housing and Living Arrangements for Seniors*. Burnaby, BC: The Gerontology Research Centre, Simon Fraser University.

11   Blackie, Norman K. 1986. "The Option of 'Staying Put.'" In Gloria Gutman and Norman Blackie, eds. *Aging in Place: Housing Adaptations and Options for Remaining in the Community*. Burnaby, BC: The Gerontology Research Centre, Simon Fraser University.

12   Blair, S.N., H.W. Kohl, and R.S. Paffenbarger. 1989. "Physical Fitness and All-Cause Mortality." *The Journal of the American Medical Association* 262:2395–2401.

11   Blakeney, M. 1992. "Canadians in Subsidized Housing." *Canadian Social Trends* (Winter): 20–24.

7   Blandford, Audrey A., and Neena L. Chappell. 1990. "Subjective Well-Being among Native and Non-Native Elderly Persons: Do Differences Exist?" *Canadian Journal on Aging* 9:386–99.

11   Blandford, Audrey A., Neena L. Chappell, and Susan Marshall. 1989. "Tenant Resource Coordinators: An Experiment in Supportive Housing." *The Gerontologist* 29:826–29.

7,13 Blau, Zena Smith. 1973. *Old Age in a Changing Society*. New York: New Viewpoints.

8   Blendon, R.J., and Taylor, H. 1989. "Views on Health Care: Public Opinion in Three Nations." *Health Affairs* 8(2):149–57.

8   Blomqvist, A. 1994. "Introduction: Economic Issues in Canadian Health Care." In A. Blomqvist and D.M. Brown, eds. *Limits to Care: Reforming Canada's Health System in an Age of Restraint*, 3–50. Ottawa: C.D. Howe Institute.

16   Blumberg, P., and Macpherson, A.S. 1993. "Increasing Geriatrics in a Family Medicine Residency Program. *Gerontology and Geriatrics Education* 14(1):57–69.

12   Bocksnick, J.G., and Hall, B.L. 1994. "Recreation Activity Programming for the Institutionalized Older Adult." *Activities, Adaptation and Aging* 19(1):1–25.

10   Bolger, Joe. 1980. "Bill C-12 and the Debate over Public Service Pension Indexing." Unpublished master's essay. Ottawa: Carleton University.

12,13 Bond, J.B., Jr. 1982. "Volunteerism and Life Satisfaction among Older Adults." *Canadian Counsellor* 16:168–72.

13   Bond, J.B., Jr., M.R. Baril, S. Axelrod, and L. Crawford. 1990. "Support to Older Parents by Middle Aged Children." *Canadian Journal of Community Mental Health* 9:163–78.

12,13 Bond, J.B., Jr., and C.D.H. Harvey. 1991. "Ethnicity and Intergenerational Perceptions of Family Solidarity." *International Journal of Aging and Human Development* 33:33–34.

12,13 Bond, J.B., Jr., C.D.H. Harvey, and E.A. Hildebrand. 1987. "Familial Support of the Elderly in a Rural Mennonite Community." *Canadian Journal on Aging* 6:7–17.

13   Bond, J.B., Jr., R.L. Penner, and P. Yellen. 1992. *The Effectiveness of Legislation Concerning Abuse of the Elderly: A Survey of Canada and the United States. Final Report*. Winnipeg: University of Manitoba.

13   Bond, J.B., Jr., R.L. Penner, and P. Yellen. 1995. "Perceived Effectiveness of Legislation Concerning Abuse of the Elderly: A Survey of Professionals in Canada and the United States." *Canadian Journal on Aging* 14(Supp. 2):118–35.

11   Borden, L., and J. McGregor. 1994. "Current Realities and Challenges in Providing Services to Seniors: The Home Care Perspective." In G. Gutman and A.V. Wister, eds. *Progressive Accommodation for Seniors: Interfacing Shelter and Services*, 47–56. Vancouver, BC: Gerontology Research Centre.

5,6 Bosman, E. 1993. "Age-Related Differences in the Motoric Aspects of Transcription Typing Skill." *Psychology and Aging* 8(1):87–102.

2,5,6 Botwinick, J. 1984. *Aging and Behavior*. 3d ed. New York: Springer.

5   Botwinick, J., J.F. Brinley, and J.S. Robbin. 1958. "The Interaction Effects of Perceptual Difficulty and Stimulus Exposure Time on Age Differences in Speed and Accuracy of Response." *Gerontologia* 2:1–10.

5   Botwinick, J., J.R. Brinley, and J.S. Robbin. 1959. "Maintaining Set in Relation to Motivation and Age." *American Journal of Psychology* 72:585–88.

6   Botwinick, J., and I.C. Siegler. 1980. "Intellectual Ability among the Elderly: Simultaneous Cross-Sectional and Longitudinal Comparisons." *Developmental Psychology* 16:49–53.

5   Botwinick, J., and L.W. Thompson. 1968. "A Research Note on Individual Differences in Reaction Time in Relation to Age." *Journal of Genetic Psychology* 112:73-75.

12   Bourdeau, Christiane. 1991. Personal correspondence.

6   Bowles, N.L., and L.W. Poon. 1982. "An Analysis of the Effect of Aging on Memory." *Journal of Gerontology* 37:212–19.

16   Boyce, M., and D. Morgan. 1982. "Educating a Government Bureaucracy in Gerontology: The Department of Veterans Affairs Experience." Paper presented at the 11th Annual Scientific and Educational Meetings of the Canadian Association on Gerontology, Winnipeg.

7   Boyd, R., and R.N. Koskela. 1970. "A Test of Erikson's Theory of Ego-Stage Development by Means of a Self-Report Instrument." *Journal of Experimental Education* 38:1–14.

3   Bradbury, Bettina. 1983. "The Family Economy and Work in an Industrializing City: Montreal in the 1970's." In W.P. Ward, comp. *The Social Development of Canada: Readings*. Richmond, BC: Open Learning Institute.

5   Branch, L.G., and A.M. Jette. 1981. "Elders' Use of Informal Long-Term Care Assistance." Paper presented at the Annual Meeting of the Gerontological Society of America, Toronto.

3   Braudel, Fernand. 1981. *The Structure of Everyday Life: Civilization and Capitalism 15th–18th Century. Vol. 1*. Trans. Sian Reynolds. New York: Harper and Row.

7   Braun, Peter, and Robert Sweet. 1983–84. "Passages: Fact or Fiction?" *International Journal of Aging and Human Development* 18:161–76.

15   Braungart, Richard G., and Margaret M. Braungart. 1986. "Life-Course and Generational Politics." *Annual Review of Sociology* 12:205–31.

7   Breytspraak, L.M. 1995. "The Development of Self in Later Life." In M. Novak, ed. *Aging and Society: A Canadian Reader*, 92–103. Toronto: Nelson Canada.

1   Brillon, Yves. 1986. "Les personnes âgées face au crime." Rapport de Recherche. Centre International de Criminologie Comparée. Montréal: Université de Montréal.

1   Brillon, Yves. 1987. *Victimization and Fear of Crime among the Elderly*. Trans. D.R. Crelinsten. Toronto: Butterworths.

8   Brillon, Y. 1992. "Editorial: The 'Right' to Age in an Institution." *Canadian Journal on Aging* 12(1):7–11.

11   Brink, S. 1994. "Social Policy Models for Shelter and Services: An International Perspective." In G. Gutman and A.V. Wister, eds. *Progressive Accommodation for Seniors: Interfacing Shelter and Services*, 101–18. Vancouver: Gerontology Research Centre.

13   Brody, Elaine M. 1981. "'Women in the Middle' and Family Help to Older People." *The Gerontologist* 18:471–80.

13   Brody, Elaine M. 1983. "Women's Changing Roles and Help to Elderly Parents: Attitudes of Three Generations of Women." *Journal of Gerontology* 38:597–607.

13   Brody, Elaine M. 1990. *Women in the Middle: Their Parent-Care Years*. New York: Springer.

13   Brody, Elaine M., and Claire B. Schoonover. 1986. "Patterns of Parent-Care When Adult Daughters Work and When They Do Not." *The Gerontologist* 26:372–81.

3   Bronowski, Jacob. 1976. *The Ascent of Man*. London: BBC Publishing.

12   Brooks, J.D. 1994. "What We Know about Exercise and Where We Should Go from Here." Paper presented at the Midwest Sociological Association annual meeting, St. Louis, March.

9,15 Bryden, Kenneth. 1974. *Old Age Pensions and Policy-Making in Canada*. Montreal: McGill-Queen's University Press.

12,14 Buckingham, R.W., III, S.A. Lack, G.M. Mount, L.D. MacLean, and J.T. Collins. 1976. "Living with the Dying." *Canadian Medical Association Journal* 115:1211–15.

7   Bühler, C. 1951. "Maturation and Motivation." *Personality* 1:184–211.

1   Bultena, Gordon L., and Edward A. Powers. 1978. "Denial of Aging: Age Identification Reference Group Orientations." *Journal of Gerontology* 33:748–54.

12,14 Burden, C., and A.J. Lee. 1992. "Older Volunteers: An Agency Perpsective." *The Journal of Volunteer Administration* 11(1):19–21.

13   Burdz, M.P., W.O. Eaton, J.B. Bond, Jr. 1988. "Effects of Respite Care on Dementia and Nondementia Patients and Their Caregivers." *Psychology and Aging* 3:38–42.

4   Burke, Mary Anne. 1991. "Implications of an Aging Society." *Canadian Social Trends* (Spring):6–8.

11   Burke, M.A., and A. Spector. 1991. "Falling through the Cracks: Women Aged 55–64 Living on Their Own." *Canadian Social Trends* (Winter):14–17.

12,14 Butler, R.N. 1968. "The Life Review: An Interpretation of Reminiscence in the Aged." In Bernice L. Neugarten, ed. *Middle Age and Aging*. Chicago: University of Chicago Press.

1   Butler, R.N. 1969. "Age-ism: Another Form of Bigotry." *The Gerontologist* 9:243–46.

6   Butler, R.N. 1974. "The Creative Life and Old Age." In E. Pfeiffer, ed. *Successful Aging*. Durham, NC: Center for the Study of Aging and Human Development, Duke University.

6,7   Butler, R.N. 1975. *Why Survive? Being Old in America*. New York: Harper and Row.

1   Butler, R.N. 1989. "Dispelling Ageism: The Cross-Cutting Intervention." *The Annals of the American Academy of Political and Social Sciences* 503:138–47.

1   Butler, R.N. 1993. "Dispelling Ageism: The Cross-Cutting Intervention." *Generations* 17(2):75–78.

11,13 Butler, R.N., and M.I. Lewis. 1976. "Sex after 60: A Guide for Men and Women for Their Later Years." New York: Harper and Row.

6   Butler, R.N., and M.I. Lewis. 1982. *Aging and Mental Health*. 3d ed. St. Louis, MO: Mosby.

8   Buzzell, Mary. 1981. "So Very Vulnerable." *Journal of Gerontological Nursing* 7:286–87.

11   Byers, Thomas O. 1982. "The Congregate-Housing Model: Integrating Facilities and Services." In Robert D. Chellis, James F. Seagle, Jr., and Barbara Mackey Eagle, eds. *Congregate Housing for Older People: A Solution for the 1980s*. Lexington, MA: Lexington Books.

7   Cain, L.D., Jr. 1964. "Life Course and Social Structure." In Robert E.L. Faris, ed. *Handbook of Modern Sociology*. Chicago: Rand McNally.

10   Calasanti, Toni M. 1988. "Participation in a Dual Economy and Adjustment to Retirement." *International Journal of Aging and Human Development* 26:13–27.

12   Caldwell, L.L., E.A. Smith, and E. Weissinger. 1992. "The Relationships of Leisure Activities and Perceived Health of College Students." *Society and Leisure* 15:545–56.

14   Callahan, Daniel. 1987. *Setting Limits: Medical Goals in an Aging Society*. New York: Simon and Schuster.

13   Callahan, James J. 1986. "Guest Editor's Perspective." *Pride Institute Journal of Long-Term Home Health Care* 5:2–3.

13   Campbell, Ruth, and Elaine Brody. 1985. "Women's Changing Roles and Help to the Elderly: Attitudes of Women in the United States and Japan." *The Gerontologist* 25:584–92.

13   Canada. 1993. *Ageing and Independence: Overview of a National Survey*. Ottawa: Supply and Services Canada.

8   *Canada Health Act*, R.S.C. 1984. Ottawa: Queen's Printer.

11   Canada Mortgage and Housing Corporation. No date. *Housing Choices for Older Canadians*. Ottawa: Minister of Supply and Services.

11   Canada Mortgage and Housing Corporation. 1978. *Housing the Elderly*. Ottawa: Minister of Supply and Services.

11   Canada Mortgage and Housing Corporation. 1982. *HIFE Microdata File and Projections*. Ottawa: Canada Mortgage and Housing Corporation.

11   Canada Mortgage and Housing Corporation. 1987. *Garden Suites: A New Housing Option for Elderly Canadians?* Ottawa: Minister of Supply and Services.

11   Canada Mortgage and Housing Corporation. 1988. *Housing for Older Canadians: New Financial and Tenure Options*. Ottawa: Canada Mortgage and Housing Corporation.

13   Canadian Advisory Council on the Status of Women. 1990. *Women and Labour Market Poverty*. Ottawa: Canadian Advisory Council on the Status of Women.

15   Canadian Association of Retired Persons. 1991. C.A.R.P. news release. Toronto: Canadian Association of Retired Persons.

10   Canadian Association of University Teachers. 1991. "Mandatory Retirement." *CAUT Bulletin* 38:1–5.

11   Canadian Broadcasting Corporation. 1986. Report on aging segment. "Midday," December 4.

1   Canadian Council on Social Development. 1973. *Beyond Shelter*. Ottawa: Canadian Council on Social Development.

11   Canadian Council on Social Development. 1976a. *Housing the Elderly*. Ottawa: Canadian Council on Social Development.

10   Canadian Council on Social Development. 1976b. *Statement on Retirement Policies*. Ottawa: Canadian Council on Social Development.

4,8   Canadian Council on Social Development. 1990. *Canada's Social Programs Are in Trouble*. Ottawa: Canadian Council on Social Development.

14,16 Canadian Medical Association. 1987. *Health Care for the Elderly: Today's Challenges, Tomorrow's Options*. Ottawa: Canadian Medical Association.

10   Canadian Pension Plan Advisory Commission. 1980. Retirement Ages. Ottawa: Minister of Supply and Services.

13   Canadian Press. 1993. "Caring for Kin Costs Workers." *Winnipeg Free Press*, March 23.

11,12   Canadian Red Cross Society. 1983. *Red Cross National Seniors' Services Needs Assessment.* Toronto: Canadian Red Cross Society.

11   *Canadian Social Trends.* 1989. "1986 Census Highlights: Changes in Living Arrangements." *Canadian Social Trends.* Cat. No. 11-008E. Spring: 27–29.

13   Canadian Study of Health and Aging. 1994. "Patterns of Caring for People with Dementia in Canada." *Canadian Journal on Aging* 13(4):470–87.

13   Cantor, M.H., and V. Little. 1985. "Aging and Social Care." In R.H. Binstock and E. Shanas, eds. *Handbook of Aging and the Social Sciences.* New York: Van Nostrand Reinhold.

12   Cape, Elizabeth. 1983. "Activity and Independence: Issues in the Implementation of Activity Programs for Institutionalized Elders." *Canadian Journal on Aging* 2:185–95.

5,8   Cape, Ronald D.T., and Philip J. Henschke. 1980. "Perspectives of Health in Old Age." *Journal of the American Geriatrics Society* 28: 295–99.

6   Cappliez, P. 1988. "Some Thoughts on the Prevalence and Etiology of Depressive Conditions in the Elderly." *Canadian Journal on Aging* 7:431–40.

6   Carswell-Opzoomer, A., J. Puxty, M. Teaffe, and W. Walop. 1993. "Dementia in Long-Term Care Facilities: A Survey of the Ottawa-Carleton Region." *Canadian Journal on Aging* 12(3): 360–72.

12   Casperson, C.J., K. Powell, and G.M. Christenson. 1985. "Psychical Activity, Exercise, and Physical Fitness: Definitions for Health Related Research." *Public Health Reports* 100:126–30

6   Cattell, R.B. 1963. "Theory of Fluid and Crystallized Intelligence: An Initial Experiment." *Journal of Educational Psychology* 54:105–11.

6   Cavanaugh, J.C. 1983. "Comprehension and Retention of Television Programs by 20- and 60-Year Olds." *Journal of Gerontology* 38:190–96.

6   Cavanaugh, J.C., J.A. Grady, and M. Perlmutter. 1983. "Forgetting and Use of Memory Aids in 20 to 70 Year-Olds' Everyday Life." *International Journal of Aging and Human Development* 17:113–22.

6   Cerella, J. 1990. "Aging and Information-Processing Rate." In James E. Birren and K. Warner Schaie, eds. *Handbook of the Psychology of Aging.* 3d ed. San Diego: Academic Press.

6   Cerella, J., J. Rybash, W. Hoyer, and M.L. Commons, eds. 1993. *Adult Information Processing: Limits on Loss.* San Diego: Academic Press.

15   Cernetig, Miro. 1985. "Plans to De-Index Old Age Pensions Mean Poverty Jump Council Says." *Globe and Mail* (June 11).

14   Chappell, Neena L. 1975. "Awareness of Death in Disengagement Theory: A Conceptualization and an Empirical Investigation." *Omega* 6: 325–43.

13   Chappell, Neena L. 1980. "Re-examining Conceptual Boundaries: Peer and Inter-generational Relationships." *Essence* 4:169–78.

13   Chappell, Neena L. 1982a. "The Future Impact of the Changing Status of Women." In Gloria Gutman, ed. *Canada's Changing Age Structure: Selected Papers.* Burnaby, BC: Simon Fraser University Publications.

2   Chappell, Neena L. 1982b. "The Value of Research to Practitioners in Work with the Elderly." *Canadian Journal on Aging* 1:62–65.

12,13   Chappell, Neena L. 1983a. "Informal Support Networks among the Elderly." *Research on Aging* 5:77–99.

8   Chappell, Neena L. 1983b. "Who Benefits from Adult Day Care? Changes in Functional Ability and Mental Functioning during Attendance." *Canadian Journal on Aging* 2:9–26.

9   Chappell, Neena L. 1987. "Canadian Income and Health-Care Policy: Implications for the Elderly." In Victor W. Marshall, ed. *Aging in Canada.* Toronto: Fitzhenry and Whiteside.

8   Chappell, Neena L. 1988. "Long-Term Care in Canada." In Eloise Rathbone-McCuan and Betty Havens, eds. *North American Elders: United States and Canadian Perspectives.* New York: Greenwood Press.

13   Chappell, Neena L. 1989a. "Health and Helping among the Elderly: Gender Differences." *Journal of Aging and Health* 1:102–20.

11,13   Chappell, Neena L. 1989b. *Formal Programs for Informal Caregivers to Elders.* Paper prepared for the Aging Policy Section, Health Policy Division, Policy, Planning and Information Branch, Health and Welfare Canada. Ottawa: Health and Welfare Canada.

13   Chappell, Neena L. 1990. "Aging and Social Care." In Robert H. Binstock and Linda K. George, eds. *Handbook of Aging and the Social Sciences.* 3d ed. San Diego: Academic Press.

13 Chappell, Neena L. 1991. "Living Arrangements and Sources of Caregiving." *Journal of Gerontology: Social Sciences* 46:S1–S8.

13 Chappell, N.L. 1992. *Social Support and Aging.* Toronto: Butterworths.

5,8 Chappell, N. 1993a. "Technology and Aging." *Journal of Canadian Studies* 28(1):45–58.

8 Chappell, N.L. 1993b. "The Future of Health Care in Canada." *International Social Policy* 22(4):487–505.

8 Chappell, N.L. 1993c. "Implications of Shifting Health Care Policy for Caregiving in Canada." *Journal of Aging and Social Policy* 5(1/2):39–55.

8 Chappell, N.L. 1994a. "Health Care in Canada." In D.G. Gill and S.R. Ingman, eds. *Eldercare, Distributive Justice, and the Welfare State: Retrenchment or Expansion?* Albany, NY: State University of New York Press.

8 Chappell, N.L. 1994b. "Home Care Research: What Does It Tell Us?" *The Gerontologist* 34(1):116–20.

2 Chappell, N.L. 1995. "Gerontological Research in the '90s: Strengths, Weaknesses and Contributions to Policy." *Canadian Journal on Aging* 14(supp. 1): 23–36.

13 Chappell, Neena L., and Mark Badger. 1989. "Social Isolation and Well-Being." *Journal of Gerontology: Social Sciences* 44:5169–76.

6 Chappell, Neena L., and G.E. Barnes. 1982. "The Practicing Pharmacist and the Elderly Client." *Contemporary Pharmacy Practice* 5:170–75.

8 Chappell, Neena L., and Audrey A. Blandford. 1987a. "Adult Day Care and Medical and Hospital Claims." *The Gerontologist* 27:773–79.

13 Chappell, Neena L., and Audrey A. Blandford. 1987b. "Health Service Utilization by Elderly Persons." *Canadian Journal of Sociology* 12:195–215.

13 Chappell, N., and A. Blandford. 1991. "Informal and Formal Care: Exploring the Complementarity." *Ageing and Society*, 11:299–317.

5 Chappell, Neena L., and Betty Havens. 1980. "Old and Female: Testing the Double Jeopardy Hypothesis." *Sociological Quarterly* 21:157–71.

13 Chappell, Neena L., and Betty Havens. 1985. "Who Helps the Elderly Person: A Discussion of Informal and Formal Care." In Warren A. Peterson and Jill Quadagno, eds. *Social Bonds in Later Life: Aging and Interdependence.* Beverly Hills, CA: Sage.

2 Chappell, Neena L., and Harold L. Ohrbach. 1986. "Socialization in Old Age: A Meadian Perspective." In Victor W. Marshall, ed. *Later Life: The Social Psychology of Aging.* Beverly Hills, CA: Sage.

8,15 Chappell, Neena L., and Margaret Penning. 1979. "The Trend Away from Institutionalization: Humanism or Economic Efficiency?" *Research on Aging* 1:361–87.

13 Chappell, N.L., and M.J. Prince. 1994. *Social Support among Today's Seniors.* Final report for the Centre on Aging, University of Victoria, Victoria, BC.

13 Chappell, Neena L., and Alexander Segall. 1989. "Health, Helping Networks and Well-Being." *Journal of Aging Studies* 3:313–24.

13 Chappell, Neena L., Alexander Segall, and Doris G. Lewis. 1990. "Gender and Helping Networks Among Day Hospital and Senior Centre Participants." *Canadian Journal on Aging* 9:220–33.

7 Chappell, Neena L., and Laurel A. Strain. 1984. *Needs Assessment of Natives 50+ Living in Winnipeg.* Winnipeg: University of Manitoba Centre on Aging.

5,8 Chappell, Neena L., Laurel A. Strain, and Audrey A. Blandford. 1986. *Aging and Health Care: A Social Perspective.* Toronto: Holt, Rinehart and Winston of Canada.

7 Chard, J. 1995. "Women in a Visible Minority." In Statistics Canada, *Women in Canada: A Statistical Report*, 3d ed., 133–46. Cat. No. 89-503E. Ottawa: Minister of Supply and Services Canada.

8 Charles, C., and C. Schalm. 1992a. "Alberta's Resident Classification System for Long-Term Care Facilities. Part I: Conceptual and Methodological Development." *Canadian Journal on Aging* 11(3):219–32.

8 Charles, C., and C. Schalm. 1992b. "Alberta's Resident Classification System for Long-Term Care Facilities. Part II: First-Year Results and Policy Implications." *Canadian Journal on Aging* 11(3):233–48.

6 Charness, Neil. 1981. "Aging and Skilled Problem Solving." *Journal of Experimental Psychology: General* 110:21–38.

6 Charness, Neil. 1982. "Problem Solving and Aging: Evidence from Semantically Rich Domains." *Canadian Journal on Aging* 1:21–28.

6 Charness, Neil. 1985. "Aging and Problem-Solving Performance." In Neil Charness, ed. *Aging and Human Performance.* Chichester, England: John Wiley and Sons.

6 Charness, Neil. 1987. "Component Processes in Bridge Bidding and Novel Problem-Solving Tasks." *Canadian Journal of Psychology* 41:223–43.

11 Charness, N.H. 1993. "Whither Technology and Aging?" *Gerontology News* April, 2ff.

2 Charness, N. 1995. "Psychological Models of Aging: How, Who, and What? A Comment." *Canadian Journal on Aging* 14(1):67–73.

5 Charness, Neil, and Elizabeth Bosman. 1989. "The Role of Human Factors in Product Design for Older Adults." Paper presented at the 18th Annual Scientific and Educational Meeting of the Canadian Association on Gerontology, Ottawa.

5 Charness, Neil, and Elizabeth A. Bosman. 1990. "Human Factors and Design for Older Adults." In James E. Birren and K. Warner Schaie, eds. *Handbook of the Psychology of Aging*. 3d ed. San Diego: Academic Press.

5 Charness, N., and E.A. Bosman. 1994. "Age-Related Changes in Perceptual and Psychomotor Performance: Implications for Engineering Design." *Experimental Aging Research* 20(1):45–59.

6 Charness, Neil, and Jamie I.D. Campbell. 1988. "Acquiring Skill at Mental Calculation in Adulthood: A Task Decomposition." *Journal of Experimental Psychology: General* 117:115–29.

4 Chawla, Raj. 1991. "Dependency Ratios." *Canadian Social Trends*. Cat. No. 11-008E (Spring):3–5.

9,13 Cheal, David. 1983. "Intergenerational Family Transfers." *Journal of Marriage and the Family* 45:805–13.

9 Cheal, David. 1985a. *Moral Economy: Gift Giving in an Urban Society*. Winnipeg Area Study Report No. 5. Winnipeg: Institute for Social and Economic Research, University of Manitoba.

9,13 Cheal, David. 1985b. "The System of Transfers to and from Households in Canada." *Western Economic Review* 4:35–39.

13 Cheal, David. 1986. "The Social Dimensions of Gift Behaviour." *Journal of Social and Personal Relationships* 3:423–39.

13 Cheal, David J. 1989–90. "Theories of Serial Flow in Intergenerational Transfers." *International Journal of Aging and Human Development* 26:261–73.

6 Checkland, D., and M. Silberfeld. 1993. "Competence and the Three A's: Autonomy, Authenticity, and Aging." *Canadian Journal on Aging* 12(4):453–68.

4 Chen, Yung-Ping. 1987. "Making Assets Out of Tomorrow's Elderly." *The Gerontologist* 27:410–16.

12 Chené, A. 1994. "Community-Based Older Learners: Being with Others." *Educational Gerontology* 20, 765–81.

12 Chené, A., and M. Fleury. 1992. "College Studies after 50 Years of Age: A Quebec Experience." *Educational Gerontology* 18: 497–510.

13 Cherlin, Andrew, and Frank F. Furstenberg. 1985. "Styles and Strategies of Grand-Parenting." In Vern L. Bengtson and Joan F. Robertson, eds. *Grandparenthood*. Beverly Hills, CA: Sage.

3 Cherry, Ralph, and Scott Magnuson-Martinson. 1981. "Modernization and the Status of the Aged in China: Decline or Equalization?" *The Sociological Quarterly* 22:253–61.

13 Chipperfield, J.G. 1994. "The Support Source Mix: A Comparison of Elderly Men and Women from Two Decades." *Canadian Journal on Aging* 13(4):434–53.

7 Chipperfield, J.G., and B. Havens. 1992. "A Longitudinal Analysis of Perceived Respect among Elders: Changing Perceptions of Some Ethnic Groups." *Canadian Journal on Aging* 11(2):15–30.

7 Chiriboga, David A. 1984. "Social Stressors as Antecedents of Change." *Journal of Gerontology* 39:468–77.

13 Chiriboga, David A., Philip G. Weiler, and Karen Nielsen. 1990. "The Stress of Caregivers." In David E. Biegel and Arthur Blum, eds. *Aging and Caregiving: Theory, Research, and Policy*. Newbury Park, CA: Sage.

16 Church, J. 1991. "Long Term Care Inservice Resource Centres." *Alberta Association of Registered Nurses* 47(11):10–11.

7 Ciaccio, N.V. 1971. "A Test of Erikson's Theory of Ego Epigenesis." *Developmental Psychology* 4:306–11.

10 Ciffin, S., and J. Martin. 1977. *Retirement in Canada: Volume I, When and Why People Retire*. Health and Welfare Canada, Policy Research and Long Range Planning (Welfare). Ottawa: Minister of Supply and Services.

15 Clark, P.G. 1993. "Moral Discourse and Public Policy in Aging: Framing Problems, Seeking Solutions, and 'Public Ethics.'" *Canadian Journal on Aging* 12(4):485–508.

12 Clarke, H.H. 1977. "Joint and Body Range of Motion." *Physical Fitness Research Digest* 7.

15 Clarke, Harold D., L. LeDuc, J. Jenson, and J. Pammett. 1980. *Political Choice in Canada*. Abridged ed. Toronto: McGraw-Hill Ryerson.

11 CMHC (Canada Mortgage and Housing Corporation). 1988. *New Made-to-Convert Housing*. Cat. No. NH15-38/1988E. Ottawa: CMHC.

11 CMHC (Canada Mortgage and Housing Corporation). 1992. *Housing Choices for Canadians with Disabilities*. Cat. No. NH15-74/1992E. Ottawa: CMHC.

2,3   Cockerham, William C. 1991. *This Aging Society.* Englewood Cliffs, NJ: Prentice Hall.

6   Cohen, C.A., D.P. Gold, K.I. Shulman, J.T. Wortley, and G. McDonald. 1993. "Factors Determining the Decision to Institutionalize Dementing Individuals: A Prospective Study." *Gerontologist* 33(6):714–20.

13   Cohen, C.A., D.P. Gold, K.I. Shulman, and C.A. Zucchero. 1994. "Positive Aspects in Caregiving: An Overlooked Variable in Research." *Canadian Journal on Aging* 13(3):378–91.

6   Cohen, Gene D. 1990. "Psychopathology and Mental Health in the Mature and Elderly Adult." In James E. Birren and K. Warner Schaie, eds. *Handbook of the Psychology of Aging.* 3d ed. San Diego: Academic Press.

3   Cohn, R. 1982. "Economic Development and Status Change of the Aged." *American Journal of Sociology* 87:1150–61.

2   Cole, T.R., D.D. Van Tassel, and R. Kastenbaum, eds. 1992. *Handbook of the Humanities and Aging.* New York: Springer.

1   Cole, T.R., and M.G. Winkler. 1994. *The Oxford Book of Aging.* Oxford: Oxford University Press.

12   Coleman, D., and S.E. Iso-Ahola. 1993. "Leisure and Health: The Role of Social Support and Self-Determination." *Journal of Leisure Research* 25: 111–28

13   Colerick, E.J., and L.K. George. 1986. "Predictors of Institutionalization among Caregivers of Patients with Alzheimer's Disease." *Journal of the American Geriatric Society* 34:493–98.

6   Collins, B., and A. Tellier. 1994. "Differences in Conceptual Flexibility with Age as Measured by a Modified Version of the Visual Verbal Test." *Canadian Journal on Aging* 13(3):368–77.

3   Colson, E., and T. Scudder. 1981. "Old Age in Gwembe District, Zambia." In P.T. Amoss and S. Harrell, eds. *Other Ways of Growing Old: Anthropological Perspectives.* Stanford, CA: Stanford University Press.

5   Colvez, A., and M. Blanchet. 1981. "Disability Trends in the United States Population 1966–1976: Analysis of Reported Causes." *American Journal of Public Health* 71:464–71.

1   Commonwealth Fund. 1993. "Commonwealth Fund Survey: Over 65 in Five Nations." *Ageing International* 20(1):43–45.

16   Connelly, J. Richard. 1981. "Education and the Future." In Gloria Gutman, ed. *Canada's Changing Age Structure: Implications for the Future.* Burnaby, BC: Simon Fraser University.

9   Connelly, M. Patricia, and Martha MacDonald. 1990. *Women and the Labour Force.* Cat. No. 98-125. Ottawa: Minister of Supply and Services.

10   Connidis, Ingrid. 1982. "Women and Retirement: The Effect of Multiple Careers on Retirement Adjustment." *Canadian Journal on Aging* 1:17–27.

11   Connidis, Ingrid. 1983a. "Living Arrangement Choices of Older Residents: Assessing Quantitative Results with Qualitative Data." *Canadian Journal of Sociology* 8:359–75.

7   Connidis, Ingrid. 1983b. "The Pros, Cons and Worries of Aging." Paper presented at the Canadian Association on Gerontology 12th Annual Scientific and Educational Meeting, Moncton.

2,13   Connidis, Ingrid Arnet. 1989a. *Family Ties and Aging.* Toronto: Butterworths.

13   Connidis, Ingrid Arnet. 1989b. "Report on Seniors' Volunteer Work and Unpaid Help to Others." Paper commissioned by the National Advisory Council on Aging for the Symposium on Social Supports, Ottawa, March 28–29.

13   Connidis, Ingrid Arnet. 1989c. "Siblings as Friends in Later Life." *American Behavioral Scientist* 33:81–93.

13   Connidis, I.A. 1994. "Sibling Support in Older Age." *Journal of Gerontology: Social Sciences* 49(6):S309–S317.

13   Connidis, Ingrid Arnet, and Lorraine Davies. 1990. "Confidants and Companions in Later Life: The Place of Family and Friends." *Journal of Gerontology: Social Sciences* 45:S141–S149.

13   Connidis, I.A., and L. Davies. 1992. "Confidants and Companions: Choices in Later Life." *Journal of Gerontology: Social Sciences* 47(3):S115–S122.

13   Connidis, I.A., and J.A. McMullin. 1992. "Getting Out of the House: The Effect of Childlessness on Social Participation and Companionship in Later Life." *Canadian Journal on Aging* 11(4):370–86.

13   Connidis, I.A., and J.A. McMullin. 1993. "To Have or Have Not: Parent Status and the Subjective Well-Being of Older Men and Women." *The Gerontologist* 33(5):630–36.

13   Connidis, I.A., and J.A. McMullin. 1994. "Social Support in Older Age: Assessing the Impact of Marital and Parent Status." *Canadian Journal on Aging* 13(4):510–27.

11   Connidis, Ingrid, and Judith Rempel. 1983. "The Living Arrangements of Older Residents: The Role of Gender, Marital Status, Age, and Family Size." *Canadian Journal on Aging* 2:91–105.

7   Constantinople, A. 1969. "An Eriksonian Measure of Personality Development in College Students." *Developmental Psychology* 1:357–72.

12   Corbeil, J-P. 1995. "Sport Participation in Canada." *Canadian Social Trends* (Spring):18–23.

13   Corby, Nan, and Judy Maes Zarit. 1983. "Old and Alone: The Unmarried in Later Life." In Ruth B. Weg, ed. *Sexuality in the Later Years: Roles and Behavior*. New York: Academic Press.

4   Corelli, Rae. 1986. "A Matter of Care." *Maclean's* (October).

13   Corin, Ellen. 1987. "The Relationship between Formal and Informal Social Support Networks in Rural and Urban Contexts." In Victor W. Marshall, ed. *Aging in Canada: Social Perspectives*. 2d ed. Toronto: Fitzhenry and Whiteside.

11   Corke, Susan. 1986a. "Granny Flats as an Intensification Option for Housing the Elderly." In Susan Corke, Gregory S. Romanick, Michael Lazarowich, Joan Simon, eds. *Granny Flats: A Housing Option for the Elderly*. Report No. 13. Winnipeg: Institute of Urban Studies.

11   Corke, Susan. 1986b. "Provincial Housing and Shelter Support Programs for the Elderly: Ontario." In Gloria Gutman and Norman Blackie, eds. *Aging in Place: Housing Adaptations and Options for Remaining in the Community*. Burnaby, BC: The Gerontology Research Centre, Simon Fraser University.

6   Cornelius, S.W., and A. Caspi. 1987. "Everyday Problem Solving in Adulthood and Old Age." *Psychology and Aging* 2: 144–53.

7   Costa, P.T., Jr., and R.R. McCrae. 1989. "Personality Continuity and the Changes of Adult Life." In M. Storandt and G. R. VandenBos, eds. *Adult Years: Continuity and Change*, 41–77. Washington, DC: American Psychological Association.

2   Coupland, J., N. Coupland, and J.D. Robinson. 1992. "'How Are You?': Negotiating Phatic Communion." *Language in Society* 21:207–30.

12   Cousins, S.O. 1993. "Turn of the Century Tomboys: Does Older Women's Efficacy for Late Life Exercise Originate in Childhood?" In E. Beregi, I.A. Gergely, and K. Rajczi, eds. *Recent Advances in Aging Science, 1911–1916*. Bologna (Italy): Monduzzi Editore.

2,12 Cousins, S.O. 1995a. "Social Support for Exercise among Elderly Women in Canada." *Health Promotion International* 10(4): 273–82.

12   Cousins, S.O. (1995b). "Anticipated Exertion for Exercise Activities among Women over 70." *Canadian Woman Studies* 15(4):74–77.

12   Cousins, S.O., and A. Burgess. 1992. "Perspectives on Older Adults in Physical Activity and Sports." *Educational Gerontology* 18:461–81.

12   Cousins, S.O., and N. Keating. 1995. "Life Cycle Patterns of Physical Activity among Sedentary and Active Older Women." *Journal of Aging and Physical Activity* 3:340–59.

12   Covey, Herbert C. 1983. "Higher Education and Older People: Some Theoretical Considerations, Part II." *Educational Gerontology* 9:95–109.

23   Cowgill, Donald O. 1972. "A Theory of Aging in Cross-Cultural Perspective." In D. Cowgill and L. Holmes, eds. *Aging and Modernization*. New York: Appleton-Century-Crofts.

3,10 Cowgill, Donald O. 1974. "Aging and Modernization: A Revision of the Theory." In Jaber F. Gubrium, ed. *Late Life*. Springfield, IL: Charles C. Thomas.

3   Cowgill, Donald O. 1986. *Aging around the World*. Belmont, CA: Wadsworth.

2,3 Cowgill, Donald O., and Lowell D. Holmes, eds. 1972. *Aging and Modernization*. New York: Appleton-Century-Crofts.

6   Craik, F.I.M. 1994. "Memory Changes in Normal Aging." *Current Directions in Psychological Science* 3(5):155–58.

11   Cranz, Galen, and Thomas L. Schumacher. 1975. *The Impact of High-Rise Housing on Older Residents*. Working Paper 18. Princeton, NJ: Research Centre for Urban and Environmental Planning, School of Architecture and Urban Planning.

13   Crawford, L.M., J.B. Bond, and R.F. Balshaw. 1994. "Factors Affecting Sons' and Daughters' Caregiving to Older Parents." *Canadian Journal on Aging* 13(4):454–69.

12   Creative Retirement Manitoba. 1992. *Annual Report*. Winnipeg: CRM.

5   Crews, D.E. 1993. "Biological Aging: Book Review Essay." *Journal of Cross-Cultural Gerontology* 8:281–90.

13   Crimmins, Eileen M., and Dominique G. Ingegneri. 1990. "Interaction and Living Arrangements of Older Parents and Their Children." *Research on Aging* 12:3–35.

3,4 Cross, D. Suzanne. 1983. "The Neglected Majority: The Changing Role of Women in Nineteenth-Century Montreal." In P.W. Ward, comp. *The Social Development of Canada: Readings*. Richmond, BC: Open Learning Institute.

6   Crosson, C.W., and E.A. Robertson-Tchabo. 1983. "Age and Preference for Complexity among Manifestly Creative Women." *Human Development* 26:149–55.

13   Crystal, S. 1986. "Social Policy and Elder Abuse." In K.A. Pillemer and R.S. Wolf, eds. *Elder Abuse: Conflict in the Family*. Dover, MA: Auburn House.

2,7   Cumming, E., and W.E. Henry. 1961. *Growing Old: The Process of Disengagement*. New York: Basic Books.

12   Cunningham, D.A., P.A. Rechnitzer, J.H. Howard, and A.P. Donner. 1987. "Exercise Training of Men at Retirement: A Clinical Trial." *Journal of Gerontology* 42:17–23.

15   Curtis, James E., and Ronald D. Lambert. 1976. "Voting, Election Interest, and Age: National Findings for English and French Canadians." *Canadian Journal of Political Science* 9:293–307.

12   Curtis, James E., and Barry D. McPherson. 1987. "Regional Differences in the Leisure Physical Activity of Canadians: Testing Some Alternative Interpretations." *Sociology of Sport Journal* 4:363–75.

2   Cusack, S.A. 1995. "Developing a Lifelong Learning Program: Empowering Seniors as Leaders in Lifelong Learning." *Educational Gerontology* 21:305–20.

3   Cutler, N.E., and R.A. Harootyan. 1975. "Demography of the Aged." In D.S. Woodruff and J.E. Birren, eds. *Aging: Scientific Perspectives and Social Issues*. New York: Van Nostrand.

12   Cutler, Stephen, and Jon Hendricks. 1990. "Leisure and Time Use across the Life Course." In Robert H. Binstock and Linda K. George, eds. *Handbook of Aging and the Social Sciences*. 3d ed. San Diego: Academic Press.

12   Cyr, J., and M.M. Schnore. 1982. "Level of Education of the Future Elderly: Demographic Characteristics and Clinical Implications." *Essence* 5:153–67.

1   Dail, P.W. 1988. "Prime-Time Television Portrayals of Older Adults in the Context of Family Life." *The Gerontologist* 28(5):700–6.

13   Damrosch, Shirley Petchel. 1984. "Graduate Nursing Students' Attitudes toward Sexually Active Older Persons." *The Gerontologist* 24:299–302.

7   d'Anglure, B.S. 1994. "Recycling the 'Elders' in the Inuit Social Life." In National Advisory Council on Aging, *Aboriginal Seniors' Issues*, 59–64. Cat. No. H71-2/1-15-1994E. Ottawa: Minister of Supply and Services Canada.

10   David, H. 1993. "Canada's Labor Market: Older Workers Need Not Apply." *Ageing International* 20(3):21–25.

1   Davies, Leland J. 1977. "Attitudes toward Old Age and Aging as Shown by Humor." *The Gerontologist* 17:220–26.

5,11 Davis, C.K. 1991. *Housing Choices for Canadians over 75 Years Old*. Ottawa: Canada Mortgage and Housing Corporation.

13   Davis, I. 1996. "Grandparenting Denied." *Maturity* (March/April):25–26.

6   Dawson, Pam, and David W. Reid. 1987. "Behavioral Dimensions of Patients at Risk of Wandering." *The Gerontologist* 27:104–7.

2   de Beauvoir, Simone. 1978. *Old Age*. Harmondsworth, England: Penguin.

8   Deber, R.B., S.L. Mhatre, and G.R. Baker. 1994. "A Review of Provincial Initiatives." In A. Blomqvist and D.M. Brown, eds. *Limits to Care: Reforming Canada's Health System in an Age of Restraint*, 91–124. Ottawa: C.D. Howe Institute.

8   Deber, R.B., and A.P. Williams. 1995. "Policy, Payment, and Participation: Long-Term Care Reform in Ontario." *Canadian Journal on Aging* 14(2):294–318.

3   DeLehr, Esther Contreras. 1988. "Today's and Tomorrow's Aging in Latin America." In *Aging around the World: A Report on the President's Symposium, 'Aging in Tomorrow's World: An International Perspective.'* The Gerontological Society of America.

7   Delisle, Marc-André. 1988. "What Does Solitude Mean to the Aged?" *Canadian Journal on Aging* 7:358–71.

13   Demers, A., and J-P Lavoie. 1996. "Effect of Support Groups on Family Caregivers to the Frail Elderly." *Canadian Journal on Aging* 15(1):129–44.

1   Demos, Vasilikie, and Ann Jache. 1981. "When You Care Enough: An Analysis of Attitudes toward Aging in Humorous Birthday Cards." *The Gerontologist* 21:209–15.

6   Denney, N.W., and A.M. Palmer. 1981. "Adult Age Differences on Traditional and Practical Problem-Solving Measures." *Journal of Gerontology* 4:144–48.

6   Dennis, Wayne. 1968. "Creative Productivity between the Ages of 20 and 80 Years." In Bernice L. Neugarten, ed. *Middle Age and Aging*. Chicago: University of Chicago Press.

4   Denton, F.T., C.H. Feaver, and B. Spencer. 1986. "Prospective Aging of the Population and Its Implications for the Labour Force and Government Expenditures." *Canadian Journal on Aging* 5:75–98.

8   Denton, F.T., S.N. Li, and B.G. Spencer. 1987. "How Will Population Aging Affect the Future Costs of Maintaining Health-Care Standards?" In Victor W. Marshall, ed. *Aging in Canada*. 2d ed. Toronto: Fitzhenry and Whiteside.

12   Denton, F.T., P.C. Pineo, and B.G. Spencer. 1988. "Participation in Adult Education by the

Elderly: A Multivariate Analysis and Some Implications for the Future." *Canadian Journal on Aging* 7:4–16.

4 Denton, Frank T., and Byron G. Spencer. 1980. "Canada's Population and Labour Force: Past, Present and Future." In Victor W. Marshall, ed. *Aging in Canada*. Toronto: Fitzhenry and Whiteside.

8 Denton, Frank T., and Byron G. Spencer. 1983. "Population Aging and Future Health Costs in Canada." *Canadian Public Policy* 9:155–63.

4,8 Denton, F.T., and B.G. Spencer. 1995. "Demographic Change and the Cost of Publicly Funded Health Care." *Canadian Journal on Aging* 14(2):174–92.

3 Dentzer, S. 1991. "The Graying of Japan." *U.S. News and World Report* (September 30):65–73.

4 Department of Indian Affairs and Northern Development. 1996. *Indian Register Population by Sex and Residence 1995*. Cat. No. R31-3/1995. Ottawa: Minister of Public Works and Government Services Canada.

6 de Santana, Hubert. 1980. "Portrait of the Artist as an Old Man." *Today Magazine* (November 29).

4 Desjardins, B. 1993. *Population Ageing and the Elderly*. Cat. No. 91-533E. Ottawa: Minister of Industry, Science and Technology.

12 Devereaux, M.S. 1985. *One in Every Five: A Survey of Adult Education in Canada*. Statistics Canada. Cat. No. SZ-139/1984E. Ottawa: Minister of Supply and Services.

12 Devereaux, M.S. 1993. "Time Use of Canadians." *Canadian Social Trends*, (Autumn):13–17.

8 Devine, Barbara A. 1980. "Old Age Stereotyping: A Comparison of Nursing Staff Attitudes toward the Elderly." *Journal of Gerontological Nursing* 6:25–32.

12 DeVries, Herbert A. 1975. "Physiology of Exercise and Aging." In Diana S. Woodruff and James E. Birren, eds. *Aging: Scientific Perspectives and Social Issues*. New York: D. Van Nostrand Co.

3 de Vries, Patricia. 1987. "Every Old Person Is Somebody: The Image of Aging in Canadian Children's Literature." *Canadian Children's Literature* 46:37–44.

12 Diamond, M. 1984. "A Love Affair with the Brain." *Psychology Today*, November, 62–73.

14 Dickinson, G.E. 1976. "Death Education in U.S. Medical Schools." *Journal of Medical Education* 51:134–36.

14 Dickinson, G.E., and A.A. Pearson. 1980–81. "Death Education and Physicians' Attitudes Towards Dying Patients." *Omega* 11:167–74.

6 Dixon, R.A., and L. Backman. 1993. "The Concept of Compensation in Cognitive Aging: The Case of Prose Processing in Adulthood." *International Journal of Aging and Human Development* 36(3):199–217.

5 Dixon, R.A., D. Kurzman, and I.C. Friesen. 1993. "Handwriting Performance in Younger and Older Adults: Age, Familiarity, and Practice Effects." *Psychology and Aging* 8(3):360–70.

6 Dobbs, Allen R., and Brendan Gail Rule. 1987. "Prospective Memory and Self-Reports of Memory Abilities in Older Adults." *Canadian Journal of Psychology* 41:209–22.

4 Dominion Bureau of Statistics. 1964. *Census of Canada* (1961 Census). Bulletin 7:1–4. Ottawa: The Queen's Printer.

1 Dooley, Stephen, and B. Gail Frankel. 1990. "Improving Attitudes toward Elderly People: Evaluation of an Intervention Program for Adolescents." *Canadian Journal on Aging* 9:400–9.

11 Doolin, Joseph. 1986. "Planning for the Special Needs of the Homeless Elderly." *The Gerontologist* 26:229–31.

14 Doutre, D., D.M. Stillwell, and I. Ajemian. 1979. "Physiotherapy in Palliative Care." *Essence* 3:69–77.

10 Dowd, J. J. 1980. *Stratification among the Aged*. Monterey, CA: Brooks/Cole.

11 Doyle, V. 1994. "Choice, Control and the Right to Age in Place." In G. Gutman and A.V. Wister, eds. *Progressive Accommodation for Seniors: Interfacing Shelter and Services*, 33–44. Vancouver, BC: Gerontology Research Centre.

13 Dranoff, L.S. 1984. "Ask a Lawyer: Do Adult Children Have a Legal Duty to Support Their Parents?" *Chatelaine* (November).

2,4,7,13 Driedger, Leo, and Neena L. Chappell. 1987. *Aging and Ethnicity: Toward an Interface*. Toronto: Butterworths.

8 Drummond, M.F. 1980. *Principles of Economic Appraisal in Health Care*. Oxford: Oxford University Press.

13 Ducharme, F. 1994. "Conjugal Support, Coping Behaviors, and Psychological Well-Being of the Edlerly Spouse: An Empirical Model." *Research on Aging* 16(2):167–90.

9,13 Dulude, Louise. 1987. "Getting Old: Men in Couples and Women Alone." In G.H. Neimiroff, ed. *Women and Men: Interdisciplinary Readings on Gender*. Toronto: Fitzhenry and Whiteside.

4 Dumas, Jean. 1990. *Current Demographic Analysis: Report on the Demographic Situation in Canada 1988*. Statistics Canada Cat. No. 91-209E. Ottawa: Minister of Supply and Services.

4   Dumas, J. 1994. *Report on the Demographic Situation in Canada 1993*. No. 91-209E. Ottawa: Minister of Industry, Science and Technology.

4,5 Dumas, J., and A. Bélanger. 1994. *Report on the Demographic Situation in Canada 1994*. Cat. No. 91-209E. Ottawa: Minister of Industry, Science and Technology.

5   Dunn, Peter A. 1990. *Barriers Confronting Seniors with Disabilities in Canada. Special Topics Series: The Health and Activity Limitation Survey*. Statistics Canada Cat. No. 82-615. Ottawa: Minister of Supply and Services.

7   Durkheim, E. 1951. *Suicide: A Study in Sociology*. New York: Free Press.

8   Eagle, D. Joan, Gordon Guyatt, Christopher Patterson, and Irene Turpie. 1987. "Day Hospitals' Cost and Effectiveness: A Summary." *The Gerontologist* 27:735–40.

14   Eakes, G.G. 1985. "The Relationship between Anxiety and Attitudes toward the Elderly among Nursing Staff." *Death Studies* 9:163–72.

8   Eakin, Joan M. 1987. "Care of the Unwanted: Stroke Patients in a Canadian Hospital." In D. Coburn, C. D'Arcy, G. Torrance, and P. New, eds. *Health and Canadian Society: Sociological Perspectives*. 2d ed. Toronto: Fitzhenry and Whiteside.

16   Earthy, A. 1993. "A Survey of Gerontological Curricula in Canada." *Journal of Gerontological Nursing* 19(12):7–13.

4   Easterlin, R.A. 1996. "Economic and Social Implications of Demographic Patterns." In R.H. Binstock and L.K. George, eds. *Handbook of Aging and the Social Sciences*, 4th ed., 73–93. San Diego: Academic Press.

2   Eastwood, R., H. Nobbs, J. Lindsay, and I. McDowell. 1992. "Canadian Study of Health and Aging." *Dementia* 3(4):209–12.

6,8 Eaton, Bill, M.J. Stones, and Ken Rockwood. 1986. "Poor Mental Status in Older Hospital Patients: Prevalence and Correlates." *Canadian Journal on Aging* 5:231–39.

14   Eaton, Joseph W. 1964. "The Art of Aging and Dying" *The Gerontologist* 4:94–112.

6   Ebly, E.M., I.M. Parhad, D.B. Hogan, and T.S. Fung. 1994. "Prevalence and Types of Dementia in the Very Old: Results from the Canadian Study of Health and Aging." *Neurology* 44(9):1593–1600.

11   Eckert, J.K. 1980. *The Unseen Elderly*. San Diego: The Companile Press.

11   Economic Council of Canada. 1981. "Reverse Mortgages: A New Way to Help Pensioners." *Au Courant* 2:21.

12   Edwards, Peggy. 1983. "New Frontier in Geriatric Science: Fitness in the 'Third Age.'" *Canadian Journal of Public Health* 74:96–99.

11   Ehrlich, I., and P. Ehrlich. 1976. *The Invisible Elderly*. Washington, DC: National Council on the Aging.

3   Eisdorfer, Carl. 1981. "Foreword." In P.T. Amoss and S. Harrell, eds. *Other Ways of Growing Old: Anthropological Perspectives*. Stanford, CA: Stanford University Press.

10   Ekerdt, David J., Raymond Bossé, and Sue Levkoff. 1985. "An Empirical Test for Phases of Retirement: Findings from the Normative Aging Study." *Journal of Gerontology* 40:95–101.

12   Elderhostel. 1981. *Annual Report*. Boston: Elderhostel.

12   Elderhostel Canada. 1987. *Welcome to Elderhostel Canada*. May to October Issue. Toronto: Elderhostel Canada.

12   Elderhostel Canada. 1991a. *Elderhostel Canada* (Summer 1991). Toronto: Elderhostel Canada.

12   Elderhostel Canada. 1991b. *This Is Elderhostel Canada/1991*. Toronto: Elderhostel Canada.

12   Elderhostel Canada. 1996. Spring Because You Live in Canada … Note circulated with Elderhostel Canada catalogue.

6   Elo, A.E. 1965. "Age Changes in Master Chess Performance." *Journal of Gerontology* 20:289–99.

8   Epp, Jake. 1986. *Achieving Health for All: A Framework for Health Promotion*. Cat. No. H39-102/1986E. Ottawa: Minister of Supply and Services.

11   Epstein, Don. 1976. *Retirement Housing in Urban Neighbourhoods: Some Inner City Options*. Winnipeg: Institute of Urban Studies.

12   Ericsson, K. Anders. 1990. "Peak Performance and Age: An Examination of Peak Performance in Sports." In Paul B. Baltes and Margaret M. Baltes, eds. *Successful Aging: Perspectives from the Behavioral Sciences*. Cambridge: Cambridge University Press.

7   Erikson, Erik H. 1950. "Growth and Crises of the Health Personality." In M.J. Senn, ed. *Symposium on the Healthy Personality, Supplement II: Problems of Infancy and Childhood*. Transaction of Fourth Conference. New York: Josiah Macy, Jr., Foundation.

7   Erikson, Erik H. 1959. "Identity and the Life Cycle: Selected Issues." *Psychological Issues* 1:50–100, Appendix.

7,14 Erikson, Erik H. 1963. *Childhood and Society*. 2d ed. New York: W.W. Norton.

7   Erikson, Erik H. 1976. "Reflections on Dr. Borg's Life Cycle." In Erik Erikson, ed. *Adulthood*. New York: W.W. Norton.

7   Erikson, Erik H. 1982. *The Life Cycle Completed.* New York: W.W. Norton.

2   Estes, C.L. 1979. *The Aging Enterprise.* San Francisco: Jossey-Bass.

2   Estes, C.L., S.P. Wallace, and E.A. Binney. 1989. "Health, Aging, and Medical Sociology." In H. Freeman and S. Levine, eds. *Handbook of Medical Sociology.* 4th ed. Englewood Cliffs, NJ: Prentice-Hall.

11   Evans, Aeron T., and G.J.M. Purdie. 1985. "Private Sector Financing for Elderly Housing." In Gloria Gutman and Norman Blackie, eds. *Innovations in Housing and Living Arrangements for Seniors.* Burnaby, BC: The Gerontology Research Centre, Simon Fraser University.

11   Evans, Leonard. 1988. "Older Driver Involvement in Fatal and Severe Traffic Crashes." *Journal of Gerontology: Social Sciences* 43:S186–93.

8   Evans, R.G. 1984. *Strained Mercy: The Economics of Canadian Health Care.* Toronto: Butterworths.

8   Evans, R.G., M.L. Barer, and G.L. Stoddart. 1995. "User Fees for Health Care: Why a Bad Idea Keeps Coming Back (or, What's Health Got to Do with It?)." *Canadian Journal on Aging* 14(2):360–90.

6   Featherman, D.L., J. Smith, and J.G. Peterson. 1990. "Successful Aging in a Post-Retired Society." In P.B. Baltes and M.M. Baltes, eds. *Successful Aging: Perspectives from the Behavioral Sciences,* 50–93. Cambridge: Cambridge University Press.

8   Federal/Provincial/Territorial Subcommittee on Continuing Care. 1992. *Future Directions in Continuing Care.* Cat. No. H39-260/1002E. Ottawa: Minister of Supply and Services Canada.

8   Federal/Provincial/Territorial Working Group on Home Care. 1990. *Report on Home Care.* Cat. No. H39-186/1990E. Ottawa: Minister of Supply and Services Canada.

8   Fedorak, Sandra A., and Carole Griffin. 1986. "Developing a Self-Advocacy Program for Seniors: The Essential Component of Health Promotion." *Canadian Journal on Aging* 5:269–77.

8   Feeny, D. 1994. "Technology Assessment and Health Policy in Canada." In A. Blomqvist and D.M. Brown, eds. *Limits to Care: Reforming Canada's Health System in an Age of Restraint,* 293–326. Ottawa: C.D. Howe Institute.

14   Feigenberg, Loma. 1980. *Terminal Care: Friendship Contracts with Dying Cancer Patients.* New York: Brunner/Mazel.

5   Fernie, G. 1994. "Technology to Assist Elderly People's Safe Mobility." *Experimental Aging Research* 20(3):219–28.

12   Ferraro, Kenneth F., and Catherine Cobb. 1987. "Participation in Multipurpose Senior Centers." *Journal of Applied Gerontology* 6:429–47.

11   Filion, P., A.V. Wister, and E.J. Coblentz. 1992. "Subjective Dimensions of Environmental Adaptation among the Elderly: A Challenge to Models of Housing Policy." *Journal of Housing for the Elderly* 10(1–2):3–32.

10   Finlayson, Ann. 1985. "The Lure of Early Retirement." *Maclean's* (February 4).

2,3 Fischer, David Hackett. 1978. *Growing Old in America.* Expanded ed. New York: Oxford University Press.

12   Fischer, Andrew A. 1977. "The Effect of Aging and Physical Activity on the Stabile Component of Arterial Distensibility." In R.H. Harris and L.J. Frankel, eds. *Guide to Fitness after 50.* New York: Plenum Press.

14   Fisher, Rory H., Grant W. Nadon, and Ralph Shedletsky. 1983. "Management of the Dying Elderly Patient." *Journal of the American Geriatric Society* 31:563–64.

14   Fisher, Rory H., and Ralph Shedletsky. 1979. "A Retrospective Study of Terminal Care of Hospitalized Elderly." *Essence* 3:91–100.

8   Fisher, Rory H., and M.L. Zorzitto. 1983. "Placement Problem: Diagnosis, Disease or Term of Denigration?" *Canadian Medical Association Journal* 129:331–33.

12   Fitness and Amateur Sport. 1982. *Fitness and Aging: Canada Fitness Survey.* Ottawa: Minister of Supply and Services Canada.

13   Fitting, M., P. Rabins, M.J. Lucas, and J. Eastham. 1986. "Caregivers for Dementia Patients: A Comparison of Husbands and Wives." *The Gerontologist* 26:248–52.

8   Flathman, D.P., and D.E. Larsen. 1976. "Evaluation of Three Geriatric Day Hospitals in Alberta." Unpublished report, Division of Community Health Services, Faculty of Medicine. Calgary: University of Calgary.

1   Fletcher, S. 1990. "Seniors in the Marketplace." *Canadian Business Review* (Winter):36–39.

11   Fletcher, Susan, and Leroy O. Stone. 1980. "The Living Arrangements of Canada's Older Women." *Essence* 4:115–33.

6   Foisy, P. 1995. "Variations in Age-Related Deficits among Episodic Memory Tasks: An Archival Study. *Canadian Journal on Aging* 14(4):686–96.

10   Foot, D.K., and K.J. Gibson. 1993. "Population Aging in the Canadian Labour Force: Changes

and Challenges." *Journal of Canadian Studies* 28(1):59–74.

8 Forbes, W.F., J.A. Jackson, and A.S. Kraus. 1987. *Institutionalization of the Elderly in Canada.* Toronto: Butterworths.

1 Forbes, W.F., B.D. McPherson, and M.A. Shadbolt-Forbes. 1989. "The Validation of Longitudinal Studies: The Case of the Ontario Longitudinal Study of Aging (LSA)." *Canadian Journal on Aging* 8:51–67.

12 Forgas, J., and S. Moylan. 1987. "After the Movies: Transient Mood and Social Judgments." *Personality and Social Psychology Bulletin* 13: 467–77.

2 Foundations Project. 1980. "Foundations for Gerontological Education." *The Gerontologist* 20:Pt. II.

11 Fox, P.L. 1995. "Environmental Modifications in the Homes of Elderly Canadians with Disabilities." *Disability and Rehabilitation: An International Multidisciplinary Journal* 17(1):3–49.

5 Fozard, J.L. 1990. "Vision and Hearing." In James E. Birren and K. Warner Schaie, eds. *Handbook of the Psychology of Aging.* 3d ed. San Diego: Academic Press.

6 France, A.I. 1990. "Psychology of Aging: Stability and Change in Intelligence and Personality." In K.F. Ferraro, ed., *Gerontology: Perspectives and Issues*, 87–109. New York: Springer.

15 Frank, J. 1992. "Voting and Contributing: Political Participation in Canada." *Canadian Social Trends* (Winter):2–6.

7 Frankl, V. 1990. "Facing the Transitoriness of Human Existence." *Generations* 15(4):7–10.

11 Fraser, D. 1982. *Defining the Parameters of a Housing Policy for the Elderly.* Ottawa: Canada Mortgage and Housing Corporation.

9 Freeman, A. 1994. "CPP Dips into Surplus Fund." *The Globe and Mail* (April 21):B1–B2.

1 Freeman, J.T. 1979. *Aging: Its History and Literature.* New York: Human Sciences Press.

9 Frenken, H. 1995. "RRSPs—Unused Opportunities." *Perspectives* (Winter):20–25.

7 Frideres, J. 1994. "The Future of Our Past: Native Elderly in Canadian Society. In National Advisory Council on Aging, *Aboriginal Seniors' Issues*, 17–37. Cat. No. H71-2/1-15-1994E. Ottawa: Minister of Supply and Services Canada.

13 Friend, Richard A. 1991. "Older Lesbian and Gay People: A Theory of Successful Aging." In John Alan Lee, ed. *Gay Midlife and Maturity.* New York: Haworth.

5 Fries, James F. 1980. "Aging, Natural Death, and the Compression of Morbidity." *New England Journal of Medicine* 303:130–36.

5 Fries, James F. 1986. "The Elimination of Premature Disease." In Ken Dychtwald and Judy MacLean, eds. *Wellness and Health Promotion for the Elderly.* Rockville, MD: Aspen.

5 Fries, James F. 1990. "Medical Perspectives upon Successful Aging." In Paul B. Baltes and Margaret M. Baltes, eds. *Successful Aging: Perspectives from the Behavioural Sciences.* Cambridge: Cambridge University Press.

5 Fries, J.F., and L.M. Crapo. 1981. *Vitality and Aging.* San Francisco: W.H. Freeman.

4 Gagan, D. 1983a. "Geographical and Social Mobility in Nineteenth-Century Ontario: A Microstudy." In P.W. Ward, comp. *The Social Development of Canada: Readings.* Richmond, BC: Open Learning Institute.

3,4 Gagan, D. 1983b. "Land, Population, and Social Change: The 'Critical Years' in Rural Canada West." In P.W. Ward, comp. *The Social Development of Canada: Readings.* Richmond, BC: Open Learning Institute.

8 Garant, L. 1994. *Summary of an Evaluation Program on the Response to the Long-Term Care Requirements of Elderly People with Functional Limitations.* Québec: Direction de l'Évaluation, Ministère de la Santé et des Services Sociaux.

2 Garfinkel, Harold. 1967. *Studies in Ethnomethodology.* Englewood Cliffs, NJ: Prentice-Hall.

13 Gatz, Margaret, Vern L. Bengtson, and Mindy J. Blum. 1990. "Caregiving Families." In James E. Birren and K. Warner Schaie, eds. *Handbook of the Psychology of Aging.* 3d ed. San Diego: Academic Press.

8 Gaudette, Leslie, and Georgia Roberts. 1988. "Trends in Cancer since 1970." *Canadian Social Trends* (Autumn):8–13.

1,10 Gauthier, Pierre. 1991. "Canada's Seniors." *Canadian Social Trends* (Autumn):16–20.

12 Gauthier, P., and A. Haman. 1992. "Physical Fitness." *Canadian Social Trends* (Summer): 18–20.

6 Gauthier, Serge, Ian McDowell, and Gerry Hill. 1990. "Canadian Study of Health and Aging (CaSHA)." *Psychiatry Journal of the University of Ottawa* 1515:227–29.

14 Gee, Ellen M. 1985. "Historical Change in the Life Course of Canadian Women." Paper presented at the Canadian Association on Gerontology 14th Annual Scientific and Educational Meeting, Hamilton.

13 Gee, Ellen M. 1986. "The Life Course of Canadian Women: An Historical and Demo-

graphic Analysis." *Social Indicators Research* 18:263–83.

13 Gee, Ellen M. 1987. "Historical Change in the Family Life Course of Canadian Men and Women." In Victor W. Marshall, ed. *Aging in Canada: Social Perspectives.* 2d ed. Toronto: Fitzhenry and Whiteside.

13 Gee, Ellen M. 1988. "The Changing Demography of Intergenerational Relations in Canada." Paper presented at the 17th Annual Scientific and Educational Meeting of the Canadian Association on Gerontology, Halifax, October.

10,13 Gee, Ellen M., and Meredith M. Kimball. 1987. *Women and Aging.* Toronto: Butterworths.

15 Gee, E.M., and S.A. McDaniel. 1995. "Social Policy for an Aging Society." In M. Novak, ed. *Aging and Society: A Canadian Reader*, 436–42. Toronto: Nelson Canada.

15 Geoffroy, C. 1994. *Communication and Information Technologies and Older Adults (Summary).* A report published by CITI, Centre for Information Technology Innovation and One Voice—The Canadian Seniors Network. February.

13 George, Linda K. 1990. "Editorials: Caregiver Stress Studies—There Really Is More to Learn." *The Gerontologist* 30:580–81.

4 George, M.V., M.J. Norris, F. Nault, S. Loh, and S.Y. Dai. 1994. *Population Projections for Canada, Provinces and Territories 1993–2016.* Ottawa: Minister of Industry, Science and Technology.

4 Gerber, Linda M. 1983. "Ethnicity Still Matters: Socio-Demographic Profiles of the Ethnic Elderly in Ontario." *Canadian Ethnic Studies* 15:60–80.

14 Gesser, Gina, Paul T.P. Wong, and Gary T. Reker. 1986. "Death Attitudes across the Life-Span: The Development and Validation of the Death Attitude Profile (DAP)." Personal communication.

1 Gfellner, Barbara M. 1982. "Case Study Analysis: A Field Placement Program in the Study of Aging." Paper presented at the Canadian Association on Gerontology 11th Annual Scientific and Educational Meeting, Winnipeg.

9 Ghalam, N.Z. 1993. "Women in the Workplace." *Canadian Social Trends* (Spring):3–6.

9 Ghalam, N. 1995. "Income and Earnings." In Statistics Canada, *Women in Canada: A Statistical Report*, 3d ed., 84–100. Cat. No. 89-503E. Ottawa: Minister of Supply and Services Canada.

10 Gibson, K.J., Zerbe, W.J., and Franken, R.E. 1993. "The Influence of Rater and Ratee Age on Judgments of Work-Related Attributes." *Journal of Psychology* 127(3):271–80.

7 Gibson, Rose C. 1988. "Minority Aging Research: Opportunity and Challenge." *The Gerontologist* 28:559–60.

6 Gibson, R.W. 1970. "Medicare and the Psychiatric Patient." *Psychiatric Opinion* 7:17–22.

15 Gifford, C.G. 1982. "Senior Power in Canada." Poster presentation at the Canadian Association on Gerontology 11th Annual Scientific and Educational Meeting, Winnipeg.

15 Gifford, C.G. 1983. "Senior Politics." *Policy Options* (September):12–15.

15 Gifford, C. 1985. "Grey Is Strong." *Policy Options* 6:16–18.

15 Gifford, C.G. 1987. Personal communication.

15 Gifford, C.G. 1990. *Canada's Fighting Seniors.* Toronto: James Lorimer and Co.

3 Gillin, C.T. 1986. "Aging in the Developing World." Paper presented at the Canadian Sociology and Anthropology Association 21st Annual Meeting, Winnipeg.

13 Gladstone, James W. 1987. "Factors Associated with Changes in Visiting between Grandmothers and Grandchildren Following an Adult Child's Marriage Breakdown." *Canadian Journal on Aging* 6:117–27.

13 Gladstone, James W. 1988. "Perceived Changes in Grandmother-Grandchild Relations Following a Child's Separation or Divorce." *The Gerontologist* 28:66–72.

13 Gladstone, James W. 1989. "Grandmother-Grandchild Contact: The Mediating Influence of the Middle Generation Following Marriage Breakdown and Remarriage." *Canadian Journal on Aging* 8:355–65.

13 Gladstone, James W. 1991. "An Analysis of Changes in Grandparent–Grandchild Visitation Following an Adult Child's Remarriage." *Canadian Journal on Aging* 10:113–26.

8 Gladstone, James W. 1992. "Identifying the Living Arrangements of Elderly Married Couples in Long-Term Care Institutions." *Canadian Journal on Aging* 11:184–96.

13 Gladstone, J.W. 1995. "The Marital Perceptions of Elderly Persons Living or Having a Spouse Living in a Long-Term Care Institution in Canada." *The Gerontologist* 35(1):52–60.

3 Glascock, A.P., and S.L. Feinman. 1981. "Social Asset or Social Burden: Treatment of the Aged in Non-industrial Societies." In C.L. Fry, ed. *Dimensions: Aging, Culture, and Health.* New York: Praeger.

14   Glaser, Barney G., and Anselm L. Strauss. 1977. "The Ritual Drama of Mutual Pretense." In Steven H. Zarit, ed. *Readings in Aging and Death: Contemporary Perspectives*. Harper and Row: New York.

14   Glass, K.C. 1993. "Ethical Principles and Age-Based Rationing of Health Care." In National Advisory Council on Aging, *Ethics and Aging*, 69–83. Cat. No. H71-3/16-1993E. Ottawa: Minister of Supply and Services Canada.

5   Glass, P-Y. 1995. "He Didn't Know She'd Live Forever." *Winnipeg Free Press* (December 29):1.

8   Glazebrook, K., K. Rockwood, P. Stolee, J. Fisk, and J.M. Gray. 1994. "A Case Control Study of the Risks for Institutionalization of Elderly People in Nova Scotia." *Canadian Journal on Aging* 13(1):104–17.

3   *Globe and Mail, The.* 1983. "Latin Americans Seek Refuge in Debtors' Club." (July 11).

15   *Globe and Mail, The.* 1985. "Seniors Urge Wilson to Drop De-Indexing Plan." (June 18).

4   *Globe and Mail, The.* 1993. "Will We Still Feed Them, When They're 64?" Editorial (November 15).

13   Globerman, J. 1994. "Balancing Tensions in Families with Alzheimer's Disease: The Self and the Family." *Journal of Aging Studies* 8(2):211–32.

8   Glor, Eleanor D. 1991. "An Effective Evaluation of a Small-Scale Seniors Health Promotion Centre: A Case Study." *Canadian Journal on Aging* 10:64–73.

13   Gnaedinger, Nancy. 1989. *Housing Alzheimer's Disease at Home*. Ottawa: Canada Mortgage and Housing Corporation.

6   Gold, D.P., D. Andres, J. Etezadi, T. Arbuckle, and A. Schwartzman. 1995. "Structural Equation Model of Intellectual Change and Continuity and Predictors of Intelligence in Older Men." *Psychology and Aging* 10(2):294–303.

7   Gold, Yhetta. 1980. "Ethnic and Cultural Aspects of Aging." Paper presented at the 9th Annual Scientific and Educational Meeting of the Canadian Association on Gerontology. Saskatoon.

5,12   Goldberg, Andrew P., and James M. Hagberg. 1990. "Physical Exercise and the Elderly." In Edward L. Schneider and John W. Rowe, eds. *Handbook of the Biology of Aging*. 3d ed. San Diego: Academic Press.

14   Goldberg, Helene S. 1981–82. "Funeral and Bereavement Rituals of Kota Indians and Orthodox Jews." *Omega* 12:117–28.

6   Goldmeier, John. 1986. "Pets or People: Another Research Note." *The Gerontologist* 26:203–6.

10   Goodwin, J.L., and M.Y.T. Chen. 1991. "From Pastor to Pensioner: A Study of Retired Canadian Protestant Clergy from the Continuity Perspective." *Journal of Religious Gerontology* 7(3):69–79.

7   Gordon, S. 1976. *Lonely in America*. New York: Simon and Schuster.

14   Gorer, Geoffrey. 1965. *Death, Grief and Mourning in Contemporary Britain*. London: Cresset.

14   Gorer, Geoffrey. 1967. *Death, Grief and Mourning*. New York: Anchor.

13   Gottlieb, Benjamin H. 1989. "A Contextual Perspective on Stress in Family Care of the Elderly." *Canadian Psychology* 30:596–606.

13   Gottlieb, B.H. 1992. "Editorial: Social Support: A Relationship Process, Not a Commodity." *Canadian Journal on Aging* 11(4):306–10.

13   Gottlieb, B.H., and K. Kelloway. 1993. "Eldercare and Employment." *Human Resources Management in Canada* (June):597–604.

13   Gottlieb, B.H., E.K. Kelloway, and M. Fraboni. 1994. "Aspects of Eldercare That Place Employees at Risk." *Gerontologist* 34(6):815–21.

7   Gould, R.L. 1978. *Transformations: Growth and Change in Adult Life*. New York: Simon and Schuster.

9   Government of Canada. 1982a. *Better Pensions for Canadians (Green Paper)*. Ottawa: Minister of Supply and Services.

9   Government of Canada. 1982b. *Better Pensions for Canadians: Focus on Women*. Ottawa: Minister of Supply and Services.

11,15   Government of Canada. 1988. *Seniors' Guide to Federal Programs and Services*. Cat. No. H71-3/8-1988E. Ottawa: Minister of National Health and Welfare.

4   Government of Canada. 1989. "Seniors—Aging in a Multicultural Canada." *Seniors Info Exchange* (Fall):10.

4,9,10   Government of Canada. 1993. "Our Aging Society—A Look at the Stats." *Seniors Info Exchange* 5(2):6.

9   Government of Canada. 1996a. "Government Proposes New Seniors Benefit." News release. March 6.

9   Government of Canada. 1996b. "Information. The Canada Pension Plan: Basic Facts." *World Wide Web* (March 26).

13   Government of Canada Seniors Secretariat. 1992. *A Shared Concern*. Cat. No. H88-3/12-1991E. Ottawa: Minister of Supply and Services Canada.

1,2   Government of Manitoba. 1973. *Aging in Manitoba*. 10 vols. Winnipeg: Department of Health and Social Development.

10   Gower, D. 1995. "Men Retiring Early: How Are They Doing?" *Perspectives* (Winter):30–34.

12   Graham, D.F., I. Graham, and M.J. MacLean. 1991. "Going to the Mall: A Leisure Activity of Urban Elderly People." *Canadian Journal on Aging* 10(4):345–58.

3   Graham, Ian D., and Paul M. Baker. 1989. "Status, Age, and Gender: Perceptions of Old and Young People." *Canadian Journal on Aging* 8:255–67.

12   Grant McEwan Community College. n.d. *Senior Studies Institute*. Pamphlet. Edmonton: Grant McEwan.

11   Grant, Peter R. 1983. "Creating a Feasible Transportation System for Rural Areas: Reflections on a Symposium." *Canadian Journal on Aging* 2:30–35.

11   Grant, Peter R., and Bruce Rice. 1983. "Transportation Problems of the Rural Elderly: A Needs Assessment." *Canadian Journal on Aging* 2:107–24.

10   Grauer, H., and N.M. Campbell. 1983. "The Aging Physician and Retirement." *Canadian Journal of Psychiatry* 28:552–54.

3   Greene, J.P., ed. 1965. *Diary of Colonel Landon Carter of Sabine Hall, 1752–1778*. 2 vols. Charlottesville, VA.

1   Greenslade, V. 1986. "Evaluation of Postgraduate Gerontological Nursing Education." Unpublished manuscript.

11   Grescoe, Audrey. 1981. "Little Old Lady in a Hard Hat." *Today Magazine* (January 17).

12   Grescoe, Audrey. 1982. "Good Old." *Today Magazine* (January 9).

8   Gross, John, and Cope Schwenger. 1981. "Health Care Costs for the Elderly in Ontario: 1976–2026." Occasional Paper 11. Toronto: Ontario Economic Council.

11   Gross, L.P. 1985. "Federal Housing Programs." In Gloria Gutman and Norman Blackie, eds. *Innovations in Housing and Living Arrangements for Seniors*. Burnaby, BC: The Gerontology Research Centre, Simon Fraser University.

13   Grube, J. 1991. "Natives and Settlers: An Ethnographic Note on Early Interaction of Older Homosexual Men with Younger Gay Liberationists." In J.A. Lee, ed. *Gay Midlife and Maturity*, 119–35. New York: Haworth Press.

5   Grundy, E. 1984. "Mortality and Morbidity among the Old." *British Medical Journal* 288:663–64.

13   Guberman, N., P. Maheu, and C. Maillé. 1992. "Women as Family Caregivers: Why Do They Care?" *The Gerontologist* 32(5):607–17.

2   Gubrium, Jaber F. 1986. *Oldtimers and Alzheimer's: The Descriptive Organization of Senility*. Greenwich, CT: JAI Press.

3   Guemple, L. 1977. "The Dilemma of the Aging Eskimo." In Christopher Beattie and Stewart Chrysdale, eds. *Sociology Canada: Readings*. 2d ed. Toronto: Butterworths.

3   Guemple, L. 1980. "Growing Old in Inuit Society." In Victor W. Marshall, ed. *Aging in Canada: Social Perspectives*. Toronto: Fitzhenry and Whiteside.

10   Guillemard, A.M. 1977. "The Call to Activity amongst the Old: Rehabilitation or Regimentation." In Blossom T. Wigdor, ed. *Canadian Gerontological Collection I*. Winnipeg: Canadian Association on Gerontology.

2   Guillemard, A.M., ed. 1983. *Old Age in the Welfare State*. Beverly Hills, CA: Sage.

10   Guppy, Neil. 1989. "The Magic of 65: Issues and Evidence in the Mandatory Retirement Debate." *Canadian Journal on Aging* 8:174–86.

6   Gurland, B.J. 1976. "The Comparative Frequency of Depression in Various Adult Age Groups." *Journal of Gerontology* 31:283–92.

6   Gurland, B.J., J. Copeland, J. Kuriansky, M. Kelleher, L. Sharpe, and L.L. Dean. 1983. *The Mind and Mood of Aging: Mental Health Problems of the Community Elderly in New York and London*. New York: Haworth Press.

6   Gurland, B.J., and J.A. Toner. 1983. "Depression in the Elderly: A Review of Recently Published Studies." *Annual Review of Gerontology and Geriatrics* 3:228–65.

3,11 Gutman, Gloria. 1978. "Issues and Findings Relating to Multi-Level Accommodation for Seniors." *Journal of Gerontology* 33:592–600.

11   Gutman, Gloria. 1983. *The Long Term Impact of Multi-Level, Multi-Service Accommodation for Seniors*. Senior Citizen Housing Study Report No. 3. Ottawa: Canada Mortgage and Housing Corporation.

11   Gutman, Gloria, and Norman Blackie, eds. 1985. *Innovations in Housing and Living Arrangements for Seniors*. Burnaby, BC: The Gerontology Research Centre, Simon Fraser University.

11   Gutman, G.M., V. Doyle, K. Melliship, and P. Baldwin. 1989. *Survey of Canadian Homesharing Agencies Serving the Elderly*. Report sponsored by Health and Welfare Canada.

8   Gutman, Gloria, and Carol P. Herbert. 1976. "Mortality Rates among Relocated Extended Care Patients." *Journal of Gerontology* 31:352–57.

12   Gutman, G., C.P. Herbert, and S.R. Brown. 1977. "Feldenkrais Versus Conventional

Exer-cises for the Elderly." *Journal of Gerontology* 32:562–72.

8   Gutman, G., C. Jackson, A.J. Stark, and B. McCashin. 1986. "Mortality Rates Five Years after Admission to a Long-Term Care Program." *Canadian Journal on Aging* 5:9–17.

3,10   Haber, Carole. 1978. "Mandatory Retirement in Nineteenth-Century America: The Conceptual Basis for a New York Cycle." *Journal of Social History* 12:77–96.

3   Haber, C. 1983. *Beyond Sixty-Five: The Dilemma of Old Age in America's Past.* Cambridge: Cambridge University Press.

3   Haber, C. 1993. "'And the Fear of the Poorhouse': Perceptions of Old Age Impoverishment in Early Twentieth-Century America." *Generations* (Spring/(Summer):46–50.

5   Haber, Paul A.L. 1986. "Technology in Aging." *The Gerontologist* 26:350–57.

13   Hadjistavropoulos, T., S. Taylor, H. Tuokko, and B.L. Beattie. 1994. "Neuropsychological Deficits, Caregivers' Perception of Deficits and Caregiver Burden." *The Journal of the American Geriatrics Society* 42:308–14.

13   Hagestad, Gunhild O. 1985. "Continuity and Connectedness." In Vern L. Bengtson and Joan F. Robertson, eds. *Grandparenthood.* Beverly Hills, CA: Sage.

13   Hagestad, Gunhild O. 1986. "The Aging Society as a Context for Family Life." *Daedalus* 115: 119–39.

7   Hagestad, Gunhild O. 1990. "Social Perspectives on the LifeCourse." In Robert H. Binstock and Linda K. George, eds. *Handbook of Aging and the Social Sciences.* 3d ed. San Diego: Academic Press.

11   Haldemann, V., and A. Wister. 1992. "Environment and Aging." *Journal of Canadian Studies* 28(1):30–44.

13   Hall, Barry L. 1989. "The Role of Adult Children in Helping Chronically Ill Hospitalized Parents." *Canadian Journal on Aging* 8:68–78.

7   Hall, B.L. 1993. "Elderly Vietnamese Immigrants: Family and Community Connections." *Community Alternatives* 5(2):81–96.

11   Hamilton, K., and T. Brehaut. 1992. *Older Women: A Study of the Housing and Support Service Needs of Older 'Single' Women.* A report for the Canada Mortgage and Housing Corporation. Charlottetown: Renaissance Communi-cations.

8   Hamilton, N., and T. Bhatti. 1996. *Population Health Promotion: An Integrated Model of Population Health and Health Promotion.* Ottawa: Health Promotion Development Division, Health Canada.

16   Hancock, Gordon. 1984. *A Study of Gerontology Activities and of Centres of Gerontology on University Campuses in the United States and Canada.* Winnipeg: Centre on Aging, University of Manitoba.

8   Hansen, Signy, and Gary Ledoux. 1985. "Developing a Health Promotion Resource for Older Adults." Paper presented at the Meeting of the International Association of Gerontology, New York.

8   Harbison, Joan, and Patricia M. Melanson. 1987. "Interdisciplinary Collaboration between the Professional Social Worker and Nurse in Planning the Care of the Older Adult Living in a Long-term Care Facility." *Canadian Journal on Aging* 6:155–69.

1   Harding, Michele, and Sheila Neysmith. 1984. "Ageism and Health Costs: Reality and Implications." Paper presented at the Canadian Association on Gerontology 13th Annual Scientific and Educational Meeting, Vancouver.

11   Harper, I. 1984. "Housing Options for the Elderly in the Capital Region: Sheltered Housing and Other Alternatives." Victoria, BC: Capital Regional Hospital District, Hospital and Health Planning Commission.

1   Harris, Louis, et al. 1975. *Myth and Reality of Aging in America.* Washington, DC: National Council on Aging.

14   Harrison, Albert A., and Neal E.A. Kroll. 1985–86. "Variations in Death Rates in the Proximity of Christmas: An Opponent Process Interpretation." *Omega* 16:181–92.

14   Harrison, Albert A., and M. Moore. 1982–83. "Birth Dates and Death Dates: A Closer Look." *Omega* 13:117–25.

6   Harrison, C. 1993. "Personhood, Dementia and Integrity of Life." *Canadian Journal on Aging* 12(4):428–40.

14   Harvard Medical School. 1968. "A Definition of Irreversible Coma: Report of the Ad Hoc Committee of the Harvard Medical School to Examine the Definition of Brain Death." *Journal of the American Medical Association* 205:337–40.

12   Harvey, A.S., K. Marshall, and J.A. Frederick. 1991. *Where Does Time Go?* Cat. No. 11-612E, No. 4. Ottawa: Ministry of Industry, Science and Technology.

12   Harvey, A.S., and J.F. Singleton. 1989. "Canadian Activity Patterns across the Life Span: A Time Budget Perspective." *Canadian Journal on Aging* 8:268–85.

13 Harvey, Carol H. 1984. "Decision-Making by Middle-Aged Widows in Winnipeg." Paper presented at the Beatrice Paolucci Symposium, Michigan State University, East Lansing, MI.

2,8,11 Havens, Betty. 1980. "Differentiation of Unmet Needs Using Analysis by Age/Sex Cohorts." In Victor W. Marshall, ed. *Aging in Canada*. Toronto: Fitzhenry and Whiteside.

8 Havens, B. 1995a. "Long-Term Care Diversity within the Care Continuum." *Canadian Journal on Aging* 14(2):245–62.

1,2 Havens, B. 1995b. "Overview of Longitudinal Research on Aging." *Canadian Journal on Aging* 14(supp. 1.):119–34.

8 Havens, B. 1995c. "Canadian Long-Term Care Use: What Is the Future?" In S.R. Ingman, X. Pei, C.D. Ekstrom, H.J. Friedsam, and K.R. Bartlett, eds. *An Aging Population, an Aging Planet, and a Sustainable Future*. Denton, TX: Texas Institute for Research and Education on Aging, University of North Texas.

7 Havens, Betty, and N.L. Chappell. 1983. "Triple Jeopardy: Age, Sex and Ethnicity." *Canadian Ethnic Studies* 15:119–32.

12 Hawkins, Terry. 1980. *Never Too Old: A Report to the Northumberland Newcastle Board of Education on the Educational Needs of Senior Adults Living in the Area Served by Its Schools*. Northumberland Newcastle, ON: Board of Education.

12 Hayashida, David. 1983. "Take a Closer Look at the National Parks." *Recreation Canada* (February):16–18.

5 Hayflick, L. 1974. "The Strategy of Senescence." *The Gerontologist* 14:37–45.

10 Haynes, Suzanne G., Anthony J. McMichael, and H.A. Tyroler. 1977. "The Relationship of Normal Involuntary Retirement to Early Mortality among U.S. Rubber Workers." *Social Science and Medicine* 11:105–14.

13 Health Canada. 1993–94. "Update on GRAND." *Seniors INFO Exchange*. Ottawa: Health Canada, 11.

7,14 Health Canada. 1994. *Suicide in Canada: Update of the Report of the Task Force on Suicide in Canada*. Cat. No. 39-107/1995E. Ottawa: Minister of National Health and Welfare.

8 Health Canada. Health Information Division. 1993. *Green Book Tables: Provincial Government Health Expenditures and Related Federal Contribution, Canada, the Provinces and the Territories 1974–75 to 1990–91*. Ottawa: Author.

8 Health Canada. Health Information Division. 1994. *Health Expenditures in Canada: Provincial/Territorial Summary Report 1987– 1991*. February. Ottawa: Author.

8 Health Care. 1980. "Restrained in Canada—Free in Britain." *Health Care* 22:22.

16 Health and Welfare Canada. 1977a. *Medical Education in Geriatrics*. Health Manpower Report No. 1/77. Ottawa: Minister of Supply and Services.

11,12 Health and Welfare Canada. 1977b. *Social Security Research Reports. Retirement in Canada: Summary Report* (Report No. 03) Ottawa: Long Range Planning Directorate, Policy Research and Long Range Planning Branch (Welfare): National Health and Welfare.

7 Health and Welfare Canada. 1977c. *Who Commits Suicide in Old Age and Why?* Ottawa: Health and Welfare Canada.

10 Health and Welfare Canada. 1979. *Retirement Age*. Ottawa: Minister of Supply and Services.

9 Health and Welfare Canada. 1982a. *Better Pensions for Canadians: Highlights*. Ottawa: Minister of Supply and Services.

1,2,8,10,11,12 Health and Welfare Canada. 1982b. *Canadian Governmental Report on Aging*. Ottawa: Minister of Supply and Services.

12 Health and Welfare Canada. 1982c. *New Horizons: First Decade*. Ottawa: Minister of Supply and Services.

14 Health and Welfare Canada. 1982d. *Palliative Care in Canada*. Ottawa: Minister of Supply and Services.

4,5,8,12,13,15,16 Health and Welfare Canada. 1983. *Fact Book on Aging in Canada*. Ottawa: Minister of Supply and Services.

6 Health and Welfare Canada. 1984a. *Alzheimer's Disease: A Family Information Handbook*. Ottawa: Minister of Supply and Services.

8 Health and Welfare Canada. 1984b. *National Health Expenditures in Canada, 1970–1982*. Ottawa: Minister of Supply and Services.

16 Health and Welfare Canada, Health Information Division. 1985. *Canada Health Manpower Inventory 1985*. Ottawa: Minister of Supply and Services.

1,8 Health and Welfare Canada. 1988a. *Active Health Report: The Active Health Report on Seniors*. Cat No. H-39-124/1988E. Ottawa: Minister of Supply and Services.

8,9 Health and Welfare Canada. 1988b. *Canada's Health Promotion Survey: Technical Report*. Cat No. H39-119/1988E. Ottawa: Minister of Supply and Services.

11 Health and Welfare Canada. 1989–90. "55 Alive: What Is It?" *Seniors Info Exchange*. Ottawa: Minister of Supply and Services.

5,6,8,12 Health and Welfare Canada and Statistics Canada. 1981. *The Health of Canadians (The*

Canada Health Survey). Cat. No. 82-538E. Ottawa: Minister of Supply and Services.

15   Heclo, H. 1988. "Generational Politics." In J.L. Palmer, T. Smeeding, and B.B. Torrey, eds. *The Vulnerable.* Washington, DC: Urban Institute Press.

16   Heinemann, G.D., E.B. Douglass, and J.C. Lobenstine. 1995. *Careers in Aging: Consider the Possibilities.* Washington, DC: Association for Gerontology in Higher Education.

1   Hendrick, J.J., V.J. Knox, W.L. Gekoski, and K.J. Dyne. 1988. "Perceived Cognitive Ability of Young and Old Targets." *Canadian Journal on Aging* 7:192–203.

2,3   Hendricks, Jon. 1982. "The Elderly in Society: Beyond Modernization." *Social Science History* 6:321–45.

2   Hendricks, Jon, and C. Davis Hendricks. 1981. *Aging in Mass Society: Myths and Realities.* 2d ed. Cambridge, MA: Winthrop.

6,15   Hendricks, Jon, and C. Davis Hendricks. 1986. *Aging in Mass Society: Myths and Realities.* 3d ed. Boston: Little, Brown and Company.

4   Henripin, J. 1972. *Trends and Factors of Fertility in Canada.* Ottawa: Statistics Canada (Dominion Bureau of Statistics).

3   Henripin, J. 1994. "The Financial Consequences of Population Aging." *Canadian Public Policy* 20(1):78–94.

4   Henripin, J., and Y. Peron. 1972. "The Demographic Transition of the Province of Quebec." In D. Glass and R. Revelle, eds. *Population and Social Change.* London: Edward Arnold.

14   Henteleff, Paul D. 1978. "Decisions in the Care of the Dying." *Essence* 2:15–17.

6   Herchak, Gail, and Brian Wilford. 1983. "The Therapy of Pets." *Alberta Report* (November 28).

6   Hermann, N. 1991. "Confusion and Dementia in the Elderly." In National Advisory Council on Aging, *Mental Health and Aging,* 31–48. Ottawa: NACA.

6, 16   Hermann, N., I.I. Shulman, and I.L. Silver. 1992. "Intensive Early Exposure to Geriatric Psychiatry in Residency Training: Impact on Career Choice and Practice." *Canadian Journal of Psychiatry* 37(8):549–52.

11,13   Hess, Beth B., and Beth J. Soldo. 1985. "Husband and Wife Networks." In W.J. Sauer and R.T. Cowards, eds. *Social Support Networks and the Care of the Elderly.* New York: Springer.

11   Heumann, L., and D. Boldy. 1982. *Housing for the Elderly.* New York: St. Martin's Press.

13   Hickey, Tom, and Richard L. Douglass. 1981. "Neglect and Abuse of Older Family Members: Professionals' Perspectives and Case Experiences." *The Gerontologist* 21:171–76.

1   Higgs, A. 1994. "Rating the Gerontology Journals." *Gerontology Research Centre News* (January): 8–9.

1,2   Hirdes, J.P., and K.S. Brown. 1994. "The Statistical Analysis of Event Histories in Longitudinal Studies of Aging." *Canadian Journal on Aging* 13(3):332–52.

8   Hirdes, J.P., K.S. Brown, W.F. Forbes, D. Vigoda, and L. Crawford. 1986. "The Association between Self-Reported Income and Perceived Health Based on the Ontario Longitudinal Study of Aging." *Canadian Journal on Aging* 6:189–204.

1,5   Hirdes, J.P., and W.F. Forbes. 1993. "Factors Associated with the Maintenance of Good Self-Rated Health." *Journal of Aging and Health* 5(1):101–22.

13   Hirdes, J.P., and L.A. Strain. 1995. "The Balance of Exchange in Instrumental Support with Network Members Outside the Household." *Journal of Gerontology: Social Sciences* 50B(3):S134–S142.

16   Hirst, S.P., J. Miller, and L. Wenger. 1992. "Factors Influencing the Selection of a Gerontology Certificate Program." *Educational Gerontology* 18:555–66.

11   Hodge, Gerald. 1984a. *Shelter and Services for the Small Town Elderly: The Role of Assisted Housing.* Ottawa: Canada Mortgage and Housing Corporation.

12   Hodge, Gerald. 1984b. "Time and the Environment of the Small Town Elderly." Paper presented at the Canadian Association on Gerontology 13th Annual Scientific and Educational Meeting, Vancouver.

11   Hodge, Gerald. 1987a. "Assisted Housing for Ontario's Rural Elderly: Shortfalls in Product and Location." *Canadian Journal on Aging* 6:141–54.

11   Hodge, G. 1987b. *The Elderly in Canada's Small Towns.* Vancouver: The Centre for Human Settlements. University of British Columbia

11   Hodge, G., and L. McKay. 1992. *Small Town Seniors and Their Freedom to Move.* Final report on Seniors' Independence Project No.4687-9-88/029. Vancouver: Simon Fraser Univer-sity Gerontology Research Centre.

3   Holmes, E.R., and L.D. Holmes. 1995. *Other Cultures, Elder Years.* 2d ed. Thousand Oaks, CA: SAGE.

7,13   Holmes, T.H., and R.H. Rahe. 1967. "The Social Readjustment Rating Scale." *Journal of Psychosomatic Research* 11:213–18.

6   Holt, J. 1978. *Never Too Late*. New York: Delacorte Press.

1,7   Holzberg, Carol S. 1981. "Cultural Gerontology: Toward an Understanding of Ethnicity and Aging." *Culture* 1:110–22.

7   Holzberg, Carol S. 1982. "Ethnicity and Aging: Anthropological Perspectives on More than Just the Minority Elderly." *The Gerontologist* 22:249–57.

2   Homans, George C. 1961. *Social Behaviour: Its Elementary Forms*. New York: Harcourt Brace Jovanovich.

12   Homebound Learning Opportunities. 1989. "1988–1989 Program Statistics and Comments About HLO." Personal communication.

13   Hooyman, Nancy R. 1990. "Women as Caregivers of the Elderly: Implications for Social Welfare Policy and Practice." In David E. Biegel and Arthur Blum, eds. *Aging and Caregiving: Theory, Research, and Policy*. Newbury Park, CA: Sage.

1   Hooyman,. N.R., and H.A. Kiyak. 1993. *Social Gerontology: A Multidisciplinary Perspective*. 3d ed. Boston: Allyn and Bacon.

6   Horn, J.L. 1978. "Human Ability Systems." In P.B. Baltes, ed. *Life-Span Development and Behavior*. Vol. 1. New York: Academic Press.

6   Horn, J.L., and R.B. Cattel. 1966. "Age Differences in Primary Mental Ability Factors." *Journal of Gerontology* 21:210–20.

6   Horn, J.L., and R.B. Cattell. 1967. "Age Differences in Fluid and Crystallized Intelligence." *Acta Psychologica* 26:107–29.

13   Horowitz, Amy. 1985. "Sons and Daughters as Caregivers to Older Parents: Differences in Role Performance and Consequences." *The Gerontologist* 25:612–17.

13   Horowitz, Amy, and L.W. Shindelman. 1981. "Reciprocity and Affection: Past Influences on Current Caregiving." Paper presented at the 34th Annual Scientific Meeting of the Gerontological Society of America.

11   Hough, George S. 1981. *Tenant Receptiveness: Family and Senior Citizen Mixing in Public Housing*. Toronto: Policy and Program Development Secretariat, Ministry of Municipal Affairs and Housing.

9   House of Commons Canada. 1983. *Report of the Parliamentary Task Force on Pension Reform (Frith Commission)*. Ottawa: Supply and Services Canada.

6   Howard, D.V., M.P. McAndrews, and M.I. Lasagna. 1981. "Semantic Priming of Lexical Decisions in Young and Old Adults." *Journal of Gerontology* 36:707–14.

3   Howells, W.W. 1960. "Estimating Population Numbers through Archaeological and Skeletal Remains." In R.F. Heizer, and C.F. Cook, eds. *The Application of Quantitative Methods to Archaeology*. Chicago: Quadrangle.

15   Hudson, R.B., and J. Strate. 1985. "Aging and Political Systems." In Robert Binstock and Ethel Shanas, eds. *Handbook of Aging and the Social Sciences*. 2d ed. New York: Van Nostrand Reinhold.

3   Hufton, O. 1975. *The Poor in Eighteenth-Century France*. Oxford: Oxford University Press.

7   Hughes, E.C., and H.M. Hughes. 1952. *Where Peoples Meet*. Glencoe, IL: Free Press.

6   Hultsch, David F., and Francine Deutsch. 1981. *Adult Development and Aging. A Life-Span Perspective*. New York: McGraw-Hill.

6   Hultsch, David F., and Roger A. Dixon. 1983. "The Role of Pre-Experimental Knowledge in Text Processing in Adulthood." *Experimental Aging Research* 9:7–22.

6   Hultsch, David F., and Roger A. Dixon. 1990. "Learning and Memory in Aging." In James E. Birren and K. Warner Schaie, eds. *Handbook of the Psychology of Aging*. 3d ed. San Diego: Academic Press.

6   Hultsch, D.F., C. Hertzog, and R.A. Dixon. 1987. "Age Differences in Metamemory: Resolving the Inconsistencies." *Canadian Journal of Psychology* 41:193–208.

6   Hultsch, D.F., C. Hertzog, B.J. Small, L. McDonald-Miszczak, and R.A. Dixon. 1992. "Short-Term Longitudinal Change in Cognitive Performance in Later Life." *Psychology and Aging* 7(4):571–84.

3   *Human Behavior Magazine*. 1977. "Retirement to the Porch." In Steven H. Zarit, ed. *Readings in Aging and Death: Contemporary Perspectives*. New York: Harper and Row.

9   Human Resources Development Canada. 1996. *Income Security Programs, April 1996*. Ottawa: Government of Canada.

6   Iglauer, Edith. 1980. "The Unsinkable Hubert Evans." *Today Magazine* (December 20).

3   Ikels, C. 1981. "The Coming of Age in Chinese Society: Traditional Patterns and Contemporary Hong Kong." In C.L. Fry, ed. *Dimensions: Aging, Culture, and Health*. New York: Praeger.

2   Inter-Council Program Directorate. 1988. *Open Letter and Call for Proposal Submissions for Networks of Centres of Excellence*. Ottawa: Government of Canada.

12   Iso-Ahola, S.E. 1989. "Motivation for Leisure." In E.L. Jackson and T. Burton, eds. *Understanding*

Leisure and Recreation. State College, PA: Venture Publishing.

12 Iso-Ahola, S.E. 1993. "Leisure Lifestyles and Health." In D. Compton and S.E. Iso-Ahola, eds. *Leisure and Mental Health.* Park City, UT: Family Development Resources Inc.

8   Jackson, J.S., T.C. Antonucci, and R.C. Gibson. 1990. "Cultural, Racial, and Ethnic Minority Influences on Aging." In J.E. Birren and K.W. Schaie, eds. *Handbook of the Psychology of Aging.* 3d ed. San Diego: Academic Press.

8   Jackson, Marilyn F. 1983. "Day Care for Handicapped Elders: An Evaluation Study." *Canadian Journal of Public Health* 74:348–51.

15 Jacobs, Bruce. 1990. "Aging and Politics." In Robert H. Binstock and Linda K. George, eds. *Handbook of Aging and the Social Sciences.* 3d ed. San Diego: Academic Press.

15 Jacobs, Ruth Harriet, and Beth B. Hess. 1980. "Panther Power: Symbol and Substance." In Jill S. Quadagno, ed. *Aging, the Individual and Society.* New York: St. Martin's Press.

6   Jacquish, G.A., and R.E. Ripple. 1981. "Cognitive Creative Abilities and Self-Esteem across the Adult Life-Span." *Human Development* 24:110–19.

12 Jahn, Penelope. 1982. "Good Old." *Today Magazine* (January 9).

1   Janelli, L.M. 1993. "Grandparents' Depictions in Children's Literature: A Revisit." *Gerontology and Geriatrics Education* 14(2):43–52.

13 Johnson, Colleen J. 1985. "Grandparenting Options in Divorcing Families: An Anthropological Perspective." In Vern L. Bengtson and Joan F. Robertson, eds. *Grandparenthood.* Beverly Hills, CA: Sage.

10 Johnson, E.S., and J.B. Williamson. 1987. "Retirement in the United States." In K.S. Markides and C.L. Cooper, eds. *Retirement in Industrialized Societies.* New York: Wiley.

5   Johnson, M.A., and D. Choy. 1987. "On the Definition of Age-Related Norms for Visual Function Testing." *Applied Optics* 26:1449–54.

6   Jones, H.E., and H.S. Conrad. 1933. "The Growth and Decline of Intelligence." *Genetic Psychology Monographs* 12:223–98.

11 Joseph, Alun E., and Anthony M. Fuller. 1991. "Towards an Integrative Perspective on the Housing, Services and Transportation Implications of Rural Aging." *Canadian Journal on Aging* 10:127–48.

2,11 Joseph, A.E., and A. Martin-Matthews. 1993. "Growing Old in Aging Communities." *Journal of Canadian Studies* 28(1):14–29.

7   Jung, C.G. 1976. "The Stages of Life." In Joseph Campbell, ed. *The Portable Jung.* Harmondsworth, England: Penguin.

13 Jutras, Sylvie. 1988. "Formal and Informal Caregivers: Towards a Partnership in Prevention." *Health Promotion* (Fall):9–12.

13 Jutras, S., and J-P Lavoie. 1995. "Living with an Impaired Elderly Person: The Informal Caregiver's Physical and Mental Health." *Journal of Aging and Health* 7(1):46–73.

13 Jutras, Sylvie, and France Veilleux. 1991. "Informal Caregiving: Correlates of Perceived Burden." *Canadian Journal on Aging* 10:40–55.

13 Kaden, Joan, and Susan A. McDaniel. 1990. "Caregiving and Care-Receiving: A Double Bind for Women in Canada's Aging Society." *Journal of Women and Aging* 2:3–26.

13 Kahana, B., and E. Kahana. 1970. "Grandparenthood from the Perspective of the Developing Grandchild." *Developmental Psychology* 3:98–105.

11 Kaill, Robert C. 1980. "Housing Canada's Aging." *Essence* 4:79–86.

4   Kalbach, Warren E., and Wayne M. McVey. 1979. *The Demographic Bases of Canadian Society.* 2d ed. Toronto: McGraw-Hill Ryerson.

14 Kalish, R.A. 1963. "An Approach to the Study of Death Attitudes." *American Behavioral Scientist* 6:68–70.

14 Kalish, R.A. 1981. *Death, Grief and Caring Relationships.* Monterey, CA: Brooks/Cole.

8   Kane, R.L. 1993. "Lessons in Long-term Care: The Benefits of a Northern Exposure." In A. Kind, T. Hyclak, and R. Thornton, eds. *North American Health Care Policy in the 1990s*, 91–109. New York: J. Wiley.

13 Kane, R.L., J.G. Evans, and D. McFadyen. 1990. *Improving the Health of Older People: A World View.* New York: Oxford University Press.

14 Kane, R.L., J. Wales, L. Bernstein, A. Leibowitz, and S. Kaplan. 1984. "A Randomized Controlled Trial of Hospice Care." *Lancet* 1:890–94.

13 Kassel, Victor. 1983. "Long-Term Care Institutions." In Ruth B. Weg, ed. *Sexuality in the Later Years: Roles and Behavior.* New York: Academic Press.

3   Kastenbaum, R., and B. Ross. 1975. "Historical Perspectives on Care." In J.G. Howells, ed. *Modern Perspectives in the Psychiatry of Old Age.* New York: Brunner/Mazel.

3   Katz, Michael B. 1975. *The People of Hamilton, Canada West: Family and Class in a Mid-Nineteenth-Century City.* Cambridge, MA: Harvard University Press.

6   Kausler, D.H. 1982. *Experimental Psychology and Human Aging.* New York: Wiley.

10 Kaye, L.W., and A. Monk. 1984. "Sex Role Traditions and Retirement from Academe." *The Gerontologist* 24:420–26.

11 Keating, N.C. 1991. *Aging in Rural Canada.* Toronto: Butterworths.

10 Keating, Norah, and Barbara Jeffrey. 1983. "Work Careers of Ever Married and Never Married Retired Women." *The Gerontologist* 23:416–21.

13 Kehoe, Monika. 1989. *Lesbians over 60 Speak for Themselves.* New York: Harrington Park Press.

5 Keith, J., and L. Landry. 1992. "Well-Being of Older Canadians." *Canadian Social Trends* (Summer):16–17.

13 Keith, Patricia M., Kathleen Hill, Willis J. Goudy, and Edward A. Powers. 1984. "Confidants and Well-Being: A Note on Male Friendship in Old Age." *The Gerontologist* 24:318–20.

8 Kelk, Doug. 1989. "CRD Quick-Response Team Keeps Woman, 89, Mobile." Victoria *Times-Colonist* (February 4).

14 Kelly, John L., G. Elphick, V. Mepham, and D.W. Molloy. 1989. *Let Me Decide.* Publisher and place of publication unknown.

12 Kelly, John R., M.W. Steinkamp, and J.R. Kelly. 1987. "Later-Life Satisfaction: Does Leisure Contribute?" *Leisure Sciences* 9:189–200.

12 Kelly, Paula. 1987. "Learning Begins at Home for Shut-In Seniors." *Seniors Today* (December 30).

1 Kennedy, Leslie W., and Robert A. Silverman. 1984–85. "Significant Others and Fear of Crime among the Elderly." *International Journal of Aging and Human Development* 20:241–56.

2 Kenyon, Gary M. 1988. "Basic Assumptions in Theories of Human Aging." In James E. Birren and Vern L. Bengtson, eds. *Emergent Theories of Aging.* New York: Springer.

1 Kenyon, G.M. 1992. "Editorial: Why Is Ageism a Serious Social Problem and What Can Be Done About It?" *Canadian Journal on Aging* 11(1):2–5.

15 Kernaghan, Kenneth. 1982. "Politics, Public Administration and Canada's Aging Population." *Canadian Public Policy* 8:69–79.

15 Kernaghan, Kenneth, and Olivia Kuper. 1983. *Coordination in Canadian Governments: A Case Study of Aging Policy.* Toronto: Institute of Public Administration of Canada.

11 Kerr, R., and Normand, R. 1992. "Independent Living and Psychomotor Performance." *Canadian Journal on Aging* 11(1):92–100.

12 Kidd, J.R. 1973. *How Adults Learn.* New York: Associated Press.

2 King, J.A. 1995. "Bringing Research to Life through Action Research Methods." *Canadian Journal on Aging* 14(supp. 1.):165–76.

8 King, R.H.T. 1994. "An Update on the Future of Medicare in Canada." *Employee Benefits Journal* 19(1):17–20.

8 King, R.H.T. 1995. "Medicare—Where Is Its Future?" *Employee Benefits Journal* 20(1):31–35.

12 Kinsley, B., and F. Graves. 1983. *The Time of Our Lives.* Ottawa: Employment and Immigration Canada.

14 Kjellstrand, C.M., and H. Moody. 1994. "Hemodialysis in Canada: A First-Class Medical Crisis." *Canadian Medical Association Journal* 150(7):1067–71.

14 Klug, Leo F., and Earle H. Waugh. 1982. "Survey of Credit Courses in Thanatology Offered by Canadian Universities: 1971–80." *Essence* 5:227–33.

1,3 Knox, V.J., and W.L. Gekoski. 1989. "The Effect of Judgement Context on Assessments of Age Groups." *Canadian Journal on Aging* 8:244–54.

1 Knox, V.J. and W.L. Gekoski, and E.A. Johnson. 1984. "The Relationship between Contact with and Perceptions of the Elderly." Paper presented at the Canadian Association on Gerontology 13th Annual Scientific and Educational Meeting, Vancouver.

6 Koch, Kenneth. 1977. *I Never Told Anybody: Teaching Poetry Writing in a Nursing Home.* New York: Random House.

6 Koch, Kenneth. 1982. "Teaching Poetry Writing in a Nursing Home." In Steven H. Zarit, ed. *Readings in Aging and Death: Contemporary Perspectives.* 2d ed. New York: Harper and Row.

5 Korba, L.W., P.J. Nelson, B.A. Turpin, and R. Joly. 1992. "Exploring Applications of Advanced Robotics Technology in a Long-Term Care Setting—Part 2: Identifying Applications." *International Journal of Technology and Aging* 5(1):21–38.

11 Kormos, W., and T.L. Horton. 1994. *Are We Spending Our Children's Inheritance?* Ottawa: National Advisory Council on Aging.

3 Koty, J. 1933. *Die Behandlung der Alten und Kranken bei den Naturvolkern.* Stuttgart.

10 Koyl, L.F. 1974. *Employing the Older Worker: Matching the Employee to the Job.* 2d ed. Washington: The National Council on the Aging, Inc.

7 Kozma, Albert, and M.J. Stones. 1978. "Some Research Issues and Findings in the Study of

Psychological Well-Being in the Aged." *Canadian Psychological Review* 19:241–49.

6 Kraus, Arthur S. 1984. "The Burden of Care for Families of Elderly Persons with Dementia." *Canadian Journal on Aging* 3:45–51.

5 Kraus, Arthur S. 1987. "The Increase in the Usual Life Span in North America." *Canadian Journal on Aging* 6:19–32.

5 Kraus, Arthur S. 1988. "Is a Compression of Morbidity in Late Life Occurring? Examination of Death Certificate Evidence." *Canadian Journal on Aging* 7:58–70.

6 Kraus, Arthur S., and C.P. McGeer. 1983. *Final Report on the Study: The Management of Elderly Persons with Dysfunctional Brain Syndrome (DBS)*. Kingston, ON: Queen's University.

12 Kraus, H., and W. Raab. 1961. *Hypokinetic Disease*. Springfield, IL: Charles C. Thomas.

7 Krause, N. 1993. "Neighborhood Deterioration and Social Isolation in Later Life." *International Journal of Aging and Human Development* 36(1):9–38.

14 Krauthammer, C. 1996. First and Last, Do No Harm." *Time* (April 15):61.

13 Krishnan, P. 1990. "Aging in Developed and Developing Countries." *University of Alberta Centre for Gerontology Newsletter* (Fall).

11 Krivo, Lauren J., and Jan E. Mutchler. 1989. "Elderly Persons Living Alone: The Effect of Community Context on Living Arrangements." *Journal of Gerontology: Social Sciences* 44:S54–S62.

8 Krueger, A. 1996. "Tories Cut Drug Benefits." *Winnipeg Free Press* (March 21):1.

13 Kruk, E. 1995. "Grandparent-Grandchild Contact Loss: Findings from a Study of 'Grandparent Rights' Members." *Canadian Journal on Aging* 14(4):737–54.

14 Kübler-Ross, Elisabeth. 1969. *On Death and Dying*. New York: Macmillan.

12 Kuehne, V.S., and H.A. Sears. 1993. "Beyond the Call of Duty: Older Volunteers Committed to Children and Families." *Journal of Applied Gerontology* 12(4):425–38.

14 Kunz, Phillip, and Jeffrey Summers. 1979–80. "A Time to Die: A Study of the Relationship of Birthdays and Time of Death." *Omega* 10:281–89.

7 Kuypers, J.A., and V.L. Bengtson. 1973. "Social Breakdown and Competence: A Model of Normal Aging." *Human Development* 16:181–201.

7 Labillois, M. 1994. "Aboriginal Housing: A Personal Perspective." In National Advisory Council on Aging, *Aboriginal Seniors' Issues*, 11–15. Cat. No. H71-2/1-15-1994E. Ottawa: Minister of Supply and Services Canada.

10 Labour Canada. 1986. *Women in the Labour Force, 1985–1986*. Cat. No. L38-30/1986. Ottawa: Minister of Supply and Services.

9 *Labour Gazette*. 1924.

6 Labouvie-Vief, G. 1977. "Adult Cognitive Development: In Search of Alternative Interpretations." *Merrill Palmer Quarterly* 23:227–63.

6 Labouvie-Vief, G. 1985. "Intelligence and Cognition." In James E. Birren and K. Warner Schaie, eds. *Handbook of the Psychology of Aging*. 2d ed. New York: Van Nostrand Reinhold.

14 Labovitz, S. 1974. "Control over Death: The Canadian Case." *Omega* 5:217–21.

5 LaBuda, Dennis R. 1990. "The Impact of Technology on Geriatric Rehabilitation." In Bryan Kemp, Kenneth Brummel-Smith, and Joseph W. Ramsdell, eds. *Geriatric Rehabilitation*. Boston: Little, Brown and Company.

4 Lachepelle, Réjean. 1988. "Changes in Fertility among Canada's Linguistic Groups." *Canadian Social Trends* (Autumn):2–8.

7 Lacy, William B., and Jon Hendricks. 1980. "Developmental Models of Adult Life: Myth or Reality." *International Journal of Aging and Human Development* 11:89–110.

8 Lalonde, Marc. 1974. *A New Perspective on the Health of Canadians*. Ottawa: Minister of Supply and Services.

7 Lam, L. 1994. "Self-Assessment of Health Status of Aged Chinese-Canadians." *Journal of Asian and African Studies* 29(1–2):77–90.

13 Laner, M.R. 1979. "Growing Older Female: Heterosexual and Homosexual." *Journal of Homosexuality* 4:267–75.

12 Lansley, J. 1991. "Continuity and Choices of Older Students: Retired Extra-Mural Students and Their Courses." *Journal of Educational Gerontology* 6:80–92.

7 Lapierre, S., L. Bouffard, and E. Bastin. 1993. "Motivational Goal Objects in Later Life." *International Journal of Aging and Human Development* 36(4):279–92.

7 Lapierre, S., J. Pronovost, M. Dube, and I. Delisle. 1992. "Risk Factors Associated with Suicide in the Community." *Canada's Mental Health* 40(3):8–12.

12 LaRocque P., and P.D. Campagna. 1983. "Physical Activity through Rhythmic Exercise for Elderly Persons Living in a Senior Citizen Residence." *Activities, Adaptations and Aging* 4:77–81.

12 Larsen, R., R. Mannell, and J. Zuzanek. 1986. "Daily Well-Being of Older Adults with Friends and Family." *Journal of Psychology and Aging* 1:117–26.

15 Laskin, Richard, and Richard Baird. 1970. "Factors in Voter Turnout and Party Preference in a Saskatchewan Town." *Canadian Journal of Political Science* 3:450–62.

3 Laslett, P. 1965. *The World We Have Lost*. New York: Charles Scribner's Sons.

3,4 Laslett, P. 1976. "Societal Development and Aging." In R.H. Binstock and E. Shanas, eds. *Handbook of Aging and the Social Sciences*. New York: Van Nostrand Reinhold.

14 Lavigne, P.C., and L. Lévesque. 1992. "Reactions of the Institutionalized Elderly upon Learning of the Death of a Peer." *Death Studies* 16(5):451–61.

3,4 Lavoie, Y. 1992. "Structure in Transition: Two Centuries of Demographic Change." In J. Dumas, *Report on the Demographic Situation in Canada 1992*, 101–53. Cat. No. 91-209E. Ottawa: Minister of Industry, Science and Technology.

4,9 Lavoie, Y., and J. Oderkirk. 1993. "Social Consequences of Demographic Change." *Canadian Social Trends* (Winter):2–5.

14 Law Reform Commission of Canada. 1982. *Euthanasia, Aiding Suicide and Cessation of Treatment*. Working Paper 28. Ottawa: Minister of Supply and Service.

11 Lawton, M. Powell. 1976. "The Relative Impact of Enriched and Traditional Housing on Elderly Tenants." *The Gerontologist* 16:237–42.

11 Lawton, M. Powell. 1980. *Environment and Aging*. Monterey, CA: Brooks/Cole.

11 Lawton, M. Powell. 1982. "Environmental Research: Issues and Methods." In Ronald Bayne and Blossom Wigdor, eds. *Research Issues in Aging: Report of a Conference, 1980*. Hamilton: Gerontology Research Council of Ontario.

11 Lawton, M. Powell. 1985. "Housing and Living Environments of Older People." In Robert H. Binstock and Ethel Shanas, eds. *Handbook of Aging and the Social Sciences*. 2d ed. New York: Van Nostrand Reinhold.

13 Lawton, M.P., E.M. Brody, and A.R. Saperstein. 1989. "A Controlled Study of Respite Services for Caregivers of Alzheimer's Patients." *The Gerontologist* 29:8–16.

7,11 Lawton, M. Powell, and Lucille Nahemow. 1973. "Ecology and the Aging Process." In Carl Eisdorfer and M. Powell Lawton, eds. *The Psychology of Adult Development and Aging*. Washington, DC: American Psychological Association.

11 Lazarowich, Michael. 1986. "The Perspective of the User in the Ontario Granny Flat Demonstration Project." In Susan Corke,

Gregory S. Romanick, Michael Lazarowich, and Joan Simon, eds. *Granny Flats: A Housing Option for the Elderly*. Report No. 13, Winnipeg: Institute of Urban Studies.

11 Lazarowich, Michael. 1990. "A Review of the Victoria, Australia Granny Flat Program." *The Gerontologist* 30:171–77.

11 Lazarowich, M., and B.W. Haley. 1982. *Granny Flats: Their Practicality and Implementation*. Ottawa: Canada Mortgage and Housing Corporation.

4 Leacy, F., ed. 1983. *Historical Statistics of Canada*. 2d ed. Ottawa: Minister of Supply and Services.

6 LeBlanc, Julia. 1985. "Combined Medical Psychiatric Day Centre." Paper presented at the Canadian Association on Gerontology 14th Annual Scientific and Educational Meeting, Hamilton.

13 Lee, J.A., ed. 1991. *Gay Midlife and Maturity*. New York: Haworth Press.

13 Lee, John Alan. 1987. "The Invisible Lives of Canada's Gray Gays." In Victor W. Marshall, ed. *Aging in Canada*. 2d ed. Toronto: Fitzhenry and Whiteside.

4 Legare, J., and B. Desjardins. 1976. "La situation des personnes âgées au Canada." *Canadian Review of Sociology and Anthropology* 13:321–36.

6 Lehman, Harvey C. 1953. *Age and Achievement*. Princeton, NJ: Princeton University Press.

6 Lehman, Harvey C. 1968. "The Creative Production Rates of Present versus Past Generations of Scientists." In Bernice L. Neugarten, ed. *Middle Age and Aging*. Chicago: University of Chicago Press.

7 Lemon, B., V. Bengtson, and J. Peterson. 1972. "Activity Types and Life Satisfaction in a Retirement Community." *Journal of Gerontology* 27:511–23.

7 Lenaars, A.A. 1992. "Suicide Notes of the Older Adult." *Suicide and Life Threatening Behavior* 22(1):62–79.

7 Lenaars, A.A., and D. Lester. 1992. "Comparison of Rates and Patterns of Suicide in Canada and the United States, 1960–1988." *Death Studies* 16(5):417–30.

3 Lenski, G., and J. Lenski. 1974. *Human Societies: An Introduction to Macrosociology*, 2d ed. New York: McGraw-Hill.

5 Leo, John, and Barbara Blonarz. 1981. "Fighting Off Old Age." *Time* (February 16).

5 Leon, J., and T. Lair. 1990. "Functional Status of the Noninstitutionalized Elderly: Estimates of ADL and IADL Difficulties." DHHS Pub. No. (PHS)90-3462. *National Medical Expenditure*

Survey Research Findings 4. Agency for Health Care Policy and Research. Rockville, MD: Public Health Service.

3   Lerner, M. 1970. "When, Why and Where People Die." In O.G. Brim, Jr., H.E. Freeman, S. Levine, and N.A. Scotch, eds. *The Dying Patient*. New York: Russell Sage Foundation.

7   Levinson, D.J. 1978. *The Seasons of a Man's Life*. New York: Knopf.

14   Levy, J.A. 1987. "A Life Course Perspective on Hospice and the Family." *Marriage and Family Review* 11:39–64.

13   Lewis, J., and B. Meredith. 1988. "Daughters Caring for Mothers." *Ageing and Society* 8:1–21.

14   Ley, Dorothy C.H. 1985. "Palliative Care in Canada: The First Decade and Beyond." *Journal of Palliative Care* 1:32–34.

7   Lieberman, M.A. 1975. "Adaptive Processes in Late Life." In N. Datan, and L.H. Ginsberg, eds. *Life-Span Developmental Psychology: Normative Life Crises*. New York: Academic Press.

6   Light, L.L. 1990. "Interactions between Memory and Language in Old Age." In J.E. Birren and K.W. Schaie, eds. *Handbook of the Psychology of Aging*. 3d ed. San Diego: Academic Press.

6   Light, L.L., and J.L. Capps. 1986. "Comprehension of Pronouns in Young and Older Adults." *Developmental Psychology* 2: 580–85.

6   Light, L.L., E.M. Zelinski, and M. Moore. 1982. "Adult Age Differences in Reasoning from New Information." *Journal of Experimental Psychology: Learning, Memory and Cognition* 8:435–47.

14   Lindemann, E. 1944. "Symptomatology and Management of Acute Grief." *American Journal of Psychiatry* 101:141–48.

9   Lindsay, Colin, and Shelley Donald. 1988. "Income of Canada's Seniors." *Canadian Social Trends* (Autumn):20–25.

7   Linton, Ralph. 1936. *The Study of Man*. New York: Appleton-Century-Crofts.

13   Litwak, E. 1985. *Helping the Elderly: The Complementary Roles of Informal Networks and Formal Systems*. New York: The Guilford Press.

4   Litwak, Eugene, and Charles F. Longino, Jr. 1987. "Migration Patterns among the Elderly: A Developmental Perspective." *The Gerontologist* 27:266–72.

11   Lo, O., and P. Gauthier. 1995. "Housing Affordability Problems among Renters." *Canadian Social Trends* (Spring):14–17.

4   Logan, Ronald. 1991. "Immigration during the 1980s." *Canadian Social Trends* (Spring):10–13.

15   Long, Cathy, and Carol Shelton, researchers and compilers. 1982. *The Directory: Programs for Senior Citizens across Canada*. Toronto: Canadian Pensioners Concerned, Ontario Division.

4   Longino, Charles F., Jr. 1988a. "The Gray Peril Mentality and the Impact of Retirement Migration." *The Journal of Applied Gerontology* 7:448–55.

4   Longino, Charles F., Jr. 1988b. "On the Nesting of Snowbirds: Canadian-Born Residents of the United States." In Larry C. Mullins and Richard D. Tucker, eds. *Snowbirds in the Sun Belt: Older Canadians in Florida*. Tampa, FL: International Exchange Center on Gerontology.

4   Longino, C.F., V.W. Marshall, L.C. Mullins, and R.D. Tucker. 1991. "On the Nesting of Snowbirds: A Question about Seasonal and Permanent Migrants." *Journal of Applied Gerontology* 10(2):157–68.

7   Lopata, H.Z. 1969. "Loneliness: Forms and Components." *Social Problems* 17:248–61.

12   Losier, G.F., P.E. Bourque, and R.J. Vallerand. 1993. "Motivational Model of Leisure Participation in the Elderly." *Journal of Psychology* 127(2):153–70.

15   Loveland, N.C. 1994. "It's Time for Older Canadians to Pay More." *The Globe and Mail* (November 22):A21.

5   Lowe, Graham S. 1990. "Computer Literacy." *Canadian Social Trends* (Winter):13–15.

10   Lowe, G.S. 1992. "Canadians and Retirement." *Canadian Social Trends* 26 (Autumn):18–21.

7   Lowenthal, M.F. 1975. "Psychosocial Variations across the Adult Life Course: Frontiers for Research and Policy." *The Gerontologist* 15:6–12.

13   Lowenthal, M.F., and C. Haven. 1968. "Interaction and Adaptation: Intimacy as a Critical Variable." In B.L. Neugarten, ed. *Middle Age and Aging*. Chicago: University of Chicago Press.

7   Lowenthal, M.F., M. Thurner, and D. Chiriboga. 1975. *Four Stages of Life*. San Francisco: Jossey-Bass.

1   Luttropp, N. 1995. "Minnie Mouse Matures." *Aging Today* 16(4):5.

7   McAdams, D.P., E. de St. Aubin, R.L. Logan. 1993. "Generativity among Young, Midlife, and Older Adults." *Psychology and Aging* 8:221–30.

10   MacBride, A. 1976. "Retirement as a Life Crisis: Myth or Reality?" *Canadian Psychiatric Association Journal* 21:547–56.

7   McCrae, R., and P. Costa, Jr. 1990. *Personality in Adulthood*. New York: Guilford.

6   McCrae, R.R., D. Arenberg, and P.T. Costa, Jr. 1987. "Declines in Divergent Thinking with

Age-Cross-Sectional, Longitudinal, and Cross-Sequential Analyses." *Psychology and Aging* 2:130–37.

2,4 McDaniel, Susan. 1986. *Canada's Aging Population*. Toronto: Butterworths.

2,10,13 McDaniel, Susan. 1989. "Women and Aging: A Sociological Perspective." In Dianne J. Garner and Susan O. Mercer, eds. *Women As They Age: Challenge, Opportunity, and Triumph*. Binghamton, NY: Haworth Press.

13 McDaniel, S. 1993. "Emotional Support and Family Contacts of Older Canadians." *Canadian Social Trends*, Spring, 30–33.

13 McDaniel, S.A. 1994a. *Family and Friends*. Statistics Canada Cat. No. 11-612E, No. 9. Ottawa: Minister of Industry, Science and Technology.

11 McDaniel, S. 1994b. "Living Arrangements and Satisfaction." In Statistics Canada. *Family and Friends*, 49–62. Cat. No. 11-612E, No. 9. Ottawa: Minister of Supply and Services Canada.

2 McDaniel, Susan, and Ben Agger. 1982. *Social Problems through Conflict and Order*. Don Mills, ON: Addison-Wesley.

13 McDaniel, S.A., and E.M. Gee. 1993. "Social Policies Regarding Caregiving to Elders: Canadian Contradictions." *Journal of Aging and Social Policy* 5(1/2):57–72.

13 McDaniel, S.A., and A.L. McKinnon. 1993. "Gender Differences in Informal Support and Coping among Elders: Findings from Canada's 1985 and 1990 General Social Surveys." *Journal of Women and Aging* 5(2):79–98.

11 MacDonald, Alison. 1989. *Transportation: Options for the Future*. National Advisory Council on Aging Cat. No. H71-2/1-5-1988E. Ottawa: Minister of Supply and Services.

8 McDonald, L., D. Badry, and C. Mueller. 1988. "The Elderly Physically and Developmentally Handicapped: An Analysis of Service Delivery." *Canadian Journal on Aging* 8:134–47.

9 McDonald, L., and M.Y.T. Chen. 1995. "The Youth Freeze and the Retirement Bulge: Older Workers and the Impending Labour Shortage." *Journal of Canadian Studies* 28(1):75–101.

13 McDonald, L., J.P. Hornick, G.B. Robertson, and J.E. Wallace. 1991. *Elder Abuse and Neglect in Canada*. Markham, ON: Butterworths.

10 McDonald, P. Lynn, and Richard A. Wanner. 1982. "Work Past Age 65 in Canada: A Socioeconomic Analysis." *Aging and Work* 5: 169–80.

10 McDonald, P. Lynn, and Richard A. Wanner. 1984. "Socioeconomic Determinants of Early Retirement in Canada." *Canadian Journal on Aging* 3:105–16.

10 McDonald, P. Lynn, and Richard A. Wanner. 1987. "Retirement in a Dual Economy: The Canadian Case." In Victor W. Marshall, ed. *Aging in Canada: Social Perspectives*, 2d ed. Toronto: Fitzhenry and Whiteside.

1,2,10 McDonald, P. Lynn, and Richard A. Wanner. 1990. *Retirement in Canada*. Toronto: Butterworths.

6 Mace, Nancy L., and Peter V. Rabins. 1981. *The Thirty-Six-Hour Day*. Baltimore: Johns Hopkins University Press.

7 McFadden, S.H. 1996. "Religion, Spirituality, and Aging." In J.E. Birren and K.W. Schaie, eds. *Handbook of the Psychology of Aging*, 4th ed. 162–77. San Diego: Academic Press.

6 MacFadgen, S. Lynne. 1987. "The Care of Irreversible Dementia Sufferers in the Toronto and Peel Regions: Perceptions of Service Providers." *Canadian Journal on Aging* 6:271–89.

12 McGuire, Francis A., F.D. Dottavio, and J.T. O'Leary. 1987. "The Relationship of Early Life Experiences to Later Life Leisure Involvement." *Leisure Sciences* 9:251–57.

4 McInnis, R.M. 1977. "Childbearing and Land Availability: Some Evidence from Individual Household Data." In R. Lee, ed. *Population Patterns in the Past*. New York: Academic Press.

6 McIntyre, John S., and Fergus I.M. Craik. 1987. "Age Differences in Memory for Item and Source Information." *Canadian Journal of Psychology* 41:175–92.

13 MacKenzie, P., and M. MacLean. 1992. "Altered Roles: The Meaning of Placement for the Spouse Who Remains in the Community." *Journal of Gerontological Social Work* 19(2): 107–20.

5 McKie, Craig. 1987. "Lifestyle Risks: Smoking and Drinking in Canada." *Canadian Social Trends* (Spring):20–26.

4 McKie, Craig. 1993. "Population Aging: Baby Boomers into the 21st Century." *Canadian Social Trends* (Summer): 2–6.

8 Maclean, Mary Beth, and Jillian Oderkirk. 1991. "Surgery among Elderly People." *Canadian Social Trends* (Summer):11–13.

7 MacLean, Michael J. 1982. "Personal Major Events and Individual Life Satisfaction in Old Age." *Essence* 5:119–266.

8 MacLean, M.J., and R. Bonar. 1983. "The Normalization Principle and the Institutionalization of the Elderly." *Canada's Mental Health* 31:16–18.

13   MacLean, M.J., and R.M. Williams. 1995. "Introduction." In M. J. MacLean, ed. *Abuse and Neglect of Older Canadians: Strategies for Change*, xi–xxii. Toronto: Thompson Educational Publishing.

8   MacLennan, Barbara A. 1983. "Some Possible Implications for Adapting the Milieu in Nursing Homes." *Activities, Adaptation and Aging* 4:33–38.

12   Macleod, Betty. 1985. "Education and Aging in Canada." *Convergence* 18:113–16.

16   Macpherson, A.S. 1995. "Exploring the Context of Educational Change." *Educational Gerontology* 21:15–22.

16   Macpherson, A.S., and P. Blumberg. 1992. "Building the Infrastructure for Educational Change." *Educational Gerontology* 18:529–40.

12   McPherson, Barry D. 1983. *Aging as a Social Process*. Toronto: Butterworths.

12   McPherson, Barry D. 1985. "The Meaning and Use of Time across the Life-Cycle: The Influence of Work, Family and Leisure." In Ellen M. Gee and Gloria M. Gutman, eds. *Canadian Gerontological Collection V: The Challenge of Time*. Winnipeg: Canadian Association on Gerontology.

10   McPherson, Barry D., and N. Guppy. 1979. "Preretirement Life-Style and Degree of Planning for Retirement." *Journal of Gerontology* 34:254–63.

12   McPherson, Barry D., and Carol Kozlik. 1980. "Canadian Leisure Patterns: Disengagement, Continuity or Ageism." In Victor W. Marshall, ed. *Aging in Canada*. Toronto: Fitzhenry and Whiteside.

12   McPherson, Barry D., and Carol Kozlik. 1987. "Age Patterns in Leisure Participation: The Canadian Case." In Victor W. Marshall, ed. *Aging in Canada*. 2d ed. Toronto: Fitzhenry and Whiteside.

3,4   McVey, Wayne. 1987. Personal communication.

7   Maddox, G.L. 1970. "Fact or Artifact: Evidence Bearing on Disengagement Theory." In Erdman Palmore, ed. *Normal Aging*. Durham, NC: Duke University Press.

2   Maddox, G.L., ed. 1987. *The Encyclopedia of Aging*. New York: Springer.

3   Maddox, G.L. 1988. "Overview." In *Aging around the World: A Report on the President's Symposium, "Aging in Tomorrow's World: An International Perspective."* The Gerontological Society of America.

2   Maddox, G.L., and R.T. Campbell. 1985. "Scope, Concepts, and Methods in the Study of Aging." In R.H. Binstock, and E. Shanas, eds.

Handbook of Aging and the Social Sciences, 2d ed., 3–31. New York: Van Nostrand Reinhold.

3   Makihara, K. 1989. "In Search of the Silver Lining." *Time* (August 28):58–59.

8   Manga, P. n.d. "Health Economics and the Current Health Care Cost Crisis: Contributions and Controversies." *Health and Canadian Society* 1(1):177–203.

8   Manitoba Health. 1992. *Quality Health for Manitobans: The Action Plan*. Winnipeg: Author.

14   Manitoba Health Organizations. No date. Bulletin. Winnipeg: Manitoba Health Organizations.

5   Manitoba Health Services Commission. 1980. *Planning Guide for Personal Care Homes in Manitoba*. Winnipeg: Manitoba Health Services Commission.

8   Manitoba Health Services Commission. 1985. "Manitoba Health Services Commission Study of Persons Age 65+ Presenting at the Emergency Departments of Three Winnipeg Hospitals." Winnipeg: Manitoba Health Services Commission.

14   Manitoba Law Reform Commission. 1990. "Discussion Paper on Advance Directives and Durable Powers of Attorney for Health Care." Winnipeg: Manitoba Law Reform Commission.

5   Mann, W.C. 1994. "Use and Potential Use of Assistive Devices by Home-Based Seniors." In G. Gutman and A.V. Wister, eds. *Progressive Accommodation for Seniors: Interfacing Shelter and Services*, 181–96. Vancouver: Gerontology Research Centre.

2   Manning, Gerald F. 1989. "Fiction and Aging: 'Ripeness Is All.'" *Canadian Journal on Aging* 8:157–63.

5   Manton, Kenneth G. 1982. "Changing Concepts of Mortality and Morbidity in the Elderly Population." *Milbank Memorial Fund Quarterly* 60:183–244.

5   Manton, Kenneth G. 1986. "Past and Future Life Expectancy Increases at Later Ages: Their Implications for the Linkage of Chronic Morbidity, Disability, and Mortality." *Journal of Gerontology* 41:672–81.

13   Marcil-Gratton, N., and J. Légaré. 1992. "Will Reduced Fertility Lead to Greater Isolation in Old Age for Tomorrow's Elderly?" *Canadian Journal on Aging* 11(1):54–71.

16   Marcus, Lotte. 1978. "Ageing and Education." In David Hobman, ed. *The Social Challenge of Aging*. London: Croom Helm.

16   Marcus, Lotte. 1980. "The Education of the Practitioner in Gerontology." Personal communication.

13   Marcus, Lotte, and Valerie Jaeger. 1984. "The Elderly as Family Caregivers." *Canadian Journal on Aging* 13:33–43.

13   Maris, R.W. 1969. *Social Forces in Urban Suicide*. Homewood, IL: Dorsey Press.

7   Markides, Kyriakos S., and Charles H. Mindel. 1987. *Aging and Ethnicity*. Newbury Park, CA: Sage.

12   Marmel, Bernice, S. Sawyer, and D. Shell. 1983. *A Study of the Needs of Tenants of Willow Centre Elderly Persons' Housing*. Study #1. Winnipeg: Nor'West Co-op Health and Social Services Centre, Inc.

15   Marmor, T.R., J.L. Mashaw, and P.L. Harvey. 1990. "Attack on Social Security." In T.R. Marmor, J.L. Mashaw, and P.L. Harvey, eds. *American's Misunderstood Welfare State: Persistent Myths, Enduring Realities*, 128–74. New York: Basic Books.

14   Marshall, Victor W. 1974. "The Last Strand: Remnants of Engagement in the Later Years." *Omega* 5:25–35.

14   Marshall, Victor W. 1975. "Age and Awareness of Finitude in Developmental Gerontology." *Omega* 6:113–29.

1   Marshall, Victor W., ed. 1980a. *Aging in Canada*. Toronto: Fitzhenry and Whiteside.

14   Marshall, Victor W. 1980b. *Last Chapters: A Sociology of Aging and Dying*. Monterey, CA: Brooks/Cole.

7   Marshall, Victor W. 1983. "Generations, Age Groups and Cohorts." *Canadian Journal on Aging* 2:51–61.

2   Marshall, Victor W. 1986. "A Sociological Perspective on Aging and Dying." In Victor W. Marshall, ed. *Later Life: The Social Psychology of Aging*. Beverly Hills, CA: Sage.

13   Marshall, Victor W. 1987. "The Health of Very Old People as a Concern of Their Children." In Victor W. Marshall, ed. *Aging in Canada: Social Perspectives*. 2d ed. Toronto: Fitzhenry and Whiteside.

13   Marshall, Victor W. 1989. *Models for Community-Based Long Term Care*. Paper prepared for the Aging Policy Section, Health Policy Division, Policy, Planning and Information Branch, Health and Welfare Canada. Ottawa: Health and Welfare Canada.

14   Marshall, Victor W., and Judith A. Levy. 1990. "Aging and Dying." In Robert H. Binstock and Linda K. George, eds. *Handbook of Aging and the Social Sciences*. 3d ed. San Diego: Academic Press.

1   Marshall, V.W., and B.D. McPherson. 1993. "Aging: Canadian Perspectives." *Journal of Canadian Studies* 28(1):3–13.

13   Marshall, Victor W., C.J. Rosenthal, and J. Synge. 1981. "The Family as a Health Service Organization for the Elderly." Paper presented at the Annual Meeting of Society for the Study of Social Problems, Toronto.

13   Marshall, V.W., C.J. Rosenthal, and J. Synge. 1983. "Concerns about Parental Health." In Elizabeth W. Markson, ed. *Older Women: Issues and Prospects*. Lexington, MA: D.C. Heath.

4   Marshall, V.W., and R.D. Tucker. 1990. "Canadian Seasonal Migrants to the Sunbelt: Boon or Burden?" *Journal of Applied Gerontology* 9(4):420–32.

4   Martin, H.W., S.K. Hoppe, V.W. Marshall, and J.F. Daciuk. 1992. "Sociodemographic and Health Characteristics of Anglophone Canadian and U.S. Snowbirds." *Journal of Aging and Health* 4(4):500–13.

9   Maser, K. 1995. "Who's Saving for Retirement?" *Perspectives* (Winter):14–19.

13   Masters, W., and V. Johnson. 1970. *Human Sexual Inadequacy*. Boston: Little, Brown.

7   Matsuoka, A.K. 1993. "Collecting Qualitative Data through Interviews with Ethnic Older People." *Canadian Journal on Aging* 12(2): 216–32.

13   Matthews, Anne Martin. 1982. "Review Essay—Canadian Research on Women as Widows: A Comparative Analysis of the State of the Art." *Resources for Feminist Research* 11:227–30.

13   Matthews, Anne Martin. 1985. "Support Systems of Widows in Canada." In Helena Z. Lopata, ed. *Widows: Other Countries/Other Places*. Durham, NC: Duke University Press.

13   Matthews, Anne Martin. 1987. "Widowhood as an Expectable Life Event." In Victor W. Marshall, ed. *Aging in Canada: Social Perspectives*. 2d ed. Toronto: Fitzhenry and Whiteside.

2   Matthews, A. Martin. 1995. "Editorial: Multifaceted and Innovative Answers to Complex Questions in Research on Aging. *Canadian Journal on Aging* 14(supp. 1):1–15.

10   Matthews, Anne Martin, and Kathleen H. Brown. 1987. "Retirement as a Critical Life Event: The Differential Experience of Women and Men." *Research on Aging* 9:548–71.

9,10,13   Matthews, Anne Martin, K.H. Brown, C.K. Davis, and M.A. Denton. 1982. "A Crisis Assessment Technique for the Evaluation of Life Events: Transition to Retirement as an Example." *Canadian Journal on Aging* 1:28–39.

13   Matthews, A.M., and L.D. Campbell. 1995. "Gender Roles, Employment and Informal Care." In S. Arber, and J. Ginn, eds. *Connecting Gender and Aging: A Sociological Approach*,

13   Matthews, A.M., and C.J. Rosenthal. 1993. "Balancing Work and Family in an Aging Society: The Canadian Experience." In G.L. Maddox and M.P. Lawton, eds. *Annual Review of Gerontology and Geriatrics: Focus on Kinship, Aging, and Social Change* 13, 96–119. New York: Springer.

129–43. Buckingham, UK: Open University Press.

10   Matthews, Anne Martin, and Joseph A. Tindale. 1987. "Retirement in Canada." In Kyriakos S. Markides and Cary L. Cooper, eds. *Retirement in Industrialized Societies: Social, Psychological and Health Factors*. Toronto: John Wiley and Sons.

1   Matthews, A.M., J.A. Tindale, and J.E. Norris. 1985. "The Facts on Aging Quiz: A Canadian Validation and Cross-Cultural Comparison." *Canadian Journal on Aging* 3:165–74.

3   Matthews, C., and J.V. Thompson. 1985. "The Aged in Canadian Fiction: No Longer Tragic Figures." Paper presented at the Canadian Association on Gerontology 14th Annual Scientific and Educational Meeting, Hamilton.

1   Matthews, Sarah H. 1979. *The Social World of Old Women: The Management of Self-Identity*. Beverly Hills, CA: Sage.

14   Mattos, J., and Sachs, A. 1996. "Defining the Right to Die." *Time* (April 15):58.

8   Maxwell, Robert J. 1981. *Health and Wealth*. Lexington, MA: Lexington Books.

3   Maxwell, Robert J,. and Philip Silverman. 1977. "Information and Esteem: Cultural Considerations in the Treatment of the Aged." In Wilbur H. Watson and Robert J. Maxwell, eds. *Human Aging and Dying: A Study in Sociocultural Gerontology*. New York: St. Martin's Press.

3   Mays, H.J. 1983. "A Place to Stand: Families, Land and Permanence in Toronto Gore Township, 1820–1890." In W.P. Ward, ed. *The Social Development of Canada: Readings*. Richmond, BC: Open Learning Institute.

5   Mazess, Richard B., and Sylvia H. Forman. 1979. "Longevity and Age Exaggeration in Vilcabamba, Ecuador." *Journal of Gerontology* 34:94–98.

1   Meadows, Rita E., and H. Thompson Fillmer. 1987. "Depictions of Aging in Basal Readers of the 1960s and 1980s." *Educational Gerontology* 13:85–100.

5   Medvedev, Z.A. 1974. "Caucasus and Altay Longevity: A Biological or Social Problem?" *The Gerontologist* 14:381–87.

10   Meier, E.L., and E.A. Kerr. 1976. "Capabilities of Middle-aged and Older Workers." *Industrial Gerontology* 3:147–56.

6   Mental Health Division, Health Services and Promotion Branch, Department of National Health and Welfare. 1988. *Guidelines for Comprehensive Services to Elderly Persons with Psychiatric Disorders*. Cat. No. H39-120/1988 E. Ottawa: Minister of Supply and Services.

10   Méthot, Suzanne. 1987. "Employment Patterns of Elderly Canadians." *Canadian Social Trends* (Autumn):7–11.

14   Metzger, Anne M. 1979–80. "A Q-Methodological Study of the Kübler-Ross Stage Theory." *Omega* 10:291–301.

15   Milbrath, Lester W. 1965. *Political Participation: How and Why Do People Get Involved in Politics?* Chicago: Rand McNally.

6   Miles, C.C., and W.R. Miles. 1932. "The Correlation of Intelligence Scores and Chronological Age from Early to Late Maturity." *American Journal of Psychology* 44:44–78

11   Minuk, M., and K. Davidson. 1981. *A Report on the Research Findings on the MHRC 1981 Shelter Allowance Program Review*. Winnipeg: Manitoba Housing and Renewal Corporation.

5   Mitchell, E. 1996. "Yo, Van Gogh! What's Up?" *Time* (February 26):60.

8   Mitchell-Pedersen, L., L. Edmund, E. Fingerote, and C. Powell. 1985. "Let's Untie the Elderly." *OAHA Quarterly* (October):10–14.

12   Mittelman, K., S. Crawford, S. Holliday, G. Gutman, and G. Bhakthan. 1989. "The Older Cyclist: Anthropometric, Physiological, and Psychosocial Changes Observed during a Trans-Canada Cycle Tour." *Canadian Journal on Aging* 8:144–56.

12   Mobily, K.E., R. Nilson, L.J. Ostiguy, R.D. MacNeil, and R.B. Wallace. 1995. "Seasonal Variation in Physical Activity in Older Adults." *Topics in Geriatric Rehabilitation* 10(3):11–22.

13   Mohide, E.A., D.M. Pringle, D.L. Streiner, J.R. Gilbert, G. Muir, and M. Tew. 1990. "A Randomized Trial of Family Caregiver Support in the Home Management of Dementia." *Journal of the American Geriatrics Society* 38:446–54.

5   Molloy, D.W., D.A. Beerschoten, M.J. Borrie, R.G. Crilly, and R.D.T. Cape. 1988. "Acute Effects of Exercise on Neuropsychological Function in Elderly Subjects." *Journal of the American Geriatrics Society* 36:29–33.

15   Montgomery, Charlotte. 1985. "Tories Retreat on De-Indexing Pensions." *The Globe and Mail* (June 28).

8   Montgomery, P.R., A.J. Kirshen, and N.P. Roos. 1988. "Long-Term Care and Impending Mortality: Influence upon Place of Death and

Hospital Utilization." *The Gerontologist* 28:351–54.

3 Moodie, S. 1853. *Life in the Clearings versus the Bush*. New York: DeWitt and Davenport.

12 Moody, Harry R. 1988a. *Abundance of Life: Human Development Policies for an Aging Society*. New York: Columbia University Press.

2 Moody, Harry R. 1988b. "Toward a Critical Gerontology: The Contribution of the Humanities to Theories of Aging." In James E. Birren and Vern L. Bengtson, eds. *Emergent Theories of Aging*. New York: Springer.

7 Moore, E. 1995. "Aboriginal Women in Canada." In Statistics Canada, *Women in Canada: A Statistical Report*, 3d ed., 147–62. Cat. No. 89-503E. Ottawa: Minister of Supply and Services Canada.

4 Moore, E.G., and M.W. Rosenberg. 1994. "Residential Mobility and Migration among Canada's Elderly." In V. Marshall and B. McPherson, eds. *Aging: Canadian Perspectives*, 51–69. Peterborough, ON: Broadview Press/Journal of Canadian Studies.

6 Morantz, A. 1990. "The Right to Decide. Today's Health." *The Globe and Mail* (September):39–44.

12 Morgan, W.P., and P.J. O'Connor. 1988. "Exercise and Mental Health." In R. Dishman, ed. *Exercise Adherence: Its Impact on Public Health*. Champaign, IL: Human Kinetics.

12 Mori, G.A., and B. Burke. 1986. *Educational Attainment of Canadians*. Statistics Canada. Cat. No. 98-134. Ottawa: Minister of Supply and Services.

14 Mori, M. 1991. *Palliative Care of the Elderly: An Overview and Annotated Bibliography*. Burnaby, BC: Gerontology Research Centre, Simon Fraser University.

13 Morris, John N., and Sylvia Sherwood. 1983–84. "Informal Support Resources for Vulnerable Elderly Persons: Can They Be Counted on, Why Do They Work?" *International Journal of Aging and Human Development* 18:81–98.

10 Morrison, M. 1984. "Retirement and Human Resource Planning for the Aging Work Force." *Personnel Administrator* (June):151–59.

6 Morse, C. K. 1993. "Does Variability Increase with Age? An Archival Study of Cognitive Measures." *Psychology and Aging* 8(2):156–64.

14 Moss, Miriam S., and Sidney Z. Moss. 1984–85. "Some Aspects of the Elderly Widow(er)'s Persistent Tie with the Deceased Spouse." *Omega* 15:195–206.

7,8 Mossey, Jana M., B. Havens, N.P. Roos, and E. Shapiro. 1981. "The Manitoba Longitudinal Study on Aging: Description and Methods." *The Gerontologist* 21:551–58.

14 Mount, B.F., and J.F. Scott. 1983. "Whither Hospice Evaluation." *Journal of Chronic Diseases* 36:731–36.

14 Mount, R.M., A. Jones, and A. Patterson. 1974. "Death and Dying: Attitudes in a Teaching Hospital." *Urology* 4:741.

13 Mullens, Harry J. 1983. "Love, Sexuality, and Aging in Nursing Homes and Public Housing." Paper presented at the Canadian Association on Gerontology 12th Annual Scientific and Educational Meeting, Moncton.

4 Mullins, Larry C., R. Tucker, C.F. Longino, Jr., and V. Marshall. 1989. "An Examination of Loneliness among Elderly Canadian Seasonal Residents in Florida." *Journal of Gerontology: Social Sciences* 44:S80–S86.

2 Murphy, Barbara. 1982. "Corporate Capital and the Welfare State: Canadian Business and Public Pension Policy in Canada Since World War II." Unpublished master's thesis. Ottawa: Carleton University.

5 Murrell, F.H. 1970. "The Effect of Extensive Practice on Age Differences in Reaction Time." *Journal of Gerontology* 25:268–74.

6 Murrell, S.A., S. Himmelfarb, and K. Wright. 1983. "Prevalence of Depression and Its Correlates in Older Adults." *American Journal of Epidemiology* 117:173–85.

7 Mussell, W.J. 1994. "First Nations Elders as Resource Persons/Educators." In National Advisory Council on Aging, *Aboriginal Seniors' Issues*, 49–58. Cat. No. H71-2/1-15-1994E. Ottawa: Minister of Supply and Services Canada.

12 Myers, Anita M., and Gail Gonda. 1986. "Research on Physical Activity in the Elderly: Practical Implications for Program Planning." *Canadian Journal on Aging* 5:175–87.

12 Myers, Anita M., and N. Hamilton. 1985. "Evaluation of the Canadian Red Cross Society's Fun and Fitness Program for Seniors." *Canadian Journal on Aging* 4:201–12.

5 Myers, George C., and Kenneth G. Manton. 1984. "Compression of Mortality: Myth or Reality?" *The Gerontologist* 24:346–53.

9 Myles, John F. 1981a. "Income Inequality and Status Maintenance." *Research on Aging* 3:123–41.

9 Myles, John. 1981b. "The Trillion Dollar Misunderstanding." *Working Papers Magazine* (July–August).

4,9 Myles, John. 1982. "Social Implications of a Changing Age Structure." In Gloria Gutman, ed. *Canada's Changing Age Structure: Implications for the Future.* Burnaby, BC: SFU Publications.

2,9,10,15 Myles, John. 1984. *Old Age in the Welfare State: The Political Economy of Public Pensions.* Boston: Little, Brown and Co.

9,15 Myles, John F. 1988. "Social Policy in Canada." In Eloise Rathbone-McEwan and Betty Havens, eds. *North American Elders: United States and Canadian Perspectives.* New York: Greenwood.

13 Myles, John. 1991. "Women, the Welfare State and Care-Giving." *Canadian Journal on Aging* 10:82–85.

4,8,12 Myles, John F., and Monica Boyd. 1982. "Population Aging and the Elderly." In Dennis Forcese and Stephen Richer, eds. *Social Issues: Sociological Views of Canada.* Scarborough, ON: Prentice-Hall.

9 Myles J., and D. Street. 1995. "Should the Economic Life Course Be Redesigned? Old Age Security in a Time of Transition." *Canadian Journal on Aging* 14(2):335–59.

9,15 Myles, J., and L. Teichroew. 1991. "The Politics of Dualism: Pension Policy in Canada." In J. Myles and J. Quadagno, eds. *States, Labor Markets, and the Future of Old-Age Policy,* 84–104. Philadelphia: Temple University Press.

6 Naglie, G., M. Silberfeld, K. O'Rourke, B. Fried, N. Durham, C. Bombardier, and A. Detsky, A. 1995. "Convening Expert Panels to Identify Mental Capacity Assessment Items." *Canadian Journal on Aging* 14(4):697–705.

4 Nagnur, Dhruva. 1986. *Longevity and Historical Life Tables 1921–1981 (Abridged) Canada and the Provinces.* Statistics Canada. Cat. No 89–506. Ottawa: Minister of Supply and Services.

13 Nagnur, Dhruva, and Owen Adams. 1987. "Tying the Knot: An Overview of Marriage Rates in Canada." *Canadian Social Trends* (Autumn):2–6.

13 Nagnur, Dhruva, and Owen Adams. 1989. "Marrying and Divorcing: A Status Report for Canada." *Canadian Social Trends* (Summer): 24–27.

4,5 Nagnur, Dhruva, and Michael Nagrodski. 1988. "Cardiovascular Disease, Cancer and Life Expectancy." *Canadian Social Trends* (Winter): 25–27.

12 Nahmiash, Daphne. 1985. "Intergenerational Relationships." Paper presented at the Canadian Association on Gerontology 14th Annual Scientific and Educational Meeting, Hamilton.

8 Nahmiash, D., and F. Lesemann. 1993. *Home Care ... A Love Affair.* North York, ON: Captus Press.

8 Nahmiash, D., and M. Reis. 1992. *An Exploratory Study of Private Home Care Services in Canada.* Cat. No. H39-248/1992E. Ottawa: Minister of Supply and Services Canada.

3 Nason, J.D. 1981. "Respected Elder or Old Person: Aging in a Micronesian Community." In P.T. Amoss and S. Harrell, eds. *Other Ways of Growing Old: Anthropological Perspectives.* Stanford, CA: Stanford University Press.

8 National Advisory Council on Aging. No date. "The Rate of Institutionalization of the Elderly in Canada Is Declining for Those below Age of 85." *Info-Age* 1(2):1.

15 National Advisory Council on Aging. 1985a. "Listen to Me!": The Technical Evaluation Report of The National Advisory Council on Aging's Consultation with Seniors. News release. Ottawa: National Advisory Council on Aging.

15 National Advisory Council on Aging. 1985b. *Seniors and Decision-Making.* Ottawa: Minister of Supply and Services.

11 National Advisory Council on Aging. 1985c. *Expression* 2(4). Ottawa: National Advisory Council on Aging.

11,13 National Advisory Council on Aging. 1986a. *Expression* 3(1). Ottawa: National Advisory Council on Aging.

11 National Advisory Council on Aging. 1986b. *Expression* 3. Ottawa: National Advisory Council on Aging.

8 National Advisory Council on Aging. 1986c. "Toward a Community Support Policy for Canadians." Ottawa: National Advisory Council on Aging.

5 National Advisory Council on Aging. 1988. "NACA's Philosophy on Technology for an Aging Population." News release. Ottawa: Government of Canada.

15,16 National Advisory Council on Aging. 1989a. *1989 and Beyond: Challenges of an Aging Canadian Society.* Cat. No. H71-3/10-1989. Ottawa: Minister of Supply and Services.

12 National Advisory Council on Aging. 1989b. "Not All Learning Takes Place in Formal Classes." *Expression* 5:4.

8 National Advisory Council on Aging. 1989c. *Understanding Seniors' Independence Report No. 1: The Barriers and Suggestions for Action.* Cat. No. H71-3/11-1-1989E. Ottawa: Minister of Supply and Services.

11 National Advisory Council on Aging. 1989d. *Understanding Seniors' Independence: The Barriers and Suggestions for Action Summary Report.* Cat. No. H71-3/11-1-1989-1. Ottawa: Minister of Supply and Services.

1 National Advisory Council on Aging. 1990a. "The Mature Marketplace." *Expression* 6(3):2–5.

13 National Advisory Council on Aging. 1990b. "Grandparents' Rights." *Expression* 6.

8 National Advisory Council on Aging. 1990c. *The NACA Position on Community Services in Health Care for Seniors*. Cat. No. H71-2/2-8-1990. Ottawa: Minister of Supply and Services.

13 National Advisory Council on Aging. 1990d. *The NACA Position on Informal Caregiving: Support and Enhancement*. Cat. No. H71-2/2-9-1990. Ottawa: Minister of Supply and Services.

12 National Advisory Council on Aging. 1990e. *The NACA Position on Lifelong Learning*. Cat. No. H71-2/2-10-1990. Ottawa: Minister of Supply and Services.

9,11 National Advisory Council on Aging. 1991. *The Economic Situation of Canada's Seniors: A Fact Book*. Cat. No. H71-3/14-1991E. Ottawa: Minister of Supply and Services.

8 National Advisory Council on Aging (NACA). 1992a. *The NACA Position on Canada's Oldest Seniors: Maintaining the Quality of Their Lives*. Cat. No. H71-2/4-1993. Ottawa: Minister of Supply and Services Canada.

7 National Advisory Council on Aging. 1992b. "Spirituality and Meaning." *Expression* 8(4):3–8.

10 National Advisory Council on Aging. 1992c. *The NACA Position on Managing an Aging Labour Force*. Cat. No. H71-2/2-12-1991. Ottawa: Minister of Supply and Services Canada.

6 National Advisory Council on Aging. 1993a. "Freedom and Responsibility: Home Alone." *Expression* 9(2):2.

6 National Advisory Council on Aging. 1993b. "Competency and Risk." *Expression* 9(2):3–4.

7,13 National Advisory Council on Aging. 1993c. *The NACA Position on Women's Life-Course Events*. Cat. No.: H71-2/2-15-1993. Ottawa: Minister of Supply and Services Canada.

11 National Advisory Council on Aging. 1993d. "The Freedom to Drive a Car." *Expression* 9(2):7.

8 National Advisory Council on Aging. 1993e. "Rights and Limits to Risk." *Expression* 9(2):1–8.

9 National Advisory Council on Aging. 1993f. "Rural and Urban 'Senior' Families' Income Patterns." *Info-Age* (April).

9 National Advisory Council on Aging. 1993g. "Thirteen Common Myths." *Expression* 10(3):2–8.

1 National Advisory Council on Aging. 1993h. The NACA Position on the Image of Aging. Ottawa: Minister of Supply and Services Canada.

13 National Advisory Council on Aging. 1994a. "We're Family." *Expression* 9(4).

8 National Advisory Council on Aging. 1994b. "A Quick Portrait on Canadian Health and Seniors." *Aging Vignettes*. Ottawa: Author.

5 National Advisory Council on Aging. 1994c. "A State of Optimal Well-Being." *Expression* 10(2):2–7.

14 National Advisory Council on Aging. 1994d. "Euthanasia and Assisted Suicide: What They Mean." *Expression* 10(1).

8 National Advisory Council on Aging. 1995a. *The NACA Position on Community Services in Health Care for Seniors: Progress and Challenges*. Ottawa: NACA.

8 National Advisory Council on Aging. 1995b. *The NACA Position on Determining Priorities in Health Care: The Seniors' Perspective*. Ottawa: NACA.

5,14 National Advisory Council on Aging. 1995c. *The NACA Position on Health Care Technology and Aging*. Cat. No. H71-2/2-18-1995. Ottawa: Minister of Supply and Services Canada.

6 National Advisory Council on Aging. 1996a. *Aging Vignette #35 and #42*. Ottawa: NACA.

5 National Advisory Council on Aging. 1996b. "Health Consequences of Inadequate Incomes." *Info-Age* 14(March).

9 National Council of Welfare. 1979. *Women and Poverty*. Ottawa: Minister of Supply and Services.

9 National Council of Welfare. 1984a. *A Pension Primer*. Ottawa: Minister of Supply and Services.

4,9 National Council of Welfare. 1984b. *Sixty-Five and Older*. Cat. No. H68-11/1984E. Ottawa: Minister of Supply and Services.

9 National Council of Welfare. 1985. *Giving and Taking: The May 1985 Budget and the Poor*. Ottawa: Minister of Supply and Services.

9 National Council of Welfare. 1988. *Poverty Profile*. Cat. No. H67-1/4-1988E. Ottawa: Minister of Supply and Services.

9 National Council of Welfare. 1989a. *The 1989 Budget and Social Policy*. Cat. No. H68-22/1989E. Ottawa: Minister of Supply and Services.

9 National Council of Welfare. 1989b. *A Pension Primer*. Cat. No. H68-23/1989E. Ottawa: Minister of Supply and Services.

9,11,13 National Council of Welfare. 1990a. *Women and Poverty Revisited*. Cat. No. H68-25/1990E. Ottawa: Minister of Supply and Services.

9 National Council of Welfare. 1990b. *Pension Reform*. Cat. No. H68-24/1990E. Ottawa: Minister of Supply and Services.

8 National Council of Welfare. 1991. *Funding Health and Higher Education: Danger Looming*.

Cat. No. H68-30/1991E. Ottawa: Minister of Supply and Services.

9   National Council of Welfare. 1994. *A Blueprint for Social Security Reform.* Cat. No. H68-35/1994E. Ottawa: Minister of Supply and Services.

9   National Council of Welfare. 1995. *Poverty Profile 1993.* Cat. No. H67-1/4-1993E. Ottawa: Minister of Supply and Services.

9   National Council of Welfare. 1996a. *A Pension Primer.* Cat. No. H68-23/1996E. Ottawa: Minister of Supply and Services Canada.

9   National Council of Welfare. 1996b. *Poverty Profile 1994.* Cat. No. H67-1/4-1994E. Ottawa: Minister of Supply and Services Canada.

9   National Health and Welfare. 1973. *Working Paper on Social Security in Canada.* 2d ed. Ottawa: Queen's Printer.

5   National Health and Welfare. 1993. *Ageing and Independence: Overview of a National Survey.* Cat. No. H88-3/13-1993E. Ottawa: Minister of Supply and Services Canada.

16   National Institute on Aging. 1987. "Personnel for Health Needs of the Elderly through Year 2020" (NIH Publication No. 87–2950). Bethseda, MD: National Institute of Health.

4   Nault, F, J. Chen, M.V. George, and M.J. Norris. 1993. *Population Projections of Registered Indians, 1991–2015.* Cat. No. R32-98/1993E. Ottawa: Minister of Supply and Services Canada.

13   Neal, M.B., N.J. Chapman, B. Ingersoll-Dayton, A.C. Emlen, and L. Boise. 1990. "Absenteeism and Stress among Employed Caregivers of the Elderly, Disabled Adults, and Children." In David E. Biegel and Arthur Blum, eds. *Aging and Caregiving: Theory, Research, and Policy.* Newbury Park, CA: Sage.

1   Nemeth, Mary. 1994. "Amazing Greys." *Maclean's* (January 10):32–33.

13   Nemeth, M., and J. Howse. 1994. "Sandwich Generation." *Maclean's* (January 10):34–35.

5   Nessner, Katherine. 1990. "Profile of Canadians with Disabilities." *Canadian Social Trends* (Autumn):2–5.

13   Nett, Emily M. 1988. *Canadian Families Past and Present.* Toronto: Butterworths.

12   The Institute Network. 1992. "We're Growing." *Network News* 14(1).

7   Neugarten, B.L. 1964. *Personality in Middle and Late Life.* New York: Atherton Press.

7   Neugarten, B.L., ed. 1968. *Middle Age and Aging.* Chicago: University of Chicago Press.

7   Neugarten, B.L. 1969. "Continuities and Discontinuities of Psychological Issues into Adult Life." *Human Development* 12:121–30.

3,10   Neugarten, B.L. 1980. "Acting One's Age: New Rules for Old" (Interview with Elizabeth Hall). *Psychology Today* (April).

3,5,15 Neugarten, B.L., and R.J. Havighurst. 1979. "Aging and the Future." In J. Hendricks and C.D. Hendricks, eds. *Dimensions of Aging: Readings.* Cambridge, MA: Winthrop.

2,7   Neugarten, B.L., R.J. Havighurst, and S. Tobin. 1968. "Personality and Patterns of Aging." In Bernice L. Neugarten, ed. *Middle Age and Aging.* Chicago: University of Chicago Press.

7   Neugarten, B.L., and J.W. Moore. 1968. "The Changing Age-status System." In Bernice L. Neugarten, ed. *Middle Age and Aging.* Chicago: University of Chicago Press.

7   Neugarten, B.L., J.W. Moore, and J.C. Lowe. 1968. "Age Norms, Age Constraints, and Adult Socialization." In Bernice L. Neugarten, ed. *Middle Age and Aging.* Chicago: University of Chicago Press.

13   Neugarten, B.L., and Karol K. Weinstein. 1964. "The Changing American Grandparent." *Journal of Marriage and the Family* 26:199–204.

13   Neysmith, Sheila M. 1982. "The Social Contributions of Old People: A Description and Assessment." Revised version of a paper presented at the 11th Annual Scientific and Educational Meeting of the Canadian Association on Gerontology, Winnipeg.

9   Neysmith, Sheila M. 1984. "Poverty in Old Age: Can Pension Reform Meet the Needs of Women?" *Canadian Woman Studies* 5:17–21.

15   Neysmith, Sheila M. 1986. "Social Policy Implications of an Aging Society." In Victor W. Marshall, ed. *Aging in Canada: Social Perspectives.* 2d ed. Toronto: Fitzhenry and Whiteside.

15   Neysmith, Sheila M. 1987. "Organizing for Influence: The Relationship of Structure to Impact." *Canadian Journal on Aging* 6:105–16.

8   Neysmith, S.M. 1993. "Developing a Home Care System to Meet the Needs of Aging Canadians and Their Families." In J. Hendricks and C. J. Rosenthal, eds. *The Remainder of Their Days: Domestic Policy and Older Families in the United States and Canada,* 145–67. New York: Garland.

13   Neysmith, S. 1995. "Power in Relationships of Trust: A Feminist Analysis of Elder Abuse." In M.J. MacLean, ed. *Abuse and Neglect of Older Canadians: Strategies for Change,* 43–54. Toronto: Thompson Educational Publishing.

3   Neysmith, Sheila M., and Joey Edwardh. 1983. "Ideological Underpinnings of the World Assembly on Aging." *Canadian Journal on Aging* 2:125–36.

13   Neysmith, S.M., and B. Nichols. 1994. Working Conditions in Home Care: Comparing Three Groups of Workers." *Canadian Journal on Aging* 13(2):169–86.

15   Ng, E. 1992. "Children and Elderly People: Sharing Public Income Resources." *Canadian Social Trends* (Summer):12–17.

11   Nicklin, Robert L. 1985. "The Role of the Canada Mortgage and Housing Corporation in the Development Process." In Gloria Gutman and Norman Blackie, eds. *Innovations in Housing and Living Arrangements for Seniors*. Burnaby, BC: The Gerontology Research Centre, Simon Fraser University.

11   Niewind, A.C., M. Krondl, and D. Lau. 1988. "Relative Impact of Selected Factors on Food Choices of Elderly Individuals." *Canadian Journal on Aging* 8:32–47.

10   Nishio, Harry K., and Heather Lank. 1987. "Patterns of Labour Participation of Older Female Workers." In Victor W. Marshall, ed. *Aging in Canada: Social Perspectives*. 2d ed. Toronto: Fitzhenry and Whiteside.

13   Noelker, L.S., and S.W. Poulshock. 1982. *The Effects on Families of Caring for Impaired Elderly in Residence*. Washington, DC: U.S. Department of Health and Human Services, Administration on Aging.

1,4,5,9,10,11,12,13   Norland, J.A. 1994. *Profile of Canada's Seniors*. Cat. No. 96-312E. Ottawa: Statistics Canada and Prentice Hall Canada.

12   Normand, J. 1995. *Women in Canada: A Statistical Report*, 3d ed. Cat. No. 89-503E. Ottawa: Minister of Supply and Services Canada.

13   Norris, J. 1980. "The Social Adjustment of Single and Widowed Older Women." *Essence* 4:134–44.

10   Norris, J.E. 1993. "'Why Not Think Carnegie Hall'? Working and Retiring among Older Professionals." *Canadian Journal on Aging* 12(2):182–99.

13   Norris, J.E., K.H. Rubin, J. Cohen, and L. Both. 1983. "Assessing Qualitative Dimensions of Adult Social Interaction: Examining Peer Relationships." Paper presented at the 12th Annual Scientific and Educational Meeting of the Canadian Association on Gerontology, Moncton.

1,7   Northcott, Herbert C. 1982. "The Best Years of Your Life." *Canadian Journal on Aging* 1:72–78.

4   Northcott, Herbert C. 1985. "The Geographic Mobility of Canada's Elderly." *Canadian Studies in Population* 12:183–202.

4   Northcott, Herbert C. 1988. *Changing Residence: The Geographic Mobility of Elderly Canadians*. Toronto: Butterworths.

4   Northcott, H.C. 1992. *Aging in Alberta: Rhetoric and Reality*. Calgary: Detselig Enterprises.

15   Northcott, H.C. 1994. "Public Perceptions of the Population Aging 'Crisis.'" *Canadian Public Policy* 20(1):66–77.

2   Novak, Mark. 1983. "Discovering a Good Age." *International Journal of Aging and Human Development* 16:231–39.

7,14   Novak, Mark. 1985. *Successful Aging: The Myths, Realities and Future of Aging in Canada*. Markham, ON: Penguin.

7   Novak, Mark. 1985–86. "Biography after the End of Metaphysics." *International Journal of Aging and Human Development* 22:189–204.

12   Novak, Mark. 1987. "The Canadian New Horizons Program." *The Gerontologist* 27: 353–55.

2   Novak, Mark. 1988. Review of "Oldtimers and Alzheimer's: The Descriptive Organization of Senility," by Jaber F. Gubrium. *Canadian Journal on Aging* 7:71–77.

14   Novak, Mark, and Charles Axelrod. 1979. "Primitive Myth and Modern Medicine: On Death and Dying, by Elisabeth Kubler-Ross." *The Psychoanalytic Review* 66:443–50.

6   Novak, M., N. Chappell, and C. Miles-Tapping. 1990. "Nursing Assistant Stress and the Cognitively Impaired Elderly." Paper presented at the 43rd Scientific Meeting of the Gerontological Society of America, Boston.

6   Novak, Mark, and Carol Guest. 1985. "Social Correlates of Caregiver Burden." Paper presented at the Canadian Association on Gerontology 14th Annual Scientific and Education Meeting, Hamilton.

13   Novak, Mark, and Carol Guest. 1989. "Application of a Multidimensional Caregiver Burden Inventory." *The Gerontologist* 29: 798–803.

13   Novak, M., and C. Guest. 1992. "A Comparison of the Impact of Institutionalization on Spouse and Nonspouse Caregivers." *Journal of Applied Gerontology* 11(4):379–94.

12   Novak, Mark, and Anne Percival. 1993. "Adult Education: A Study of Motivations, Preferences, and Financial Support in a Winnipeg Sample." Winnipeg Area Study Research Reports Series. Winnipeg: WAS.

13   Novak, Mark, and Leroy O. Stone. 1985. "Changing Patterns of Aging." Paper presented at the annual meeting of the Canadian Sociology and Anthropology Association, Montreal.

1   Nuessel, F.H., Jr. 1982. "Language of Ageism." *The Gerontologist* 22:273–76.

3   Nusberg, C. 1982. "World Assembly Seeks to Alert Developing Countries about Their Aging Populations." *Ageing International* 9:7–9.

13   O'Brien, J.E., and D.L. Wagner. 1980. "Help-Seeking by the Frail Elderly: Problems in Network Analysis." *The Gerontologist* 20:78–83.

12   O'Brien, S.J., and P.R. Conger. 1991. "No Time to Look Back: Approaching the Finish Line of Life's Course." *International Journal of Aging and Human Development* 33(1):75–87.

5,12 O'Brien, Sandra J., and Patricia A. Vertinsky. 1991. "Unfit Survivors: Exercise as a Resource for Aging Women." *The Gerontologist* 31:347–57.

12   O'Brien, S.J., and P.A. Vertinsky. 1991. "Unfit Survivors: Exercise as a Resource for Aging Women." *The Gerontologist* 31:347–57.

13   O'Connor, B.P. 1995. "Family and Friend Relationships among Older and Younger Adults: Interaction Motivation, Mood, and Quality." *International Journal of Aging and Human Development* 40(1):9–29.

8   O'Connor, B.P., and R.J. Vallerand. 1994. "Motivation, Self-Determination, and Person-Environment Fit as Predictors of Psychological Adjustment among Nursing Home Residents." *Psychology and Aging* 9(2):189–94.

13   Oderkirk, J. 1994. "Marriage in Canada: Changing Beliefs and Behaviours, 1600–1990." *Canadian Social Trends* (Summer):2–7.

8   OECD (Organization for Economic Co-operation and Development). 1988. *Ageing Populations: The Social Policy Implications*. Paris: Author.

8   OECD (Organization for Economic Co-operation and Development). 1993. *OECD Health Data, Software Package, Version 1.5*. Paris: Author.

8, 11 Okraku, Ishmael O. 1987. "Age and Attitudes toward Multigenerational Residence, 1973 to 1983." *Journal of Gerontology* 42:280–87.

12   One Voice, The Canadian Seniors Network. 1989. *Illiteracy and Older Canadians: An Unrecognized Problem: A Literature Review*. Ottawa: One Voice, the Seniors Network (Canada).

12   One Voice, the Canadian Seniors Network. 1990a. *Learning—That's Life: Conference Report and Recommendations*. Ottawa: One Voice, the Seniors Network (Canada).

12   One Voice, the Canadian Seniors Network. 1990b. "Illiteracy a Major Threat to Seniors' Independence, Conference Reveals." Press release. Ottawa: One Voice, the Seniors Network (Canada).

11   Ontario Advisory Council on the Physically Handicapped and Ontario Advisory Council on Senior Citizens. 1987. *The Freedom to Move Is Life Itself: A Report on Transportation in Ontario*. Toronto.

11   Ontario Advisory Council on Senior Citizens. 1978. *Through the Eyes of Others*. Toronto: Ontario Advisory Council on Senior Citizens.

11   Ontario Advisory Council on Senior Citizens. 1980–81. *Seniors Tell All*. Toronto: Ontario Advisory Council on Senior Citizens.

7   Ontario Advisory Council on Senior Citizens. 1993. *Denied Too Long*. Toronto: Ontario Advisory Council on Senior Citizens.

11   Ontario Ministry of Municipal Affairs and Housing, Research and Special Projects Branch. 1983. *Towards Community Planning for an Aging Society*. Toronto: Queen's Printer for Ontario.

4   Ontario Ministry of Treasury and Economics. 1979. *Issues in Pension Policy: Demographic and Economic Aspects of Canada's Ageing Population*. Ontario Treasury Studies 16. Toronto: Ministry of Treasury and Economics, Taxation and Fiscal Policy Branch.

6,8 Ontario Public Health Association. 1983. "Creating a Healthy Ontario: Health Care in the 80's and Beyond." Toronto: Ontario Public Health Association.

3,10 O'Rand, Angela M. 1990. "Stratification and the Life Course." In Robert H. Binstock and Linda K. George, eds. *Handbook of Aging and the Social Sciences*. 3d ed. San Diego: Academic Press.

10   Orbach, Harold L. 1981. "Mandatory Retirement and the Development of Adequate Retirement Provisions for Older Persons." In George Gasek, ed. *Canadian Gerontological Collection II: Retirement Income Systems*. Winnipeg: Canadian Association on Gerontology.

8   Organization for Economic Co-operation and Development. 1985. *Measuring Health Care, 1960–1983*. Social Policy Studies No. 2. Paris: Organization for Economic Co-operation and Development.

7   Osgood, N.J., B.A. Brant, and A. Lipman. 1991. *Suicide among the Elderly in Long-Term Care Facilities*. New York: Greenwood Press.

12   Ouellet, Pierre. 1986. "The Leisure Participation and Enjoyment Patterns of French and English-Speaking Members of Senior Citizens' Clubs in New Brunswick, Canada." *Canadian Journal on Aging* 5:257–68.

13   Paletta, A. 1992. "Today's Extended Families." *Canadian Social Trends* (Winter):26–28.

7 Palmore, Erdman B. 1970. "The Effects of Aging on Activities and Attitudes." In Erdman Palmore, ed. *Normal Aging*. Durham, NC: Duke University Press.

1 Palmore, Erdman B. 1971. "Attitudes toward Aging as Shown in Humor." *The Gerontologist* 11:181–86.

1 Palmore, Erdman B. 1977. "Facts on Aging: A Short Quiz." *The Gerontologist* 17:315–20.

13 Palmore, Erdman B. 1981. *Social Patterns in Normal Aging: Findings from the Duke Longitudinal Study*. Durham, NC: Duke University Press.

5 Palmore, Erdman B. 1984. "Longevity in Abkhazia: A Re-evaluation." *The Gerontologist* 24:95–96.

5 Palmore, E.B. 1987. Centenarians. In G.L. Maddox, ed. *The Encyclopedia of Aging*, 107–8. New York: Springer.

1 Palmore, Erdman B. 1988. *The Facts on Aging Quiz: A Handbook of Uses and Results*. New York: Springer.

3 Palmore, Erdman B., and K. Manton. 1974. "Modernization and the Status of the Aged: International Correlations." *Journal of Gerontology* 29:205–10.

3 Palmore, Erdman B., and F. Whittington. 1971. "Trends in the Relative Status of the Aged." *Social Forces* 50:84–91.

8 Parboosingh, Jean E., and Donald E. Larsen. 1987. "Factors Influencing Frequency and Appropriateness of Utilization of the Emergency Room by the Elderly." *Medical Care* 25:1139–47.

10 Paris, H. 1989. The Corporate Response to Workers with Family Responsibilities. Report 43–89. Ottawa: The Conference Board of Canada.

16 Parker, Brant. 1991. "Bridging the Generation Gap." Paper presented at the National Institute for Educational Innovation, Winnipeg (August).

4,5 Parliament, Jo-Anne. 1987. "Increased Life Expectancy, 1921–1986." *Canadian Social Trends* (Summer):15–19.

4 Parliament, Jo-Anne. 1989. "The Decline in Cardio-Vascular Disease Mortality." *Canadian Social Trends* (Autumn):28–29.

11 Parmelee, Patricia A., and M. Powell Lawton. 1990. "The Design of Special Environments for the Aged." In James E. Birren and K. Warner Schaie, eds. *Handbook of the Psychology of Aging*. 3d ed. San Diego: Academic Press.

2 Parsons, Talcott. 1937. *The Structure of Social Action*. New York: McGraw-Hill.

2 Parsons, Talcott. 1951. *The Social System*. New York: Free Press.

2 Passuth, Patricia M., and Vern L. Bengtson. 1988. In James E. Birren and Vern L. Bengtson, *Emergent Theories of Aging*. New York: Springer.

8 Paterson, Jody. 1989. "New Services Help Seniors Convalesce in Own Home." Victoria *Times-Colonist* (November 28).

5 Paul, A. 1994. "AIDS Stalking the Elderly." *Winnipeg Free Press* (October 15):A17.

13 Payne, B. J. 1994. Separation and Divorce in Later Adult Life. In National Advisory Council on Aging, *Marital Disruption in Later Life*, 47–63. Cat. No. H71-3/17-1994E. Ottawa: Minister of Supply and Services Canada.

7,14 Peck, Robert C. [1955] 1968. "Psychological Aspects of Aging." In John E. Anderson, ed. Proceedings of a Conference on Planning Research, Bethesda, MD, April 24–27, 1955; Washington, DC: American Psychological Association. Excerpted as "Psychological Developments in the Second Half of Life." In Bernice L. Neugarten, ed. *Middle Age and Aging*. Chicago: University of Chicago Press, 1968.

7 Penning, Margaret J. 1983. "Multiple Jeopardy: Age, Sex, and Ethnic Variations." *Canadian Ethnic Studies* 15:81–105.

13 Penning, Margaret J. 1990. "Receipt of Assistance by Elderly People: Hierarchical Selection and Task Specificity." *The Gerontologist* 30:220–27.

8 Penning, Margaret J., and Neena L. Chappell. 1982. "Mental Health Status: A Comparison of Different Socio-Cultural Environments for the Elderly." *Essence* 5:169–82.

8 Penning, M.J., and N.L. Chappell. 1993. "Age-Related Differences." In T. Stephens, and D.F. Graham, eds. *Canada's Health Promotion Survey 1990: Technical Report*, 248–61. Cat. No. H39-263/2-1990E. Ottawa: Minister of Supply and Services Canada.

5 Penning, M.J., and L.A. Strain. 1994. "Gender Differences in Disability, Assistance, and Subjective Well-Being in Later Life." *Journals of Gerontology* 49(4):S202–S208.

12 Penning, M.J., and D. Wasyliw. 1992. "Homebound Learning Opportunities: Reaching Out to Older Short-Ins and Their Caregivers." *The Gerontologist* 32: 704–7.

7 Perlman, Daniel, A.C. Gerson, and B. Spinner. 1978. "Loneliness among Senior Citizens: An Empirical Report." *Essence* 2:239–48.

6 Perlmutter, Marion. 1988. "Cognitive Potential throughout Life." In James E. Birren and Vern

L. Bengtson, eds. *Emergent Theories of Aging.* New York: Springer.

4   Perreault, J. 1990. *Population Projections for Canada, Provinces and Territories 1989–2011.* Cat. No. 91-520. Ottawa: Minister of Supply and Services.

12   Perri, Samuel, II, and Donald I. Templer. 1984–85. "The Effects of Aerobic Exercise Program on Psychological Variables in Older Adults." *International Journal of Aging and Human Development* 20:167–72.

10   Pesando, James, and S. Rea. 1977. *Public and Private Pensions in Canadian Economic Analysis.* Toronto: University of Toronto Press.

16   Peterson, D.A. 1987. *Career Paths in the Field of Aging: Professional Gerontology.* Lexington, MA: Lexington Books.

16   Peterson, D.A., E.B. Douglass, C.R. Botton, J.R. Connelly, and D. Bergstone. 1987. *A National Survey of Gerontology Instruction in American Institutions of Higher Education.* Washington, DC: AGHE.

16   Peterson, D.A., E.B. Douglass, and J.C. Lobenstine. 1996. *Careers in Aging: Opportunities and Options.* Washington, DC: The Association for Gerontology in Higher Education.

13   Pfeiffer, E., A. Verwoerdt, and H.S. Wang. 1968. "Sexual Behavior in Aged Men and Women, I: Observations on 254 Community Volunteers," *Archives of General Psychiatry* 19:753–58.

6   Phifer, J.F., and S.A. Murrell. 1986. "Etiologic Factors in the Onset of Depressive Symptoms in Older Adults." *Journal of Abnormal Psychology* 95:282–91.

14   Phillips, D.P., and K.A. Feldman. 1973. "A Dip in Deaths before Ceremonial Occasions: Some New Relationships between Social Integration and Mortality." *American Sociological Review* 38:678–96.

4   Philpot, H.J. 1871. *Guide Book to the Canadian Dominion Containing Full Information for the Emigrant, the Tourist, the Sportsman and the Small Capitalist.* London.

13   Pihlblad, C.T., D.L. Adams, and D.L. Rosencranz. 1972. "Socio-Economic Adjustment to Widowhood." *Omega* 3:295–305.

12   Pihlchyn, P. 1995. "Seniors Set Up Shop on Internet." *Winnipeg Free Press,* March 14:C6.

13   Pillemer, Karl, and David Finkelhor. 1988. "The Prevalence of Elder Abuse: A Random Sample Survey." *The Gerontologist* 28:51–57.

5   Pitskhelauri, G.Z. 1982. *The Longliving of Soviet Georgia.* Trans. and ed. G. Lesnoff-Caravaglia. New York: Human Sciences.

13   Pittaway, E., and E. Gallagher. 1995. *A Guide to Enhancing Service for Abused Older Canadians.* Victoria, BC: Centre on Aging, University of Victoria.

13   Pittaway, E., E. Gallagher, M. Stones, J. Kosberg, D. Nahmiash, E. Podnieks, L. Strain, and J. Bond. 1995. *Services for Abused Older Canadians.* Report for The Interministry Committee on Elder Abuse, Office for Seniors, Province of British Columbia. Victoria, BC: Minisry of Health and Ministry Responsible for Seniors.

13   Pittaway, E.D., and A. Westhues. 1993. "The Prevalence of Elder Abuse and Neglect of Older Adults Who Access Health and Social Services in London, Ontario, Canada." *Journal of Elder Abuse and Neglect* 5(4):77–93.

13   Pittaway, E.D., A. Westhues, and T. Peressini. 1995. "Risk Factors for Abuse and Neglect among Older Adults." *Canadian Journal on Aging* 14(Supp. 2):20–44.

3   Plath, D.W. 1972. "Japan: The After Years." In D.O. Cowgill and L.D. Holmes, eds. *Aging and Modernization.* New York: Appleton-Century-Crofts.

1   Plouffe, L. 1991. *Consumer Fraud and Seniors.* Ottawa: NACA.

1,13 Podnieks, E., K. Pillemer, J.P. Nicholson, T. Shillington, and A. Frizzell. 1989. *National Survey of Abuse of the Elderly in Canada: Preliminary Findings.* Toronto: Ryerson Office of Research and Innovation.

13   Podnieks, E., K. Pillemer, J.P. Nicholson, T. Shillington, and A. Frizzel. 1990. *National Survey on Abuse of the Elderly in Canada.* Toronto: Ryerson Polytechnical Institute.

8   Poirier, D. 1992. "Power of Social Workers in the Creation and Application of Elder Protection Statutory Norms in New Brunswick and Nova Scotia." *Journal of Elder Abuse and Neglect* 4:13–33.

8   Poirier, D., and G. Thériault. 1992. "Les normes juridiques et adminstratives en matière de droits des résidents de foyers de soins." *Canadian Journal on Aging* 12(1):16–32.

8   Policy, Planning and Information Branch. 1993. *Health Expenditures in Canada: Fact Sheets.* (March). Ottawa: Health Canada.

6   Poon, Leonard W. 1985. "Differences in Human Memory with Aging: Nature, Causes, and Clinical Implications." In James E. Birren and K. Warner Schaie, eds. *Handbook of the Psychology of Aging.* 2d ed. New York: Van Nostrand Reinhold.

6 Poon, Leonard W., J.L. Fozard, D.R. Paulshock, and J.C. Thomas. 1979. "A Questionnaire Assessment of Age Differences in Retention of Recent and Remote Events." *Experimental Aging Research* 5:401–11.

3 Population Reference Bureau, Inc. 1980. *1980 World Population Data Sheet*. Washington, DC: Population Reference Bureau, Inc.

13 Poulin, N., and B.L. Mishara. 1994. "A Comparison of Adult Attitudes toward Their Parents' Sexuality and Their Parents' Attitudes." *Canadian Journal on Aging* 13(1):96–103.

15 Powell, G.B. 1987. "Comparative Voting Behavior: Cleavages, Partisanship and Accountability." *Research in Micropolitics* 2:233–64.

13 Powers, Edward A., and Gordon L. Bultena. 1980. "Sex Differences in Intimate Friendships of Old Age." In Marie Marschall Fuller and Cora Ann Martin, eds. *The Older Woman: Lavender Rose or Gray Panther*. Springfield, IL: Charles C. Thomas.

15 Pratt, Henry J. 1979. "Politics of Aging." *Research on Aging* 1:155–86.

15 Pratt, Henry J. 1983. "National Interest Groups among the Elderly: Consolidation and Constraint." In William P. Browne and Laura Katz Olson, eds. *Aging and Public Policy*. Westport, CT: Greenwood Press.

15 Pratt, Henry J. 1984. "Aging in Canada: The Challenge to Political Science." *Canadian Journal on Aging* 3:55–61.

15 Pratt, H.J. 1993. *Gray Agendas: Interest Groups and Public Pensions in Canada, Britain, and the United States*. Ann Arbor, MI: The University of Michigan Press.

3 Press, I., and M. McKool. 1972. "Social Structure and Status of the Aged: Toward Some Valid Cross-Cultural Generalizations." *Aging and Human Development* 3:297–306.

6 Pressey, S.L., and A.D. Pressey. 1967. "Genius at 80; and Other Oldsters." *The Gerontologist* 7:183–87.

11 Priest, Gordon E. 1988. "Living Arrangements of Canada's 'Older Elderly' Population." *Canadian Social Trends* Cat. No. 11-008E. (Autumn):26–30.

11 Priest, G.E. 1994. "Current Demographics and Living Arrangements of Canada's Elderly." In G. Gutman and A.V. Wister, eds. *Progressive Accommodation for Seniors: Interfacing Shelter and Services*, 13–32. Vancouver, BC: Gerontology Research Centre.

12 Prince, M.J., and N.L. Chappell. 1994. "Voluntary Action by Seniors in Canada: Executive Summary." A report published by the Centre on Aging, University of Victoria, Victoria, BC.

11 Pritchard, David C. 1983. "The Art of Matchmaking: A Case Study in Shared Housing." *The Gerontologist* 23:174–79.

1 Proby, Joscelyn. 1984. "Combat Skills Put to Use." *Winnipeg Free Press* (April 10).

12 Program Audit and Review Directorate. 1989. *Evaluation Study of the New Horizons Program: Executive Summary*. Ottawa: Health and Welfare Canada.

5 Prohaska, T., R. Mermelstein, B. Miller, and S. Jack. 1993. "Functional Status and Living Arrangements." In J.F. Van Nostrand, S.E. Turner, and R. Suzman, eds. *Health Data on Older Americans: United States, 1992*. Hyattsville, MD: National Center for Health Statistics.

15 Pross, A. Paul. 1975. "Canadian Pressure Groups in the 1970's: Their Role and Their Relations with the Public Service." *Canadian Public Administration* 18:121–35.

13 Pruchno, Rachel A. 1990. "The Effects of Help Patterns on the Mental Health of Spouse Caregivers." *Research on Aging* 12:57–71.

13 Pruchno, R., and N. Resch. 1989. "Husbands and Wives as Caregivers: Antecedents of Depression and Burden." *Journals of Gerontology* 29(2):159–65.

8 Psychogeriatric Clinic. No date. "A Telephone Reassurance Service: An Evaluation." Ottawa: Ottawa General Hospital.

6 Puner, M. 1979. *Vital Maturity*. New York: Universe Books.

16 Puxty, J. 1995. "Goals, Development, and Strategies of a Coalition of Ontario Universities." *Educational Gerontology* 21:23–33.

3 Quadagno, J. 1980. "The Modernization Controversy: A Socio-Historical Analysis of Retirement in Nineteenth Century England." Paper presented at the meeting of the American Sociological Association, New York.

15 Quadagno, J. 1991. "Interest-Group Politics and the Future of U.S. Social Security." In J. Myles and J. Quadagno, eds. *States, Labor Markets, and the Future of Old-Age Policy*, 36–58. Philadelphia: Temple University Press.

8 Quick Response Team. No date. A Report on the Capital Regional District Quick Response Team. Victoria, BC: Quick Response Team.

10 Quinn, Joseph F. 1981. "The Extent and Correlates of Partial Retirement." *The Gerontologist* 21:634–43.

10 Quinn, Joseph F., and Richard V. Burkhauser. 1990. "Work and Retirement." In Robert H. Binstock and Linda K. George, eds. *Handbook of*

Aging and the Social Sciences. 3d ed. San Diego: Academic Press.

12 Radcliffe, David. 1982. "U3A: A French Model for the Later Years." A working paper prepared for the Annual Conference of the Comparative and International Education Society, New York.

11 Rahder, B., and B. Farge. 1990. *Share and Care: A Literature Review and Needs Assessment on Homesharing with a Service Component.* A report for Sharing, Toronto.

11 Rahder, B., B. Farge, and R. Todres. 1992. "A Review of the Canadian and American Literature on Homesharing Agencies with a Service Component." *Home Health Care Services Quarterly* 13(1–2):71–90.

8   Randhawa, J., and R. Riley. 1995. "Trends in Hospital Utilization, 1982–83 to 1992–93." *Health Reports* 7(1):41–49.

11 Rapelje, Douglas H. 1985. "A Canadian Example: The Home Sharing Program for Older Adults in Regional Niagara." In Gloria Gutman and Norman Blackie, eds. *Innovations in Housing and Living Arrangements for Seniors.* Burnaby, BC: The Gerontology Research Centre, Simon Fraser University.

13 Rapelje, D.H. 1992. "Respite Care: What Are the Options?" In G. Gutman, ed. *Shelter and Care of Persons with Dementia,* 243–50. Vancouver, BC: Simon Fraser University Gerontology Research Centre.

12 Rapelje, Douglas H., B. Goodman, and P. Swick. 1986. "Volunteer Opportunities for Senior Citizens: Part of the Continuum of Care." Paper presented at the Canadian Association on Gerontology 15th Annual Scientific and Educational Meeting, Quebec City.

8   Rattenbury, C., and M.J. Stones. 1989. "A Controlled Evaluation of Reminiscence and Current Topics Discussion Groups in a Nursing Home Context." *The Gerontologist* 29:768–71.

12 Rauschi, T.M. 1989. "Older Students and Higher Education." *Gerontology Review* 2:55–64.

15 Regenstreif, Peter. 1965. *The Diefenbaker Interlude: Parties and Voting in Canada.* Toronto: Longmans.

7   Reker, G.T., E.J. Peacock, and P.T.P. Wong. 1987. "Meaning and Purpose in Life and Well-Being: A Life-Span Perspective." *Journal of Gerontology* 42:44–49.

13 Rempel, Judith. 1985. "Childless Elderly: What Are They Missing?" *Journal of Marriage and the Family* 47:343–48.

1   Rempel, J.D. 1987. *Annotated Bibliography of Papers, Articles, and Other Documents Resulting from the Aging in Manitoba 1971, 1976, 1983*

Cross-sectional and Panel Studies. Winnipeg: Government of Manitoba.

11 Renaud, François, and Martin Wexler. 1986. "Housing the Elderly in the Community: A Review of Existing Programs in Quebec." In Gloria Gutman and Norman Blackie, eds. *Aging in Place: Housing Adaptations and Options for Remaining in the Community.* Burnaby, BC: The Gerontology Research Centre, Simon Fraser University.

8   Research and Planning Unit, Family and Community Support Services Division, Social Services Department. 1983. "A Profile of the Elderly in Calgary: A Demographic Profile and Needs Assessment." Calgary: City of Calgary.

13 Resnick, H., and J. Cantor. 1970. "Suicide and Aging." *Journal of the American Geriatric Society* 18:152–58.

6   Rhodes, Ann. 1983. "Five Women Who Defy the Stereotypes of Aging." *Chatelaine* (February).

6,7 Riegel, Klaus F. 1975. "Adult Life Crises: A Dialectic Interpretation of Development." In Nancy Datan and Leon H. Ginsberg, eds. *Life-Span Developmental Psychology: Normative Life Crisis.* New York: Academic Press.

7   Riegel, Klaus F. 1976. "The Dialectics of Human Development." *American Psychologist* 31:689–700.

2   Riley, Matilda White. 1971. "Social Gerontology and the Age Stratification of Society." *The Gerontologist* 11:79–87.

2   Riley, Matilda White. 1987. "On the Significance of Age in Sociology." *American Sociological Review* 52:1–14.

5   Riley, M.W. 1989. "AIDS and Older People: The Overlooked Segment of the Population." In M.W. Riley, M.G. Ory, and D. Zablotsky, eds. *AIDS in an Aging Society,* 3–26. New York: Springer.

7   Riley, M.W., and A. Foner, eds. 1968. *Aging and Society.* Volume I: *An Inventory of Research Findings.* New York: Russell Sage Foundation.

2   Riley, M.W., A. Foner, and J. Waring. 1988. "Sociology of Age." In N. Smelser, ed. *Handbook of Sociology.* Beverly Hills, CA: Sage.

2,7,10 Riley, M.W., M.E. Johnson, and A. Foner, eds. 1972. *Aging and Society. Volume III: A Sociology of Age Stratification.* New York: Russell Sage Foundation.

13 Riordan, R. 1994. "Two by Two: Sex Ratios of Unattached Canadians." *Canadian Social Trends* (Spring):26–29.

7   Ritzer, G. 1992. *Contemporary Sociological Theory,* 3d ed. New York: McGraw-Hill.

10,12 Roadburg, Alan. 1985. *Aging: Retirement, Leisure and Work in Canada*. Toronto: Methuen.

8 Roberge, Roger, and René Beausejour. 1988. "Use of Restraints in Chronic Care Hospitals and Nursing Homes." *Canadian Journal on Aging* 8:377–81.

5,8 Roberge, R., J-M Berthelot, and M. Wolfson. 1995. "Health and Socio-Economic Inequalities." *Canadian Social Trends* (Sum-mer):15–19.

16 Robertson, Duncan. 1981. "Undergraduate Medical Education in Geriatric Medicine." *Annals Royal College of Physicians and Surgeons of Canada* 14:371–73.

6 Robertson, D., K. Rockwood, and P. Stolee. 1982. "Prevalence of Cognitive Impairment in an Elderly Population." Paper presented at the Canadian Association on Gerontology 11th Annual Scientific and Education Meeting, Winnipeg.

6,7 Robertson, Ian. 1981. *Sociology*. 2d ed. New York: Worth.

13 Robertson, Joan F. 1977. "Grandmotherhood: A Study of Role Conceptions." *Journal of Marriage and the Family* 39:165–74.

10 Robinson, P.K., S. Coberly, and C.E. Paul. 1985. "Work and Retirement." In Robert H. Binstock and Ethel Shanas, eds. *Handbook of Aging and the Social Sciences*. 2d ed. New York: Van Nostrand Reinhold.

11 Romanick, Gregory S. 1986. "Municipal Mechanisms for the Implementation of Granny Flats." In Susan Corke, Gregory S. Romanick, Michael Lazarowich, and Joan Simon, eds. *Granny Flats: A Housing Option for the Elderly, Report No. 13*. Winnipeg: Institute of Urban Studies.

4 Romaniuc, Anatole. 1984. *Current Demographic Analysis: Fertility in Canada: From Baby-Boom to Baby-Bust*. Statistics Canada Cat. No. 91-524E Occasional. Ottawa: Minister of Supply and Services Canada.

5 Roos, Noralou P., and Betty Havens. 1991. "Predictors of Successful Aging: A Twelve-Year Study of Manitoba Elderly." *American Journal of Public Health* 81:63–68.

5 Roos, N.P., B. Havens, and C.D. Black. 1993. "Living Longer but Doing Worse: Assessing Health Status in Elderly Persons at Two Points in Time in Manitoba, Canada, 1971 and 1983." *Social Science and Medicine* 36(3):273–82.

8 Roos, N.P., and Evelyn Shapiro. 1981. "The Manitoba Longitudinal Study on Aging." *Medical Care* 19:644–57.

7,8 Roos, N. P., E. Shapiro, and L.L. Roos, Jr. 1984. "Aging and the Demand for Health Services: Which Aged and Whose Demand?" *The Gerontologist* 24:31–36.

12 Rootman, I., R. Warren, R. Stephens, and L. Peters. 1988. *Canada's Health Promotion Survey: Technical Report*. Cat. No. H39-119/1988E. Ottawa: Minister of Supply and Services Canada.

11 Rose, Albert, and J. Grant Macdonald. 1984. *Factors Influencing the Quality of Life of Community-Based Elderly, Part II: Housing Conditions of the Elderly in Ontario*. Research paper No. 152.

5 Rose, M.R. 1993. "Evolutionary Gerontology and Critical Gerontology: Let's Just Be Friends." In T.R. Cole, W.A. Achenbaum, P.L. Jakobi, and R. Kastenbaum, eds. *Voices and Visions of Aging: Toward a Critical Gerontology*, 64–75. New York: Springer.

11 Rosenmayr, L., and E. Kockeis. 1963. "Propositions for a Sociological Theory of Aging and the Family." *International Social Science Journal* 15:410–26.

7 Rosenthal, Carolyn J. 1983. "The Anglo-Canadian Family: A Perspective on Ethnicity and Support to the Elderly." Paper presented at the 12th Annual Scientific and Educational Meeting of the Canadian Association on Gerontology, Moncton.

13 Rosenthal, Carolyn J. 1985. "Kinkeeping in the Familial Division of Labor." *Journal of Marriage and the Family* 47:965–74.

7 Rosenthal, Carolyn J. 1986a. "Family Supports in Later Life: Does Ethnicity Make a Difference?" *The Gerontologist* 26:19–24.

7 Rosenthal, Carolyn J. 1986b. *Intergenerational Solidarity in Later Life: Ethnic Contrasts in Jewish and Anglo Families*. Program in Gerontology, University of Toronto Research Paper Series, Research paper No. 4.

13 Rosenthal, Carolyn J. 1987a. "Aging and Intergenerational Relations in Canada." In Victor W. Marshall, ed. *Aging in Canada: Social Perspectives*. 2d ed. Toronto: Fitzhenry and Whiteside.

13 Rosenthal, Carolyn J. 1987b. "The Comforter: Providing Personal Advice and Emotional Support to Generations in the Family." *Canadian Journal on Aging* 6:228–39.

13 Rosenthal, C.J. 1994. "Editorial: Long-term Care Reform and 'Family' Care: A Worrisome Combination." *Canadian Journal on Aging* 13(4):419–27.

13   Rosenthal, C., and P. Dawson. 1991. "Wives of Institutionalized Husbands." *Journal of Aging and Health* 3(3):315–34.

13   Rosenthal, C., and P. Dawson. 1992. "Caregiving after Institutionalization: The Needs of Older Wives." In B. Bauer, ed. *Conceptual and Methodological Issues in Family Caregiving Research*, 62–68. Proceedings of the Invitational Conference on Family Caregiving Research, June 21–22, 1990, Toronto. Toronto: University of Toronto Press.

13   Rosenthal, C. J., and J. Gladstone. 1993. "Family Relationships and Support in Later Life." *Journal of Canadian Studies* 28(1):122–38.

13   Rosenthal, C.J., V.W. Marshall, and J. Synge. 1980. "The Succession of Lineage Roles as Families Age." *Essence* 4:179–93.

13   Rosenthal, C.J., S.H. Matthews, and V.W. Marshall. 1989. "Is Parent Care Normative? The Experiences of a Sample of Middle-Aged Women." *Research on Aging* 11(2):244–60.

13   Rosenthal, C.J., J. Sulman, and V.W. Marshall. 1993. "Depressive Symptoms in Family Caregivers of Long-Stay Patients." *The Gerontologist* 33(2):249–57.

15   Rosenzweig, Robert M. 1991. "Generational Conflict Brewing, GSA Members Warned." *Gerontology News* (January).

3   Rosow, Irving. 1965. "And Then We Were Old." *Transaction* 2:20–26.

7   Rosow, Irving. 1976. "Status and Role Change Through the Life Span." In R.H. Binstock and E. Shanas, eds. *Handbook of Aging and the Social Sciences*. New York: Van Nostrand Reinhold.

6   Ross, E. 1968. "Effects of Challenging and Supportive Instructions in Verbal Learning in Older Persons." *Journal of Educational Psychology* 59:261–66.

16   Ross, Elsie. 1990. "Computers Bridge Age Gap." *Calgary Herald*, 30 April.

14   Ross, M.M., and B. McDonald. 1994. "Providing Palliative Care to Older Adults: Context and Challenges." *Journal of Palliative Care* 10(4):5–10.

13   Ross, M.M., C.J. Rosenthal, and P. Dawson. 1994. "The Continuation of Caregiving Following the Institutionalization of Elderly Husbands." In National Advisory Council on Aging. *Marital Disruption in Later Life*, 23–32. Cat. No. H71-3/17-1994E. Ottawa: Minister of Supply and Services Canada.

5   Rowe, John W., and Robert L. Kahn. 1991. "Human Aging: Usual and Successful." In Harold Cox, ed. *Aging*, 7th ed. Guilford, CT: Dushkin. Originally published in *Science* 237(1987):143–49.

9   Royal Commission on the Status of Pensions in Ontario. 1980. *Report. Vol. II. Design for Retirement*. Toronto: Government of Ontario.

13   Rushing, W.A. 1968. "Individual Behaviour and Suicide." In J. Gibbs, ed. *Suicide*. New York: Harper and Row.

7   Ruth, J., and P. Coleman. 1996. "Personality and Aging: Coping and Management of the Self in Later Life." In J.E. Birren and K.W. Schaie, eds. *Handbook of the Psychology of Aging*, 4th ed., 308–22. San Diego: Academic Press.

11   Rutman, Deborah, and Jonathan L. Freedman. 1988. "Anticipating Relocation: Coping Strategies and the Meaning of Home for Older People." *Canadian Journal on Aging* 7:17–31.

1   Ryan, E.B., and R.K.B. Heaven. 1988. "The Impact of Situational Context on Age-Based Attitudes." *Social Behaviour* 3:105–18.

6   Ryan, E.B., and S.K. See. 1993. "Age-Based Beliefs about Memory Changes for Self and Others across Adulthood." *Journals of Gerontology* 48(4):199–201.

6   Rybash, J. M., W.J. Hoyer, and P.A. Roodin. 1986. *Adult Cognition and Aging: Developmental Changes in Processing, Knowing, and Thinking*. New York: Pergamon Press.

10   Sadavoy, J. 1994. "The Aging Physician." In V.W. Marshall and B.D. McPherson, eds. *Aging: Canadian Perpsectives*. Peterborough, ON: Broadview Press/*Journal of Canadian Studies*.

6   Sainsbury, Robert S., and Marjorie Coristine. 1986. "Affective Discrimination in Moderately to Severely Demented Patients." *Canadian Journal on Aging* 5:99–104.

6,14   Saint-Arnaud, J. 1993. "Autonomy, Self-Determination and the Decision-Making Process Concerning End-of-Life Treatment." In National Advisory Council on Aging, *Ethics and Aging*, 33–49. Cat. No. H71-3/16-1993E. Ottawa: Minister of Supply and Services Canada.

3   Salas, Rafael. 1982. "Aging: A Universal Phenomenon." *Populi* 9:3–7.

5   Salthouse, T.A. 1984. "Effects of Age and Skill in Typing." *Journal of Gerontology* 113:345–71.

10   Salthouse, T.A., and T.J. Maurer. 1996. "Aging, Job Performance, and Career Development." In J.E. Birren and K.W. Schaie, eds. *Handbook of the Psychology of Aging*, 4th ed., 353–64. San Diego: Academic Press.

10   Sammartino, F.J. 1987. "The Effect of Health on Retirement." *Social Security Bulletin* 50:31–47.

14 Sanders, C.M. 1980–81. "Comparison of Younger and Older Spouses in Bereavement Outcome." *Omega* 11:217–32.

6 Sanders, R.E., M.D. Murphy, F.A. Schmitt, and K.K. Walsh. 1980. "Age Differences in Free Recall Rehearsal Strategies." *Journal of Gerontology* 35:550–58.

6 Sanders, R.E., and J.A. Sanders. 1978. "Long-Term Durability and Transfer of Enhanced Conceptual Performance in the Elderly." *Journal of Gerontology* 33:408–12.

11 Saskatchewan Housing Corporation. 1984. *Housing Need in Saskatchewan*. Regina: Saskatchewan Housing Corporation.

11 Saskatchewan Housing Corporation. No date. *Enriched Housing*. Regina: Saskatchewan Housing Corporation.

14 Saunders, Cicely. 1984. "St. Christopher's Hospice." In Edwin S. Shneidman, ed. *Death: Current Perspectives*. 3d ed. Palo Alto, CA: Mayfield.

6 Schaie, K. Warner. 1959. "Cross-Sectional Methods in the Study of Psychological Aspects of Aging." *Journal of Gerontology* 14:208–15.

2,7 Schaie, K. Warner. 1968. "Age Changes and Age Differences." In Bernice L. Neugarten, ed. *Middle Age and Aging*. Chicago: University of Chicago Press.

6 Schaie, K. Warner. 1975. "Age Changes in Adult Intelligence." In Diana S. Woodruff and J.E. Birren, eds. *Aging: Scientific Perspectives and Social Issues*. New York: D. Van Nostrand.

6 Schaie, K. Warner. 1990a. "Intellectual Development in Adulthood." In James E. Birren and K. Warner Schaie, eds. *Handbook of the Psychology of Aging*. 3d ed. San Diego: Academic Press.

6 Schaie, K. Warner. 1990b. "The Optimization of Cognitive Functioning in Old Age: Predictions Based on Cohort-Sequential and Longitudinal Data." In Paul B. Baltes and Margaret M. Baltes, eds. *Successful Aging: Perspectives from the Behavioral Sciences*. Cambridge: Cambridge University Press.

6 Schaie, K.W. 1996. "Intellectual Development in Adulthood." In J.E. Birren and K.W. Schaie, eds. *Handbook of the Psychology of Aging*, 4th ed., 266–86. San Diego: Academic Press.

2,6 Schaie, K. Warner, and G. Labouvie-Vief. 1974. "Generational Versus Ontogenetic Components of Change in Adult Cognitive Behavior: A Fourteen-Year Cross-Sequential Study." *Development Psychology* 10:305–20.

6 Scheibel, A.B. 1996. "Structural and Functional Changes in the Aging Brain." In J.E. Birren and K.W. Schaie, eds. *Handbook of the Psychology of Aging*, 4th ed., 105–28. San Diego: Academic Press.

10 Schellenberg, G. 1994. *Older Workers and Canada's Aging Labour Force*. Ottawa: One Voice—Seniors Network (Canada) Ltd.

13 Schlesinger, Benjamin. 1983. "Institutional Life: The Canadian Experience." In Ruth B. Weg, ed. *Sexuality in the Later Years: Roles and Behavior*. New York: Academic Press.

13 Schlesinger, B., and D. Raphael. 1992. "The Sandwich Generations; The Jewish Woman in the Middle: Stresses and Satisfaction." *Journal of Psychology and Judaism* 16(2):77–96.

3 Schmidt, W.E. 1993. "Why Europe Fears Its Future." *The Globe and Mail* (July 14):A7.

5 Schneider, E.L., and J.A. Brody. 1983. "Aging, Natural Death and the Compression of Morbidity: Another View." *New England Journal of Medicine* 309:854–56.

5 Schneider, E.L., and J.D. Reed. 1985. "Modulations of Aging Processes." In Caleb E. Finch and Edward L. Schneider, eds. *Handbook of the Biology of Aging*. 2d ed. New York: Van Nostrand Reinhold.

2 Schneider, E.L., and J.W. Rowe, eds. 1990. *Handbook of the Biology of Aging*, 3d ed. San Diego: Academic Press.

5,8 Schoenborn, C.A. 1993. "Trends in Health Status and Practices: Canada and the United States." *Canadian Social Trends* (Winter):16–21.

12 Scholz, W.D. 1993. "New Prospects at the Third Stage of Life: Older People at University." *Journal of Educational Gerontology* 8:33–46.

1 Schonfield, David. 1982. "Who Is Stereotyping Whom and Why?" *The Gerontologist* 22:267–72.

6,11 Schooler, Carmi. 1990. "Psychosocial Factors and Effective Cognitive Functioning in Adulthood." In James E. Birren and K. Warner Schaie, eds. *Handbook of the Psychology of Aging*. 3d ed. San Diego: Academic Press.

13 Schorr, A. 1980. "'… thy father and thy mother …' A Second Look at Filial Responsibility and Social Policy." Social Security Administration Publication 13-11953. Washington, DC: U.S. Department of Health and Human Services.

2 Schroots, Johannes J.F. 1988. "On Growing, Formative Change, and Aging." In James E. Birren and Vern L. Bengtson, eds. *Emergent Theories of Aging*. New York: Springer.

6   Schroots, J.J.F. 1995. "Psychological Models of Aging." *Canadian Journal on Aging* 14(1):44–66.

11   Schull, Christiane. 1981. "Bag Ladies." *Today Magazine* (April 15).

3,10   Schulz, James H. 1980. *The Economics of Aging.* 2d ed. Belmont, CA: Wadsworth.

10   Schulz, James H. 1985. *The Economics of Aging.* 3d ed. Belmont, CA: Wadsworth.

10   Schulz, J. 1991. "Epilogue: The 'Buffer Years': Market Incentives and Evolving Retirement Policies." In J. Myles and J. Quadagno, eds. *States, Labor Markets, and the Future of Old-Age Policy*, 295–308. Philadelphia: Temple University Press.

14   Schulz, Richard. 1978. *The Psychology of Death, Dying, and Bereavement.* Reading, MA: Addison-Wesley.

2   Schutz, Alfred. 1967. *The Phenomenology of the Social World.* Evanston, IL: Northwestern University Press.

13   Schwartz, A.N. 1979. "Psychological Dependency: An Emphasis on the Later Years." In P.K. Ragan, ed. *Aging Parents.* Los Angeles: University of Southern California.

6   Schwartzman, A.E., D. Gold, D. Andres, T.Y. Arbuckle, and J. Chaikelson. 1987. "Stability of Intelligence: A 40-Year Follow-Up." *Canadian Journal of Psychology* 41:244–56.

8   Schwenger, Cope, and M. Gross. 1980. "Institutional Care and Institutionalization of the Elderly in Canada." In Victor W. Marshall, ed. *Aging in Canada.* Toronto: Fitzhenry and Whiteside.

12   Searle, Mark S. 1987. *Leisure and Aging in Manitoba: A Report to Manitoba Culture, Heritage and Recreation.* Winnipeg: Faculty of Physical Education and Recreation Studies, University of Manitoba.

12   Searle, Mark S., and Michael J. Mahon. 1991. "Leisure Education in a Day Hospital: The Effects of Selected Social-Psychological Variables among Older Adults." Paper presented at the 1990 National Recreation and Park Association Leisure Research Symposium.

12   Searle, M.S., M.J. Mahon, S.E. Iso-Ahola, and H.A. Sdrolias. 1995. "Enhancing a Sense of Independence and Psychological Well-Being among the Elderly: A Field Experiment." *Journal of Leisure Research* 27(2):107–24.

3   Secretariat of the Economic Commission for Europe. 1992. "Aging, the Public Sector and Age Profiles." In G.J. Stolnitz, ed., *Demographic Causes and Economic Consequences of Population Aging: Europe and North America*, 383–96. New York: United Nations.

8   Segall, Alexander. 1987. "Age Differences in Lay Conceptions of Health and Self-Care Responses to Illness." *Canadian Journal on Aging* 6:47–65.

1   Senate of Canada. 1966. *Final Report of the Special Committee of the Senate on Aging.* Ottawa: Queen's Printer.

1,9,10,15 Senate of Canada. 1979. *Retirement Without Tears: A Report of the Special Senate Committee on Retirement Age Policies (Croll Commission).* Ottawa: Minister of Supply and Services.

14   Senate of Canada. 1995. *Of Life and Death.* Report of the Special Senate Commmittee on Euthanasia and Assisted Suicide. Ottawa: Queen's Printer of Canada.

11   Senior Citizens' Provincial Council. 1981. *Regina Social Support Survey.* Regina: Senior Citizens' Provincial Council.

11   Senior Citizens' Provincial Council. 1982. *A Survey of the Transportation Needs of the Rural Elderly.* Regina: Senior Citizens' Provincial Council.

8,12,13 Senior Citizens' Provincial Council. 1983. *Profile '83: The Senior Population in Saskatchewan. 3: Social Resources.* Regina: Senior Citizens' Provincial Council.

7   Senior Citizens' Provincial Council. 1988. *A Study of Unmet Needs of Off-Reserve Indian and Metis Elderly in Saskatchewan.* Regina: Senior Citizens' Provincial Council.

6   *Seniors Today.* 1995. "National Alzheimer Registry Created." *Seniors Today* (July 1):3.

3   Sennott-Miller, L. 1994. "Research on Aging in Latin America: Present Status and Future Directions." *Journal of Cross-Cultural Gerontology* 9:87–97.

7   Sermat, Vello. 1978. "Sources of Loneliness." *Essence* 2:271–76.

13   Shanas, Ethel. 1967. "Family Help Patterns and Social Class in Three Societies." *Journal of Marriage and the Family* 29:257–66.

13   Shanas, Ethel. 1979. "The Family as a Social Support System in Old Age." *The Gerontologist* 19:169–74.

13   Shanas, E., P. Townsend, D. Wedderburn, H. Friis, P. Milhoj, and J. Stehouwer. 1968. *Older People in Three Industrial Societies.* New York: Atherton Press.

7,8,14 Shapiro, Evelyn. 1983. "Impending Death and the Use of Hospitals by the Elderly." *Journal of the American Geriatrics Society* 31:348–51.

5,8   Shapiro, E. 1991. *Manitoba Health Care Studies and Their Policy Implications.* Winnipeg: Manitoba Centre for Health Policy and Evalaution.

8 Shapiro, E. 1992. "Editorial: We've Come a Long Way but Are We There?" *Canadian Journal on Aging* 11(3):206–9.

8 Shapiro, E. 1994. "Community and Long-Term Health Care in Canada." In A. Blomqvist and D.M. Brown, eds. *Limits to Care: Reforming Canada's Health System in an Age of Restraint*, 327–62. Ottawa: C.D. Howe Institute.

8 Shapiro, E. 1995. "Long-Term Care and Population Aging." In M. Novak, ed. *Aging and Society: A Canadian Reader*, 154–60. Toronto: Nelson Canada.

8 Shapiro, E., R.B. Tate, and N.P. Roos. 1987. "Do Nursing Homes Reduce Hospital Use?" *Medical Care* 25:1–8.

10 Shapiro, Evelyn, and Noralou P. Roos. 1982. "Retired and Employed Elderly Persons: Their Utilization of Health Care Services." *The Gerontologist* 22:187–93.

8 Shapiro, Evelyn, and Noralou P. Roos. 1986. "High Users of Hospital Days." *Canadian Journal on Aging* 5:165–74.

8 Shapiro, Evelyn, and N.P. Roos. 1987. "Predictors, Patterns and Consequences of Nursing-Home Use in One Canadian Province." In Victor W. Marshall, ed. *Aging in Canada: Social Perspectives*. 2d ed. Toronto: Fitzhenry and Whiteside.

8 Shapiro, Evelyn, and Robert B. Tate. 1985. "Predictors of Long Term Care Facility Use among the Elderly." *Canadian Journal on Aging* 4:11–19.

8 Shapiro, Evelyn, and Robert Tate. 1988a. "Survival Patterns of Nursing Home Admissions and Their Policy Implications." *Canadian Journal of Public Health* 79:268–74.

8 Shapiro, Evelyn, and Robert Tate. 1988b. "Who Is Really at Risk of Institutionalization?" *The Gerontologist* 28:237–45.

8 Shapiro, Evelyn, and Linda M. Webster. 1984. "Nursing Home Utilization Patterns for All Manitoba Admissions, 1974–1981." *The Gerontologist* 24:610–15.

3 Sharp, H.S. 1981. "Old Age among the Chipewyan." In P.T. Amoss and S. Harrell, eds. *Other Ways of Growing Old: Anthropological Perspectives*. Stanford, CA: Stanford University Press.

14 Shedletsky, Ralph, and Rory Fisher. 1986. "Terminal Illness: Attitudes in Both an Acute and an Extended Care Teaching Hospital." *Journal of Palliative Care* 2:16–21.

13,14 Shedletsky, R., R. Fisher, and G. Nadon. 1982. "Assessment of Palliative Care for Dying Hospitalized Elderly." *Canadian Journal on Aging* 1:11–15.

12 Shephard, Roy J. 1978. *Physical Activity and Aging*. London: Croom Helm.

12 Shephard, Roy J. 1986. "Physical Activity and Aging in a Post-Industrial Society." In Barry D. McPherson, ed. *Sport and Aging: The 1984 Olympic Scientific Congress Proceedings, Vol. 5*. Champaign, IL: Human Kinetics.

12 Shephard, Roy J. 1990. "Measuring Physical Activity in the Elderly: Some Implications for Nutrition." *Canadian Journal on Aging* 9:188–203.

10 Shephard, R.J. 1995. "A Personal Perspective on Aging and Productivity, with Particular Reference to Physically Demanding Work." *Ergonomics* 38(4):617–36.

10 Sheppard, H.L. 1991. "Early Retirement: Questions and Speculations. In J. Myles and J. Quadagno, eds. *States, Labor Markets, and the Future of Old-Age Policy*, 290–94. Philadelphia: Temple University Press.

3 Sheppard, H.L., and G.F. Streib. 1985. *Aging in China*. Tampa, FL: International Exchange Center on Gerontology University of South Florida.

14 Shneidman, Edwin S. 1984. "Malignancy: Dialogues with Life-Threatening Illnesses." In Edwin S. Shneidman, ed. *Death: Current Perspectives*. 3d ed. Palo Alto, CA: Mayfield.

12 Sidney, K.H., and Shephard, R.J. 1978. *Exercise and Aging: The Scientific Basis*. Hillsdale, NJ: Enslow Publishers.

12 Sijpkes, P., M. MacLean, and D. Brown. 1983. "Hanging around the Mall." *Recreation Canada* (February).

6 Silberfeld, M. 1992. "The Use of 'Risk' in Decision-Making." *Canadian Journal on Aging* 11(2):124–36.

6 Silberfeld, M. 1994. "Evaluating Decisions in Mental Capacity Assessments." *International Journal of Geriatric Psychiatry* 9:365–71.

11 Silver, C., and R. Van Diepen. 1995. "Housing Tenure Trends 1951–1991." *Canadian Social Trends* (Spring):8–12.

3 Simmons, L.W. 1960. "Aging in Preindustrial Societies." In C. Tibbitts, ed. *Handbook of Social Gerontology: Societal Aspects of Aging*. Chicago: University of Chicago Press.

3 Simmons, L.W. 1970. *The Role of the Aged in Primitive Society*. New Haven, CT: Yale University.

5 Simmons-Tropea, Daryl, and Richard Osborn. 1987. "Disease, Survival and Death: The Health Status of Canada's Elderly." In Victor W.

Marshall, ed. *Aging in Canada*. 2d ed. Toronto: Fitzhenry and Whiteside.

6   Simonton, D.K. 1977. "Creative Productivity, Age, and Stress: A Biographical Time-Series Analysis of 10 Classical Composers." *Journal of Personality and Social Psychology* 35:791–804.

6   Simonton, D.K. 1988a. "Age and Outstanding Achievement: What Do We Know after over a Century of Research?" *Psychological Bulletin* 104: 251–67.

6   Simonton, D.K. 1988b. *Scientific Genius: A Psychology of Science*. Cambridge, MA: Cambridge University Press.

6   Simonton, Dean Keith. 1990. "Creativity and Wisdom in Aging." In James E. Birren and K. Warner Schaie, eds. *Handbook of the Psychology of Aging*. 3d ed. San Diego: Academic Press.

10 Simpson, I.H., K.W. Back, and J.C. McKinney. 1966. "Continuity of Work and Retirement Activities, and Self-Evaluation." In Ida H. Simpson and John C. McKinney, eds. *Social Aspects of Aging*. Durham, NC: Duke University Press.

8   Sinclair, Douglas. 1984. "A New Approach to Geriatric Institutional Care." *Canadian Family Physician* 30:1373–76.

12 Singleton, J.F., W.F. Forbes, and N. Agwani. 1993. "Stability of Activity across the Lifespan." *Activities, Adaptation and Aging* 18(1):19–27.

2   SIRP. 1991. *Inventory of Funded Research Projects*. Cat. No. H39-215/1991. Ottawa: Minister of Supply and Services Canada.

6   Ska, Bernadette, and Jean-Luc Nespoulous. 1988. "Encoding Strategies and Recall Performance of a Complex Figure by Normal Elderly Subjects." *Canadian Journal on Aging* 7:408–16.

14 Skelton, David. 1982. "The Hospice Movement: A Human Approach to Palliative Care." *Canadian Medical Association Journal* 126:556–58.

16 Skelton, David. 1986. "Future of Geriatric Medicine in Canada." *Gerontion* 1:19–23.

6   Skinkle, Randy R., and P.R. Grant. 1988. "Outcome Evaluation of an In-Service Training Program for Nursing Home Aides." *Canadian Journal on Aging* 7:48–57.

1   Slaughter-Defoe, D.T., V.S. Kuehne, and J.K. Straker. 1992. "African-American, Anglo-American, and Anglo-Canadian Grade 4 Children's Concepts of Old People and of Extended Family." *International Journal of Aging and Human Development* 35(3): 161–78.

6   Smith, A.D. 1996. "Memory." In J.E. Birren and K.W. Schaie, eds. *Handbook of the Psychology of Aging*, 4th ed., 236–50. San Diego: Academic Press.

12 Smith, E.L. 1982. "Exercise for Prevention of Osteoporosis: A Review." *Physician and Sportsmedicine* 10:72–83.

13 Smith, G., and Dumas, J. 1994. "The Sandwich Generation: Myths and Reality." In J. Dumas and A. Bélanger, eds. *Report on the Demographic Situation in Canada 1994*, 111–48. Cat. No. 91-209E. Ottawa: Minister of Industry, Science and Technology.

11 Smith, Wendy. 1979. *Single Old Men on Main Street: An Evaluation of Jack's Hotel*. Winnipeg: Canada Mortgage and Housing Corporation.

6   Smyer, M.A., S.H. Zarit, and S.H. Qualls. 1990. "Psychological Intervention with the Aging Individual." In James E. Birren and K. Warner Schaie, eds. *Handbook of the Psychology of Aging*, 3d ed. San Diego: Academic Press.

13 Snell, James G. 1990. "Filial Responsibility Laws in Canada: An Historical Study." *Canadian Journal on Aging* 9:268–77.

9   Snell, J.G. 1993. "The Gendered Construction of Elderly Marriage, 1900–1950." *Canadian Journal on Aging* 12(4):509–23.

10 Snell, M. Leslie, and Kathleen Brown. 1987. "Financial Strategies of the Recently Retired." *Canadian Journal on Aging* 6:290–303.

13 Snider, Earle L. 1981. "The Role of Kin in Meeting Health Care Needs of the Elderly." *Canadian Journal of Sociology* 6:325–36.

3   Sokolovsky, Jay, ed. 1990. *The Cultural Context of Aging: Worldwide Perspectives*. New York: Bergin and Garvey.

11 Sokolovsky, J., and C. Cohen. 1981. "Measuring Social Interaction of the Urban Elderly: A Methodological Synthesis." *International Journal of Aging and Human Development* 12:233–44.

10 Solem, Per Erik. 1976. *Paid Work after Retirement Age, and Mortality in Retirement: Norwegian Experience*. Oslo: Norwegian Institute of Gerontology.

1   Solicitor General of Canada. 1983. *Canadian Urban Victimization Survey. Bulletin 1: Victims of Crime*. Ottawa: Minister of Supply and Services.

14 Somerville, M.S. 1989. "Legal Issues in Surgical Care of Elderly Persons." *Canadian Journal on Aging* 8:128–43.

14 Southall, H. 1982. *A Survey of Palliative Care Programs and Services in Canada*. Toronto: Palliative Care Foundation.

11 Spence, David. 1986. "Granny Flats: The Ontario Demonstration." In Gloria Gutman and Norman Blackie, eds. *Aging in Place: Housing Adaptations and Options for Remaining in the Community*. Burnaby, BC: The Gerontology Research Centre, Simon Fraser University.

5   Spirduso, W.W. 1980. "Physical Fitness, Aging, and Psychomotor Speed: A Review." *Journal of Gerontology* 35:850–65.

5   Spirduso, W.W. 1982. "Physical Fitness in Relation to Motor Aging." In J.A. Mortimer, F.J. Pirozzolo, and G.J. Maletta, eds. *The Aging Motor System*. New York: Praeger.

5   Spirduso, W.W., and P.G. MacRae. 1990. "Motor Performance and Aging." In James E. Birren and K. Warner Schaie, eds. *Handbook of the Psychology of Aging*. 3d ed. San Diego: Academic Press.

12   Spirduso, W.W., and P.G. MacRae. 1991. "Physical Activity and Quality of Life in the Frail Elderly." In J.E. Birren, D.E. Deutchman, J. Lubben, and J. Rowe, eds. *The Concept and Measurement of the Quality of Life in the Frail Elderly*. New York: Academic Press.

12   Stacey, C., A. Kozma, and M.J. Stones. 1985. "Simple Cognitive and Behavioral Changes Resulting from Improved Physical Fitness in Persons over 50 Years of Age." *Canadian Journal on Aging* 4:67–74.

13   Staff. 1985. "Volunteer Granny Becomes 'Friend' to All of the Family." *Winnipeg Sun* (December 22).

8   Staff. 1991. *Seniors Today* (January 21):3.

10   Stagner, Ross. 1985. "Aging in Industry." In James E. Birren and K. Warner Schaie, eds. *Handbook of the Psychology of Aging*. 2d ed. New York: Van Nostrand Reinhold.

12,13 Starr, Bernard D., and Marcella Bakur Weiner. 1981. *The Starr-Weiner Report on Sex and Sexuality in the Mature Years*. New York: Stein and Day.

4   Statistics Canada. 1968. *1966 Census of Canada, Vol. 1 (1–11)*. Ottawa: Queen's Printer.

4   Statistics Canada. 1973. *Census of Canada. Bulletin 1: 2–3. 1971 Census*. Ottawa: Minister of Supply and Services.

11   Statistics Canada. 1978a. *Family, Expenditure in Canada. Volume I. Preliminary Estimates: Eight Cities*. Cat. No. 62-549. Ottawa: Minister of Supply and Services.

4   Statistics Canada. 1978b. *1976 Census of Canada. Advanced Release*. Ottawa: Minister of Supply and Services.

4   Statistics Canada. 1978c. *Vital Statistics. Vol. I. Births. 1975 and 1976*. Cat. No. 84–204. Ottawa: Statistics Canada.

4,10 Statistics Canada. 1979. *Canada's Elderly*. Cat. No. 98-800E. Ottawa: Minister of Supply and Services.

11   Statistics Canada. 1980a. *Expenditure Patterns and Income Adequacy for the Elderly. 1969–1976*. Cat. No. 13–575. Ottawa: Minister of Supply and Services.

13   Statistics Canada. 1980b. *Perspectives Canada III*. Cat. No. 11–511E. Ottawa: Minister of Supply and Services.

8   Statistics Canada. 1980c. *Surgical Procedures and Treatments 1976*. Cat. No. 82–208. Ottawa: Minister of Supply and Services Canada.

4   Statistics Canada. 1981. *Canada Year Book 1980–81*. Ottawa: Minister of Supply and Services.

8   Statistics Canada. 1981c. *Surgical Procedures and Treatments 1977*. Cat. No. 82–208. Ottawa: Minister of Supply and Services.

7   Statistics Canada. 1984a. *Canada's Immigrants*. Cat. No. 99–936 Ottawa: Minister of Supply and Services.

4,7 Statistics Canada. 1984b. *The Elderly in Canada*. Cat. No. 99–932. Ottawa: Minister of Supply and Services.

11   Statistics Canada. 1984c. *Household Facilities by Income and Other Characteristics*. 1983. Cat. No. 13–567. Ottawa: Minister of Supply and Services.

13   Statistics Canada. 1984d. *Life Tables. Canada and Provinces. 1980–82*. Cat. No. 84–532. Ottawa: Minister of Supply and Services.

4   Statistics Canada. 1986a. *Ethnic Diversity in Canada*. Cat. No. 98–132. Ottawa: Minister of Supply and Services.

10   Statistics Canada. 1986b. *The Labour Force–August, 1986*. Cat. No. 71–001. Ottawa: Minister of Supply and Services.

2,4,5,8,12 Statistics Canada. 1987. *Health and Social Support, 1985: General Social Survey Analysis Series*. Cat. No. 11–612E, No. 1. Ottawa: Minister of Supply and Services.

4   Statistics Canada. 1987c. *Special Projections 1991–2031*. Unpublished data. September. Supplied to Statistics Canada, Health Division, Social Security Section. Ottawa: Minister of Supply and Services.

5   Statistics Canada. 1988. *Health and Activity Limitation Survey (HALS)*. Ottawa: Minister of Supply and Services.

4,5,12 Statistics Canada. 1989a. *Canada Year Book 1990*. Cat. No. 11–402E/1990. Ottawa: Minister of Supply and Services.

12   Statistics Canada. 1989b. *Family Expenditure in Canada, 1986*. Cat. No. 62–555. Ottawa: Minister of Supply and Services.

12   Statistics Canada. 1989c. *Survey of Literacy Skills Used in Daily Activities*. Ottawa: Minister of Supply and Services.

8,15   Statistics Canada. 1990a. *Canada Year Book*. Ottawa: Minister of Supply and Services Canada.

5   Statistics Canada. 1990b. *Highlights: Disabled Persons in Canada*. Cat. No. 82–602. Ottawa: Minister of Supply and Services.

9   Statistics Canada. 1990c. *Income Distribution by Size in Canada 1989*. Cat. No. 13–207. Ottawa: Minister of Supply and Services.

9   Statistics Canada. 1990d. *Pension Plans in Canada 1988*. Cat. No. 74–401. Ottawa: Minister of Supply and Services.

2,4,6,8–13,15 Statistics Canada. 1990e. *A Portrait of Seniors in Canada*. Cat. No. 89–519. Ottawa: Minister of Supply and Services.

4   Statistics Canada. 1991. "Life Tables, Canada and Provinces 1985–1987." Cat. No. 82–0038. *Health Reports*, Supplement No. 13. Vol. 2., No. 4. Ottawa: Minister of Supply and Services.

4,8,10,11 Statistics Canada. 1993. *Canada Year Book*. Cat. No. 11-402E/1994. Ottawa: Minister of Industry, Science and Technology.

5,6   Statistics Canada. 1994a. *Health Status of Canadians: Report of the 1991 General Social Survey*. Cat. No. 11-612E, No. 8. Ottawa: Ministry of Industry, Science and Technology.

1   Statistics Canada. 1994b. *Canadian Crime Statistics*. Cat. No. 85-205. Ottawa: Minister of Industry, Science and Technology.

8   Statistics Canada. 1994c. *General Social Survey Analysis Series*. Cat. No. 11-612 E, No. 8. Ottawa: Minister of Industry, Science and Technology.

5   Statistics Canada. 1995a. *Women in Canada: A Statistical Report*, 3d ed. Cat. No. 89–503E. Ottawa: Minister of Industry.

9   Statistics Canada. 1995b. *Earnings of Men and Women 1993*. Cat. No. 13-217. Ottawa: Minister of Industry, Science and Technology.

9   Statistics Canada. 1996. *Canada's Retirement Income Programs: A Statistical Overview*. Cat. No. 74-507-XPB. Ottawa: Minister of Industry.

3   Stearns, Peter N. 1967. *European Society in Upheaval*. New York: Macmillan.

3   Stearns, Peter N. 1977. *Old Age in European Society: The Case of France*. London: Croom Helm.

13   Stearns, P. 1986. "Old Age Family Conflict: The Perspective of the Past." In K.A. Pillemer and R.S. Wolf, eds. *Elder Abuse: Conflict in the Family*. Dover, MA: Auburn House.

12   Steptoe, A., and D.S. Cox. 1988. "Acute Effects of Aerobic Exercise on Mood." *Health Psychology* 7: 329–40.

13   Stevenson, C. 1985. "Family Abuse of the Elderly in Alberta." Unpublished manuscript

prepared for the Senior Citizens Bureau, Alberta Social Services and Community Health.

11,12   Stewart, G. 1982. "Programme Principles." In Fitness and Amateur Sport, *National Conference on Fitness in the Third Age: Workshop Discussion Papers*. Ottawa: Government of Canada.

2,12   Stirling, D.R., G. Miller, P. Barker, G. Rowden, S. Meehan, and M. Ralston. 1986. "Exercise: An Effective Strategy to Activate Seniors." In Barry D. McPherson, ed. *Sport and Aging: The 1984 Olympic Scientific Congress Proceedings, Vol. 5*. Champaign, IL: Human Kinetics.

8   Stockwell, H., and E. Vayda. 1979. "Variations in Surgery in Ontario." *Medical Care* 17:390–96.

13   Stolar, G.E., M.A. Hill, and A. Tomblin. 1986. "Family Disengagement—Myth or Reality: A Follow-Up Study after Geriatric Assessment." *Canadian Journal on Aging* 5:113–23.

13   Stolar, G.E., M.I. MacIntee, and P. Hill. 1993. "The Elderly: Their Perceived Supports and Reciprocal Behaviors." *Journal of Gerontological Social Work* 19(3/4):15–33.

6   Stone, Leroy O. 1986. "On the Demography of Dementia." In M.R. Easterwood, chair. *Alzheimer's Disease and Other Dementias: The Magnitude and Management of the Problem*. Symposium presented at the Clarke Institute of Psychiatry, Toronto.

13   Stone, Leroy O. 1987. "Cohort Aging and Support Network Help Capacity." In George Maddox and E.W. Busse, eds. *Aging: The Universal Human Experience*. New York: Springer.

2,12,13 Stone, Leroy O. 1988. *Family and Friendship Ties among Canada's Seniors*. Cat. No. 89–508. Ottawa: Minister of Supply and Services.

10   Stone, L.O. 1994. "Men's Work over the Life Course." *Info-Age* 10(March).

4   Stone, Leroy O., and Susan Fletcher. 1980. *A Profile of Canada's Older Population*. Montreal: Institute for Research on Public Policy.

5,8,13,15 Stone, Leroy O., and Susan Fletcher. 1986. *The Seniors Boom*. Statistics Canada. Cat. No. 89–515E. Ottawa: Minister of Supply and Services.

1,4,8,11 Stone, Leroy O., and Hubert Frenken. 1988. *Canada's Seniors*. Cat. No. 98–121. Ottawa: Minister of Supply and Services.

9   Stone, Leroy O., and Michael MacLean. 1979. *Future Income Prospects for Canada's Senior Citizens*. Toronto: Butterworths.

13   Stones, M.J. 1994. *Rules and Tools: The Meaning and Measurement of Elder Abuse*. A manual for Milestones (Newfoundland).

12   Stones, M.J., and D. Dawe. 1993. "Acute Exercise Facilitates Semantically Cued Memory

in Nursing Home Residents." *Journal of the American Geriatrics Society* 41(5):531–34.

8 Stones, M.J., B. Dornan, and A. Kozma. 1989. "The Prediction of Mortality in Elderly Institution Residents." *Journal of Gerontology*: Social Sciences 44:P72–P79.

12 Stones, M.J., and A. Kozma. 1980. "Adult Age Trends in Record Running Performances." *Experimental Aging Research* 6:407–16.

12 Stones, M.J., and A. Kozma. 1982. "Cross-Sectional, Longitudinal, and Secular Age Trends in Athletic Performance." *Experimental Aging Research* 8:185–88.

8 Strain, L.A. 1991. "Use of Health Services in Later Life: The Influence of Health Beliefs." *Journal of Gerontology: Social Sciences* 46(3):S143–50.

5 Strain, L.A. 1993. "Good Health: What Does It Mean in Later Life?" *Journal of Aging and Health* 5(3):338–64.

13 Strain, Laurel A., and Neena L. Chappell. 1982a. "Confidants: Do They Make a Difference in Quality of Life?" *Research on Aging* 4:479–502.

12 Strain, Laurel A., and Neena L. Chapell. 1982b. "Outdoor Recreation and the Rural Elderly: Participation, Problems and Needs." *Therapeutic Recreation Journal* 16:42–48.

7 Strain, Laurel A., and Neena L. Chappell. 1984. "Social Support among Elderly Canadian Natives: A Comparison with Elderly Non-Natives." Paper presented at the Canadian Association on Gerontology 13th Annual Scientific and Educational Meetings, Vancouver.

5 Strain, L.A., N.L. Chappell, and M.J. Penning. 1993. "The Need for Social Science Research on Technology and Aging." *Technology and Disability* 2(1):56–64.

2,13 Strain, L.A., and B.J. Payne. 1992. "Social Networks and Patterns of Social Interaction among Ever-Single and Separated/Divorced Elderly Canadians." *Canadian Journal on Aging* 11(1):31–53.

2 Streib, Gordon F., and Robert H. Binstock. 1990. "Aging and the Social Sciences: Changes in the Field." In Robert H. Binstock and Linda K. George, eds. *Handbook of Aging and the Social Sciences*. 3d ed. San Diego: Academic Press.

2 Streib, Gordon F., and Carroll J. Bourg. 1984. "Age Stratification Theory, Inequality, and Social Change." *Comparative Social Research* 7:63–77.

11 Streib, Gordon F., N.E. Folts, and A.J. LaGreca. 1985. "Autonomy, Power, and Decision-Making in 36 Retirement Communities." *The Gerontologist* 25:403–9.

1 Streib, Gordon, and Clement Schneider. 1971. *Retirement in American Society*. Ithaca, NY: Cornell University Press.

8 Strike, Carol. 1989. "Residential Care." *Canadian Social Trends* (Autumn):25–26.

10 Stryckman, Judith. 1987. "Work Sharing and the Older Worker in a Unionized Setting." In Victor W. Marshall, ed. *Aging in Canada: Social Perspectives*. 2d ed. Toronto: Fitzhenry and Whiteside.

13 Stull, Donald E., and Annemarie Scarisbrick-Hauser. 1989. "Never-Married Elderly: A Reassessment with Implications for Long-Term Care Policy." *Research on Aging* 11:124–39.

8 Sturdy, Catherine, and Joseph A. Tindale. 1985. "The Social Organization of Health Care Provision to the Elderly in Ontario." Paper presented to the Conference of the Canadian Association on Gerontology 14th Annual Scientific and Educational Meetings, Hamilton.

14 Subcommittee on Institutional Program Guidelines. 1989. *Palliative-Care Services*. Health and Welfare Canada. Cat. No. H39-32/1989E. Ottawa: Minister of Supply and Services.

14 Sudnow, David. 1967. *Passing On*. Englewood Cliffs, NJ: Prentice-Hall.

8 Sulman, Joanne, and Sue Wilkinson. 1989. "An Activity Group for Long-Stay Elderly Patients in an Acute Care Hospital: Program Evaluation." *Canadian Journal on Aging* 8:34–50.

5 Surwillo, W. 1963. "The Relation of Simple Response Time to Brain-Wave Frequency and the Effects of Age." *Electroencephalography and Clinical Neurophysiology* 15:105–14.

12 Swedburg, R.B. 1993. "Educational Institutes: Models for and by Seniors." Report for Elderhostel Canada sponsored by Health and Welfare Canada and the Seniors Independence Program, Ottawa.

13 Synergistics Consulting. 1993. *The Elder Monitor: Survey of Older Canadians*. Toronto: Synergistics Consulting.

3 Synge, Jane. 1980. "Work and Family Support Patterns of the Aged in the Early Twentieth Century." In Victor W. Marshall, ed. *Aging in Canada: Social Perspectives*. Toronto: Fitzhenry and Whiteside.

13 Synge, Jane. No date. "Women as Telephoners: On the Importance of Phoning and Writing in Maintaining Kin and Friendship Ties in Middle and Old Age." Personal communication.

13 Synge, Jane, and M. Luxton. 1984. "Patterns of Sociability and Companionship among the Middle Aged and the Aged with Special Reference to Elderly Women." Paper presented

at the 13th Annual Meeting of the Canadian Sociology and Anthropology Association.

13   Szasz, George. 1980. "The Sexual Consequences of Aging." In John Crawford, ed. *The Family in Later Life: Canadian Gerontological Collection III. Selected Papers 1980*. Winnipeg: Canadian Association on Gerontology.

10   Szinovacz, M.E. 1982. "Introduction: Research on Women's Retirement." In M. Szinovacz, ed. *Women's Retirement*. Beverly Hills, CA: Sage.

10   Szinovacz, M.E. 1983. "Beyond the Hearth: Older Women and Retirement." In Elizabeth W. Markson, ed. *Older Women: Issues and Prospects*. Lexington, MA: D.C. Heath.

5   Tait, H. 1992. "Sleep Problems: Whom Do They Affect? *Canadian Social Trends* (Winter): 8–10.

3   Takahashi, T. 1994. "Home Care System." *Pacific Friend* 22(2)(June):14–15.

7   Task Force on Suicide in Canada. 1994. *Suicide in Canada*. Cat. No. H39-107/1995E. Ottawa: Minister of National Health and Welfare.

7   Tasse, L. 1993. "Promised Lands: The Social Role and Filiation of Elderly Algonquins of Kitigan Zibi." *International Review of Community Development* 29(69):25–36.

6   Taub, H.A. 1979. "Comprehension and Memory of Prose Materials by Young and Old Adults." *Experimental Aging Research* 5:3–13.

10,15 Taylor, P.S. 1995. "Grandma! Grandpa! Back to Work!" *Saturday Night* (June): 18+.

1   Taylor, S.C. 1995. "Primetime's Big Sleep." *Modern Maturity* (November/December):38–43.

12   Thacker, Charlene, and Mark Novak. 1991. "Middle-Aged Re-Entry Women and Student Role Supports: Application of a Life Event Model." *Canadian Journal of Higher Education*. 21:13–36.

8   Tholl, W.G. 1994. "Health Care Spending in Canada: Skating Faster on Thinner Ice." In A. Blomqvist and D.M. Brown, eds. *Limits to Care: Reforming Canada's Health System in an Age of Restraint*, 53–89. Ottawa: C.D. Howe Institute.

14   Thompson, Edward H. 1985–86. "Palliative and Curative Care: Nurses' Attitudes toward Dying and Death in the Hospital Setting." *Omega* 16:233–42.

1,13 Thompson, J. Victor. 1989. "The Elderly and Their Informal Social Networks." *Canadian Journal on Aging* 8:319–32.

5   Thompson, M.E. and W.F. Forbes. 1990. "The Various Definitions of Biological Aging." *Canadian Journal on Aging* 9:91–94.

16   Thornton, J.E. 1992. "Educational Gerontology in Canada." *Educational Gerontology* 18:415–31.

8   Thurston, N.E., D.E. Larsen, A.W. Rademaker, and J.C. Kerr. 1982. "Health Status of the Rural Elderly: A Picture of Health." Paper presented at the 11th Annual Scientific and Educational Meetings of the Canadian Association on Gerontology, Winnipeg.

7   Tindale, J. 1980. "Identity Maintenance Processes of Old Poor Men." In Victor W. Marshall, ed. *Aging in Canada*. Toronto: Fitzhenry and Whiteside.

10   Tindale, J. 1991. *Older Workers in an Aging Work Force*. Cat. No. H71-2/1-10-1991E. Ottawa: Minister of Supply and Services.

4   Tindale, J., and V.W. Marshall. 1980. "A Generational Conflict Perspective for Gerontology." In Victor W. Marshall ed. *Aging in Canada*. Toronto: Fitzhenry and Whiteside.

4   Torrance, George M. 1981. "Introduction: Socio-Historical Overview: The Development of the Canadian Health System." In D. Coburn, C. D'Arcy, P. New, and G. Torrance, eds. *Health and Canadian Society: Sociological Perspectives*. Toronto: Fitzhenry and Whiteside.

8   Torrance, George M. 1987. "Socio-Historical Overview." In D. Coburn, C. D'Arcy, G. Torrance, and P. New, eds. *Health and Canadian Society: Sociological Perspectives*. 2d ed. Toronto: Fitzhenry and Whiteside.

13   Toseland, R.W., M.S. Labrecque, S.T. Goebel, and M.H. Whitney. 1992. "An Evaluation of a Group Program for Spouses of Frail Elderly Veterans." *The Gerontologist* 32(3):382–90.

5   Toufexis, Anastasia. 1986. "New Rub for the Skin Game." *Time* (March 31).

10   Tournier, Paul. 1972. *Learning to Grow Old*. London: SCM Press.

1   Towler, John C. 1983. "Ageism in Children's Popular Literature and Television." Paper presented at the Canadian Association on Gerontology 12th Annual Scientific and Educational Meeting, Moncton.

15   Townson, M. 1994. *The Social Contract and Seniors: Preparing for the 21st Century*. Ottawa: National Advisory Council on Aging.

1   Trainor, C., J. Normand, and L. Verdon. 1995. "Women and the Criminal Justice System. In Statistics Canada, *Women in Canada: A Statistical Report*, 3d ed., 101–27. Cat. No. 89-503E. Ottawa: Statistics Canada.

13   Treas, J. 1977. "Family Support Systems for the Aged, Some Social and Demographic Considerations." *The Gerontologist* 17:486–91.

4   Treasury Board Secretariat. 1977. *Changing Population and the Impact on Government Age-Specific Expenditures*. Ottawa: Planning Branch

Effectiveness Evaluation Division, Treasury Board Secretariat.

15 Trela, James. 1976. "Status Inconsistency and Political Action in Old Age." In Jaber Gubrium, ed. *Time, Roles, and Self in Old Age*. New York: Human Sciences Press.

3 Trexler, Richard C. 1982. "A Widows' Asylum of the Renaissance: The Orbatello of Florence." In Peter N. Stearns, ed. *Old Age in Preindustrial Society*. New York: Holmes and Meier.

11 Trickey, F., Maltais, D., Gosselin, C., Robitaille, Y. 1993. "Adapting Older Persons' Homes to Promote Independence." *Physical and Occupational Therapy in Geriatrics* 12(1):1–14.

12 Trombo, B. 1995. *Seniors Computer Information Projects, Spring 1995, Survey Results*. Report of Creative Retirement Manitoba. Winnipeg.

7 Trovato, Frank. 1988. "Suicide in Canada: A Further Look at the Effects of Age, Period and Cohort." *Canadian Journal of Public Health* 79:37–44.

4 Tucker, Richard D., and Victor Marshall. 1988. "Descriptive Overview of Older Anglophone Canadians in Florida." In Larry C. Mullins and Richard D. Tucker, eds. *Snowbirds in the Sun Belt: Older Canadians in Florida*. Tampa, FL: International Exchange Center on Gerontology.

4 Tucker, Richard D., Victor W. Marshall, Charles F. Longino, Jr., and Larry C. Mullins. 1988. "Older Anglophone Canadian Snowbirds in Florida: A Descriptive Profile." *Canadian Journal on Aging* 7:218–32.

4 Tucker, R.D., L.C. Mullins, F. Beland, C.F. Longino, Jr., and V.W. Marshall. 1992. "Older Canadians in Florida: A Comparison of Anglophone and Francophone Seasonal Migrants." *Canadian Journal on Aging* 11(3):281–97.

3 Turnbull, Colin. 1961. *The Forest People*. New York: Simon and Schuster.

13 Turner, Barbara F., and Catherine Adams. 1983. "The Sexuality of Older Women." In Elizabeth W. Markson, ed. *Older Women: Issues and Prospects*. Lexington, MA: D.C. Heath.

11 Turner, L., and E. Mangum. 1982. *Report on Housing Choice of Older Americans. Summary of Survey Findings and Recommendations for Practitioners*. Bryn Mawr, PA: The Graduate School of Social Work and Social Research, Bryn Mawr College.

7 Ujimoto, V.K. 1983. "Introduction: Ethnicity and Aging in Canada." *Canadian Ethnic Studies* 15:iii–vii.

4 United Nations. 1984. *Periodical on Aging* 1(1): Tables 3, 10, 17, 24, 31, 38. New York: Department of International Economic and Social Affairs.

3 United Nations. 1992. "Asia Faces Era of Population Ageing." *Bulletin on Ageing* 1992(3):2–3.

11 United Senior Citizens of Ontario. 1985. "Elderly Residents in Ontario: Their Current Housing Situation and Their Interest in Various Housing Options." Ontario: Minister for Senior Citizen Affairs.

4 U.S. Census Bureau. 1987. *An Aging World*. Washington, DC: U.S. Government Printing Office.

13 Vachon, M.L.S. 1981. "The Importance of Social Relationships and Social Support in Widowhood." Paper presented to the Joint Meeting of the Canadian Association on Gerontology and the Gerontological Society of America, Toronto.

13 Vachon, M.L.S., A. Formo, K. Freedman, A. Lyall, J. Rogers, and S. Freeman. 1976. "Stress Reactions to Bereavement." *Essence* 1:23–33.

7 Vanderburgh, Rosamund M. 1988. "The Impact of Government Support for Indian Culture on Canada's Aged Indians." In Eloise Rathbone-McEwan and Betty Havens, eds. *North American Elders: United States and Canadian Perspectives*. New York: Greenwood.

12 Van der Veen, R. 1990. "Third Age or Inter-Age Universities?" *Journal of Educational Gerontology* 5: 96–105.

5 Vandervoort, A.A., K.C. Hayes, and A.Y. Belanger. 1986. "Strength and Endurance of Skeletal Muscle in the Elderly." *Physiotherapy Canada* 38:167–73.

8 Van Horne, Ron. 1986. *A New Agenda: Health and Social Service Strategies for Ontario's Seniors*. Toronto: Government of Ontario.

15 Van Loon, R. 1970. "Political Participation in Canada: The 1965 Election." *Canadian Journal of Political Science* 3:376–99.

3 Vatuk, Sylvia. 1982. "Old Age in India." In Peter N. Stearns, ed. *Old Age in Preindustrial Society*. New York: Holmes and Meier.

11 Veevers, Jean E. 1987. "The 'Real' Marriage Squeeze: Mate Selection, Mortality and the Mating Gradient." Paper presented at the Annual Meeting of the Pacific Sociological Association.

15 Verba, Sidney, and Norman H. Nie. 1972. *Participation in America: Political Democracy and Social Equality*. New York: Harper and Row.

15 Verba, Sidney, Norman H. Nie, and Jae-on Kim. 1971. *The Modes of Democratic Participation*. Beverly Hills, CA: Sage.

12 Verduin, John R., and Douglas N. McEwen. 1984. *Adults and Their Leisure: The Need for*

Lifelong Learning. Springfield, IL: Charles C. Thomas.

13 Verwoerdt, A., E. Pfeiffer, and H.S. Wang. 1969. "Sexual Behavior in Senescence—Changes in Sexual Activity and Interest of Aging Men and Women." *Journal of Geriatric Psychiatry* 2:163–80.

12 Vigoda, Debby, L. Crawford, and J. Hirdes. 1985. "The Continuity Theory: Empirical Support." In Norman K. Blackie, Sister Anne Robichaud, and Shawn MacDonald, eds. *Aging, Mirror of Humanity: Canadian Gerontological Collection IV.* Winnipeg: Canadian Association on Gerontology.

12 Waldron, M.K., and G.A.B. Moore. 1991. *Helping Adults Learn.* Toronto: Thompson Educational Publishers.

13 Walker, Alan. 1991. "The Relationship between the Family and the State in the Care of Older People." *Canadian Journal on Aging* 10:94–112.

14 Walton, Douglas N., and W.H. Fleming. 1980. "Responsibility for the Discontinuation of Treatment." *Essence* 4:57–61.

12 Wannell, T., and C. McKie. 1986a. "Expanding the Choices." *Canadian Social Trends* (Summer):13–18.

7,9 Wanner, Richard A., and P. Lynn McDonald. 1986. "The Vertical Mosaic in Later Life: Ethnicity and Retirement in Canada." *Journal of Gerontology* 41:662–71.

16 Watt, S., and S. Meredith. 1995. "Integrating Gerontology into Social Work Education Programs." *Educational Gerontology* 21:55–68.

8 Watzke, J.R., and A.V. Wister. 1993. "Staff Attitudes: Monitoring Technology in Long-Term Care." *Journal of Gerontological Nursing* 19(11):23–29.

6 Waugh, Nancy C., and Robin A. Barr. 1982. "Encoding Deficits in Aging." In F.I.M. Craik and Sandra Trehub, eds. *Aging and Cognitive Processes.* New York: Plenum Press.

2 Weber, M. 1978. *Economy and Society: An Outline of Interpretive Sociology.* 2 vols. G. Roth and C. Wittich, eds. Berkeley: University of California Press.

6 Wechsler, D. 1939. *A Measurement of Adult Intelligence.* Baltimore: Williams and Wilkins.

6 Wechsler, D. 1981. *WAIS-R Manual* (Wechsler Adult Intelligence Scale Revised). New York: Harcourt Brace Jovanovich.

13 Weg, Ruth B. 1983. "The Physiological Perspective." In Ruth B. Weg, ed. *Sexuality in the Later Years: Roles and Behavior.* New York: Academic Press.

13 Weinberg, Martin S. 1969. "The Aging Male Homosexual." *Medical Aspects of Human Sexuality* 3:66–72.

14 Weisman, Avery. 1972. *On Dying and Denying.* New York: Behavioral Press.

7 Weiss, R.S., ed. 1973. *Loneliness: The Experience of Emotional and Social Isolation.* Cambridge, MA: MIT Press.

6 Welford, A.T. 1958. *Aging and Human Skill.* London: Oxford University Press.

5 Welford, A.T. 1984. "Psychomotor Performance." In Carl Eisdorfer, ed. *Annual Review of Gerontology and Geriatrics.* New York: Springer.

4 Weller, Robert H., and Leon F. Bouvier. 1981. *Population: Demography and Policy.* New York: St. Martin's Press.

12 Werner, Lawrence. 1976. "Functional Analysis of Viewing for Older Adults." *Journal of Broadcasting* 20:77–87.

8 Wershow, H. 1976. "The Four Percent Fallacy: Some Further Evidence and Policy Implications." *The Gerontologist* 16:52–55.

6 White, K. 1993. "How the Mind Ages. *Psychology Today* 26(6):38–42, 80.

13 Wigdor, B. T. 1991. *Elder Abuse: Major Issues from a National Perspective.* Ottawa: National Advisory Council on Aging.

14 Wilcox, Sandra G., and Marilyn Sutton. 1985. *Understanding Death and Dying.* 3d ed. Palo Alto, CA: Mayfield.

6 Willis, S.L. 1990. "Contributions of Cognitive Training Research to Understanding Late Life Potential." In M. Perlmutter, ed., *Late Life Potential,* 25–42. Washington, DC: The Gerontological Society of America.

2 Wilson, T.P. 1970. "Normative and Interpretive Paradigms in Sociology." In J.D. Douglas, ed. *Understanding Everyday Life.* Chicago: Aldine.

13 *Winnipeg Sun.* 1985. "Volunteer Granny Becomes 'Friend' to All of the Family." *Winnipeg Sun* (December 22).

15 Wisensale, S.K. 1993. "Generational Equity." In R. Kastenbaum, ed. *Encyclopedia of Adult Development,* 175–80. Phoenix, AZ: Oryx.

11 Wister, Andrew V. 1985. "Living Arrangement Choices among the Elderly." *Canadian Journal on Aging* 4:127–44.

13 Wister, Andrew V. 1986. "Living Arrangements and Informal Social Support among the Elderly." Personal communication.

8 Wister, A.V. 1992. "Residential Attitudes and Knowledge, Use, and Future Use of Home Support." *Journal of Applied Gerontology* 11(1):84–100.

13 Wister, Andrew V., and Laurel A. Strain. 1986. "Social Support and Well-Being: A Comparison of Older Widows and Widowers." Paper presented at the 21st Annual Meeting of the Canadian Sociology and Anthropology Association, Winnipeg.

13 Wolf, R.S., and K.A. Pillemer. 1989. *Helping Elderly Victims: The Reality of Elder Abuse*. New York: Columbia University Press.

13 Wolfson, C., R. Handfield-Jones, K.C. Glass, J. McClaran, and E. Keyserlingk. 1993. "Adult Children's Perceptions of Their Responsibility to Provide Care for Dependent Elderly Parents." *The Gerontologist* 33(3):315–23.

5 Wolfson, M., G. Rowe, J.F. Gentleman, and M. Tomiak. 1993. "Career Earnings and Death: A Longitudinal Analysis of Older Canadian Men." *Journal of Gerontology: Social Sciences* 48(4): S167–S179.

9,10 Women's Bureau, Labour Canada. 1990. *Women in the Labour Force, 1990-91 Edition*. Labour Canada Cat. No. L016-1728/90E Ottawa: Minister of Supply and Services Canada.

7 Wong, Paul T.P., and Gary T. Reker. 1985. "Stress, Coping, and Well-Being in Anglo and Chinese Elderly." *Canadian Journal on Aging* 4:29–38.

7 Wood, Linda A. 1978. "Loneliness, Social Identity and Social Structure." *Essence* 2:259–70.

7 Wood, Linda, and A. Guest. 1978. "Perspectives on Loneliness." *Essence* 2:199–201.

1 Woodruff, D.S. 1975. "Introduction: Multi-Disciplinary Perspectives of Aging." In D.S. Woodruff and J. E. Birren, eds. *Aging: Scientific Perspectives and Social Issues*. New York: D. Van Nostrand.

5 Woodruff, Diana S. 1982. "The Life Expectancy Test: Can You Live to Be 100?" In Steven H. Zarit, ed. *Readings in Aging and Death*. 2d ed. New York: Harper and Row.

13 Woodward, T.S. 1994. *French-Language Literature in Canada on Social Support*. Report for the Centre on Aging, University of Victoria, Victoria, BC.

8 World Health Organization. 1984. "Health Promotion: A World Health Organization Document on the Concept and Principles." *Canadian Public Health Association Digest* 8:101–2.

14 Wortman, Camille B., and Roxane Cohen Silver. 1990. "Successful Mastery of Bereavement and Widowhood: A Life-Course Perspective." In Paul B. Baltes and Margaret M. Baltes, eds. *Successful Aging*. Cambridge: Cambridge University Press.

13 Wu, Z. 1995. "Remarriage after Widowhood: A Marital History Study of Older Canadians." *Canadian Journal on Aging* 14(4):719–36.

13 Wylie, Betty Jane. 1981. "Coping with Survival: The Quiet Agony of the Widower." *Quest* (Spring):34–38.

15 Yelaja, Shankar A. 1981. "Gray Power: A Study on Political Attitudes and Behaviour of Older People in a Canadian City." Paper presented at the 12th International Congress of Gerontology, Hamburg.

15 Yelaja, Shankar A. 1989. "Gray Power: Agenda for Future Research." *Canadian Journal on Aging* 8:118–27.

8 Young, J.E., W.F. Forbes, and J.P. Hirdes. 1994. "The Association of Disability with Long-Term Care Institutionalization of the Elderly." *Canadian Journal on Aging* 13(1):15–29.

11 Zamprelli, Jim. 1985. "Shelter Allowances for Older Adults: Programs in Search of a Policy." In Gloria Gutman and Norman Blackie, eds. *Innovations in Housing and Living Arrangements for Seniors*. Burnaby, BC: The Gerontology Research Centre, Simon Fraser University.

11 Zamprelli, Jim. 1986. "Housing and Support Service Programs for Older Manitobans." In Gloria Gutman and Norman Blackie, eds. *Aging in Place: Housing Adaptations and Options for Remaining in the Community*. Burnaby, BC: The Gerontology Research Centre, Simon Fraser University.

5 Zandri, Elaine, and Neil Charness. 1989. "Training Older and Younger Adults to Use Software." *Educational Gerontology* 15:615–31.

13 Zarit, S.H., K.E. Reever, and J. Bach-Peterson. 1980. "Relatives of the Impaired Elderly: Correlates of Feelings of Burden." *The Gerontologist* 20:649–55.

1 Zay, N., D. Carrier, A. Grandmaison, L. Lévesque, and C. Sicotte. 1984. "Profil de la recherche en gérontologie au Québec." *Le Gérontophile* 6:1–23.

5 Zimmer, Z., and N.L. Chappell. 1994. "Mobility Restriction and the Use of Devices." *Journal of Aging and Health* 6(2):185–208.

11 Zimmer, Z., and Chappell, N. Forthcoming. "Rural–Urban Differences in Seniors' Neighborhood Preferences." *Journal of Housing for the Elderly*.

6 Zivian, M.T., W. Larsen, V.J. Knox, and W.L. Gekoski. 1992. "Psychotherapy for the Elderly: Psychotherapists' Preferences." *Psychotherapy* 29(4):668–74.

14   Zorza, Victor, and Rosemary Zorza. 1979. "Hospice—Death with Dignity? Or Giving Up on Life." *Texas Medicine* 75:35–37.

6   Zuckerman, H. 1977. *Scientific Elite: Studies of Nobel Laureates in the United States*. New York: Free Press.

12   Zuzanek, Jiri, and Sheila J. Box. 1988. "Life Course and the Daily Lives of Older Adults in Canada." In Karen Altergott, ed. *Daily Life in Later Life: Comparative Perspectives*. Newbury Park, CA: Sage.

Index

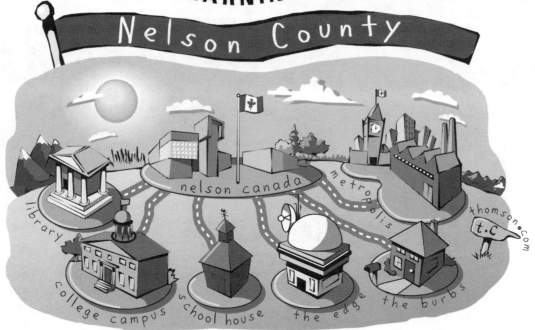

Visit us on the Web at **http://www.nelson.com/nelson.html**
You can also send your comments to us by e-mail at **college_arts_hum@nelson.com**

To the owner of this book

We hope that you have enjoyed *Aging and Society,* and we would like to know as much about your experiences with this text as you would care to offer. Only through your comments and those of others can we learn how to make this a better text for future readers.

School _____ Your instructor's name _____

Course _____ Was the text required? _____ Recommended? _____

1. What did you like the most about *Aging and Society?*

_____
_____
_____

2. How useful was this text for your course?

_____
_____
_____

3. Do you have any recommendations for ways to improve the next edition of this text?

_____
_____
_____

4. In the space below or in a separate letter, please write any other comments you have about the book. (For example, please feel free to comment on reading level, writing style, terminology, design features, and learning aids.)

_____
_____
_____
_____

Optional

Your name _____ Date _____

May ITP Nelson quote you, either in promotion for *Aging and Society* or in future publishing ventures?

Yes _____ No _____

Thanks!

You can also send your comments to us via e-mail at
college_arts_hum@nelson.com

PLEASE TAPE SHUT. DO NOT STAPLE.

TAPE SHUT

TAPE SHUT

FOLD HERE

MAIL POSTE
Canada Post Corporation
Société canadienne des postes
Postage paid   Port payé
if mailed in Canada si posté au Canada
Business Reply   Réponse d'affaires

0066102399   01

Nelson

TAPE SHUT

TAPE SHUT

0066102399-M1K5G4-BR01

ITP NELSON
MARKET AND PRODUCT DEVELOPMENT
PO BOX 60225 STN BRM B
TORONTO ON M7Y 2H1